Black American Literature

Essays   Poetry   Fiction   Drama

Edited by

Darwin T. Turner

University of Michigan

Charles E. Merrill Publishing Company
A Bell & Howell Company
Columbus, Ohio

CHARLES E. MERRILL LITERARY TEXTS

Under the General Editorship of
Matthew J. Bruccoli and Joseph Katz

Anthologies by genre, period, theme, or other significant principle for the study of American Literature. Each volume provides reliable texts introduced by a noted authority.

Textual Note

This volume presents authoritative texts for all material. The selections are reprinted from their original appearances as specified in each case.

ISBN: 0-675-09279-5 Clothbound edition
0-675-09278-7 Paperbound edition

Library of Congress Catalog Card Number: 73-132399

1 2 3 4 5 6 7 8 9 10 — 76 75 74 73 72 71 70

Printed in the United States of America

General Preface

The following anthology is a composite of three volumes, previously published separately, and a new section on drama.* It has been assembled in this manner for the convenience of readers who desire a single volume which includes representative samples of the writings of Afro-Americans in several genres. Because the anthology has been developed in this manner, the reader will discover some repetitions in introductions and headnotes. Furthermore, because the criteria for selecting representative works differed for each genre, the reader is advised to examine carefully in the separate introductions the principles governing the selection of works in that genre. Finally, I wish to emphasize a fact stated in the introductions. This volume is not intended to be a definitive anthology of the best short literature by Afro-Americans. Instead, it is intended to introduce readers to Afro-American writers, well-known and less well-known, who exemplify styles and thoughts representative of the literary culture of Afro-Americans.

Elsewhere in this anthology, I express my gratitude to individuals who assisted with the preparation of the sections. I wish here to express appreciation to Mrs. Claudia Weston and Miss Bonnie Floyd, who helped prepare this final volume.

---

*Black American Literature: Essays, Black American Literature: Poetry, and Black American Literature: Fiction — all published by the Charles E. Merrill Publishing Company.

Preface

A word, perhaps, needs to be said about the title. When James Baldwin wrote, "Nobody knows my name," he could not have foreseen the violent dispute which would be incited a decade later by those who, rejecting the term "Negro," wish to be described as "black." The title of this volume indicates my awareness of and sympathy with that group even if I cannot totally agree with their argument.

The controversy is not trivial. It reflects a troubled, sometimes desperate search for identity by a people who have lived in a society which consciously stripped their racial identity from them. Originally, we were African, but we were taken from Africa. Voluntarily or involuntarily, we mixed with people of other nations and other races; but, as long as our skin remained dark and our features Negroid, we were identified as Negroes rather than as members of any other ethnic or political group. And, despite our three-century existence in America, we have never been recognized fully as Americans. Because of such a history, we have sought to retain or regain our identity and to proclaim that identity with a meaningful name.

Early in the twentieth century, the term "colored" linked the causes of the black American with other dark-skinned peoples of the world. To others, "Afro-American" seemed a more accurate description of our identity. Then, a solution seemed to lie in a crusade to capitalize "negro" and thus change it from a sometimes derogatory description to the name of a racially proud group. Now, rejecting "Negro" as a term which they identify with slavery and servility, many members of the group insist upon "black."

In this work I shall use "black" generally to contrast with "white" and most often to identify individuals of African ancestry who wrote in this country before the United States gained its identity as a nation. I shall also use "black" specifically to refer to writers identified with Black Nationalism or with the Black Arts Movement. Frequently, however, I shall use "black," "Afro-American," and "Negro" interchangeably. My reason — if I need one — is not that I am too old to change my habits but that I have struggled too diligently to discover my own identity to permit it to be dislodged by the mere question of whether I am called "Negro" or "black."

D.T.

iv

Acknowledgments

"On being brought from Africa to America," "To the University of Cambridge in New-England," and "Goliath of Gath" from *Poems on Various Subjects, Religious and Moral* by Phillis Wheatley (London: A. Bell, 1773).

"The Swan-Vain Pleasures," "The Powers of Love," "To a Departing Favorite," "The Eye of Love," and "The Setting Sun" from *The Poetical Works of George M. Horton, The Colored Bard of North Carolina* by George M. Horton (Hillsborough, North Carolina: D. Heartt, 1845).

"Frederick Douglass," "Ode to Ethiopia," "Ere Sleep Comes Down to Soothe the Weary Eyes," and "An Ante-Bellum Sermon," originally from *Lyrics of Lowly Life* by Paul Laurence Dunbar (New York: Dodd, Mead and Company, 1896). Reprinted by permission of Dodd, Mead & Company, Inc. from *The Complete Poems of Paul Laurence Dunbar*.

"When a Feller's Itchin' to be Spanked" from *Lyrics of Sunshine and Shadow* by Paul Laurence Dunbar (New York: Dodd, Mead and Company, 1905).

"Rhapsody," "Hymn for the Slain in Battle," "To ———," "If I Could Touch," and "Two Questions" from *Lyrics of Life and Love* by W. S. Braithwaite (Boston: Herbert B. Turner, 1904).

"Sence You Went Away" from *Fifty Years and Other Poems* (Boston: Cornhill, 1917), by permission of The Viking Press, Inc. Copyright © 1917 by James Weldon Johnson. All rights reserved.

"The Creation" from *God's Trombones* by James Weldon Johnson (New York: Viking, 1927), by permission of The Viking Press, Inc. Copyright © 1927 by The Viking Press, Inc., renewed 1955 by Grace Nail Johnson.

"Black Woman," "Credo," "The Suppliant," and "To William Stanley Braithwaite" from *Bronze: A Book of Verse* by Georgia Douglas Johnson (Boston: B. J. Brimmer, 1922).

"Outcast," "Enslaved," "Africa," "America," "The Lynching," "If We Must Die," "Flame-Heart," "The Harlem Dancer," and "Flower of Love" from *Harlem Shadows* by Claude McKay (New York: Harcourt, Brace & Co., 1922). Copyright © 1922 by Harcourt, Brace & Company. Reprinted by permission of Twayne Publishers.

Last 119 lines from *The Blue Meridian* , "Five Vignettes," "The Lost Dancer," and "At Sea" published here for the first time by permission of Liveright Publishing Corporation. Copyright © 1969 by Marjorie C. Toomer.

"Heritage," "From the Dark Tower," "Song in Spite of Myself," "Magnets," and "For Paul Laurence Dunbar" from *On These I Stand* by Countee Cullen (New York: Harper & Brothers, 1947); "Heritage" and "For Paul Laurence Dunbar," copyright 1925 by Harper & Brothers, renewed 1953 by Ida M. Cullen; "From the Dark Tower," copyright 1927 by Harper & Brothers, renewed 1955 by Ida M. Cullen; "Magnets," copyright 1935 by Harper & Brothers, renewed 1963 by Ida M. Cullen. Reprinted by permission of Harper & Row, Publishers.

"Dream Variation," "Epilogue," and "The Weary Blues": Copyright © 1926 by Alfred A. Knopf, Inc. and renewed 1954 by Langston Hughes. Reprinted from *Selected Poems,* by Langston Hughes, by permission of the publisher. (The three texts used in this volume were taken from *The Weary Blues* by Langston Hughes.)

"Theme for English B" and "College Formal: Renaissance Casino" from *Montage of a Dream Deferred* by Langston Hughes. Reprinted by permission of Harold Ober Associates Incorporated. Copyright © 1951 by Langston Hughes.

"Madam and Her Madam," copyright 1948 by Alfred A. Knopf, Inc. Reprinted from *Selected Poems,* by Langston Hughes, by permission of the publisher. (The text used in this volume was taken from *One-Way Ticket* by Langston Hughes.)

"Southern Mansion," and "Nocturne at Bethesda" from *Personals* by Arna Bontemps (London: Paul Breman, 1963), by permission of Harold Ober Associates Incorporated. Copyright © 1963 by Arna Bontemps.

"Slim Greer," "Long Gone," "Return," and "Southern Road" from *Southern Road* by Sterling A. Brown (New York: Harcourt, Brace, 1932), by permission of the author. Copyright © 1932 by Harcourt, Brace and Company.

"Dark Symphony" from *Rendezvous with America* by Melvin B. Tolson (New York: Dodd, Mead, 1944), by permission of Dodd, Mead, & Company, Inc. Copyright © 1944 by Dodd, Mead, & Company, Inc."

"Runagate, Runagate" and "The Ballad of Nat Turner" from *Selected Poems* by Robert Hayden (New York: October House, 1966). Reprinted by permission of the October House, Inc. Copyright © 1966 by Robert Hayden.

"Sorrow Is the Only Faithful One," "For My Brother: VII," and "Open Letter" from *Powerful Long Ladder* by Owen Dodson. Copyright © 1946 by Farrar, Straus & Giroux, Inc. Reprinted by permission of Farrar, Strauss & Giroux, Inc.

"For My People" from *For My People* by Margaret Walker (New Haven: Yale University Press, 1942), by permission of Yale University Press. Copyright © 1942 by Yale University Press.

"Kitchenette Apartment," from *Selected Poems* (1963) by Gwendolyn Brooks, copyright 1945 by Gwendolyn Brooks Blakely; "The Womanhood: I. 2," copyright 1949 by Gwendolyn Brooks Blakely. Reprinted by permission of Harper & Row, Publishers. (The texts used in this volume are the following: "Kitchenette Building" from *A Street in Bronzeville* by Gwendolyn Brooks, "The Womanhood: I. 2" from *The Bean Eaters* by Gwendolyn Brooks.) Reprinted by permission of Harper & Row, Publishers.

"The Womanhood: XV" is from *Annie Allen* by Gwendolyn Brooks, copyright 1949 by Gwendolyn Brooks Blakely. Reprinted by permission of Harper & Row, Publishers.

From *In the Mecca* (1968) by Gwendolyn Brooks: "Malcolm X," copyright © 1967 by Gwendolyn Brooks Blakely; "The Blackstone Rangers," copyright © 1968 by Gwendolyn Brooks Blakely. Reprinted by permission of Harper & Row, Publishers.

"Primitives" and "The Melting Pot" from *Cities Burning* by Dudley Randall. Copyright © 1968 by Dudley Randall. Reprinted by permission of the author and the publisher, Broadside Press.

"Nocturne" and "Alabama Centennial" from *Star by Star* by Naomi Long Madgett, copyright © 1965 by Naomi Long Madgett. Reprinted by permission of the author.

"The Sit-In," "Death," "Love," and "Sonnet Sequence: I and Finale" are from *Katharsis* by Darwin T. Turner, copyright © 1964 by Darwin T. Turner.

"Guest Lecturer" by Darwin T. Turner is published here for the first time. Copyright © 1969 by Darwin T. Turner.

"An Agony. As Now" and "The end of man is his beauty" from the *Dead Lecturer* by LeRoi Jones, copyright © 1964 by LeRoi Jones. Reprinted by permission of The Sterling Lord Agency.

"The Idea of Ancestry" and "He Sees Through Stone" from *Poems form Prison* by Etheridge Knight, copyright © 1968 by Etheridge Knight, Detroit, Michigan. Reprinted by permission of the publisher, Dudley Randall and Broadside Press, Detroit, Michigan.

"Education" and "Back Again, Home" from *Think Black* by Don L. Lee, copyright © by Don L. Lee. Reprinted by permission of the publisher, Dudley Randall and Broadside Press, Detroit, Michigan.

Contents

Essays

Poetry

Contents   xi

Fiction

Drama

Essays

Introduction

Unlike the essayists most frequently studied in literature courses, black essayists were created by need rather than by desire. White Joseph Addison and Richard Steele established *The Tatler* and *The Spectator* periodicals to provide a medium for their polished, witty comments about the manners, morals, customs, and activities of eighteenth-century Londoners. In 1827, black David Russwurm published the first issue of *Freedom's Journal* to voice black men's cries for liberation. In nineteenth-century England, white Charles Lamb and Robert Louis Stevenson momentarily escaped from thoughts of personal troubles by writing charming, humorous, or sentimental essays. In 1829, black David Walker in a pamphlet, *Appeal*, urged slaves to rebel.

There are obvious reasons for the more utilitarian motives of black writers. First, because literate black men were scarce, most who could write effectively assumed — or were forced to assume — the responsibility of speaking for Negroes, individually or as a group. Second, publishers — whether nineteenth-century Abolitionists or twentieth-century editors — most often have been interested in publicizing the words of a black writer if he addressed himself to "The Negro Problem." Through the centuries, the specific issues have varied: protests against slavery; biographical or historical presentations of the cultural achievements of black men; protests against lynching; arguments about education, job opportunities, voting rights, legal rights, civil rights, housing. Despite the seeming variety, always there is "The Cause," developed in two dominant themes — (1) protests against unjust treatment of Negroes and (2) defenses of Negroes based on their contributions to America.

Because of this sustained emphasis upon purpose, the short nonfiction writings of black Americans have been judged more frequently according to the popular appeal of the subject-matter

1

rather than the literary skill of the writer. Nevertheless, during the nineteenth century, and increasingly during the twentieth, black writers have demonstrated rhetorical skill in short, nonfiction works. This slim volume offers a collection of works from some of the best-known and most talented Afro-American essayists of those two centuries.

"Essay," of course, is a vague term, which may describe many different forms of writing. Here, it is restricted to any short, nonfiction development of a single theme. As such, it includes pamphlets and letters, which, in the eighteenth and nineteenth centuries, were a popular form of literature. In the sense in which it is used, however, "essay" does not include speeches, designed for oral rather than written presentation. Nor does it include sections of longer works, such as histories and biographies, unless those longer works are merely collections of disparate essays rather than unified compositions. These criteria, therefore, exclude the works of some individuals who have been important as orators, historians, political leaders, religious leaders, intellectual leaders, poets, novelists, or dramatists, but who have not earned reputations for artistic excellence as essayists.

Such a collection serves four main purposes. First, by furnishing samples of the styles of the best-known black essayists, it affords a comparison of their work with that of their more frequently anthologized white contemporaries. Second, it provides opportunity for examination of the changes in style from the nineteenth to the twentieth century. Third, the personal and cultural essays offer glimpses into the thoughts of individual men about subjects other than the social, economic, and political struggles of Negroes. In all of these, this collection reflects, in miniature, the history of essay writing by black Americans.

The earliest essay known to have been published is *Address to Negroes in the State of New York* (1787), a pamphlet by Jupiter Hammon, who twenty-seven years earlier had become the first black American to publish a poem. Undistinguished in style or thought, Hammon's address urged Negroes to conduct themselves well.

This admonitory tone did not set a pattern for the essays which followed in pre-Civil War America. As has been stated earlier, most either protested against unjust treatment of Negroes or defended Negroes, primarily by pointing out their achievements and contributions.

One style of defense is apparent in *A Narrative of the Proceedings of the Black People during the Late Awful Calamity in*

Philadelphia; and a Refutation of Some Censures Thrown upon Them in Some Late Publications (1794). This pamphlet, written by Absalom Jones and Richard Allen, organizers of the Free African Society, praised Negroes for helping during an epidemic of yellow fever. In a similar vein are pamphlets by James Forten and Russell Parrott (1818), by Lydia Child (1833), and by Robert Purvis (1838). All call attention to unjust treatment of Negroes.

Another style of defense is typified by William Wells Brown's *The Black Man: His Antecedents, His Genius and His Achievements* (1863), which was expanded into *The Rising Son* (1874). Each work is a collection of essays praising the achievements of both famous and almost unknown individuals of African descent.

Most essayists writing prior to the Civil War preferred to attack slavery rather than to defend Negroes. Possibly the earliest, certainly the best-known of these, was David Walker, author of *Appeal,* an incendiary treatise urging slaves to rebel. Equally bold, if less well-known, were David Ruggles, who defended the New York Anti-Slavery Society by attacking its attackers, and Reverend Hosea Eaton, who, tracing the cultural heritage of black men, sought to prove the inferiority of white men.

Many of the attacks on slavery appeared in newspapers and periodicals edited by Negroes. The earliest of these, *Freedom's Journal* (1827), was edited by Samuel E. Cornish, a minister, and John B. Russwurm, the first black man to graduate from a college in the United States. It was followed in 1829 by *Rights for All,* edited by Cornish, and by *The Colored American* (1837–41), which included among its several editors Cornish and James McCune Smith, a graduate of the University of Glasgow, who is described by the editors of *The Negro Caravan* as "the most learned Negro of the antebellum period." Of the 100 newspapers which Smith estimated that Negroes attempted prior to 1855, the best-known and most enduring was Frederick Douglass's *The North Star,* published as a weekly from 1847 to 1860.

Not all black writers were polarized to attack or defense. In 1831, Maria W. Stewart published her first collection of devotional essays, *Religion and the Pure Principles of Morality.* In 1851 and again in 1855, William C. Nell published biographical sketches of Negroes who had served in the armed forces. In 1852, Martin R. Delany, a physician, scientist, novelist, and political writer, wrote *The Condition, Elevation, Emigration, and Destiny of the Colored People of the United States, Politically Considered.* Like Hammon before him, Delany concerned himself more with the question of what Negroes could do to improve themselves than with the problem of what was being done to them. In the same year, William Wells Brown, who wrote the first novel and the first drama by a black American, published a collection of letters, *Three Years in Europe; or, Places I Have Seen and People I Have Met*. Brown concentrated on lyric or entertaining descriptions of his observations and activities, but he never fully escaped awareness of the problems of enslaved Americans. In 1862, Alexander Crummell, one of the most learned men of his time, published *The Future of Africa*, a collection of essays and sermons objectively examining the future possibilities for Africans.

The patterns established prior to the Civil War also characterized essay writing by Negroes in the last half of the nineteenth century. For example, although he had supposed that Emancipation would relieve him from the need to continue to champion the Negro cause, Frederick Douglass kept his pen busy during Reconstruction, first joining with others to urge the passage of a Civil Rights bill, then participating in the protests against the Supreme Court decision which declared the bill unconstitutional.

Two issues in particular stimulated the interest of black essayists during the last decade of the nineteenth century and the first decade of the twentieth. One was the Booker T. Washington–W. E. B. DuBois controversy. In 1895, at the Atlanta Exposition, one of the featured speakers was Booker T. Washington, founder of Tuskegee Institute. While urging whites to grant additional economic opportunities to blacks, Washington promised that Negroes would renounce their interests in social or political equality. In addition, he stressed the need for industrial education to a degree which seemed to minimize the desirability of any other kind of education for Negroes. W. E. B. DuBois, who led the objections to Washington's conciliatory policy, was joined by such writers as Kelly Miller, a professor at Howard University, and William Monroe Trotter, a Boston journalist.

The second issue was the abusive treatment of Negroes at the end of the century. Finding sufficient support in Booker T. Washington's endorsement of social separation, Southern legislators passed laws to enforce segregation and to deprive Negroes of all political rights. And the North acquiesced. The federal government could not defend the equality of American Negroes when, to justify its foreign policy in Latin America and the Philippines, it implied that all dark-skinned people are inferior creatures who need masters. The intensified discrimination and increasing acts of violence produced such collections of essays as *The Negro Problem* (1903), to which Chesnutt, Dunbar, Washington, and DuBois contributed, and *How to Solve the Race Problem* (1904).

Despite the continuing emphasis on racial problems, three significant changes are evident in essays written between 1900 and 1960. First, improving educational opportunities so expanded the number of competent essayists that no brief history can include all of the works and writers who might be mentioned. Second, particularly after 1920, the tone of essays shifted from defense to presentation. That is, no longer feeling inferior, Negro essayists sensed no compulsion to disprove their inferiority. Instead, they concentrated on explaining their needs and their desires. Third, as pride and confidence have developed among Negro writers and other intellectuals, there has been a diminution of the tendency to overpraise members of the race. Exaltation has been replaced by critical evaluation.

The most significant collections of essays written between 1900 and 1940 are W. E. B. DuBois's *The Souls of Black Folk* (1903) and Alain Locke's *The New Negro* (1925). Both are important interpretations of the character and spirit of Negroes. DuBois's work, which is evidenced later in this book, is, despite its age, an extremely perceptive presentation of the nature and sentiments and aspirations of black people, particularly those who live in the South. *The New Negro* interprets a different group — the young Negro writers and artists who clustered in Harlem during the 1920's.

Inspired by the enthusiasm and the idealism which pervaded America in the decade following World War I, numbers of talented artists earned their first national fame. "King" Oliver, Louis Armstrong, and Duke Ellington organized their orchestras. Several Negro writers and performers collaborated on *Shuffle Along* (1921), a musical comedy, which became so popular that it was moved from Harlem to Broadway — the first time that a Broadway theatre had ever presented a musical written, produced, and performed by Negroes. Florence Mills and Josephine Baker appeared professionally for the first time.

Literary artists also flourished. Claude McKay, Jean Toomer, Jessie Fauset, Countee Cullen, Langston Hughes, Wallace Thurman, Zora Neale Hurston, and Arna Bontemps published their first significant works. James Weldon Johnson edited the first anthology of poetry by Negroes, *The Book of American Negro Poetry* (1922). Within the decade, Cullen edited a second, and

Locke co-edited a collection of plays about Negro life. *The Crisis*
and *Opportunity* magazines encouraged and published young
black writers. Benjamin Brawley continued to publicize the
achievements of Negroes, and Carter G. Woodson finished the
first edition of *The Negro in Our History*. In the midst of this
exciting decade, Locke, a professor of philosophy at Howard
University, published his record of the achievements and his
interpretation of the spirit of the "new" Negro.

Everyone, it seems, was writing essays during the Twenties.
Negro periodicals needed writers: Jessie Fauset and Dorothy West,
novelists of the Thirties, and Countee Cullen, a talented poet,
were contributing editors. Negro newspapers needed writers. *The
Baltimore Afro-American, The Chicago Defender, The Atlanta
Daily World, The Pittsburgh Courier* were merely a few which
offered space to young writers such as the satirical, outspoken
George Schuyler, who became associate editor of *The Courier*.
One-man newspapers flourished. An excellent example is Wendell
P. Dabney's *The Union*, published in Cincinnati, Ohio. Magazines
edited by whites sought black writers. They did not seek to hide
the racial identities as earlier editors had concealed those of
Charles Chesnutt and James Weldon Johnson. Instead, they
advertised the racial heritage of such a talented writer as Langston
Hughes. All these offered opportunity to the brash young Negroes,
who, exuding confidence and pride, irreverently laughed at the
old idols and ideals.

The Thirties and Forties were dominated by academic and political essayists. Such academicians as Sterling Brown and E. Frank-
lin Frazier of Howard were evaluating the literary and social
conditions of Negroes. Brown, in fact, succeeded Brawley as the
major literary historian for Negroes. *Phylon* (Atlanta University),
The Journal of Negro Education, and *The Journal of Negro
History* were only a few of the scholarly journals established to
give voice to the black academic community. Like many other
intellectuals during the Depression, several Negro writers tempo-
rarily espoused Communism: Richard Wright, W. E. B. DuBois,
and Langston Hughes were among these. Excellent histories,
biographies, and other books of nonfiction abound, and individual
essays are excellent. But in the twenty-year period, no significant
collection of essays was produced. Perhaps the most famous
individual essay is "The Ethics of Living Jim Crow" (1937),
Richard Wright's recollections of incidents which taught him the
behavior which is expected from a Southern Negro.

The past two decades have produced a spate of talented essayists and brilliant essays at a time at which critical issues have required spokesmen. At the beginning of the period is Saunders Redding's *On Being Negro in America* (1951), a collection of personal essays in which he defines and describes the black experience. The political leaders have communicated with the vast audience which reads newspapers and periodicals. Roy Wilkins, executive secretary of the National Association for the Advancement of Colored People, writes editorials published regularly in Negro newspapers, but these editorials generally are valued more for their ideas than for their style. Civil rights leaders, such as James Farmer, formerly head of the Congress on Racial Equality (CORE), and Stokely Carmichael, formerly head of the Student Non-violent Coordinating Committee (SNCC), have written articles, but their remarkable talents are best demonstrated in their speeches. Even more, Malcolm X, a brilliant leader, was an orator rather than a writer. The exception was Martin Luther King, Jr. An eloquent and moving speaker — as a minister should be, he was also a polished writer. "Letter from a Birmingham Jail," in particular, is a model of rhetoric.

Professional writers also have revitalized the essay to explain their reactions to critical issues. In *White Man, Listen!* (1964), Richard Wright examined the culture and aspirations of black people. Calvin Hernton, in *White Papers for White Americans* (1967), has interpreted current inter-racial issues and has analyzed the artistic and racial stances of Sidney Poitier and James Baldwin. Poet LeRoi Jones has set forth thoughts on various subjects in *Home: Social Essays* (1966). In *Shadow and Act* (1966) Ralph Ellison published a collection of intelligent, philosophical comments about literature and music. The most gifted professional writer and essayist, however, is James Baldwin who, more effectively than any writer since DuBois, has expressed the meaning of existence as a black man in America.

Since 1960, the work of the younger black writers has been characterized by a new awareness of the Black identity. Like the New Negro Movement of the Twenties and the Negro Revolution of the Fifties, the present Black Revolution is an effort by black Americans to clarify their identity and to determine the appropriate bases for the pride and dignity essential to the moral survival of human beings. The significant difference is that, for the first time in America, black intellectuals do not merely admit cultural differences which distinguish them from white countrymen; instead, they reject the cultural standards evolved for the white community. The distinction is sometimes subtle but significant. Young blacks do not defend the achievements of black Americans in the manner of William Wells Brown. They do not exaggerate their differences as exotic qualities in the manner of essayists of the Renaissance. Unlike Redding and Martin Luther King, they do not solicit understanding and compassion for black Americans. They even seem to reject James Baldwin's habit of criticizing Americans with the hope of reforming them. Instead, they tell Americans what is wrong with Americans, and they use individualized vocabularies and styles rather than those approved by literary tradition. This is the style of LeRoi Jones, after 1960, and of Eldridge Cleaver.

From Hammon's labored admonition to Cleaver's throbbing condemnation is less than two hundred years in time but more than two hundred light years in thought. Black essayists came of age, then rejected the age.

Like the turbulent years of the Civil War and Reconstruction, the times seem to call for men who can articulate the issues of the day, and the men are here. Each year seems to bring more essayists into view. It is not surprising. Articulate black writers exist. They are hidden only from a literary public which is hostile or indifferent to their existence. Their ideas have meaning for American readers; and, as this book illustrates, their styles can be rhetorical models in a study of the art of the essay.

William Wells Brown (1816-1884)

Letter XI

Born a slave in Lexington, Kentucky, William Wells Brown became the most productive, versatile, and popular Negro writer of his generation. When he was nineteen, he escaped from slavery, took the name "Wells Brown" in honor of a Quaker who had befriended him, and turned his attention to ways to help those who were still enslaved. As a steward on a Lake Erie steamer, he arranged for many fugitives to flee to Canada. In 1844, he became an agent of the Western New York Anti-Slavery Society and later replaced Frederick Douglass with the Massachusetts Anti-Slavery Society. Sent to Europe as a delegate to the Paris Peace Conference, he remained for several years because of the harsh fugitive slave law which Congress passed while he was abroad. While in Europe, he studied medicine, and, after manumission, returned to America to practice medicine and to write.

In his own time, Brown was well-known for lectures and letters attacking slavery. These, however, represent only part of his voluminous and varied work. His first literary work was an autobiography, *The Narrative of William W. Brown* (1847), which sold eight thousand copies within the first eight months after publication. A year later, he published a book of poems, *The Anti-Slavery Harp*. In 1852, he collected his letters into *My Three Years in Europe*, the first travel book by an Afro-American, and the following year, he published in London the first novel by a Negro

From *Three Years in Europe; or, Places I Have Seen and People I Have Met* (London: Gilpin, 1852).

9

American — *Clotel, or The President's Daughter,* the story of one
of the mulatto daughters of Thomas Jefferson's housekeeper.
Revised and published in America in 1864 as *Clotelle: A Tale of
the Southern States,* with no mention of Jefferson, the novel
became very popular among Union soldiers. In 1858, he wrote *The
Escape, or a Leap for Freedom,* the first play by a Negro American. His last published works were collections of biographical-
historical sketches: *The Black Man: His Antecedents, His Genius,
and His Achievements* (1863), *The Negro in the American Rebellion: His Heroism and His Fidelity* (1867), *The Rising Son*
(1874), and *My Southern Home, or The South and Its People*
(1880).

The following is one of a series of letters which Brown wrote
while traveling in Europe. Although Brown concerned himself
largely with lyric descriptions of people and places, he could not
forget the slavery from which he had escaped.

Letter XI

*York Minster — The Great Organ — Newcastle-on-
Tyne — The Labouring Classes — The American Slave
— Sheffield — James Montgomery.*

January, 1850.

Some days since, I left the Metropolis to fulfill a few engage-
ments to visit provincial towns; and after a ride of nearly eight
hours, we were in sight of the ancient city of York. It was night,
the moon was in her zenith, and there seemed nothing between
her and the earth but glittering gold. The moon, the stars, and
the innumerable gas-lights, gave the city a panoramic appearance.
Like a mountain starting out of a plain, there stood the Cathedral
in all its glory, looking down upon the surrounding buildings, with
all the appearance of a Gulliver standing over the Lilliputians.
Night gave us no opportunity to view the Minster. However, we
were up the next morning before the sun, and walking round the
Cathedral with a degree of curiosity seldom excited within us.
It is thought that a building of the same dimensions would take
fifty years to complete it at the present time, even with all the
improvements of the nineteenth century, and would cost no less
than the enormous sum of two millions of pounds sterling. From
what I had heard of this famous Cathedral, my expectations

were raised to the highest point; but it surpassed all the ideas that
I had formed of it. On entering the building, we lost all thought
of the external appearance by the matchless beauty of the interior. The echo produced by the tread of our feet upon the floor
as we entered, resounding through the aisles, seemed to say "Put
off your shoes, for the place whereon you tread is holy ground."
We stood with hat in hand, and gazed with wonder and astonishment down the incomparable vista of more than five hundred
feet. The organ, which stands near the centre of the building, is
said to be one of the finest in the world. A wall, in front of which
is a screen of the most gorgeous and florid architecture and executed in solid stone, separates the nave from the service choir.
The beautiful workmanship of this makes it appear so perfect,
as almost to produce the belief that it is tracery work of wood.
We ascended the rough stone steps through a winding stair to
the turrets, where we had such a view of the surrounding country,
as can be obtained from no other place. On the top of the centre
and highest turret, is a grotesque figure of a fiddler; rather a
strange looking object, we thought, to occupy the most elevated
pinnacle on the house of God. All dwellings in the neighborhood
appear like so many dwarfs couching at the feet of the Minster;
while its own vastness and beauty impress the observer with feelings of awe and sublimity. As we stood upon the top of this stu-
pendous mountain of ecclesiastical architecture, and surveyed the
picturesque hills and valleys around, imagination recalled the
tumult of the sanguinary battles fought in sight of the edifice.
The rebellion of Octavius near three thousand years ago, his
defeat and flight to the Scots, his return and triumph over the
Romans and being crowned king of all Britain; the assassination of
Oswald king of the Northumbrians; the flaying alive of Osbert;
the crowning of Richard III; the siege by William the Conqueror;
the siege by Cromwell, and the pomp and splendour with which
the different monarchs had been received in York, all appeared to
be vividly before me. While we were thus calling to our aid our
knowledge of history, a sweet peal from the lungs of the ponderous organ below cut short our stay among the turrets, and we
descended to have our organ of tune gratified, as well as to finish
the inspection of the interior.

I have heard the sublime melodies of Handel, Hayden, and
Mozart, performed by the most skilful musicians; I have listened
with delight and awe to the soul-moving compositions of those
masters, as they have been chaunted in the most magnificent

churches; but never did I hear such music, and played upon such
an instrument, as that sent forth by the great organ in the Cathedral of York. The verger took much delight in showing us the
Horn that was once mounted with gold, but is now garnished with
brass. We viewed the monuments and tombs of the departed, and
then spent an hour before the great north window. The designs
on the painted glass, which tradition states was given to the
church by five virgin sisters, is the finest thing of the kind in Great
Britain. I felt a relief on once more coming into the open air and
again beholding Nature's own sun-light. The splendid ruins of
St. Mary's Abbey, with its eight beautiful light gothic windows,
next attracted our attention. A visit to the Castle finished our
stay in York; and as we were leaving the old city we almost
imagined that we heard the chiming of the bells for the celebration
of the first Christian Sabbath, with Prince Arthur as the presiding
genius.

      *   *   *   *   *   *

England stands pre-eminently the first government in the world
for freedom of speech and of the press. Not even in our own
beloved America, can the man who feels himself oppressed speak
as he can in Great Britain. In some parts of England, however,
the freedom of thought is tolerated to a greater extent than in
others; and of the places favourable to reforms of all kinds,
calculated to elevate and benefit mankind, Newcastle-on-Tyne
doubtless takes the lead. Surrounded by innumerable coal mines,
it furnishes employment for a large labouring population, many
of whom take a deep interest in the passing events of the day,
and, consequently, are a reading class. The public debater or
speaker, no matter what may be his subject, who fails to get
an audience in other towns, is sure of a gathering in the Music Hall,
or Lecture Room in Newcastle. Here I first had an opportunity
of coming in contact with a portion of the labouring people of
Britain. I have addressed large and influential meetings in Newcastle and the neighboring towns, and the more I see and learn
of the condition of the working-classes of England the more I am
satisfied of the utter fallacy of the statements often made that
their condition approximates to that of the slaves of America.
Whatever may be the disadvantages that the British peasant
labours under, he is free; and if he is not satisfied with his
employer he can make choice of another. He also has the right
to educate his children; and he is the equal of the most wealthy

person before an English Court of Justice. But how is it with the American Slave? He has no right to himself, no right to protect his wife, his child, or his own person. He is nothing more than a living tool. Beyond his field or workshop he knows nothing. There is no amount of ignorance he is not capable of. He has not the least idea of the face of this earth, nor of the history or constitution of the country in which he dwells. To him the literature, science, and art — the progressive history, and the accumulated discoveries of byegone ages, are as if they had never been. The past is to him as yesterday, and the future scarcely more than to-morrow. Ancestral monuments, he has none; written documents fraught with cogitations of other times, he has none; and any instrumentality calculated to awaken and expound the intellectual activity and comprehension of a present or approaching generation, he has none. His condition is that of the leopard of his own native Africa. It lives, it propagates its kind; but never does it indicate a movement towards that all but angelic intelligence of man. The slave eats, drinks, and sleeps — all for the benefit of the man who claims his body as his property. Before the tribunals of his country he has no voice. He has no higher appeal than the mere will of his owner. He knows nothing of the inspired Apostles through their writings. He has no Sabbath, no Church, no Bible, no means of grace, — and yet we are told that he is as well off as the labouring classes of England. It is not enough that the people of my country should point to their Declaration of Independence which declares that "all men are created equal." It is not enough that they should laud to the skies a constitution containing boasting declarations in favour of freedom. It is not enough that they should extol the genius of Washington, the patriotism of Henry, or the enthusiasm of Otis. The time has come when nations are judged by the acts of the present instead of the past. And so it must be with America. In no place in the United Kingdom has the American Slave warmer friends than in Newcastle.

*   *   *   *   *   *

I am now in Sheffield, and have just returned from a visit to James Montgomery, the poet. In company with James Wall, Esq., I proceeded to The Mount, the residence of Mr. Montgomery; and our names being sent in, we were soon in the presence of the "Christian Poet." He held in his left hand the *Eclectic Review* for the month, and with the right gave me a hearty shake, and

bade me "Welcome to old England." He was anything but like
the portraits I had seen of him, and the man I had in my mind's
eye. I had just been reading his "Pelican Island," and I eyed
the poet with no little interest. He is under the middle size, his
forehead high and well formed, the top of which was a little bald;
his hair of a yellowish colour, his eyes rather small and deep set,
the nose long and slightly acquiline, his mouth rather small, and
not at all pretty. He was dressed in black, and a large white
cravat entirely hid his neck and chin: his having been afflicted
from childhood with saltrhum, was doubtless the cause of his chin
being so completely buried in the neckcloth. Upon the whole,
he looked more like one of our American Methodist parsons, than
any one I have seen in this country. He entered freely into conversation with us. He said he should be glad to attend my lecture
that evening, but that he had long since quit going out at night.
He mentioned having heard William Lloyd Garrison some years
before, and with whom he was well pleased. He said it had long
been a puzzle to him, how Americans could hold slaves and still
retain their membership in churches. When we rose to leave, the
old man took my hand between his two, and with tears in his
eyes said, "Go on your Christian mission, and may the Lord
protect and prosper you. Your enslaved countrymen have my
sympathy, and shall have my prayers." Thus ended our visit to
the Bard of Sheffield. Long after I had quitted the presence of the
poet, the following lines of his were ringing in my ears: —

> "Wanderer, whither dost thou roam?
> Weary wanderer, old and grey,
> Wherefore has thou left thine home,
> In the sunset of thy day.
> Welcome wanderer as thou art,
> All my blessings to partake;
> Yet thrice welcome to my heart,
> For thine injured people's sake.
> Wanderer, whither would'st thou roam?
> To what region far away?
> Bend thy steps to find a home,
> In the twilight of thy day.
> Where a tyrant never trod,
> Where a slave was never known —
> But where Nature worships God
> In the wilderness alone."

Mr. Montgomery seems to have thrown his entire soul into his
meditations on the wrongs of Switzerland. The poem from which

we have just quoted, is unquestionably one of his best productions, and contains more of the fire of enthusiasm than all his other works. We feel a reverence almost amounting to superstition, for the poet who deals with nature. And who is more capable of understanding the human heart than the poet? Who has better known the human feelings than Shakspere; better painted than Milton, the grandeur of Virtue; better sighed than Byron over the subtle weaknesses of Hope? Who ever had a sounder taste, a more exact intellect than Dante? or who has ever tuned his harp more in favour of Freedom, than our own Dante?

Frederick Douglass (1817-1895)

A Letter to Mrs. Stowe

Born a slave on the Eastern Shore of Maryland, Frederick Bailey became the best-known Negro of his generation. After escaping from slavery, Bailey, who had taught himself to read and to write, assumed the name of Douglass and was persuaded to work as an agent for the Massachusetts Anti-Slavery Society. One of the most gifted orators in a century which produced Daniel Webster and William Jennings Bryan, the handsome, muscular Douglass was so articulate that pro-slavery skeptics doubted that he had ever been a slave. To refute the allegation, he wrote *Narrative of the Life of Frederick Douglass* (1845), which he later expanded into *My Bondage and My Freedom* (1855) and *The Life and Times of Frederick Douglass* (1891). After a trip to England in 1845, where he was lionized, Douglass became increasingly disenchanted with William Lloyd Garrison and other members of the Massachusetts Anti-Slavery Society. He opposed their attempts to reject the Constitution as a pro-slavery document, and he argued for the use of direct political action as the most effective means of overthrowing slavery. Above all, however, he resented their attempts to restrict his speeches to a mere recitation of his experiences as a slave; he wanted the freedom to assist the Abolitionists in shaping the policy of the movement. In 1847,

From *The Mind of the Negro as Reflected in Letters Written during the Crisis,* edited by Carter G. Woodson (Lancaster, Pa.: Association for the Study of Negro Life and History, Inc., 1926). Reprinted with the permission of The Association for the Study of Negro Life and History.

he separated from the Massachusetts Society, and began publication of a weekly, *The North Star*, later known as *Frederick Douglass's Paper*, which lasted until 1860. From 1858 to 1863, he produced *Douglass's Monthly*, and from 1869 to 1872 he wrote another weekly, *New National Era*.

Although his major talent was his oratory, his many editorials and letters evidence his ability as a writer. In the following selection, somewhat atypical in its mildness, Douglass urges for the welfare of Negroes an industrial education, comparable to that advocated by Booker T. Washington later.

Letter to Mrs. Stowe

ROCHESTER, March 8, 1853

MY DEAR MRS. STOWE:

You kindly informed me, when at your house a fortnight ago, that you designed to do something which would permanently contribute to the improvement and elevation of the free coloured people in the United States. You especially expressed interest in such of this class as had become free by their own exertions, and desired most of all to be of service to them. In what manner and by what means you can assist this class most successfully, is the subject upon which you have done me the honour to ask my opinion. . . I assert then that *poverty, ignorance* and *degradation* are the combined evils; or in other words, these constitute the social disease of the free coloured people of the United States.

To deliver them from this triple malady, is to improve and elevate them, by which I mean, simply to put them on an equal footing with their white fellow countrymen in the sacred right to *"Life, Liberty*, and the pursuit of happiness." I am for no fancied or artificial elevation, but only ask fair play. How shall this be obtained? I answer, first, not by establishing for our use high schools and colleges. Such institutions are, in my judgment, beyond our immediate occasions and are not adapted to our present most pressing wants. High schools and colleges are excellent institutions, and will in due season be greatly subservient to our progress; but they are the result, as well as they are the demand of a point of progress, which we as a people have not yet attained. Accustomed as we have been, to the rougher and harder modes of living, and of gaining a livelihood, we cannot, and we ought not to hope that in a single leap from our low condition, we can reach that of

Minister, Lawyers, Doctors, Editors, Merchants, etc. These will doubtless be attained by us; but this will only be, when we have patiently and laboriously, and I may add, successfully, mastered and passed through the intermediate gradations of agriculture and the mechanical arts. Besides, there are — and perhaps this is a better reason for my view of this case — numerous institutions of learning in this country, already thrown open to coloured youth. To my thinking, there are quite as many facilities now afforded to the coloured people, as they can spare the time from the sterner duties of life, to avail themselves of. In their present condition of poverty, they cannot spare their sons and daughters two or three years at boarding-schools or colleges, to say nothing of finding the means to sustain them while at such institutions. I take it, therefore, that we are well provided for in this respect; and that it may be fairly inferred from the fact, that the facilities for our education, so far as schools and colleges in the Free States are concerned, will increase quite in proportion with our future wants. Colleges have been open to coloured youth in this country during the last dozen years. Yet few comparatively, have acquired a classical education; and even this few have found themselves educated far above a living condition, there being no methods by which they could turn their learning to account. Several of this latter class have entered the ministry; but you need not be told that an educated people is needed to sustain an educated ministry. There must be a certain amount of cultivation among the people to sustain such a ministry. At present we have not that cultivation amongst us; and therefore, we value in the preacher, strong lungs, rather than high learning. I do not say, that educated ministers are not needed amongst us, far from it! I wish there were more of them! but to increase their number, is not the largest benefit you can bestow upon us.

We have two or three coloured lawyers in this country; and I rejoice in the fact; for it affords very gratifying evidence of our progress. Yet it must be confessed, that in point of success, our lawyers are as great failures as our ministers. White people will not employ them to the obvious embarrassment of their causes, and the blacks, taking their *cue* from the whites, have not sufficient confidence in their abilities to employ them. Hence educated coloured men, among the coloured people, are at a very great discount.

It would seem that education and emigration go together with us, for as soon as a man rises amongst us, capable, by his genius and learning, to do us great service, just so soon he finds that he can serve himself better by going elsewhere. In proof of this, I might instance the Russwurms, the Garnets, the Wards, the Crummells and others, all men of superior ability and attainments, and capable of removing mountains of prejudice against their race, by their simple presence in the country; but these gentlemen, finding themselves embarrassed here by the peculiar disadvantages to which I have referred, disadvantages in part growing out of their education, being repelled by ignorance on the one hand, and prejudice on the other, and having no taste to continue a contest against such odds, they have sought more congenial climes, where they can live more peaceable and quiet lives. I regret their election, but I cannot blame them; for with an equal amount of education and the hard lot which was theirs, I might follow their example. . . .

There is little reason to hope that any considerable number of the free coloured people will ever be induced to leave this country; even if such a thing were desirable. This black man — *un*like the Indian — loves civilization. He does not make very great progress in civilization himself but he likes to be in the midst of it, and prefers to share its most galling evils, to encountering barbarism. Then the love of the country, the dread of isolation, the lack of adventurous spirit, and the thought of seeming to desert their "brethren in bonds," are a powerful check upon all schemes of colonization, which look to the removal of the coloured people, without the slaves. The truth is, dear madam, we are *here*, and here we are likely to remain. Individuals emigrate—nations never. We have grown up with this republic, and I see nothing in her character, or even in the character of the American people as yet, which compels the belief that we must leave the United States. If then, we are to remain here, the question for the wise and good is precisely that you have submitted to me — namely: What can be done to improve the condition of the free people of colour in the United States?

The plan which I humbly submit in answer to this inquiry—and in the hope that it may find favour with you, and with the many friends of humanity who honour, love, and cooperate with you—is the establishment in Rochester, N. Y., or in some other part of the United States equally favourable to such an enterprise, of an INDUSTRIAL COLLEGE in which shall be taught several important branches of the mechanical arts. This college to be opened to coloured youth. I will pass over the details of such an institution as I propose. . . . Never having had a day's schooling in all my life I may not be expected to map out the details of a plan so comprehensive as that involved in the idea of a college. I repeat, then,

I leave the organisation and administration to the superior wisdom of yourself and the friends who second your noble efforts.

The argument in favour of an Industrial College — a college to be conducted by the best men — and the best workmen which the mechanical arts can afford; a college where coloured youth can be instructed to use their hands, as well as their heads; where they can be put into possession of the means of getting a living whether their lot in after life may be cast among civilized or uncivilized men; whether they choose to stay here, or prefer to return to the land of their fathers — is briefly this: Prejudice against the free coloured people in the United States has shown itself nowhere so invincible as among mechanics. The farmer and the professional man cherish no feeling so bitter as that cherished by these. The latter would starve us out of the country entirely. At this moment I can more easily get my son into a lawyer's office to learn law than I can into a blacksmith's shop to blow the bellows and to wield the sledge-hammer. Denied the means of learning useful trades we are pressed into the narrowest limits to obtain a livelihood. In times past we have been the hewers of wood and the drawers of water for American society, and we once enjoyed a monopoly in menial enjoyments, but this is so no longer. Even these enjoyments are rapidly passing away out of our hands. The fact is — every day begins with the lesson, and ends with the lesson—that coloured men must learn trades; and must find new employment; new modes of usefulness to society, or that they must decay under the pressing wants to which their condition is rapidly bringing them.

We must become mechanics; we must build as well as live in houses; we must make as well as use furniture; we must construct bridges as well as pass over them, before we can properly live or be respected by our fellow men. We need mechanics as well as ministers. We need workers in iron, clay, and leather. We have orators, authors, and other professional men, but these reach only a certain class, and get respect for our race in certain select circles. To live here as we ought we must fasten ourselves to our country-men through their every day cardinal wants. We must not only be able to *black* boots, but to *make* them. At present we are un-known in the Northern States as mechanics. We give no proof of genius or skill at the county, State, or national fairs. We are unknown at any of the great exhibitions of the industry of our fellow-citizens, and being unknown we are unconsidered.

The fact that we make no show of our ability is held conclusive of our inability to make any, hence all the indifference and con-tempt with which incapacity is regarded, fall upon us, and that too, when we have had no means of disproving the infamous opinion of our natural inferiority. I have during the last dozen years denied before the Americans that we are an inferior race; but this has been done by arguments based upon admitted principles rather than by the presentation of facts. Now, firmly believing, as I do, that there are skill, invention, power, industry, and real mechanical genius, among the coloured people, which will bear favourable testimony for them, and which only need the means to develop them, I am decidedly in favour of the establishment of such a college as I have mentioned. The benefits of such an institution would not be confined to the Northern States, nor to the free coloured people. They would extend over the whole Union. The slave not less than the freeman would be benefited by such an institution. It must be confessed that the most powerful arguments now used by the Southern slaveholder, and the one most soothing to his conscience, is that derived from the low condition of the free coloured people of the North. I have long felt that too little attention has been given by our truest friends in this country to removing this stumbling block out of the way of the slave's liberation.

The most telling, the most killing refutation of slavery, is the presentation of an industrious, enterprising, thrifty, and intelligent free black population. Such a population I believe would rise in the Northern States under the fostering care of such a college as that supposed.

To show that we are capable of becoming mechanics I might adduce any amount of testimony; but dear madam, I need not ring the changes on such a proposition. There is no question in the mind of any prejudiced person that the negro is capable of making a good mechanic. Indeed, even those who cherish the bitterest feelings towards us have admitted that the apprehension that negroes might be employed in their stead, dictated the policy of excluding them from trades altogether. But I will not dwell upon this point as I fear I have already trespassed too long upon your precious time, and written more than I ought to expect you to read.

Allow me to say in conclusion, that I believe every intelligent coloured man in America will approve and rejoice at the establishment of some such institution as that now suggested. There are many respectable coloured men, fathers of large families, having boys nearly grown up, whose minds are tossed by day and by night with the anxious enquiry, "what shall I do with my boys?" Such an institution would meet the wants of such persons. Then, too, the establishment of such an institution would be in character with the eminently practical philanthropy of your trans-Atlantic friends. America could scarcely object to it as an attempt to agitate the public mind on the subject of slavery, or to *dissolve the Union*. It could not be tortured into a cause for hard words by the American people, but the noble and good of all classes would see in the effort an excellent motive, a benevolent object, temperately, wisely, and practically manifested.

Wishing, you, dear madam, renewed health, a pleasant passage, and safe return to your native land.

I am most truly, your grateful friend,

FREDERICK DOUGLASS.

Alexander Crummell (1819-1898)

The Negro Race not under a Curse

Alexander Crummell, an Episcopalian minister, was one of the intellectual leaders of Negroes during the last decades of the nineteenth century. His fame has diminished since his death, and today he is almost unknown, even among historians. In his time, however, he earned lavish praise from such distinguished contemporaries as William Wells Brown, who, in *Three Years in Europe*, recorded their meeting at Cambridge, and W. E. B. DuBois, whose eloquent tribute is printed in a later section of this book.

Born in New York City and educated in theology in Boston, Crummell received a Bachelor of Arts from Cambridge University (England) in 1853. After spending the next twenty years in Liberia, he returned to America to become rector at St. Paul's Episcopal Church in Washington, D. C.

Crummell's literary reputation depends largely upon three collections of essays and sermons — *The Future of Africa* (1862), *The Greatness of Christ, and Other Sermons* (1882), and *Africa and America* (1892). As a theologian, Crummell urged young Negroes to develop the moral strength to become teachers and leaders of the race. Frequently, however, topical issues compelled him to defend Negroes against unjust attacks.

In the following selection, which reveals his characteristic logic, directness, and precise style, Crummell refutes a popular justifi-

---

From *The Future of Africa*. (New York: Charles Scribner, 1862).

cation of slavery — the belief that it was a curse which Noah
placed on Ham.

The Negro Race not under a Curse*

The chief object of this paper is to show the falsity of the
opinion that the sufferings and the slavery of the Negro race are
the consequence of the curse of Noah, as recorded in Genesis
ix. 25. That this is a general, almost universal, opinion in the
Christian world, is easily proven. During the long controversy
upon the slavery question which has agitated Christendom, no
argument has been so much relied upon, and none more frequently
adduced. It was first employed in vindication of the lawfulness
of the slave trade. When the slave trade was abolished, and
philanthropists commenced their warfare against the system of
slavery, the chief pro-slavery argument brought forward in support of that system was this text. The friends of the Negro race
have had to meet it when asserted by statesmen in the Legislature,
and they have had to contend against the earnest affirmation of
it by learned divines. And now, although both slavery and the
slave trade are condemned by the general sentiment of the
Christian world, yet the same interpretation is still given to this
text, and the old opinion which was founded on it still gains
credit and receives support. Its insidious influence relaxes the
missionary zeal of even many pious persons, who can see no hope
for Africa, nor discover any end to the slavery of its sons. It is
found in books written by learned men; and it is repeated in
lectures, speeches, sermons, and common conversation. So strong
and tenacious is the hold which it has taken upon the mind of
Christendom, that it seems almost impossible to uproot it. Indeed,

---

*This paper was originally written as a letter, in reply to another from an
eminent philanthropic lady in Cheltenham, England. She communicated it to
the then Editor of the London "Christian Observer," in which monthly it was
published in September, 1852. Subsequent to this, in compliance with the
request of many persons, it was rewritten and prepared, in its present form,
for publication as a tract. Perhaps the Author may be permitted to say here,
that it has had the advantage of being read by the late Rev. G. Stanley
Faber, D.D., of Sherburne, the distinguished author of many learned works,
who expressed his approbation of it, and presented the writer with his
learned and able work, "PROPHETICAL DISSERTATIONS," in which the writer
found that Mr. Faber had, several years ago, taken the same view of Gen.
ix. 25, as is contained in this article.

it is an almost foregone conclusion, that the Negro race is an accursed race, weighed down, even to the present, beneath the burden of an ancestral malediction. The prejudice against this race seems as wide, as absolute, and as decided, as that entertained by the Jews against the Samaritans.

2. The Opinions of Commentators and Theological Writers.

A very few references to writers in the past and at the present will show the prejudiced views of even eminently good men upon this topic. POOLE admits the primary and pointed application of the curse to Canaan; he also acknowledges the subsequent power and greatness of the other three sons of Ham, and the spiritual blessedness which ultimately attended them; yet, with singular inconsistency, in another place, he involves Ham, the father, in the curse, which he declares to have been pointed at his son Canaan. He says: "When Canaan is mentioned, *Ham* is not exempted from the curse, but rather more deeply plunged into it; whilst he is pronounced accursed, not only in his person, (which is manifestly supposed by his commission of that sin for which the curse was inflicted,) but also in his posterity, which doubtless was a great aggravation of his grief."*

The learned and pious MATTHEW HENRY says: "He (that is, Noah) pronounces a curse on Canaan, the son of Ham, in whom Ham himself is cursed; either because this son of his was now more guilty than the rest, or because the posterity of this son were afterward to be rooted out of their land, to make room for Israel."† Again, in another place, speaking of the division of the families of the earth, he says: "The birthright was now to be divided between Shem and Japheth, *Ham being utterly discarded.*"

BISHOP NEWTON, in the first place, applies this prophecy to Canaan and his descendants; but he afterward gives a fanciful correction of the text, on the authority of the Septuagint and the Arabic version; and then asks: "May we not suppose that the copyist, by mistake, wrote only *Canaan,* instead of *Ham, the father of Canaan,* and that the whole passage was originally thus: And Ham, the father of Canaan, saw the nakedness of his father,

---

*Poole on Gen. ix. 25.
†See Henry's Commentary on Gen. ix. 25.

&c. &c. And he said, Cursed be Ham, the father of Canaan, &c.?"
He then goes on to remark: "By this reading all the three sons
of Noah are included in the prophecy, whereas otherwise Ham,
who was the offender, is excluded, or is only punished in one of
his children. . . . . . . The whole continent of Africa was peopled
principally by the children of Ham; and for how many ages have
the better parts of that country lain under the dominion of the
Romans, and then of the Saracens, and now of the Turks! In
what wickedness, ignorance, barbarity, slavery, misery, live most
of the inhabitants! And of the poor Negroes, how many hundreds
every year are sold and bought like beasts in the market, and are
conveyed from one quarter of the world to do the work of beasts
in another! Nothing can be more complete than the execution of
the sentence upon *Ham*, as well as upon Canaan."*

The excellent Rev. THOMAS SCOTT says: "The frequent mention
of Ham as the father of Canaan, suggests the thought that the
latter was also criminal. . . . . . . Ham must have felt it a very
mortifying rebuke, when his own father was inspired, on this
occasion, to predict the durable oppression and slavery of his
posterity; Canaan was also rebuked by learning that the curse
would especially rest on that branch of the family which would
descend from him; for his posterity were no doubt *principally*,
though not *exclusively*, intended. . . . . . . True religion has hith-
erto flourished very little among Ham's descendants; they remain
to this day almost entire strangers to Christianity, and their
condition, in every age, has remarkably coincided with this
prediction."†

Similar views are expressed by KEITH, who remarks: "The
unnatural conduct of Ham, and the dutiful and respectful behavior of Shem and Japheth toward their aged father, gave rise
to the prediction of the future fate of their posterity, without
being at all assigned as the cause of that fate. . . . . Though long
banished from almost all Europe, slavery still lingers in Africa.
That country is distinguished, above every other, as the land of
slavery. Slaves at home, and transported for slavery, the poor
Africans, the descendants of Ham, are the servants of servants,
or slaves to others."‡

In a popular work much used in the schools and the universities
of England, this comment upon the curse of Noah is found:
These prophecies (Gen. ix. 25–27) have since been wonderfully

---

*See Newton on Prophecies, Dissertation I.

†Scott on Gen. ix. 24, 25.

‡See Keith on the Prophecies.

fulfilled; the Egyptians were afflicted with various plagues; the land of *Canaan*, eight hundred years afterward, was delivered by God into the hands of the Israelites under Joshua, who destroyed great numbers and obliged the rest to fly, some into Africa, and others into various countries; what their condition is in Africa, we know at this day."*

The Rev. Dr. CUMMING, of London, thus discourses upon this subject:

"Read the predictions respecting *Ham*, that his descendants, the children of Africa, should be bondsmen of bondsmen. England nobly sacrificed twenty millions, in order to wash her hands of the heinous crime and horrible abominations of slavery, and sent her cruisers to sweep the seas of every craft that ventured to encourage the inhuman traffic. But while God is not the author of sin, nor man irresponsible for his crimes, slavery has grown under all the attempts to extinguish it, and shot up in spite of the power of Britain and the piercing protest of outraged humanity, the hour of its extinction not having yet come; thereby showing that heaven and earth may pass away, but that one jot or tittle of God's word cannot pass away."†

3. The Real State of the Case.

The writer of this paper differs from the distinguished persons here referred to. He regards the prevalent opinions upon this subject a sad preversion of Biblical history on the part of the intelligent minds that have stereotyped them, during the last century and a half, in the literature and theology of the English language.

In considering this subject, there is one material point which should be carefully noticed — a point upon which nearly all writers upon the subject have greatly erred: THE CURSE WAS PRONOUNCED UPON CANAAN, NOT UPON HAM. "And he said, Cursed be Canaan, a servant of servants shall he be unto his brethren." Gen. ix. 25. This is the utterance of the Divine word, clear, plain, distinct. There may be differences of opinion as to the cause, the nature, the extent, the justice, and the influence of this judgment; but as it respects *the person* who is cursed, the word of God is

---

*Analysis of Scripture History, by Rev. W. H. Pinnock, B. C. L. *"What their condition is in Africa, we know at this day."* Whose* condition? Some would suppose that Africa was peopled in the mass by Canaanites. Surely this is loose writing, and inaccurate history.

†Exeter Hall Lecture.

specific and pointed: "CURSED BE CANAAN;" and in this we have the curse, *direct.*

No one, indeed, can deny that learned and distinguished divines have thought that *Ham* fell under the dire influence of this strong malediction. The suppositions of such most eminent divines as Poole, and Henry, and Newton, have already been presented. But what are they when contrasted with the distinct and emphatic word of God? They *suppose* that Ham was cursed; the word of God says, "CURSED BE CANAAN."

But, as though the Holy Spirit intended that there should be no error or mistake in the matter, we find the curse upon Canaan repeated, that is, by implication, again and again, in this same chapter, (chap. ix.,) both in the context and sub-text. In the 18th verse of this (ix.) chapter it is written: "And the sons of Noah, that went forth of the ark, were Shem, and Ham, and Japheth; and *Ham is the father of Canaan.*" Why are Shem and Japheth spoken of *individually,* while Ham is mentioned *in relation to his son Canaan?** Why, there can be no doubt that this form of expression was *designed* to point out *Canaan* as a marked individual.

In verses 26 and 27 we find the same form of expression *twice,* "and Canaan shall be his servant." We now have the curse *indirect.* In both cases, however, it is manifest that Canaan was the person subjected to this curse. Neither directly nor indirectly is Ham, the father, denounced by Noah; and therefore we have the authority of the word of God, for the affirmation that the curse was *not* pronounced upon Ham.†

Now, in order to involve the Negro race in this malediction, one of two things must be proven: either,

1st. That Noah, in mentioning Canaan, intended to include *all* the children of Ham; or,

2d. That the Negro race, in Africa, are the descendants of Canaan.

---

* Mr. Faber asks, "Why Ham should be specially distinguished as the father of Canaan, while, *in the very same prophecy,* his two brothers are simply mentioned as Shem and Japheth, without any parallel genealogical adjunct to their names." See "Prophetical Dissertations:" Dis. ii. p. 102, note.

†In an old work entitled "The General History of the World," I find the following sentence: "Some have believed that Noah cursed Canaan because he could not well have cursed Ham himself, whom God had not long before blessed." And he refers to Sermon 29, Chrysostom in Genesis.

4. The Whole Family of Ham not Accursed.

It cannot be proven that *all* the sons of Ham were included in the curse pronounced upon Canaan. Ham had four sons: "And the sons of Ham, Cush, and Mizraim, and Phut, and Canaan." Gen. x. 6. Canaan, it is evident, was the *youngest* of these sons, and Cush the *eldest*.

Now, the common rule among men is that "THE GREATER IN-CLUDES THE LESS." If, therefore, Cush, the *eldest* of the sons of Ham, had been the person cursed, then there would have been some strength and plausibility in the plea, that, according to this principle, a curse upon him, that is, Cush, as the head and representative of the family, involved a curse upon his three younger brothers. But the curse was upon the youngest, *Canaan*. And there is no received rule among men, the reverse of that here quoted, that is, that "the less includes the greater."

So, also, if Ham himself had been the person designated by Noah, then all disputation upon this matter would be, at once, at an end; for then the inference would be natural, legitimate, and indisputable, that *all* his posterity were implicated in the curse which fell upon himself. But this fact is nowhere stated in Scripture. IT DOES, INDEED, RECORD GOD'S BLESSING UPON HAM AND HIS POSTERITY;* although this is universally passed over and ignored; but that he was cursed by Noah is only one of the con-jectures of men. In the sacred record we find Canaan's name, and his only, mentioned as the person cursed.

It is mentioned, moreover, in such a way as though the Divine mind intended there should be a marked significance connected with it. For why, when the Scripture narrative is so careful to

---

* It is objected to the view taken, in this paper, of Gen. ix. 25, that Ham is left neither blessed nor cursed; and hence divines include him in the curse on Canaan. But it is a singular fact, that all the commentators neglect to notice the fact that Ham had just received a blessing from God.

In Genesis ix, 1, we read: "And God blessed Noah and his sons, and said unto them, Be fruitful," &c., &c. And in verses 8 and 12 it reads: "And God spake unto Noah, and to his sons *with him*, saying, And I, behold, I establish my covenant with you, and with your seed after you. . . . . . And God said, This is the token of the covenant which I make between me and you, and every living creature that is with you, *for perpetual generations.*"

The question here arises "Does Noah's curse (*incidental to Ham's young-est son*) override the blessing of God, for perpetual generations, to Ham and his seed, in the general and particular blessings of Gen. ix. 9 and 12? Does the cure of *man* supersede and set aside the *covenanted* blessings of God?

give the names of Ham's four sons, according to seniority, why
is *Canaan's name* — the name of the youngest — selected, singled
out, and repeated, no less than *five* different times, in the brief
narrative which records this remarkable event?* Surely for no
other reason than to mark HIM distinctly as *the* individual referred to, and to separate his three elder brothers from the curse.

The argument of an American writer upon this point is of great
force, and deserves notice. He adduces "two rules of law and
logic, viz.: enumeration weakens, in cases not enumerated; exceptions strengthen, in cases not excepted. In the curse Canaan is
enumerated, and therefore the probability of its application to
his brothers is *weakened* by this enumeration, and in the blessings
bestowed upon Shem and Japheth, in the next two verses, Canaan,
and not Ham and his posterity, is excepted; and therefore the
probability of the exclusive application of the curse to Canaan
is strengthened by this exception."†

The testimony of Josephus accords with this theory. He says:
"Noah spared Ham by reason of his nearness of blood, but
cursed his posterity; and when the rest of them (*i. e.*, of the children of Ham) escaped that curse, God inflicted it on the children
of Canaan.‡

This argument is strengthened and confirmed by a reference
to the counterpart of this curse, which is seen in God's dealings
with the Canaanites. It is seen in those severe commands to the
Hebrews on their entrance into the promised land, to expel and
destroy the devoted Canaanites. The indictment against this
wicked and profane people is written, in fearfully descriptive
terms, in the 18th chapter of Leviticus, which enumerates the
aggravated crimes on account of which the Almighty was about
calling them to judgment.§ The events which followed, in consequence of the commands of Jehovah to the Hebrews, have
always been taken as the fulfilment of this prediction of Noah.
By Jew and Christian Gentile, in the early periods of the Church,
and in more recent times by writers upon prophecy, and by
commentators upon the Bible, the havoc and destruction visited
upon the Canaanites have been regarded, not only as a punishment for their wickedness, but also as the counterpart to the

---

* See Genesis ix, 18, 22, 25, 26, 27.

†I cannot give the name of the writer of the above. I found this extract in
the fragment of a newspaper.

‡Josephus, "Antiquities of the Jews," B. i. Ch. vi.

§See Lev. xviii. 24–28.

prediction of Noah, and as a complete fulfilment of his prophetic curse upon Canaan.

To sum up, then, we have, for the application and *limitation* of this curse to Canaan and his posterity only, the following facts and arguments:

1. The text of Genesis.
2. Two fundamental rules of law and logic.
3. The testimony of Josephus.
4. The Scriptural account of the fate of the Canaanites.

5. The Negro Race not the Descendants of Canaan.

But, in reply to the above arguments, it may be said that, granting that the three elder sons of Ham were not under the curse, nevertheless the Negro race may be the descendants of Canaan, and hence under the infliction of this prophetic judgment.

The facts of the case warrant the most positive denial of the assertion that the Negro race are the descendants of Canaan. In fact, of all the sons of Ham, *Canaan was the only one who never entered Africa.* Of this there is abundant evidence, sacred and profane.

The evidence, so far as *Scripture* is concerned, is given us in Gen. x. 19: "And the border of the Canaanites was from Sidon, as thou comest to Gerar, unto Gaza; as thou goest unto Sodom and Gomorrah, and Admah, and Zeboim, even unto Lasha." The locality here designated is evidently the land of Palestine, and in Asia; and in the Pentateuch, this region is frequently called the land of Canaan.

A reference to the names of the descendants of Canaan will tend to place this still more distinctly before us. In Gen. x. 15–18, we find the following statement: "And Canaan begat Sidon, his first-born, and Heth, and the Jebusite, and the Amorite, and the Girgasite, and the Hivite, and the Arkite," &c., &c. These names, most surely, are not African, nor do they indicate African localities. We recognize in SIDON the name of that city, celebrated in history for its commerce and luxury, which stood on the Mediterranean, at the north of Palestine. The Hittites were the descendants of Heth, and lived in nearly the same quarter. The Jebusites were the descendants of JEBUS, and their locality was the spot on which Jerusalem was built. And the Amorites, Girgasites, &c., are frequently mentioned in the Old Testament as inhabitants of the land of Canaan.

The *profane* historical evidence is brief, but clear, weighty, and decisive: it is the evidence of Josephus, who says: "Canaan, the fourth son of Ham, inhabited the country now called Judea, and called it, from his own name, Canaan."*

It appears, then, from the evidence adduced, that this curse, in its *significance* and LOCALITY, is altogether Asiatic, and not African. Asia was the field on which the Canaanites moved, and whence their history is derived. The Canaanites of old were Asiatics, that is, so far as residence is concerned; and the mass of their descendants, if existing anywhere, are the modern Syrians.

Again, the above facts and arguments may be opposed by some, by the fact that *some* of the Canaanites established themselves on the north coast of Africa, in a colony. But it is quite evident that the Negro race, which mostly peoples that vast continent, could not have proceeded from them: —

1. Because the establishment of Carthage, the great Phœnician (Canaanitish) colony, was at a late period in the history of the world;† but the permanent division of races had been formed centuries anterior to this event; and the Negro race, as a race, had long before sprung into existence.

2. If this were not the case, the probability is that the great desert would have prevented their being mingled with the mass of the aborigines who live south of the desert; and it is almost certain that the interior of Africa was first reached by the way of Egypt.

3. History informs us that Carthage, a colony, grew up, *by itself*, in one locality; flourished for a space, and then sank to decay; while it does *not* inform us that Carthage was the mother of nations, the founder of a race.

Moreover, the fact should not be forgotten that the blood of the Canaanites was more mingled with that of Europeans than with Africans; for they formed *more* colonies in Europe than in Africa, and their influence was stronger in Europe than in Africa; and they have left behind more numerous marks and monuments of their power in Europe than in Africa. Indeed, almost every vestige of their former might, in Africa, has been obliterated.

When the Israelites entered the promised land, they broke up the political establishment of the Canaanites, destroyed large

---

* Josephus, "Antiquities of the Jews," B. i. Ch. vi.

†The foundation of Carthage, Utica, Septis, &c., took place, according to Heeren, between 1000–500 B. C. See "Heeren's Historical Researches," Vol. i. Ch. ii.

numbers of them, and drove many of them out of the land. These
latter went northward, and at first settled in the country called
Phœnicia; and from this they received the name Phœnicians. And
here it was that the Canaanites gave evidence of being a wonderfully active, enterprising, ingenious, and intellectual people — as
much, if not more so, than any people of ancient times. They were
a maritime nation, and their adventurous spirit led to the far
regions of the North, and southward around the Cape of Good
Hope, which they doubled, traversing thence the countries border-
ing on the Indian Ocean.* They had commercial intercourse all
through the Mediterranean Sea. Their ships aand trade reached
all along the coast of Europe, even beyond the pillars of Hercules,
to Britain and Ireland. In many of these places they planted
colonies, on both sides of the Mediterranean; carrying with them
arts, letters, commerce, and civilization, to people yet rude and
uncultivated. It appears to be an established fact that one of
their colonies was planted on the coasts of both Spain and Ireland; and thus some of the Celts of the present day may now have
some of the blood of the Canaanites flowing through their veins.†

"The establishment of a Canaanitish colony on the coast of
Africa is no more evidence that the African race proceeded from
Canaan, than the similar fact in Ireland and Spain is evidence
that Europeans had such an origin.

6. Whence is the Origin of the Negro Race?

Here it may be well to give a passing notice to the question,
Who were the progenitors of the Negro race?

The writer of this paper does not pretend to speak with certainty upon this question. The following, he thinks, is a true statement of the matter.

Africa was originally settled by the descendants of Ham, *excepting his son Canaan.* Ham himself is supposed to have emigrated
to Egypt; and Egypt, in Scripture, is called the "land of Ham."‡
There he attained to state and eminence; and after his death, it is
said, was deified by his descendants. The supreme deity AM of the
Egyptians, it is stated, signifies his name; e. g., (H)AM; and the
Jupiter AMMON, in honor of whom a temple was erected, is supposed to indicate HAM.

---

* See Heeren's Historical Researches, Vol. i. Ch. iii.
† See Heeren's Historical Researches, Vol. i. Ch. ii. Also, Ezekiel xxvii.
‡Ps. cvi. 22.

Africa was peopled by Ham in the line of his *three* sons, CUSH, MIZRAIM, and PHUT.

1. Cush, the eldest, and undoubtedly the most distinguished of all the sons of Ham, appears to have been the great progenitor of the Negro race. His name is also associated, with distinction, with Asia. The records of these early periods of the world's history are by no means clear and distinct; but Cush appears to have gone, at first, into Arabia, between the Euphrates and the Tigris, the country sometimes called Chaldea, and in Scripture, Shiraz. Thence his descendants spread themselves abroad through the beautiful and luxuriant region of "Araby the blest," and eastward, by the Persian Gulf, to the Orient. Here, in the first place, Cush and his children distinguished themselves. Here Nimrod, his son, became the first of kings, and reared up the mighty city of Babylon, and founded Nineveh. In the course of time some of the descendants of Cush crossed the Straits of Babelmandel, turned their steps southward toward the source of the Nile, and settled in the land south of the Mountains of the Moon; and from them the Negro race has sprung, although the Cushites were, undoubtedly, greatly mingled in blood with the children of Mizraim and Phut.

2. Mizraim was the father of the Egyptians. Wherever, in our version, we find the name Egypt, in the original it is Mizraim.

3. Of Phut, the *third* son of Ham, we have but little more than conjecture. It is the generally received opinion that his descendants settled on the northern Atlantic coast of Africa — Libya, and the adjacent parts, the country of the Moors.

7. Slavery not Peculiar to the Negro Race.

But there may be persons who will still object that the severities of the African slave trade, and the horrors of Negro slavery, are peculiar and significant, indicate something special in their inflictions, outweigh all theory and argument, and give strength and authority to the opinion that the curse was pronounced upon Ham, and that the children of Africa have participated in its consequences. The reply to this is:

1st. That the severities of the African slave trade, and the horrors of Negro slavery, as exhibited in European colonies and possessions, are entirely *modern* — confined to a short period in the history of the world, and therefore not a true exemplification of the *general* condition of the Negro race.

2dly. That while it is true that servitude and slavery have existed in some form throughout Africa, in every stage of its history, it is also true that *servitude and slavery have been the general condition of society, in all nations, in all countries, at all periods of time,* and are not in any manner peculiar to the black man, or the Negro race.

In connection with this fact:

3dly. That if the general existence of slavery in a race, or among a people, is to be taken as an indication that a curse has descended upon them, then the mass of the Turks, Poles, Russians, Circassians, are lineal descendants of Canaan, and therefore "doomed races." And in the same category the larger portion of even Anglo-Saxons must be placed; for, but a short time since, a multitude of Britons were absolutely "goods and chattels," under the name of "villeins."

8. The Universal Prevalence of Slavery.

Those persons, surely, display great ignorance, who associate the system of slavery, specially and alone, with the Negro race, and who are not aware of its existence in other races, and in all periods of history. There are no people, whether ancient or modern, with whom slavery has not been, at one period or other, a national institution. Indeed, how very little freedom has ever been enjoyed in this sin-ridden world of ours! Among the various evils to which society has been subjected, none have been more general or more deadly than slavery. No portion of the globe has been exempt from this curse. Slavery existed among all the nations of antiquity of whom we have any knowledge. It was maintained among the Assyrians and Babylonians. That slavery existed among the Egyptians is evidenced by the testimony of the Bible. Joseph was sold by his brethren; and sold again to an officer of Pharaoh's household. The Canaanites, after they were driven from the land of Canaan, and set up empire in Tyre and Sidon, trafficked in the bodies of men. The Greeks and Romans held vast numbers of slaves; they were great traders in human flesh, and distinguished themselves beyond all other people as cruel slave-holders; they kept their slaves in the deepest subjection, and visited upon them the most horrible cruelties, as is instanced in the condition of the Helots.

In more recent times, we see the same prevalence of slavery among the nations. The whole western part of Europe, not long since, was in a state of abject vassalage. In Russia, twenty millions of serfs, even *now*, in wretchedness and poverty, suffer the infliction of the knout, and are subject to irresponsible power and unrestrained tyranny. And if all the truth were known, it would, no doubt, be seen, that some of the convulsions which have recently occurred on the continent, were, in fact, insurrections of slaves battling for personal freedom.

The same state of things has existed even in England. A few centuries since, Saxons were bought and sold in Ireland and Rome. At one time slaves and cattle were a kind of currency in the land; and down to the period of the Reformation, human beings were "marketable commodities."

In the light of these facts, how ignorant and idle is it to regard the children of Africa as the subjects of a peculiar curse, because, in the mysterious providence of God, they have participated in the miseries and the sufferings of a cruel system, which has existed from the dawn of history, *in every quarter of the globe*, among every people under the sun.*

9. The Cause of the Slave Trade, and of Negro Slavery in Christian Countries.

It was the discovery of America, and the development of the treasures of the New World, which led to all the accumulated horrors of the slave trade, and the dreadful barbarities of Negro slavery, in Christian lands. The system took its rise in the sixteenth century. Since then the shameful fact has been witnessed, by earth and by heaven, of men, civilized men, men born and reared in Christian lands and under Christian influences, tearing their fellow-creatures from home, and friends, and country; carrying them across the wide ocean; trading in the flesh and blood of human beings! The system of slavery, *as thus marked and distinguished*, is a MODERN affair—was unknown anterior to the discovery of America; and therefore, as such, not a fact of history —not the general, universal state of the Negro race.

10. The Slave Trade Doubly Disastrous.

But it should be remembered that this event did not bring distress and slavery upon the Negro race only; it struck at once,

---

* With reference to the general prevalence of the system of slavery, see a very able article in the "Life and Remains of Rev. B. B. Edwards, D. D.," late of Andover Theological Seminary.

with deadly, blasting influence, upon two races of men,—the Indian as well as the Negro; and if, because of its destructive and enslaving influence, we are to infer a people's descent from Canaan, then the American Indian is of his seed, as well as the Negro. So soon as the European planted his foot upon the western continent, he seized upon the aborigine as his instrument and property. Before there was any thought of stealing the African and making him a slave, the Indian was enslaved and over-worked; until, at last, he sank down, spent and overwearied, into the grave. And then, when the Indian was exterminated, the Negro was torn from his native land, brought across the water, and made to supply the red man's place. It is difficult to tell which has suffered the more from the discovery, and the slavery which has grown out of it—the Indian or the African. "In the West Indies," to use the words of another, "the whole native population became speedily extinct; the ten millions of that almost unearthly race, the gentle Caribs, vanished like a morning mist before their oppressors. They bled in war; they wasted away in the mines; they toiled to death in the sugar mills."* And then, when their spirits had fled from earthly thraldom, the "conquerors of the New World" turned toward the vast African continent for new victims to fill up the places they had made vacant by their murderous treatment of the natives.

11. Whence this Perversion of Scripture?

A consideration of this subject would be altogether incomplete, without an attempt to account for the origin of this perversion of the word of God, that is, that the Negro race is under a curse, and devoted to slavery. The writer of this article is fully aware of the responsibility he assumes in making the assertions which follow; but it is his deliberate conviction that this perversion of Scripture originated,

1st. In the unscriptural dogma, still maintained by Christian men, and even ministers, that slavery is consistent with, nay,

---

*Rev. J. S. Stone, D.D.

"Las Casas and Vieyra might be quoted to show the cruelties which stimulated them in their unwearied efforts to save the original inhabitants from servitude. The Indians vanished from the scene, giving way to a more enduring race, who were thenceforward to monopolize the miseries of slavery."—"Friends in Council," p. 121.

authorized by, the word and will of God, and that it existed among the Jews under the divine sanction.*

2d. In the natural disposition of our corrupt nature to justify a committed wrong, and, if possible, to claim the authority of God's word for it; and this is the peculiarity which characterizes this great and deep-seated error. It had its origin in the rise and influence of the system of slavery; and this system has appropriated for itself no stronger support than this, and those other staple arguments, wrenched from the Scripture to vindicate and sustain the whole fabric of Negro slavery.

Christianity, in the abstract, is a pure and perfect gift from God to man. But Christianity is a deposit from heaven, in the hands of sinful men; and consequently, in all its ages, Christianity has suffered the loss which is the natural result of being entrusted to this agency, and of being transmitted through this medium. History proves this; for no one need be told that Christianity, in every age, has partaken of the prevailing spirit of that age, whatever it might be. In a philosophical age, it has been influenced by the philosophical spirit and dogmas of that age. In the middle ages, Christianity was influenced by scholasticism. In the age of wars and crusades, she produced Peter the Hermit, and her prelates led forth mighty armies to battle. In an age of luxury, its rigid tone has been relaxed by the enervating influence of wealth, and ease, and refinement. That Christianity has suffered in a like manner, in a slave-trading and a slave-holding age, no one need wonder who looks at the wide and withering influence which the slave trade and slavery have exerted, in all the countries of Christendom, during the last three hundred years. During this period, nearly all the literature of the chief European nations was a Negro-hating and a pro-slavery literature. The institution of slavery, wielding a most potent and commanding authority, brought every thing, in politics, science, philosophy, and letters, to bear in support of the slave trade, in maintenance of the institution of slavery, and to uphold the dogma that the Negro was but

---

*The mind of God upon this subject, so far as the *Old Testament* is concerned, is thus expressed in Exodus xxi. 16: "He that stealeth a man, and selleth him, or if he be found in his hand, he shall surely be put to death." Can any thing be more explicit?

So far as the *New Testament* is concerned, one distinct, unambiguous and positive utterance would seem to be sufficient. St. Paul furnishes us with such an one in 1 Timothy i. 9, 10: "Knowing this, that the law is not made for a righteous man, but for . . . . . . MENSTEALERS"—$\alpha\nu\delta\rho o\pi\alpha\delta\iota\sigma\tau\alpha\iota s$. See "Conybeare and Howson" upon this verse.

an inferior animal. The aid of science was invoked; philosophy trimmed her lamps; literature poured forth whatever treasures she could possibly command. The period has but recently passed since distinguished men in England and France exercised the keenest wit and the subtlest genius to prove that the Negro differed physically from the rest of the human species, and had a *distinct* organization. The puzzling questions concerning the cuticle, the coloring membrane, the "woolly" hair, the facial angle, the pelvis, and all the other supposed characteristic differences of the Negro race, have only recently been settled in a sensible, reasonable manner. In such a state of public sentiment in the Christian world, what wonder that the Church herself should have become tainted and infected by the deadly touch of slavery? And she did not escape; she, too, fell into the common sentiment of the age; and has not yet entirely unschooled herself from it;* and hence it was that, to a very considerable extent, for nigh three centuries, the black man has had a pro-slavery theology pressing him to the earth, as well as the all-grasping cupidity of man:

> "Trade, wealth, and fashion asked him still to bleed,
> And holy men gave Scripture for the deed."

To this prevailing sentiment we owe the fact that nearly all interpretations of Scripture, commentaries, works on prophecy, dissertations on Jewish servitude, sermons and theological treatises elicited by the anti-slavery struggle in England and America, nearly all are pervaded by a pro-slavery tone.

In legal matters it is an assumed principle "that in doubtful cases the advantage of the law shall be in favor of the prisoner;" but Christian men have reversed this principle, and in their treatises have assumed, as a foregone conclusion, that the spirit of the Bible was in favor of slavery, and *not* for freedom, and hence ingenuity has been exhausted in order to show the exact similitude between Jewish servitude and Negro slavery; and to prove that when Noah cursed Canaan he was looking right down the track of time upon some fine specimens of "Ebony," in the barracoons of the Gallinas, or some "fat and sleek" Negroes in the slave-shambles of Virginia!

---

* See, as a most lamentable instance, a recent scriptural defense of Negro slavery, by the venerable Rt. Rev. Bishop Hopkins, of Vermont.

Conclusion.

In conclusion, the author submits that the preceding examination authorizes the following conclusions:

1. That the curse of Noah was *pronounced* upon Canaan, *not* upon Ham.

2. That it *fell* upon Canaan, and was designed to fall upon him only.

3. That neither Ham, nor any of his three sons, was involved in this curse.

4. That the Negro race have not descended from Canaan; were never involved in the curse pronounced upon him; and their peculiar sufferings, during the last three centuries, are not the results or evidences of *any* specific curse upon them.

5. That the fact of slavery in the Negro race is not peculiar to them as a people; but a *general* evil existing in the whole human family; in which, in God's providence, the Negro family have latterly been called to suffer greatly, and doubtless for some high and important ends.

6. That the geographical designations of Scripture are to be taken in good faith; and that when the *"land of Canaan"* is mentioned in the Bible, it was not intended to include the Gold Coast, the Gaboon, Goree, or Congo.

This examination furnishes us with suggestions upon a few *collateral* subjects which have been more or less associated with, or deduced from, the false interpretation thus noticed:

1. We see that *whatever* may be the significance of Gen. ix. 25, *it does not imply mental degradation and intellectual inaptitude.* The curse of Noah did not rob Canaan and his descendents of their brains. The history of the Phœnicians gives evidence of as great creative faculty, and of as much mental force and energy, as that of any other people in the world. It would seem that they, of all the ancient world, were only *second* to the Romans in that commanding national influence which begets life in distant quarters, starts enterprise in new regions, and reproduces its own force and energy among other peoples. Of course, it follows legitimately from the above, that the *whole* Hamitic family are under no Divine doom to perpetual ignorance or endless moral benightedness.

2. The history of the Canaanites serves to show that the *"principle of chattelism" is not the correlative of the curse of Canaan;* this was neither their doom nor their destiny. Neither

in sacred nor profane history do we find them bought and sold like cattle. Driven out of Canaan, they themselves traded in "the bodies and souls" of men, but *not* so others with them.* The nearest approach to any thing of this character is the condition of the Gibeonites, who deceived Joshua; but their condition was that of *servants*.† Although subjugated and humbled, yet their personal and family rights were preserved intact, and none of the aggravations of slavery were permitted to reach themselves or their children. When set upon, at times, by lawless and ruthless men, both Divine and human power interposed for their protection and preservation.

3. This examination *nullifies the foolish notion that the curse of Canaan carried with it the sable dye which marks the Negro races of the world.* The descendants of Canaan in Palestine, Phœnicia, Carthage, and in their various colonies, were not black. They were not Negroes, either in lineage or color.

---

* See Ezekiel xxvii.
† See Joshua ix. 21. 2 Samuel xxi, 3, 4, 5, 6.

Paul Laurence Dunbar (1872-1906)

Negro Life in Washington

At the beginning of the twentieth century, Paul Laurence Dunbar was one of America's most popular poets. The first Negro American to earn and sustain an international reputation as a creative writer, he was highly praised by critics who pointed to him as a symbol of the intellectual and creative potential of the Negro race.

Born in Dayton, Ohio, a son of former slaves, Dunbar was educated at the same high school attended by Orville and Wilbur Wright. There he was elected president of the literary society and editor of the school newspaper. After graduation, he took a job as elevator operator, the best paying position he could obtain. While holding that position, he published his first book of poetry, *Oak and Ivy* (1892). In 1896, he attracted national attention with the publication of *Lyrics of Lowly Life*, his third book of poetry, for which William Dean Howells wrote an introduction in which he praised Dunbar as the first American Negro to evidence innate talent as a writer. In the ten remaining years of his life, Dunbar published three additional collections of poems, four novels, four collections of stories, and numerous articles and sketches.

Although his interest and talents were best revealed in his poetry, Dunbar, like many other celebrated personalities, frequently was asked to write his impressions of places, people, and events. He professed to dislike such work, but accepted it because it frequently paid better than poetry did. Despite his aesthetic

From *Harper's Weekly,* XLIV (January 13, 1900).

disinterest in essays, Dunbar generally infused them with the light touches of satire and sentiment which characterize his best writing.

The following selection reveals Dunbar's deftness in word portraits and his desire to preserve the character traits which he identified with the racial identity of the Negro.

Negro Life in Washington

Washington is the city where the big men of little towns come to be disillusioned. Whether black or white, the little great soon seek their level here. It matters not whether it is Ezekiel Corncray of Podunk Center, Vermont, or Isaac Johnson of the Alabama black belt—in Washington he is apt to come to a realization of his true worth to the world.

In a city of such diverse characteristics it is natural that the life of any portion of its people should be interesting. But when it is considered that here the experiment of sudden freedom has been tried most earnestly, and, I may say, most successfully, upon a large percentage of the population, it is to the lives of these people that one instinctively turns for color, picturesqueness, and striking contrast.

It is the delicately blended or boldly differentiated light and shade effects of Washington negro life that are the despair of him who tries truthfully to picture it.

It is the middle-class negro who has imbibed enough of white civilization to make him work to be prosperous. But he has not partaken of civilization so deeply that he has become drunk and has forgotten his own identity. The church to him is still the centre of his social life, and his preacher a great man. He has not—and I am not wholly sorry that he has not—learned the repression of his emotions, which is the mark of a high and dry civilization. He is impulsive, intense, fervid, and—himself. He has retained some of his primitive ingenuousness. When he goes to a party he goes to enjoy himself and not to pose. If there be onlookers outside his own circle, and he be tempted to pose, he does it with such childlike innocence and good-humor that no one is for a moment anything but amused, and he is forgiven his little deception.

Possibly in even the lower walks of life a warmer racial color is discoverable. For instance, no other race can quite show the counterpart of the old gentleman who passes me on Sunday on his way to church. An ancient silk hat adorns a head which I know instinctively is bald and black and shiny on top; but the edges are fringed with a growth of crisp white hair, like a frame around the mild old face. The broadcloth coat which is buttoned tightly around the spare form is threadbare, and has faded from black to gray-green; but although bent a little with the weight of his years, his glance is alert, and he moves briskly along, like a character suddenly dropped out of one of Page's stories. He waves his hand in salute, and I have a vision of Virginia of fifty years ago.

A real bit of the old South, though, as one sees it in Washington, is the old black mammy who trundles to and fro a little baby-carriage with its load of laundry-work, but who tells you, with manifest pride, "Yes, suh, I has nussed, off'n on, mo'n a dozen chillun of de X fambly, an' some of de men dat's ginuls now er in Cong'ess was jes nachully raised up off'n me." But she, like so many others, came to Washington when it was indeed the Mecca for colored people, where lay all their hopes of protection, of freedom, and of advancement. Perhaps in the old days, when labor brought better rewards, she saved something and laid it by in the ill-fated Freedman's Savings Bank. But the story of that is known; so the old woman walks the streets to-day, penniless, trundling her baby-carriage, a historic but pathetic figure.

Some such relic of the past, but more prosperous withal, is the old lady who leans over the counter of a tiny and dingy restaurant on Capitol Hill and dispenses coffee and rolls and fried pork to her colored customers. She wears upon her head the inevitable turban or handkerchief in which artists delight to paint the old mammies of the South. She keeps unwavering the deep religious instinct of her race, and is mighty in her activities on behalf of one or the other of the colored churches. Under her little counter she always has a contribution-book, and not a customer, white or black, high or low, who is not levied upon to "he'p de chu'ch outen hits 'stress." But one who has sat and listened to her, as, leaning chin on hand, she recounted one of her weird superstitious stories of the night-doctors and their doings, or the "awful jedgement on a sinnah man," is not unwilling to be put at some expense for his pleasure.

The old lady and her stories are of a different cast from that part of the Washington life which is the pride of her proudest people. It is a far cry from the smoky little restaurant on the Hill, with its genial and loquacious old owner, to the great business

block on Fourteenth Street and its wealthy, shrewd, and cultivated proprietor.

Colored men have made money here, and some of them have
known how to keep it. There are several of them on the Board
of Trade—five, I think—and they are regarded by their fellows
as solid, responsible, and capable business men. The present assess-
ment law was drafted by a colored member of the board, and
approved by them before it was submitted to Congress.

As for the professions, there are so many engaged in them that
it would keep one busy counting or attempting to count the dark-
skinned lawyers and doctors one meets in a day.

The cause of this is not far to seek. Young men come here to
work in the departments. Their evenings are to a certain extent
free. It is the most natural thing in the world that they should
improve their time by useful study. But why such a preponder-
ance in favor of the professions, you say. Are there not other useful pursuits—arts and handicrafts? To be sure there are. But then
your new people dearly love a title, and Lawyer Jones sounds well,
Dr. Brown has an infinitely more dignified ring, and as for Professor—well, that is the acme of titular excellence, and there are
more dark professors in Washington than one could find in a
day's walk through a European college town.

However, it is well that these department clerks should carry
something away with them when they leave Washington, for their
condition is seldom financially improved by their sojourn here.
This, though, is perhaps apart from the aim of the present article,
for it is no more true of the negro clerks than of their white
confrères. Both generally live up to the limit of their salaries.

The clerk has much leisure, and is in consequence a society
man. He must dress well and smoke as good a cigar as an Eastern
Congressman. It all costs money, and it is not unnatural that at
the end of the year he is a little long on unreceipted bills and short
on gold. The tendency of the school-teachers, now, seems to be
entirely different. There are a great many of them here, and on
the average they receive less than the government employés. But
perhaps the discipline which they are compelled to impart to their
pupils has its salutary effect upon their own minds and impulses.
However that may be, it is true that the banks and building
associations receive each month a part of the salaries of a large
proportion of these instructors.

The colored people themselves have a flourishing building association and a well-conducted bank, which do part—I am sorry
I cannot say the major part—of their race's business.

The influence which the success of a few men will have upon a whole community is indicated in the spirit of venture which actuates the rising generation of this city. A few years ago, if a man secured a political position, he was never willing or fit to do anything else afterward. But now the younger men, with the example of some of their successful elders before them, are beginning to see that an easy berth in one of the departments is not the best thing in life, and they are getting brave enough to do other things. Some of these ventures have proven failures, even disasters, but it has not daunted the few, nor crushed the spirit of effort in them.

It has been said, and not without some foundation in fact, that a colored man who came to Washington never left the place. Indeed, the city has great powers of attracting and holding its colored population; for, belong to whatever class or condition they may, they are always sure to find enough of that same class or condition to make their residence pleasant and congenial. But this very spirit of enterprise of which I have spoken is destroying the force of this dictum, and men of color are even going so far as to resign government positions to go away and strike out for themselves. I have in mind now two young men who are Washingtonians of the Washingtonians, and who have been in office here for years. But the fever has taken them, and they have voluntarily given up their places to go and try their fortunes in the newer and less crowded West.

Such things as these are small in themselves, but they point to a condition of affairs in which the men who have received the training and polish which only Washington can give to a colored man can go forth among their fellows and act as leaveners to the crudity of their race far and wide.

That the pleasure and importance of negro life in Washington are overrated by the colored people themselves is as true as that it is underrated and misunderstood by the whites. To the former the social aspect of this life is a very dignified and serious drama. To the latter it is nothing but a most amusing and inconsequential farce. But both are wrong: it is neither the one thing nor the other. It is a comedy of the period played out by earnest actors, who have learned their parts well, but who on that very account are disposed to mouth and strut a little and watch the gallery.

Upon both races the truth and significance of the commercial life among the negroes have taken a firmer hold, because the sight of their banks, their offices, and places of business are evidences which cannot be overlooked or ignored.

As for the intellectual life, a university set on a hill cannot be hid, and the fact that about this university and about this excellent high-school clusters a community in which people, unlike many of the educational fakirs which abound, have taken their degrees from Cambridge, Oxford, Edinburgh, Harvard, Yale, Cornell, Wellesley, and a score of minor colleges, demands the recognition of a higher standard of culture among people of color than obtains in any other city.

But, taking it all in all and after all, negro life in Washington is a promise rather than a fulfilment. But it is worthy of note for the really excellent things which are promised.

William Edward Burghardt
DuBois (1868-1963)

Of the Passing of the First-Born *and* Of Alexander Crummell

Frequently a controversial figure, W. E. B. DuBois was a perceptive interpreter and outspoken champion of Negroes. Born in Great Barrington, Massachusetts, DuBois received the Bachelor of Arts degree from Fisk, and the Doctor of Philosophy from Harvard (1895), where his dissertation was *The Suppression of the African Slave Trade to the United States of America.* In 1896, he became professor of history and economics at Atlanta University, where he initiated and edited *Studies of Negro Problems,* which earned him recognition as the first Negro scientific student of history and sociology. More overtly aggressive than Booker T. Washington, DuBois gained national attention by leading opposition to Washington's conciliatory political and educational philosophies. One of the founders of the National Association for the Advancement of Colored People and the first editor of *The Crisis,* the official publication of that organization, DuBois, throughout his life, attempted to promote unity among all the colored peoples of the world. In his later years, he renounced his American citizenship and moved to Ghana, where he died.

Although he wrote novels, autobiographies, and histories, DuBois's literary talent is most effectively displayed in his essays, which range in style from lucid, tightly organized arguments to lyric and rambling expressions of personal emotions. The extensive range of his mind and style appears in the many editorials and articles which he wrote for *The Crisis,* in *The Gift of Black Folk*

From *The Souls of Black Folk.* (New York: McClurg, 1903).

(1924), and in *Dusk of Dawn* (1940). His major literary achieve-ment, however, is *The Souls of Black Folk,* a very perceptive presentation of the temperaments and culture of Negroes. In the following selection from that work, DuBois, grieving over the loss of his son, reaches a bitter consolation.

Of the Passing of the First-Born

O sister, sister, thy first-begotten,
The hands that cling and the feet that follow,
The voice of the child's blood crying yet,
Who hath remembered me? who hath forgotten?
Thou hast forgotten, O summer swallow,
But the world shall end when I forget.

SWINBURNE.

"Unto you a child is born," sang the bit of yellow paper that fluttered into my room one brown October morning. Then the fear of fatherhood mingled wildly with the joy of creation; I wondered how it looked and how it felt, — what were its eyes, and how its hair curled and crumpled itself. And I thought in awe of her, — she who had slept with Death to tear a man-child from underneath her heart, while I was unconsciously wandering. I fled to my wife and child, repeating the while to myself half wonderingly, "Wife and child? Wife and child?" — fled fast and faster than boat and steam-car, and yet must ever impatiently await them; away from the hard-voiced city, away from the flickering sea into my own Berkshire Hills that sit all sadly guard-ing the gates of Massachusetts.

Up the stairs I ran to the wan mother and whimpering babe, to the sanctuary on whose altar a life at my bidding had offered itself to win a life, and won. What is this tiny formless thing,

this newborn wail from an unknown world, — all head and voice?
I handle it curiously, and watch perplexed its winking, breathing,
and sneezing. I did not love it then; it seemed a ludicrous thing
to love; but her I loved, my girl-mother, she whom now I saw
unfolding like the glory of the morning — the transfigured woman.
Through her I came to love the wee thing, as it grew strong; as
its little soul unfolded itself in twitter and cry and half-formed
word, and as its eyes caught the gleam and flash of life. How
beautiful he was, with his olive-tinted flesh and dark gold ringlets,
his eyes of mingled blue and brown, his perfect little limbs, and
the soft voluptuous roll which the blood of Africa had moulded
into his features! I held him in my arms, after we had sped far
away to our Southern home, — held him, and glanced at the hot
red soil of Georgia and the breathless city of a hundred hills, and
felt a vague unrest. Why was his hair tinted with gold? An evil
omen was golden hair in my life. Why had not the brown of his
eyes crushed out and killed the blue? — for brown were his
father's eyes, and his father's father's. And thus in the Land of
the Color-line I saw, as it fell across my baby, the shadow of
the Veil.

Within the Veil was he born, said I; and there within shall he
live, — a Negro and a Negro's son. Holding in that little head —
ah, bitterly! — the unbowed pride of a hunted race, clinging with
that tiny dimpled hand — ah, wearily! — to a hope not hopeless
but unhopeful, and seeing with those bright wondering eyes that
peer into my soul a land whose freedom is to us a mockery and
whose liberty a lie. I saw the shadow of the Veil as it passed over
my baby, I saw the cold city towering above the blood-red land.
I held my face beside his little cheek, showed him the star-
children and the twinkling lights as they began to flash, and
stilled with an even-song the unvoiced terror of my life.

So sturdy and masterful he grew, so filled with bubbling life,
so tremulous with the unspoken wisdom of a life but eighteen
months distant from the All-life, — we were not far from wor-
shipping this revelation of the divine, my wife and I. Her own
life builded and moulded itself upon the child; he tinged her
every dream and idealized her every effort. No hands but hers
must touch and garnish those little limbs; no dress or frill must
touch them that had not wearied her fingers; no voice but hers
could coax him off to Dreamland, and she and he together spoke
some soft and unknown tongue and in it held communion. I too
mused above this little white bed; saw the strength of my own arm

stretched onward through the ages through the newer strength of
his; saw the dream of my black fathers stagger a step onward in
the wild phantasm of the world; heard in his baby voice the voice
of the Prophet that was to rise within the Veil.

And so we dreamed and loved and planned by fall and winter,
and the full flush of the long Southern spring, till the hot winds
rolled from the fetid Gulf, till the roses shivered and the still stern
sun quivered its awful light over the hills of Atlanta. And then
one night the little feet pattered wearily to the wee white bed, and
the tiny hands trembled; and a warm flushed face tossed on the
pillow, and we knew baby was sick. Ten days he lay there, — a
swift week and three endless days, wasting, wasting away.
Cheerily the mother nursed him the first days, and laughed into
the little eyes that smiled again. Tenderly then she hovered round
him, till the smile fled away and Fear crouched beside the little bed.

Then the day ended not, and night was a dreamless terror, and
joy and sleep slipped away. I hear now that Voice at midnight
calling me from dull and dreamless trance,—crying, "The Shadow
of Death! The Shadow of Death!" Out into the starlight I crept,
to rouse the gray physician, — the Shadow of Death, the Shadow
of Death. The hours trembled on; the night listened; the ghastly
dawn glided like a tired thing across the lamplight. Then we two
alone looked upon the child as he turned toward us with great
eyes, and stretched his stringlike hands, — the Shadow of Death!
And we spoke no word, and turned away.

He died at eventide, when the sun lay like a brooding sorrow
above the western hills, veiling its face; when the winds spoke
not, and the trees, the great green trees he loved, stood motionless. I saw his breath beat quicker and quicker, pause, and then
his little soul leapt like a star that travels in the night and left
a world of darkness in its train. The day changed not; the same
tall trees peeped in at the windows, the same green grass glinted
in the setting sun. Only in the chamber of death writhed the
world's most piteous thing — a childless mother.

I shirk not. I long for work. I pant for a life full of striving. I
am no coward, to shrink before the rugged rush of the storm, nor
even quail before the awful shadow of the Veil. But hearken, O
Death! Is not this my life hard enough, — is not that dull land
that stretches its sneering web about me cold enough, — is not
all the world beyond these four little walls pitiless enough, but
that thou must needs enter here, — thou, O Death? About my
head the thundering storm beat like a heartless voice, and the

crazy forest pulsed with the curses of the weak; but what cared
I, within my home beside my wife and baby boy? Wast thou so
jealous of one little coign of happiness that thou must needs
enter there, — thou, O Death?

A perfect life was his, all joy and love, with tears to make it
brighter, — sweet as a summer's day beside the Housatonic. The
world loved him; the women kissed his curls, the men looked
gravely into his wonderful eyes, and the children hovered and
fluttered about him. I can see him now, changing like the sky
from sparkling laughter to darkening frowns, and then to wondering thoughtfulness as he watched the world. He knew no color-line,
poor dear, — and the Veil, though it shadowed him, had not yet
darkened half his sun. He loved the white matron, he loved his
black nurse; and in his little world walked souls alone, uncolored
and unclothed. I — yea, all men — are larger and purer by the
infinite breadth of that one little life. She who in simple clearness
of vision sees beyond the stars said when he had flown, "He will
be happy There; he ever loved beautiful things." And I, far more
ignorant, and blind by the web of mine own weaving, sit alone
winding words and muttering, "If still he be, and he be There,
and there be a There, let him be happy, O Fate!"

Blithe was the morning of his burial, with bird and song and
sweet-smelling flowers. The trees whispered to the grass, but the
children sat with hushed faces. And yet it seemed a ghostly
unreal day, — the wraith of Life. We seemed to rumble down
an unknown street behind a little white bundle of posies, with
the shadow of a song in our ears. The busy city dinned about us;
they did not say much, those pale-faced hurrying men and
women; they did not say much, — they only glanced and said,
"Niggers!"

We could not lay him in the ground there in Georgia, for the
earth there is strangely red; so we bore him away to the northward, with his flowers and his little folded hands. In vain, in vain!
— for where, O God! beneath thy broad blue sky shall my dark
baby rest in peace, — where Reverence dwells, and Goodness, and
a Freedom that is free?

All that day and all that night there sat an awful gladness in
my heart, — nay, blame me not if I see the world thus darkly
through the Veil, — and my soul whispers ever to me, saying,
"Not dead, not dead, but escaped; not bond, but free." No bitter
meanness now shall sicken his baby heart till it die a living death,
no taunt shall madden his happy boyhood. Fool that I was to

think or wish that this little soul should grow choked and de-
formed within the Veil! I might have known that yonder deep
unworldly look that ever and anon floated past his eyes was
peering far beyond this narrow Now. In the poise of his little curl-
crowned head did there not sit all that wild pride of being which
his father had hardly crushed in his own heart? For what, for-
sooth, shall a Negro want with pride amid the studied humiliations of fifty million fellows? Well sped, my boy, before the world
had dubbed your ambition insolence, had held your ideals unat-
tainable, and taught you to cringe and bow. Better far this nameless void that stops my life than a sea of sorrow for you.

Idle words; he might have borne his burden more bravely than
we, — aye, and found it lighter too, some day; for surely, surely
this is not the end. Surely there shall yet dawn some mighty
morning to lift the Veil and set the prisoned free. Not for me,
— I shall die in my bonds, — but for fresh young souls who have
not known the night and waken to the morning; a morning when
men ask of the workman, not "Is he white?" but "Can he work?"
When men ask artists, not "Are they black?" but "Do they
know?" Some morning this may be, long, long years to come.
But now there wails, on that dark shore within the Veil, the
same deep voice, *Thou shalt forego!* And all have I foregone at
that command, and with small complaint, — all save that fair
young form that lies so coldly wed with death in the nest I had
builded.

If one must have gone, why not I? Why may I not rest me
from this restlessness and sleep from this wide waking? Was not
the world's alembic, Time, in his young hands, and is not my time
warning? Are there so many workers in the vineyard that the
fair promise of this little body could lightly be tossed away? The
wretched of my race that line the alleys of the nation sit fatherless and unmothered; but Love sat beside his cradle, and in his
ear Wisdom waited to speak. Perhaps now he knows the All-love,
and needs not to be wise. Sleep, then, child, — sleep till I sleep
and waken to a baby voice and the ceaseless patter of little feet
— above the Veil.

In the following selection, W. E. B. DuBois paid eloquent
tribute to Alexander Crummell, whose achievements are represented earlier in this book.

Of Alexander Crummell

Then from the Dawn it seemed there came, but faint
As from beyond the limit of the world,
Like the last echo born of a great cry,
Sounds, as if some fair city were one voice
Around a king returning from his wars.

TENNYSON.

This is the history of a human heart, — the tale of a black boy who many long years ago began to struggle with life that he might know the world and know himself. Three temptations he met on those dark dunes that lay gray and dismal before the wonder-eyes of the child: the temptation of Hate, that stood out against the red dawn; the temptation of Despair, that darkened noonday; and the temptation of Doubt, that ever steals along with twilight. Above all, you must hear of the vales he crossed, — the Valley of Humiliation and the Valley of the Shadow of Death.

I saw Alexander Crummell first at a Wilberforce commencement season, amid its bustle and crush. Tall, frail, and black he stood, with simple dignity and an unmistakable air of good breeding. I talked with him apart, where the storming of the lusty young orators could not harm us. I spoke to him politely, then curiously, then eagerly, as I began to feel the fineness of his character, — his calm courtesy, the sweetness of his strength, and his fair blending of the hope and truth of life. Instinctively I bowed before this man, as one bows before the prophets of the world. Some seer he seemed, that came not from the crimson Past or the gray To-come, but from the pulsing Now, — that mocking world which seemed to me at once so light and dark, so splendid and sordid. Four-score years had he wandered in this same world of mine, within the Veil.

He was born with the Missouri Compromise and lay a-dying amid the echoes of Manila and El Caney: stirring times for living, times dark to look back upon, darker to look forward to. The black-faced lad that paused over his mud and marbles seventy years ago saw puzzling vistas as he looked down the world. The slave-ship still groaned across the Atlantic, faint cries burdened the Southern breeze, and the great black father whispered mad tales of cruelty into those young ears. From the low doorway the mother silently watched her boy at play, and at nightfall sought him eagerly lest the shadows bear him away to the land of slaves.

So his young mind worked and winced and shaped curiously a vision of Life; and in the midst of that vision ever stood one dark figure alone, — ever with the hard, thick countenance of that bitter father, and a form that fell in vast and shapeless folds. Thus the temptation of Hate grew and shadowed the growing child, — gliding stealthily into his laughter, fading into his play, and seizing his dreams by day and night with rough, rude turbulence. So the black boy asked of sky and sun and flower the never-answered Why? and loved, as he grew, neither the world nor the world's rough ways.

Strange temptation for a child, you may think; and yet in this wide land to-day a thousand thousand dark children brood before this same temptation, and feel its cold and shuddering arms. For them, perhaps, some one will some day lift the Veil, — will come tenderly and cheerily into those sad little lives and brush the brooding hate away, just as Beriah Green strode in upon the life of Alexander Crummell. And before the bluff, kind-hearted man the shadow seemed less dark. Beriah Green had a school in Oneida County, New York, with a score of mischievous boys. "I'm going to bring a black boy here to educate," said Beriah Green, as only a crank and an abolitionist would have dared to say. "Oho!" laughed the boys. "Ye-es," said his wife; and Alexander came. Once before, the black boy had sought a school, had travelled, cold and hungry, four hundred miles up into free New Hampshire, to Canaan. But the godly farmers hitched ninety yoke of oxen to the abolition schoolhouse and dragged it into the middle of the swamp. The black boy trudged away.

The nineteenth was the first century of human sympathy, — the age when half wonderingly we began to descry in others that transfigured spark of divinity which we call Myself; when clodhoppers and peasants, and tramps and thieves, and millionaires

and — sometimes — Negroes, became throbbing souls whose warm
pulsing life touched us so nearly that we half gasped with surprise,
crying, "Thou too! Hast Thou seen Sorrow and the dull waters
of Hopelessness? Hast Thou known Life?" And then all helplessly
we peered into those Other-worlds, and wailed, "O World of
Worlds, how shall man make you one?"

So in that little Oneida school there came to those schoolboys
a revelation of thought and longing beneath one black skin, of
which they had not dreamed before. And to the lonely boy came
a new dawn of sympathy and inspiration. The shadowy, formless
thing — the temptation of Hate, that hovered between him and
the world — grew fainter and less sinister. It did not wholly fade
away, but diffused itself and lingered thick at the edges. Through
it the child now first saw the blue and gold of life, — the sun-
swept road that ran 'twixt heaven and earth until in one far-off
wan wavering line they met and kissed. A vision of life came to
the growing boy,—mystic, wonderful. He raised his head, stretched
himself, breathed deep of the fresh new air. Yonder, behind the
forests, he heard strange sounds; then glinting through the trees
he saw, far, far away, the bronzed hosts of a nation calling, —
calling faintly, calling loudly. He heard the hateful clank of their
chains; he felt them cringe and grovel, and there rose within him
a protest and a prophecy. And he girded himself to walk down
the world.

A voice and vision called him to be a priest, — a seer to lead
the uncalled out of the house of bondage. He saw the headless
host turn toward him like the whirling of mad waters, — he
stretched forth his hands eagerly, and then, even as he stretched
them, suddenly there swept across the vision the temptation of
Despair.

They were not wicked men, — the problem of life is not the
problem of the wicked, — they were calm, good men, Bishops of
the Apostolic Church of God, and strove toward righteousness.
They said slowly, "It is all very natural—it is even commendable;
but the General Theological Seminary of the Episcopal Church
cannot admit a Negro." And when that thin, half-grotesque
figure still haunted their doors, they put their hands kindly, half
sorrowfully, on his shoulders, and said, "Now, — of course, we —
we know how *you* feel about it; but you see it is impossible, —
that is — well — it is premature. Sometime, we trust — sincerely
trust — all such distinctions will fade away; but now the world
is as it is."

This was the temptation of Despair; and the young man fought it doggedly. Like some grave shadow he flitted by those halls, pleading, arguing, half angrily demanding admittance, until there came the final *No:* until men hustled the disturber away, marked him as foolish, unreasonable, and injudicious, a vain rebel against God's law. And then from that Vision Splendid all the glory faded slowly away, and left an earth gray and stern rolling on beneath a dark despair. Even the kind hands that stretched themselves toward him from out the depths of that dull morning seemed but parts of the purple shadows. He saw them coldly, and asked, "Why should I strive by special grace when the way of the world is closed to me?" All gently yet, the hands urged him on, — the hands of young John Jay, that daring father's daring son; the hands of the good folk of Boston, that free city. And yet, with a way to the priesthood of the Church open at least before him, the cloud lingered there; and even when in old St. Paul's the venerable Bishop raised his white arms above the Negro deacon — even then the burden had not lifted from that heart, for there had passed a glory from the earth.

And yet the fire through which Alexander Crummell went did not burn in vain. Slowly and more soberly he took up again his plan of life. More critically he studied the situation. Deep down below the slavery and servitude of the Negro people he saw their fatal weaknesses, which long years of mistreatment had emphasized. The dearth of strong moral character, of unbending righteousness, he felt, was their great shortcoming, and here he would begin. He would gather the best of his people into some little Episcopal chapel and there lead, teach, and inspire them, till the leaven spread, till the children grew, till the world hearkened, till — till — and then across his dream gleamed some faint after-glow of that first fair vision of youth — only an after-glow, for there had passed a glory from the earth.

One day — it was in 1842, and the springtide was struggling merrily with the May winds of New England — he stood at last in his own chapel in Providence, a priest of the Church. The days sped by, and the dark young clergyman labored; he wrote his sermons carefully; he intoned his prayers with a soft, earnest voice; he haunted the streets and accosted the wayfarers; he visited the sick, and knelt beside the dying. He worked and toiled, week by week, day by day, month by month. And yet month by month the congregation dwindled, week by week the hollow walls echoed more sharply, day by day the calls came fewer and fewer, and day by day the third temptation sat clearer and still more clearly within the Veil; a temptation, as it were, bland and smiling, with just a shade of mockery in its smooth tones. First it came casually, in the cadence of a voice: "Oh, colored folks? Yes." Or perhaps more definitely: "What do you *expect?*" In voice and gesture lay the doubt — the temptation of Doubt. How he hated it, and stormed at it furiously! "Of course they are capable," he cried; "of course they can learn and strive and achieve — " and "Of course," added the temptation softly, "they do nothing of the sort." Of all the three temptations, this one struck the deepest. Hate? He had outgrown so childish a thing. Despair? He had steeled his right arm against it, and fought it with the vigor of determination. But to doubt the worth of his life-work, — to doubt the destiny and capability of the race his soul loved because it was his; to find listless squalor instead of eager endeavor; to hear his own lips whispering, "They do not care; they cannot know; they are dumb driven cattle, — why cast your pearls before swine?" — this, this seemed more than man could bear; and he closed the door, and sank upon the steps of the chancel, and cast his robe upon the floor and writhed.

The evening sunbeams had set the dust to dancing in the gloomy chapel when he arose. He folded his vestments, put away the hymn-books, and closed the great Bible. He stepped out into the twilight, looked back upon the narrow little pulpit with a weary smile, and locked the door. Then he walked briskly to the Bishop, and told the Bishop what the Bishop already knew. "I have failed," he said simply. And gaining courage by the confession, he added: "What I need is a large constituency. There are comparatively few Negroes here, and perhaps they are not of the best. I must go where the field is wider, and try again." So the Bishop sent him to Philadelphia, with a letter to Bishop Onderdonk.

Bishop Onderdonk lived at the head of six white steps, — corpulent, red-faced, and the author of several thrilling tracts on Apostolic Succession. It was after dinner, and the Bishop had settled himself for a pleasant season of contemplation, when the bell must needs ring, and there must burst in upon the Bishop a letter and a thin, ungainly Negro. Bishop Onderdonk read the letter hastily and frowned. Fortunately, his mind was already clear on this point; and he cleared his brow and looked at Crummell. Then he said, slowly and impressively: "I will receive you into this diocese on one condition: no Negro priest can sit in my church convention, and no Negro church must ask for representation there."

I sometimes fancy I can see that tableau: the frail black figure, nervously twitching his hat before the massive abdomen of Bishop Onderdonk; his threadbare coat thrown against the dark woodwork of the bookcases, where Fox's "Lives of the Martyrs" nested happily beside "The Whole Duty of Man." I seem to see the wide eyes of the Negro wander past the Bishop's broadcloth to where the swinging glass doors of the cabinet glow in the sunlight. A little blue fly is trying to cross the yawning keyhole. He marches briskly up to it, peers into the chasm in a surprised sort of way, and rubs his feelers reflectively; then he essays its depths, and, finding it bottomless, draws back again. The dark-faced priest finds himself wondering if the fly too has faced its Valley of Humiliation, and if it will plunge into it, — when lo! it spreads its tiny wings and buzzes merrily across, leaving the watcher wingless and alone.

Then the full weight of his burden fell upon him. The rich walls wheeled away, and before him lay the cold rough moor winding on through life, cut in twain by one thick granite ridge, — here, the Valley of Humiliation; yonder, the Valley of the Shadow of Death. And I know not which be darker, — no, not I. But this I know: in yonder Vale of the Humble stand to-day a million swarthy men, who willingly would

> "... bear the whips and scorns of time,
> The oppressor's wrong, the proud man's contumely,
> The pangs of despised love, the law's delay,
> The insolence of office, and the spurns
> That patient merit of the unworthy takes,"—

all this and more would they bear did they but know that this were sacrifice and not a meaner thing. So surged the thought within that lone black breast. The Bishop cleared his throat suggestively; then, recollecting that there was really nothing to say, considerately said nothing, only sat tapping his foot impatiently. But Alexander Crummell said, slowly and heavily: "I will never enter your diocese on such terms." And saying this, he turned and passed into the Valley of the Shadow of Death. You might have noted only the physical dying, the shattered frame and hacking cough; but in that soul lay deeper death than that. He found a chapel in New York, — the church of his father; he labored for it in poverty and starvation, scorned by his fellow priests. Half in despair, he wandered across the sea, a beggar with outstretched hands. Englishmen clasped them, — Wilberforce and Stanley, Thirwell and Ingles, and even Froude and Macaulay; Sir Benjamin Brodie bade him rest awhile at Queen's College in Cambridge, and there he lingered, struggling for health of body and mind, until he took his degree in '53. Restless still and unsatisfied, he turned toward Africa, and for long years, amid the spawn of the slave-smugglers, sought a new heaven and a new earth.

So the man groped for light; all this was not Life, — it was the world-wandering of a soul in search of itself, the striving of one who vainly sought his place in the world, ever haunted by the shadow of a death that is more than death, — the passing of a soul that has missed its duty. Twenty years he wandered, — twenty years and more; and yet the hard rasping question kept gnawing within him, "What, in God's name, am I on earth for?" In the narrow New York parish his soul seemed cramped and smothered. In the fine old air of the English University he heard the millions wailing over the sea. In the wild fever-cursed swamps of West Africa he stood helpless and alone.

You will not wonder at his weird pilgrimage, — you who in the swift whirl of living, amid its cold paradox and marvellous vision, have fronted life and asked its riddle face to face. And if you find that riddle hard to read, remember that yonder black boy finds it just a little harder; if it is difficult for you to find and face your duty, it is a shade more difficult for him; if your heart sickens in the blood and dust of battle, remember that to him the dust is thicker and the battle fiercer. No wonder the wanderers fall! No wonder we point to thief and murderer, and haunting prostitute, and the never-ending throng of unhearsed dead! The Valley of the Shadow of Death gives few of its pilgrims back to the world.

But Alexander Crummell it gave back. Out of the temptation of Hate, and burned by the fire of Despair, triumphant over Doubt, and steeled by Sacrifice against Humiliation, he turned at last home across the waters, humble and strong, gentle and determined. He bent to all the gibes and prejudices, to all hatred and discrimination, with that rare courtesy which is the armor of pure souls. He fought among his own, the low, the grasping, and the wicked, with that unbending righteousness which is the sword of the just. He never faltered, he seldom complained; he simply worked, inspiring the young, rebuking the old, helping the weak, guiding the strong.

So he grew, and brought within his wide influence all that was best of those who walk within the Veil. They who live without knew not nor dreamed of that full power within, that mighty inspiration which the dull gauze of caste decreed that most men should not know. And now that he is gone, I sweep the Veil away and cry, Lo! the soul to whose dear memory I bring this little tribute. I can see his face still, dark and heavy lined beneath his snowy hair; lighting and shading, now with inspiration for the future, now in innocent pain at some human wickedness, now with sorrow at some hard memory from the past. The more I met Alexander Crummell, the more I felt how much that world was losing which knew so little of him. In another age he might have sat among the elders of the land in purple-bordered toga; in another country mothers might have sung him to the cradles.

He did his work, — he did it nobly and well; and yet I sorrow that here he worked alone, with so little human sympathy. His name to-day, in this broad land, means little, and comes to fifty million ears laden with no incense of memory or emulation. And herein lies the tragedy of the age: not that men are poor, — all men know something of poverty; not that men are wicked, — who is good? not that men are ignorant, — what is Truth? Nay, but that men know so little of men.

He sat one morning gazing toward the sea. He smiled and said, "The gate is rusty on the hinges." That night at star-rise a wind came moaning out of the west to blow the gate ajar, and then the soul I loved fled like a flame across the Seas, and in its seat sat Death.

I wonder where he is to-day? I wonder if in that dim world beyond, as he came gliding in, there rose on some wan throne a King, — a dark and pierced Jew, who knows the writhings of the earthly damned, saying, as he laid those heart-wrung talents down, "Well done!" while round about the morning stars sat singing.

Kelly Miller (1863-1939)

Frederick Douglass

For a generation, Kelly Miller was an intellectual champion of Negro Americans. Born in Winnsboro, South Carolina, he was educated at Howard University and at Johns Hopkins (A.M., 1901; LL.D 1903). He was a member of the faculty of Howard University, where he taught mathematics and sociology and served as dean of the College of Arts and Sciences. A frequent lecturer and essayist on controversial subjects, he collected his writings in *Race Adjustment* (1908), *Out of the House of Bondage* (1914), *An Appeal to Conscience* (1918), *History of the World War and the Important Part Taken by the Negroes* (1919), and *The Everlasting Stain* (1924).

The following selection is not in Miller's most characteristic vein of defense or attack. Instead, in an essay which is a model for organization and direct presentation of an idea, Miller explains the significance of Frederick Douglass, whose work is represented earlier in this book.

Frederick Douglass

The highest function of a great name is to serve as an example and as a perpetual source of inspiration to the young who are to come after him. By the subtle law known as "consciousness of

From *Race Adjustment*: *Essays on the Negro in America*. (New York: Neale, 1908).

kind" a commanding personality incites the sharpest stimulus and exerts the deepest intensity of influence among the group from which he springs. We gather inspiration most readily from those of our class who have been touched with the feeling of our infirmities and have been subject to like conditions as ourselves. Every class, every race, every country, and indeed every well-defined group of social interests has its own glorified names whose fame and following are limited to the prescribed sphere of influence. Indeed, human relations are so diverse and human interests and feelings so antagonistic that the names which command even a fanatical following among one class may be despised and rejected by another. He who serves his exclusive class may be great in the positive degree; the man who serves a whole race or country may be considered great in the comparative degree; but it is only the man who breaks the barrier of class and creed and country and serves the human race that is worthy to be accounted great in the superlative degree. We are so far the creatures of local and institutional environment, and so disposed to borrow our modes of thought and feeling from our social medium, that even an appeal to the universal heart must be adapted to the spirit and genius of the time and people to whom it is first made. Even the Saviour of the world offered the plan of salvation first to the Jews in the traditional guise of the Hebrew cult.

It is essential that any isolated, proscribed class should honor its illustrious names. They serve not only as a measure of their possibilities, but they possess greater inspirational power by virtue of their close sympathetic and kindly touch. Small wonder that such people are wont to glorify their distinguished men out of proportion to their true historical setting on the scale of human greatness.

Frederick Douglass is the one commanding historic character of the colored race in America. He is the model of emulation of those who are struggling up through the trials and difficulties which he himself suffered and subdued. He is illustrative and exemplary of what they might become — the first fruit of promise of a dormant race. To the aspiring colored youth of this land Mr. Douglass is, at once, the inspiration of their hopes and the justification of their claims.

I do not on this occasion intend to dwell upon the well-known facts and circumstances in the life and career of Mr. Douglass, but deem it more profitable to point out some of the lessons to be derived from that life.

In the first place, Mr. Douglass began life at the lowest possible level. It is only when we understand the personal circumstances of his early environment that we can appreciate the pathos and power with which he was wont to insist upon the true measure of the progress of the American Negro, not by the height already attained, but by the depth from which he came. It has been truly said that it required a greater upward move to bring Mr. Douglass to the status in which the ordinary white child is born than is necessary on the part of the latter to reach the presidency of the United States. The early life of this gifted child of nature was spent amid squalor, deprivation and cruel usage. Like Melchizedek of old, it can be said of him that he sprang into existence without father or mother, or beginning of days. His little body was unprotected from the bitter, biting cold, and his vitals griped with the gnawing pangs of hunger. We are told that he vied with the dogs for the crumbs that fell from his master's table. He tasted the sting of a cruel slavery, and drank the cup to its very dregs. And yet he arose from this lowly and degraded estate and gained for himself a place among the illustrious names of his country.

We hear much in this day and time about the relative force of environment and heredity as factors in the formation of character. But, as the career of Mr. Douglass illustrates, there is a subtle power of personality which, though the product of neither, is more potential than both. God has given to each of us an irrepressible inner something, which, for want of better designation, the old philosophy used to call the freedom of the will, which counts for most in the making of manhood.

In the second place, I would call attention to the tremendous significance of a seemingly trifling incident in his life. When he was about thirteen years of age he came into possession of a copy of the "Columbian Orator," abounding in dramatic outbursts and stirring episodes of liberty. It was the ripened fruit of the choicest spirits, upon which the choicest spirits feed. This book fired his whole soul and kindled an unquenchable love for liberty. It is held by some that at the age of puberty the mind is in a state of unstable equilibrium, and, like a pyramid on its apex, may be thrown in any direction by the slightest impression of force. The instantaneity of religious conversions, which the Methodists used to acclaim with such triumphant outbursts of hallelujah, may rest upon some such psychological foundation. When the child nature stands at the parting of the ways, between youth and adolescence, it yields to some quickening touch, as the fuse to the spark, or as the sensitized plate to the impressions of sunlight. There are "psychological moments" when the revealed idea rises sublimely above the revealing agent. According to the theory of harmonies, if two instruments are tuned in resonant accord the vibrations of the one will wake up the slumbering chords of the other. Young Douglass's soul was in sympathetic resonance with the great truth of human brotherhood and equality, and needed only the psychological suggestion which the "Columbian Orator" supplied. In a moment, in the twinkling of an eye, it burned deep into his soul and made an ineffaceable impression upon his consciousness of the gospel of brotherhood and equality of man. It was the same truth which could only be impressed upon the Apostle Peter in the rhapsodies of a heavenly vision. The age of revelation is not past, and will not pass so long as there remains one soul that yearns for spiritual illumination. There comes at times into our lives some sudden echo of the heavenly harmony from the unseen world, and happy is that soul which beats in vibrant harmony with that supernal sound. When the gospel of liberty first dawned upon the adolescent Douglass, as he perused the pages of the "Columbian Orator," there is no rendition of either the old or the new school of psychology that can analyze the riot of thought and sentiment that swept through his turbulent soul. This was indeed his new birth, his baptism with fire from on high. From that moment he was a possessed man. The love of liberty bound him with its subtle cords and did not release him until the hour of his death on Anacostia's mist-clad height.

Our educational philosophers are ransacking their brains to prescribe wise curricula of study for colored youth. There is not so much need of that which gives information to the mind or cunning to the fingers as that which touches the soul and quickens the spirit. There must be first aroused dormant consciousness of manhood with its inalienable rights, privileges, and dignity. The letter killeth, the spirit maketh alive. The "Columbian Orator" contributed more toward arousing the manhood of Mr. Douglass than all the traditional knowledge of all the schools. Of what avail is the mastery of all branches of technical and refined knowledge unless it touches the hidden springs of manhood? The value of any curriculum of study for a suppressed class that is not pregnant with moral energy, and that does not make insistent and incessant appeal to the half-conscious manhood within is seriously questionable. The revelation to a young man of the dignity, I had almost said the divinity, of his own selfhood is worth more to him in the development of character and power than all the knowledge in all the de luxe volumes in the gilded Carnegie libraries.

In the third place, Negro youth should study Mr. Douglass as a model of manly courage. In order to acquire a clear conception of principles let us discriminate sharply in the use of terms. Courage is that quality which enables one to encounter danger and difficulties with firmness and resolution of spirit. It is the swell of soul which meets outward pressure with inner resistance. Fortitude, on the other hand, is the capacity to endure, the ability to suffer and be strong. It is courage in the passive voice. True courage sets up an ideal and posits a purpose; it calculates the cost and is economic of means, though never faltering in determination to reach that end. Bravery is mere physical daring in the presence of danger, and responds to temporary physical and mental excitation. He who is eager to fight every evil which God allows to exist in society does not display rational courage. Even our Saviour selected the evils against which He waged war. The caged eagle which beats his wings into insensibility against the iron bars of his prison-house is accounted a foolish bird. On the other hand, "the linnet void of noble raze" has gained the everlasting seal of poetic disapproval. It is not genuine courage to go through the world like the knight in the tale with sword in hand and challenge on lips to offer mortal combat to every windmill of opposition.

Mr. Douglass was courageous in the broadest and best significance of the term. He set before him as the goal of his ambition his own personal freedom and that of his race, and he permitted neither principalities nor powers, nor height nor depth, nor things present nor things to come, to swerve him from the pursuit of that purpose.

When we speak of moral courage we indulge in tautology of terms; for all courage is essentially moral. It does not require courage to go with your friends or against your enemies; it is a physical impulse to do so. But true moral courage is shown when we say no to our friends.

Mr. Douglass reached the climax of moral courage when he parted with William Lloyd Garrison, his friend and benefactor, because of honest difference of judgment, and when for the same motive he refused to follow John Brown to the scaffold at Harper's Ferry. It required an iron resolution and sublime courage for

Douglass to deny the tender, pathetic, paternal appeal of the man
who was about to offer up himself as a sacrifice for an alien race.
John Brown on the scaffold dying for an alien and defenseless
race is the most sublime spectacle that this planet has seen since
Christ hung on the cross. That scaffold shall be more hallowed
during the ages to come than any throne upon which king ever
sat. Who but Douglass would decline a seat on his right hand?

In the fourth place, Mr. Douglass stands out as a model of
self-respect. Although he was subject to all of the degradation
and humiliation of his race, yet he preserved the integrity of his
own soul. It is natural for a class that is despised, rejected and
despitefully used to accept the estimate of their contemners, and
to conclude that they are good for nothing but to be cast out and
trodden under foot. In a civilization whose every feature serves to
impress a whole people with a sense of their inferiority, small
wonder if the more timid and resigned spirits are crushed beneath
the cruel weight. It requires the philosophic calm and poise to
stand upright and unperturbed amid such irrational things.

It is imperative that the youth of the colored race have impressed upon them the lesson that it is not the treatment that a
man receives that degrades him, but that which he accepts. It
does not degrade the soul when the body is swallowed up by
the earthquake or overwhelmed by the flood. We are not humiliated by the rebuffs of nature. No more should we feel humiliated
and degraded by violence and outrage perpetrated by a powerful
and arrogant social scheme. As a man thinketh in his heart, so
is he. The inner freedom of soul is not subject to assault and
battery. Mr. Douglass understood this principle well. He was
never in truth and in deed a slave; for his soul never accepted
the gyves that shackled his body.

It is related that Mr. Douglass was once ordered out of a first-
class coach into a "Jim Crow" car by a rude and ill-mannered
conductor. His white companion followed him to the prescribed
department, and asked him how he felt to be humiliated by such
a coarse fellow. Mr. Douglass let himself out to the full length
of his robust manhood and replied, "I feel as if I had been kicked
by an ass." If one will preserve his inner integrity, the ill-usage
and despiteful treatment others may heap upon him can never
penetrate to the holy of holies, which remains sacred and inviol-
able to an external assault.

The fifth lesson which should be emphasized in connection with
the life of Mr. Douglass is that he possessed a ruling passion out-

side the narrow circle of self-interest and personal well being. The love of liberty reigned supreme in his soul. All great natures are characterized by a passionate enthusiasm for some altruistic principle. Its highest manifestation is found in the zeal for the salvation of men on the spiritual side. All great religious teachers belong to this class. Patriots and philanthropists are ardently devoted to the present well-being of man. The poet, the painter, and the sculptor indulge in a fine frenzy over contemplative beauty or its formal expression. The philosopher and the scientist go into ecstasy over the abstract pursuit of truth. Minds of smaller caliber get pure delight from empty pleasure, sportsmanship or the collection of curios and bric-à-brac. Even the average man is at his highest level when his whole soul goes out in love for another. The man who lives without altruistic enthusiasm goes through the world wrapped in a shroud.

There have been few members of the human race that have been characterized by so intense and passionate a love for liberty as Frederick Douglass. His love for liberty was not limited by racial, political or geographical boundaries, but included the whole round world. He believed that liberty, like religion, applied to all men "without one plea." He championed liberty for black men, liberty for white men, liberty for Americans, liberty for Europeans, liberty for Asiatics, liberty for the wise, liberty for the simple; liberty for the weak, liberty for the strong; liberty for men, liberty for women; liberty for all the sons and daughters of men. I do not know whether he permitted his thoughts to wander in planetary space or speculated as to the inhabitability of other worlds than ours; but if he did, I am sure that his great soul took them all in his comprehensive scheme of liberty. In this day and time, when the spirit of commercialism and selfish greed command the best energies of the age, the influence of such a life to those who are downtrodden and overborne is doubly significant. Greed for gain has never righted any wrong in the history of the human race. The love of money is the root, and not the remedy of evil.

In the sixth and last place, I would call attention of the young to the danger of forgetting the work and worth of Frederick Douglass and the ministrations of his life. We live in a practical age when the things that are seen overshadow the things that are invisible.

What did Douglass do? ask the crass materialists. He built no institutions and laid no material foundations. True, he left us no showy tabernacles of clay. He did not aspire to be the mechanic of the colored race. The greatest things of this world are not made with hands, but reside in truth and righteousness and love. Douglass was the moral leader and spiritual prophet of his race. Unless all signs of the times are misleading, the time approaches, and is even now at hand, which demands a moral renaissance. Then, O for a Douglass, to arouse the conscience of the white race, to awaken the almost incomprehensible lethargy of his own people, and to call down the righteous wrath of Heaven upon injustice and wrong.

James Weldon Johnson (1871-1938)

Detroit

A man of many talents, James Weldon Johnson at various times was a school teacher, a principal, a lawyer, a leading song writer, a poet, a novelist, a consul for the United States, secretary for the National Association for the Advancement of Colored People, and a college professor. Born in Jacksonville, Florida, he received a Bachelor's degree from Atlanta University. After passing the Florida bar examinations, Johnson, a high-school principal, abandoned both law and education to join his brother Rosamond in New York, where, for several years, the two collaborated in writing successful musical comedies presented on Broadway. From 1906 to 1913 he served as Consul in Venezuela and Nicaragua. After leaving government service, he worked first as field secretary, then as general secretary, for the NAACP from 1916 to 1930. While teaching at Fisk University, whose faculty he joined in 1930, Johnson was killed in an automobile accident.

Although Johnson is best known to literary historians for his novel, *Autobiography of an Ex-Coloured Man* (1912), for his book of poetic folk sermons, *God's Trombones* (1927), for his cultural and social history of Negroes in New York, *Black Manhattan* (1930), or for *Book of American Negro Poetry*, the first anthology of poetry by black Americans, his position as secretary for the NAACP required him to write extensively on contemporary, political, social, and economic issues. In the following selection, he

From *The Crisis* XXXII (July 1926). Reprinted by permission of publishers of *The Crisis*.

describes the trial of Dr. Henry Sweet, who was charged with murder because, after moving into a white residential neighborhood in Detroit, he defended his home against a mob led by individuals organized to prevent Negroes from living in white neighborhoods. The chief defense attorney for Henry Sweet was Clarence Darrow, one of America's most famous trial lawyers.

Detroit

For eight months the National Office has been steeped in the Sweet case. It has whipped up every energy and drawn upon every recourse to carry the fight through to victory. All of us at the office realized the responsibility involved, and carried the whole matter on our hearts.

But when I entered the Recorder's Court of Detroit on Monday morning, May 3, in the midst of the second trial, I felt myself thrust suddenly, as an individual, into an arena of vital conflict and personally engaged in the struggle. I was at once so gripped by the tense drama being enacted before my eyes that I became a part of the tragedy. And tragedy it was. The atmosphere was tragic. The serried rows of colored faces that packed the courtroom from the rail to the back wall, watching and waiting, were like so many tragic masks. The mild, softspoken boy being tried for murder in the first degree and, for the time, carrying the onus of the other ten defendants, and upon whose fate hung the right of the black man to defend himself in his home, was an extremely tragic figure. The twelve white men sitting over against him, under oath to disregard prejudice and to render a true and just verdict between black and white in a land where race prejudice is far more vital than religion, also became tragic figures. The rugged face of Clarence Darrow, more haggard and lined by the anxious days, with the deep, brooding eyes, heightened the intense effect of the whole.

For a week I listened to testimony and the examination of witnesses. Each day the courtroom on the other side of the rail was packed as tightly as the space would permit. First, the witnesses for the prosecution, most of them members of the police force, evading the truth, distorting the truth, actually lying. And why? Because they were opposed to a Negro moving into a white neighborhood? Not primarily. The policemen who testified felt, even though a man's liberty was at stake, that they had to justify the course which the police had followed in the case. And so policeman after policeman, under oath, testified that on the night of the shooting, the streets around the Sweet house were almost deserted. From their description of the scene the vicinity was like Goldsmith's "Deserted Village". And thus they showed themselves willing to swear away a man's liberty for life in order to save the face of the Police Department. For if it was shown that there was a mob around the Sweet home on that fateful night the Police Department would become responsible for all the consequences, because it allowed that mob to assemble. But it was proven that there was a mob of five hundred persons or more. This was proven by disinterested witnesses for the defense; and the police did nothing to prevent the gathering of that mob. From their own testimony they did not ask a single person what he was doing there or to move away.

The witnesses for the prosecution who were not policemen were admittedly prejudiced against colored people and opposed to their living in white neighborhoods. They were for the most part members of the Waterworks Improvement Association, organized for the purpose of keeping colored people out of white neighborhoods, and home owners in the vicinity in which Dr. Sweet had purchased. And so, like the policemen, they were interested witnesses. They did not have their faces to save but they felt that they had their property to save. One of these witnesses with a Germanic name and the face of a moron, on Mr. Darrow's cross-examination, stated that he and his neighbors were organized to keep "undesirables" out of the neighborhood. He, of course, listed Negroes at the head of the "undesirables". When further pressed by Mr. Darrow he added "Italians". When still further pressed he stated that they did not want anybody but Americans. When Mr. Darrow asked him if he knew that Negroes had been in America for more than three hundred years, longer than any of his ancestors, and that America was discovered by a great Italian, he had no words for answer.

Witnesses for the defense restored my faith in human nature — and not because they were for the defense but because they were telling the truth. The white witnesses for the defense were absolutely without interest. It was plain that they could have no motive for testifying that there was a mob around the Sweet house on that eventful night, except in behalf of truth. And although racial interest might have been imputed to the colored witnesses, nevertheless, because they were speaking the truth they

carried conviction. And perhaps more impressive still was the
fact that the colored witnesses who testified showed themselves
far superior intellectually, culturally and socially, to the white
witnesses who were among those opposed to the Sweets moving
into their neighborhood.

During all the days of the testimony the court and the crowd
listened intently to every word that fell from the lips of the witnesses. The crowd was sensitive, like a barometer, to the ups and
downs of the testimony. Whenever Darrow or Chawke scored in
their cross-examination a ray of light lit the sea of dark faces,
and when the prosecutors won a point sombre tragedy would
again settle down.

On Saturday night, May 8, both sides rested.

On Monday morning the attorneys for the defense made the
motions for dismissal or a directed verdict and, as was expected,
the motions were denied. The argument for the State was then
opened by the Assistant Prosecuting Attorney who made a fierce
attack upon the Sweets and their motives. He closed by drawing
for the jury a picture of the cold, stark body of Leon Breiner,
the white man who had been killed. He stressed the words, "I
hold a brief for Leon Breiner". He was followed in the afternoon
by Mr. Chawke for the Defense. Mr. Chawke spoke with all of
the skill and power of the great criminal lawyer that he is.

On Tuesday morning every available space in the courtroom was
taken up. Even within the railing spectators were closely packed
together. There were hundreds of colored people and a large
number of interested whites. There were prominent lawyers and
jurists of Detroit. When the court opened not another person
could be squeezed into the courtroom. Clarence Darrow was to
speak.

For nearly seven hours he talked to the jury. I sat where I
could catch every word and every expression of his face. It was
the most wonderful flow of words I ever heard from a man's lips.
Clarence Darrow, the veteran criminal lawyer, the psychologist,
the philosopher, the great humanist, the great apostle of liberty,
was bringing into play every bit of skill, drawing upon all the
knowledge, and using every power that he possessed. Court and
jury and spectators had unrolled before them a complete panorama of the experiences, physical and spiritual, of the American
Negro, beginning with his African background, down to the
present — a panorama of his sufferings, his struggles, his achievements, his aspirations. Mr. Darrow's argument was at once an
appeal for the Negro because of the injustice he has suffered, a

tribute to him for what he has achieved in spite of handicaps and obstacles, and an indictment of the morality and civilization of America because of the hypocrisies and brutalities of race prejudice. At times his voice was as low as though he were coaxing a reluctant child. At such times the strain upon the listeners to catch his words made them appear almost rigid. At other times his words came like flashes of lightning and crashes of thunder. He closed his agrument with an appeal that did not leave a dry eye in the courtroom. When he finished I walked over to him to express in behalf of the National Association for the Advancement of Colored People my appreciation and thanks. His eyes were shining and wet. He placed his hands on my shoulders. I stammered out a few words but broke down and wept, and I was not ashamed of my tears.

On the following morning the Prosecutor closed the argument for the State. He began as though he intended to rival Mr. Darrow in paying a tribute to the Negro race, but his beginning was only a background to set off what he really meant to say. Some of the things he said brought quick and firm objections from our lawyers. He spoke in rather high terms of the National Association for the Advancement of Colored People and then added that if he had a mind like some people he would say it was an organization for the purpose of foistering colored people into white neighborhoods, for the purpose of promoting social equality, and for the purpose of bringing about an amalgamation of the races. The defense attorneys objected and the Judge admonished, but this appeal to prejudice the jury had already heard. At another time he virtually asked the jury what would they as twelve white men, if they brought in a verdict of not guilty, answer to white men who asked them about their verdict. Here again the defense lawyers objected, but the jury again had heard. In his zeal to convict, the Prosecutor overstepped legal lines and called the jury's attention to the fact that the defendant had not taken the stand and testified in his own behalf to contradict certain statements which had been made. Mr. Chawke was immediately on his feet and objected. The objection was sustained and the grounds were laid for a reversible error. The point was one which has been several times sustained by the Supreme Court of Michigan and the courts of various other states. When the Prosecutor finished the court adjourned for the day.

The next morning, Thursday, the courtroom was again crowded, to hear the charge of the Judge. For two and a half hours Judge Murphy charged the jury. The charge contemplated the law

involved from every point and yet it was not the dry dust of the
law books. It was eloquent and moving. In his charge, as in presiding over the case, Judge Murphy showed himself absolutely fair
and impartial. Indeed, he was in the highest degree the just judge.
The jury went into deliberation immediately after lunch. We were
hopeful but not sanguine. We counted that the worst we could get
would be another mistrial. It was commonly expressed that a
mistrial was the probable verdict. We were heartened by the
fact that, in case of a verdict of guilty in any degree, we held in
our hands the ace of a reversible error.

I left the courtroom after the charge to the jury and sent a
telegram to the National Office. I walked over to Judge Jayne's
court and talked with him for a while. Then, feeling not at all
like eating, I went back to the courtroom to wait. The crowd that
had waited patiently for days was still waiting. Suddenly there
was a pounding on the jury room door. The officer in charge of the
jury answered and found that the jury wanted further instructions. Neither the Judge nor the attorneys had yet returned from
lunch. There was nothing to indicate the need of hurry. Everybody expected the jury would ask for further instructions and be
locked up for the night. A little later the Judge and the attorneys
returned to the court. The attorneys began to draft instructions
that would be acceptable to both sides on the point raised by the
jury. I sat in the Judge's ante-chamber and watched them while
they worked. Mr. Chawke made the first draft on a yellow pad.
The Prosecuting Attorney revised and amended. Mr. Darrow and
the Assistant Prosecuting Attorney expressed their views. The
draft was at last agreed upon by the four attorneys. The Prosecutor had just torn from the pad the sheets that contained the
written words to pass them in to the Judge when the officer in
charge of the jury entered the room and announced that a verdict
had been reached. Everybody in the room was amazed. We for the
defense, in spite of ourselves, were seized with apprehension. The
probabilities were that a verdict so quickly reached was a compromise verdict. There was even the possibility of a verdict of guilty
as charged. These thoughts ran through all our minds. They
showed themselves in the quickly changing expressions of the
Prosecutors. Both attorneys for the prosecution, perhaps unconsciously, assumed a magnanimous air. It was as much as to say,
"We are sorry; it is too bad; but we had to do our official duty".
These thoughts were quickly transmitted to the waiting crowd in

the courtroom and with the crowd the fears and apprehensions were magnified.

The court re-convened. The judge ascended to the bench. Mr. Chawke came over and whispered a word of encouragement to Henry Sweet. I sat next to Henry Sweet. I put my hand on his arm and said, "No matter what happens the National Association will stand by you to the end."

The jury was called in. They filed in solemnly and took their places facing the bench. The clerk asked, "Gentlemen, have you arrived at a verdict?" The answer was, "We have". I then began to live the most intense thirty seconds of my whole life. The verdict was pronounced by the foreman in a strong, clear voice which filled the courtroom, "Not Guilty".

The effect is electrical. We are transported in a flash from the depths to the heights. Someone starts to applaud but brings his hands together only once. A simultaneous sigh of relief goes up from the hundreds outside the rail. I look around. Women are sobbing convulsively, and tears are running down the cheeks of men. I get a confused vision of Henry Sweet, Dr. Sweet and his wife shaking hands with the jury and thanking them, shaking hands with Mr. Darrow and Mr. Chawke and thanking them. They are followed by others. It seems that everybody is shaking hands and giving thanks.

The verdict was recorded upon the oath of the jury and thus was reached what we believe to be the end of the most dramatic court trial involving the fundamental rights of the Negro in his whole history in this country.

Langston Hughes (1902-1967)

Fooling Our White Folks

Langston Hughes has been described as the most versatile Negro American writer who ever lived. Born in Joplin, Missouri, reared in Kansas and Ohio, he entered Columbia University in 1922 but dropped out after a year of studying. For several years, he worked his way through Europe and Africa before he returned to America, where he became a part of the Harlem Renaissance. After returning to college to earn an undergraduate degree from Lincoln University (Pa.), Hughes became a professional writer and lecturer.

No other Negro writer has matched the variety of Hughes's achievements. Well-known for his attempts to reproduce "jazz" rhythms and "blues" in poetry, he published nine volumes of poems, two novels, and three collections of stories. Fascinated by theater, he established several all-Negro theatrical companies and wrote several plays. Three of his plays were produced on Broadway, and one — *Mulatto* (1934) — enjoyed the longest continuous run of any play written by a Negro before Lorraine Hansberry. In addition, Hughes wrote the libretto for the musical version of Elmer Rice's *Street Scene*, an opera, stories for children, and two autobiographies. He also translated poetry, edited or co-edited anthologies of folklore and poetry, and publicized the musical and literary achievements of Africans and Afro-Americans. Perhaps his most significant literary achievement lies in the many stories, sketches, and essays about Jesse B. Semple ("Simple").

From *Negro Digest* (April, 1950). ©Copyright, 1950 by the Johnson Publishing Company, Inc. Reprinted by permission of publisher.

A migrant from Virginia to Harlem, Simple is a memorable character in American literature. Lacking formal education, but richly endowed with intelligence, wit, and pride, he rejoices in the excitement of living while he simultaneously denounces white men who repress Negroes and middle-class Negroes who attempt to escape their racial identity.

As he continued to write for more than thirty years after the Renaissance ended, Hughes, better than any other writer, kept alive the confidence, the laughter, and the zest for living which had characterized the Harlem writers during that exuberant decade. The following selection is characteristic of the manner in which Hughes frequently satirized subjects which other writers have viewed with serious, often excessively serious, concern.

Fooling Our White Folks

I never was one for pushing the phrase "social equality" to the nth degree. I concur with those persons, white or colored, who wish to reserve the right of inviting whom they choose into the house as friends, or as dinner guests. I do not believe civil rights should encroach on personal privacy or personal associations. But health, wealth, work, the ballot, the armed services, are another matter. Such things should be available to whites and Negroes alike in this American country.

But, because our American whites are stupid in so many ways, racially speaking, and because there are many things in this U.S.A. of ours which Negroes may achieve only by guile, I have great tolerance for persons of color who deliberately set out to fool our white folks. I remember the old slave story of the mistress who would not allow her house servants to have any biscuits. She was so particular on this point that she would cut the biscuits out herself and count them. But the cook went her one better. When the mistress left the kitchen, the cook would trim a narrow rim off every biscuit — with the result that the Negroes had in the end a pan of biscuits, too.

A great many Negroes in America are daily engaged in slyly trimming off the biscuits of race prejudice. Most Negroes feel that bigoted white persons deserve to be cheated and fooled since the way they behave toward us makes no moral sense at all. And many Negroes would be way behind the eight ball had they not devised surreptitious means of escape. For those who are able to do it, passing for white is, of course, the most common means of escaping color handicaps. Every large Negro section has many residents who pass for white by day, but come home to their various Harlems at night. I know dozens of colored whites in downtown offices or shops. But at night they are colored again.

Then there are those Negroes who go white permanently. This is perhaps a more precarious game than occupational passing during work hours only. Some break down under the strain and go native again or go to pieces. But hundreds of others pass blithely into the third and fourth generations — entirely losing their dusky horizons by intermarriage. There is one quite well-known Negro family in the East with an equally well-known brother out West who has been "white" for forty years, and whose children's children are "white" — now, no doubt, beyond recall. A famous Negro educator told me recently of having lost track of one of his most brilliant students, only to be asked to address a large and wealthy congregation in the Midwest and to find as pastor of this church his long lost colored graduate, now the "white" shepherd of a white flock. The educator was delighted at his former student's ministerial success in fooling our white folks.

The consensus of opinion among Negroes seems to be approval of those who can get by with it. Almost all of as know Negroes of light complexion who, during the war, were hustled through their draft boards so fast that they were unwittingly put into white units and did their service entirely without the humiliations of the military color bar. One young Negro of my acquaintance took his basic training in Mississippi in a white unit, lived with the white boys, went to all the local dances and parties, and had a wonderful time without the army or Rankin being any the wiser. He is back now in the Negro college from which the draft took him. The army policy being stupid anyway, all his family and friends applaud his having so thoroughly fooled our white folks in the deep South.

Negroes are even more pleased when persons of *obviously* colored complexion succeed in calling white America's bluff. Those young ladies who, in spite of golden or brown complexions, take foreign names and become Hollywood starlets, delight us. And the men who go to Mexico as colored and come back as Spanish to marry wealthy white debutantes gain a great deal of admiration from the bulk of the Negro race. Negroes feel it is good

enough for Nordic debutantes to be thusly fooled. Besides, nothing
is too good for those with nerve enough to take it. Anyhow, hasn't
the army a strange way of classifying black Puerto Ricans as
"white" while quite white American Negroes are put down as
"colored"? Simple, our white folks: so why not fool them?

When the Waldorf-Astoria first opened in New York, Negroes
were not served in its main dining rooms. In a spirt of fun, a
well-known Harlem journalist of definitely colored cast, put on
a turban and went into the hotel. He was served with the utmost
courtesy. During the war a fine Negro chemist, quite brownskin,
applied for a position in a war plant and was given a blank to
fill out. He truthfully put down his nationality as American, his
race as Negro. He received a letter saying no openings were
available, in spite of the fact that every day the firm advertised
for chemists. He simply procured another blank. Instead of putting
down Negro as his race, he wrote Puerto Rican — and was hired
at once. Silly, our white folks!

Some Negroes make sport of them all the time. There is a
very dark gentleman in a large Midwestern city where prejudice
in public places is rampant, who delights in playing upon white
gullibility. Being truly African in complexion, he does not pretend
to pass for white. He can't. But since many of the restaurants
and theatres are owned or managed by foreign-born Americans,
or Jewish Americans, he simply passes for whatever the nationality
of the management might be at the time. He will tell a Jewish
theatre manager who wishes him to sit in the Negro section, "Do
you not know that I am a black Hebrew?" Usually the man will
be so taken aback that he will say no more. Such sport this patron
enjoys more than the films.

He once went into a Greek restaurant at the edge of the Negro
section, but which, nevertheless, had a custom of not serving
Negroes. He was told he could not eat therein. He said, "but did
you never hear of Socrates? He was a black Greek. Many noble
Greeks of old were colored. I am descended from such ancient
Greeks. What do you mean, *I*, a black Greek, cannot eat here?"
He was served without further ado. Funny, our white folks —
even those not yet Americanized! They, too, act right simple
sometimes.

In the early days of the war, reading my poems at various
U.S.O.'s in the South, one day between Nashville and Chattanooga
I went into the buffet section of a parlor car coach for luncheon.
The Filipino steward-waiter looked at me askance as I sat down.

He made several trips into the kitchen before he finally came up to me and said, "The cook wants to see you." I said, "Please send the cook out here, then." He did. The cook was a Negro. The cook said, "That Filipino wants me to tell you that you can't eat in here, but I am not going to tell you no such thing. I am going to send your lunch out." He did. I ate.

Another time during the war, before they had those curtained-off tables for colored folk in Southern diners, passing through Alabama, I went to dinner and sat down in the very center of the car. The white steward leaned over and whispered politely in my ear, "Are you Negro or foreign, sir?" I said, "I'm just hungry!" The colored waiters laughed. He went away. And I was served. Sometimes a little nerve will put discrimination to rout. A dignified lady of color one day walked into a white apartment house elevator whose policy was not to take Negroes upstairs except on the servant's lift. The elevator man directed her, "Take the service car, please." She drew herself up to her full height and said, "How dare you?" He did not dare further. He took her up without a word to the white friends on whom she was calling.

A little daring with languages, too, will often go a long way. *"Dame un boletto Pullman to Chicago,"* will get you a berth in Texas when often plain English, "Give me a Pullman ticket to Chicago," will not. Negroes do not always have to change color to fool our white folks. Just change tongues. Upon returning from Europe one summer, a mulatto lady I know decided to live downtown for the winter. So, using her French, she registered at a Fifth Avenue hotel that has never before nor since been known to house a Negro guest. But she stayed there several months before moving back to Harlem. A little, *"S'il vous plait"* did it. I once knew a West Indian Negro darker than I am who spent two weeks at the Beverly-Wiltshire Hotel in the movie colony simply by registering as a Chinese from Hong Kong.

Our white folks are very easily fooled. Being so simple about race, why shouldn't they be? They have no business being prejudiced with so much democracy around. But since they are prejudiced, there's no harm in fooling the devil, is there? That old mistress in slavery time with plenty of dough, had no business denying her house servants a few biscuits. That they got them in the end served her right. Most colored folks think that as long as white folks remain foolish, prejudiced and racially selfish, they deserve to be fooled. No better for them!

George S. Schuyler (1895-   )

What the Negro
Thinks of the South

No anthology of essays by black Americans is complete without a sample of the work of one of the many columnists who have published in the Negro newspapers. One of the better-known columnists is George Schuyler, who was born in Providence, Rhode Island, and educated in the public schools of Syracuse, New York. A member of the editorial staff of *The Messenger*, from 1923 to 1928, and assistant editor from 1926 to 1928, Schuyler became more widely known as associate editor and regular columnist for *The Pittsburgh Courier*, whose editorial staff he joined in 1924. He also wrote *Slaves, Today: A History of Liberia* (1931) and *Black No More*, a satirical novel about the confusions resulting from the discovery of a drug which enables Negroes to become white.

A journalist of strong convictions, Schuyler spared neither blacks nor whites from his vitriolic ridicule. His increasing conservatism late in his career alienated many black readers who had admired his early work. In the following selection, Schuyler, a Northerner, turns his attention to Negroes' attitudes about Southern white people.

What the Negro Thinks of the South

Wide circulation has been given to the opinion of the white South about the Negro but the latter's opinion of the white South has enjoyed far less currency, except in the Negro press.

From *Negro Digest* (1945). ©Copyright, 1945 by the Johnson Publishing Company, Inc. Reprinted by permission of publishers.

Accordingly, many of our native Caucasians who have recently begun reading Negro newspapers have been quite shocked by the bitterness with which Dixie is customarily discussed, and professional Southerners of the Rankin stripe have hastened to reassert with emotional conviction the Negrophobic faiths which motivate them.

Just what do Negroes, by and large, think about the South?

Well, their thoughts about Dixie are similar to the opinion of Jews about Germany. They love the South (especially if they are Southern-born) for its beauty, its climate, its fecundity and its better ways of life; but they hate, with a bitter, corroding hatred, the color prejudice, the discrimination, the violence, the crudities, the insults and humiliations, and the racial segregation of the South, and they hate all those who keep these evils alive.

As a young Florida bootblack once told me, "The South sure would be a fine place if there wasn't no white folks there!"

I know a colored woman, a Georgia-born graduate of Spelman College who has resided in New York City for ten years. When she recently returned from a brief visit to her native State, I asked her what she thought of the South. Grimly she replied, "I would like to see it blasted by robot bombs until not a building was left standing!"

This is a rather extreme expression of the hatred of Dixie which I believe to be characteristic of most Southern Negroes living outside the South. Because of this feeling they have left there in droves and have no intention of returning except for brief visits to their families.

When these Negroes left the South they were through with it forever. They hate it for what they suffered physically and spiritually, and they are eager contributors to all efforts to fight the things for which the South stands in their opinion. In the main their paramount desire is to get their families and friends out of the South to freer territory where they will no longer be "boys," "gals" and "niggers"; where they will be free of the atmosphere of restriction, proscription and terror; where they can escape the maddeningly smug assumption of white superiority, and the oily and transparent condescension of "good" white folks who have "always loved the Negro."

Most Southern whites would be surprised to know that the Negroes who live in the South are similarly detestful of the "institutions" of Dixie. They bitterly resent having to swallow their pride, having perforce to plead and fawn for a measure of justice and fair play, having to be ever watchful of word and

action for fear of swift reprisal, having forever to play second
fiddle and pretend to like it.

And they loathe those Negroes in the vulnerable position of
leadership who, for various reasons, pretend to like it and are
sometimes wont to console themselves with the baseless belief
that those who have escaped to freer soil are actually worse off,
voluminous statistics to the contrary notwithstanding.

Most of these Southern Negroes feel themselves in a battle as
important as any struggles of the various European Undergrounds
— a battle which thy have fought in various ways for three
centuries, first by poison, fire, bullet and flight, and latterly by
education and organization.

For this reason they have flocked to the National Association
for the Advancement of Colored People, some of whose largest
and most militant branches today are below "The Line." They
have rallied enthusiastically to the fight for equalization of teachers' salaries, for a free ballot, for economic advantages, and against
insult, humiliation and terrorism.

The Southern Negro today regards most of the white South
as his enemy, and all his scheming, planning, organizing and
fighting is with the aim of worsting this enemy about whom he
is far more bitter than he is against either the Germans or the
Japanese.

He does not think of the white Southerners as in any way
superior, save in military, political and economic power, and he
has no desire to take advantage of them, assuming he could. In
fact my observation has been that the Southern Negro wants
as little as possible to do with the Southern white man — he
simply wants the same rights, privileges and duties, and hates
those who deny them to him.

As for Northern-born Negroes, they think of the South as an
outlandish and barbaric area to be shunned as one would the
plague, and to never visit except as a school teacher or on business.
A Negro who migrates South is as rare as a Jew seeking transportation to Berlin.

They hate the white South from afar and contribute to all
attacks against it with grim and fanatical zeal. For decades they
fostered and sustained the attack against the enemy until their
Southern brethren were prepared to join in the attack, as they
have done in increasing numbers since World War I.

The average Negro does not think that *all* Southern whites
are ignorant, prejudiced, cruel and unfair. He knows there are
notable exceptions, but he also thinks they are a microscopic

minority having little or no effect on Southern traditions and institutions.

He would like to see the South change but he is none too optimistic. He is hopeful but not gullible.

He is bitterly militant and determined, sore and resentful, and what he privately thinks of the South is usually unprintable.

Saunders Redding (1906-   )

American Negro Literature

In the period since World War II, Saunders Redding has been one of the more distinguished scholar-critics among Negro writers. Born in Delaware in 1906, he earned a Bachelor of Philosophy degree from Brown University. A member of Phi Beta Kappa Honor Society and a former college professor, he is currently Director of the Division of Research and Publication of the National Foundation on the Arts and the Humanities. Recipient of Guggenheim and Rockefeller Awards and the Mayflower Award from the North Carolina Literary and Historical Society for his autobiographical *No Day of Triumph*, Redding has published a novel, *Stranger and Alone* (1950); an excellent critical history of literature by Negroes, *To Make a Poet Black* (1939); a collection of essays, *On Being Negro in America* (1951); and three histories of Negroes in America. His most recent book is *The Negro* (1967).

As a frequent contributor to periodicals, Redding has earned a reputation as a perceptive and knowledgeable historian of literature by Afro-Americans. The following selection summarizes their literary development during the first half of the twentieth century.

American Negro Literature

There is this about literature by American Negroes — it has uncommon resilience. Three times within this century it has been

Reprinted from *The American Scholar,* Volume 18, Number 2, Spring, 1949. Copyright ©1949 by the United Chapters of Phi Beta Kappa. By permission of the publishers.

done nearly to death: once by indifference, once by opposition, and once by the unbounded enthusiasm of its well-meaning friends.

By 1906, Charles W. Chesnutt, the best writer of prose fiction the race had produced, was silent; Paul Laurence Dunbar, the most popular poet, was dead. After these two, at least in the general opinion, there were no other Negro writers. Booker Washington had published *Up from Slavery,* but Washington was no writer — he was the orator and the organizer of the march to a questionable new Canaan. The poetic prose of DuBois, throbbing in *The Souls of Black Folk,* had not yet found its audience. Polemicists like Monroe Trotter, Kelly, Miller and George Forbes were faint whispers in a lonesome wood. Indifference had stopped the ears of all but the most enlightened who, as often as not, were derisively labeled "nigger lovers."

But this indifference had threatened even before the turn of the century. Dunbar felt it, and the purest stream of his lyricism was made bitter and all but choked by it. Yearning for the recognition of his talent as it expressed itself in the pure English medium, he had to content himself with a kindly, but condescending praise of his dialect pieces. Time and again he voiced the sense of frustration brought on by the neglect of what he undoubtedly considered his best work. Writing dialect, he told James Weldon Johnson, was "the only way he could get them to listen to him." His literary friend and sponsor, William D. Howells, at that time probably the most influential critic in America, passing over Dunbar's verse in pure English with only a glance, urged him to write "of his own race in its own accents of our English."

During Dunbar's lifetime, his pieces in pure English appeared more or less on sufferance. The very format of the 1901 edition of *Lyrics of the Hearthside,* the book in which most of his non-dialect poetry was published, suggests this. No fancy binding on this book, no handsome paper, no charming, illustrative photographs. *Lyrics of the Hearthside* was the least publicized of all his books of poetry, and four lines from his "The Poet" may tell why.

> He sang of love when earth was young,
>   And love itself was in his lays,
>   But, ah, the world it turned to praise
> A jingle in a broken tongue.

Enough has been said about the false concepts, the stereotypes which were effective — and to some extent are still effective — in white America's thinking about the Negro for the point not to be labored here. History first, and then years of insidious labor to perpetuate what history had wrought, created these stereotypes. According to them, the Negro was a buffoon, a harmless child of nature, a dangerous despoiler (the concepts were contradictory), an irresponsible beast of devilish cunning — soulless, ambitionless and depraved. The Negro, in short, was a higher species of some creature that was not quite man.

What this had done to writing by American Negroes could easily be imagined, even without the documentation, which is abundant. No important critic of writing by American Negroes has failed to note the influence of the concept upon it. Sterling Brown, one of the more searching scholars in the field, gives it scathing comment in "The Negro Author and His Publisher." James Weldon Johnson touches upon it in his preface to the 1931 edition of his anthology, but he does so even more cogently in "The Negro Author's Dilemma." The introduction to Countee Cullen's *Caroling Dusk* is a wry lament over it. In *The New Negro*, Alain Locke expresses the well-founded opinion that the Negro "has been a stock figure perpetuated as an historical fiction partly in innocent sentimentalism, partly in deliberate reactionism."

There can be no question as to the power of the traditional concepts. The Negro writer reacted to them in one of two ways. Either he bowed down to them, writing such stories as would do them no violence; or he went to the opposite extreme and wrote for the purpose of invalidating, or at least denying, the tradition. Dunbar did the former. Excepting only a few, his short stories depict Negro characters as whimsical, simple, folksy, not-too-bright souls, all of whose social problems are little ones, and all of whose emotional cares can be solved by the intellectual or spiritual equivalent of a stick of red peppermint candy. It is of course significant that three of his four novels are not about Negroes at all; and the irony of depicting himself as a white youth in his spiritual autobiography, *The Uncalled*, needs no comment.

Charles Chesnutt's experience is also to the point. When his stories began appearing in the *Atlantic Monthly* in 1887, it was not generally known that their author was a Negro. Stories like "The Gray Wolf's Ha'nt" and "The Goophered Grapevine" were so detached and objective that the author's race could not have been detected from a reading of them. The editor of the *Atlantic Monthly*, Walter H. Page, fearing that public acknowledgment of it would do the author's work harm, was reluctant to admit that Chesnutt was a Negro, and the fact of his race was kept a closely guarded secret for a decade.

It was this same fear that led to the rejection of Chesnutt's first novel, *The House Behind The Cedars*, for "a literary work by an American of acknowledged color was a doubtful experiment . . . entirely apart from its intrinsic merit." The reception of Chesnutt's later books — those that came after 1900 — was to prove that literary works by an "American of color" were more than doubtful experiments. *The Colonel's Dream* and *The Marrow of Tradition* did not pay the cost of the paper and the printing. They were honest probings at the heart of a devilish problem; they were, quite frankly, propaganda. But the thing that made the audience of the day indifferent to them was their attempt to override the concepts that were the props of the dialect tradition. Had Chesnutt not had a reputation as a writer of short stories (which are, anyway, his best work), it is likely that his novels would not have been published at all.

The poetry of Dunbar and the prose of Chesnutt proved that even with the arbitrary limitations imposed upon them by historical convention, Negro writers could rise to heights of artistic expression. They could even circumvent the convention, albeit self-consciously, and create credible white characters in a credible white milieu.

II

After about 1902, indifference began to crystallize into opposition to the culture-conscious, race-conscious Negro seeking honest answers to honest questions. It was opposition to the Negro's democratic ambitions which were just then beginning to burgeon. It was opposition to the Negro who was weary of his role of clown, scapegoat, doormat. And it was, of course, opposition to the Negro writer who was honest and sincere and anxious beyond the bounds of superimposed racial polity.

There is danger here of over-simplifying a long and complex story. Even with the advantage of hindsight, it is hard to tell what is cause and what effect. But let us have a look at some of the more revealing circumstances. In 1902 came Thomas Dixon's *The Leopard's Spots*, and three years later *The Clansman*. They were both tremendously popular. In 1906 there were race riots in Georgia and Texas, in 1908 in Illinois. . . . By this later year, too, practically all of the Southern states had disfranchised the Negro and made color caste legal. . . . The Negro's talent for monkeyshines had been exploited on the stage, and coon songs (some by James Weldon Johnson and his brother!) had attained wide popularity. Meantime, in 1904, Thomas Nelson Page had published the bible of reactionism, *The Negro, The Southerner's Problem*. And, probably most cogent fact of all, Booker Washington had reached the position of undisputed leader of American Negroes by advocating a racial policy strictly in line with the traditional concept.

There had been a time when the old concept of the Negro had served to ease his burden. He had been laughed at, tolerated, and genially despaired of as hopeless in a modern, dynamic society. White Americans had become used to a myth — had, indeed, convinced themselves that myth was reality. All the instruments of social betterment — schools, churches, lodges — adopted by colored people were the subjects of ribald jokes and derisive laughter. Even the fact that the speeches which Booker Washington was making up and down the country could have been made only by a really intelligent and educated man did not strike them as a contradiction of the concept. And anyway, there was this about Washington: he was at least half-white, and white blood in that proportion excused and accounted for many a thing, including being intelligent, lunching with President Theodore Roosevelt, and getting an honorary degree from Harvard.

Today any objective judgment of Booker Washington's basic notion must be that it was an extension of the old tradition framed in new terms. He preached a message of compromise, of humility, of patience. Under the impact of social change the concept was modified to include the stereotype of the Negro as satisfied peasant, a docile servitor under the stern but kindly eye of the white boss; a creature who had a place, knew it, and would keep it unless he got *bad* notions from somewhere. The merely laughable coon had become also the cheap laborer who could be righteously exploited for his own good and to the greater glory of God. By this addition to the concept, the Negro-white status quo — the condition of inferior-superior caste — could be maintained in the face of profound changes in the general society.

What this meant to the Negro artist and writer was that he must, if he wished an audience, adhere to the old forms and the acceptable patterns. It meant that he must work within the limitations of the concept, or ignore his racial kinship altogether and leave unsounded the profoundest depths of the peculiar experiences which were his by reason of his race. But fewer and fewer Negro writers were content with the limitations. The number of dialect pieces (the term includes the whole tradition) written after 1907 is very small indeed. Among Negro writers the tradition had lost its force and its validity. White writers like Julia Peterkin and Gilmore Millen, and, in a different way, Carl Van Vechten and DuBose Heyward, were to lend it a spurious strength down through the 1920's.

Negro writers of unmistakable talent chose the second course, and some of them won high critical praise for their work in non-racial themes. Their leader was William Stanley Braithwaite. Save only a few essays written at the behest of his friend, W. E. B. DuBois, nothing that came from his pen had anything about it to mark it as Negro. His leading essays in the Boston *Transcript*, his anthologies of magazine verse, and his own poetry, might just as well have been written by someone with no background in the provocative experience of being colored in America.

Though the other Negro poets of this genre (which was not entirely a genre) developed a kind of dilettantist virtuosity, none carried it to Braithwaite's amazing lengths of self-conscious contrivance. They were simpler and more conventional in their apostasy. Alice Dunbar, the widow of Paul, wrote sonnets of uncommon skill and beauty. Georgia Johnson and Anne Spenser were at home in the formal lyric, and James Weldon Johnson in "The White Witch" and "My City" set a very high standard for his fellow contributors to the *Century Magazine*.

But given the whole web of circumstance — empirical, historic, racial, psychological — these poets must have realized that they could not go on in this fashion. With a full tide of race-consciousness bearing in upon them individually and as a group, they could not go on forever denying their racehood. To try to do this at all was symptomatic of neurotic strain. They could not go on, and they did not. The hardiest of them turned to expression of another kind the moment the pressure was off.

The pressure was not off for another decade and a half. As a matter of fact, it mounted steadily. For all of Booker Washington's popularity and ideological appeal among whites, who had set him up as *the* leader of the Negro race, and for all of his power, there was rebellion against him in the forward ranks of Negroes. Rebellion against Washington meant dissatisfaction with the social and economic goals which he had persuaded white Americans were the proper goals for the Negro race. The whites had not counted on this disaffection, and their reaction to it was willful, blind opposition.

What had happened was that Booker Washington, with the help of the historic situation and the old concept, had so thoroughly captured the minds of most of those white people who were kindly disposed to Negroes that not another Negro had a chance to be heard. Negro schools needing help could get it from rich and powerful whites only through Booker Washington. Negro social thought wanting a sounding board could have it only with the sanction of the principal of Tuskegee. Negro politicians were helpless without his endorsement. Negro seekers after jobs of any consequence in either public or private capacities begged recommendations from Booker Washington.

This despotic power — and there is scarcely another term for it — was stultifying to many intelligent Negroes, especially in the North. White editors, who would have published anything under the signature of Booker Washington, consistently rejected all but the most innocuous work of other Negroes. Publishers were not interested in the ideas of Negroes unless those ideas conformed to Washington's, or in creative work by and about Negroes unless they fell into the old pattern.

So intelligent, articulate Negroes grew insurgent, and the leader of this insurgence was W. E. B. DuBois. Nor was his the only voice raised in protest. Charles Chesnutt spoke out, and so did John Hope and Kelly Miller. In 1900 the *Chicago Defender* had been founded, and in 1901 Monroe Trotter's *Boston Guardian.* Courageous as these polemical organs were, they had not yet grown into full effectiveness. Neither had DuBois, but he was growing fast. By 1903 the Atlanta University Studies of the Negro were coming out regularly under his editorship. In that year he published *The Souls of Black Folk,* which contained the essay "Of Mr. Booker T. Washington and Others," sharply critical of the Tuskegee leader. DuBois was in on the founding of the National Association for the Advancement of Colored People, and in 1910 he became editor of the new monthly, the *Crisis.*

From the very first the *Crisis* was much more than the official organ of the N.A.A.C.P. It was a platform for the expression of all sorts of ideas that ran counter to the notion of Negro inferiority. Excepting such liberal and nonpopular journals as the *Atlantic Monthly* and *World's Work* and the two or three Negro newspapers that had not been bought or throttled by the "Tuskegee Machine," the *Crisis* was the only voice the Negro had. The opposition to that voice was organized around the person and the philosophy of Booker Washington, and there were times when this opposition all but drowned out the voice.

Nevertheless protestation and revolt were becoming bit by bit more powerful reagents in the social chemistry that produced the New Negro. Year by year more Negroes were transformed — and a lot of them needed transforming. Once James Weldon Johnson himself had written "coon songs" and been content to carol with sweet humility "Lift Every Voice and Sing." When Johnson wrote it in 1900, it had the approval of Booker Washington and became the "Negro National Anthem." Then followed Johnson's period of apostasy and such jejune pieces as "The Glory of the Day Was in Her Face," among others. But in 1912, when he was already forty-one, he wrote the novel *The Autobiography of an Ex-Colored Man,* and in 1917 he cried out bitterly that Negroes must cease speaking "servile words" and must "stand erect and without fear."

III

Other factors than simple protest contributed to the generation of the New Negro. In the first place, the notions regarding the Old Negro were based on pure myth. The changes occurring at the onset of war in Europe sloughed off some of the emotional and intellectual accretions, and the Negro stood partially revealed for what he was — a fellow whose opportunities had been narrowed by historical fallacies, "a creature of moral debate," but a man pretty much as other men. The war, which made him an inter-sectional migrant, proved that he, too, sought more economic opportunities, the protection of laws even-handedly administered, the enlargement of democracy. He, too, was a seeker for the realities in the American dream.

But when in 1917 the Negro was called upon to protect that dream with his blood, he revealed himself more fully. He asked questions and demanded answers. Whose democracy? he wanted to know; and why, and wherefore? There followed the promises, which were certainly sincerely meant in the stress of the times. Then came the fighting and dying — and, finally, came a thing called Peace. But in 1919 and after, there were the race riots in the nation's capital, in Chicago, in Chester, Pennsylvania, and in East St. Louis.

By this time the New Negro movement was already stirring massively along many fronts. In the 1920's Negroes cracked through the prejudices that had largely confined them to super-numerary roles on Broadway. *Shuffle Along* was praised as "a sparkling, all-Negro musical of unusual zest and talent." Charles Gilpin's portrayal of the Emperor Jones was the dramatic triumph of 1921. The Garvey Movement, fast getting out of bounds, swept the country like a wildfire. James Weldon Johnson published an anthology of Negro verse. The monumental historical studies of the Negro were begun by Carter Woodson. *The Gift of Black Folk, Color, Fire in the Flint, Weary Blues, God's Trombones, Walls of Jericho,* and *Home to Harlem* had all been published, read, discussed, praised or damned by 1928.

Fortunately some of the talents that produced these works were genuine. Had this not been so, the New Negro movement in art and literature would surely have come to nothing. The best of Johnson, Hughes, Cullen, McKay, Fisher and DuBois would have lived without the movement, but the movement without them would have gone the way of mah-jongg. Their work considerably furthered the interest of white writers and critics in Negro material and Negro art expression. Whatever else Eugene O'Neill, Paul Rosenfeld and DuBose Heyward did, they gave validity to the new concept of the Negro as material for serious artistic treatment.

Writing by Negroes beginning with this period and continuing into the early thirties had two distinct aspects. The first of these was extremely arty, self-conscious and experimental. Jean Toomer's *Cane* and the "racial-rhythm" and jazz-rhythm poetry of Langston Hughes represent it most notably, while the magazines *Harlem* and *Fire,* which published a quantity of nonsense by writers unheard of since, were its special organs. But the times were themselves arty and experimental. That Negro writers could afford to be touched by these influences was a good sign. It was healthy for them to be blown upon by the winds of literary freedom—even of license — that blew upon e. e. cummings, Dos Passos and Hemingway. If their self-conscious experimentation proved nothing lasting, it at least worked no harm.

One searches in vain for a phrase to characterize the exact impulses behind the second aspect, which is the one best remembered. It was chock-full of many contradictory things. It showed itself naive and sophisticated, hysterical and placid, frivolous and sober, free and enslaved. It is simple enough to attribute this contrariety to the effects of the war; but the atavistic release of certain aberrant tendencies in writing by Negroes in this period cannot be matched in all the rest of contemporary writing. The period produced the poignant beauty of Johnson's *God's Trombones* and the depressing futility of Thurman's *The Blacker The Berry.* Within a span of five years McKay wrote the wholesome

Banjo and the pointlessly filthy *Banana Bottom*. The Hughes who wrote "I've Known Rivers" and "Mother to Son" could also find creative satisfaction in the bizarre "The Cat and the Saxophone."

The mass mind of white America fastened upon the exotic and the atavistic elements and fashioned them into a fad, the commercialized products of which were manufactured in Harlem. That that Harlem itself was largely synthetic did not seem to matter. It was "nigger heaven." There, the advertised belief was, Dullness was dethroned: Gaiety was king! The rebels from Sauk Center and Winesburg, Main Street and Park Avenue, sought carnival in Harlem. "Life," the burden of the dithyrambics ran, "had surge and sweep there, and blood-pounding savagery."

Commercialism was the bane of the Negro renaissance of the twenties. Jazz music became no longer the uninhibited expression of unlearned music-makers, but a highly sophisticated pattern of musical sounds. The "Charleston" and the "Black Bottom" went down to Broadway and Park Avenue. Losing much of its folk value, the blues became the "torch song" eloquently sung by Ruth Etting and Helen Morgan. Negro material passed into the less sincere hands of white artists, and Negro writers themselves, from a high pitch of creation, fell relatively and pathetically silent.

IV

When Richard Wright's *Uncle Tom's Children* was published in 1938, only the least aware did not realize that a powerful new pen was employing itself in stern and terrible material; when *Native Son* appeared in 1940, even the least aware realized it. The first book is a clinical study of human minds under the stress of violence; the second is a clinical study of the social being under the cumulative effects of organized repression. The two books complement each other. The theme of both is prejudice, conceptual prejudgment — the effects of this upon the human personality. For Wright deals only incidentally — and for dramatic purposes, and because of the authenticity of empiricism — with *Negro* and *white*. "Bigger Thomas was not black all the time," Wright wrote in "How Bigger Was Born." "He was white, too, and there were literally millions of him, *everywhere*. . . . Certain modern experiences were creating types of personalities whose existence ignored racial and national lines. . . ."

Some critics have said that the wide appeal of Wright's work (it has been translated into a dozen languages) is due to the sensationalism in it, but one can have serious doubts that the sensationalism comes off well in translation. What does come off well is the concept of the primary evil of prejudice. This all peoples would understand, and a delineation of its effects, particular though it be, interests them in the same way and for the same reason that love interests them. *Black Boy,* which does not prove the point, does not deny it either. Even here it may be argued that Wright delineates and skewers home the point that "to live habitually as a superior among inferiors . . . is a temptation and a hubris, inevitably deteriorating."

So Wright is a new kind of writer in the ranks of Negroes. He has extricated himself from the dilemma of writing exclusively for a Negro audience and limiting himself to a glorified and race-proud picture of Negro life, and of writing exclusively for a white audience and being trapped in the old stereotypes and fixed opinions that are bulwarks against honest creation. Negro writers traditionally have been impaled upon one or the other horn of this dilemma, sometimes in spite of their efforts to avoid it. Langston Hughes was sincere when he declared, back in the twenties, that Negro writers cared nothing for the pleasure or displeasure of either a white or a colored audience — he was sincere, but mistaken.

A writer writes for an audience. Until recently Negro writers have not believed that the white audience and the colored audience were essentially alike, because, in fact, they have not been essentially alike. They have been kept apart by a wide sociocultural gulf, by differences of concept, by cultivated fears, ignorance, race- and caste-consciousness. Now that gulf is closing, and Negro writers are finding it easier to appeal to the two audiences without being either false to the one or subservient to the other. Thus Margaret Walker, writing for the two audiences now becoming one, can carry away an important poetry prize with her book *For My People.* No longer fearing the ancient interdiction, Chester Himes in *If He Hollers Let Him Go* and *Lonely Crusade* writes of the sexual attraction a white woman feels for a Negro man. In *Knock On Any Door* Willard Motley can concern himself almost entirely with white characters. On the purely romantic and escapist side, Frank Yerby's *The Foxes of Harrow* sells over a million copies, and *The Vixens* and *The Golden Hawk* over a half-million each. Anthologists no longer think it risky to collect, edit and issue the works of Negro writers.

Facing up to the tremendous challenge of appealing to two audiences, Negro writers are extricating themselves from what has sometimes seemed a terrifying dilemma. Working honestly in the material they know best, they are creating for themselves a new freedom. Though what is happening seems very like a miracle, it has been a long, long time preparing. Writing by American Negroes has never before been in such a splendid state of health, nor had so bright and shining a future before it.

Ralph Ellison (1914-   )

On Becoming A Writer

Ralph Ellison is widely known in the academic world as the author of *Invisible Man* (1952), a work which some critics consider the most artistic novel written by a Negro American. In 1964 a group of 200 American writers and editors voted it the most distinguished novel written by any American in the past twenty years.

Born in Oklahoma, Ellison studied music at Tuskegee Institute; but, after going to New York in the summer following his junior year, he never returned to college. In New York, he worked at various jobs, for a time performed as a professional jazz musician, and began writing articles and reviews for various magazines. Despite his continuous productivity as a writer, he did not earn critical attention until he published *Invisible Man*, on which he had labored for seven years. Since then, he has taught at various colleges, worked on a second novel, and continued to produce essays. In 1964 he published *Shadow and Act*, a collection of essays and interviews.

Ironically, although Ellison's literary reputation derives from his novel, the bulk of his writing is essay — reviews, critical appraisals of writers and musicians, analyses and discussions of jazz, and reminiscences. In these, especially in "Richard Wright's Blues," he has revealed his keen insights into aesthetics, jazz,

Originally published in *Commentary* (October 1964). ©Copyright 1964 by Ralph Ellison. Another version appears in *Shadow and Act* by Ralph Ellison. Reprinted by permission of Random House.

blues, and literature, always phrased in a style suggestive of the academic scholar rather than the professional writer. In his most recent writing, Ellison frequently has stressed two themes: the necessity that America recognize and respect the cultural identity of black Americans and the need for Negroes to understand the labor that is required for success.

In the following selection, he recalls his search for and discovery of identity as a writer.

On Becoming A Writer

In the beginning writing was far from a serious matter; it was a reflex of reading, an extension of a source of pleasure, escape, and instruction. In fact, I had become curious about writing by way of seeking to understand the aesthetic nature of literary power, the devices through which literature could command my mind and emotions. It was not, then, the *process* of writing which initially claimed my attention, but the finished creations, the artifacts, poems, plays, novels. The act of learning writing technique was, therefore, an amusing investigation of what seemed at best a secondary talent, an exploration, like dabbling in sculpture, of one's potentialities as a "Renaissance Man." This, surely, would seem a most unlikely and even comic concept to introduce here; and yet, it is precisely because I come from where I do (the Oklahoma of the years between World War I and the Great Depression) that I must introduce it, and with a straight face.

Anything and everything was to be found in the chaos of Oklahoma; thus the concept of the Renaissance Man has lurked long within the shadow of my past, and I shared it with at least a half dozen of my Negro friends. How we actually acquired it I have never learned, and since there is no true sociology of the dispersion of ideas within the American democracy, I doubt if I ever shall. Perhaps we breathed it in with the air of the Negro community of Oklahoma City, the capital of that state whose Negroes were often charged by exasperated white Texans with not knowing their "place." Perhaps we took it defiantly from one of them. Or perhaps I myself picked it up from some transplanted New Englander whose shoes I had shined of a Saturday afternoon. After all, the most meaningful tips do not always come in the form of money, nor are they intentionally extended. Most likely, however, my friends and I acquired the idea from some book or from some idealistic Negro teacher, some dreamer seeking to function responsibly in an environment which at its most normal took on some of the mixed character of nightmare and of dream.

One thing is certain, ours was a chaotic community, still characterized by frontier attitudes and by that strange mixture of the naive and sophisticated, the benign and malignant, which makes the American past so puzzling and its present so confusing; that mixture which often affords the minds of the young who grow up in the far provinces such wide and unstructured latitude, and which encourages the individual's imagination — up to the moment "reality" closes in upon him — to range widely and, sometimes, even to soar.

We hear the effects of this in the Southwestern jazz of the 30's, that joint creation of artistically free and exhuberantly creative adventurers, of artists who had stumbled upon the freedom lying within the restrictions of their musical tradition as within the limitations of their social background, and who in their own unconscious way have set an example for any Americans, Negro or white, who would find themselves in the arts. They accepted themselves and the complexity of life as they knew it, they loved their art and through it they celebrated American experience definitively in sound. Whatever others thought or felt, this was their own powerful statement, and only non-musical assaults upon their artistic integrity — mainly economically inspired changes of fashion — were able to compromise their vision.

Much of so-called Kansas City jazz was actually brought to perfection in Oklahoma by Oklahomans. It is an important circumstance for me as a writer to remember, because while these musicians and their fellows were busy creating out of tradition, imagination, and the sounds and emotions around them, a freer, more complex, and driving form of jazz, my friends and I were exploring an idea of human versatility and possibility which went against the barbs or over the palings of almost every fence which those who controlled social and political power had erected to restrict our roles in the life of the country. Looking back, one might say that the jazzmen, some of whom we idolized, were in their own way better examples for youth to follow than were most judges and ministers, legislators and governors (we were stuck with the notorious Alfalfa Bill Murray). For as we viewed these pillars of society from the confines of our segregated community we almost always saw crooks, clowns, or hypocrites. Even the best were revealed by their attitudes toward us as lacking the respectable qualities to which they pretended and for which they were accepted outside by others, while despite the outlaw nature of their art, the jazzmen were less torn and damaged by the moral compromises and insincerities which have so sickened the life of our country.

Be that as it may, our youthful sense of life, like that of many Negro children (though no one bothers to note it — especially the specialists and "friends of the Negro" who view our Negro-American life as essentially non-human) was very much like that of Huckleberry Finn, who is universally so praised and enjoyed for the clarity and courage of his moral vision. Like Huck, we observed, we judged, we imitated and evaded as we could the dullness, corruption, and blindness of "civilization." We were undoubtedly comic because, as the saying goes, we weren't supposed to know what it was all about. But to ourselves we were "boys," members of a wild, free, outlaw tribe which transcended the category of race. Rather we were Americans born into the forty-sixth state, and thus, into the context of Negro-American post-Civil War history, "frontiersmen." And isn't one of the implicit functions of the American frontier to encourage the individual to a kind of dreamy wakefulness, a state in which he makes — in all ignorance of the accepted limitations of the possible — rash efforts, quixotic gestures, hopeful testings of the complexity of the known and the given?

Spurring us on in our controlled and benign madness was the voracious reading of which most of us were guilty and the vicarious identification and empathetic adventuring which it encouraged. This was due, in part, perhaps to the fact that some of us were fatherless — my own father had died when I was three — but most likely it was because boys are natural romantics. We were seeking examples, patterns to live by, out of a freedom which for all its being ignored by the sociologists and subtle thinkers, was implicit in the Negro situation. Father and mother substitutes also have a role to play in aiding the child to help create himself. Thus we fabricated our own heroes and ideals catch-as-catch-can; and with an outrageous and irreverent sense of freedom. Yes, and in complete disregard of ideas of respectability or the surreal incongruity of some of our projections. Gamblers and scholars, jazz musicians and scientists, Negro cowboys and soldiers from the Spanish-American and First World Wars, movie stars and stunt men, figures from the Italian Renaissance and literature, both classical and popular, were combined with the special virtues of some local bootlegger, the eloquence of some Negro preacher, the strength and grace of some local athlete, the ruthlessness of some businessman-physician, the elegance in dress and manners of some head-waiter or hotel doorman.

Looking back through the shadows upon this absurd activity, I realize now that we were projecting archetypes, recreating folk figures, legendary heroes, monsters even, most of which violated all ideas of social hierarchy and order and all accepted conceptions of the hero handed down by cultural, religious, and racist tradition. But we, remember, were under the intense spell of the early movies, the silents as well as the talkies; and in our community, life was not so tightly structured as it would have been in the traditional South — or even in deceptively "free" Harlem. And our imaginations processed reality and dream, natural man and traditional hero, literature and folklore, like maniacal editors turned loose in some frantic film-cutting room. Remember, too, that being boys, yet in the play-stage of our development, we were dream-serious in our efforts. But serious nevertheless, for *culturally* play is a preparation, and we felt that somehow the human ideal lay in the vague and constantly shifting figures — sometimes comic but always versatile, picaresque, and self-effacingly heroic — which evolved from our wildly improvisatory projections: figures neither white nor black, Christian nor Jewish, but representative of certain desirable essences, of skills and powers, physical, aesthetic, and moral.

The proper response to these figures was, we felt, to develop ourselves for the performance of many and diverse roles, and the fact that certain definite limitations had been imposed upon our freedom did not lessen our sense of obligation. Not only were we to prepare but we were to perform — not with mere competence but with an almost reckless verve; with, may we say (without evoking the quaint and questionable notion of *négritude*) Negro-American style? Behind each artist there stands a traditional sense of style, a sense of the felt tension indicative of expressive completeness; a mode of humanizing reality and of evoking a feeling of being at home in the world. It is something which the artist shares with the group, and part of our boyish activity expressed a yearning to make any and everything of quality

Negro-American; to appropriate it, possess it, recreate it in our own group and individual images.

And we recognized and were proud of our group's own style wherever we discerned it, in jazzmen and prize-fighters, ballplayers, and tap dancers; in gesture, inflection, intonation, timbre, and phrasing. Indeed, in all those nuances of expression and attitude which reveal a culture. We did not fully understand the cost of that style, but we recognized within it an affirmation of life beyond all question of our difficulties as Negroes.

Contrary to the notion currently projected by certain specialists in the "Negro problem" which characterizes the Negro American as self-hating and defensive, we did not so regard ourselves. We felt, among ourselves at least, that we were supposed to be whoever we would and could be and do anything and everything which other boys did, and do it better. Not defensively, because we were ordered to do so; nor because it was held in the society at large that we were naturally, as Negroes, limited — but because we demanded it of ourselves. Because to measure up to our own standards was the only way of affirming our notion of manhood.

Hence it was no more incongruous, as seen from our own particular perspective in this land of incongruities, for young Negro Oklahomans to project themselves as Renaissance men than for white Mississippians to see themselves as ancient Greeks or noblemen out of Sir Walter Scott. Surely our fantasies have caused far less damage to the nation's sense of reality, if for no other reason than that ours were expressive of a more democratic ideal. Remember, too, as William Faulkner made us so vividly aware, that the slaves often took the essence of the aristocratic ideal (as they took Christianity) with far more seriousness than their masters, and that we, thanks to the tight telescoping of American history, were but two generations from that previous condition. Renaissance men, indeed!

I managed, by keeping quiet about it, to cling to our boyish ideal during three years in Alabama, and I brought it with me to New York, where it not only gave silent support to my explorations of what was then an unknown territory, but served to mock and caution me when I became interested in the Communist ideal. And when it was suggested that I try my hand at writing it was still with me.

The act of writing requires a constant plunging back into the shadow of the past where time hovers ghostlike. When I began writing in earnest I was forced, thus, to relate myself consciously and imaginatively to my mixed background as American, as Negro-American, and as a Negro from what in its own belated way was a pioneer background. More important, and inseparable from this particular effort, was the necessity of determining my true relationship to that body of American literature to which I was most attracted and through which, aided by what I could learn from the literatures of Europe, I would find my own voice and to which I was challenged, by way of achieving myself, to make some small contribution, and to whose composite picture of reality I was obligated to offer some necessary modifications.

This was no matter of sudden insight but of slow and blundering discovery, of a struggle to stare down the deadly and hypnotic temptation to interpret the world and all its devices in terms of race. To avoid this was very important to me, and in light of my background far from simple. Indeed, it was quite complex, involving as it did, a ceaseless questioning of all those formulas which historians, politicians, sociologists, and an older generation of Negro leaders and writers — those of the so-called "Negro Renaissance" — had evolved to describe my group's identity, its predicament, its fate, and its relation to the larger society and the culture which we share.

Here the question of reality and personal identity merge. Yes, and the question of the nature of the reality which underlies American fiction and thus the human truth which gives fiction viability. In this quest, for such it soon became, I learned that nothing could go unchallenged; especially that feverish industry dedicated to telling Negroes who and what they are, and which can usually be counted upon to deprive both humanity and culture of their complexity. I had undergone, not too many months before taking the path which led to writing, the humiliation of being taught in a class in sociology at a Negro college (from Park and Burgess, the leading textbook in the field) that Negroes represented the "lady of the races." This contention the Negro instructor passed blandly along to us without even bothering to wash his hands, much less his teeth. Well, I had no intention of being bound by any such humiliating definition of my relationship to American literature. Not even to those works which depicted Negroes negatively. Negro Americans have a highly developed ability to abstract desirable qualities from those around them, even from their enemies, and my sense of reality could reject bias while appreciating the truth revealed by achieved art. The pleas-

ure which I derived from reading had long been a necessity, and
in the *act* of reading, that marvelous collaboration between the
writer's artful vision and the reader's sense of life, I had become
acquainted with other possible selves; freer, more courageous and
ingenuous and, during the course of the narrative at least, even
wise.

At the time I was under the influence of Ernest Hemingway,
and his description, in *Death in the Afternoon,* of his thinking
when he first went to Spain became very important as translated
in my own naïve fashion. He was trying to write, he tells us,

> and I found the greatest difficulty aside from knowing truly what
> you really felt, rather than what you were supposed to feel, and
> had been taught to feel, was to put down what really happened in
> action; what the actual things were which produced the emotion
> that you experienced. . . .

His statement of moral and aesthetic purpose which followed
focused my own search to relate myself to American life through
literature. For I found the greatest difficulty for a Negro writer
was the problem of revealing what he truly felt, rather than serving up what Negroes were supposed to feel, and were encouraged
to feel. And linked to this was the difficulty, based upon our
long habit of deception and evasion, of depicting what really happened within our areas of American life, and putting down with
honesty and without bowing to ideological expediencies the attitudes and values which give Negro-American life its sense of
wholeness and which render it bearable and human and, when
measured by our own terms, desirable.

I was forced to this awareness through my struggles with the
craft of fiction; yes, and by my attraction (soon rejected) to
Marxist political theory, which was my response to the inferior
status which society sought to impose upon me (I did not then,
now, or ever *consider* myself inferior).

I did not know my true relationship to America — what citizen
of the U.S. really does? — but I did know and accept how I felt
inside. And I also knew, thanks to the old Renaissance Man,
what I expected of myself in the matter of personal discipline and
creative quality. Since by the grace of the past and the examples
of manhood picked willy-nilly from the continuing-present of my
background, I rejected all negative definitions imposed upon me
by others, there was nothing to do but search for those relationships which were fundamental.

In this sense fiction became the agency of my efforts to answer the questions, Who am I, what am I, how did I come to be? What shall I make of the life around me, what celebrate, what reject, how confront the snarl of good and evil which is inevitable? What does American society *mean* when regarded out of my *own* eyes, when informed by my *own* sense of the past and viewed by my *own* complex sense of the present? How, in other words, should I think of myself and my pluralistic sense of the world, how express my vision of the human predicament, without reducing it to a point which would render it sterile before that necessary and tragic — though enhancing — reduction which must occur before the fictive vision can come alive? It is quite possible that much potential fiction by Negro Americans fails precisely at this point: through the writers' refusal (often through provincialism or lack of courage or through opportunism) to achieve a vision of life and a resourcefulness of craft commensurate with the complexity of their actual situation. Too often they fear to leave the uneasy sanctuary of race to take their chances in the world of art.

James Baldwin (1924-   )

The Discovery of What
It Means to be an American

James Baldwin is the best-known Negro writer today and one of the most distinguished essayists writing in the English language. Born in New York City and educated in the schools of that city, Baldwin, at the age of fourteen, became a minister after a religious awakening which he described in his first novel, *Go Tell It on the Mountain* (1953). After three years as a minister, Baldwin experienced disillusionment which caused him to reject Christianity. Leaving home, working at odd jobs while learning to be a writer, Baldwin finally migrated to France to search for his identity and for a new faith.

His first novel earned praise from critics who believed that they had discovered a Negro capable of writing artistically about life without revealing bitterness about the black experience. His two collections of essays, *Notes of a Native Son* (1955) and *Nobody Knows My Name* (1961) informed critics of their error but firmly established his reputation as a major essayist. In essays, Baldwin has articulated the Negro experience more effectively than any black writer since W. E. B. DuBois. Simultaneously, he has compelled many white readers to re-examine their beliefs and their attitudes.

In the early sixties, Baldwin completed three highly controversial, financially successful works on racial themes — *Another Coun-*

try (1962), a novel; *The Fire Next Time* (1963), a long essay; and *Blues for Mr. Charlie* (1964), a drama. His most recent works of fiction — *Going to Meet the Man* (1965) and *Tell Me How Long the Train's Been Gone* (1968) — have been received more ambivalently by critics, who, willing to acknowledge his stylistic excellence as an essayist, argue that he has not fulfilled his artistic promise as a writer of fiction.

The following selection is taken from Baldwin's second collection of essays. In it, Baldwin recalls how experiences in Europe helped him to understand that he was not merely Negro but also American.

The Discovery of What It Means to be an American

"It is a complex fate to be an American," Henry James observed, and the principal discovery an American writer makes in Europe is just how complex this fate is. America's history, her aspirations, her peculiar triumphs, her even more peculiar defeats, and her position in the world — yesterday and today — are all so profoundly and stubbornly unique that the very word "America" remains a new, almost completely undefined and extremely controversial proper noun. No one in the world seems to know exactly what it describes, not even we motley millions who call ourselves Americans.

I left America because I doubted my ability to survive the fury of the color problem here. (Sometimes I still do.) I wanted to prevent myself from becoming *merely* a Negro; or, even, merely a Negro writer. I wanted to find out in what way the *specialness* of my experience could be made to connect me with other people instead of dividing me from them. (I was as isolated from Negroes as I was from whites, which is what happens when a Negro begins, at bottom, to believe what white people say about him.)

In my necessity to find the terms on which my experience could be related to that of others, Negroes and whites, writers and non-writers, I proved, to my astonishment, to be as American as any Texas G.I. And I found my experience was shared by every American writer I knew in Paris. Like me, they had been divorced from their origins, and it turned out to make very little difference that the origins of white Americans were European and mine were African — they were no more at home in Europe than I was.

The fact that I was the son of a slave and they were the sons of free men meant less, by the time we confronted each other on European soil, than the fact that we were both searching for our separate identities. When we had found these, we seemed to be saying, why, then, we would no longer need to cling to the shame and bitterness which had divided us so long.

It became terribly clear in Europe, as it never had been here, that we knew more about each other than any European ever could. And it also became clear that, no matter where our fathers had been born, or what they had endured, the fact of Europe had formed us both, was part of our identity and part of our inheritance.

I had been in Paris a couple of years before any of this became clear to me. When it did, I, like many a writer before me upon the discovery that his props have all been knocked out from under him, suffered a species of breakdown and was carried off to the mountains of Switzerland. There, in that absolutely alabaster landscape, armed with two Bessie Smith records and a typewriter, I began to try to re-create the life that I had first known as a child and from which I had spent so many years in flight.

It was Bessie Smith, through her tone and her cadence, who helped me to dig back to the way I myself must have spoken when I was a pickaninny, and to remember the things I had heard and seen and felt. I had buried them very deep. I had never listened to Bessie Smith in America (in the same way that, for years, I would not touch watermelon), but in Europe she helped to reconcile me to being a "nigger."

I do not think that I could have made this reconciliation here. Once I was able to accept my role — as distinguished, I must say, from my "place" — in the extraordinary drama which is America, I was released from the illusion that I hated America.

The story of what can happen to an American Negro writer in Europe simply illustrates, in some relief, what can happen to any American writer there. It is not meant, of course, to imply that it happens to them all, for Europe can be very crippling, too; and, anyway, a writer, when he has made his first breakthrough, has simply won a crucial skirmish in a dangerous, unending and unpredictable battle. Still, the breakthrough is important, and the point is that an American writer, in order to achieve it, very often has to leave this country.

The American writer, in Europe, is released, first of all, from the necessity of apologizing for himself. It is not until he *is* released from the habit of flexing his muscles and proving that he is just a "regular guy" that he realizes how crippling this habit has been. It is not necessary for him, there, to pretend to be something he is not, for the artist does not encounter in Europe the same suspicion he encounters here. Whatever the Europeans may actually think of artists, they have killed enough of them off by now to know that they are as real — and as persistent — as rain, snow, taxes or businessmen.

Of course, the reason for Europe's comparative clarity concerning the different functions of men in society is that European society has always been divided into classes in a way that American society never has been. A European writer considers himself to be part of an old and honorable tradition — of intellectual activity, of letters — and his choice of a vocation does not cause him any uneasy wonder as to whether or not it will cost him all his friends. But this tradition does not exist in America.

On the contrary, we have a very deep-seated distrust of real intellectual effort (probably because we suspect that it will destroy, as I hope it does, that myth of America to which we cling so desperately). An American writer fights his way to one of the lowest rungs on the American social ladder by means of pure bull-headedness and an indescribable series of odd jobs. He probably *has* been a "regular fellow" for much of his adult life, and it is not easy for him to step out of that lukewarm bath.

We must, however, consider a rather serious paradox: though American society is more mobile than Europe's, it is easier to cut across social and occupational lines there than it is here. This has something to do, I think, with the problem of status in American life. Where everyone has status, it is also perfectly possible, after all, that no one has. It seems inevitable, in any case, that a man may become uneasy as to just what his status is.

But Europeans have lived with the idea of status for a long time. A man can be as proud of being a good waiter as of being a good actor, and in neither case feel threatened. And this means that the actor and the waiter can have a freer and more genuinely friendly relationship in Europe than they are likely to have here. The waiter does not feel, with obscure resentment, that the actor has "made it," and the actor is not tormented by the fear that he may find himself, tomorrow, once again a waiter.

This lack of what may roughly be called social paranoia causes the American writer in Europe to feel — almost certainly for the first time in his life — that he can reach out to everyone, that he is accessible to everyone and open to everything. This is an extraordinary feeling. He feels, so to speak, his own weight, his own value.

It is as though he suddenly came out of a dark tunnel and found himself beneath the open sky. And, in fact, in Paris, I began to see the sky for what seemed to be the first time. It was borne in on me — and it did not make me feel melancholy — that this sky had been there before I was born and would be there when I was dead. And it was up to me, therefore, to make of my brief opportunity the most that could be made.

I was born in New York, but have lived only in pockets of it. In Paris, I lived in all parts of the city — on the Right Bank and the Left, among the bourgeoisie and among *les misérables*, and knew all kinds of people, from pimps and prostitutes in Pigalle to Egyptian bankers in Neuilly. This may sound extremely unprincipled or even obscurely immoral: I found it healthy. I love to talk to people, all kinds of people, and almost everyone, as I hope we still know, loves a man who loves to listen.

This perpetual dealing with people very different from myself caused a shattering in me of preconceptions I scarcely knew I held. The writer is meeting in Europe people who are not American, whose sense of reality is entirely different from his own. They may love or hate or admire or fear or envy this country — they see it, in any case, from another point of view, and this forces the writer to reconsider many things he had always taken for granted. This reassessment, which can be very painful, is also very valuable.

This freedom, like all freedom, has its dangers and its responsibilities. One day it begins to be borne in on the writer, and with great force, that he is living in Europe as an American. If he were living there as a European, he would be living on a different and far less attractive continent.

This crucial day may be the day on which an Algerian taxi-driver tells him how it feels to be an Algerian in Paris. It may be the day on which he passes a café terrace and catches a glimpse of the tense, intelligent and troubled face of Albert Camus. Or it may be the day on which someone asks him to explain Little Rock

and he begins to feel that it would be simpler — and, corny as the
words may sound, more honorable — to *go* to Little Rock than sit
in Europe, on an American passport, trying to explain it.

This is a personal day, a terrible day, the day to which his entire
sojourn has been tending. It is the day he realizes that there are no
untroubled countries in this fearfully troubled world; that if he has
been preparing himself for anything in Europe, he has been preparing himself — for America. In short, the freedom that the American writer finds in Europe brings him, full circle, back to himself,
with the responsibility for his development where it always was:
in his own hands.

Even the most incorrigible maverick has to be born somewhere.
He may leave the group that produced him — he may be forced
to — but nothing will efface his origins, the marks of which he
carries with him everywhere. I think it is important to know this
and even find it a matter for rejoicing, as the strongest people
do, regardless of their station. On this acceptance, literally, the
life of a writer depends.

The charge has often been made against American writers that
they do not describe society, and have no interest in it. They
only describe individuals in opposition to it, or isolated from it.
Of course, what the American writer is describing is his own
situation. But what is *Anna Karenina* describing if not the tragic
fate of the isolated individual, at odds with her time and place?

The real difference is that Tolstoy was describing an old and
dense society in which everything seemed — to the people in it,
though not to Tolstoy — to be fixed forever. And the book is a
masterpiece because Tolstoy was able to fathom, and make us
see, the hidden laws which really governed this society and made
Anna's doom inevitable.

American writers do not have a fixed society to describe. The
only society they know is one in which nothing is fixed and in
which the individual must fight for his identity. This is a rich
confusion, indeed, and it creates for the American writer unprec-
edented opportunities.

That the tensions of American life, as well as the possibilities,
are tremendous is certainly not even a question. But these are
dealt with in contemporary literature mainly compulsively; that
is, the book is more likely to be a symptom of our tension than an
examination of it. The time has come, God knows, for us to
examine ourselves, but we can only do this if we are willing to free

ourselves of the myth of America and try to find out what is really happening here.

Every society is really governed by hidden laws, by unspoken but profound assumptions on the part of the people, and ours is no exception. It is up to the American writer to find out what these laws and assumptions are. In a society much given to smashing taboos without thereby managing to be liberated from them, it will be no easy matter.

It is no wonder, in the meantime, that the American writer keeps running off to Europe. He needs sustenance for his journey and the best models he can find. Europe has what we do not have yet, a sense of the mysterious and inexorable limits of life, a sense, in a word, of tragedy. And we have what they sorely need: a new sense of life's possibilities.

In this endeavor to wed the vision of the Old World with that of the New, it is the writer, not the statesman, who is our strongest arm. Though we do not wholly believe it yet, the interior life is a real life, and the intangible dreams of people have a tangible effect on the world.

John O. Killens (1916-   )

The Black Psyche

Born in Macon, Georgia, John O. Killens studied law at Columbia University and at New York University. He has worked with the National Labor Relations Board, and presently is a writer-in-residence at Fisk University.

Best known for his novels — *Youngblood* (1954), *And Then We Heard the Thunder* (1964), and *'Sippi* (1967), Killens insists that the black writer has the responsibility to search for his subject matter within the experiences of his race and to present those experiences with full consciousness of his racial identity. In other words, a black writer is not merely a writer who is black; instead, he is a black man who is a writer.

The title of Killens's collection of essays is, of course, an ironic reversal of the philosophy by which white colonials justified their subjugation of dark-skinned people. They argued that it was the white man's burden to advise and provide for dark-skinned natives, who, incapable of directing their own destiny, would not survive without such assistance. Rejecting paternalistic philosophy, Killens examines interracial relationships in language and style which frequently suggest a deliberate rejection of the traditional formal literary idiom.

The Black Psyche

When I was a boy in Macon, Georgia, one of the greatest compliments a benevolent white man could give a Negro was usually found in the obituary column of the local newspaper: "He was a black man, but he had a white heart." And the burden of every black man was supposedly just a little easier to bear that day. It was a time when many of us black folk laughed at the antics of *Amos 'n' Andy* and wept copious tears at a ridiculous movie very aptly titled *Imitation of Life*. Most of us looked at life through the eyes of white America.

The great fictional (and film) masterpieces on the American racial theme usually fell into two categories. One theme dealt with the utter heartbreak of the mulatto, who rejected his black blood and was in turn rejected by his white blood. A variation of this theme was the shattering experience of "passing." The other theme was the "Uncle Tom," or what I prefer to call the "Gunga Din," theme. This one also had many variations, but over all there was the image created by that great apologist for colonialism, Rudyard Kipling, of a man who

> . . . For all 'is dirty 'ide
> 'E was white, clear white, inside
> When 'e went to tend the wounded
> under fire!

With some "additional touches" by Hollywood, dear old "white inside" Gunga evolved as a marvelous figment of Western man's wistful imagination, the personification of his wish fulfillment. Remember Gunga? He was a water boy for the British regiment and in the movie version, finally blew the bugle against his own people. And how "whiter" inside could a "noble savage" be?

I am waging a quiet little campaign at the moment to substitute the term "Gunga Din" for that much maligned character "Uncle Tom" in designating the contemporary water boys who still blow the bugles for old Massa. For although Mrs. Stowe's beloved "Uncle Tom" was indeed an Uncle Tom, as we understand the term today, he nevertheless, in the final confrontation, chose death rather than blow the whistle on his people.

Variations of the Gunga Din theme were seen in a rash of movie epics, like *Gone with the Wind* and *Virginia* and *Kentucky*, etc., ad infinitum, *ad nauseam*, always played magnificently with tongue in cheek by such stalwarts as Hattie McDaniel and Louise Beavers. In the great emotional scene the black "mammy" was usually in the big house, weeping and moaning over little pure-white-as-the-driven-snow Missy Anne, who had just sneezed, while Mammy's own young-un was dying of double pneumonia, unattended, down in the cabins. All in all, the slaves were presented as carefree and contented in their idyllic degradation. If the black man really believed in this romantic version of American slavery, he would have long since wasted away, pining for those good old happy-go-lucky days of bondage.

Last year I did considerable research on that bygone "utopian" era, and I got a very different picture, slightly less romantic. I found that the slaves were so happy that most of the plantation owners couldn't afford the astronomical rates of fire insurance. These rapturous slaves kept setting fire to the cotton patches, burning down the plantation, every day the good Lord sent them. They organized countless insurrections, killed their masters, poisoned their mistresses, even put spiders in the Big House soup. They demonstrated their contentment in most peculiar ways.

The point is, most white Americans cling desperately to these wish-fulfillment fantasies, but most of us Negroes have become unbelievers. We don't break into cheers any more when the cowboys chase the Indians across the movie screen, or when the Army finally captures old John Brown. Indeed, our favorite epic of the west has become Custer's Last Stand. Sitting Bull is a colored hero. Many black folk wish that this mighty warrior had been an American Negro.

I shall never forget an evening I spent in a movie house in Hollywood watching the closed-circuit television broadcast of the first Patterson-Johannson fight, and the great shame I felt for my white countrymen that night as they began to sense a possible victory for the white foreigner over the black American. Forgotten entirely was the fact that softhearted Floyd Patterson was fellow countryman. Color superseded patriotism. As I sat there hearing shouted exhortations, like "Kill the nigger!", I felt that Patterson and I were aliens in a strange and hostile country, and that Ingemar was at home among his people. In fairness to my countrymen in the closed circuits of America that night, their reactions were not intellectual, not even willful. They were spontaneous, not unlike a conditioned reflex. This ecstasy at the sudden emergence of a new white hope came from their hearts, their souls, their bellies. It was their white insides reacting.

I have been told that this incident had no racial implications at all, that these rabid Johannson fans were merely upholding the old American tradition of rooting for the underdog. Well, I was also rooting for the underdog, and I knew that, win or lose, the underdog in America was Floyd Patterson, Harry Belafonte, Emmett Till, Rosa Parks, Meredith, Poitier, the black American, I, *me*. The words "Kill the nigger!" could not possibly have come screaming from my throat, subconsciously, unconsciously, or otherwise. Nor could they from any other black man's throat.

Just as surely as East is East and West is West, there is a "black" psyche in America and there is a "white" one, and the sooner we face up to this psychological, social, and cultural reality, the sooner the twain shall meet. Our emotional chemistry is different from white America's. Your joy is very often our anger, and your despair our hope. Most of us came here in chains, and many of you came here to escape your chains. Your freedom was our slavery, and therein lies the bitter difference in the way we look at life. You created the myth of the faithful slave, but we know that the "loyal slave" is a contradiction in terms. We understand, though, that the master must always make himself believe in the undying love of his slave.

Ironically enough, the fathers of our magnificent Revolution, Washington and Jefferson, themselves owned hundreds of human chattels, and even though the great Thomas Jefferson made many speeches against the peculiar institution, he was never able to convince himself to the extent of manumitting his own slaves during his lifetime. Surely the great irony of the situation did not escape my ancestors back in the days of the Revolution. And now, today, it does not escape their great-great-grandchildren. When we hear some white statesman use the phrase "the Free World," even though the same white statesman may very well be the Governor of the State of Mississippi or Alabama, or even President of these United States, for that matter, we — as the slaves of Washington and Jefferson must have done — stare at him incredulously and cannot believe our ears. And we wonder how this word "freedom" can have such vastly different meanings, such conflicting connotations.

But the time has come for you (white America) and me (black America) to work this thing out once and for all, to examine and evaluate the differences between us and the differences inside us. Time is swiftly running out, and a new dialogue is indispensable. It is so long overdue it is already half past midnight.

And let us be clear on one thing. My fight is not to be a white man in a black skin, but to inject some black blood, some black intelligence, some black humaneness, into the pallid mainstream of American life — culturally, socially, psychologically, philosophically. This is the truer, deeper meaning of the Negro revolt which is not yet a revolution — to get America ready for the middle of the twentieth century, which is already magnificently here.

This new epoch has caught our country (yours and mine) dozing in a sweet nostalgia of the good old days. Our country slumbers in a world of yesteryears, before Africa and Asia got up off their knees and threw off the black man's burden. The good old days when you threw pennies to the "natives." And there were gunboats in the China Sea and Big Stick policies and Monroe Doctrines and "Gold Coasters" from the U.K. sipped their gin-and-tonics in Accra and Lagos and talked about the "natives," as they basked in their roles of Great White Fathers in that best of all possible worlds.

That world is gone forever, and black and brown men everywhere are glad, deep in their hearts, though most Western men are chagrined, which may be the understatement of the century. The title of the great Duke Ellington's song has come true: "Things Ain't What They Used to Be." And the good news, or the bad news, depending on your point of view, is: Things ain't never going to be anything like they used to be. This is why the world is becoming too much for Western men, however liberal, even some radical Western men, whoever you are, and wherever. But the world is becoming more and more to my liking, to my taste and in my image. It gladdens my heart to see black and brown men and women walk with dignity in the United Nations, in affirmation of the manhood and the selfhood of the entire human race.

The American Negro, you see, is an Anglo-Saxon invention, a role the Anglo-Saxon gentleman created for the black man in this drama known euphemistically as the American Way of Life. It began as an economic expedient, frankly, because you wanted somebody to work for nothing. It is still that, but now it is much more than that. It has become a way of life within a way of life, socially, economically, psychologically, philosophically. The Negro Invention, hatched in the brave New World, ultimately and rapidly became a rationalization for the colonializing of three-quarters of the earth's peoples. All non-whites throughout the world became "niggers" and therefore proper material for "civilizing" and "Christianizing" (cruel euphemisms for colonization, exploitation, genocide, and slavery).

And now, in the middle of the twentieth century, I, the Negro, like my counterparts in Asia and Africa and South America and on the islands of the many seas, am refusing to be your "nigger" any longer. Even some of us "favored," "talented," "unusual," ones are refusing to be your educated, sophisticated, split-leveled "niggers" any more. We refuse to look at ourselves through the eyes of white America.

We are not fighting for the right to be like you. We respect ourselves too much for that. When we advocate freedom, we mean freedom for us to be black, or brown, and you to be white and yet live together in a free and equal society. This is the only way that integration can bring dignity for both of us. I, for one, am growing weary of those well-meaning white liberals who are forever telling me they don't know what color I am. The very fact that they always single me out at every cocktail party to gratuitously make me the beneficiary of their blessed assurances gives the lie to their pronouncements.

My fight is not for racial sameness but for racial equality and against racial prejudice and discrimination. I work for the day when black people will be free of the racist pressures to be white like you; a day when "good hair" and "high yaller" and bleaching cream and hair straighteners will be obsolete. What a tiresome place America would be if freedom meant we all had to think alike or be the same color or wear that same gray flannel suit! That road leads to the conformity of the graveyard.

If relationships are to improve between us Americans, black and white and otherwise, if the country is to be changed and saved, we will have to face up to the fact that differences do exist between us. All men react to life through man-made symbols. Even our symbolic reactions are different from yours. To give a few examples:

In the center of a little Southern town near the border of Mississippi there is a water tower atop which sits a large white cross, illumined at night with a lovely (awesome to Negroes) neon brightness, which can be seen for miles. To most white Americans, seeing it for the first time, it is a beacon that symbolizes the Cross upon which Jesus died, and it gives them a warm feeling. But it puts an angry knot in a black man's belly. To him it symbolizes the very "Christian" K.K.K. Just as to the average white man, a courthouse, even in Mississippi, is a place where justice is dispensed. Yet to me, the black man, it is a place where justice is dispensed with.

We even have a different historical perspective. Most white Americans, even today, look upon the Reconstruction period as a horrible time of "carpetbagging," and "black politicians," and "black corruption," the absolutely lowest ebb in the Great American Story. Oh, the oceans of bitter tears American writers have wept for that ill-begotten era. Oh, the shame of it all, the way those Southern patriots were treated after that unfortunate war, that horrendous misunderstanding.

We black folk, however, look upon Reconstruction as the most democratic period in the history of this nation; a time when the dream the founders dreamed was almost within reach and right there for the taking; a time of democratic fervor the like of which was never seen before and never since. For all we know, it was a time when America could have won the world but lost it, probably forever. We don't share your feeling that the Negro was not ready for the franchise. We think that the first slaves on that first slave ship were men and women and therefore capable of being citizens anywhere. This is our understanding of democracy. We are not impressed with the mess white Americans (educated and illiterate ones) have made of this Republic, and apparently, because of their whiteness, they were born ready. Apparently, they were endowed by "their creator."

For us, Reconstruction was the time when two black men were Senators in the Congress of the United States from the State of Mississippi; when black men served in the legislatures of all the states in Dixie; and when those "corrupt" legislatures gave to the South its first public-school education. And the lowest ebb for us black folk came on the heels of the Great Betrayal, when the government in Washington turned us over to the benevolent Ku Klux Klan and the Knights of the Camellias.

Nor do we share your romantic view of Rob Lee and Jeff Davis. Certainly, to most of us who have thought about the matter, they were traitors, pure and simple. We put them in the same inglorious category as the infamous Benedict Arnold.

I shall never forget the feeling I had one morning in the fall of 1957, in a Hollywood hotel, when I awoke and tuned into the outside world of television. There before my eyes were American soldiers, black and white, rolling into Little Rock, Arkansas, with their rifles at the ready. I cried that morning. I unashamedly wept. Wept for the moment that had been so long in the coming, the moment when for the first time in my life I felt that the nation gave a damn about *me*. One courageous black woman and eight innocent beautiful black children had laid down the gauntlet and brought the nation to the brink of human decency.

Whatever the political considerations that dictated the move, I felt that the nation had committed itself again, in a way it had not done since Reconstruction. When I saw the Star-Spangled Banners waving from those jeeps and tanks as they rolled endlessly into Little Rock that morning, Old Glory meant more to me, the black American, *me*, than ever before in my life's brief span, including the forty-one months I spent in the service of my country during World War II. Oh yes, we black folk find it difficult to understand the nation's hesitation about sending troops to Mississippi to guarantee free elections when we read of American boys dying thousands of miles from home to ensure freedom for the Vietnamese. The subtlety escapes us.

Even our white hero symbols are different from yours. You give us moody Abe Lincoln, but many of us prefer John Brown, whom most of you hold in contempt as a fanatic; meaning, of course, that the firm dedication of any white man to the freedom of the black man is *prima-facie* evidence of perversion or insanity.

You look upon these times as the Atomic Age, the Space Age, the Cold War Era. But I believe that when the history of our times is written, it will not be so important who reached the moon first or who made the largest bomb. I believe the great significance will be that this was the century when most of mankind achieved freedom and human dignity, the age when racial prejudices became obsolete. For me, this is the Freedom Century.

So now it is time for you to understand us, because it is becoming increasingly hazardous for you not to. Dangerous for both of us. As Richard Wright said in his *Twelve Million Black Voices*, voices you chose not to heed: "Each day when you see us black folk upon the dusty land of your farms or upon the hard pavement of your city streets, you usually take us for granted and think you know us, but our history is far stranger than you suspect, and we are not what we seem." The Rev. Ralph Abernathy of Montgomery put it more humorously when he said that the new Negro of Montgomery had stopped laughing when he wasn't tickled and scratching when he didn't itch.

At the turn of the century, Negro prophet William Edward Burghardt DuBois warned the Western world: "The problem of the twentieth century is the problem of the color line." But who listens to a black prophet at such a time of endless frontiers for the white pioneers and missionaries? Now, in the middle of that same century, we are bringing down the curtain on this role you cast us in, and we will no longer be a party to our own degradation. We have become unbelievers, no longer believing in the absolute superiority of the white man's juju. You have never practiced what you preached. Why should we believe in you? Why would we want to be like you?

Yes, we are different from you and we are not invisible men, Ralph Ellison notwithstanding. We are the most visible of Americans.

Last spring, Charles Harris, Negro editor for Doubleday, and I had drinks at the Playboy Club in New York. We were so visible, everybody who came into the place stared at us more than they did the semi-naked bunnies. "Who're they? Ralph Bunche and Sonny Liston, or Joe Louis and Sammy Davis, Junior? Or maybe Willie Mays and Martin Luther King?" Oh yes, we have a very high degree of visibility.

But white Americans are great pretenders. Millions of you wish we were invisible, and so you make believe we are. You'd like to wish us out of existence so that the whole world would not see us, because our very life in this country, as black people, gives the lie before the world to your protestations of freedom and human brotherhood. The white man's juju is powerful stuff, but it cannot wish the Negro into invisibility. So you try the next best thing, pretending you can't tell one of us from the other.

The point is: Since we no longer look at ourselves through *your* eyes, our visibility, to *your* eyes, is a total irrelevance, to *us*. We no longer look to you for our identity. But this self-delusion on *your* part (that you don't see us and that you can't tell us one from the other) is dangerous for you and for *our* country. You always knew the difference between the "field" slave and the "house" one; between the "bad nigger" and the "good" one; between Gunga Din and old Nat Turner, between Dubois and Booker Washington.

In the summer and fall of 1961 I traveled in a Land Rover 12,000 miles through Africa. I talked to people in the cities, on the farms, in the villages. I talked with workers, farmers, artists, market women, ministers of state, politicians, teachers, and the same question was asked me everywhere I went: "How can we believe your country's professions of good will to us, with whom they have not lived, when they deny human dignity to you who come from us and have lived with them for centuries and helped to build their great civilization?"

It is a question that America has to answer to the entire New World of Africa and Asia. The only way we Americans, black and white, can answer it affirmatively is to make freedom and democracy work at home, here and now. Most Negroes still believe that the ultimate solution for us is in America, and I am as firmly convinced that the ultimate salvation of America is in the Negro.

The Negro loves America enough to criticize her fundamentally. Most white Americans simply can't be bothered. Ironically enough, in the middle of the twentieth century, the Negro is the new white hope. To live castrated in a great white harem and yet somehow maintain our black manhood and humanity — this is the essence of the new man created out of the Negro Invention. History may render the verdict that this was the greatest legacy handed to the New World by the West.

There are glaring exceptions to every rule, but it is a truism that American Negroes are the only people in America who, as a people, are for change. This is true, again, not innately because of our color, but because of what America made of our color. The *status quo* has ever been the bane of black existence.

We black folk have learned many lessons during our sojourn in this place. One of them is the truth of the Ghana proverb, "Only a fool points to his origin with his left hand." We are becoming prouder and prouder of our origins. And we know the profound difference between pride and arrogance; the difference, if you will, between James Meredith and Ross Barnett, both of Mississippi. Our dialogue will not be protest but affirmation of the human dignity of all people everywhere. Yes, our aim is to create a dialogue in full vindication of every lonesome disinherited "nigger," every black and brown man born of woman who ever dwelt upon this alien earth, which means, of course, that all mankind would be vindicated regardless of race, color, or religion. Our dialogue is anti-racist.

Sure, I know that there are white folk who want America to be the land of the free and home of the brave, but there are far too few of them, and many of them are rarely brave. I cherish old John Brown and Garrison and William Moore and Mike Schwerner and Andy Goodman and all the other winter soldiers. Let the winter patriots increase their ranks. Let those who truly love America join the valiant Negro Revolt and change and save our country.

LeRoi Jones (1934-   )

City of Harlem *and* Cold, Hurt, and Sorrow (Streets of Despair)

LeRoi Jones has become a spokesman and a leader for many young black people who are rebelling against traditions of society and art. Born in Newark, New Jersey, he attended the Newark branch of Rutgers University before transferring to Howard to complete his undergraduate education. After serving in the Army Air Force, Jones returned to civilian life as a teacher and a writer.

Jones first attracted attention with *Preface to a Twenty-Volume Suicide Note* (1961), a volume of poems which exhibited his talent in vigorous language and powerful imagery. Since that time, Jones has become increasingly controversial. His interpretation of the history of black people through their experience — *Blues People* — is a persuasive one. His plays — *Dutchman, The Slave, The Baptism, The Toilet* — have created sensation either because of their language or their thought. His most recent collection, *Tales* (1967), mingles sketches, essays, stories in what some young writers believe to be a significant and successful experiment to achieve greater flexibility for the short-story form.

The following selections from *Home* summarize the history of Harlem and sing its blues.

City of Harlem

In a very real sense, Harlem is the capital of Black America. And America has always been divided into black and white, and the substance of the division is social, economic, and cultural. But even the name Harlem, now, means simply Negroes (even though some other peoples live there too). The identification is international as well: even in Belize, the capital of predominantly Negro British Honduras, there are vendors who decorate their carts with flowers and the names or pictures of Negro culture heroes associated with Harlem like Sugar Ray Robinson. Some of the vendors even wear t-shirts that say "Harlem, U.S.A." and they speak about it as a black Paris. In Havana a young Afro-Cuban begged me to tell him about the "big leg ladies" of Lenox Avenue, hoping, too, that I could provide some way for him to get to that mystic and romantic place.

There are, I suppose, contained within the central mythology of Harlem, almost as many versions of its glamour, and its despair, as there are places with people to make them up. (In one meaning of the name, Harlem is simply a place white cab drivers will not go.) And Harlem means not only Negroes, but, of course, whatever other associations one might connect with them. So in one breath Harlem will be the pleasure-happy center of the universe, full of loud, hippy mamas in electric colors and their fast, slick-head papas, all of them twisting and grinning in the streets in a kind of existential joyousness that never permits of sadness or responsibility. But in another breath this same place will be the gathering place for every crippling human vice, and the black men there simply victims of their own peculiar kind of sloth and childishness. But perhaps these are not such different versions after all; chances are both these stereotypes come from the same kinds of minds.

But Harlem, as it is, as it exists for its people, as an actual place where actual humans live — that is a very different thing. Though, to be sure, Harlem is a place — a city really — where almost anything any person could think of to say goes on, probably does go on, or has gone on, but like any other city, it must escape *any* blank generalization simply because it is alive, and changing each second with each breath any of its citizens take.

When Africans first got to New York, or New Amsterdam as the Dutch called it, they lived in the farthest downtown portions of the city, near what is now called The Bowery. Later, they shifted, and were shifted, as their numbers grew, to the section known as Greenwich Village. The Civil War Draft Riots in 1863 accounted for the next move by New York's growing Negro population.

After this violence (a few million dollars' worth of property was destroyed, and a Negro orphanage was burned to the ground) a great many Negroes moved across the river into Brooklyn. But many others moved farther uptown to an area just above what was known as Hell's Kitchen. The new Negro ghetto was known as Black Bohemia, and later, after the success of an all black regiment in the Spanish-American war, this section was called San Juan Hill. And even in the twenties when most Negroes had made their move even further uptown to Harlem, San Juan Hill was still a teeming branch office of black night life.

Three sections along the east side of Manhattan, The Tenderloin, Black Bohemia, and San Juan Hill or The Jungle featured all kinds of "sporting houses," cabarets, "dancing classes," afterhours gin mills, as well as the Gumbo Suppers, Fish Fries, Egg Nog Parties, Chitterlin' Struts, and Pigfoot Hops, before the Negroes moved still farther uptown.

The actual move into what is now Harlem was caused by quite a few factors, but there are a few that were particularly important as catalysts. First, locally, there were more race riots around the turn of the century between the white poor (as always) and the Negroes. Also, the Black Bohemia section was by now extremely overcrowded, swelled as it was by the influx of Negroes from all over the city. The section was a notorious red light district (but then there have only been two occupations a black woman could go into in America without too much trouble: the other was domestic help) and the overcrowding made worse by the moral squalor that poverty encourages meant that the growing local black population had to go somewhere. The imigrant groups living on both sides of the black ghetto fought in the streets to keep their own ghettos autonomous and pure, and the Negro had to go elsewhere.

At this time, just about the turn of the century, Harlem (an area which the first Africans had helped connect with the rest of the Dutch city by clearing a narrow road — Broadway — up into the woods of Nieuw Haarlem) was still a kind of semi-suburban area, populated, for the most part, by many of the city's wealthiest families. The elaborate estates of the eighteenth century, built by men like Alexander Hamilton and Roger Morris, were still being lived in, but by the descendants of wealthy merchants. (The Hamilton house still stands near Morningside Heights, as an historic landmark called The Grange. The Morris house, which was once lived in by Aaron Burr, is known as The Jumel House, and it still stands at the northern part of Harlem, near the Polo Grounds, as a museum run by the D.A.R. George Washington used it as his headquarters for a while during the Revolutionary War.) So there was still the quiet elegance of the nineteenth century brownstones and spacious apartment buildings, the wide drives, rolling greens, and huge-trunked trees.

What made the area open up to Negroes was the progress that America has always been proud of — an elevated railway went up in the nineties, and the very rich left immediately and the near rich very soon after. Saint Philips Church, after having its old site bought up by a railroad company, bought a large piece of property, with large apartment buildings, in the center of Harlem, and, baby, the panic was on. Rich and famous Negroes moved into the vacated luxury houses very soon after, including the area now known as "Strivers Row," which was made up of almost one hundred brick mansions designed by Stanford White. The panic was definitely on — but still only locally.

What really turned that quiet suburb into "Black Paris," was the coming of the First World War and the mass exodus of Negroes from the South to large urban centers. At the turn of the century most Negroes still lived in the South and were agricultural laborers, but the entrance of America into the War, and the desperate call for cheap unskilled labor, served to start thousands of Negroes scrambling North. The flow of immigrants from Europe had all but ceased by 1914, and the industrialists knew immediately where to turn. They even sent recruiters down into the South to entice the Negroes north. In 1900 the Negro population of New York City was 60,000; by 1920 it was 152,467; by 1930 it was 327,706. And most of these moved, of course, uptown.

It was this mass exodus during the early part of the century that was responsible for most of the black cities of the North — the huge Negro sections of New York, Chicago, Philadelphia, Detroit, etc. It was also responsible for what these sections would very shortly become, as the masses of Southern Negroes piled into their new Jordans, thinking to have a go at an innocent America.

The twenties are legend because they mark America's sudden insane entrance into the 20th century. The war had brought about a certain internationalism and prosperity (even, relatively speaking, for Negroes). During the twenties Harlem was the mecca of the good time and in many ways even came to symbolize the era called the Jazz Age. Delirious white people made the trip uptown to hear Negro musicians and singers, and watch Negro dancers, and even Negro intellectuals. It was, I suppose, the black man's debut into the most sophisticated part of America. The old darkies of the plantation were suddenly all over the North, and making a whole lot of noise.

There were nightclubs in Harlem that catered only to white audiences, but with the best Negro entertainers. White intellectuals made frequent trips to Harlem, not only to find out about a newly emerging black America, but to party with an international set of swinging bodies. It was the era of Ellington at The Cotton Club for the sensual, and The New Negro for the intellectual. Everyone spoke optimistically of the Negro Renaissance, and The New Negro, as if, somehow, the old Negro wasn't good enough. Harlem sparkled then, at least externally, and it took the depression to dull that sparkle, and the long lines of unemployed Negroes and the longer lines at the soup kitchens and bread queues brought reality down hard on old and new Negroes alike. So the tourist trade diminished, and colorful Harlem became just a social liability for the white man, and an open air jail for the black.

The cold depression thirties, coupled with the decay of old buildings and ancient neighborhoods, and, of course, the seeming inability of the "free enterprise" system to provide either jobs or hope for a great many black people in the city of Harlem, have served to make this city another kind of symbol. For many Negroes, whether they live in Harlem or not, the city is simply a symbol of naked oppression. You can walk along 125th Street any evening and meet about one hundred uniformed policemen, who are there, someone will tell you, to protect the people from themselves.

For many Negroes Harlem is a place one escapes from, and lives in shame about for the rest of his life. But this is one of the weirdest things about the American experience, that it can oppress a man, almost suck his life away, and then make him so ashamed that he was among the oppressed rather than the oppressors, that he will never offer any protest.

The legitimate cultural tradition of the Negro in Harlem (and America) is one of wild happiness, usually at some black man's own invention — of speech, of dress, of gait, the sudden twist of a musical phrase, the warmness or hurt of someone's voice. But that culture is also one of hatred and despair. Harlem must contain all of this and be capable of producing all of these emotions.

People line the streets in summer — on the corners or hanging out the windows — or head for other streets in winter. Vendors go by slowly . . . and crowds of people from movies or church. (Saturday afternoons, warm or cold, 125th is jammed with shoppers and walkers, and the record stores scream through loudspeakers at the street.) Young girls, doctors, pimps, detectives, preachers, drummers, accountants, gamblers, labor organizers, postmen, wives, Muslims, junkies, the employed, and the unemployed: all going someplace — an endless stream of Americans, whose singularity in America is that they are black and can never honestly enter into the lunatic asylum of white America.

Harlem for this reason is a community of nonconformists, since any black American, simply by virtue of his blackness, is weird, a nonconformist in this society. A community of nonconformists, not an artists' colony — though blind "ministers" still wander sometimes along 137th Street, whispering along the strings of their guitars — but a colony of old-line Americans, who can hold out, even if it is a great deal of the time in misery and ignorance, but still hold out, against the hypocrisy and sterility of big-time America, and still try to make their own lives, simply because of their color, but by now, not so simply, because that color now does serve to identify people in America whose feelings about it are not broadcast every day on television.

Cold, Hurt, and Sorrow (Streets of Despair)

These streets stretch from one end of America to the other and connect like a maze from which very few can fully escape. Despair sits on this country in most places like a charm, but there is a special gray death that loiters in the streets of an urban Negro slum. And the men who walk those streets, tracing and retracing their steps to some hopeless job or a pitiful rooming house or apartment or furnished room, sometimes stagger under the weight of that gray, humiliated because it is not even "real."

Sometimes walking along among the ruined shacks and lives of the worst Harlem slum, there is a feeling that just around the corner you'll find yourself in South Chicago or South Philadelphia, maybe even Newark's Third Ward. In these places life, and its possibility, has been distorted almost identically. And the distortion is as old as its sources: the fear, frustration, and hatred that Negroes have always been heir to in America. It is just that in the cities, which were once the black man's twentieth century "Jordan," *promise* is a dying bitch with rotting eyes. And the stink of her dying is a deadly killing fume.

The blues singers know all this. They knew before they got to the cities. "I'd rather drink muddy water, sleep in a hollow log, than be in New York City treated like a dirty dog." And when they arrived, in those various cities, it was much worse than even they had imagined. The city blues singers are still running all that down. Specifically, it's what a man once named for me unnatural adversity. It is social, it is economic, it is cultural and historical. Some of its products are emotional and psychological; some are even artistic, as if Negroes suffered better than anyone else. But it's hard enough to be a human being under any circumstances, but when there is an entire civilization determined to stop you from being one, things get a little more desperately complicated. What do you do then?

You can stand in doorways late nights and hit people in the head. You can go to church Saturday nights and Sundays and three or four times during the week. You can stick a needle in your arm four or five times a day, and bolster the economy. You can buy charms and herbs and roots, or wear your hat backwards to keep things from getting worse. You can drink till screaming is not loud enough, and the coldest night is all right to sleep outside in. You can buy a big car . . . if the deal goes down. There's so much, then, you can do, to yourself, or to somebody else. Another man sings, "I'm drinkin' t.n.t., I'm smokin dynamite, I hope some screwball starts a fight."

One can never talk about Harlem in purely social terms, though there are ghetto facts that make any honest man shudder. It is the tone, the quality of suffering each man knows as his own that finally must be important, but this is the most difficult thing to get to. (There are about twenty young people from one small Southern town, all friends, all living within the same few blocks of the black city, all of whom are junkies, communally hooked. What kind of statistic is *that?* And what can you say when you read it?)

The old folks kept singing, there will be a better day . . . or, the sun's gonna shine in my back door some day . . . or, I've had my fun if I don't get well no more. What did they want? What would that sun turn out to be?

Hope is a delicate suffering. Its waste products vary, but most of them are meaningful. And as a cat named Mean William once said, can you be glad, if you've never been sad?

Eldridge Cleaver (1934-   )

The White Race and Its Heroes

In prison Eldridge Cleaver wrote the essays of *Soul on Ice*, which has been praised by critics and scholars. Literary historian Maxwell Geismar wrote, "Cleaver's is one of the distinctive new literary voices to be heard." Kenneth Clark, a psychologist, praised "the explicit and implicit diagnoses of the moral dry rot which mocks our democracy." Novelist Norman Mailer wrote, "His style has the clarity and strength of someone talking to you about a subject he understands, a tone which very few writers ever achieve, no matter how long they've been working at it."

Born in Little Rock, Arkansas, Cleaver received his formal education in the black ghetto of Los Angeles. In prison, however, he gained a better education. There he did not merely learn to write more effectively than most people learn in sixteen years of formal education; more importantly, he learned to look deeply into individuals and society. His essays describe "the forces which shaped his life and which are currently molding our national destiny." Influenced first by the Muslims, Cleaver later rejected their philosophy of racial hatred to assume a position closer to that of Malcolm X.

In the following selection, Cleaver explores the psychological forces currently motivating the actions of young white people.

The White Race and Its Heroes

White people cannot, in the generality, be taken as models of how
to live. Rather, the white man is himself in sore need of new standards, which will release him from his confusion and place him once
again in fruitful communion with the depths of his own being.

James Baldwin
— *The Fire Next Time*

Right from the go, let me make one thing absolutely clear: I am
not now, nor have I ever been, a white man. Nor, I hasten to add,
am I now a Black Muslim — although I used to be. But I *am* an
Ofay Watcher, a member of that unchartered, amorphous league
which has members on all continents and the islands of the seas.
Ofay Watchers Anonymous, we might be called, because we exist
concealed in the shadows wherever colored people have known
oppression by whites, by white enslavers, colonizers, imperialists,
and neo-colonialists.

Did it irritate you, compatriot, for me to string those epithets
out like that? Tolerate me. My intention was not necessarily to
sprinkle salt over anyone's wounds. I did it primarily to relieve
a certain pressure on my brain. Do you cop that? If not, then we're
in trouble, because we Ofay Watchers have a pronounced tendency
to slip into that mood. If it is bothersome to you, it is quite a task
for me because not too long ago it was my way of life to preach, as
ardently as I could, that the white race is a race of devils, created
by their maker to do evil, and make evil appear as good; that the
white race is the natural, unchangeable enemy of the black man,
who is the original man, owner, maker, cream of the planet Earth;
that the white race was soon to be destroyed by Allah, and that
the black man would then inherit the earth, which has always, in
fact, been his.

I have, so to speak, washed my hands in the blood of the martyr,
Malcolm X, whose retreat from the precipice of madness created
new room for others to turn about in, and I am now caught up in
that tiny space, attempting a maneuver of my own. Having renounced the teachings of Elijah Muhammad, I find that a rebirth
does not follow automatically, of its own accord, that a void is left
in one's vision, and this void seeks constantly to obliterate itself by
pulling one back to one's former outlook. I have tried a tentative
compromise by adopting a select vocabulary, so that now when I
see the whites of *their* eyes, instead of saying "devil" or "beast"

I say "imperialist" or "colonialist," and everyone seems to be happier.

In silence, we have spent our years watching the ofays, trying to understand them, on the principle that you have a better chance coping with the known than with the unknown. Some of us have been, and some still are, interested in learning whether it is *ultimately* possible to live in the same territory with people who seem so disagreeable to live with; still others want to get as far away from ofays as possible. What we share in common is the desire to break the ofays' power over us.

At times of fundamental social change, such as the era in which we live, it is easy to be deceived by the onrush of events, beguiled by the craving for social stability into mistaking transitory phenomena for enduring reality. The strength and permanence of "white backlash" in America is just such an illusion. However much this rear-guard action might seem to grow in strength, the initiative, and the future, rest with those whites and blacks who have liberated themselves from the master/slave syndrome. And these are to be found mainly among the youth.

Over the past twelve years there has surfaced a political conflict between the generations that is deeper, even, than the struggle between the races. Its first dramatic manifestation was within the ranks of the Negro people, when college students in the South, fed up with Uncle Tom's hat-in-hand approach to revolution, threw off the yoke of the NAACP. When these students initiated the first sit-ins, their spirit spread like a raging fire across the nation, and the technique of non-violent direct action, constantly refined and honed into a sharp cutting tool, swiftly matured. The older Negro "leaders," who are now all die-hard advocates of this tactic, scolded the students for sitting-in. The students rained down contempt upon their hoary heads. In the pre-sit-in days, these conservative leaders had always succeeded in putting down insurgent elements among the Negro people. (A measure of their power, prior to the students' rebellion, is shown by their success in isolating such great black men as the late W. E. B. DuBois and Paul Robeson, when these stalwarts, refusing to bite their tongues, lost favor with the U.S. government by their unstinting efforts to link up the Negro revolution with national liberation movements around the world.)

The "Negro leaders," and the whites who depended upon them to control their people, were outraged by the impudence of the students. Calling for a moratorium on student initiative, they were greeted instead by an encore of sit-ins, and retired to their ivory towers to contemplate the new phenomenon. Others, less prudent because held on a tighter leash by the whites, had their careers brought to an abrupt end because they thought they could lead a black/white backlash against the students, only to find themselves in a kind of Bay of Pigs. Negro college presidents, who expelled students from all-Negro colleges in an attempt to quash the demonstrations, ended up losing their jobs; the victorious students would no longer allow them to preside over the campuses. The spontaneous protests on southern campuses over the repressive measures of their college administrations were an earnest of the Free Speech upheaval which years later was to shake the UC campus at Berkeley. In countless ways, the rebellion of the black students served as catalyst for the brewing revolt of the whites.

What has suddenly happened is that the white race has lost its heroes. Worse, its heroes have been revealed as villains and its greatest heroes as the arch-villains. The new generations of whites, appalled by the sanguine and despicable record carved over the face of the globe by their race in the last five hundred years, are rejecting the panoply of white heroes, whose heroism consisted in erecting the inglorious edifice of colonialism and imperialism; heroes whose careers rested on a system of foreign and domestic exploitation, rooted in the myth of white supremacy and the manifest destiny of the white race. The emerging shape of a new world order, and the requisites for survival in such a world, are fostering in young whites a new outlook. They recoil in shame from the spectacle of cowboys and pioneers — their heroic forefathers whose exploits filled earlier generations with pride — galloping across a movie screen shooting down Indians like Coke bottles. Even Winston Churchill, who is looked upon by older whites as perhaps the greatest hero of the twentieth century — even he, because of the system of which he was a creature and which he served, is an arch-villain in the eyes of the young white rebels.

At the close of World War Two, national liberation movements in the colonized world picked up new momentum and audacity, seeking to cash in on the democratic promises made by the Allies during the war. The Atlantic Charter, signed by President Roosevelt and Prime Minister Churchill in 1941, affirming "the right of all people to choose the form of government under which they may live," established the principle, although it took years of postwar struggle to give this piece of rhetoric even the appearance of reality. And just as world revolution has prompted the oppressed to re-evaluate their self-image in terms of the changing conditions, to slough off the servile attitudes inculcated by long years of subordination, the same dynamics of change have prompted the white people of the world to re-evaluate their self-image as well, to disabuse themselves of the Master Race psychology developed over centuries of imperial hegemony.

It is among the white youth of the world that the greatest change is taking place. It is they who are experiencing the great psychic pain of waking into consciousness to find their inherited heroes turned by events into villains. Communication and understanding between the older and younger generations of whites has entered a crisis. The elders, who, in the tradition of privileged classes or races, genuinely do not understand the youth, trapped by old ways of thinking and blind to the future, have only just begun to be vexed — because the youth have only just begun to rebel. So thoroughgoing is the revolution in the psyches of white youth that the traditional tolerance which every older generation has found it necessary to display is quickly exhausted, leaving a gulf of fear, hostility, mutual misunderstanding, and contempt.

The rebellion of the oppressed peoples of the world, along with the Negro revolution in America, have opened the way to a new evaluation of history, re-examination of the role played by the white race since the beginning of European expansion. The positive achievements are also there in the record, and future generations will applaud them. But there can be no applause now, not while the master still holds the whip in his hand! Not even the master's own children can find it possible to applaud him — he cannot even applaud himself! The negative rings too loudly. Slave-catchers, slaveowners, murderers, butchers, invaders, oppressors — the white heroes have acquired new names. The great white statesmen whom school children are taught to revere are revealed as the architects of systems of human exploitation and slavery. Religious leaders are exposed as condoners and justifiers of all these evil deeds. Schoolteachers and college professors are seen as a clique of brainwashers and whitewashers.

The white youth of today are coming to see, intuitively, that to escape the onus of the history their fathers made they must face and admit the moral truth concerning the works of their fathers. That such venerated figures as George Washington and Thomas Jefferson owned hundreds of black slaves, that all of the Presidents up to Lincoln presided over a slave state, and that every President since Lincoln connived politically and cynically with the issues affecting the human rights and general welfare of the broad masses of the American people — these facts weigh heavily upon the hearts of these young people.

The elders do not like to give these youngsters credit for being able to understand what is going on and what has gone on. When speaking of juvenile delinquency, or the rebellious attitude of today's youth, the elders employ a glib rhetoric. They speak of the "alienation of youth," the desire of the young to be independent, the problems of "the father image" and "the mother image" and their effect upon growing children who lack sound models upon which to pattern themselves. But they consider it bad form to connect the problems of the youth with the central event of our era — the national liberation movements abroad and the Negro revolution at home. The foundations of authority have been blasted to bits in America because the whole society has been indicted, tried, and convicted of injustice. To the youth, the elders are Ugly Americans; to the elders, the youth have gone mad.

The rebellion of the white youth has gone through four broadly discernible stages. First there was an initial recoiling away, a rejection of the conformity which America expected, and had always received, sooner or later, from its youth. The disaffected youth were refusing to participate in the system, having discovered that America, far from helping the underdog, was up to its ears in the mud trying to hold the dog down. Because of the publicity and self-advertisements of the more vocal rebels, this period has come to be known as the beatnik era, although not all of the youth affected by these changes thought of themselves as beatniks. The howl of the beatniks and their scathing, outraged denunciation of the system — characterized by Ginsberg as Moloch, a bloodthirsty Semitic deity to which the ancient tribes sacrificed their firstborn children — was a serious, irrevocable declaration of war. It is revealing that the elders looked upon the beatniks as mere obscene misfits who were too lazy to take baths and too stingy to buy a haircut. The elders had eyes but couldn't see, ears but couldn't hear — not even when the message came through as clearly as in this remarkable passage from Jack Kerouac's *On the Road:*

At lilac evening, I walked with every muscle aching among the lights of 27th and Welton in the Denver colored section, wishing I were a Negro, feeling that the best the white world had offered was not enough ecstasy for me, not enough life, joy, kicks, darkness, music, not enough night. I wished I were a Denver Mexican, or even a poor overworked Jap, anything but what I so drearily was, a "white man" disillusioned. All my life I'd had white ambitions. . . . I passed the dark porches of Mexican and Negro homes; soft voices were there, occasionally the dusky knee of some mysterious sensuous gal; the dark faces of the men behind rose arbors. Little children sat like sages in ancient rocking chairs.

The second stage arrived when these young people, having decided emphatically that the world, and particularly the U.S.A., was unacceptable to them in its present form, began an active search for roles they could play in changing the society. If many of these young people were content to lay up in their cool beat pads, smoking pot and listening to jazz in a perpetual orgy of esoteric bliss, there were others, less crushed by the system, who recognized the need for positive action. Moloch could not ask for anything more than to have its disaffected victims withdrawn into safe, passive, apolitical little nonparticipatory islands, in an economy less and less able to provide jobs for the growing pool of unemployed. If all the unemployed had followed the lead of the beatniks, Moloch would gladly have legalized the use of euphoric drugs and marijuana, passed out free jazz albums and sleeping bags, to all those willing to sign affidavits promising to remain "beat." The non-beat disenchanted white youth were attracted magnetically to the Negro revolution, which had begun to take on a mass, insurrectionary tone. But they had difficulty understanding their relationship to the Negro, and what role "whites" could play in a "Negro revolution." For the time being they watched the Negro activists from afar.

The third stage, which is rapidly drawing to a close, emerged when white youth started joining Negro demonstrations in large numbers. The presence of whites among the demonstrators emboldened the Negro leaders and allowed them to use tactics they never would have been able to employ with all-black troops. The racist conscience of America is such that murder does not register as murder, really, unless the victim is white. And it was only when the newspapers and magazines started carrying pictures and stories of white demonstrators being beaten and maimed by mobs and police that the public began to protest. Negroes have become so used to this double standard that they, too, react differently to the death of a white. When white freedom riders were brutalized along with blacks, a sigh of relief went up from the black masses, because the blacks knew that white blood is the coin of freedom in a land where for four hundred years black blood has been shed unremarked and with impunity. America has never truly been outraged by the murder of a black man, woman, or child. White politicians may, if Negroes are aroused by a particular murder, say with their lips what they know with their minds they should feel with their hearts — but don't.

It is a measure of what the Negro feels that when the two white and one black civil rights workers were murdered in Mississippi in 1964, the event was welcomed by Negroes on a level of understanding beyond and deeper than the grief they felt for the victims and their families. This welcoming of violence and death to whites can almost be heard — indeed it can be heard — in the inevitable words, oft repeated by Negroes, that those whites, and blacks, do not die in vain. So it was with Mrs. Viola Liuzzo. And much of the anger which Negroes felt toward Martin Luther King during the Battle of Selma stemmed from the fact that he denied history a great moment, never to be recaptured, when he turned tail on the Edmund Pettus Bridge and refused to all those whites behind him what they had traveled thousands of miles to receive. If the police had turned them back by force, all those nuns, priests, rabbis, preachers, and distinguished ladies and gentlemen old and young — as they had done the Negroes a week earlier — the violence and brutality of the system would have been ruthlessly exposed. Or if, seeing King determined to lead them on to Montgomery, the troopers had stepped aside to avoid precisely the confrontation that Washington would not have tolerated, it would have signaled the capitulation of the militant white South. As it turned out, the March on Montgomery was a show of somewhat dim luster, stage-managed by the Establishment. But by this time the young whites were already active participants in the Negro revolution. In fact they had begun to transform it into something broader, with the potential of encompassing the whole of America in a radical re-ordering of society.

The fourth stage, now in its infancy, sees these white youth taking the initiative, using techniques learned in the Negro struggle to attack problems in the general society. The classic example of this new energy in action was the student battle on the UC campus at Berkeley, California — the Free Speech Movement. Leading the revolt were veterans of the civil rights movement, some of whom spent time on the firing line in the wilderness of Mississippi/ Alabama. Flowing from the same momentum were student demonstrations against U.S. interference in the internal affairs of Vietnam, Cuba, the Dominican Republic, and the Congo and U.S. aid to apartheid in South Africa. The students even aroused the intellectual community to actions and positions unthinkable a few years ago: witness the teach-ins. But their revolt is deeper than single-issue protest. The characteristics of the white rebels which most alarm their elders — the long hair, the new dances, their love for Negro music, their use of marijuana, their mystical attitude toward sex — are all tools of their rebellion. They have turned these tools against the totalitarian fabric of American society — and they mean to change it.

From the beginning America has been a schizophrenic nation. Its two conflicting images of itself were never reconciled, because never before has the survival of its most cherished myths made a reconciliation mandatory. Once before, during the bitter struggle between North and South climaxed by the Civil War, the two images of Amercia came into conflict, although whites North and South scarcely understood it. The image of America held by its most alienated citizens was advanced neither by the North nor by the South; it was perhaps best expressed by Frederick Douglass, who was born into slavery in 1817, escaped to the North, and became the greatest leader-spokesman for the blacks of his era. In words that can still, years later, arouse an audience of black Americans, Frederick Douglass delivered, in 1852, a scorching indictment in his Fourth of July oration in Rochester:

What to the American slave is your Fourth of July? I answer: a day that reveals to him, more than all other days in the year, the gross injustic and cruelty to which he is the constant victim. To him your celebration is a sham; your boasted liberty, an unholy license; your national greatness, swelling vanity; your sounds of rejoicing are empty and heartless; your denunciation of tyrants, brass-fronted impudence; your shouts of liberty and equality, hollow mockery; your prayers and hymns, your sermons and thanksgivings, with all your religious parade and solemnity, are, to him, more bombast, fraud, deception, impiety and hypocrisy — a thin veil to cover up crimes which would disgrace a nation of savages. . . .

You boast of your love of liberty, your superior civilization, and your pure Christianity, while the whole political power of the nation (as embodied in the two great political parties) is solemnly pledged to support and perpetuate the enslavement of three millions of your countrymen. You hurl your anathemas at the crown-headed tyrants of Russia and Austria and pride yourselves on your democratic institutions, while you yourselves consent to be the mere *tools* and *bodyguards* of the tyrants of Virginia and Carolina.

You invite to your shores fugitives of oppression from abroad, honor them with banquets, greet them with ovations, cheer them, toast them, salute them, protect them, and pour out your money to them like water; but the fugitive from your own land you advertise, hunt, arrest, and kill. You glory in your refinement and your universal education; yet you maintain a system as barbarous and dreadful as ever stained the character of a nation — a system begun in avarice, supported in pride, and perpetuated in cruelty.

You shed tears over fallen Hungary, and make the sad story of her wrongs the theme of your poets, statesmen and orators, till your gallant sons are ready to fly to arms to vindicate her cause against the oppressor; but, in regard to the ten thousand wrongs of the American slave, you would enforce the strictest silence, and would hail him as an enemy of the nation who dares to make these wrongs the subject of public discourse!

This most alienated view of America was preached by the Abolitionists, and by Harriet Beecher Stowe in her *Uncle Tom's Cabin*. But such a view of America was too distasteful to receive wide attention, and serious debate about America's image and her reality was engaged in only on the fringes of society. Even when confronted with overwhelming evidence to the contrary, most white Americans have found it possible, after steadying their rattled nerves, to settle comfortably back into their vaunted belief that America is dedicated to the proposition that all men are created equal and endowed by their Creator with certain inalienable rights — life, liberty and the pursuit of happiness. With the Constitution for a rudder and the Declaration of Independence as its guiding star, the ship of state is sailing always toward a brighter vision of freedom and justice for all.

Because there is no common ground between these two contradictory images of America, they had to be kept apart. But the moment the blacks were let into the white world — let out of the voiceless and faceless cages of their ghettos, singing, walking, talking, dancing, writing, and orating *their* image of America and of Americans — the white world was suddenly challenged to match its practice to its preachments. And this is why those whites who abandon the *white* image of America and adopt the *black* are greeted with such unmitigated hostility by their elders.

For all these years whites have been taught to believe in the myth they preached, while Negroes have had to face the bitter reality of what America practiced. But without the lies and distortions, white Americans would not have been able to do the things they have done. When whites are forced to look honestly upon the objective proof of their deeds, the cement of mendacity holding white society together swiftly disintegrates. On the other hand, the core of the black world's vision remains intact, and in fact begins to expand and spread into the psychological territory vacated by the non-viable white lies, i.e., into the minds of young whites. It is remarkable how the system worked for so many years, how the majority of whites remained effectively unaware of any contradiction between their view of the world and that world itself. The mechanism by which this was rendered possible requires examination at this point.

Let us recall that the white man, in order to justify slavery and, later on, to justify segregation, elaborated a complex, all-pervasive myth which at one time classified the black man as a subhuman beast of burden. The myth was progressively modified, gradually elevating the blacks on the scale of evolution, following their slowly changing status, until the plateau of separate-but-equal was reached at the close of the nineteenth century. During slavery, the black was seen as a mindless Supermasculine Menial. Forced to do the backbreaking work, he was conceived in terms of his ability to do such work — "field niggers," etc. The white man administered the plantation, doing all the thinking, exercising omnipotent power over the slaves. He had little difficulty dissociating himself from the black slaves, and he could not conceive of their positions being reversed or even reversible.

Blacks and whites being conceived as mutually exclusive types, those attributes imputed to the blacks could not also be imputed to the whites — at least not in equal degree — without blurring the line separating the races. These images were based upon the social function of the two races, the work they performed. The ideal white man was one who knew how to use his head, who knew how to manage and control things and get things done. Those whites who were not in a position to perform these functions nevertheless aspired to them. The ideal black man was one who did exactly as he was told, and did it efficiently and cheerfully. "Slaves," said Frederick Douglass, "are generally expected to sing as well as to work." As the black man's position and function became more varied, the images of white and black, having become stereotypes, lagged behind.

The separate-but-equal doctrine was promulgated by the Supreme Court in 1896. It had the same purpose domestically as the Open Door Policy toward China in the international arena: to stabilize a situation and subordinate a non-white population so that racist exploiters could manipulate those people according to their own selfish interests. These doctrines were foisted off as *the epitome of enlightened justice, the highest expression of morality*. Sanctified by religion, justified by philosophy and legalized by the Supreme Court, separate-but-equal was enforced by day by agencies of the law, and by the KKK & Co. under cover of night. Booker T. Washington, the Martin Luther King of his day, accepted separate-but-equal in the name of all Negroes. W. E. B. DuBois denounced it.

Separate-but-equal marked the last stage of the white man's flight into cultural neurosis, and the beginning of the black man's frantic striving to assert his humanity and equalize his position with the white. Blacks ventured into all fields of endeavor to which they could gain entrance. Their goal was to present in all fields a performance that would equal or surpass that of the whites. It was long axiomatic among blacks that a black had to be twice as competent as a white in any field in order to win grudging recognition from the whites. This produced a pathological motivation in the blacks to equal or surpass the whites, and a pathological motivation in the whites to maintain a distance from the blacks. This is the rack on which black and white Americans receive their delicious torture! At first there was the color bar, flatly denying the blacks entrance to certain spheres of activity. When this no longer worked, and blacks invaded sector after sector of American life and economy, the whites evolved other methods of keeping their distance. The illusion of the Negro's inferior nature had to be maintained.

One device evolved by the whites was to tab whatever the blacks did with the prefix "Negro." We had *Negro* literature, *Negro* athletes, *Negro* music, *Negro* doctors, *Negro* politicians, *Negro* workers. The malignant ingeniousness of this device is that although it accurately describes an objective biological fact — or, at least, a sociological fact in America — it concealed the paramount psychological fact: that to the white mind, prefixing anything with "Negro" automatically consigned it to an inferior category. A well-known example of the white necessity to deny due credit to blacks is in the realm of music. White musicians were famous for going to Harlem and other Negro cultural centers literally to steal the black man's music, carrying it back across the color line into the Great White World and passing off the watered-down loot as their own original creations. Blacks, meanwhile, were ridiculed as *Negro* musicians playing inferior coon music.

The Negro revolution at home and national liberation movements abroad have unceremoniously shattered the world of fantasy in which the whites have been living. It is painful that many do not yet see that their fantasy world has been rendered uninhabitable in the last half of the twentieth century. But it is away from this world that the white youth of today are turning. The "paper tiger" hero, James Bond, offering the whites a triumphant image of themselves, is saying what many whites want desperately to hear reaffirmed: *I am still the White Man, lord of the land, licensed to kill, and the world is still an empire at my feet.* James Bond feeds on that secret little anxiety, the psychological white backlash, felt in some degree by most whites alive. It is exasperating to see little brown men and little yellow men from the mysterious Orient, and the opaque black men of Africa (to say nothing of these impudent American Negroes!) who come to the UN and talk smart to us, who are scurrying all over *our* globe in their strange modes of dress — much as if they were new, unpleasant arrivals from another planet. Many whites believe in their ulcers that it is only a matter of time before the Marines get the signal to round up these truants and put them back securely in their cages. But it is away from this fantasy world that the white youth of today are turning.

In the world revolution now under way, the initiative rests with people of color. That growing numbers of white youth are repudiating their heritage of blood and taking people of color as their heroes and models is a tribute not only to their insight but to the resilience of the human spirit. For today the heroes of the initiative are people not usually thought of as white: Fidel Castro, Che Guevara, Kwame Nkrumah, Mao Tse-tung, Gamal Abdel Nasser, Robert F. Williams, Malcolm X, Ben Balla, John Lewis, Martin Luther King, Jr., Robert Parris Moses, Ho Chi Minh, Stokely Carmichael, W. E. B. DuBois, James Forman, Chou En-lai.

The white youth of today have begun to react to the fact that the "American Way of Life" is a fossil of history. What do they care if their old baldheaded and crew-cut elders don't dig their caveman mops? They couldn't care less about the old, stiffassed honkies who don't like their new dances: Frug, Monkey, Jerk, Swim, Watusi. All they know is that it feels good to swing to way-out body-rhythms instead of dragassing across the dance floor like zombies to the dead beat of mind-smothered Mickey Mouse music. Is it any wonder that the youth have lost all respect for their elders, for law and order, when for as long as they can remember all they've witnessed is a monumental bickering over the Negro's place in American society and the right of people around the world to be left alone by outside powers? They have witnessed the law, both domestic and international, being spat upon by those who do not like its terms. Is it any wonder, then, that they feel justified, by sitting-in and freedom riding, in breaking laws made by lawless men? Old funny-styled, zipper-mouthed political night riders know nothing but to haul out an investigating committee to *look into the disturbance* to find the cause of the unrest among the youth. Look into a mirror! The cause is you, Mr. and Mrs. Yesterday, you with your forked tongues.

A young white today cannot help but recoil from the base deeds of his people. On every side, on every continent, he sees racial arrogance, savage brutality toward the conquered and subjugated people, genocide; he sees the human cargo of the slave trade; he sees the systematic extermination of American Indians; he sees the civilized nations of Europe fighting in imperial depravity over the lands of other people — and over possession of the very people themselves. There seems to be no end to the ghastly deeds of which his people are guilty. *GUILTY.* The slaughter of the Jews by the Germans, the dropping of atomic bombs on the Japanese people — these deeds weigh heavily upon the prostrate souls and tumultuous consciences of the white youth. The white heroes, their hands dripping with blood, are dead.

The young whites know that the colored people of the world, Afro-Americans included, do not seek revenge for their suffering. They seek the same things the white rebel wants: an end to war and exploitation. Black and white, the young rebels are free people, free in a way that Americans have never been before in the history of their country. And they are outraged.

There is in America today a generation of white youth that is truly worthy of a black man's respect, and this is a rare event in the foul annals of American history. From the beginning of the contact between blacks and whites, there has been very little reason for a black man to respect a white, with such exceptions as John Brown and others lesser known. But respect commands itself and it can neither be given nor withheld when it is due. If a man like Malcolm X could change and repudiate racism, if I myself and other former Muslims can change, if young whites can change, then there is hope for America. It was certainly strange to find myself, while steeped in the doctrine that all whites were devils by nature, commanded by the heart to applaud and acknowledge respect for these young whites — despite the fact that they are descendants of the masters and I the descendant of slave. The sins of the fathers are visited upon the heads of the children — but only if the children continue in the evil deeds of the fathers.

A. Significant Collections of Essays by Individual Black Writers

Baldwin, James. *The Fire Next Time*. New York: Dial, 1963.

————*Nobody Knows My Name*. New York: Dial, 1961.

————*Notes of a Native Son*. Boston: Beacon, 1955.

Bennett, Lerone, Jr. *The Negro Mood*. Chicago: Johnson, 1965.

Brown, William Wells. *The Black Man: His Antecedents, His Genius, and His Achievements*. New York: Thomas Hamilton; Boston: Wallcut, 1863.

Cleaver, Eldridge. *Soul on Ice*. New York: McGraw-Hill, 1968.

DuBois, W. E. B. *The Souls of Black Folk: Essays and Sketches*. Chicago: McClurg, 1903; Blue Heron, 1953.

Ellison, Ralph. *Shadow and Act*. New York: Random House, 1964.

Hernton, Calvin C. *White Papers for White Americans*. Garden City, New York: Doubleday, 1967.

Jones, LeRoi. *Home: Social Essays*. New York: Morrow, 1966.

Killens, John O. *Black Man's Burden*. New York: Trident, 1965.

King, Martin Luther, Jr. *Why We Can't Wait*. New York: Harper, 1964.

Miller, Kelly. *An Appeal to Conscience*. New York: Macmillan, 1918.

————*The Everlasting Stain*. Washington: Associated Publishers, 1924.

————*Out of the House of Bondage*. New York: Crowell, 1914.

————*Race Adjustment; Essays on the Negro in America*. New York: Schocken, 1968. (Originally pub. by Neale, 1908.)

Redding, Saunders. *On Being Negro in America*. Indianapolis: Bobbs-Merrill, 1951.

Williams, John A. *This Is My Country Too*. New York: New American Library, 1965.

Wright, Richard. *White Man; Listen!* New York: Doubleday, 1957.

B. Other Anthologies Including Essays by Black Writers

The American Negro Writer and His Roots. New York: American Society of African Culture, 1960.

Brown, Sterling A., Arthur P. Davis, and Ulysses Lee, eds. *The Negro Caravan.* New York: Dryden, 1941.

Calverton, Victor F., ed. *An Anthology of American Negro Literature.* New York: Modern Library, 1929.

Chapman, Abraham, ed. *Black Voices.* New York: Dell, 1968.

Cromwell, Otelia; Lorenzo D. Turner, and Eva B. Dykes, eds. *Readings from Negro Authors.* New York: Harcourt, Brace, 1931.

Culp, Daniel, ed. *Twentieth Century Negro Literature or a Cyclopedia of Thought.* Naperville, Illinois: Nichols, 1902.

Dreer, Herman. *American Literature by Negro Authors.* New York: Macmillan, 1950.

Ebony Magazine Editors, eds. *The White Problem in America.* Chicago: Johnson, 1967.

Hill, Herbert. *Soon, One Morning: New Writings by American Negroes, 1940–1962.* New York: Knopf, 1963.

Locke, Alain, ed. *The New Negro; an Interpretation.* New York: Boni, 1925.

Turner, Darwin T., and Jean M. Bright, eds. *Images of the Negro in Literature.* Boston: Heath, 1965.

Watkins, Sylvester C., ed. *Anthology of American Negro Literature.* New York: Modern Library, 1944.

Williams, John A., ed. *The Angry Black.* New York: Lancer, 1962.

_____*Beyond the Angry Black.* New York: Cooper Square, 1966.

Poetry

Introduction

A study of poetic creativity by Afro-Americans should begin not with compositions by individual writers but with the folk songs — the spirituals, the ballads, the work songs, and the secular songs. Folk songs do not depend upon the niceties of civilization — the formal education which lends literary models and the finances which permit the purchase of pen, ink, and paper. Folk singing requires only people who can voice their emotions rhythmically, melodiously, and imaginatively. Thus, it is the natural vehicle for poetic expression by people who are talented but illiterate and impoverished, as were the majority of black slaves and freedmen.

The songs deserve study. They reveal the artistic talent, the ideas, and the emotions of black Americans. Too often, consideration of this early art work has been restricted to those spirituals which obviously indicate the black man's reliance upon religion for comfort during his days of adversity. Other songs should be considered: those spirituals whose ambiguous phrasings may have signaled the slaves' intention to escape ("Steal Away"), those spirituals whose religious guise thinly veils their abolitionist content ("Go Down Moses" and "Oh, Mary, Don't You Weep"), those work songs which protest against drudgery and unjust abuse, and those ballads which create folk heroes like wicked Stackalee and proud John Henry.

Folk songs, however, reflect the art of an entire group. To examine the artistic talent of individuals one must concentrate on works which can be credited to individual authors. This present collection, therefore, is restricted to the work of representative black artists who have published volumes of poetry in the United States of America. Such a collection cannot pretend to demonstrate fully the artistic potential of a race: it does not include those unknown singers who never learned to write; it does not include those unknowns whose alien styles and thoughts dissuaded publishers from accepting their works. This collection does, however, offer a representative sampling of the kinds and quality of poetry written by black Americans.

It is not surprising that the first written poetry by black Americans issued from Northern and Eastern states, where slaves enjoyed greater freedom of educational opportunity than they experienced in the South. In 1746 Lucy Terry, a slave in Deerfield, Massachusetts, poetically described an Indian attack in "Bars Fight," the first poem known to have been composed by an African-American. Fourteen years later Jupiter Hammon, a slave on Long Island, published a poem entitled "An Evening Thought: Salvation by Christ, with Penitential Cries." And in 1773, Phillis Wheatley, a teenaged slave in Boston, published the first volume of black American poetry — *Poems on Various Subjects, Religious and Moral.*

Although Phillis Wheatley's poetry compares favorably with that which other Americans were writing at the time, these early poets in general are memorable only as historical curiosities, distinguished neither in style nor in thought. Undoubtedly, the conciliatory tone of Hammon's work and the non-racial attitude of much of Phillis Wheatley's poetry reflect the poets' awareness that their opportunities to learn and to publish depended upon the good will of their masters.

A slightly stronger cry for liberty sounded in the poetry of George Moses Horton who, in 1829, published *Hope of Liberty,* the first collection by a Southern slave. The title is appropriate for a work which Horton hoped would bring sufficient income to enable him to purchase his freedom. Nevertheless, most of the poems are not cries for liberty but sentimental songs like the love lyrics which he wrote on commission from students of the University of North Carolina at Chapel Hill. Like Hammon and Phillis Wheatley, Horton may have restrained himself from giving public offense to those upon whom his fortunes depended.

No such restriction troubled several free blacks who denounced slavery in their poetry during the generation preceding the Civil War. The most significant among this group were Frances E. W. Harper, James Whitfield, and James Madison Bell. The most popular was Frances Harper, abolitionist lecturer, temperance lecturer, and author of four books, the first — *Poems on Various Subjects* — published in 1854.

The first Afro-American to earn and maintain a national reputation as a poet, however, was Paul Laurence Dunbar, whom William Dean Howells described as the first American Negro to reveal innate artistic talent. One of the most popular American poets in the early years of the twentieth century, Dunbar became known chiefly for comic or sentimental dialect poems about slaves and freedmen — even though he also occasionally wrote poems of protest, and often wrote eloquent tributes to the Negro people and to individual Negroes. The reputation has persisted even though most of Dunbar's poetry was written in standard English. Dunbar was depressed that his "graceful lyrics," as he called them, were ignored while his "jingles in a broken tongue" were remembered; for he, like most black writers of his time, wished to demonstrate the cultural respectability of black Americans. They believed that America denied opportunity to black Americans only because, considering them slaves and savages, it failed to recognize their potential. Therefore, such men as Dunbar, Charles W. Chesnutt, and W. E. B. DuBois sought to prove, by reason and by example, that Afro-Americans were capable of moral responsibility, educated behavior, and cultural creativity in the approved traditions of America.

In Dunbar's poetry can be found the framework and the impulse for the three distinctive attitudes which Sterling Brown, Arthur Davis, and Ulysses Lee, in *The Negro Caravan* (1941), have identified among Afro-American poets during the first two decades of the twentieth century. One group of writers, including James E. Campbell and J. Mord Allen, continued the dialect tradition with its emphasis on rural life, sentimentality, and good humor. A second group used poetry as a vehicle for racial protest and defense. The most notable figures of this group were Joseph S. Cotter, Sr., Joseph S. Cotter, Jr., and Fenton Johnson. A third group echoed Dunbar's philosophy that the best poetry presents noble sentiments in beautiful language. W. S. Braithwaite, Leslie P. Hill, Georgia D. Johnson and others wrote lyrically about traditional subjects.

The third decade of the century featured the most exciting explosion of cultural activity which black Americans had ever experienced. Some observers found the character of the activity so distinctive that they described it as the "New Negro" movement. Others called it the "Negro Renaissance" or the "Harlem Renaissance." The term "Renaissance," however, may imply falsely that the culture of black Americans had died at some previous point. To the contrary, as must be evident from this brief history, black artists had not stopped working in the decade preceding the Twenties. But, during the Twenties, black artists were sought out, encouraged, supported, published, and honored by white Americans. In a sense then, black culture was not reborn but merely rediscovered or remembered.

Diverse merging forces produced this new era. After World War I, a wave of enthusiasm and idealism inspired black and white Americans. Afro-Americans had migrated North during the war; they had found jobs. Some black Americans had gone to England and to France, where they had found dignity and freedom. Some Americans looked enviously to the blacks as symbols of the joy, uninhibited emotion, and sexual freedom which young white Americans wanted, or thought they wanted. Others redirected towards their black countrymen the humanitarian sentiments which had been awakened by the war fought "to preserve democracy."

Black culture was the rage. Performers and non-performers crowded into dim clubs to hear the new sounds of jazz from "King" Oliver, Louis Armstrong, and Duke Ellington. White writers such as Eugene O'Neill, Sherwood Anderson, Carl van Vechten, Gertrude Stein, Dubose Heyward, and William Faulkner interpreted the Negro. Wealthy patrons supported black talent. Publishers accepted their works.

But, perhaps most important of all, such men as Alain Locke and Carl van Vechten brought black artists together. In America, black artists generally have been isolated. Social custom has restricted their relationships with their white contemporaries, and physical distance often has limited association with other black artists. Thus, separated from and often unfamiliar with the avant-garde ideas being discussed and practiced in their society, they have been forced to imitate the traditional style or to invent something novel. And, aware of the reluctance of white publishers to risk financial loss in experiments by black writers, they generally have clung to the traditional. From a historian's point of view, consequently, they often appear at the end of a literary tradition and rarely in the early stages of a new one. The mingling of black artists in Harlem during the Twenties, however, at least afforded them immediate awareness of the ideas circulating among artists of their own race. Significantly, the most avant-garde black poet of the Twenties was Jean Toomer, who gained access to the world of Hart Crane, Waldo Frank, Kenneth Burke, Gorham Munson, and *Dial* magazine.

Young poets responded to these forces with pride and confidence rarely evidenced by earlier Afro-Americans. They sought their individual identities in their racial heritage and their ancestral origins: Claude McKay wrote proudly of his Jamaican home; Countee Cullen boasted of the African impulses surging through his veins; Jean Toomer found his people in the red soil of Georgia. The poets explored their artistic heritage for new modes of expression: Langston Hughes experimented with ways to reproduce the soul and rhythm of jazz and the blues; James Weldon Johnson, an older poet, experimented with ways to reproduce the idiom, rhythm, and fervor of Negro sermons. Above all, they felt no shame in their color or their race. Countee Cullen and Waring Cuney described the rhythm and beauty of dark-skinned Americans. More significantly, some not only created characters resembling the comic stereotypes of white authors but even ridiculed their Negro protagonists with a freedom which comes only with self-assurance.

In reality, despite the proclamations that everything was new, the three dominant attitudes of the earlier decades shine through the transformations. Instead of imitating the tradition of satirical dialect poems about Southern Negroes, Langston Hughes wrote satirical poems about Northerners who spoke the dialect of Harlem. Claude McKay protested against racism as bitterly as any earlier writer had. And Countee Cullen and Arna Bontemps excelled the "graceful lyrics" of Dunbar and Braithwaite.

Therefore, one should not be blinded by the apparent aura of novelty in the poetry of the Harlem Renaissance. What is more important to recognize is the developing tendency towards realistic portraiture. Despite a number of idealized characterizations prompted by atavism, actual Afro-Americans are described in the poems of Countee Cullen and Langston Hughes.

The Harlem Renaissance was an era of poetic wealth in a decade of economic prosperity. For most of America, the Thirties were a decade of economic deprivation which, in poetry and other literary genres, inspired social protest, regionalism, and interest in workers and farmers. The new spirit is reflected in the work of Sterling Brown and Frank M. Davis, author of *Black Man's Verse* (1935) and *I Am the American Negro* (1937).

The late Thirties and early Forties were apprentice years for five major poets—Melvin B. Tolson, Robert Hayden, Margaret Walker, Owen Dodson, and Gwendolyn Brooks — whose work reflects a significant change in the focus of black writers. In fiction, black protest had been carried to its pinnacle by Richard Wright in *Uncle Tom's Children* (1938) and *Native Son* (1940). He had not only brought the sound of the ghetto to American critics but had informed them that literature by black writers was competent to be judged according to the criteria used for white writers. From this point on, shrill, sincere protest or naive, humorous exoticism was not sufficient to win laurels for the black writer; he earned distinction only if he mastered his craft.

It is no wonder then that the poets who stand out in the Forties and the Fifties are those who abandoned the old methods and demonstrated their competence in handling the techniques currently in favor among the established critics. Poets who longingly imitated the soft lyricism of John Keats and A. E. Housman were not those who would win praise. Critics looked for traces of T. S. Eliot and Ezra Pound, for free verse, for symbolism, for imagism, for myth and ritual, for experimental syntax.

And they found these new modes and techniques in the work of black writers. The most brilliant, in the opinion of the American critical establishment, was Melvin B. Tolson, who earned accolades from such poets as Robert Frost and Karl Shapiro. Progressing from more conventional protest in his first collection, *Rendezvous with America* (1944), Tolson demonstrated his competence in the Eliot-Pound style in *Libretto for the Republic of Liberia* (1953), which Allen Tate praised for its mastery of "the language of the Anglo-American poetic tradition." Tolson concluded his work with the complex, imaginative, humorous, elusive *Harlem Gallery* (1965), which, Shapiro predicted, would give a new language to American poetry. Starting with a more traditional lyricism in *Heart-Shape in the Dust* (1940), Robert Hayden became progressively symbolic and experimental in his subsequent works, *Figure of Time* (1955) and *A Ballad of Remembrance* (1962). Margaret Walker gave fresh, free expression to black songs of pride in *For My People* (1942). In *Powerful Long Ladder* (1946), Owen Dodson demonstrated the skillful impressionism which characterizes his subsequent novel, *Boy at the Window* (1951). Gwendolyn Brooks achieved recognition as the first Negro author to win a Pulitzer Prize, for *Annie Allen* (1949), a presentation of the mind and emotions of a black woman. In that collection Miss Brooks demonstrated excellent craftsmanship in varying modes from those as old as the ballad to the most recent. In *Montage of a Dream Deferred* (1951), Langston Hughes replaced his jazz and blues with the newer musical idioms of boogie-woogie and bebop, and continued to search for even newer techniques in *Ask Your Mama* (1961).

During the 1960's a new tradition began in black culture — the Black Arts Movement. Inspired by identity and pride derived from black nationalism, young black artists have repudiated the traditions which they identify with the culture of Western Europe. In vestiges of African heritage and in the soul of black ghettoes in America they seek subject-matter, idiom, cadence, and style for art which will inspire black people to liberate themselves from the various forms of bondage — cultural, psychological, spiritual, political, emotional, and economic — which have determined their unequal existence in a society oriented to the values of the white middle-class. Unlike earlier Afro-American protest, it is not a plea for submersion in a melting pot. Instead, it is a demand that black people identify, respect, and free themselves.

The leader of the movement, the most influential black writer since Richard Wright, is LeRoi Jones, who in his first volume, *Preface to a Twenty-Volume Suicide Note* (1961), demonstrated his talent in the more conventional modes. Another respected writer of the decade is Conrad Kent Rivers, who, in his last work, was moving along the path traced by Jones after earlier work — *Perchance to Dream, Othello* (1959) and *These Black Bodies and This Sunburned Face* (1962) — in which he examined his identity. Other voices are too new for a judgment about who will excel. Some of the more promising are Don L. Lee, Etheridge Knight, A. B. Spellman (*The Beautiful Day and Others*, 1964) and Calvin C. Hernton (*The Coming of Chronos to the House of Night Song*, 1964). Many of the younger poets have not yet collected their works. Some are publishing in *Negro Digest, Black Expression* (edited by Don Lee), *Journal of Black Poetry*, and less well-known periodicals. Others are still reading their work to audiences in Newark, Chicago, San Francisco, Brooklyn, and other centers, where college-trained listeners mingle with high school dropouts.

It is dangerous to predict the influence of an artistic revolution which is in its initial stages. Two characteristics, however, are significant. One, the black writers, for the first time in American history, have the advantage of being in the vanguard of an artistic revolt. Now they are the avant-garde writers benefiting from their mutual sharing of ideas. Second, their readings reveal that they are looking back to an oral tradition in which they are perhaps more skilled than their white countrymen. Much of this new poetry depends for its eloquence upon intonation, rhythm, and gesture — qualities which have enriched the folk art of black Americans but which cannot be reproduced adequately in writing. This very strength may conceal its art from those able to approach it only on a printed page. But this fact matters little to the black poets who, indifferent to older and estranged readers, seek to please the new critics who are learning to describe the current work so that they may prescribe for the future. In two hundred years, black singers have moved from folk art dependent on oral presentation, through imitation of obsolescing traditions, through mastery of a present tradition, to a revolutionary art dependent on oral presentation.

Phillis Wheatley (1753?-1784)

Kidnapped from Senegal, West Africa, in the early 1760's, Phillis Wheatley was sold in Boston to John Wheatley, a tailor. After learning to read scriptures within sixteen months, she was encouraged to continue her studies. Within a few years she mastered the education customary for a girl of that time. In 1770, she published her first poem, commemorating the death of a local minister. Three years later, no longer a slave, she published in London *Poems on Various Subjects, Religious and Moral*. After an unhappy marriage with a black man named Peters, she died in 1784.

Imitating the styles of eighteenth-century poetry, especially the style of Alexander Pope, Phillis Wheatley generally wrote tributes, elegies, and lyric poems on noble themes. Judged according to present standards, her poetry is stilted and artificial; but it equals the quality of the work of her fellow Americans in the late eighteenth century. Attention has been called frequently to the absence of racial protest in her work. Richard Wright assumed that the non-racial tone attested to the fact that she was accepted completely within her community. It is equally possible, however, that she did not wish to offend her benevolent master with complaints about her fortune.

The following poems typify her style and thought. In the first two, it is not surprising that she expresses preference for America above her homeland, which was part of dim childhood memories; it is significant, however, that she urges greater respect for the potential of Africans. Her advice to Harvard students was written in 1767. Much longer than her usual lyrics, "Goliath of Gath" is a smooth narration of the familiar Biblical story of David and Goliath.

165

On being brought from Africa to America

'Twas mercy brought me from my *Pagan* land,
Taught my benighted soul to understand
That there's a God, that there's a *Saviour* too:
Once I redemption neither sought nor knew.
Some view our sable race with scornful eye,
"Their colour is a diabolic die."
Remember, *Christians*, *Negros*, black as *Cain*,
May be refin'd, and join th' angelic train.

To the University Of Cambridge, in New-England.

While an intrinsic ardor prompts to write,
The muses promise to assist my pen;
'Twas not long since I left my native shore
The land of errors, and *Egyptian* gloom:
Father of mercy, 'twas thy gracious hand
Brought me in safety from those dark abodes.

Students, to you 'tis giv'n to scan the heights
Above, to traverse the ethereal space,
And mark the systems of revolving worlds.
Still more, ye sons of science, ye receive
The blissful news by messengers from heav'n
How *Jesus*' blood for your redemption flows.
See him with hands out-strecht upon the cross;
Immense compassion in his bosom glows;
He hears revilers, nor resents their scorn:
What matchless mercy in the Son of God!
When the whole human race by sin had fall'n,
He deign'd to die that they might rise again,
And share with him in the sublimest skies,
Life without death, and glory without end.

Improve your privileges while they stay,
Ye pupils, and each hour redeem, that bears
Or good or bad report of you to heav'n.
Let sin, that baneful evil to the soul,

By you be shunned, nor once remit your guard;
Suppress the deadly serpent in its egg.
Ye blooming plants of human race divine,
An *Ethiop* tells you 'tis your greatest foe;
Its transient sweetness turns to endless pain,
And in immense perdition sinks the soul.

Goliath of Gath
I. Sam. Chap. xvii.

Ye martial pow'rs, and all ye tuneful nine,
Inspire my song, and aid my high design.
The dreadful scenes and toils of war I write,
The ardent warriors, and the fields of fight:
You best remember, and you best can sing
The acts of heroes to the vocal string:
Resume the lays with which your sacred lyre,
Did then the poet and the sage inspire.

Now front to front the armies were display'd,
Here *Israel* rang'd, and there the foes array'd;
The hosts on two opposing mountains stood,
Thick as the foliage of the waving wood;
Between them an extensive valley lay,
O'er which the gleaming armour pour'd the day,
When from the camp of the *Philistine* foes,
Dreadful to view, a mighty warrior rose;
In the dire deeds of bleeding battle skill'd,
The monster stalks the terror of the field.
From *Gath* he sprung, *Goliath* was his name,
Of fierce deportment, and gigantic frame:
A brazen helmet on his head was plac'd,
A coat of mail his form terrific grac'd,
The greaves his legs, the targe his shoulders prest:
Dreadful in arms high-tow'ring o'er the rest
A spear he proudly wav'd, whose iron head,
Strange to relate, six hundred shekels weigh'd;
He strode along and shook the ample field,
While *Phoebus* blaz'd refulgent on his shield:
Through *Jacob's* race a chilling horror ran,
When thus the huge, enormous chief began:

"Say, what the cause that in this proud array
"You set your battle in the face of day?
"One hero find in all your vaunting train,
"Then see who loses, and who wins the plain:
"For he who wins, in triumph may demand
"Perpetual service from the vanquish'd land:
"Your armies I defy, your force despise,
"By far inferior in *Philistia's* eyes:
"Produce a man, and let us try the fight,
"Decide the contest, and the victor's right."

Thus challeng'd he; all *Israel* stood amaz'd,
And ev'ry chief in consternation gaz'd;
But *Jesse's* son in youthful bloom appears,
And warlike courage far beyond his years:
He left the folds, he left the flow'ry meads,
And soft recesses of the sylvan shades.
Now *Israel's* monarch, and his troops arise, ⎫
With peals of shouts ascending to the skies; ⎬
In *Elah's* vale the scene of combat lies, ⎭

When the fair morning blush'd with orient red,
What *David's* sire enjoin'd the son obey'd,
And swift of foot towards the trench he came,
Where glow'd each bosom with the martial flame.
He leaves his carriage to another's care,
And runs to greet his brethren of the war.
While yet they spake the giant-chief arose,
Repeats the challenge, and insults his foes:
Struck with the sound, and trembling at the view,
Affrighted *Israel* from its post withdrew.
"Observe ye this tremendous foe, they cry'd,
"Who in proud vaunts our armies hath defy'd:
"Whoever lays him prostrate on the plain,
"Freedom in *Israel* for his house shall gain;
"And on him wealth unknown the king will pour,
"And give his royal daughter for his dow'r."

Then *Jesse's* youngest hope: "My brethren say,
"What shall be done for him who takes away
"Reproach from *Jacob*, who destroys the chief,
"And puts a period to his country's grief.

"He vaunts the honours of his arms abroad,
"And scorns the armies of the living God."

Thus spoke the youth, th' attentive people ey'd
The wond'rous hero, and again reply'd:
"Such the rewards our monarch will bestow,
"On him who conquers, and destroys his foe,"

Eliab heard, and kindled into ire
To hear his shepherd brother thus inquire,
And thus begun? "What errand brought thee? say
"Who keeps thy flock? or does it go astray?
"I know the base ambition of thine heart,
"But back in safety from the field depart,"

Eliab thus to *Jesse's* youngest heir,
Express'd his wrath in accents most severe.
When to his brother mildly he reply'd,
"What have I done? or what the cause to chide?"

The words were told before the king, who sent
For the young hero to his royal tent:
Before the monarch dauntless he began,
"For this *Philistine* fail no heart of man:
"I'll take the vale, and with the giant fight:
"I dread not all his boasts, nor all his might."
When thus the king: "Dar'st thou a stripling go,
"And venture combat with so great a foe?
"Who all his days has been inur'd to fight,
"And made its deeds his study and delight:
"Battles and bloodshed brought the monster forth,
"And clouds and whirlwinds usher'd in his birth."
When David thus: "I kept the fleecy care,
"And out there rush'd a lion and a bear;
"A tender lamb the hungry lion took,
"And with no other weapon than my crook
"Bold I pursu'd, and chas'd him o'er the field,
"The prey deliver'd, and the felon kill'd:
"As thus the lion and the bear I slew,
"So shall *Goliath* fall, and all his crew:
"The God, who sav'd me from these beasts of prey,
"By me this monster in the dust shall lay."

So *David* spoke: "The wond'ring king reply'd;
"Go thou with heav'n and victory on thy side;
"This coat of mail, this sword gird on," he said,
And plac'd a mighty helmet on his head:
The coat, the sword, the helm he laid aside,
Nor chose to venture with those arms untry'd,
Then took his staff, and to the neighb'ring brook
Instant he ran, and thence five pebbles took,
Mean time descended to *Philistia's* son
A radiant cherub, and he thus begun:
"*Goliath*, well thou know'st thou hast defy'd
"Yon Hebrew armies, and their God deny'd:
"Rebellious wretch! audacious worm! forbear,
"Nor tempt the vengeance of their God too far:
"Them, who with his omnipotence contend,
"No eye shall pity, and no arm defend:
"Proud as thou art, in short liv'd glory great,
"I come to tell thee thine approaching fate.
"Regard my words. The judge of all the gods,
"Beneath whose steps the tow'ring mountain nods,
"Will give thine armies to the savage brood,
"That cut the liquid air, or range the wood.
"Thee too a well-aim'd pebble shall destroy,
"And thou shalt perish by a beardless boy:
"Such is the mandate from the realms above, ⎫
"And should I try the vengeance to remove, ⎬
"Myself a rebel to my king would prove. ⎭
"*Goliath* say, shall grace to him be shown,
"Who dares heav'ns monarch, and insults his throne?"

   "Your words are lost on me," the giant cries, ⎫
While fear and wrath contended in his eyes, ⎬
When thus the messenger from heav'n replies: ⎭
"Provoke no more *Jehovah's* awful hand
"To hurl its vengeance on thy guilty land:
"He grasps the thunder, and, he wings the storm,
"Servants their sov'reign's orders to perform."
The angel spoke, and turn'd his eyes away,
Adding new radiance to the rising day.

   Now *David* comes. The fatal stones demand
His left, the staff engag'd his better hand:
The giant mov'd, and from his tow'ring height

Survey'd the stripling, and disdain'd the fight,
And thus began: "Am I a dog with thee?
"Bring'st thou no amour, but a staff to me?
"The gods on thee their vollied curses pour,
"And beasts and birds of prey thy flesh devour,"

David undaunted thus, "Thy spear and shield
"Shall no protection to thy body yield:
"*Jehovah's* name — — no other arms I bear,
"I ask no other in this glorious war.
"To-day the Lord of Hosts to me will give
"Vict'ry, to-day thy doom thou shalt receive;
"The fate you threaten shall your own become,
"And beasts shall be your animated tomb,
"That all the earth's inhabitants may know
"That there's a God, who governs all below:
"This great assembly too shall witness stand,
"That needs nor sword, nor spear, th' Almighty's hand:
"The battle his, the conquest he bestows,
"And to our pow'r consigns our hated foes."

Thus *David* spoke; *Goliath* heard and came
To meet the hero in the field of fame.
Ah! fatal meeting to thy troops and thee,
But thou wast deaf to the divine decree;
Young *David* meets thee, meets thee not in vain;
'Tis thine to perish on th' ensanguin'd plain.

And now the youth the forceful pebble flung,
Philistia trembled as it whizz'd along:
In his dread forehead, where the helmet ends,
Just o'er the brows the well-aim'd stone descends,
It pierc'd the skull, and shatter'd all the brain,
Prone on his face he tumbled to the plain:
Goliath's fall no smaller terror yields
Than riving thunders in aerial fields:
The soul still ling'red in its lov'd abode,
Till conq'ring *David* o'er the giant strode:
Goliath's sword then laid its master dead,
And from the body hew'd the ghastly head;
The blood in gushing torrents drench'd the plains,
The soul found passage through the spouting veins.

And now aloud the illustrious victor said,
"Where are your boastings now your champion's dead?"
Scarce had he spoke when the *Philistines* fled:
But fled in vain; the conqu'ror swift pursu'd:
What scenes of slaughter! and what seas of blood!
There *Saul* thy thousands grasp'd th' impurpled sand
In pangs of death the conquest of thine hand;
And *David* there were thy ten thousands laid:
Thus *Israel's* damsels musically play'd.

   Near *Gath* and *Ekron* many an hero lay,
Breath'd out their souls, and curs'd the light of day;
Their fury quench'd by death, no longer burns,
And *David* with *Goliath's* head returns,
To *Salem* brought, but in his tent he plac'd
The load of armour which the giant grac'd,
His monarch saw him coming from the war,
And thus demanded of the son of *Ner*.
"Say, who is this amazing youth?" he cry'd,
When thus the leader of the host reply'd;
"As lives thy soul I know not whence he sprung,
"So great in prowess though in years so young:"
"Inquire whose son is he," the sov'reign said,
"Before whose conq'ring arm *Philistia* fled."
Before the king behold the stripling stand,
Goliath's head depending from his hand:
To him the king: "Say of what martial line
"Art thou, young hero, and what sire was thine?"
He humbly thus: "The son of *Jesse* I:
"I came the glories of the field to try,
"Small is my tribe, but valiant in the fight;
"Small is my city, but thy royal right."
"Then take the promis'd gifts," the monarch cry'd,
Conferring riches and the royal bride;
"Knit to my soul for ever thou remain
"With me, nor quit my regal roof again."

George Moses Horton
(1797-1883)

A slave in Northhampton County, North Carolina, George Moses Horton was a black Cyrano for hundreds of male students at the University of North Carolina at Chapel Hill, who commissioned him to write love lyrics to their sweethearts. Although Horton's poetry is not distinguished by protests against slavery, the cry for liberty occasionally appears, particularly in *The Hope of Liberty* (1829), from which he hoped to earn enough money to purchase his freedom. Even a reprinting of this volume, as *Poems by a Slave* (1837), failed to raise the required sum; therefore, Horton remained a slave until 1865, when he was freed by the Union troops. In the same year he published his final collection, *Naked Genius*.

The following reveal Horton's characteristic themes of conventional moralizing, appreciation of nature, and sentimentalizing of love.

The Swan — Vain Pleasures

The Swan which boasted mid the tide,
Whose nest was guarded by the wave,
Floated for pleasure till she died,
And sunk beneath the flood to lave.

The bird of fashion drops her wing,
The rose-bush now declines to bloom;
The gentle breezes of the spring
No longer waft a sweet perfume.

Fair beauty with those lovely eyes,
Withers along her vital stream;
Proud fortune leaves her throne, and flies
From pleasure, as a flattering dream.

The eagle of exalted fame,
Which spreads his pinions far to sail,
Struggled to fan his dying flame,
Till pleasure pall'd in every gale.

And gaudy mammon, sordid gain,
Whose plume has faded, once so gay,
Languishes mid the flowery train,
Whilst pleasure flies like fumes away.

Vain pleasures, O how short to last!
Like leaves which quick to ashes burn;
Which kindle from the slightest blast,
And slight to nothing hence return.

The Powers of Love

It lifts the poor man from his cell
    To fortune's bright alcove;
Its mighty sway few, few can tell,
Mid envious foes it conquers ill;
    There's nothing half like love.

Ye weary strangers, void of rest,
    Who late through life have strove,
Like the late bird which seeks its nest,
If you would hence in truth be blest,
    Light on the bough of love.

The vagrant plebeian, void of friends,
    Constrain'd through wilds to rove,
On this his safety whole depends,
One faithful smile his trouble ends,
    A smile of constant love.

Thus did a captured wretch complain,
    Imploring heaven above,
Till one with sympathetic pain,
Flew to his arms and broke the chain,
    And grief took flight from love.

Let clouds of danger rise and roar,
    And hope's firm pillars move,
With storms behind and death before,
O grant me this, I crave no more,
    There's nothing half like love.

When nature wakes soft pity's coo
    The hawk deserts the dove,
Compassion melts the creature through,
With palpitations felt by few,
    The wrecking throbs of love.

Let surly discord take its flight
    From wedlock's peaceful grove,
While union breaks the arm of fight,
With darkness swallow'd up in light,
    O what is there like love.

To a Departing Favorite

Thou mayst retire, but think of me
    When thou art gone afar,
Where'er in life thy travels be,
If tost along the brackish sea,
    Or borne upon the car.

Thou mayst retire, I care not where,
    Thy name my theme shall be;
With thee in heart I shall be there,
Content thy good or ill to share,
    If dead to lodge with thee.

Thou mayst retire beyond the deep,
    And leave thy sister train,
To roam the wilds where dangers sleep,
And leave affection sad to weep
    In bitterness and pain.

Thou mayst retire, and yet be glad
    To leave me thus alone,
Lamenting and bewailing sad;
Farewell, thy sunk deluded lad
    May rise when thou art gone.

The Eye of Love

I know her story-telling eye
   Has more expression than her tongue;
And from that heart-extorted sigh,
   At once the peal of love is rung.

When that soft eye lets fall a tear
   Of doating fondness as we part,
The stream is from a cause sincere,
   And issues from a melting heart.

What shall her fluttering pulse restrain,
   The life-watch beating from her soul,
When all the power of hate is slain,
   And love permits it no control.

When said her tongue, I wish thee well,
   Her eye declared it must be true;
And every sentence seem'd to tell
   The tale of sorrow told by few.

When low she bow'd and wheel'd aside,
   I saw her blushing temples fade;
Her smiles were sunk in sorrow's tide,
   But love was in her eye betray'd.

The Setting Sun

'Tis sweet to trace the setting sun
   Wheel blushing down the west;
When his diurnal race is run,
The traveller stops the gloom to shun,
   And lodge his bones to rest.

Far from the eye he sinks apace,
   But still throws back his light
From oceans of resplendant grace,
Whence sleeping vesper paints her face,
   And bids the sun good night.

To those hesperian fields by night
  My thoughts in vision stray,
Like spirits stealing into light,
From gloom upon the wing of flight,
  Soaring from time away.

Our eagle, with his pinions furl'd,
  Takes his departing peep,
And hails the occidental world,
Swift round whose base the globes are whirl'd,
  Whilst weary creatures sleep.

Paul Laurence Dunbar
(1872-1906)

Born in Dayton, Ohio, Paul Laurence Dunbar, the son of former slaves, became one of the most popular American poets of his time. Although he published his first collection, *Oak and Ivy*, in 1892 while working as an elevator operator, Dunbar did not gain national attention until William Dean Howells favorably reviewed *Majors and Minors* (1896) and followed with a laudatory introduction to *Lyrics of Lowly Life* (1896), in which he described Dunbar as the first American Negro to "evince innate artistic talent." Despite poor health Dunbar published three additional collections of original poems: *Lyrics of the Hearthside* (1899), *Lyrics of Love and Laughter* (1903), and *Lyrics of Sunshine and Shadow* (1905).

Although he wrote four novels and four collections of stories, Paul Laurence Dunbar should be remembered as a poet rather than a writer of fiction. Because he is known best as a writer of comic or sentimental monologues in Negro dialect, modern readers have overlooked his conscious artistry and experimentation with meter and rhyme, his skillful imitations of the dialects of Caucasian inhabitants of Ohio and Indiana, his many tributes to Afro-American heroes, the characteristic melancholy of much of his standard-English poetry, and the fact that he wrote more poetry in standard English than in dialect. Nevertheless, his chief talents — rhythm, narrative skill, and satirical characterization — are best revealed in his dialect poems, his major contribution to American literature.

The first two of the following selections illustrate Dunbar's eloquent tributes to Afro-American heroes and ancestry. The third selection is one of Dunbar's earliest and most highly praised meditations. The fourth, in Negro dialect, reveals Dunbar's humor, the characteristic rhythm which he developed for these monologues, and his understanding of the indirect protests of slaves. The final selection exhibits both the charm of Dunbar's many poems about children and his imitation of non-Negro dialect.

179

Frederick Douglass

A hush is over all the teeming lists,
    And there is pause, a breath-space in the strife;
A spirit brave has passed beyond the mists
    And vapors that obscure the sun of life.
And Ethiopia, with bosom torn,
Laments the passing of her noblest born.

She weeps for him a mother's burning tears —
    She loved him with a mother's deepest love.
He was her champion thro' direful years,
    And held her weal all other ends above.
When Bondage held her bleeding in the dust,
He raised her up and whispered, "Hope and Trust."

For her his voice, a fearless clarion, rung
    That broke in warning on the ears of men;
For her the strong bow of his power he strung,
    And sent his arrows to the very den
Where grim Oppression held his bloody place
And gloated o'er the mis'ries of a race.

And he was no soft-tongued apologist;
    He spoke straightforward, fearlessly uncowed;
The sunlight of his truth dispelled the mist,
    And set in bold relief each dark-hued cloud;
To sin and crime he gave their proper hue,
And hurled at evil what was evil's due.

Through good and ill report he cleaved his way
    Right onward, with his face set toward the heights,
Nor feared to face the foeman's dread array, —
    The lash of scorn, the sting of petty spites.
He dared the lightning in the lightning's track,
And answered thunder with his thunder back.

Ode to Ethiopia

O Mother Race! to thee I bring
This pledge of faith unwavering,
    This tribute to thy glory.

I know the pangs which thou didst feel,
When Slavery crushed thee with its heel,
  With thy dear blood all gory.

Sad days were those — ah, sad indeed!
But through the land the fruitful seed
  Of better times was growing.
The plant of freedom upward sprung,
And spread its leaves so fresh and young —
  Its blossoms now are blowing.

On every hand in this fair land,
Proud Ethiope's swarthy children stand
  Beside their fairer neighbor;
The forests flee before their stroke,
Their hammers ring, their forges smoke, —
  They stir in honest labour.

They tread the fields where honour calls;
Their voices sound through senate halls
  In majesty and power.
To right they cling; the hymns they sing
Up to the skies in beauty ring,
  And bolder grow each hour.

Be proud, my Race, in mind and soul;
Thy name is writ on Glory's scroll
  In characters of fire.
High 'mid the clouds of Fame's bright sky
Thy banner's blazoned folds now fly,
  And truth shall lift them higher.

Thou hast the right to noble pride,
Whose spotless robes were purified
  By blood's severe baptism.
Upon thy brow the cross was laid,
And labour's painful sweat-beads made
  A consecrating chrism.

No other race, or white or black,
When bound as thou wert, to the rack,
  So seldom stooped to grieving;

No other race, when free again,
Forgot the past and proved them men
    So noble in forgiving.

Go on and up! Our souls and eyes
Shall follow thy continuous rise;
    Our ears shall list thy story
From bards who from thy root shall spring,
And proudly tune their lyres to sing
    Of Ethiopia's glory.

Ere Sleep Comes Down to Soothe the Weary Eyes

Ere sleep comes down to soothe the weary eyes,
    Which all the day with ceaseless care have sought
The magic gold which from the seeker flies;
    Ere dreams put on the gown and cap of thought,
And make the waking world a world of lies, —
    Of lies most palpable, uncouth, forlorn,
That say life's full of aches and tears and sighs, —
    Oh, how with more than dreams the soul is torn,
Ere sleep comes down to soothe the weary eyes.

Ere sleep comes down to soothe the weary eyes,
    How all the griefs and heartaches we have known
Come up like pois'nous vapors that arise
    From some base witch's caldron, when the crone,
To work some potent spell, her magic plies.
    The past which held its share of bitter pain,
Whose ghost we prayed that Time might exorcise,
    Comes up, is lived and suffered o'er again,
Ere sleep comes down to soothe the weary eyes.

Ere sleep comes down to soothe the weary eyes,
    What phantoms fill the dimly lighted room;
What ghostly shades in awe-creating guise
    Are bodied forth within the teeming gloom.
What echoes faint of sad and soul-sick cries,
    And pangs of vague inexplicable pain

That pay the spirit's ceaseless enterprise,
   Come thronging through the chambers of the brain,
Ere sleep comes down to soothe the weary eyes.

Ere sleep comes down to soothe the weary eyes,
   Where ranges forth the spirit far and free?
Through what strange realms and unfamiliar skies
   Tends her far course to lands of mystery?
To lands unspeakable — beyond surmise,
   Where shapes unknowable to being spring,
Till, faint of wing, the Fancy fails and dies
   Much wearied with the spirit's journeying,
Ere sleep comes down to soothe the weary eyes.

Ere sleep comes down to soothe the weary eyes,
   How questioneth the soul that other soul, —
The inner sense which neither cheats nor lies,
   But self exposes unto self, a scroll
Full writ with all life's acts unwise or wise,
   In characters indelible and known;
So, trembling with the shock of sad surprise,
   The soul doth view its awful self alone,
Ere sleep comes down to soothe the weary eyes.

When sleep comes down to seal the weary eyes,
   The last dear sleep whose soft embrace is balm,
And whom sad sorrow teaches us to prize
   For kissing all our passions into calm,
Ah, then, no more we heed the sad world's cries,
   Or seek to probe th' eternal mystery,
Or fret our souls at long-withheld replies,
   At glooms through which our visions cannot see,
When sleep comes down to seal the weary eyes.

An Ante-Bellum Sermon

   We is gathahed hyeah, my brothahs,
      In dis howlin' wildaness,
   Fu' to speak some words of comfo't
      To each othah in distress.

An' we chooses fu' ouah subjic'
   Dis — we'll 'splain it by an' by;
"An' de Lawd said, 'Moses, Moses,'
   An' de man said, 'Hyeah am I.' "

Now ole Pher'oh, down in Egypt,
   Was de wuss man evah bo'n,
An' he had de Hebrew chillun
   Down dah wukin' in his co'n;
'T well de Lawd got tiahed o' his foolin',
   An' sez he: "I'll let him know —
Look hyeah, Moses, go tell Pher'oh
   Fu' to let dem chillun go."

"An' ef he refuse to do it,
   I will make him rue de houah,
Fu' I'll empty down on Egypt
   All de vials of my powah."
Yes, he did — an' Pher'oh's ahmy
   Was n't wuth a ha'f a dime;
Fu' de Lawd will he'p his chillun,
   You kin trust him evah time.

An' yo' enemies may 'sail you
   In de back an' in de front;
But de Lawd is all aroun' you,
   Fu' to ba' de battle's brunt.
Dey kin fo'ge yo' chains an' shackles
   F'om de mountains to de sea;
But de Lawd will sen' some Moses
   Fu' to set his chillun free.

An' de lan' shall hyeah his thundah,
   Lak a blas' f'om Gab'el's ho'n,
Fu' de Lawd of hosts is mighty
   When he girds his ahmor on.
But fu' feah some one mistakes me,
   I will pause right hyeah to say,
Dat I'm still a-preachin' ancient,
   I ain't talkin' 'bout to-day.

But I tell you, fellah christuns,
   Things 'll happen mighty strange;
Now, de Lawd done dis fu' Isrul,
   An' his ways don't nevah change,
An' de love he showed to Isrul
   Was n't all on Isrul spent;
Now don't run an' tell yo' mastahs
   Dat I's preachin' discontent.

'Cause I is n't; I'se a-judgin'
   Bible people by deir ac's;
I'se a-givin' you de Scriptuah,
   I'se a-handin' you de fac's.
Cose ole Pher'oh b'lieved in slav'ry
   But de Lawd he let him see,
Dat de people he put bref in, —
   Evah mothah's son was free.

An' dahs othahs thinks lak Pher'oh,
   But dey calls de Scriptuah liar,
Fu' de Bible says "a servant
   Is a-worthy of his hire."
An' you cain't git roun' nor thoo dat,
   An' you cain't git ovah it,
Fu' whatevah place you git in,
   Dis hyeah Bible too 'll fit.

So you see de Lawd's intention,
   Evah sence de worl' began,
Was dat His almighty freedom
   Should belong to evah man,
But I think it would be bettah,
   Ef I'd pause agin to say,
Dat I'm talkin' 'bout ouah freedom
   In a Bibleistic way.

But de Moses is a-comin',
   An' he's comin', suah and fas'
We kin hyeah his feet a-trompin',
   We kin hyeah his trumpit blas'.

But I want to wa'n you people,
    Don't you git too brigity;
An' don't you git to braggin'
    'Bout dese things, you wait an' see.

But when Moses wif his powah
    Comes an' sets us chillun free,
We will praise de gracious Mastah
    Dat has gin us liberty;
An' we'll shout ouah halleluyahs,
    On dat mighty reck'nin' day,
When we'se reco'nised ez citiz' —
    Huh uh! Chillun, let us pray!

When a Feller's Itchin' to be Spanked

W'en us fellers stomp around, makin' lots o' noise,
Gramma says, "There's certain times comes to little boys
W'en they need a shingle or the soft side of a plank;"
She says "we're a-itchin' for a right good spank."
    An' she says, "Now thes you wait,
    It's a-comin' — soon or late,
W'en a fellers itchin' fer a spank."

W'en a feller's out o' school, you know how he feels,
Gramma says we wriggle 'roun like a lot o' eels.
W'y it's like a man that's thes home from out o' jail.
What's the use o' scoldin' if we pull Tray's tail?
    Gramma says, tho', "thes you wait,
    It's a-comin' — soon or late,
You'se the boys that's itchin' to be spanked."

Cats is funny creatures an' I like to make 'em yowl,
Gramma alwus looks at me with a awful scowl
An' she says, "Young gentlemen, mamma should be thanked
Ef you'd get your knickerbockers right well spanked."
    An' she says, "Now thes you wait,
    It's a-comin' — soon or late,"
W'en a feller's itchin' to be spanked.

Ef you fin' the days is gettin' awful hot in school
An' you know a swimmin' place where it's nice and cool,
Er you know a cat-fish hole brimmin' full o' fish,
Whose a-goin' to set around school and wish?
   'Tain't no use to hide your bait,
   It's a-comin' — soon or late,
W'en a feller's itchin' to be spanked.

Ol' folks know most ever-thing 'bout the world, I guess,
Gramma does, we wish she knowed thes a little less,
But I alwus kind o' think it 'ud be as well
Ef they wouldn't alwus have to up an' tell;
   We kids wish 'at they'd thes wait,
   It's a-comin' — soon or late,
W'en a feller's itchin' to be spanked.

W[illiam] S[tanley] Braithwaite (1878-1961)

W.S. Braithwaite, of West Indian ancestry, was born and reared in Boston, Massachusetts. Although he worked several years on the editorial staff of the Boston *Transcript* and served as Professor of Creative Literature at Atlanta University, Braithwaite is remembered more widely as an anthologist and a poet. From 1913 to 1929 he edited an annual anthology of magazine verse, in which he included early works of such important poets as Vachel Lindsay and Carl Sandburg. He also edited anthologies of Restoration, Georgian, and Victorian verse.

As a critic, he encouraged experimental poets. But in his own writing — collected in *Lyrics of Life and Love* (1904), *The House of Falling Leaves* (1908), and *Selected Poems* (1948), he imitated the traditions of nineteenth-century lyric poetry and wrote chiefly on non-racial themes, as is evidenced in the following selections.

Rhapsody

I am glad daylong for the gift of song,
    For time and change and sorrow;
For the sunset wings and the world-end things
    Which hang on the edge of to-morrow.
I am glad for my heart whose gates apart
    Are the entrance-place of wonders,
Where dreams come in from the rush and din
    Like sheep from the rains and thunders.

189

To——

Half in the dim light from the hall
I saw your fingers rise and fall
Along the pale, dusk-shadowed keys,
And heard your subtle melodies.

The magic of your mastery leant
Your soul unto the instrument;
Strange-wise, its spell of power seemed
To voice the visions that you dreamed.

The music gave my soul such wings
As bore me through the shadowings
Of mortal bondage; flight on flight
I circled dreams' supremest height.

Above were tender twilight skies,
Where stars were dreams and memories —
The long forgotten raptures of
My youth's dead fires of hope and love.

If I Could Touch

If I could touch your hand to-night
    And hear you speak one little word,
I then might understand your flight
    Up the star steps, unseen, unheard.

If through the mists of gold and gray
    That tint the weary sunset skies,
There shone two stars across the bay
    That thrilled me like your passionate eyes —

If only some small part of you
    Would speak, or touch, or rise in sight,
Death would be then between us two
    The passing of a summer's night.

Hymn for the Slain in Battle

Lord, God of all in Life and Death,
The winter's storm, the summer's breath,
Of fragrant bloom, — whose Mighty hand
Decrees the pow'r of sea and land,
Hear, Lord, this prayer for those who are
Slain in the hour of thund'rous war.
Have mercy, Lord, on those who fall
Rent by the iron-splintered ball.
Reck not their cause was right or wrong,
'Twas Duty led them blind and strong.
They shaped not what to war gave rise —
They make the greatest sacrifice.

Two Questions

Heart of the soft, wild rose
Hid in a forest close
Far from the world away,
Sweet for a night and day.
Rose, is it good to be sweet,
Sun and the dews to greet?

Life that is mine to keep
In travail, play and sleep
Firm on a tossing ball,
Drilled to march at a call;
Work, love, death — these three —
Life, is there more for me?

James Weldon Johnson
(1871-1938)

A man of diverse talents, James Weldon Johnson, at various times, was a public school teacher, a principal, a lawyer, a leading song writer, a consul for the United States, a novelist, secretary of the National Association for the Advancement of Colored People, a poet, an anthologist, and a college professor. Born in Jacksonville, Florida, he earned a bachelor's degree from Atlanta University. After passing the examination permitting him to practice law in Florida, Johnson, then a high school principal, left both law and education to join his brother Rosamond in New York, where, for several years, the two collaborated in writing successful musical comedies presented on Broadway. From 1906 to 1913 he served as Consul in Venezuela and Nicaragua. After leaving government service, he took a position first as field secretary, later as general secretary for the National Association for the Advancement of Colored People, with which he worked from 1916 to 1930. While a professor at Fisk University, whose faculty he joined in 1930, Johnson was killed in an automobile accident.

Johnson's contributions to black literature are equally varied and impressive. In 1912 he wrote *The Autobiography of an Ex-Coloured Man,* which some critics describe as the most artistic novel by an American Negro prior to the 1920's. In 1922 he edited *The Book of American Negro Poetry* (revised and enlarged in 1931), the first anthology of poetry by black Americans. He also co-edited *The Book of Negro Spirituals* (1925, 1926, 1940). His *Black Manhattan* (1930) is an interesting, highly informative social and cultural history of Afro-Americans in New York. His song, "Lift Every Voice and Sing," was accepted for many years as a national anthem for Negro Americans.

In his early lyrics, written on the traditional themes of musical comedy, Johnson generally used dialect to comply with the images which audiences expected from the Negro characters. "Sence You

193

Went Away" illustrates this practice. When he attempted the more serious task of writing verse sermons, however, Johnson rejected dialect. He feared that dialect supported only comic or pathetic scenes and evoked laughter or pity from readers and audiences. In *God's Trombones: Seven Old-Time Negro Sermons in Verse*, from which "The Creation" is taken, Johnson wished to suggest the nobility as well as the emotional fervor of the sermons of Negro preachers. He believed that, rather than lending realism, dialect would merely distract the reader from the major theme.

Sence You Went Away

Seems lak to me de stars don't shine so bright,
Seems lak to me de sun done loss his light,
Seems lak to me der's nothin' goin' right,
        Sence you went away.

Seems lak to me de sky ain't half so blue,
Seems lak to me dat ev'ything wants you,
Seems lak to me I don't know what to do,
        Sence you went away.

Seems lak to me dat ev'ything is wrong,
Seems lak to me de day's jes twice es long,
Seems lak to me de bird's forgot his song,
        Sence you went away.

Seems lak to me I jes can't he'p but sigh,
Seems lak to me ma th'oat keeps gittin' dry,
Seems lak to me a tear stays in ma eye,
        Sence you went away.

The Creation

And God stepped out on space,
And he looked around and said:
I'm lonely —
I'll make me a world.

And far as the eye of God could see
Darkness covered everything,
Blacker than a hundred midnights
Down in a cypress swamp.

Then God smiled,
And the light broke,
And the darkness rolled up on one side,
And the light stood shining on the other,
And God said: That's good!

Then God reached out and took the light in his hands,
And God rolled the light around in his hands
Until he made the sun;
And he set that sun a-blazing in the heavens.
And the light that was left from making the sun
God gathered it up in a shining ball
And flung it against the darkness,
Spangling the night with the moon and stars.
Then down between
The darkness and the light
He hurled the world;
And God said: That's good!

Then God himself stepped down —
And the sun was on his right hand,
And the moon was on his left;
The stars were clustered about his head,
And the earth was under his feet.
And God walked, and where he trod
His footsteps hollowed the valleys out
And bulged the mountains up.

Then he stopped and looked and saw
That the earth was hot and barren.
So God stepped over to the edge of the world
And he spat out the seven seas —
He batted his eyes, and the lightnings flashed —
He clapped his hands, and the thunders rolled —
And the waters above the earth came down,
The cooling waters came down.

Then the green grass sprouted,
And the little red flowers blossomed,
The pine tree pointed his finger to the sky,
And the oak spread out his arms,
The lakes cuddled down in the hollows of the ground,
And the rivers ran down to the sea;
And God smiled again,
And the rainbow appeared,
And curled itself around his shoulder.

Then God raised his arm and he waved his hand
Over the sea and over the land,
And he said: Bring forth! Bring forth!
And quicker than God could drop his hand,
Fishes and fowls
And beasts and birds
Swam the rivers and the seas,
Roamed the forests and the woods,
And split the air with their wings.
And God said: That's good!

Then God walked around,
And God looked around
On all that he had made.
He looked at his sun,
And he looked at his moon,
And he looked at his little stars;
He looked on his world
With all its living things,
And God said: I'm lonely still.

Then God sat down —
On the side of a hill where he could think;
By a deep, wide river he sat down;
With his head in his hands,
God thought and thought,
Till he thought: I'll make me a man!

Up from the bed of the river
God scooped the clay;
And by the bank of the river
He kneeled him down;

And there the great God Almighty
Who lit the sun and fixed it in the sky,
Who flung the stars to the most far corner of the night,
Who rounded the earth in the middle of his hand;
This Great God,
Like a mammy bending over her baby,
Kneeled down in the dust
Toiling over a lump of clay
Till he shaped it in his own image;

Then into it he blew the breath of life,
And man became a living soul.
Amen. Amen.

Georgia Douglas Johnson
(1886-   )

Born in Atlanta, Georgia, and educated at Atlanta University and Oberlin Conservatory in Ohio, Georgia Douglas Johnson is probably the best-known female Afro-American poet of the several between Frances E. W. Harper, whose last poems were published in 1872, and Margaret Walker, whose collection appeared in 1942. She wrote four volumes of poems: *The Heart of a Woman and Other Poems* (1918), *Bronze: A Book of Verse* (1922), *An Autumn Love Cycle* (1928), and *Share My World* (1962). Although her first book appeared only shortly before the Harlem Renaissance, it is difficult to identify her with that decade of colorful, frequently exotic literature. Despite her treatment of themes of racial identity and social protest, her lyrics are characterized by a quietness and a simplicity evocative of an earlier age.

Black Woman

Don't knock at my door, little child,
    I cannot let you in,
You know not what a world this is
    Of cruelty and sin.
Wait in the still eternity
    Until I come to you,
The world is cruel, cruel, child,
    I cannot let you in!

Don't knock at my door, little one,
    I cannot bear the pain
Of turning deaf-ear to your call
    Time and time again!

199

You do not know the monster men
    Inhabiting the earth,
Be still, be still, my precious child,
    I must not give you birth!

Credo

I believe in the ultimate justice of Fate;
That the races of men front the sun in their turn;
That each soul holds the title to infinite wealth
In fee to the will as it masters itself;
That the heart of humanity sounds the same tone
In impious jungle, or sky-kneeling fane.
I believe that the key to the life-mystery
Lies deeper than reason and further than death.
I believe that the rhythmical conscience within
Is guidance enough for the conduct of men.

The Suppliant

Long have I beat with timid hands upon life's leaden door,
Praying the patient, futile prayer my fathers prayed before,
Yet I remain without the close, unheeded and unheard,
And never to my listening ear is borne the waited word.

Soft o'er the threshold of the years there comes this counsel cool:
The strong demand, contend, prevail; the beggar is a fool!

To William Stanley Braithwaite

When time has rocked the present age to sleep,
And lighter hearts are lilting to the sway
Of rhythmic poesy's enhanced lay,
Recurring sequences shall fitly keep
Your fame eternal, as they lightly sweep
Aside the curtain to that potent day
When you in primal fervor led the way
Unto Apollo's narrow winding steep.

None shall forget your travail, utter, sore,
That oped the golden avenue of song,
When, like a knight, so errantly you bore
The mantled children valiantly along,
Their homage as a rising incense sweet
Shall permeate the heavens at your feet!

Claude McKay (1891-1948)

Although he was born in Jamaica, British West Indies, where he published his first book of poems, *Songs of Jamaica* (1911), Claude McKay is identified with the Harlem Renaissance of the 1920's. Arriving in the United States in 1912, he studied at Tuskegee Institute and Kansas State University. In 1920 he became associate editor of *The Liberator*, and in 1922 he published *Harlem Shadows*, his third collection of poems but the first issued in the United States.

Today McKay is probably best-known for such novels as *Home to Harlem* (1928) and *Banjo* (1929). He was perhaps even more talented as a poet. His poems are colorful, evocative, and powerful, whether he was writing nostalgically about his boyhood or bitterly about the rejection and the abuse of black Americans.

"If We Must Die," one of the following selections, has an ironic history. During World War II, Prime Minister Winston Churchill read this poem publicly to encourage supporters of democracy in what, at that time, seemed an almost hopeless war against Fascists. Claude McKay, however, had written the poem in reaction to a massacre of Afro-Americans in the United States.

The other selections offer a medley of themes characterizing McKay's work: feeling of alienation and loss of ancestral identity, hatred of an oppressive land, interest in Africa, admiration for America, protest against white Americans' abuse of black Americans, nostalgia for Jamaica, compassion for the ordinary people of Harlem, and love.

Outcast

For the dim regions whence my fathers came
My spirit, bondaged by the body, longs.
Words felt, but never heard, my lips would frame;

203

My soul would sing forgotten jungle songs.
I would go back to darkness and to peace,
But the great western world holds me in fee,
And I may never hope for full release
While to its alien gods I bend my knee.
Something in me is lost, forever lost,
Some vital thing has gone out of my heart,
And I must walk the way of life a ghost
Among the sons of earth, a thing apart;
For I was born, far from my native clime,
Under the white man's menace, out of time.

Enslaved

Oh when I think of my long-suffering race,
For weary centuries despised, oppressed,
Enslaved and lynched, denied a human place
In the great life line of the Christian West;
And in the Black Land disinherited,
Robbed in the ancient country of its birth,
My heart grows sick with hate, becomes as lead,
For this my race that has no home on earth.
Then from the dark depths of my soul I cry
To the avenging angel to consume
The white man's world of wonders utterly:
Let it be swallowed up in earth's vast womb,
Or upward roll as sacrificial smoke
To liberate my people from its yoke!

Africa

The sun sought thy dim bed and brought forth light,
The sciences were sucklings at thy breast;
When all the world was young in pregnant night
Thy slaves toiled at thy monumental best.
Thou ancient treasure-land, thou modern prize,
New peoples marvel at thy pyramids!
The years roll on, thy sphinx of riddle eyes
Watches the mad world with immobile lids.
The Hebrews humbled them at Pharaoh's name.

Cradle of Power!   Yet all things were in vain!
Honor and Glory, Arrogance and Fame!
They went.   The darkness swallowed thee again.
Thou art the harlot, now thy time is done,
Of all the mighty nations of the sun.

America

Although she feeds me bread of bitterness,
And sinks into my throat her tiger's tooth,
Stealing my breath of life, I will confess
I love this cultured hell that tests my youth!
Her vigor flows like tides into my blood,
Giving me strength erect against her hate.
Her bigness sweeps my being like a flood.
Yet as a rebel fronts a king in state,
I stand within her walls with not a shred
Of terror, malice, not a word of jeer.
Darkly I gaze into the days ahead,
And see her might and granite wonders there,
Beneath the touch of Time's unerring hand,
Like priceless treasures sinking in the sand.

The Lynching

His Spirit in smoke ascended to high heaven.
His father, by the cruelest way of pain,
Had bidden him to his bosom once again;
The awful sin remained still unforgiven.
All night a bright and solitary star
(Perchance the one that ever guided him,
Yet gave him up at last to Fate's wild whim)
Hung pitifully o'er the swinging char.
Day dawned, and soon the mixed crowds came to view
The ghastly body swaying in the sun
The women thronged to look, but never a one
Showed sorrow in her eyes of steely blue;
And little lads, lynchers that were to be,
Danced round the dreadful thing in fiendish glee.

If We Must Die

If we must die, let it not be like hogs
Hunted and penned in an inglorious spot,
While round us bark the mad and hungry dogs,
Making their mock at our accursèd lot.
If we must die, O let us nobly die,
So that our precious blood may not be shed
In vain; then even the monsters we defy
Shall be constrained to honor us though dead!
O kinsmen! we must meet the common foe!
Though far outnumbered let us show us brave,
And for their thousand blows deal one deathblow!
What though before us lies the open grave?
Like men we'll face the murderous, cowardly pack,
Pressed to the wall, dying, but fighting back!

Flame-Heart

So much have I forgotton in ten years,
　　So much in ten brief years!　I have forgot
What time the purple apples come to juice,
　　And what month brings the shy forget-me-not.
I have forgot the special, startling season
　　Of the pimento's flowering and fruiting;
What time of year the ground doves brown the fields
　　And fill the noonday with their curious fluting.
I have forgotten much, but still remember
The poinsettia's red, blood-red in warm December.

I still recall the honey-fever grass,
　　But cannot recollect the high days when
We rooted them out of the ping-wing path
　　To stop the mad bees in the rabbit pen.
I often try to think in what sweet month
　　The languid painted ladies used to dapple
The yellow by-road mazing from the main,
　　Sweet with the golden threads of the rose-apple.
I have forgotten — strange — but quite remember
The poinsettia's red, blood-red in warm December.

The Harlem Dancer

Applauding youths laughed with young prostitutes
And watched her perfect, half-clothed body sway;
Her voice was like the sound of blended flutes
Blown by black players upon a picnic day.
She sang and danced on gracefully and calm,
The light gauze hanging loose about her form;
To me she seemed a proudly-swaying palm
Grown lovelier for passing through a storm.
Upon her swarthy neck black shiny curls
Luxuriant fell; and tossing coins in praise,
The wine-flushed, bold-eyed boys, and even the girls,
Devoured her shape with eager, passionate gaze;
But looking at her falsely-smiling face,
I knew her self was not in that strange place.

Flower of Love

The perfume of your body dulls my sense.
    I want nor wine nor weed; your breath alone
Suffices.   In this moment rare and tense
    I worship at your breast.   The flower is blown,
The saffron petals tempt my amorous mouth,
    The yellow heart is radiant now with dew
Soft-scented, redolent of my loved South;
    O flower of love! I give myself to you.
Uncovered on your couch of figured green,
    Here let us linger indivisible.
The portals of your sanctuary unseen
    Receive my offering, yielding unto me.
Oh, with our love the night is warm and deep!
    The air is sweet, my flower, and sweet the flute
Whose music lulls our burning brain to sleep,
    While we lie loving, passionate and mute.

Jean Toomer (1894-1967)

In 1923 Jean Toomer seemed destined to be a major American writer. His poems and stories were eagerly sought by editors, and he had received accolades from such writers and critics as Sherwood Anderson, Waldo Frank, Gorham Munson, and W. S. Braithwaite. Except for a privately printed collection of aphorisms, however, Jean Toomer published no books after 1923. He remains, therefore, an important but tragic figure in black American literature.

Born in Washington, D. C., Nathan Eugene Toomer was the grandson of P. B. S. Pinchback, who, during Reconstruction, served briefly as Acting Governor of Louisiana. After enrolling briefly at the University of Wisconsin, the American College of Physical Training, the University of Chicago, the City College of New York, and New York University, where he considered and rejected studies in agriculture, physical education, medicine, sociology, and history, Jean Toomer settled on a career as a writer. Following an apprenticeship as a writer in New York City and Washington, he accepted a position as acting principal in Sparta, Georgia, in the fall of 1922. Inspired with the belief that he had located his roots in the ancestral home of his people, Toomer wrote poems, stories, and sketches, especially about Southern women whose quests for identity brought them into conflict with the prevalent moral attitudes of American society. When he returned to Washington, he added stories, poems, and sketches about the more inhibited black people of Washington and Chicago. He collected and published all of these as *Cane* (1923), a classic in black American literature.

Toomer's personal search for identity, however, did not end with *Cane*. A student of Eastern philosophies, he found a spiritual leader in George Gurdjieff and dedicated himself to teaching the Gurdjieffan ideas to the American people. Thus, he smothered his lyricism under a shroud of satire and didacticism as he substituted psychological case studies for sympathetic sketches. When publishers rejected these works, he accused them of restricting him to

Negro subjects. Searching for freedom to develop, he argued that he should be judged as an American rather than a Negro; subsequently, he denied that he had any Negro ancestors. Americans refused to accept his racial stance. A national magazine made national scandal of his marriage to Caucasian Margery Latimer, a promising writer who had been his disciple in a Gurdjieffan experiment, which the newspapers characterized as a "free love" colony. Toomer attempted to answer his critics by writing novels about his marriage and about the Gurdjieffan philosophy. Publishers continued to reject them. He also wrote essays in which he explained the philosophy and his belief that America would give birth to a new race — neither white nor black but American.

The tragic death of his wife in childbirth, the Depression, and rejections by publishers made the Thirties a decade of tragedy relieved only by a second marriage. For the remainder of his life, Toomer searched for spiritual understanding through the Society of Friends, psychiatry, and Indian mysticism. Occasionally he lectured to college students and to gatherings of the Friends. He continued to write plays, novels, poems, and stories; but, except for an occasional poem or sketches, his efforts went unpublished. He died in a rest home in 1967.

Jean Toomer's best writing is a lyric impressionism which suggests poetry even when he used the medium of prose. Speaking from this point of view, one can say that Toomer's actual verse, consequently, represents only a small sampling of his poetry.

The following four selections represent his later writing. *The Blue Meridian,* Toomer's longest poem, presents his social philosophy that the intermingling of various races on this continent has produced a new race. *The Blue Meridian* was never published in entirety; only the first eighty-eight lines have been published previously, as "Brown River, Smile." In the lines selected here Toomer concludes his tribute to the individual races and to the new world which their fusion will create. All four of the following selections are published for the first time.

from The Blue Meridian

Each new American
The old gods, led by an inverted Christ,
A shaved Moses, a blanched Lemur,
And a moulting dollar,

Withdrew into the distance and soon died,
Their dust and seed falling down
To fertilize the five regions of America.

We are waiting for a new God.

The old peoples —
The great European races sent wave after wave
That washed the forests, the earth's rich loam,
Grew towns with the seeds of giant cities,
Made roads, laid golden rails,
Factoried superb machines,
Sang once of the swift achievement,
And died because it ceased to feel.

> Late minstrels of the restless earth,
> No muteness can be granted thee,
> Lift thy laughing energies
> To that white point which is a star.

The great African races sent a single wave
And singing riplets to sorrow in red fields,
Sing a swan song, to break rocks
And immortalize a hiding water boy.

> I'm leaving the shining ground, brothers,
> I sing because I ache,
> I go because I must,
> Brothers, I am leaving the shining ground;
> Don't ask me where,
> I'll meet you there,
> I'm leaving the shining ground.

The great red race was here.
In a land of flaming earth and torrent-rains,
Of red sea-plains and majestic mesas,
At sunset from a purple hill
The Gods came down;
They serpentined into pueblo,
And a white-robed priest
Danced with them five days and nights;
But pueblo, priest, and Shalikoo

Sank into the sacred earth
To fertilize the five regions of America.

> Hi-ye, hi-yo, hi-yo,
> Hi-ye, hi-yo, hi-yo,
> A lone eagle feather,
> An untamed Navajo,
> The ghosts of buffaloes,
> Hi-ye, hi-yo, hi-yo,
> Hi-ye, hi-yo, hi-yo.

We who exist today are the new people,
Born of elevated rock and lifted branches,
A race called the Americans;
And we are the old people; we are witnesses
That behind us there extends
An unbroken chain of ancestors;
Of millions of fathers through a million years
We are the breathing receptacles.
Mankind is a cross —
The solid stream sourcing in the remote past,
Ending in far off distant years,
Is the perpendicular;
The planetary wash of those new living
Forms the transverse bar. . . .

O thou, Relentless Stream, . . .
The Mississippi, sister of the Ganges,
Main artery of earth in the western world,
Is waiting to become
In the spirit of America, a sacred river.
Whoever lifts the Mississippi
Lifts himself and all America;
Whoever lifts himself
Makes that great brown river smile.
The blood of earth and the blood of man
Course swifter and rejoice when we spiritualize.

The east coast is masculine,
The west coast is feminine,
The middle region is the child —
Force of reconciling

And generator of symbols,
Source of a new force —
It not another it will be Al Capone.

So split spirit can divide,
No dead soul can undermine thee,
Thou, great coasts and harbors,
Mountains, lakes, and plains,
Thou art the majestic base
Of cathedral people,
The seed which started thee has grown.

The prairie's sweep is flat infinity,
The city's rise is perpendicular to farthest star,
I stand where the two directions intersect,
At Michigan Avenue and Walton Place,
Parallel to my countrymen,
Right-angled to the universe.

Blue Meridian, banded-light,
Dynamic atom-aggregate,
Awoke and danced upon the earth;
In his left hand he held elevated rock,
In his right hand he held lifted branches,
He danced the dance of the Blue Meridian
And dervished with the five regions of America.

Lift, lift, thou waking forces!
Let us feel the energy of animals,
The energy of rumps and bull-bent heads
Crashing the barrier to man.
It must spiral on!
A million million men, or twelve men,
Must crash the barrier to the next higher form.

Beyond plants are animals,
Beyond animals is man,
Beyond man is God.

The Big Light,
Let the Big Light in!

O thou, Radiant Incorporeal,
The I of earth and of mankind, hurl
Down these seaboards, across this continent,
The thousand-rayed discus of thy mind,
And, above our walking limbs unfurl
Spirit-torsos of exquisite strength!

Five Vignettes

1

The red-tiled ships you see reflected,
Are nervous,
And afraid of clouds.

2

There, on the clothes-line
Still as she pinned them,
Pieces now the wind may wear.

3

The old man, at ninety,
Eating peaches,
Is he not afraid of worms?

4

Wear my thimble of agony
And when you sew,
No needle points will prick you.

5

In Y. Don's laundry
A Chinese baby fell
And cried as any other.

The Lost Dancer

Spatial depths of being survive
The birth to death recurrences

Of feet dancing on earth of sand;
Vibrations of the dance survive
The sand; the sand, elect, survives
The dancer. He can find no source
Of magic adequate to bind
The sand upon his feet, his feet
Upon his dance, his dance upon
The diamond body of his being.

At Sea

Once I saw large waves
Crested with white-caps;
A driving wind
Transformed the caps
Into scudding spray —
"Swift souls," I addressed them —
They turned towards me
Startled
Sea-descending faces;
But I, not they,
Felt the pang of transience.

Countee Cullen (1903-1946)

A native of New York City, Countee Cullen was popularly acclaimed the "poet laureate" of the Harlem Renaissance. He published his first collection of poems — *Color* (1925) — while still a student at New York University. Within the next two years, he earned a master's degree in English from Harvard, published two additional volumes of poetry — *The Ballad of the Brown Girl* (1927) and *Copper Sun* (1927), edited an anthology of poetry (1927), and wrote literary columns for *Opportunity* magazine. A Guggenheim fellowship enabled him to spend several months in France, where he completed *The Black Christ and Other Poems* (1929). Although his productivity slowed during his years as a high school teacher, he produced two additional volumes of poetry, one novel (*One Way to Heaven*, 1932), and two books for children.

Even though Cullen's early work earned praise for his use of Afro-American themes, his stylistic models were John Keats and A. E. Housman, and his poems sang of love and roses as often as of the Afro-American spirit. As he matured, Cullen frequently complained about critics' efforts to restrict him to subjects related to the Afro-American experience. Increasingly, he lamented the disillusionment of lost love and the sorrows of world's outcasts. When he abstained from Afro-American themes, however, his smooth, pure melodies on conventional subjects proved insufficient to distinguish him in a generation expecting vivid imagery and marked originality in poetry.

The following selections illustrate characteristic themes: affirmation of African heritage, the sorrow of love, and sympathy for the rejected.

217

Heritage
(*For Harold Jackman*)

What is Africa to me:
Copper sun or scarlet sea,
Jungle star or jungle track,
Strong bronzed men, or regal black
Women from whose loins I sprang
When the birds of Eden sang?
One three centuries removed
From the scenes his fathers loved,
Spicy grove, cinnamon tree,
What is Africa to me?

So I lie, who all day long
Want no sound except the song
Sung by wild barbaric birds
Goading massive jungle herds,
Juggernauts of flesh that pass
Trampling tall defiant grass
Where young forest lovers lie,
Plighting troth beneath the sky.
So I lie, who always hear,
Though I cram against my ear
Both my thumbs, and keep them there,
Great drums throbbing through the air.
So I lie, whose fount of pride,
Dear distress, and joy allied,
Is my somber flesh and skin,
With the dark blood dammed within
Like great pulsing tides of wine
That, I fear, must burst the fine
Channels of the chafing net
Where they surge and foam and fret.

Africa? A book one thumbs
Listlessly, till slumber comes.
Unremembered are her bats
Circling through the night, her cats
Crouching in the river reeds,
Stalking gentle flesh that feeds
By the river brink; no more

Does the bugle-throated roar
Cry that monarch claws have leapt
From the scabbards where they slept.
Silver snakes that once a year
Doff the lovely coats you wear,
Seek no covert in your fear
Lest a mortal eye should see;
What's your nakedness to me?
Here no leprous flowers rear
Fierce corollas in the air;
Here no bodies sleek and wet,
Dripping mingled rain and sweat,
Tread the savage measures of
Jungle boys and girls in love.
What is last year's snow to me,
Last year's anything? The tree
Budding yearly must forget
How its past arose or set —
Bough and blossom, flower, fruit,
Even what shy bird with mute
Wonder at her travail there,
Meekly labored in its hair.
One three centuries removed
From the scenes his fathers loved,
Spicy grove, cinnamon tree,
What is Africa to me?

So I lie, who find no peace
Night or day, no slight release
From the unremittant beat
Made by cruel padded feet
Walking through my body's street.
Up and down they go, and back,
Treading out a jungle track.
So I lie, who never quite
Safely sleep from rain at night —
I can never rest at all
When the rain begins to fall;
Like a soul gone mad with pain
I must match its weird refrain;
Ever must I twist and squirm,

Writing like a baited worm,
While its primal measures drip
Through my body, crying, "Strip!
Doff this new exuberance.
Come and dance the Lover's Dance!"
In an old remembered way
Rain works on me night and day.

Quaint, outlandish heathen gods
Black men fashion out of rods,
Clay, and brittle bits of stone,
In a likeness like their own,
My conversion came high-priced;
I belong to Jesus Christ,
Preacher of humility;
Heathen gods are naught to me.

Father, Son, and Holy Ghost,
So I make an idle boast;
Jesus of the twice-turned cheek,
Lamb of God, although I speak
With my mouth thus, in my heart
Do I play a double part.
Ever at Thy glowing altar
Must my heart grow sick and falter,
Wishing He I served were black,
Thinking then it would not lack
Precedent of pain to guide it,
Let who would or might deride it;
Surely then this flesh would know
Yours had borne a kindred woe.
Lord, I fashion dark gods, too,
Daring even to give You
Dark despairing features where,
Crowned with dark rebellious hair,
Patience wavers just so much as
Mortal grief compels, while touches
Quick and hot, of anger, rise
To smitten cheek and weary eyes.
Lord, forgive me if my need
Sometimes shapes a human creed.
All day long and all night through,

One thing only must I do:
Quench my pride and cool my blood,
Lest I perish in the flood.
Lest a hidden ember set
Timber that I thought was wet
Burning like the dryest flax,
Melting like the merest wax,
Lest the grave restore its dead.
Not yet has my heart or head
In the least way realized
They and I are civilized.

From the Dark Tower
(To Charles S. Johnson)

We shall not always plant while others reap
The golden increment of bursting fruit,
Not always countenance, abject and mute,
That lesser men should hold their brothers cheap;
Not everlastingly while others sleep
Shall we beguile their limbs with mellow flute,
Not always bend to some more subtle brute;
We were not made eternally to weep.

The night whose sable breast relieves the stark,
White stars is no less lovely being dark,
And there are buds that cannot bloom at all
In light, but crumple, piteous, and fall;
So in the dark we hide the heart that bleeds,
And wait, and tend our agonizing seeds.

Song in Spite of Myself

Never love with all your heart,
    It only ends in aching;
And bit by bit to the smallest part
    That organ will be breaking.

Never love with all your mind,
    It only ends in fretting;

In musing on sweet joys behind,
    Too poignant for forgetting.

Never love with all your soul,
    For such there is no ending,
Though a mind that frets may find control,
    And a shattered heart find mending.

Give but a grain of the heart's rich seed,
    Confine some under cover,
And when love goes, bid him God-speed.
    And find another lover.

Magnets

The straight, the swift, the debonair,
Are targets on the thoroughfare
For every kind appraising eye;
Sweet words are said as they pass by.
But such a strange contrary thing
My heart is, it will never cling
To any bright unblemished thing.
Such have their own security,
And little need to lean on me.
The limb that falters in its course,
And cries, "Not yet!" to waning force;
The orb that may not brave the sun;
The bitter mouth, its kissing done;
The loving heart that must deny
The very love it travels by;
What most has need to bend and pray,
These magnets draw my heart their way.

For Paul Laurence Dunbar

Born of the sorrowful of heart,
    Mirth was a crown upon his head;
Pride kept his twisted lips apart
    In jest, to hide a heart that bled.

Langston Hughes (1902-1967)

Langston Hughes has been described as the most versatile Afro-American writer who ever lived. Born in Joplin, Missouri, reared in Kansas and Ohio, he entered Columbia University in 1922 but dropped out after a year of studying. For several years, he worked his way through Europe and Africa before returning to America, where he soon became a part of the Harlem Renaissance. After completing undergraduate study at Lincoln University (Pa.), Hughes became a professional writer and lecturer.

No other Negro writer has matched the variety of Hughes' achievements. Among his more than thirty books are nine volumes of poems, two novels, and three collections of stories. Fascinated by theater, he established several all-Negro theatrical companies. Three of his plays were produced on Broadway, and one — *Mulatto* (1934) — enjoyed the longest continuous run of any play written by a Negro before Lorraine Hansberry. In addition, Hughes wrote the libretto for the musical version of Elmer Rice's *Street Scene,* an opera, stories for children, and two autobiographies. He also translated poetry, edited or co-edited anthologies of folklore and poetry, and publicized the musical and literary achievements of Africans and Afro-Americans. Perhaps his most significant literary achievement lies in the many stories, sketches, and essays about Jesse B. Semple ("Simple").

Although he developed all of the conventional themes in poetry, Langston Hughes most often concerned himself with the Afro-American as subject. Forty years before the present generation's proclamation that "Black is beautiful," Langston Hughes was emphasizing the theme, encouraging black people to be proud of their identity, evoking sympathy for victims of racial discrimination, promoting closer relationships among all classes of black people, ridiculing the assininities of bigotry, revealing the mixtures of gaiety and melancholy in the Harlem he loved, and celebrating the

223

common man. Because he continued to write for more than forty
years, Hughes, better than any other writer of the Harlem Renaissance, kept alive the gaiety and exuberance of that period; but he
also revealed the underlying sorrow for which laughter was both a
scab and a shield.

From his earliest poetry to the last, Hughes sought to reproduce
the rhythms characteristic of the Afro-American music. In the
Twenties and the Thirties, he became known for his "blues" and
his imitations of jazz rhythms. As musical styles changed, Hughes
experimented with boogie-woogie and be-bop. Frequently, in his
later years, he read to the accompaniment of jazz, and a recent
book of poems, *Ask Your Mama*, provides notes for musical effects
to underscore the reading.

The first two of the following selections illustrate the rhythms
and racial pride of Hughes' early poetry. "The Weary Blues," a
sympathetic portrait, reveals in the song of musician the characteristic style of Hughes' blues poetry — a long line; the line repeated,
possibly with variation; and a third line rhyming with the first two.
In the next selections, written twenty-five years later than the first,
new rhythms support the familiar themes.

The final selection presents one incident in the life of Madam
Alberta K. Johnson, a soul sister of Jesse B. Semple.

Dream Variation

To fling my arms wide
In some place of the sun,
To whirl and to dance
Till the white day is done.
Then rest at cool evening
Beneath a tall tree
While night comes on gently,
    Dark like me, —
That is my dream!

To fling my arms wide
In the face of the sun,
Dance! whirl! whirl!
Till the quick day is done.
Rest at pale evening. . . .
A tall, slim tree. . . .

Night coming tenderly
Black like me.

Epilogue

I, too, sing America.

I am the darker brother.
They send me to eat in the kitchen
When company comes,
But I laugh,
And eat well,
And grow strong.

Tomorrow,
I'll sit at the table
When company comes.
Nobody'll dare
Say to me,
"Eat in the kitchen,"
Then.

Besides,
They'll see how beautiful I am
And be ashamed, —

I, too, am America.

The Weary Blues

Droning a drowsy syncopated tune,
Rocking back and forth to a mellow croon,
    I heard a Negro play.
Down on Lenox Avenue the other night
By the pale dull pallor of an old gas light
    He did a lazy sway. . . .
    He did a lazy sway. . . .
To the tune o' those Weary Blues.
With his ebony hands on each ivory key
He made that poor piano moan with melody.
    O Blues!

Swaying to and fro on his rickety stool
He played that sad raggy tune like a musical fool.
  Sweet Blues!
Coming from a black man's soul.
  O Blues!
In a deep song voice with a melancholy tone
I heard that Negro sing, that old piano moan —
  "Ain't got nobody in all this world,
  Ain't got nobody but ma self.
  I's gwine to quit ma frownin'
  And put ma troubles on the shelf."
Thump, thump, thump, went his foot on the floor.
He played a few chords then he sang some more —
  "I got the Weary Blues
  And I can't be satisfied.
  Got the Weary Blues
  And can't be satisfied —
  I ain't happy no mo'
  And I wish that I had died."
And far into the night he crooned that tune.
The stars went out and so did the moon.
The singer stopped playing and went to bed
While the Weary Blues echoed through his head.
He slept like a rock or a man that's dead.

Theme For English B

The instructor said,

  Go home and write
  a page tonight.
  And let that page come out of you ——
  Then, it will be true.

I wonder if it's that simple?

I am twenty-two, colored, born in Winston-Salem.
I went to school there, then Durham, then here
to this college on the hill above Harlem.
I am the only colored student in my class.
The steps from the hill lead down into Harlem,
through a park, then I cross St. Nicholas,

Eighth Avenue, Seventh, and I come to the Y,
the Harlem Branch Y, where I take the elevator
up to my room, sit down, and write this page:

It's not easy to know what is true for you or me
at twenty-two, my age. But I guess I'm what
I feel and see and hear. Harlem, I hear you:
hear you, hear me — we two — you, me, talk on this page.
(I hear New York, too.) Me — who?

Well, I like to eat, sleep, drink, and be in love.
I like to work, read, learn, and understand life.
I like a pipe for a Christmas present,
or records — Bessie, bop, or Bach.
I guess being colored doesn't make me *not* like
the same things other folks like who are other races.
So will my page be colored that I write?
Being me, it will not be white.
But it will be
a part of you, instructor.
You are white ——
yet a part of me, as I am a part of you.
That's American.
Sometimes perhaps you don't want to be a part of me.
Nor do I often want to be a part of you.
But we are, that's true!
As I learn from you,
I guess you learn from me ——
although you're older — and white ——
and somewhat more free.

This is my page for English B.

College Formal: Renaissance Casino

Golden girl
in a golden gown
in a melody night
in Harlem town
lad tall and brown
tall and wise
college boy smart

eyes in eyes
the music wraps
them both around
in mellow magic
of dancing sound
till they're the heart
of the whole big town
gold and brown

Madam and Her Madam

I worked for a woman,
She wasn't mean —
But she had a twelve-room
House to clean.

Had to get breakfast,
Dinner, and supper, too —
Then take care of her children
When I got through.

Wash, iron, and scrub,
Walk the dog around —
It was too much,
Nearly broke me down.

I said, Madam,
Can it be
You trying to make a
Pack-horse out of me?

She opened her mouth.
She cried, Oh, no!
You know, Alberta,
I love you so!

I said, Madam,
That may be true —
But I'll be dogged
If I love you!

Arna Bontemps (1902-   )

Novelist, poet, editor, historian, biographer, librarian, teacher, Arna Bontemps, like his friend Langston Hughes, has distinguished himself in a variety of literary fields. Born in Louisiana, but reared in California, where he graduated from Pacific Union College in 1923, Bontemps, who studied further at Columbia and the University of Chicago, was librarian at Fisk University from 1943 to 1966. Since then he has taught at the University of Illinois at Chicago Circle and at Yale University.

One of the bright young writers who migrated to Harlem during the Renaissance, Bontemps achieved his first significant publication as a novelist — *God Sends Sunday* (1932); *Black Thunder* (1936), a history of the slave Gabriel's abortive rebellion in Virginia in 1800; and *Drums at Dusk* (1939), the story of the successful revolution of Haitian slaves. Dissatisfied with the literature available for his children and other Afro-American children, Bontemps wrote juvenile literature (biography, fiction, poetry, and history), more in fact than any other Negro author, and has received the Jane Addams Children's Book Award. Recipient of Guggenheim and Rosenwald fellowships and of various other awards for writing, Bontemps has edited poetry and co-edited folklore. His best-known works of non-fiction for adults are *Any Place But Here* (1966), originally entitled *They Seek a City* and written in collaboration with Jack Conroy, and *100 Years of Negro Freedom* (1961).

Although his collection of poetry was not published until 1963, the poems were written during the Harlem Renaissance.

Southern Mansion

Poplars are standing there still as death
and ghosts of dead men

229

meet their ladies walking
two by two beneath the shade
and standing on the marble steps.

There is a sound of music echoing
through the open door
and in the field there is
another sound tinkling in the cotton:
chains of bondmen dragging on the ground.

The years go back with an iron clank,
a hand is on the gate,
a dry leaf trembles on the wall.
Ghosts are walking.
They have broken roses down
and poplars stand there still as death.

Nocturne at Bethesda

I thought I saw an angel flying low.
I thought I saw the flicker of a wing
above the mulberry trees — but not again.
Bethesda sleeps. This ancient pool that healed
a host of bearded Jews does not awake.
This pool that once the angels troubled does not move.
No angel stirs it now, no Saviour comes
with healing in His hands to raise the sick
and bid the lame man leap upon the ground.

The golden days are gone. Why do we wait
so long upon the marble steps, blood
falling from our open wounds? And why
do our black faces search the empty sky?
Is there something we have forgotten? some precious thing
we have lost, wandering in strange lands?

There was a day, I remember now,
I beat my breast and cried 'Wash me God,
wash me with a wave of wind upon
the barley; O quiet One, draw near, draw near!

walk upon the hills with lovely feet
and in the waterfall stand and speak.

Dip white hands in the lily pool and mourn
upon the harps still hanging in the trees
near Babylon along the river's edge,
but oh, remember me, I pray, before
the summer goes and rose leaves lose their red.'

The old terror takes my heart, the fear
of quiet waters and of faint twilights.
There will be better days when I am gone
and healing pools where I cannot be healed.
Fragrant stars will gleam forever and ever
above the place where I lie desolate.

Yet I hope, still I long to live.
And if there can be returning after death
I shall come back. But it will not be here:
if you want me you must search for me
beneath the palms of Africa. Or if
I am not there then you may call to me
across the shining dunes, perhaps I shall
be following a desert caravan.

I may pass through centuries of death
with quiet eyes, but I'll remember still
a jungle tree with burning scarlet birds.
There is something I have forgotten, some precious thing.
I shall be seeking ornaments of ivory,
I shall be dying for a jungle fruit.

You do not hear, Bethesda.
O still green water in a stagnant pool!
Love abandoned you and me alike.
There was a day you held a rich full moon
upon your heart and listened to the words
of men now dead and saw the angels fly.
There is a simple story on your face:
years have wrinkled you. I know, Bethesda!
You are sad. It is the same with me.

Sterling Brown (1901-   )

Born in Washington, D. C., Sterling Brown is a major authority on the Negro as writer and as character in American literature. Educated at Williams College and at Harvard University, where he received a Master of Arts degree, Brown has written extensively on the literature, language, drama, poetry, and music of Afro-Americans. His best-known book-length studies are *The Negro in American Fiction* (1937) and *Negro Poetry and Drama* (1937). He also served as senior editor of *The Negro Caravan* (1941), the most comprehensive anthology prior to the present decade.

Brown earned his early literary reputation, however, for satiric and lyric poetry on racial themes. Zestfully he satirized white-black relationships in the South; but, with the spirit of the Harlem Renaissance, he also realistically revealed the foibles of black people.

Slim Greer

Listen to the tale
Of Ole Slim Greer,
Waitines' devil
Waitin' here;

Talkinges' guy
An' biggest liar,
With always a new lie
On the fire.

Tells a tale
Of Arkansaw
That keeps the kitchen
In a roar;

Tells in a long-drawled
Careless tone,
As solemn as a Baptist
Parson's moan.

How he in Arkansaw
Passed for white,
An' he no lighter
Than a dark midnight.

Found a nice white woman
At a dance,
Thought he was from Spain
Or else from France;

Nobody suspicioned
Ole Slim Greer's race
But a Hill Billy, always
Roun' the place,

Who called one day
On the trustful dame
An' found Slim comfy
When he came.

The whites lef' the parlor
All to Slim
Which didn't cut
No ice with him,

An' he started a-tinklin'
Some mo'nful blues,
An' a-pattin' the time
With No. Fourteen shoes.

The cracker listened
An' then he spat
An' said, "No white man
Could play like that. . . ."

The white jane ordered
The tattler out;

Then, female-like,
Began to doubt,

Crept into the parlor
Soft as you please,
Where Slim was agitatin'
The ivories.

Heard Slim's music —
An' then, hot damn!
Shouted sharp — "Nigger!"
An' Slim said, "Ma'am?"

She screamed and the crackers
Swarmed up soon,
But found only echoes
Of his tune;

'Cause Slim had sold out
With lightnin' speed;
"Hope I may die, sir —
Yes, indeed. . . ."

Long Gone

I laks yo' kin' of lovin',
    Ain't never caught you wrong,
But it jes' ain' nachal
    Fo' to stay here long;

It jes' ain' nachal
    Fo' a railroad man,
With a itch fo' travelin'
    He cain't understan'. . . .

I looks at de rails,
    An' I looks at de ties,
An' I hears an ole freight
    Puffin' up de rise,

An' at nights on my pallet,
   When all is still,
I listens fo' de empties
   Bumpin' up de hill;

When I oughta be quiet,
   I is got a itch
Fo' to hear de whistle blow
   Fo' de crossin' or de switch,

An' I knows de time's a-nearin'
   When I got to ride,
Though it's homelike and happy
   At yo' side.

You is done all you could do
   To make me stay;
'Tain't no fault of yours I'se leavin' —
   I'se jes dataway.

I don't know which way I'm travelin' —
   Far or near,
All I knows fo' certain is
   I cain't stay here.

Ain't no call at all, sweet woman,
   Fo' to carry on —
Jes' my name and jes' my habit
   To be Long Gone. . . .

Return

I have gone back in boyish wonderment
To things that I had foolishly put by. . . .
Have found an alien and unknown content
In seeing how some bits of cloud-filled sky
Are framed in bracken pools; through chuckling hours
Have watched the antic frogs, or curiously
Have numbered all the unnamed, vagrant flowers,
That fleck the unkempt meadows, lavishly.

Or where a headlong toppling stream has stayed
Its racing, lulled to quiet by the song
Bursting from out the thick-leaved oaken shade,
There I have lain while hours sauntered past —
I have found peacefulness somewhere at last,
Have found a quiet needed for so long.

Southern Road

Swing dat hammer — hunh —
Steady, bo';
Swing dat hammer — hunh —
Steady, bo';
Ain't no rush, bebby,
Long ways to go.

Burner tore his — hunh —
Black heart away;
Burner tore his — hunh —
Black heart away;
Got me life, bebby,
An' a day.

Gal's on Fifth Street — hunh —
Son done gone;
Gal's on Fifth Street — hunh —
Son done gone;
Wife's in de ward, bebby,
Babe's not bo'n.

My ole man died — hunh —
Cussin' me;
My ole man died — hunh —
Cussin' me;
Ole lady rocks, bebby,
Huh misery.

Doubleshackled — hunh —
Guard behin';
Doubleshackled — hunh —

Guard behin';
Ball an' chain, bebby,
On my min'.

White man tells me — hunh —
Damn yo' soul;
White man tells me — hunh —
Damn yo' soul;
Got no need, bebby,
To be tole.

Chain gang nevah — hunh —
Let me go;
Chain gang nevah — hunh —
Let me go;
Po' los' boy, bebby,
Evahmo'. . . .

Melvin B. Tolson (1900-1966)

Melvin B. Tolson elicited accolades from critics and poets. Upon reading a section of Tolson's *Libretto for the Republic of Liberia* (1953), Allen Tate declared, "For the first time . . . a Negro poet has assimilated completely the full poetic language of his time and, by implication, the language of the Anglo-American poetic tradition." With even more enthusiasm though contrasting evaluation, Karl Shapiro, in the introduction to Tolson's final book, *Harlem Gallery* (1965), described Tolson as a poet who "writes and thinks in Negro" and, thus, would expand the poetic language. Despite similar approbation by such poets as John Ciardi, Langston Hughes, and Robert Frost, M. B. Tolson's general recognition as a poet has been limited.

Born in Moberly, Missouri, he was educated at Fisk University, Lincoln University in Pennsylvania (B.A.), and Columbia University (M.A.). For many years, he taught English, coached debating, and directed drama at Wiley College and Langston University, where he developed extraordinary popularity among students. His ability to charm voters enabled him to win election four times to the position of mayor of Langston, Oklahoma.

Although Tolson also wrote drama, he achieved his excellence in poetry. In 1944 he published his first volume of verse, *Rendezvous with America*. In 1947, he was commissioned poet laureate of Liberia to compose a poem, which was published in 1953—*Libretto for the Republic of Liberia*. His last book was *The Harlem Gallery: Book I, The Curator* (1965).

An admirer of Hart Crane and Ezra Pound, Tolson achieved increasing complexity in his use of language and allusion. Written in a style far simpler than that of his late work, "Dark Symphony" was his first poem to gain significant attention. It traces the history of the black man in America and concludes with a prophecy of triumph for the New Negro.

Melvin B. Tolson

Dark Symphony

I

Allegro Moderato

Black Crispus Attucks taught
                Us how to die
Before white Patrick Henry's bugle breath
Uttered the vertical
                Transmitting cry:
"Yea, give me liberty or give me death."

Waifs of the auction block,
                Men black and strong
The juggernauts of despotism withstood,
Loin-girt with faith that worms
                Equate the wrong
And dust is purged to create brotherhood.

No Banquo's ghost can rise
                Against us now,
Aver we hobnailed Man beneath the brute,
Squeezed down the thorns of greed
                On Labor's brow,
Garroted lands and carted off the loot.

II

Lento Grave

The centuries-old pathos in our voices
Saddens the great white world,
And the wizardry of our dusky rhythms
Conjures up shadow-shapes of ante-bellum years:

Black slaves singing *One More River to Cross*
In the torture tombs of slave-ships,
Black slaves singing *Steal Away to Jesus*
In jungle swamps,
Black slaves singing *The Crucifixion*
In slave-pens at midnight,
Black slaves singing *Swing Low, Sweet Chariot*

In cabins of death,
Black slaves singing *Go Down, Moses*
In the canebrakes of the Southern Pharaohs.

III

Andante Sostenuto

They tell us to forget
The Golgotha we tread . . .
We who are scourged with hate,
A price upon our head.
They who have shackled us
Require of us a song,
They who have wasted us
Bid us condone the wrong.

They tell us to forget
Democracy is spurned.
They tell us to forget
The Bill of Rights is burned.
Three hundred years we slaved,
We slave and suffer yet:
Though flesh and bone rebel,
They tell us to forget!

Oh, how can we forget
Our human rights denied?
Oh, how can we forget
Our manhood crucified?
When Justice is profaned
And plea with curse is met,
When Freedom's gates are barred,
Oh, how can we forget?

IV

Tempo Primo

The New Negro strides upon the continent
In seven-league boots . . .
The New Negro
Who sprang from the vigor-stout loins

Of Nat Turner, gallows-martyr for Freedom,
Of Joseph Cinquez, Black Moses of the Amistad Mutiny,
Of Frederick Douglass, oracle of the Catholic Man,
Of Sojourner Truth, eye and ear of Lincoln's legions,
Of Harriet Tubman, Saint Bernard of the Underground Railroad.

The New Negro
Breaks the icons of his detractors,
Wipes out the conspiracy of silence,
Speaks to *his* America:
"My history-moulding ancestors
Planted the first crops of wheat on these shores,
Built ships to conquer the seven seas,
Erected the Cotton Empire,
Flung railroads across a hemisphere,
Disemboweled the earth's iron and coal,
Tunneled the mountains and bridged rivers,
Harvested the grain and hewed forests,
Sentineled the Thirteen Colonies,
Unfurled Old Glory at the North Pole,
Fought a hundred battles for the Republic."

The New Negro:
His giant hands fling murals upon high chambers,
His drama teaches a world to laugh and weep,
His music leads continents captive,
His voice thunders the Brotherhood of Labor,
His science creates seven wonders,
His Republic of Letters challenges the Negro-baiters.

The New Negro,
Hard-muscled, Fascist-hating, Democracy-ensouled,
Strides in seven-league boots
Along the Highway of Today
Toward the Promised Land of Tomorrow!

V

Larghetto

None in the Land can say
To us black men Today:

You send the tractors on their bloody path,
And create Okies for *The Grapes of Wrath.*
You breed the slum that breeds a *Native Son*
To damn the good earth Pilgrim Fathers won.

None in the Land can say
To us black men Today:
You dupe the poor with rags-to-riches tales,
And leave the workers empty dinner pails.
You stuff the ballot box, and honest men
Are muzzled by your demagogic din.

None in the Land can say
To us black men Today:
You smash stock markets with your coined blitzkriegs,
And make a hundred million guinea pigs.
You counterfeit our Christianity,
And bring contempt upon Democracy.

None in the Land can say
To us black men Today:
You prowl when citizens are fast asleep,
And hatch Fifth Column plots to blast the deep
Foundations of the State and leave the Land
A vast Sahara with a Fascist brand.

VI

Tempo di Marcia

Out of abysses of Illiteracy,
Through labyrinths of Lies,
Across waste lands of Disease . . .
We advance!

Out of dead-ends of Poverty,
Through wildernesses of Superstition,
Across barricades of Jim Crowism . . .
We advance!

With the Peoples of the World . . .
We advance!

Robert E. Hayden (1913-   )

At the World Festival of Negro Arts, held in Dakar, Senegal, in 1965, Robert Hayden won the Grand Prize for poetry, awarded for *A Ballad of Remembrance* (1962), his fourth volume of poetry. Born in Detroit, he attended Wayne State University and earned a Master's degree from the University of Michigan, where in 1938 and 1942, he received Avery Hopwood awards for poetry. A teacher at Fisk University from 1946 to 1968, he is presently on the faculty at the University of Michigan. In addition to *A Ballad of Remembrance*, he has published four volumes of poetry: *Heart-Shape in the Dust* (1940), *The Lion and the Archer* (with Myron O'Higgins, 1949), *Figure of Time* (1955), and *Selected Poems* (1966). He has also written drama and edited *Kaleidoscope: Poems by American Negro Poets* (1967).

An admirer of the verbal dexterities of William Butler Yeats, Hayden has provoked reaction from some recent black critics by insisting that a black poet should not be restricted to racial utterance. Despite the rhetoric of the debate, Robert Hayden, sensitively aware of his heritage, often has recreated incidents from the black man's history, paying eloquent tribute to Frederick Douglass, Nat Turner, Harriet Tubman, and the slaves who overthrew their jailors aboard the Spanish vessel, *The Amistad.*

In "Runagate, Runagate" he reproduces the yearning for liberty which motivated the slaves who followed the North Star and Harriet Tubman to freedom. The poem is a medley of voices: the narrator, the escaping slaves (their hopes expressed in spirituals), the slave masters advertising for their return, one slave who recalls Harriet Tubman, and the slave masters advertising a reward for her capture.

In "The Ballad of Nat Turner," Hayden focuses upon the vision which inspired Nat Turner to lead a slave rebellion in Virginia.

Runagate Runagate

I

Runs falls rises stumbles on from darkness into darkness
and the darkness thicketed with shapes of terror
and the hunters pursuing and the hounds pursuing
and the night cold and the night long and the river
to cross and the jack-muh-lanterns beckoning beckoning
and blackness ahead and when shall I reach that somewhere
morning and keep on going and never turn back and keep on going

       Runagate
          Runagate
             Runagate

Many thousands rise and go
many thousands crossing over
                O mythic North
           O star-shaped yonder Bible city

Some go weeping and some rejoicing
some in coffins and some in carriages
some in silks and some in shackles

       Rise and go or fare you well

No more auction block for me
no more driver's lash for me

       If you see my Pompey, 30 yrs of age,
       new breeches, plain stockings, negro shoes;
       if you see my Anna, likely young mulatto
       branded E on the right cheek, R on the left,
       catch them if you can and notify subscriber.
       Catch them if you can, but it won't be easy.
       They'll dart underground when you try to catch them,
       plunge into quicksand, whirlpools, mazes,
       turn into scorpions when you try to catch them.

And before I'll be a slave
I'll be buried in my grave

North star and bonanza gold
I'm bound for the freedom, freedom-bound
and oh Susyanna don't you cry for me

Runagate

Runagate

II

Rises from their anguish and their power,

Harriet Tubman,

woman of earth, whipscarred,
a summoning, a shining

Mean to be free

And this was the way of it, brethren brethren,
way we journeyed from Can't to Can.
Moon so bright and no place to hide,
the cry up and the patterollers riding,
hound dogs belling in bladed air.
And fear starts a-murbling, Never make it,
we'll never make it. *Hush that now,*
and she's turned upon us, levelled pistol
glinting in the moonlight:
Dead folks can't jaybird-talk, she says;
you keep on going now or die, she says.

Wanted   Harriet Tubman   alias The General
alias Moses   Stealer of Slaves

In league with Garrison   Alcott   Emerson
Garrett   Douglass   Thoreau   John Brown

Armed and known to be Dangerous

Wanted   Reward   Dead or Alive

Tell me, Ezekiel, oh tell me do you see
mailed Jehovah coming to deliver me?

Hoot-owl calling in the ghosted air,
five times calling to the hants in the air.
Shadow of a face in the scary leaves,
shadow of a voice in the talking leaves:

Come ride-a my train

Oh that train, ghost-story train
through swamp and savanna movering movering,
over trestles of dew, through caves of the wish,
Midnight Special on a sabre track movering movering,
first stop Mercy and the last Hallelujah.

Come ride-a my train

Mean mean mean to be free.

The Ballad of Nat Turner

Then fled, O brethren, the wicked juba
and wandered wandered far
from curfew joys in the Dismal's night.
Fool of St. Elmo's fire

In scary night I wandered, praying,
Lord God my harshener,
speak to me now or let me die;
speak, Lord, to this mourner.

And came at length to livid trees
where Ibo warriors
hung shadowless, turning in wind
that moaned like Africa,

Their belltongue bodies dead, their eyes
alive with the anger deep
in my own heart. Is this the sign,
the sign forepromised me?

The spirits vanished. Afraid and lonely
I wandered on in blackness.

Speak to me now or let me die.
  Die, whispered the blackness.

And wild things gasped and scuffled in
  the night; seething shapes
of evil frolicked upon the air.
  I reeled with fear, I prayed.

Sudden brightness clove the preying
  darkness, brightness that was
itself a golden darkness, brightness
  so bright that it was darkness.

And there were angels, their faces hidden
  from me, angels at war
with one another, angels in dazzling
  combat. And oh the splendor,

The fearful splendor of that warring.
  Hide me, I cried to rock and bramble.
Hide me, the rock, the bramble cried. . . .
  How tell you of that holy battle?

The shock of wing on wing and sword
  on sword was the tumult of
a taken city burning. I cannot
  say how long they strove,

For the wheel in a turning wheel which is time
  in eternity had ceased
its whirling, and owl and moccasin,
  panther and nameless beast

And I were held like creatures fixed
  in flaming, in fiery amber.
But I saw I saw oh many of
  those mighty beings waver,

Waver and fall, go streaking down
  into swamp water, and the water
hissed and steamed and bubbled and locked
  shuddering shuddering over

The fallen and soon was motionless.
  Then that massive light
began a-folding slowly in
  upon itself, and I

Beheld the conqueror faces and, lo,
  they were like mine, I saw
they were like mine and in joy and terror
  wept, praising praising Jehovah.

Oh praised my honer, harshener
  till a sleep came over me,
a sleep heavy as death. And when
  I awoke at last free

And purified, I rose and prayed
  and returned after a time
to the blazing fields, to the humbleness.
  And bided my time.

Owen Dodson (1914-   )

A native of Brooklyn, New York, Owen Dodson was educated at Bates College and at Yale University, where he earned the Master of Fine Arts degree. A teacher at Spelman College and at Howard University, where he is currently head of the Drama Department, Owen Dodson has contributed significantly in Negro college theatre, a little-known but important training ground for black playwrights and performers. As a director, he has developed several of the black actors who are currently winning recognition in the professional theatre. Of the several plays he has written, the best-known is *Divine Comedy*, first produced at Yale University in 1938. Based on the story of Father Divine, it is probably the best verse drama written by a black playwright. His novel, *Boy at the Window* (1951), reprinted as *When Trees Were Green*, is distinguished by sensitive characterization and imaginative, sensuous description presented through the young protagonist. Both in his drama and in his fiction, Mr. Dodson has suggested rich poetic talent, revealed fully in his collection *Powerful Long Ladder* (1946). Taken from that volume, the following selections, written during World War II, consider the anguish of war and the hoped-for profits of peace.

For My Brother

VII

Sleep late with your dream.
The morning has a scar
To mark on the horizon
With the death of the morning star.

The color of blood will appear
And wash the morning sky,

251

Aluminum birds flying with fear
Will scream to your waking,
Will send you to die;

Sleep late with your dream.
Pretend that the morning is far,
Deep in the horizon country,
Unconcerned with the morning star.

Open Letter

Brothers, let us discover our hearts again,
Permitting the regular strong beat of humanity there
To propel the likelihood of other terror to an exit.

For at last it is nearly ended: the daily anguish needles
Probing in our brains when alarms crust the air
And planes stab over us.

(Tears screamed from our eyes,
Animals moaned for death, gardens were disguised,
Stumps strained to be whole again.)

For at last it is nearly ended, grass
Will be normal, hillsides
Pleased with boys roaming their bellies.

All the mourning children
Will understand the long word, hallelujah,
Each use for joy will light for them.

The torn souls and broken bodies will be restored,
Primers circulate for everlasting peace,
The doors to hope swung open.

Brothers, let us enter that portal for good
When peace surrounds us like a credible universe.
Bury that agony, bury this hate, take our black hands in yours.

Sorrow is the Only
Faithful One

Sorrow is the only faithful one:
The lone companion clinging like a season
To its original skin no matter what the variations.

If all the mountains paraded
Eating the valleys as they went
And the sun were a coiffure on the highest peak,

Sorrow would be there between
The sparkling and the giant laughter
Of the enemy when the clouds come down to swim.

But I am less, unmagic, black,
Sorrow clings to me more than to doomsday mountains
Or erosion scars on a palisade.

Sorrow has a song like a leech
Crying because the sand's blood is dry
And the stars reflected in the lake

Are water for all their twinkling
And bloodless for all their charm.
I have blood, and a song.

Sorrow is the only faithful one.

Margaret Walker Alexander
(1915-   )

Born in Birmingham, Alabama, Margaret Walker received a B.A. from Northwestern University and completed her graduate study at the University of Iowa, where, instead of the usual theses, she submitted a collection of poems for the Master's degree and *Jubilee*, a historical novel about the Civil War period, for the doctorate. Both volumes have been published. A wife, a mother, a teacher of English at Livingstone College, West Virginia State College, and Jackson State College in Mississippi, a visiting professor at Northwestern University, and a recipient of a Rosenwald Fellowship, Margaret Walker Alexander is widely known for her volume of poetry, *For My People* (1942), which includes personal anguish, interest in Africa, racial pride, denunciations of the betrayers of black believers, and Negro folklore. The title poem of this volume is one of the most eloquent and understanding love poems ever addressed to black Americans.

For My People

For my people everywhere singing their slave songs repeatedly: their dirges and their ditties and their blues and
jubilees, praying their prayers nightly to an unknown
god, bending their knees humbly to an unseen power;

For my people lending their strength to the years, to the gone
years and the now years and the maybe years, washing
ironing cooking scrubbing sewing mending hoeing
plowing digging planting pruning patching dragging
along never gaining never reaping never knowing and
never understanding;

For my playmates in the clay and dust and sand of Alabama
backyards playing baptizing and preaching and doctor and jail and soldier and school and mama and
cooking and playhouse and concert and store and hair
and Miss Choomby and company;

For the cramped bewildered years we went to school to learn
to know the reasons why and the answers to and the
people who and the places where and the days when,
in memory of the bitter hours when we discovered we
were black and poor and small and different and
nobody cared and nobody wondered and nobody
understood;

For the boys and girls who grew in spite of these things to be
man and woman, to laugh and dance and sing and
play and drink their wine and religion and success, to
marry their playmates and bear children and then die
of consumption and anemia and lynching;

For my people thronging 47th Street in Chicago and Lenox
Avenue in New York and Rampart Street in New
Orleans, lost disinherited dispossessed and happy
people filling the cabarets and taverns and other
people's pockets needing bread and shoes and milk
and land and money and something — something all
our own;

For my people walking blindly spreading joy, losing time
being lazy, sleeping when hungry, shouting when
burdened, drinking when hopeless, tied and shackled
and tangled among ourselves by the unseen creatures
who tower over us omnisciently and laugh;

For my people blundering and groping and floundering in
the dark of churches and schools and clubs and
societies, associations and councils and committees
and conventions, distressed and disturbed and deceived and devoured by money-hungry glory-craving
leeches, preyed on by facile force of state and fad and
novelty, by false prophet and holy believer;

For my people standing staring trying to fashion a better
way from confusion, from hypocrisy and misunderstanding, trying to fashion a world that will hold all
the people, all the faces, all the adams and eves and
their countless generations;

Let a new earth rise. Let another world be born. Let a bloody
peace be written in the sky. Let a second generation
full of courage issue forth; let a people loving freedom come to growth. Let a beauty full of healing
and a strength of final clenching be the pulsing in
our spirits and our blood. Let the martial songs be
written, let the dirges disappear. Let a race of men
now rise and take control.

Gwendolyn Brooks (1917-   )

In 1950, Gwendolyn Brooks became the first Afro-American poet to receive a Pulitzer Prize for poetry (for *Annie Allen*, 1949). Born in Topeka, Kansas, she was reared in Chicago, where she completed her formal education at Wilson Junior College. For many years a housewife, she recently has accepted teaching positions at several colleges in Chicago and at the University of Wisconsin.

Her first volume of poetry, *A Street in Bronzeville*, was published in 1945. Subsequent volumes are *Bronzeville Boys and Girls* (poems for children, 1956), *The Bean Eaters* (1960), *Selected Poems* (1963), and *In the Mecca* (1968). In 1953, she published *Maud Martha*, a poetic novel about the maturing of a Negro girl.

Gwendolyn Brooks has earned praise both for technical artistry and for her sympathetic revelations of the Afro-American experience. A careful artist, she has experimented successfully with all of the traditional forms of short poetry, including the traditional ballad. Increasingly, in her later work, she has moved from relatively simple, suggestive, but grammatically complete, poetic statements to compressed phrases stripped of all words which can be spared. This development can be discerned from the stylistic differences between the first two of the following selections, taken from her first volume, and the last two, from her latest. As her style has changed, her thought has developed from emphasis upon the attitudes of a black *woman* to emphasis upon the ideas of black people in general.

Kitchenette Building

We are things of dry hours and the involuntary plan,
Grayed in, and gray. "Dream" makes a giddy sound, not strong
Like "rent," "feeding a wife," "satisfying a man."

257

But could a dream send up through onion fumes
Its white and violet, fight with fried potatoes
And yesterday's garbage ripening in the hall,
Flutter, or sing an aria down these rooms

Even if we were willing to let it in,
Had time to warm it, keep it very clean,
Anticipate a message, let it begin?

We wonder. But not well! not for a minute!
Since Number Five is out of the bathroom now,
We think of lukewarm water, hope to get in it.

The Womanhood

I. 2

What shall I give my children? who are poor,
Who are adjudged the leastwise of the land,
Who are my sweetest lepers, who demand
No velvet and no velvety velour;
But who have begged me for a brisk contour,
Crying that they are quasi, contraband
Because unfinished, graven by a hand
Less than angelic, admirable or sure.
My hand is stuffed with mode, design, device.
But I lack access to my proper stone.
And plenitude of plan shall not suffice
Nor grief nor love shall be enough alone
To ratify my little halves who bear
Across an autumn freezing everywhere.

The Womanhood

XV

Men of careful turns, haters of forks in the road,
The strain at the eye, that puzzlement, that awe —
Grant me that I am human, that I hurt,
That I can cry.

Not that I now ask alms, in shame gone hollow,
Nor cringe outside the loud and sumptuous gate.
Admit me to our mutual estate.

Open my rooms, let in the light and air.
Reserve my service at the human feast.
And let the joy continue. Do not hoard silence
For the moment when I enter, tardily,
To enjoy my height among you. And to love you
No more as a woman loves a drunken mate,
Restraining full caress and good My Dear,
Even pity for the heaviness and the need —
Fearing sudden fire out of the uncaring mouth,
Boiling in the slack eyes, and the traditional blow.
Next, the indifference formal, deep and slow.

Comes in your graceful glider and benign,
To smile upon me bigly; now desires
Me easy, easy; claims the days are softer
Than they were; murmurs reflectively "Remember
When cruelty, metal, public, uncomplex,
Trampled you obviously and every hour. . . ."
(Now cruelty flaunts diplomas, is elite,
Delicate, has polish, knows how to be discreet):
    Requests my patience, wills me to be calm,
    Brings me a chair, but the one with broken straw,
    Whispers "My friend, no thing is without flaw.
    If prejudice is native — and it is — you
    Will find it ineradicable — not to
    Be juggled, not to be altered at all,
    But left unvexed at its place in the properness
    Of things, even to be given (with grudging) honor.
        What
We are to hope is that intelligence
Can sugar up our prejudice with politeness.
Politeness will take care of what needs caring.
For the line is there.
And has a meaning. So our fathers said —
And they were wise — we think — At any rate,
They were older than ourselves. And the report is
What's old is wise. At any rate, the line is

Long and electric. Lean beyond and nod.
Be sprightly. Wave. Extend your hand and teeth.
But never forget it stretches there beneath."
The toys are all grotesque
And not for lovely hands; are dangerous,
Serrate in open and artful places. Rise.
Let us combine. There are no magics or elves
Or timely godmothers to guide us. We are lost, must
Wizard a track through our own screaming weed.

The Blackstone Rangers

I

AS SEEN BY DISCIPLINES

There they are.
Thirty at the corner.
Black, raw, ready.
Sores in the city
that do not want to heal.

II

THE LEADERS

Jeff. Gene. Geronimo. And Bop.
They cancel, cure and curry.
Hardly the dupes of the downtown thing
the cold bonbon,
the rhinestone thing. And hardly
in a hurry.
Hardly Belafonte, King,
Black Jesus, Stokely, Malcolm X or Rap.
Bungled trophies.
Their country is a Nation on no map.

Jeff, Gene, Geronimo and Bop
in the passionate noon,
in bewitching night

are the detailed men, the copious men.
They curry, cure,
they cancel, cancelled images whose Concerts
are not divine, vivacious; the different tins
are intense last entries; pagan argument;
translations of the night.

The Blackstone bitter bureaus
(bureaucracy is footloose) edit, fuse
unfashionable damnations and descent;
and exulting, monstrous hand on monstrous hand,
construct, strangely, a monstrous pearl or grace.

III

GANG GIRLS

A Rangerette

Gang Girls are sweet exotics.
Mary Ann
uses the nutrients of her orient,
but sometimes sighs for Cities of blue and jewel
beyond her Ranger rim of Cottage Grove.
(Bowery Boys, Disciples, Whip-Birds will
dissolve no margins, stop no savory sanctities.)

Mary is
a rose in a whiskey glass.

Mary's
Februaries shudder and are gone. Aprils
fret frankly, lilac hurries on.
Summer is a hard irregular ridge.
October looks away.
And that's the Year!
        Save for her bugle-love.
Save for the bleat of not-obese devotion.
Save for Somebody Terribly Dying, under
the philanthropy of robins. Save for her Ranger
bringing

an amount of rainbow in a string-drawn bag.
"Where did you get the diamond?" Do not ask:
but swallow, straight, the spirals of his flask
and assist him at your zipper; pet his lips
and help him clutch you.

Love's another departure.
Will there be any arrivals, confirmations?
Will there be gleaning?

Mary, the Shakedancer's child
from the rooming-flat, pants carefully, peers at
her laboring lover. . . .
          Mary! Mary Ann!
Settle for sandwiches! settle for stocking caps!
for sudden blood, aborted carnival,
the props and niceties of non-loneliness —
the rhymes of Leaning.

Malcolm X

For Dudley Randall

Original.
Ragged-round.
Rich-robust.

He had the hawk-man's eyes.
We gasped. We saw the maleness.
The maleness raking out and making guttural the air
and pushing us to walls.

And in a soft and fundamental hour
a sorcery devout and vertical
beguiled the world.

He opened us —
who was a key,

who was a man.

Dudley Randall (1914-   )

Dudley Randall, founder of the Broadside Press, has written poetry, fiction, and articles. Born in Washington, D. C., he received his Bachelor's degree from Wayne State University and a Master's in library science from the University of Michigan. Winner of the Tompkins Award for poetry, he has published two collections: *Poem Counterpoem* (1966), in collaboration with Margaret Danner, and *Cities Burning* (1968).

Primitives

Paintings with stiff
homuncules, flat in iron
draperies, with distorted
bodies against spaceless
landscapes.

Poems of old
poets in stiff
metres whose harsh
syllables
drag like
dogs with
crushed
backs.

We go back to
them, spurn difficult
grace and
symmetry,
paint tri-faced

monsters,
write lines that
do not sing, or
even croak, but that
bump,
jolt, and are hacked
off in the mid-
dle, as if by these dis-
tortions, this
magic, we can
exorcise
horror, which we
have seen and fear to
see again:

hate deified,
fears and
guilt conquering,
turning cities to
gas, powder and a
little rubble.

The Melting Pot

There is a magic melting pot
where any girl or man
can step in Czech or Greek or Scot,
step out American.

Johann and **Jan** and **Jean** and **Juan,**
Giovanni and **Ivan**
step in and then step out again
all freshly christened **John.**

Sam, watching, said, "Why, I was here
even before they came,"
and stepped in too, but was tossed out
before he passed the brim.

And every time Sam tried that pot
they threw him out again.
"Keep out. This is our private pot.
We don't want your black stain."

At last, thrown out a thousand times,
Sam said, "I don't give a damn.
Shove your old pot. You can like it or not,
but I'll be just what I am."

Naomi Long Madgett (1923-   )

Born in Norfolk, Virginia, reared in New Jersey and Missouri, Naomi Long Madgett received a Bachelor's from Virginia State College and a Master's from Wayne State University. A teacher of English in high school and college, recipient of fellowships for writing and once honored as "English Teacher of the Year" in Detroit, she has published three volumes of poetry: *Songs to a Phantom Nightingale, One and the Many,* and *Star by Star.*

Nocturne

See how dark the night settles on my face,
How deep the rivers of my soul
Flow imperturbable and strong.

Rhythms of unremembered jungles
Pulse through the untamed shadows of my song,
And my cry is the dusky accent of secret midnight birds.

Above the sable valleys of my sorrow
My swarthy hands have fashioned
Pyramids of virgin joy.

See how tenderly God pulls His blanket of blackness over the earth.
You think I am not beautiful?
You lie!

Alabama Centennial

They said, "Wait." Well, I waited.
For a hundred years I waited

In cotton fields, kitchens, balconies,
In bread lines, at back doors, on chain gangs,
In stinking "colored" toilets
And crowded ghettos,
Outside of schools and voting booths.
And some said, "Later."
And some said, "Never!"

Then a new wind blew, and a new voice
Rode its wings with quiet urgency,
Strong, determined, sure.
"No," it said. "Not 'never,' not 'later,'
Not even 'soon.'
Now.
Walk!"

And other voices echoed the freedom words,
"Walk together, children don't get weary,"
Whispered them, sang them, prayed them, shouted them.
"Walk!"
And I walked the streets of Montgomery
Until a link in the chain of patient acquiescence broke.

Then again: Sit down!
And I sat down at the counters of Greensboro.
Ride! And I rode the bus for freedom.
Kneel! And I went down on my knees in prayer and faith.
March! And I'll march until the last chain falls
Singing, "We shall overcome."

Not all the dogs and hoses in Birmingham
Nor all the clubs and guns in Selma
Can turn this tide.
Not all the jails can hold these young black faces
From their destiny of manhood,
Of equality, of dignity,
Of the American Dream
A hundred years past due.
Now!

Darwin T. Turner (1931-   )

The grandson of Dr. Charles Henry Turner, an eminent biologist, Darwin T. Turner, born and reared in Cincinnati, Ohio, graduated, Phi Beta Kappa, from the University of Cincinnati in 1947 with a B.A. in English. He earned an M.A. (English, 1949) from the same institution and a Ph.D. (English, 1956) from the University of Chicago. He has taught English at Clark College and Morgan State College; has chaired English departments at Florida A. and M. University and North Carolina A. and T. State University; and has served as visiting professor at the University of Wisconsin. Presently he is Dean of the Graduate School of North Carolina A. and T. State University.

In addition to serving as president or a member of governing boards of several professional societies, Darwin Turner has published critical studies on drama, Afro-American literature, American literature, and literary criticism in various journals. He has co-edited *Images of the Negro in America* and is the author of *Nathaniel Hawthorne's The Scarlet Letter*. He has also written short stories, drama, and poetry. *Katharsis* is his only published volume of poetry.

The Sit-in

Patient, we pray and wait and weep and pray.
Our faces are ridged; our faces are black —
Black mirrors of a cancerous, imbedded rack
Of festered hate stretching our souls today.
Our stomachs knot in ulcered, entrailed clay;
Our eyes flame pain of sleepless, voiceless fears;
Our song has choked on spittle of shame and tears.

269

But patient we weep, and patient we pray:
"Teach us, God, in this moment's hate and pain
To taste the Judas kiss and cry, 'Forgive,'
To wear the centuries' crown of thorns and live
In grace to know our wait was not in vain."

But louder surges thought incessantly,
"He died for us. For what in hell do we?"

Death

Death is not a dream; death lives:
the shadow at the corner of the eye,
the steps that trail along a dawn-damp street,
the window's sudden face.

The young — warm-blanketed, head poked out —
the young can damn Death:
a playmate
carelessly cast into dim and distant corners
with geese of golden eggs
and giants of steps of seven leagues
and magic swords and witches' candy houses
that fret and fright and swirl into
a tucking-in, feet-warm, goodnight kiss.

Youth can yearn Death:
laurel seized to shake in spite
at the forehead-furrowed alive and left behind;
Elysian fields of peace for the alone,
the not-understood,
the first feet in new snow along the worn path.

Age knows Death.
One day a friend, an offered cigarette,
a laugh and idle compliment,
a breathing-in and breathing-out of life;
the next, a hushed report,
a solemn shaking of the head,
a line or two of type —
another gone before the shock has time to thaw.

And then we pray
and think
and fear
and backward crawl
into the magnet of indifferent Night.

Love

I have known what it is to love:
to walk among the midday mob,
and share the friendship of the faceless throng;
to laugh with children on the paths,
and chatter at a bright-eyed squirrel.
I have known what it is to love:
afraid to speak,
fearing it would be thought a lie;
afraid to breathe a smoke-ring dream
and watch it fade,
or see it ground beneath a careless toe.
I have known what it is to love
and hear a sigh —
soft as worn string that parts —
and not to know it as my own.
I have known what it is to love:
to walk the tower-shadowed streets
and seek one face;
to shudder at cacophony of horns and brakes,
and listen for one voice.
I have known what it is to love:
to seek to hide the thought
in Lethal wine and laughing eyes
and kisses from a dozen pairs
of painted lips.
I have known what it is to love,
and tongue the alum of
a lonely heart.

Sonnet Sequence

I

You are but these to me: a freckled face,
Soft-lighted by a fragile smile, from lips

And eyes that shade a sorrow's ghost; a grace
As lightly balanced as a lark that dips
In restless pause before he seeks the stars;
A childyoung voice, that lullabies me peace,
Secure and warm, from life's diurnal wars
That fret the lonely mind without surcease.
You are remembered scent, imprinted on
A chair; a careless touch that burns within;
A glance that kisses from a table's length;
A subtle difference that you bring into
A room. But most, you are the woman
Who has taught me what it is to love.

FINALE

How carelessly the poet sings love's pains.
Sure-cushioned in a flint-cased mind, he sighs
The tears that trickle from the loveblind eyes;
The purifying grief that purging, drains
The sin-sick soul, and cleanses it of stains,
As rain gentles soot from wan winter's dawn;
The "glad-girl" heart that smiles, when storms have gone,
"It's better to have loved," the ancient strains.
Much grimmer is the weary gardener's fate,
When first he finds the heart, in wayward yield,
Has trampled flowers nursed through patient years:
No time to chide the mind, nor time for tears;
Time but to mend the wall, re-seed the field,
And hire a sterner will to guard the gate.

Guest Lecturer

The evening, ending.
          Already only memory:
The lights upon his face and hair;
The human shapes which nodded, laughed,
          And breathed on tonal cue;
Applause that chattered for a second bow;
Crowding, clutching compliments;
The thrust of challenge;

The tongues and hands and eyes
   Of Adoration presumed.
      Now:
A caterer crumbs the folded cloth
   And drains the silver urn
While he,
   Clinging to a question,
Evades the fretting host,
   Charon to the dreaded end:
A needed, not wanted, lingered
   Bourbon;
The room —
Which has no stage.

LeRoi Jones (1934-   )

LeRoi Jones has become a spokesman and a leader for many young black people who are rebelling against traditions of society and art. Born in Newark, New Jersey, he attended the Newark branch of Rutgers University before transferring to Howard University to complete his undergraduate education. After serving in the Army Air Force, Jones returned to civilian life as a teacher and a writer. He founded the Black Arts Repertory Theatre in Harlem and has directed Spirit House in Newark.

The recipient of a Guggenheim fellowship, Jones first attracted attention with *Preface to a Twenty-Volume Suicide Note* (1961), a volume of poems characterized by vigorous language and powerful imagery. His subsequent work has been influential and controversial. The techniques of *The System of Dante's Hell*, a novel, are studied by many young writers. His interpretation of the history of black people through their experience — *Blues People* — is a persuasive one. His plays have created sensation because of their revolutionary thought, violent language, and fervent denunciations of white racism. *Dutchman*, the best-known, was judged the best off-Broadway production of 1963-64. *The Slave, The Baptism*, and *The Toilet* are other well-known plays. His most recent collection — *Tales* (1967) — mingles sketches, essays, and stories in what some writers believe to be a laudable effort to achieve greater flexibility for the short-story form. In 1968, he co-edited *Black Fire*, an anthology of black revolutionary literature.

Since 1964, Jones has concentrated on the use of literature — poetry and drama especially — as the force of revolution. To this end, he has revised his poetic style to make it more meaningful for community residents who have found little relevance in the traditional, formal language of American poetry. His success is evidenced in the extreme popularity of his frequent public readings in community assemblies. Thus, Jones has revitalized poetry for many people.

The following selections, however, are from Jones' second book and mark a stage at which, still using traditional style and language, he was exploring his own psyche.

An Agony. As Now.

I am inside someone
who hates me. I look
out from his eyes. Smell
what fouled tunes come in
to his breath. Love his
wretched women.

Slits in the metal, for sun. Where
my eyes sit turning, at the cool air
the glance of light, or hard flesh
rubbed against me, a woman, a man,
without shadow, or voice, or meaning.

This is the enclosure (flesh,
where innocence is a weapon. An
abstraction. Touch. (Not mine.
Or yours, if you are the soul I had
and abandoned when I was blind and had
my enemies carry me as a dead man
(if he is beautiful, or pitied.

It can be pain. (As now, as all his
flesh hurts me.) It can be that. Or
pain. As when she ran from me into
that forest.
      Or pain, the mind
silver spiraled whirled against the
sun, higher than even old men thought
God would be. Or pain. And the other. The
yes. (Inside his books, his fingers. They
are withered yellow flowers and were never
beautiful.) The yes. You will, lost soul, say
'beauty.' Beauty, practiced, as the tree. The
slow river. A white sun in its wet sentences.

The end of man is his beauty

And silence
which proves / but
a referent
to my disorder.
              Your world shakes

cities die
beneath your shape.

   The single shadow

at noon
like a live tree
whose leaves
are like clouds
Weightless soul
at whose love faith moves
as a dark and
withered day.

They speak of singing who
have never heard song; of living
whose deaths are legends
for their kind.

         A scream
gathered in wet fingers,
at the top of its stalk.

— They have passed
and gone
whom you thot your lovers

In this perfect quiet, my friend,
their shapes
are not unlike
night's

Etheridge Knight (1933-   )

In her introduction to Etheridge Knight's *Poems from Prison*, Gwendolyn Brooks called attention to their masculinity, centers of softness, warmth, music, and blackness — "freed and terrible and beautiful." Born in Corinth, Mississippi, a veteran of the United States Army, Knight was sentenced to Indiana State Prison in 1960. His poems and stories written there have established his reputation as one of the promising new black writers.

The Idea of Ancestry

1

Taped to the wall of my cell are 47 pictures: 47 black
faces: my father, mother, grandmothers (1 dead), grand
fathers (both dead), brothers, sisters, uncles, aunts,
cousins (1st & 2nd), nieces, and nephews. They stare
across the space at me sprawling on my bunk. I know
their dark eyes, they know mine. I know their style,
they know mine. I am all of them, they are all of me;
they are farmers, I am a thief, I am me, they are thee.

I have at one time or another been in love with my mother,
1 grandmother, 2 sisters, 2 aunts (1 went to the asylum),
and 5 cousins. I am now in love with a 7 yr old niece
(she sends me letters written in large block print, and
her picture is the only one that smiles at me).

I have the same name as 1 grandfather, 3 cousins, 3 nephews,
and 1 uncle. The uncle disappeared when he was 15, just took
off and caught a freight (they say). He's discussed each year
when the family has a reunion, he causes uneasiness in

279

the clan, he is an empty space. My father's mother, who is 93 and who keeps the Family Bible with everybody's birth dates (and death dates) in it, always mentions him. There is no place in her Bible for "whereabouts unknown."

He Sees Through Stone

He sees through stone
he has the secret
eyes this old black one
who under prison skies
sits pressed by the sun
against the western wall
his pipe between purple gums

the years fall
like overripe plums
bursting red flesh
on the dark earth

his time is not my time
but I have known him
in a time gone

he led me trembling cold
into the dark forest
taught me the secret rites
to take a woman
to be true to my brothers
to make my spear drink
the blood
of my enemies

now black cats circle him
flash white teeth
snarl at the air
mashing green grass beneath
shining muscles
ears peeling his words
he smiles
he knows
the hunt   the enemy
he has the secret eyes
he sees through stone

Don L. Lee (1942-   )

Born in 1942, Don Lee, author of three slim volumes of poetry and a broadside, is particularly well-known in Chicago, where he has taught at Roosevelt University, and throughout Illinois, Michigan, and Wisconsin, where audiences have been excited by his poems and his dramatic readings of them. Although he has written lyrics on traditional themes, most of his poetry exemplifies the revolutionary creed of the Black Arts Movement, with emphasis on black language, nontraditional structure, and thought which is immediately relevant to black people. His latest collection is *Don't Cry! Scream!* (1969). The following selections are from his second book, *Think Black* (1968).

Education

I had a good teacher,
He taught me everything I know;
how to lie,
  cheat,
  and how to strike the softest blow.

My teacher thought himself to be wise and right
He taught me things most people consider nice;
 such as to pray,
   smile,
   and how not to fight.

My teacher taught me other things too,
Things that I will be forever looking at;
 how to berate.
   segregate,
   and how to be inferior without hate.

My teacher's wisdom forever grows,
He taught me things every child will know;
   how to steal,
      appeal,
         and accept most things against my will.

All these acts take as facts,
The mistake was made in teaching me
How not to be BLACK.

Back Again, Home
(confessions of an ex-executive)

Pains of insecurity surround me;
   shined shoes,
   conservative suits,
   button down shirts with silk ties.
   bi-weekly payroll.

Ostracized, but not knowing why;
   executive haircut,
   clean shaved,
   "yes" instead of "yeah" and "no" instead of "naw",
   hours, nine to five. (after five he's alone)

"Doing an excellent job, keep it up;"
   promotion made — semi-monthly payroll,
   very quiet — never talks,
   budget balanced — saved the company money,
   quality work — production tops.
   He looks sick. (but there is a smile in his eyes)

He resigned, we wonder why;
   let his hair grow — a mustache too,
   out of a job — broke and hungry,
   friends are coming back — bring food,
   not quiet now — trying to speak,
   what did he say?

"Back Again,

     BLACK AGAIN,

        Home."

A. Selected Collections by Individual Authors

Bontemps, Arna. *Personals*. London: Breman, 1963.

Braithwaite, William Stanley. *The House of Falling Leaves*. Boston: Luce, 1908.

Braithwaite, William Stanley. *Lyrics of Life and Love*. Boston: Turner, 1904.

Braithwaite, William Stanley. *Selected Poems*. New York: Coward-McCann, 1948.

Brooks, Gwendolyn. *Annie Allen*. New York: Harper and Bros., 1949.

Brooks, Gwendolyn. *The Bean Eaters*. New York, Harper and Bros., 1960.

Brooks, Gwendolyn. *Bronzeville Boys and Girls*. New York: Harper and Bros., 1956.

Brooks, Gwendolyn. *In the Mecca*. New York: Harper and Bros., 1968.

Brooks, Gwendolyn. *Selected Poems*. New York: Harper and Bros., 1963.

Brooks, Gwendolyn. *A Street in Bronzeville*. New York: Harper and Bros., 1945.

Brown, Sterling A. *Southern Road*. New York: Harcourt, Brace, 1932.

Cotter, Joseph Seamon, Jr. *The Band of Gideon and Other Lyrics*. Boston: Cornhill, 1918.

Cotter, Joseph Seamon, Sr. *Collected Poems of Joseph S. Cotter Sr.* New York: Harrison, 1938.

Cotter, Joseph Seamon, Sr. *Sequel to the "Pied Piper of Hamelin," and Other Poems*. New York: Harrison, 1939.

Cotter, Joseph Seamon, Sr. *A White Song and a Black One*. Louisville, Ky.: Bradley and Gilbert, 1909.

Cullen, Countee. *The Ballad of the Brown Girl; an Old Ballad Retold*. New York: Harper, 1927.

Cullen, Countee. *The Black Christ and Other Poems*. New York: Harper, 1929.

Cullen, Countee. *Color*. New York: Harper, 1925.

Cullen, Countee. *Copper Sun*. New York: Harper, 1927.

Cullen, Countee. *The Lost Zoo; by Countee Cullen and Christopher Cat*. New York: Harper, 1940. [For children.]

Cullen, Countee. *The Medea and Some Poems*. New York: Harper, 1935.

Cullen, Countee. *On These I Stand*. New York: Harper, 1947.

Cuney, Waring. *Puzzles*. Selected and introduced by Paul Breman. Utrecht, Holland: Breman, 1961.

Davis, Frank Marshall. *Black Man's Verse*. Chicago: Black Cat, 1935.

Davis, Frank Marshall. *47th Street Poems*. Prairie City, Ill.: Decker, 1948.

Dodson, Owen. *Powerful Long Ladder*. New York: Farrar, Straus, 1946.

Dunbar, Paul Laurence. *The Complete Poems of Paul Laurence Dunbar*. New York: Dodd, Mead, 1913.

Dunbar, Paul Laurence. *Lyrics of the Hearthside*. New York: Dodd, Mead, 1899.

Dunbar, Paul Laurence. *Lyrics of Love and Laughter*. New York: Dodd, Mead, 1903.

Dunbar, Paul Laurence. *Lyrics of Lowly Life*. New York: Dodd, Mead, 1896.

Dunbar, Paul Laurence. *Lyrics of Sunshine and Shadow*. New York: Dodd, Mead, 1905.

Dunbar, Paul Laurence. *Majors and Minors*. Toledo, Ohio: Hadley and Hadley, 1895. [Actually pub. 1896]

Dunbar, Paul Laurence. *Oak and Ivy*. Dayton, Ohio: United Brethren, 1893 [Actually pub. 1892]

Emanuel, James A. *The Treehouse and Other Poems*. Detroit: Broadside, 1968.

Harper, Frances Ellen Watkins. *Poems*. Philadelphia: Ferguson, 1895.

Harper, Frances Ellen Watkins. *Poems on Miscellaneous Subjects*. Philadelphia: Merrihew, 1874.

Hayden, Robert E. *A Ballad of Remembrance*. London: Breman, 1962.

Hayden, Robert E. *Figure of Time*. Nashville: Hemphill, 1955.

Hayden, Robert E. *Heart-Shape in the Dust*. Detroit: Falcon, 1940.

Hayden, Robert E. *The Lion and the Archer*. New York: Hemphill, 1949.

Hayden, Robert E. *Selected Poems*. New York: October House, 1966.

Hill, Roy L. *49 Poems*. Manhattan, Kansas: Agsic Press, 1968.

Hill, Leslie Pinckney. *Wings of Oppression and Other Poems*. Boston: Stratford, 1921.

Hughes, Langston. *Ask Your Mama: 12 Moods for Jazz*. New York: Knopf, 1961.

Hughes, Langston. *The Dream Keeper and Other Poems*. New York: Knopf, 1932.

Hughes, Langston. *Fields of Wonder*. New York: Knopf, 1947.

Hughes, Langston. *Fine Clothes to the Jew*. New York: Knopf, 1927.

Hughes, Langston. *Montage of a Dream Deferred*. New York: Holt, 1951.

Hughes, Langston. *One-Way Ticket*. New York: Knopf, 1949.

Hughes, Langston. *The Panther and the Lash: Poems of Our Times*. New York: Knopf, 1967.

Hughes, Langston. *Scottsboro Limited: Four Poems and A Play in Verse*. New York: Golden Stair, 1932.

Hughes, Langston. *The Selected Poems of Langston Hughes*. New York: Knopf, 1965.

Hughes, Langston. *Shakespeare in Harlem*. New York: Knopf, 1942.

Hughes, Langston. *The Weary Blues*. New York: Knopf, 1926.

Johnson, Fenton. *A Little Dreaming*. Chicago: Peterson, 1913.

Johnson, Fenton. *Vision of the Dusk*. New York: [the author] 1915.

Johnson, Georgia Douglas. *An Autumn Love Cycle*. New York: Neal, 1938.

Johnson, Georgia Douglas. *Bronze: A Book of Verse*. Boston: Brimmer, 1922.

Johnson, Georgia Douglas. *The Heart of a Woman and Other Poems*. Boston: Cornhill, 1918.

Johnson, James Weldon. *Fifty Years and Other Poems*. Boston: Cornhill, 1917.

Johnson, James Weldon. *God's Trombones; Seven Negro Sermons in Verse*. New York: Viking, 1927.

Johnson, James Weldon. *Saint Peter Relates an Incident; Selected Poems*. New York: Viking, 1935.

Jones, LeRoi. *The Dead Lecturer*. New York: Grove, 1964.

Jones, LeRoi. *Preface to a Twenty-Volume Suicide Note*. New York: Corinth, 1961.

Knight, Etheridge. *Poems from Prison*. Detroit: Broadside, 1968.

Lee, Don. *Black Pride*. Detroit: Broadside, 1968.

Lee, Don. *Don't Cry! Scream!* Detroit: Broadside, 1969.

Lee, Don. *Think Black*. Detroit: Broadside, 1968.

Lorde, Audre. *The First Cities*. New York: Poets, 1967.

McGirt, James E. *Avenging the Maine*. Raleigh, N.C.: Edward & Broughton, 1899.

McKay, Claude. *Harlem Shadows*. New York: Harcourt, Brace, 1922.

McKay, Claude. *Selected Poems*. New York: Bookman, 1953.

McKay, Claude. *Spring in New Hampshire and Other Poems*. London: Richards, 1920.

Madgett, Naomi Long. *One and the Many*. New York: Exposition, 1956

Madgett, Naomi Long. *Songs to a Phantom Nightingale*. New York: Fortuny's, 1941.

Madgett, Naomi Long. *Star by Star*. Detroit, Mich.: Harlo, 1965.

Randall, Dudley. *Cities Burning*. Detroit: Broadside, 1968.

Rivers, Conrad Kent. *The Black Bodies and This Sunburnt Face*. Cleveland: Free Lance, 1963.

Spellman, A. B. *The Beautiful Days*. New York: Poet's Press, 1965.

Tolson, Melvin B. *Harlem Gallery, Book I: The Curator*. New York: Twayne, 1965.

Tolson, Melvin B. *Libretto for the Republic of Liberia*. New York: Twayne, 1953.

Tolson, Melvin B. *Rendezvous with America*. New York: Dodd, Mead, 1944.

Turner, Darwin T. *Katharsis*. Wellesley, Mass.: Wellesley P., 1964.

Walker, Margaret. *For My People*. New Haven, Conn.: Yale U P, 1942.

Whitman, Albery Allson. *An Idyl of the South: An Epic Poem in Two Parts*. Metaphysical, 1901.

Whitman, Albery Allson. *Not a Man, and Yet a Man*. Springfield, Ohio: Republic, 1877.

Whitman, Albery Allson. *The Rape of Florida*. 3rd ed. St. Louis: Nixon-Jones, 1890.

B. Selected Anthologies Including Poems

Brown, Sterling A., Arthur P. Davis, and Ulysses Lee, eds. *The Negro Caravan.* New York: Dryden, 1941.

Calverton, Victor F., ed. *An Anthology of American Negro Literature.* New York: Random, 1929.

Chapman, Abraham, ed. *Black Voices.* New York: Dell, 1968.

Emanuel, James A., and Gross, Theodore L. *Dark Symphony: Negro Literature in America.* New York: The Free Press, 1968.

Hughes, Langston, and Arna Bontemps, eds. *The Poetry of the Negro, 1746-1949.* Garden City, N.Y.: Doubleday, 1949.

Johnson, Charles S., ed. *Ebony and Topaz: A Collectanea.* New York: National Urban League, 1927.

Johnson, James W., ed. *The Book of American Negro Poetry.* Rev. ed. New York: Harcourt, Brace, 1931.

Jones, LeRoi, and Larry Neal, eds. *Black Fire.* New York: Morrow, 1968.

Kerlin, Robert T., ed. *Contemporary Poetry of the Negro.* Hampton, Va.: Hampton Institute P, 1923.

Kerlin, Robert T., ed. *Negro Poets and Their Poems.* 2nd ed. Washington: Associated Pub., 1935.

Lanussee, Armand, ed. *Creole Voices: Poems in French by Free Men of Color.* Centennial ed. Washington: Associated Pub., 1945.

Locke, Alain, ed. *Four Negro Poets.* New York: Simon and Schuster, 1927.

Major, Clarence, ed. *The New Black Poetry.* New York: International Pub., 1969.

Marcus, Samuel, ed. *Anthology of Revolutionary Poetry.* New York: Active, 1929.

Murphy, Beatrice, ed. *Ebony Rhythm.* New York: Exposition, 1948.

Murphy, Beatrice, ed. *Negro Voices; An Anthology of Contemporary Verse.* New York: Harrison, 1938.

Perez Echavarria, Miguel Ramon, ed. *La poesia negra en America.* Buenos Aires: Nocito & Rano, 1946.

Perkins, Eugene, ed. *Black Expressions: An Anthology of New Black Poets.* Chicago: Conda, 1967.

Pool, Rosey E., ed. *Beyond the Blues: New Poems by American Negroes.* Lympne, Kent, England: Hand and Flower, 1962.

Pool, Rosey E., ed. *Black and Unknown Bards.* Aldington, Kent, England: Hand and Flower, 1958.

Schulmann, R. Baird, ed. *Nine Black Poets.* Durham, N. C.: Moore, 1968.

Ten: Anthology of Detroit Poets. Fort Smith, Ark.: South and West, 1968.

Watkins, Sylvester C., ed. *Anthology of American Negro Literature.* New York: Random, 1944.

White, Newman and W. C. Jackson, eds. *An Anthology of Verse by American Negroes.* Durham, N. C.: Moore, 1968.

Fiction

Introduction

This book is a collection of short works by black Americans who have earned recognition as writers of fiction. The choice of selections is a major problem for any editor who proposes such a collection. Talented authors frequently abandon the short story form after they have published favorably received novels. Consequently, an editor who wishes to include short works from the best-known writers of fiction may be forced to select pieces which fail to exemplify the style and thought which characterize the more mature work of those authors. In some instances, in fact, the early work of a famous novelist may be inferior to stories of writers who are less well known. But because most students need to become more familiar with the history of literature by black Americans, it seems more important to offer a collection of stories by the best-known writers than to prepare a collection of the best stories.

Even the term "best-known" must be qualified. If only the writers most familiar to contemporary readers were selected, the collection probably would be limited to those published during the past thirty years. To provide a reasonably representative picture of the literary achievements throughout the twentieth century, however, I have included works from the best-known writers of each decade. If it seems that too much space has been given to the early writers, the reason is my belief that, because works of the past decade are available in libraries and paperbacked books, it is important in an anthology to provide readers with selections which may be more difficult to obtain.

Despite these apologies for the uneven quality of the selections, I believe that this anthology provides models for the study of the short story as an art form and, simultaneously, provides representative materials for a history of short fiction by black writers.

The first Afro-American makers of fiction were the slaves who retold and adapted to the new world the tales which their fathers had brought from Africa. These were folk tales which no individual proclaimed to be his unique creation. Certainly, individuals invented them, but later narrators felt free to modify them; for these stories about heroes—animal and human—whose character traits were well known to the listeners were the product of the race. They reflected the imagination, the aspirations, and the ideals of the black men of America. And, because they were imaginative departures from Anglo-Saxon tradition, they became an important addition to American culture, as Joel Chandler Harris realized after the enthusiastic reception of the first volume of Uncle Remus tales.

Folk tales were circulated orally. The Afro-American's development as a *writer* of short stories, however, proceeded more slowly for a number of reasons. First, and most obvious, is the fact that relatively few slaves and freemen knew how to write; most Southern states forbade the education of black Americans. Second, the popular medium for the short story in America is the periodical, but few early nineteenth-century editors desired material written by Afro-Americans. Those few were abolitionists looking for "true," horrifying autobiographies to win converts to their cause.

Consequently, even though Afro-Americans repeated African tales in the seventeenth century and published poetry as early as 1760, the first serious short story writers did not appear until more than twenty years after the Emancipation Proclamation. In 1887, *The Atlantic Monthly* published Charles Waddell Chesnutt's "The Goophered Grapevine," the story of the conjuring or enchanting of a vineyard, told by a former slave who wants to prevent the sale of the vineyard. Although *The Atlantic* continued to publish Chesnutt's work, the editor, possibly fearing criticism or cancellation of subscriptions, avoided identifying the writer as Negro.

In contrast, the publishers of Paul Laurence Dunbar's stories wanted to identify him. By 1897, Dunbar had earned national fame as a poet, but he was still crude and inexperienced as a writer of fiction. Hoping to capitalize on his popularity, publishers not only accepted his stories but even collected them, in *Folks from Dixie* (1898), a year before the more experienced, more artistic Chesnutt could persuade anyone to accept *The Conjure Woman and Other Tales*.

The success of Dunbar and Chesnutt did not encourage boldness from publishers. Some Afro-Americans, such as James McGirt and

Fenton Johnson, published their own work; but black writers of short fiction remained unknown until the Harlem Renaissance.

The Harlem Renaissance is the name popularly assigned to that decade during which white Americans rediscovered the culture of black Americans. A combination of circumstances produced the Renaissance. First, white writers became interested in black people. In 1917, Ridgely Torrence issued *Three Plays for a Negro Theatre*, and four years later Eugene O'Neill wrote *The Emperor Jones*. For Afro-American readers, the four plays are limited because they concentrate on primitive aspects of Negro life and psychology; nevertheless, the four helped awaken artists to awareness of the Negro as subject for serious realistic presentation. Before the Twenties ended, the subject was explored significantly by such writers as Carl van Vechten (*Nigger Heaven*), Gertrude Stein (*Melanctha*), Waldo Frank (*Holiday*), Sherwood Anderson (*Dark Laughter*), William Faulkner (*The Sound and the Fury*), and Dubose Heyward (*Porgy* and *Mamba's Daughters*). A second cause of the Renaissance was the popularity of jazz. The post-war generation danced to a jazz tempo, set by such black artists as King Oliver, Louis Armstrong, and Duke Ellington and imitated by white musicians. Third, in a generation seeking freedom, the Afro-American symbolized the uninhibited man. Although the image was false, it aroused curiosity about black Americans.

Fourth, and probably most important, were the efforts of black men anxious to inform the nation about the contributions and potential of black Americans. The National Association for the Advancement of Colored People, more than a decade old, formed a platform on which W. E. B. DuBois and James Weldon Johnson, both literary artists, brought Negroes to American attention. Pushing back the curtains of historical research, Carter G. Woodson revealed the black man's role in building the nation. Alain Locke—Ph.D. from Harvard, Rhodes Scholar, aesthetician, philosopher—persuaded young black writers, painters, and dancers to seek their subjects and styles in their African and Afro-American heritage. Charles S. Johnson, editor of *Opportunity* magazine, sought black writers.

These four forces combined to cast a spotlight on Afro-Americans. And a young, confident, educated generation of black writers was prepared to meet the challenge.

Needless to say, short story writers want and need to be published. Outlets appeared during the Twenties. *The Crisis*, official organ of the NAACP, and *Opportunity*, the organ of the National

Urban League, encouraged literary attention through book reviews, literary columns, and annual contests. Little magazines such as *Fire* and *Palms* came into existence, lasted an issue or two, then died, but not before they had introduced new writers. And the more prestigious magazines not only accepted works by Negroes but, capitalizing on the rage, even requested such materials. For instance, *Survey Graphic* devoted an entire issue to a presentation of the culture of the "new" Negro. For three successive years, *The Carolina*, literary magazine of the University of North Carolina, reserved a spring issue for literature by Negroes.

The young black writers responded. Two generations removed from slavery, bolstered by their education, flattered by the attention, they wrote. Jean Toomer lyrically sketched life in Georgia, Washington, and Chicago. Wallace Thurman satirized Negroes; Langston Hughes satirized both whites and blacks. Eric Walrond wrote sultry stories revealing the emotions of Caribbean natives; Rudolph Fisher depicted the people of Harlem. Zora Neale Hurston told about black people of Florida. John Matheus, Claude McKay, and Arna Bontemps were among others.

These new writers freed themselves from some psychological restrictions which had repressed Dunbar and Chesnutt. In many stories Dunbar had written humorously of stereotyped Southern darkies; these characters appealed to his editors and publishers. Even more often, however, he had stressed the virtues of Afro-Americans—their generosity, their charity, their love, their loyalty, their sense of duty, their honor; his purpose had been to persuade his white readers that black Americans were worthy to share the opportunities granted to other Americans. Chesnutt too had written with a purpose. Contemptuous of the slaves who remained loyal to their masters, he wrote instead about free mulattoes who equalled or surpassed the intelligence and honor of their white neighbors.

Young blacks of the Twenties, however, saw less need to "put forward the best foot of the race." They laughed at and with their amoral, irresponsible protagonists. Sometimes in the opinion of older and more conservative critics, such as W. E. B. DuBois and Benjamin Brawley, they seemed to go too far in reporting publicly the human frailties which the race had concealed for fear of further criticism by white America.

The Twenties rocketed young black short story writers into public prominence, but the Thirties dropped them into the reality of depression. It is true that they were not neglected as completely as they had been between 1910 and 1920: *Crisis* and *Opportunity* continued to publish creative works; Langston Hughes collected his stories into *The Ways of White Folks* (1934); such reputable journals as *The New Republic* and *Esquire* published Ted Poston and Chester Himes among others; new novelists emerged; and helpful assistance came from the Federal Workers Project and new left-wing magazines. The American public was interested in writings by Afro-Americans, but it did not seek them as eagerly as it had during the Twenties.

The pendulum reversed its swing with the advent of Richard Wright, who, in 1938, published *Uncle Tom's Children,* a collection of short stories about people trapped by the violence which Wright believed to be continuously surrounding the Southern black man. Wright wrote obvious propaganda in his stories; some critics have even accused him of being overly melodramatic. Nevertheless, he demonstrated an unmistakable power and artistry which won new respect for the Afro-American writers.

Wright was soon imitated by others. Chester Himes wrote colorful, violent stories about the people of Harlem. Willard Motley and Ann Petry earned praise as short story writers before they concentrated their talents on novels. Frank Yerby wrote protest in the Wright tradition before he too moved on to fame and fortune as a novelist.

In the late Forties and Fifties the list of significant short story writers grew to proportions which cannot be encompassed within a brief introduction. The most prominent are probably Ralph Ellison, James Baldwin, Mary Ellen Vroman ("See How They Run," the story of a school teacher and her pupils), William Melvin Kelley, John Killens, John A. Williams, Julian Mayfield, Ernest Gaines, Kristin Hunter, and Le Roi Jones.

The increase can be attributed to several causes. A first is education. More black Americans than ever before are attending school, where they are probably receiving a better quality of education—as are non-black Americans. From numbers alone, even if the percentage remained constant, one might expect to find more black writers coming from the schools of America. Nevertheless, improved education should not be emphasized to the extreme reflected by scholars who write as though black authors did not exist before World War II or as though black Americans were disinterested in their economic, political, and social conditions before 1950.

There are more important causes. One, the generation of writers after Wright understood that their success depended upon the quality rather than the subject of their work. Instead of hoping to sell a story merely because it was about Negroes, they struggled to develop themselves as artists. An even more important reason is that black men now perceive that the writing of fiction can lead to fame and fortune. As long as chances for success seem impossible in literature or any other activity, talented individuals will concentrate their efforts in more promising areas. But, once the opportunity becomes apparent, many will try. The success of Richard Wright inspired Ellison, Yerby, Motley, and Baldwin. These, in turn, encouraged the present generation. As long as the opportunity continues, talented black Americans will try their hand at stories, and many will succeed.

Charles Waddell Chesnutt
(1858-1932)

Po' Sandy

Charles Waddell Chesnutt was the first Afro-American to master the short story as an art form. Born in Cleveland, Ohio, he was reared in North Carolina, where he became a school teacher at the age of sixteen. After training himself in stenography, he moved North to work briefly as a typist, write fiction, and practice law.

According to popular tradition, Chesnutt's desire to be a writer was inspired by his reading of a novel by Albion Tourgée (*A Fool's Errand*, 1880). Not knowing about William Wells Brown's *Clotel* (1852), Chesnutt decided to be the first Afro-American to write a novel about his race. Although his first story, "The Goophered Grapevine," appeared in *The Atlantic Monthly* in 1887, thirteen years passed before he realized his ambition to publish a novel.

A mulatto, Chesnutt was deeply concerned with the psychological and social problems of Negroes in the North and the South. He examined these problems in *The Wife of His Youth and Other Stories of the Color Line* (1899) and in such novels as *The House Behind the Cedars* (1900), *The Marrow of Tradition* (1901), and *The Colonel's Dream* (1905). His most significant contribution to American literature, however, may be the tales of *The Conjure Woman*, based on folklore which he had heard in North Carolina. The tales are narrated by Uncle Julius, a shrewd ex-slave, who uses them as a means of instructing and manipulating his Northern employer.

From *The Conjure Woman and Other Tales* (Boston: Houghton Mifflin, 1899).

Po' Sandy

On the northeast corner of my vineyard in central North Carolina, and fronting on the Lumberton plank-road, there stood a small
frame house, of the simplest construction. It was built of pine
lumber, and contained but one room, to which one window gave
light and one door admission. Its weather-beaten sides revealed a
virgin innocence of paint. Against one end of the house, and
occupying half its width, there stood a huge brick chimney: the
crumbling mortar had left large cracks between the bricks; the
bricks themselves had begun to scale off in large flakes, leaving
the chimney sprinkled with unsightly blotches. These evidences of
decay were but partially concealed by a creeping vine, which
extended its slender branches hither and thither in an ambitious
but futile attempt to cover the whole chimney. The wooden shut-
ter, which had once protected the unglazed window, had fallen
from its hinges, and lay rotting in the rank grass and jimson-weeds
beneath. This building, I learned when I bought the place, had
been used as a schoolhouse for several years prior to the breaking
out of the war, since which time it had remained unoccupied, save
when some stray cow or vagrant hog had sought shelter within its
walls from the chill rains and nipping winds of winter.

One day my wife requested me to build her a new kitchen. The
house erected by us, when we first came to live upon the vineyard,
contained a very conveniently arranged kitchen; but for some
occult reason my wife wanted a kitchen in the back yard, apart
from the dwelling-house, after the usual Southern fashion. Of
course I had to build it.

To save expense, I decided to tear down the old schoolhouse,
and use the lumber, which was in a good state of preservation, in
the construction of the new kitchen. Before demolishing the old
house, however, I made an estimate of the amount of material
contained in it, and found that I would have to buy several
hundred feet of lumber additional, in order to build the new
kitchen according to my wife's plan.

One morning old Julius McAdoo, our colored coachman, har-
nessed the gray mare to the rockaway, and drove my wife and me
over to the sawmill from which I meant to order the new lumber.
We drove down the long lane which led from our house to the
plank-road; following the plank-road for about a mile, we turned
into a road running through the forest and across the swamp to

the sawmill beyond. Our carriage jolted over the half-rotten corduroy road which traversed the swamp, and then climbed the long
hill leading to the sawmill. When he reached the mill, the foreman
had gone over to a neighboring farmhouse, probably to smoke or
gossip, and we were compelled to await his return before we could
transact our business. We remained seated in the carriage, a few
rods from the mill, and watched the leisurely movements of the
mill-hands. We had not waited long before a huge pine log was
placed in position, the machinery of the mill was set in motion,
and the circular saw began to eat its way through the log, with a
loud whir which resounded throughout the vicinity of the mill. The
sound rose and fell in a sort of rhythmic cadence, which, heard
from where we sat, was not unpleasing, and not loud enough to
prevent conversation. When the saw started on its second journey
through the log, Julius observed, in a lugubrious tone, and with a
perceptible shudder:—

"Ugh! but dat des do cuddle my blood!"

"What's the matter, Uncle Julius?" inquired my wife, who is of
a very sympathetic turn of mind. "Does the noise affect your
nerves?"

"No, Mis' Annie," replied the old man, with emotion, "I ain'
narvous; but dat saw, a-cuttin' en grindin' thoo dat stick er timber, en moanin', en groanin', en sweekin', kyars my 'memb'ance
back ter ole times, en 'min's me er po' Sandy." The pathetic
intonation with which he lengthened out the "po' Sandy" touched
a responsive chord in our own hearts.

"And who was poor Sandy?" asked my wife, who takes a deep
interest in the stories of plantation life which she hears from the
lips of the older colored people. Some of these stories are quaintly
humorous; others wildly extravagant, revealing the Oriental cast
of the negro's imagination; while others, poured freely into the
sympathetic ear of a Northern-bred woman, disclose many a tragic
incident of the darker side of slavery.

"Sandy," said Julius, in reply to my wife's question, "was a
nigger w'at useter b'long ter ole Mars Marrabo McSwayne. Mars
Marrabo's place wuz on de yuther side'n de swamp, right nex' ter
yo' place. Sandy wuz a monst'us good nigger, en could do so many
things erbout a plantation, en alluz 'ten' ter his wuk so well, dat
w'en Mars Marrabo's chilluns growed up en married off, dey all un
'em wanted dey daddy fer ter gin 'em Sandy fer a weddin' present.
But Mars Marrabo knowed de res' would n' be satisfied ef he gin
Sandy ter a'er one un 'em; so w'en day wuz all done married, he fix

it by 'lowin' one er his chilluns ter take Sandy fer a mont' er so, en den ernudder for a mont' er so, en so on dat erway tel dey had all had 'im de same lenk er time; en den dey would all take him roun' ag'in, 'cep'n' oncet in a w'ile w'en Mars Marrabo would len' 'im ter some er his yuther kinfolks 'roun' de country, w'en dey wuz short er han's; tel bimeby it got so Sandy did n' hardly knowed whar he wuz gwine ter stay fum one week's een' ter de yuther.

"One time w'en Sandy wuz lent out ez yushal, a spekilater come erlong wid a lot er niggers, en Mars Marrabo swap' Sandy's wife off fer a noo 'oman. W'en Sandy come back, Mars Marrabo gin 'im a dollar, en 'lowed he wuz monst'us sorry fer ter break up de fambly, but de spekilater had gin 'im big boot, en times wuz hard en money skase, en so he wuz bleedst ter make de trade. Sandy tuk on some 'bout losin' his wife, but he soon seed dey want no use cryin' ober spilt merlasses; en bein' ez he lacked de looks er de noo 'oman, he tuk up wid her atter she'd be'n on de plantation a mont' er so.

"Sandy en his noo wife got on mighty well tergedder, en de niggers all 'mence' ter talk about how lovin' dey wuz. W'en Tenie wuz tuk sick oncet, Sandy useter set up all night wid 'er, en den go ter wuk in de mawnin' des lack he had his reg'lar sleep; en Tenie would 'a' done anythin' in de worl' for her Sandy.

"Sandy en Tenie had n' be'n libbin' tergedder fer mo' d'n two mont's befo' Mars Marrabo's old uncle, w'at libbed down in Robeson County, sent up ter fin' out ef Mars Marrabo could n' len' 'im er hire 'im a good han' fer a mont' er so. Sandy's marster wuz one er dese yer easy-gwine folks w'at wanter please eve'ybody, en he says yas, he could len' 'im Sandy. En Mars Marrabo tol' Sandy fer ter git ready ter go down ter Robeson nex' day, fer ter stay a mont' er so.

"It wuz monst'us hard on Sandy fer ter take 'im 'way fum Tenie. It wuz so fur down ter Robeson dat he did n' hab no chance er comin' back ter see her tel de time wuz up; he would n' 'a' mine comin' ten er fifteen mile at night ter see Tenie, but Mars Marrabo's uncle's plantation wuz mo' d'n forty mile off. Sandy wuz mighty sad en cas' down atter w'at Mars Marrabo tol' 'im en he says ter Tenie, sezee:—

" 'I'm gittin' monst'us ti'ed er dish yer gwine roun' so much. Here I is lent ter Mars Jeems dis mont', en I got ter do so-en-so; en ter Mars Archie de nex' mont', en I got ter do so-en-so; den I got ter go ter Miss Jinnie's: en hit's Sandy dis en Sandy dat, en Sandy yer en Sandy dere, tel it 'pears ter me I ain' got no home, ner no marster, ner no mistiss, ner no nuffin. I can't eben keep a wife: my yuther ole 'oman wuz sol' away widout my gittin' a chance fer ter tell her good-by; en now I got ter go off en leab you, Tenie, en I dunno whe'r I'm eber gwine ter see you ag'in er no. I wisht I wuz a tree, er a stump, er a rock, er sump'n w'at could stay on de plantation fer a w'ile.'

"Atter Sandy got thoo talkin', Tenie did n' say naer word, but des sit dere by de fier, studyin' en studyin'. Bimeby she up'n' says:—

" 'Sandy, is I eber tol' you I wuz a cunjuh 'omen?'

"Co'se Sandy had'n nebber dremp' er nuffin lack dat, en he made a great 'miration w'en he hear w'at Tenie say. Bimeby Tenie went on:—

" 'I ain' goophered nobody, ner done no cunjuh wuk, fer fifteen year er mo'; en w'en I got religion I made up my mine I would n' wuk no mo' goopher. But dey is some things I doan b'lieve it's no sin fer ter do; en ef you doan wanter be sent roun' fum pillar ter pos', en ef you doan wanter go down ter Robeson, I kin fix things so you won't haf ter. Ef you'll des say de word, I kin turn you ter w'ateber you wanter be, en you kin stay right whar you wanter, ez long ez you mineter.'

"Sandy say he doan keer: he's willin' fer ter do anythin' fer ter stay close ter Tenie. Den Tenie ax 'im ef he doan wanter be turnt inter a rabbit.

"Sandy say, 'No, de dogs mought git atter me.'

" 'Shill I turn you ter a wolf?' sez Tenie.

" 'No, eve'ybody's skeered er a wolf, en I doan want nobody ter be skeered er me.'

" 'Shill I turn you ter a mawkin'bird?'

" 'No, a hawk mought ketch me. I wanter be turnt inter sump'n w'at'll stay in one place.'

" 'I kin turn you ter a tree', sez Tenie. 'You won't hab no mouf ner years, but I kin turn you back oncet in a w'ile, so you kin git sump'n ter eat, en hear w'at's gwine on.'

"Well, Sandy say dat'll do. En so Tenie tuk 'im down by de aidge er de swamp, not fur fum de quarters, en turnt 'im inter a big pine-tree, en sot 'im out 'mongs' some yuther trees. En de nex' mawnin', ez some er de fiel' han's wuz gwine long dere, dey seed a tree w'at dey did'n 'member er habbin' seed befo'; it wuz monst'us quare, en dey wuz bleedst ter 'low dat dey had n' 'membered right er e'se one er de saplin's had be'n growin' monst'us fas'.

"W'en Mars Marrabo 'skiver' dat Sandy wuz gone, he 'lowed Sandy had runned away. He got de dogs out, but de las' place dey could track Sandy ter wuz de foot er dat pine-tree. En dere de dogs stood en barked, en bayed, en pawed at de tree, en tried ter climb up on it; en w'en dey wuz tuk roun' thoo de swamp ter look fer de scent, dey broke loose en made fer dat tree ag'in. It wuz de beatenis' thing de w'ite folks eber hearn of, en Mars Marrabo 'lowed dat Sandy must 'a' clim' up on de tree en jump' off on a mule er sump'n, en rid fur ernuff fer ter spile de scent. Mars Marrabo wanted ter 'cuse some er de yuther niggers er heppin' Sandy off, but dey all 'nied it ter de las'; en eve'ybody knowed Tenie sot too much sto' by Sandy fer ter he'p 'im run away whar she could n' nebber see 'im no mo'.

"W'en Sandy had be'n gone long ernuff fer folks ter think he done got clean away, Tenie useter go down ter de woods at night en turn 'im back, en den dey'd slip up ter de cabin en set by de fire en talk. But dey ha' ter be monst'us keerful, er e'se somebody would 'a' seed 'em, en dat would 'a' spile' de whole thing; so Tenie alluz turnt Sandy back in de mawnin' early, befo' anybody wuz a-stirrin'.

"But Sandy did n' git erlong widout his trials en tribberlations. One day a woodpecker come erlong en 'mence' ter peck at de tree; en de nex' time Sandy wuz turnt back he had a little roun' hole in his arm, des lack a sharp stick be'n stuck in it. Atter dat Tenie sot a sparrer-hawk fer ter watch de tree; en w'en de woodpecker come erlong nex' mawnin' fer ter finish his nes', he got gobble' up mos' 'fo' he stuck his bill in de bark.

"Nudder time, Mars Marrabo sent a nigger out in de woods fer ter chop tuppentime boxes. De man chop a box in dish yer tree, en hack' de bark up two er th'ee feet, fer ter let de tuppentime run. De nex' time Sandy wuz turnt back he had a big skyar on his lef' leg, des lack it be'n skunt; en it tuk Tenie nigh 'bout all night fer ter fix a mixtry ter kyo it up. Atter dat, Tenie sot a hawnet fer ter watch de tree; en w'en de nigger come back ag'in fer ter cut ernudder box on de yuther side'n de tree, de hawnet stung 'im so hard dat de ax slip en cut his foot nigh 'bout off.

"W'en Tenie see so many things happenin' ter de tree, she 'cluded she'd ha' ter turn Sandy ter sump'n e'se; en atter studyin' de matter ober, en talkin' wid Sandy one ebenin', she made up her mine fer ter fix up a goopher mixtry w'at would turn herse'f en Sandy ter foxes, er sump'n, so dey could run away en go some'rs whar dey could be free en lib lack w'ite folks.

"But dey ain' no tellin' w'at's gwine ter happen in dis worl'. Tenie had got de night sot fer her en Sandy ter run away, w'en dat ve'y day one er Mars Marrabo's sons rid up ter de big house in his buggy, en say his wife wuz monst'us sick, en he want his mammy ter len' 'im a 'oman fer ter nuss his wife. Tenie's mistiss say sen' Tenie; she wuz a good nuss. Young mars wuz in a tarrible hurry fer ter git back home. Tenie wuz washin' at de big house dat day, en her mistiss say she should go right 'long wid her young marster. Tenie tried ter make some 'scuse fer ter git away en hide 'tel night, we'n she would have eve'ything fix' up fer her en Sandy; she say she wanter go ter her cabin fer ter git her bonnet. Her mistiss say it doan matter 'bout de bonnet; her head-hankcher wuz good ernuff. Den Tenie say she wanter git her bes' frock; her mistiss say no, she doan need no mo' frock, en w'en dat one got dirty she could git a clean one whar she wuz gwine. So Tenie had ter git in de buggy en go 'long wid young Mars Dunkin ter his plantation, w'ich wuz mo' d'n twenty mile away; en dey wa'n't no chance er her seein' Sandy no mo' 'tel she come back home. De po' gal felt monst'us bad 'bout de way things wuz gwine on, en she knowed Sandy mus' be a wond'rin' why she did n' come en turn 'im back no mo'.

"W'iles Tenie wuz away nussin' young Mars Dunkin's wife, Mars Marrabo tuk a notion fer ter buil' 'im a noo kitchen; en bein' ez he had lots er timber on his place, he begun ter look 'roun' fer a tree ter hab de lumber sawed out'n. En I dunno how it come to be so, but he happen fer ter hit on de ve'y tree w'at Sandy wuz turnt inter. Tenie wuz gone, en dey wa'n't nobody ner nuffin fer ter watch de tree.

"De two men w'at cut de tree down say dey nebber had sech a time wid a tree befo': dey axes would glansh off, en did n' 'pear ter make no prōgress thoo de wood; en of all de creakin', en shakin', en wobblin' you eber see, dat tree done it w'en it commence' ter fall. It wuz de beatenis' thing!

"W'en dey got de tree all trim' up, dey chain it up ter a timber waggin, en start fer de sawmill. But dey had a hard time gittin' de log dere: fus' dey got stuck in de mud w'en day wuz gwine crosst de swamp, en it wuz two er th'ee hours befo' dey could git out. W'en dey start' on ag'in, de chain kep' a-comin' loose, en dey had ter keep a-stoppin' en a-stoppin' fer ter hitch de log up ag'in. W'en dey commence' ter climb de hill ter de sawmill, de log broke loose, en roll down de hill en in 'mongs' de trees, en hit tuk nigh 'bout half a day mo' ter git it haul' up ter de sawmill.

"De nex' mawnin' atter de day de tree wuz haul' ter de sawmill, Tenie come home. W'en she got back ter her cabin, de fus' thing she done wuz ter run down ter de woods en see how Sandy wuz gittin' on. W'en she seed de stump standin' dere, wid de sap runnin' out'n it, en de limbs layin' scattered roun', she night 'bout went out'n her min'. She run ter her cabin, en got her goopher mixtry, en den follered de track er de timber waggin ter de saw-mill. She knowed Sandy could n' lib mo' d'n a minute er so ef she turnt him back, fer he wuz all chop' up so he 'd 'a' be'n bleedst ter die. But she wanted ter turn 'im back long ernuff fer ter 'splain ter 'im dat she had n' went off a-purpose, en lef' 'im ter be chop' down en sawed up. She did n' want Sandy ter die wid no hard feelin's to'ds her.

"De han's at de sawmill had des got de big log on de kerridge, en wuz startin' up de saw, w'en dey seed a 'oman runnin' up de hill, all out er bref, cryin' en gwine on des lack she wuz plumb 'stracted. It wuz Tenie; she come right inter de mill, en th'owed herse'f on de log, right in front er de saw, a-hollerin' en cryin' ter her Sandy ter fergib her, en not ter think hard er her, fer it wa'n't no fault er hern. Den Tenie 'membered de tree did n' hab no years, en she wuz gittin' ready fer ter wuk her goopher mixtry so ez ter turn Sandy back, w'en de mill-hands kotch holt er her en tied her arms wid a rope, en fasten' her to one er de posts in de sawmill; en den dey started de saw up ag'in, en cut de log up inter bo'ds en scantlin's right befo' her eyes. But it wuz mighty hard wuk; fer of all de sweekin', en moanin', en groanin', dat log done it w'iles de saw wuz a-cuttin' thoo it. De saw wuz one er dese yer old-timey, up-en-down saws, en hit tuk longer dem days ter saw a log 'en it do now. Dey greased de saw, but dat did n' stop de fuss; hit kep' right on, tel fin'ly dey got de log all sawed up.

"W'en de oberseah w'at run de sawmill come fum breakfas', de han's up en tell him 'bout de crazy 'oman—ez dey s'posed she wuz—w'at had come runnin' in de sawmill, a-hollerin' en gwine on, en tried ter th'ow herse'f befo' de saw. En de oberseah sent two er th'ee er de han's fer ter take Tenie back ter her marster's plantation.

"Tenie 'peared ter be out'n her min' fer a long time, en her marster ha' ter lock her up in de smoke-'ouse 'tel she got ober her spells. Mars Marrabo wuz monst'us mad, en hit would 'a' made yo' flesh crawl fer ter hear him cuss, 'caze he say de spekilater w'at he got Tenie fum had fooled 'im by wukkin' a crazy 'oman off on him. W'iles Tenie wuz lock up in de smoke-'ouse, Mars Marrabo tuk 'n' haul de lumber fum de sawmill, en put up his noo kitchen.

"W'en Tenie got quiet' down, so she could be 'lowed ter go 'round' de plantation, she up'n' tole her marster all erbout Sandy en de pine-tree; en w'en Mars Marrabo hearn it, he 'lowed she wuz de wuss 'stracted nigger he eber hearn of. He did n' know w'at ter do wid Tenie: fus' he thought he'd put her in de po'-house; but fin'ly, seein' ez she did n' do no harm ter nobody ner nuffin, but des went 'roun' moanin', en groanin', en shakin' her head, he 'cluded ter let her stay on de plantation en nuss de little nigger chilluns w'en dey mammies wuz ter wuk in de cotton-fiel'.

"De noo kitchen Mars Marrabo buil' wuz n' much use, fer it had n' be'n put up long befo' de niggers 'mence' ter notice quare things erbout it. Dey could hear sump'n moanin' en groanin' 'bout de kitchen in de night-time, en w'en de win' would blow dey could hear sump'n a-hollerin' en sweekin' lack it wuz in great pain en sufferin'. En it got so atter a w'ile dat it wuz all Mars Marrabo's wife could do ter git a 'oman ter stay in de kitchen in de daytime long ernuff ter do de cookin'; en dey wa'n't naer nigger on de plantation w'at would n' rudder take forty dan ter go 'bout dat kitchen atter dark,—dat is, 'cep'n' Tenie; she did n' 'pear ter min' de ha'nts. She useter slip 'roun' at night, en set on de kitchen steps, en lean up agin de do'-jamb, en run on ter herse'f wid some kine er foolishness w'at nobody could n' make out; fer Mars Marrabo had th'eaten' ter sen' her off'n de plantation ef she say anything ter any er de yuther niggers 'bout de pine-tree. But somehow er 'nudder de niggers foun' out all erbout it, en dey all knowed de kitchen wuz ha'nted by Sandy's sperrit. En bimeby hit got so Mars Marrabo's wife herse'f wuz skeered ter go out in de yard atter dark.

"W'en it come ter dat, Mars Marrabo tuk en to' de kitchen down, en use' de lumber fer ter buil' dat ole school'ouse w'at you er talkin' 'bout pullin' down. De school'ouse wuz n' use' 'cep'n' in de daytime, en on dark nights folks gwine 'long de road would hear quare soun's en see quare things. Po' ole Tenie useter go down dere at night, en wander 'roun' de school'ouse; en de niggers all 'lowed she went fer ter talk wid Sandy's sperrit. En one winter mawnin', w'en one er de boys went ter school early fer ter start de fire, w'at should he fin' but po' ole Tenie, layin' on de flo', stiff en col', en dead. Dere did n' 'pear ter be nuffin pertickler de matter wid her,—she had des grieve' herse'f ter def fer her Sandy. Mars Marrabo did n' shed no tears. He thought Tenie wuz crazy, en dey wa'n't no tellin' w'at she mought do nex'; en dey ain' much room in dis worl' fer crazy w'ite folks, let 'lone a crazy nigger.

"Hit wa'n't long atter dat befo' Mars Marrabo sol' a piece er his track er lan' ter Mars Dugal' McAdoo,—*my* old marster,—en dat's how de ole school'ouse happen to be on yo' place. W'en de wah broke out, de school stop', en de ole school'ouse be'n stannin' empty ever sence,—dat is, 'cep'n' fer de ha'nts. En folks sez dat de ole school'ouse, er any yuther house w'at got any er dat lumber in it w'at wuz sawed out'n de tree w'at Sandy wuz turnt inter, is gwine ter be ha'nted tel de las' piece er plank is rotted en crumble' inter dus'."

Annie had listened to this gruesome narrative with strained attention.

"What a system it was," she exclaimed, when Julius had finished, "under which such things were possible!"

"What things?" I asked, in amazement. "Are you seriously considering the possibility of a man's being turned into a tree?"

"Oh, no," she replied quickly, "not that;" and then she murmured absently, and with a dim look in her fine eyes, "Poor Tenie!"

We ordered the lumber, and returned home. That night, after we had gone to bed, and my wife had to all appearances been sound asleep for half an hour, she startled me out of an incipient doze by exclaiming suddenly,—

"John, I don't believe I want my new kitchen built out of the lumber in that old schoolhouse."

"You wouldn't for a moment allow yourself," I replied, with some asperity, "to be influenced by that absurdly impossible yarn which Julius was spinning to-day?"

"I know the story is absurd," she replied dreamily, "and I am not so silly as to believe it. But I don't think I should ever be able to take any pleasure in that kitchen if it were built out of that lumber. Besides, I think the kitchen would look better and last longer if the lumber were all new."

Of course she had her way. I bought the new lumber, though not without grumbling. A week or two later I was called away from home on business. On my return, after an absence of several days, my wife remarked to me,—

"John, there has been a split in the Sandy Run Colored Baptist Church, on the temperance question. About half the members have come out from the main body, and set up for themselves. Uncle Julius is one of the seceders, and he came to me yesterday and asked if they might not hold their meetings in the old schoolhouse for the present."

"I hope you didn't let the old rascal have it," I returned, with some warmth. I had just received a bill for the new lumber I had bought.

"Well," she replied, "I couldn't refuse him the use of the house for so good a purpose."

"And I'll venture to say," I continued, "that you subscribed something toward the support of the new church?"

She did not attempt to deny it.

"What are they going to do about the ghost?" I asked, somewhat curious to know how Julius would get around this obstacle.

"Oh," replied Annie, "Uncle Julius says that ghosts never disturb religious worship, but that if Sandy's spirit *should* happen to stray into meeting by mistake, no doubt the preaching would do it good."

Paul Laurence Dunbar
(1872-1906)

The Mortification of the Flesh *and* Mr. Cornelius Johnson, Office-Seeker

The son of former slaves, Paul Laurence Dunbar, born in Dayton, Ohio, was the best known and most popular Afro-American writer of his generation. While working as an elevator operator (the best job he could find as a black man with a high school education), he published two books of poetry—*Oak and Ivy* (1892) and *Majors and Minors* (1896). The second impressed William Dean Howells, who enthusiastically praised him as "the first American Negro to evince innate artistic talent." The success of *Lyrics of Lowly Life* (1896) prompted Dunbar to concentrate on a career as a writer and public reader. Despite failing health, which caused an early death, he published three additional volumes of poetry, four novels, four collections of stories, lyrics for musical shows, and numerous articles and stories which have not been collected.

Dunbar's literary reputation is based upon his poetry, which is superior to his fiction. Nevertheless, his stories often reveal the perceptive characterization and the light satire which constitute a major part of his talent as a writer. In fiction Dunbar is best known for stories about life on the plantations either before or shortly after the Civil War. The following stories, however, reveal Dunbar's interest in other themes too frequently ignored by his critics.

"The Mortification of the Flesh" from *Lippincott's Magazine,* LXVII (September, 1901).

"Mr. Cornelius Johnson, Office-seeker" from *The Strength of Gideon and Other Stories* (New York: Dodd, Mead, 1900).

"The Mortification of the Flesh" is one of a series of "Ohio Pastorals," which Dunbar wrote for *Lippincott's Magazine*. The characters in the stories are white.

The Mortification of the Flesh

First in a Series of Ohio Pastorals

Nathan Foster and his life-long friend and neighbor, Silas Bollender, sat together side by side upon the line fence that separated their respective domains. They were both whittling away industriously, and there had been a long silence between them. Nathan broke it, saying, " 'Pears to me like I've had oncommon good luck this year."

Silas paused and carefully scrutinized the stick he was whittling into nothing at all, and then resumed operations on it before he returned: "Well, you have had good luck, there ain't no denyin' that. It 'pears as though you've been ee-specially blest."

"An' I know I ain't done nothin' to deserve it."

"No, of course not. Don't take no credit to yoreself, Nathan. We don't none of us deserve our blessin's, however we may feel about our crosses: we kin be purty shore o' that."

"Now look," Nathan went on; "my pertater vines was like little trees, an' nary a bug on 'em."

"An' you had as good a crop o' corn as I've ever seen raised in this part o' Montgomery County."

"Yes, an' I sold it, too, jest before that big drop in the price."

"After givin' away all the turnips you could, you had to feed 'em to the hogs."

"My fruit-trees jest had to be propped up, an' I've got enough perserves in my cellar to last two er three winters, even takin' into consideration the drain o' church socials an' o' cherity."

"Yore chickens air fat an' sassy, not a sign o' pip among 'em."

"Look at them cows in the fur pasture. Did you ever seen anything to beat 'em fur sleekness?"

"Well, look at the pasture itself: it's most enough to make human bein's envy the critters. You didn't have a drop o' rain on you while you was gettin' yore hay in, did you?"

"Not a drop."

"An' I had a whole lot ruined jest as I was about to rick it."

So, alternately, they went on enumerating Nathan's blessings, until it seemed that there was nothing left for him to desire.

"Silas," he said solemnly, "sich luck as I'm a-havin' is achilly skerry; it don't seem right."

Silas had a droll humor of his own, and his eyes twinkled as he said: "No, it don't seem right fur a religious man like you, Nathan. Ef you was a hard an' graspin' sinner it 'u'd be jest what a body'd 'spect. You could understand it then: the Lord 'u'd jest be makin' you topheavy so's yore fall 'u'd be the greater."

"I do' know but what that's it anyhow. Mebbe I'm a-gittin' puffed up over my goods without exactly knowin' it."

"Mebbe so, mebbe so. Them kind o' feelin's is mighty sneaky comin' on a body. O' course, I ain't seen no signs of it yit in you; but it 'pears to me you'll have to mortify yore flesh yit to keep from bein' purse-proud."

"Mortify the flesh," repeated Nathan seriously.

"O' course, you can't put peas in yore shoes er git any of yore friends to lash you, so you'll have to find some other way o' mortifyin' yore flesh. Well, fur my part, I don't need to look fur none, fur I never had too many blessin's in my life, less'n you'd want to put the children under that head."

Silas shut up his jack-knife with a snap and, laughing, slid down on his side of the fence. In serious silence Nathan Foster watched him go stumping up the path towards his house. "Silas seems to take everything so light in this world," he breathed half aloud. "I wonder how he can do it."

With Nathan, now, it was just the other way. Throughout his eight-and-forty years he had taken every fact of life with ponderous seriousness. Entirely devoid of humor, he was a firm believer in signs, omens, tokens, and judgments. Though the two men had grown up together and been friends from a boyhood spent upon their fathers' adjoining farms, their lives had been two very different stories. Silas, looking on everything cheerily, had married early and was the father of a houseful of children. His wife ruled him with a rod of iron, but he accepted her domination quite as a matter of course and went merrily on his way. He had never been a very successful man, but he had managed to hold the old homestead and feed and clothe his family. This seemed entirely to satisfy him.

On the other hand, to Nathan marriage had always seemed an undertaking fraught with so much danger that he had feared to embark upon it, and although in his younger days his heart had often burned within him when he contemplated some charming damsel, these heart-burnings had gone unknown to anyone but himself until someone else had led the girl to the altar. So he was set down as not a marrying man. He was essentially a cautious man, and through caution and industry his means had grown until from being well-to-do the people of Montgomery County spoke of him as a rich old bachelor. He was a religious man, and with the vision of Dives in his mind his wealth oppressed and frightened him. He gave to his church and gave freely. But he had the instinct for charity without the faculty for it. And he was often held back from good deeds by a modesty which told him that his gifts would be looked upon as "Alms to be seen of men."

As usual, he had taken his friend's bantering words in hard earnest and was turning them over in his mind. When the bell rang, calling him in to supper, he flung the stick which he had been whittling into the middle of the potato patch and stood watching abstractedly where it fell. Then, as if talking to it, he murmured, "Mortification of the flesh," and started moving slowly to the kitchen.

The next morning, when Nathan and Silas met to compare notes, the former began, "I been thinking over what you said last night, Silas, about me mortifying my flesh, and it seems to me like a good idee."

Silas looked at him quizzically from beneath bent brows, but Nathan went on, "I wrasseled in prayer last night, and it was shown to me that it wa'n't no more'n right fur me to make some kind o' sacrifice fur the mercies that's been bestowed upon me."

"Well, I do' know, Nathan; burnt offerings air a little out now."

"I don't mean nothin' like that; I mean some sacrifice of myself; some——"

His sentence was broken in upon by a shrill voice that called from Silas Bollender's kitchen door: "Si, you'd better be gittin' about yore work instid o' standin' over there a-gassin' all the mornin'. I'm shore I don't have no time to stand around."

"All right, Mollie," he called back to his wife, and then, turning to Nathan, he said, "Speakin' of mortifyin' the flesh an' makin' a sacrifice of yoreself, why don't you git married?"

Nathan started.

"Then, you see," Silas continued, "you'd be shore to accomplish both. Fur pure mortification of the flesh, I don't know of nothin' more thorough-goin' er effectiver than a wife. Also she is a vex-

ation of the sperrit. Look at me an' Mis' Bollender, fur instance.
Do you think I need a hair shirt when I think I'm gittin' over-fed?
No. Mis' Bollender keeps me with a meek an' subdued sperrit. You
raaly ought to marry, Nathan."

"Do you think so?"

"It looks like to me that that 'u'd be about as good a sacrifice as
you could make, an' then it's sich a lastin' one."

"I don't believe that you realize what you air a-sayin', Silas. It's
a mighty desprit step that you're advisin' me to take."

Again Mrs. Bollender's voice broke in, "Si, air you goin' to git
anything done this mornin', er air you goin' to stand there an' hold
up that fence fur the rest o' the day?"

"Nathan," said Silas, "kin you stand here an' listen to a voice
an' a speech like that an' then ask me ef I realize the despritness
of marriage?"

"It's desprit," said Nathan pensively, "but who'd you advise me
to marry, Silas, ef I did,—that is, ef I did make up my mind to
marry,—an' I don' jest see any other way."

"Oh, I ain't pickin' out wives fur anybody, but it seems to me
that you might be doin' a good turn by marryin' the Widder
Young. The Lord 'u'd have two special reasons fur blessin' you
then; fur you'd be mortifyin' yore flesh an' at the same time
a-helpin' the widder an' orphans."

Nathan turned his honest gray eyes upon his friend, but there
was a guilty flush upon his sunburned cheek as he said, "That's
so." For the world, he couldn't admit to Silas that he had been
thinking hard of the Widow Young even before he had thought of
mortifying his flesh with a wife. Now that he had an added excuse
for keeping her in his mind, he was guiltily conscious of trying to
cheat himself,—of passing off a pleasure for a penance. But his
wavering determination was strengthened by the reflection that it
was about Mrs. Young, not as a widow, but as a wife and a means
of grace, that he was concerned, and the memory of what Silas had
said about wives in general had put him right with his conscience
again.

The widow was a lively, buxom woman who had seen forty busy
summers pass. She had been one of the prettiest and most industrious girls of the village, and it had seemed that Nathan, when a
young man, had serious intentions towards her. But his extreme
caution had got the better of his inclination, and she had been
retired to that limbo where he kept all his secret heart-burnings.

She had married a ne'er-do-weel, and until the day of his death, leaving her with two children on her hands, she had had need of all her thrift.

Nathan thought of all these things and a lively satisfaction grew up in his mind. He thought of the good his money would do the struggling woman, of the brightness it would bring into her life. "Well, it's good," he murmured; "I'll be killin' two birds with one stone."

Once decided, it did not take him long to put his plans into execution. But he called Silas over to the fence that evening after he had dressed to pay a visit to the widow.

"Well, Silas," he began, "I've determined to take the step you advised."

"Humph, you made up yore mind quick, Nathan."

Nathan blushed, but said, "I do' know as it's any use a-waitin'; ef a thing's to be done, it ought to be done an' got through with."

"I'll have to ask you, now, ef you realize what a desprit step you're a-takin'?"

"I've thought it over prayerfully."

"I don't want nothin' that I said in lightness of mind to influence you. I do' know as I take sich things as serious as I ought."

"Well, I own up you did start the idee in my head, but I've thought it all over sence an' made up my mind fur myself, an' I ain't to be turned now. What I want partic'lar to know now is, whether it wouldn't be best to tell Lizzie—I mean the widder— that I want her as a means of mortification."

"Well, no, Nathan, I do' know as I would do that jest yit; I don't believe it 'u'd be best."

"But ef she don't know, wouldn't it be obtainin' her under false pertenses ef she said yes?"

"Not exactly the way I look at it, fur you've got more motives fur marryin' than one."

"What! Explain yoreself, Silas, explain yoreself."

"I mean you want to do her good as well as subdue yore own sperrit."

"Oh, yes, that's so."

"Now, no woman wants to know at first that she's a vexation to a man's sperrit. It sounds scriptural, but it don't sound nooptial. Now look at me an' Mis' Bollender. I never told her untell we'd been married more'n six months. Fact is, it never occurred to me before. But she didn't believe it then, an' she won't believe it tell this day. She admits that she's my salvation, but not in that way."

Silas chuckled and his friend chewed a straw and thought long. Finally he said: "Well, I'll agree not to tell her right away, but ef she consents, I must tell her a week er so after we're married. It'll ease my conscience. If I could tell her now, it 'ud be a heap easier in gittin' 'round to the question. I don't know jest how to do it without."

"Oh, you won't have no trouble in makin' her understand. Matrimony's a subjic' that women air mighty keen on. They can see that a man's poppin' the question ef he only half tries. You'll git through all right."

Somewhat strengthened, Nathan left his friend and sought the widow's house. He found her stitching merrily away under the light of a coal-oil lamp with a red shade. Even in his trepidation he found secret satisfaction in the red glow that filled the room and glorified the widow's brown hair.

"La, Nathan," said the widow when he was seated, "who'd 'a' expected to see you up here? You've got to be sich a home body that no one don't look to see you outside o' yore own field an' garden."

"I jest thought I'd drop in," said Nathan.

"Well, it's precious kind o' you, I'm shore. I was a-feelin' kind o' lonesome. The children go to bed with the chickens."

For an instant there was a picture in his mind of just such another evening as this, with the children all in bed and the widow sitting across from him or even beside him in another room than this. His heart throbbed, but the picture vanished before his realization of the stern necessity of saying something.

"I jest thought I'd drop in," he said. Then his face reddened as he remembered that he had said that before. But the widow was fully equal to the occasion.

"Well, it does remind me of old times to see you jest droppin' in informal-like, this way. My, how time does fly!"

"It is like old times, ain't it?"

Here they found a common subject, and the talk went on more easily, aided by story and reminiscence. When Nathan began to take account of the time, he found with alarm that two hours had passed without his getting any nearer to his object. From then he attempted to talk of one thing while thinking of another and failed signally. The conversation wavered, recovered itself, wavered again, and then it fell flat.

Nathan saw that his time had come. He sighed, cleared his throat, and began: "Widder, I been thinkin' a good deal lately, an'

I been talkin' some with a friend o' mine." He felt guiltily conscious of what that friend had counselled him to keep back. "I've been greatly prospered in my day; in fact, 'my cup runneth over.' "

"You have been prospered, Nathan."

"Seems's ef—seems's ef I'd ought to sheer it with somebody, don't it?"

"Well, Nathan, I do' know nobody that's more generous in givin' to the pore than you air."

"I don't mean jest exactly that way: I mean—widder, you're the morti—I mean the salvation of my soul. Could you—would you—er—do you think you'd keer to sheer my blessin's with me—an' add another one to 'em?"

The Widow Young looked at him in astonishment; then, as she perceived his drift, the tears filled her eyes and she asked, "Do you mean it, Nathan?"

"I wouldn't 'a' spent so much labor on a joke, widder."

"No, it don't seem like you would, Nathan. Well, it's sudden, mighty sudden, but I can't say no."

"Fur these an' all other blessin's make us truly thankful, oh Lord, we ask fur His name's sake—Amen!" said Nathan devoutly. And he sat another hour with the widow, making plans for the early marriage, on which he insisted.

The marriage took place very soon after the brief wooing was done. But the widow had been settled in Nathan's home over a month before he had even thought of telling her of the real motive of his marriage, and every day from the time it occurred to him it grew harder for him to do.

The charm and comfort of married life had wrapped him about as with a mantle, and he was at peace with the world. From this state his conscience pricked him awake, and on a night when he had been particularly troubled he sought his friend and counsellor with a clouded brow. They sat together in their accustomed place on the fence.

"I'm bothered, Silas," said Nathan.

"What's the matter?"

"Why, there's several things. First off, I ain't never told the widder that she was a mortification, an' next, she ain't. I look around at that old house o' mine that ain't been a home sence mother used to scour the hearth an' it makes me feel like singing fur joy. An' I hear them children playin' round me—they're the beatenest children; that youngest one called me daddy yistiddy— well, I see them playin' around an' my eyes air opened, an' I see that the widder's jest another blessin' added to the rest. It looks to me like I had tried to cheat the Almighty."

With a furtive glance in the direction of his house, Silas took out his pipe and filled it, then between whiffs he said: "Well, now, Nathan, I do' know as you've got any cause to feel bothered. You've done yore duty. Ef you've tried to mortify yore flesh an' it refused to mortify, why, that's all you could do, an' I believe the Lord'll take the will fur the deed an' credit you accordin'ly."

"Mebbe so, Silas, mebbe so; but I've got to do more o' my duty, I've got to tell her."

He slipped down from the fence.

"Nathan," called his crony, but Nathan hurried away as if afraid to trust time with his will. "That's jest like him," said Silas, "to go an' spoil it all;" and he walked down his field-path grumbling to himself.

When the new husband reached the house his courage almost failed him, but he rushed in exclaiming, "Widder, I've got to tell you, you're a mortification of the flesh an' a vexation to the sperrit; long may you continuer fur the good of my soul."

Then, his duty being done and his conscience quieted, he kissed her and took one of the children on his knee.

Critics often accuse Dunbar of refusing to protest publicly against unjust treatment of Negroes. Actually, he could not write realistically about conditions of black Americans in the South because he was unfamiliar with that region. Dunbar, however, understood and described the economic and political problems of black men in the North. "Mr. Cornelius Johnson" is one of several stories in which Dunbar castigated the Republican party for victimizing Negroes.

Mr. Cornelius Johnson, Office-Seeker

It was a beautiful day in balmy May and the sun shone pleasantly on Mr. Cornelius Johnson's very spruce Prince Albert suit of grey as he alighted from the train in Washington. He cast his eyes about him, and then gave a sigh of relief and satisfaction as he took his bag from the porter and started for the gate. As he went along, he looked with splendid complacency upon the less fortunate mortals who were streaming out of the day coaches. It was a Pullman sleeper on which he had come in. Out on the pavement he hailed a cab, and giving the driver the address of a hotel, stepped in and was rolled away. Be it said that he had cautiously inquired about the hotel first and found that he could be accommodated there.

As he leaned back in the vehicle and allowed his eyes to roam over the streets, there was an air of distinct prosperity about him. It was in evidence from the tips of his ample patent-leather shoes to the crown of the soft felt hat that sat rakishly upon his head. His entrance into Washington had been long premeditated, and he had got himself up accordingly.

It was not such an imposing structure as he had fondly imagined, before which the cab stopped and set Mr. Johnson down. But then he reflected that it was about the only house where he could find accommodation at all, and he was content. In Alabama one learns to be philosophical. It is good to be philosophical in a place where the proprietor of a café fumbles vaguely around in the region of his hip pocket and insinuates that he doesn't want one's custom. But the visitor's ardor was not cooled for all that. He signed the register with a flourish, and bestowed a liberal fee upon the shabby boy who carried his bag to his room.

"Look here, boy," he said, "I am expecting some callers soon. If they come, just send them right up to my room. You take good care of me and look sharp when I ring and you'll not lose anything."

Mr. Cornelius Johnson always spoke in a large and important tone. He said the simplest thing with an air so impressive as to give it the character of a pronouncement. Indeed, his voice naturally was round, mellifluous and persuasive. He carried himself always as if he were passing under his own triumphal arch. Perhaps, more than anything else, it was these qualities of speech and bearing that had made him invaluable on the stump in the recent campaign in Alabama. Whatever it was that held the secret of his power, the man and principles for which he had labored triumphed, and he had come to Washington to reap his reward. He had been assured that his services would not be forgotten, and it was no intention of his that they should be.

After a while he left his room and went out, returning later with several gentlemen from the South and a Washington man. There is some freemasonry among these office-seekers in Washington that throws them inevitably together. The men with whom he returned were such characters as the press would designate as "old wheel-horses" or "pillars of the party." They all adjourned to the bar, where they had something at their host's expense. Then they repaired to his room, whence for the ensuing two hours the bell and the bell-boy were kept briskly going.

The gentleman from Alabama was in his glory. His gestures as he held forth were those of a gracious and condescending prince. It was his first visit to the city, and he said to the Washington man: "I tell you, sir, you've got a mighty fine town here. Of course, there's no opportunity for anything like local pride, because it's the outsiders, or the whole country, rather, that makes it what it is, but that's nothing. It's a fine town, and I'm right sorry that I can't stay longer."

"How long do you expect to be with us, Professor?" inquired Col. Mason, the horse who had bent his force to the party wheel in the Georgia ruts.

"Oh, about ten days, I reckon, at the furthest. I want to spend some time sight-seeing. I'll drop in on the Congressman from my district tomorrow, and call a little later on the President."

"Uh, huh!" said Col. Mason. He had been in the city for some time.

"Yes, sir, I want to get through with my little matter and get back home. I'm not asking for much, and I don't anticipate any trouble in securing what I desire. You see, it's just like this, there's no way for them to refuse us. And if any one deserves the good things at the hands of the administration, who more than we old campaigners, who have been helping the party through its fights from the time that we had our first votes?"

"Who, indeed?" said the Washington man.

"I tell you, gentlemen, the administration is no fool. It knows that we hold the colored vote down there in our vest pockets and it ain't going to turn us down."

"No, of course not, but sometimes there are delays——"

"Delays, to be sure, where a man doesn't know how to go about the matter. The thing to do, is to go right to the centre of authority at once. Don't you see?"

"Certainly, certainly," chorused the other gentlemen.

Before going, the Washington man suggested that the newcomer join them that evening and see something of society at the capital. "You know," he said, "that outside of New Orleans, Washington is

the only town in the country that has any colored society to speak
of, and I feel that you distinguished men from different sections of
the country owe it to our people that they should be allowed to see
you. It would be an inspiration to them."

So the matter was settled, and promptly at 8:30 o'clock Mr.
Cornelius Johnson joined his friends at the door of his hotel. The
grey Prince Albert was scrupulously buttoned about his form, and
a shiny top hat replaced the felt of the afternoon. Thus clad, he
went forth into society, where he need be followed only long
enough to note the magnificence of his manners and the enthusiasm of his reception when he was introduced as Prof. Cornelius
Johnson, of Alabama, in a tone which insinuated that he was the
only really great man his state had produced.

It might also be stated as an effect of this excursion into Vanity
Fair, that when he woke the next morning he was in some doubt as
to whether he should visit his Congressman or send for that individual to call upon him. He had felt the subtle flattery of attention
from that section of colored society which imitates—only imitates,
it is true, but better than any other, copies—the kindnesses and
cruelties, the niceties and deceits, of its white prototype. And for
the time, like a man in a fog, he had lost his sense of proportion
and perspective. But habit finally triumphed, and he called upon
the Congressman, only to be met by an under-secretary who told
him that his superior was too busy to see him that morning.

"But——"

"Too busy," repeated the secretary.

Mr. Johnson drew himself up and said: "Tell Congressman
Barker that Mr. Johnson, Mr. Cornelius Johnson, of Alabama,
desires to see him. I think he will see me."

"Well, I can take your message," said the clerk, doggedly, "but
I tell you now it won't do you any good. He won't see any one."

But, in a few moments an inner door opened, and the young
man came out followed by the desired one. Mr. Johnson couldn't
resist the temptation to let his eyes rest on the underling in a
momentary glance of triumph as Congressman Barker hurried up
to him, saying: "Why, why, Cornelius, how'do? how'do? Ah, you
came about that little matter, didn't you? Well, well, I haven't
forgotten you; I haven't forgotten you."

The colored man opened his mouth to speak, but the other
checked him and went on: "I'm sorry, but I'm in a great hurry
now. I'm compelled to leave town to-day, much against my will,

but I shall be back in a week; come around and see me then. Always glad to see you, you know. Sorry I'm so busy now; good-morning, good-morning."

Mr. Johnson allowed himself to be guided politely, but decidedly, to the door. The triumph died out of his face as the reluctant good-morning fell from his lips. As he walked away, he tried to look upon the matter philosophically. He tried to reason with himself—to prove to his own consciousness that the Congressman was very busy and could not give the time that morning. He wanted to make himself believe that he had not been slighted or treated with scant ceremony. But, try as he would, he continued to feel an obstinate, nasty sting that would not let him rest, nor forget his reception. His pride was hurt. The thought came to him to go at once to the President, but he had experience enough to know that such a visit would be vain until he had seen the dispenser of patronage for his district. Thus, there was nothing for him to do but to wait the necessary week. A whole week! His brow knitted as he thought of it.

In the course of these cogitations, his walk brought him to his hotel, where he found his friends of the night before awaiting him. He tried to put on a cheerful face. But his disappointment and humiliation showed through his smile, as the hollows and bones through the skin of a cadaver.

"Well, what luck?" asked Col. Mason, cheerfully.

"Are we to congratulate you?" put in Mr. Perry.

"Not yet, not yet, gentlemen. I have not seen the President yet. The fact is—ahem—my Congressman is out of town."

He was not used to evasions of this kind, and he stammered slightly and his yellow face turned brick-red with shame.

"It is most annoying," he went on, "most annoying. Mr. Barker won't be back for a week, and I don't want to call on the President until I have had a talk with him."

"Certainly not," said Col. Mason, blandly. "There will be delays." This was not his first pilgrimage to Mecca.

Mr. Johnson looked at him gratefully. "Oh, yes; of course, delays," he assented; "most natural. Have something."

At the end of the appointed time, the office-seeker went again to see the Congressman. This time he was admitted without question, and got the chance to state his wants. But somehow, there seemed to be innumerable obstacles in the way. There were certain other men whose wishes had to be consulted; the leader of one of the

party factions, who, for the sake of harmony, had to be appeased.
Of course, Mr. Johnson's worth was fully recognized, and he would
be rewarded according to his deserts. His interests would be looked
after. He should drop in again in a day or two. It took time, of
course, it took time.

Mr. Johnson left the office unnerved by his disappointment. He
had thought it would be easy to come up to Washington, claim
and get what he wanted, and, after a glance at the town, hurry
back to his home and his honors. It had all seemed so easy—before
election; but now——

A vague doubt began to creep into his mind that turned him
sick at heart. He knew how they had treated Davis, of Louisiana.
He had heard how they had once kept Brotherton, of Texas—a
man who had spent all his life in the service of his party—waiting
clear through a whole administration, at the end of which the
opposite party had come into power. All the stories of disappointment and disaster that he had ever heard came back to him, and
he began to wonder if some one of these things was going to
happen to him.

Every other day for the next two weeks, he called upon Barker,
but always with the same result. Nothing was clear yet, until one
day the bland legislator told him that considerations of expediency
had compelled them to give the place he was asking for to another
man.

"But what am I to do?" asked the helpless man.

"Oh, you just bide your time. I'll look out for you. Never fear."

Until now, Johnson had ignored the gentle hints of his friend,
Col. Mason, about a boardinghouse being more convenient than a
hotel. Now, he asked him if there was a room vacant where he was
staying, and finding that there was, he had his things moved
thither at once. He felt the change keenly, and although no one
really paid any attention to it, he believed that all Washington
must have seen it, and hailed it as the first step in his degradation.

For a while the two together made occasional excursions to a
glittering palace down the street, but when the money had grown
lower and lower Col. Mason had the knack of bringing "a little
something" to their rooms without a loss of dignity. In fact, it was
in these hours with the old man, over a pipe and a bit of something, that Johnson was most nearly cheerful. Hitch after hitch
had occurred in his plans, and day after day he had come home
unsuccessful and discouraged. The crowning disappointment,
though, came when, after a long session that lasted even up into
the hot days of summer, Congress adjourned and his one hope

went away. Johnson saw him just before his departure, and listened ruefully as he said: "I tell you, Cornelius, now, you'd better go on home, get back to your business and come again next year. The clouds of battle will be somewhat dispelled by then and we can see clearer what to do. It was too early this year. We were too near the fight still, and there were party wounds to be bound up and little factional sores that had to be healed. But next year, Cornelius, next year we'll see what we can do for you."

His constituent did not tell him that even if his pride would let him go back home a disappointed applicant, he had not the means wherewith to go. He did not tell him that he was trying to keep up appearances and hide the truth from his wife, who, with their two children, waited and hoped for him at home.

When he went home that night, Col. Mason saw instantly that things had gone wrong with him. But here the tact and delicacy of the old politician came uppermost and, without trying to draw his story from him—for he already divined the situation too well—he sat for a long time telling the younger man stories of the ups and downs of men whom he had known in his long and active life.

They were stories of hardship, deprivation and discouragement. But the old man told them ever with a touch of cheeriness and the note of humor that took away the ghastly hopelessness of some of the pictures. He told them with such feeling and sympathy that Johnson was moved to frankness and told him his own pitiful tale.

Now that he had some one to whom he could open his heart, Johnson himself was no less willing to look the matter in the face, and even during the long summer days, when he had begun to live upon his wardrobe, piece by piece, he still kept up; although some of his pomposity went, along with the Prince Albert coat and the shiny hat. He now wore a shiny coat, and less showy head-gear. For a couple of weeks, too, he disappeared, and as he returned with some money, it was fair to presume that he had been at work somewhere, but he could not stay away from the city long.

It was nearing the middle of autumn when Col. Mason came home to their rooms one day to find his colleague more disheartened and depressed than he had ever seen him before. He was lying with his head upon his folded arm, and when he looked up there were traces of tears upon his face.

"Why, why, what's the matter now?" asked the old man. "No bad news, I hope."

"Nothing worse than I should have expected," was the choking answer. "It's a letter from my wife. She's sick and one of the babies is down, but"—his voice broke—"she tells me to stay and fight it out. My God, Mason, I could stand it if she whined or accused me or begged me to come home, but her patient, long-suffering bravery breaks me all up."

Col. Mason stood up and folded his arms across his big chest. "She's a brave little woman," he said, gravely. "I wish her husband was as brave a man." Johnson raised his head and arms from the table where they were sprawled, as the old man went on: "The hard conditions of life in our race have taught our women a patience and fortitude which the women of no other race have ever displayed. They have taught the men less, and I am sorry, very sorry. The thing, that as much as anything else, made the blacks such excellent soldiers in the civil war was their patient endurance of hardship. The softer education of more prosperous days seems to have weakened this quality. The man who quails or weakens in this fight of ours against adverse circumstances would have quailed before—no, he would have run from an enemy on the field."

"Why, Mason, your mood inspires me. I feel as if I could go forth to battle cheerfully." For the moment, Johnson's old pomposity had returned to him, but in the next, a wave of despondency bore it down. "But that's just it; a body feels as if he could fight if he only had something to fight. But here you strike out and hit—nothing. It's only a contest with time. It's waiting—waiting—waiting!"

"In this case, waiting is fighting."

"Well, even that granted, it matters not how grand his cause, the soldier needs his rations."

"Forage," shot forth the answer like a command.

"Ah, Mason, that's well enough in good country; but the army of office-seekers has devastated Washington. It has left a track as bare as lay behind Sherman's troopers." Johnson rose more cheerfully. "I'm going to the telegraph office," he said as he went out.

A few days after this, he was again in the best of spirits, for there was money in his pocket.

"What have you been doing?" asked Mr. Toliver.

His friend laughed like a boy. "Something very imprudent, I'm sure you will say. I've mortgaged my little place down home. It did not bring much, but I had to have money for the wife and the children, and to keep me until Congress assembles; then I believe that everything will be all right."

Col. Mason's brow clouded and he sighed.

On the reassembling of the two Houses, Congressman Barker was one of the first men in his seat. Mr. Cornelius Johnson went to see him soon.

"What, you here already, Cornelius?" asked the legislator.

"I haven't been away," was the answer.

"Well, you've got the hang-on, and that's what an office-seeker needs. Well, I'll attend to your matter among the very first. I'll visit the President in a day or two."

The listener's heart throbbed hard. After all his waiting, triumph was his at last.

He went home walking on air, and Col. Mason rejoiced with him. In a few days came word from Barker: "Your appointment was sent in to-day. I'll rush it through on the other side. Come up to-morrow afternoon."

Cornelius and Mr. Toliver hugged each other.

"It came just in time," said the younger man; "the last of my money was about gone, and I should have had to begin paying off that mortgage with no prospect of ever doing it."

The two had suffered together, and it was fitting that they should be together to receive the news of the long-desired happiness; so arm in arm they sauntered down to the Congressman's office about five o'clock the next afternoon. In honor of the occasion, Mr. Johnson had spent his last dollar in redeeming the grey Prince Albert and the shiny hat. A smile flashed across Barker's face as he noted the change.

"Well, Cornelius," he said, "I'm glad to see you still prosperous-looking, for there were some alleged irregularities in your methods down in Alabama, and the Senate has refused to confirm you. I did all I could for you, but——"

The rest of the sentence was lost, as Col. Mason's arms received his friend's fainting form.

"Poor devil!" said the Congressman. "I should have broken it more gently."

Somehow Col. Mason got him home and to bed, where for nine weeks he lay wasting under a complete nervous give-down. The little wife and the children came up to nurse him, and the woman's ready industry helped him to such creature comforts as his sickness demanded. Never once did she murmur; never once did her faith in him waver. And when he was well enough to be moved back, it was money that she had earned, increased by what Col. Mason, in his generosity of spirit, took from his own narrow means, that paid their second-class fare back to the South.

During the fever-fits of his illness, the wasted politician first begged piteously that they would not send him home unplaced, and then he would break out in the most extravagant and pompous boasts about his position, his Congressman and his influence.

When he came to himself, he was silent, morose, and bitter. Only once did he melt. It was when he held Col. Mason's hand and bade him good-bye. Then the tears came into his eyes, and what he would have said was lost among his broken words.

As he stood upon the platform of the car as it moved out, and gazed at the white dome and feathery spires of the city, growing into grey indefiniteness, he ground his teeth, and raising his spent hand, shook it at the receding view. "Damn you! damn you!" he cried. "Damn your deceit, your fair cruelties; damn you, you hard, white liar!"

Jean Toomer (1894-1967)

Fern

In 1923 Jean Toomer seemed destined to be a major American writer. His poems and stories were eagerly sought by editors, and he had received accolades from such writers and critics as Sherwood Anderson, Waldo Frank, Gorham Munson, and W. S. Braithwaite. Except for a privately printed collection of aphorisms, however, Jean Toomer published no books after 1923. He remains, therefore, an important but tragic figure in black American literature.

Born in Washington, D. C., Nathan Eugene Toomer was the grandson of P. B. S. Pinchback, who, during Reconstruction, served as Acting Governor of Louisiana. After enrolling briefly at the University of Wisconsin, the American School of Physical Education in Chicago, the University of Chicago, the City College of New York, and New York University, where he considered and rejected studies in agriculture, physical education, medicine, sociology, and history, Jean Toomer settled on a career as a writer, which he interrupted by accepting a position as acting principal in Sparta, Georgia, in the fall of 1922. Inspired with the belief that he had located his roots in the ancestral home of his people, Toomer wrote poems, stories, and sketches, especially about Southern women whose gropings for self-realization forced them into conflict with the dominant moral attitudes of American society. When he returned to Washington, he wrote stories, poems, and sketches about more inhibited black people in Washington and

Chicago. He collected and published these as *Cane* (1923), a classic in black American literature.

Toomer's personal search for identity, however, did not end with *Cane*. A student of Eastern philosophies, he discovered a spiritual leader in George Gurdjieff and dedicated himself to teaching the Gurdjieffan ideas to the American people. In the process he smothered his lyricism under satire and didacticism by offering psychological case studies rather than sympathetic sketches. When publishers rejected these works, he accused them of restricting him to Negro subjects because they identified him as a Negro. Instead, he argued, he should be judged as an American rather than a Negro; subsequently, he even denied that he had any Negro ancestors. America refused to accept his attitudes about race. A weekly magazine made national scandal of his marriage to Caucasian Margery Latimer, a promising writer who had been his disciple in a Gurdjieffan experiment which the newspapers had characterized as a "free love" colony. Toomer attempted to answer his critics by writing novels about his marriage and about the Gurdieffan philosophy. Publishers continued to reject them. He succeeded only in publishing essays, in which he explained his belief that America would give birth to a new race—neither white nor black, but American.

The tragic death of his wife in childbirth, the Depression, and rejections by publishers turned the Thirties into a decade of tragedy relieved only by a second marriage. For the remainder of his life, Toomer searched for spiritual understanding through the Friends Society, psychiatry, and Indian mysticism. Occasionally he lectured to college students and to gatherings of the Friends. He continued to write plays, novels, poems, and stories; but, except for an occasional poem or story, his efforts went unpublished. He died in a rest home in 1967.

"Fern" reveals both the strengths and weaknesses of Toomer's early work. The style is lyric; the characterization is haunting; yet the piece is a sketch rather than a well-developed story.

Fern

Face flowed into her eyes. Flowed in soft cream foam and plaintive ripples, in such a way that wherever your glance may momentarily have rested it immediately thereafter wavered in the direction of her eyes. The soft suggestion of down slightly darkened, like the shadow of a bird's wing might, the creamy brown color of her upper lip. Why after noticing it you sought her eyes, I cannot tell you. Her nose was aquiline, Semitic. If you have heard a Jewish cantor sing, if he has touched you and made your own sorrow seem trivial when compared with his, you will know my feeling when I follow the curves of her profile, like mobile rivers, to their common delta. They were strange eyes. In this, that they sought nothing—that is, nothing that was obvious and tangible and that one could see, and they gave the impression that nothing was to be denied. When a woman seeks, you will have observed, her eyes deny. Fern's eyes desired nothing that you could give her; there was no reason why they should withhold. Men saw her eyes and fooled themselves. Fern's eyes said to them that she was easy. When she was young, a few men took her, but got no joy from it. And then, once done, they felt bound to her (quite unlike their hit and run with other girls), felt as though it would take them a lifetime to fulfill an obligation which they could find no name for. They became attached to her, and hungered after finding the barest trace of what she might desire. As she grew up, new men who came to town felt as almost everyone did who ever saw her: that they would not be denied. Men were everlastingly bringing her their bodies. Something inside of her got tired of them, I guess, for I am certain that for the life of her she could not tell why or how she began to turn them off. A man in fever is no trifling thing to send away. They began to leave her, baffled and ashamed, yet vowing to themselves that someday they would do some fine thing for her: send her candy every week and not let her know whom it came from, watch out for her wedding day and give her a magnificent something with no name on it, buy a house and deed it to her, rescue her from some unworthy fellow who had tricked her into marrying him. As you know, men are apt to idolize or fear that which they cannot understand, especially if it be a woman. She did not deny them, yet the fact was that they were denied. A sort of superstition crept into their consciousness of her being somehow above them. Being above them meant that she was not to be approached by anyone. She became a virgin. Now a virgin in a small Southern town is by no means the usual thing, if you will believe me. That the sexes were made to mate is the practice of the South. Particularly, black folks were made to mate. And it is black folks whom I have been talking about thus far. What white men thought of Fern I can arrive at only by analogy. They let her alone.

Anyone of course could see her, could see her eyes. If you walked up the Dixie Pike most any time of day, you'd be most like to see her resting listless-like on the railing of her porch, back propped against a post, head tilted a little forward because there was a nail in the porch post just where her head came which for some reason or other she never took the trouble to pull out. Her eyes, if it were sunset, rested idly where the sun, molten and glorious, was pouring down between the fringe of pines. Or maybe they gazed at the gray cabin on the knoll from which an evening folksong was coming. Perhaps they followed a cow that had been turned loose to roam and feed on cotton stalks and corn leaves. Like as not they'd settle on some vague spot above the horizon, though hardly a trace of wistfulness would come to them. If it were dusk, then they'd wait for the searchlight of the evening train which you could see miles up the track before it flared across the Dixie Pike, close to her home. Wherever they looked, you'd follow them and then waver back. Like her face, the whole countryside seemed to flow into her eyes. Flowed into them with the soft listless cadence of Georgia's South. A young Negro, once, was looking at her spellbound from the road. A white man passing in a buggy had to flick him with his whip if he was to get by without running him over. I first saw her on her porch. I was passing with a fellow whose crusty numbness (I was from the North and suspected of being prejudiced and stuck-up) was melting as he found me warm. I asked him who she was. "That's Fern," was all that I could get from him. Some folks already thought I was given to nosing around; I let it go at that, so far as questions were concerned. But at first sight of her I felt as if I heard a Jewish cantor sing. As if his singing rose above the unheard chorus of a folksong. And I felt bound to her. I too had my dreams: something I would do for her. I have knocked about from town to town too much not to know the futility of mere change of place. Besides, picture if you can this cream-colored solitary girl sitting at a tenement window looking down on the indifferent throngs of Harlem. Better that she listen to folksongs at dusk in Georgia, you would say, and so would I. Or suppose she came up North and married. Even a doctor or a lawyer, say, one who would be sure to get along—that is, make money. You and I know, who have had experience in such things, that love is not a thing like prejudice which can be bettered by changes of town. Could men in Washington, Chicago, or New York, more than the men of Georgia, bring her something left vacant by the bestowal of their bodies? You and I who know men

in these cities will have to say, they could not. See her out and out
a prostitute along State Street in Chicago. See her move into a
Southern town where white men are more aggressive. See her
become a white man's concubine. . . . Something I must do for her.
There was myself. What could I do for her? Talk, of course. Push
back the fringe of pines upon new horizons. To what purpose? and
what for? Her? Myself? Men in her case seem to lose their selfish-
ness. I lost mine before I touched her. I ask you, friend (it makes
no difference if you sit in the Pullman or the Jim Crow as the train
crosses her road), what thoughts would come to you—that is, after
you'd finished with the thoughts that leap into men's minds at the
sight of a pretty woman who will not deny them; what thoughts
would come to you, had you seen her in a quick flash, keen and
intuitively, as she sat there on her porch when your train thundered by? Would you have got off at the next station and come
back for her to take her, where? Would you have completely
forgotten her as soon as you reached Macon, Atlanta, Augusta,
Pasadena, Madison, Chicago, Boston, or New Orleans? Would you
tell your wife or sweetheart about a girl you saw? Your thoughts
can help me, and I would like to know. Something I would do for
her. . . .

One evening I walked up the Pike on purpose, and stopped to
say hello. Some of her family were about, but they moved away to
make room for me. Damn if I knew how to begin. Would you? Mr.
and Miss So-and-So, people, the weather, the crops, the new
preacher, the frolic, the church benefit, rabbit and possum hunting, the new soft drink they had at old Pap's store, the schedule
of the trains, what kind of town Macon was, Negro's migration
north, boll weevils, syrup, the Bible—to all these things she gave a
yassur or nassur, without further comment. I began to wonder if
perhaps my own emotional sensibility had played one of its tricks
on me. "Let's take a walk," I at last ventured. The suggestion,
coming after so long an isolation, was novel enough, I guess, to
surprise. But it wasn't that. Something told me that men before
me had said just that as a prelude to the offering of their bodies. I
tried to tell her with my eyes. I think she understood. The thing
from her that made my throat catch, vanished. Its passing left her
visible in a way I'd thought, but never seen. We walked down the
Pike with people on all the porches gaping at us. "Doesn't it make
you mad?" She meant the world. Through a canebrake that was
ripe for cutting, the branch was reached. Under a sweet-gum tree,
and where reddish leaves had dammed the creek a little, we sat

down. Dusk, suggesting the almost imperceptible procession of giant trees, settled with a purple haze about the cane. I felt strange, as I always do in Georgia, particularly at dusk. I felt that things unseen to men were tangibly immediate. It would not have surprised me had I had a vision. People have them in Georgia more often then you would suppose. A black woman once saw the mother of Christ and drew her in charcoal on the courthouse wall. . . . When one is on the soil of one's ancestors, most anything can come to one. . . . From force of habit, I suppose, I held Fern in my arms—that is, without at first noticing it. Then my mind came back to her. Her eyes, unusually weird and open, held me. Held God. He flowed in as I've seen the countryside flow in. Seen men. I must have done something—what, I don't know, in the confusion of my emotion. She sprang up. Rushed some distance from me. Fell to her knees, and began swaying, swaying. Her body was tortured with something it could not let out. Like boiling sap it flooded arms and fingers till she shook them as if they burned her. It found her throat, and spattered inarticulately in plaintive, convulsive sounds, mingled with calls to Christ Jesus. And then she sang, brokenly. A Jewish cantor singing with a broken voice. A child's voice, uncertain, or an old man's. Dusk hid her; I could hear only her song. It seemed to me as though she were pounding her head in anguish upon the ground. I rushed to her. She fainted in my arms.

There was talk about her fainting with me in the canefield. And I got one or two ugly looks from town men who'd set themselves up to protect her. In fact, there was talk of making me leave town. But they never did. They kept a watch out for me, though. Shortly after, I came back North. From the train window I saw her as I crossed her road. Saw her on her porch, head tilted a little forward where the nail was, eyes vaguely focused on the sunset. Saw her face flow into them, the countryside and something that I call God, flowing into them. . . . Nothing ever really happened. Nothing ever came to Fern, not even I. Something I would do for her. Some fine unnamed thing. . . . And, friend, you? She is still living, I have reason to know. Her name, against the chance that you might happen down that way, is Fernie May Rosen.

Wallace Thurman (1902-1934)

Cordelia the Crude

Born in Salt Lake City, Utah, and educated at the University of Southern California, Wallace Thurman was a leader among the young black intelligensia who earned their literary reputations during the Harlem Renaissance. A magazine writer and a member of the editorial staffs of *The Messenger* and the Macaulay Publishing Company, Thurman is best known to contemporary readers for *The Blacker the Berry* (1929), a novel examining the problem of a young woman who feels inferior and alienated because she has dark skin. In the same year Thurman collaborated with W. J. Rapp on *Harlem*, a play which ran briefly on Broadway. Two years before he died from tuberculosis, he wrote a second novel, *Infants of the Spring*, which satirizes black artists of the Twenties.

"Cordelia the Crude," taken from *Fire*, a short-lived periodical which Thurman helped found, is one of his earliest stories. It demonstrates the irony which he later sharpened in his novels.

Cordelia the Crude

Physically, if not mentally, Cordelia was a potential prostitute, meaning that although she had not yet realized the moral import of her wanton promiscuity nor become mercenary, she had, nevertheless, become quite blasé and bountiful in the matter of bestowing sexual favors upon persuasive and likely young men. Yet,

From *Fire,* I (November, 1926).

despite her seeming lack of discrimination, Cordelia was quite
particular about the type of male to whom she submitted, for
numbers do not necessarily denote a lack of taste, and Cordelia
had discovered after several months of active observation that one
could find the qualities one admires or reacts positively to in a
varied hodge-podge of outwardly different individuals.

The scene of Cordelia's activities was The Roosevelt Motion
Picture Theatre on Seventh Avenue near 145th Street. Thrice
weekly the program changed, and thrice weekly Cordelia would
plunk down the necessary twenty-five cents evening admission fee,
and saunter gaily into the foul-smelling depths of her favorite
cinema shrine. The Roosevelt Theatre presented all of the latest
pictures, also, twice weekly, treated its audiences to a vaudeville
bill, then too, one could always have the most delightly physical
contacts . . . hmm. . . .

Cordelia had not consciously chosen this locale nor had there
been any conscious effort upon her part to take advantage of the
extra opportunities afforded for physical pleasure. It had just
happened that the Roosevelt Theatre was more close to her home
than any other neighborhood picture palace, and it had also just
happened that Cordelia had become almost immediately initiated
into the ways of a Harlem theatre chippie soon after her discovery
of the theatre itself.

It is the custom of certain men and boys who frequent these
places to idle up and down the aisle until some female is seen
sitting alone, to slouch down into a seat beside her, to touch her
foot or else press her leg in such a way that it can be construed as
accidental if necessary, and then, if the female is wise or else shows
signs of willingness to become wise, to make more obvious approaches until, if successful, the approached female will soon be
chatting with her baiter about the picture being shown, lolling in
his arms, and helping to formulate plans for an after-theatre rendezvous. Cordelia had, you see, shown a willingness to become wise
upon her second visit to The Roosevelt. In a short while she had
even learned how to squelch the bloated, lewd faced Jews and
eager middle aged Negroes who might approach as well as how to
inveigle the likeable little yellow or brown half men, embryo avenue sweetbacks, with their well modeled heads, stickily plastered
hair, flaming cravats, silken or broadcloth shirts, dirty underwear,
low cut vests, form fitting coats, bell-bottom trousers and shiny
shoes with metal cornered heels clicking with a brave, brazen

rhythm upon the bare concrete floor as their owners angled and searched for prey.

Cordelia, sixteen years old, matronly mature, was an undisciplined, half literate product of rustic South Carolina, and had come to Harlem very much against her will with her parents and her six brothers and sisters. Against her will because she had not been at all anxious to leave the lackadaisical life of the little corn pone settlement where she had been born, to go trooping into the unknown vastness of New York, for she had been in love, passionately in love with one John Stokes who raised pigs, and who, like his father before him, found the raising of pigs so profitable that he could not even consider leaving Lintonville. Cordelia had blankly informed her parents that she would not go with them when they decided to be lured to New York by an older son who had remained there after the demobilization of the war time troops. She had even threatened to run away with John until they should be gone, but of course John could not leave his pigs, and John's mother was not very keen on having Cordelia for a daughter-in-law—those Joneses have bad mixed blood in 'em—so Cordelia had had to join the Gotham bound caravan and leave her lover to his succulent porkers.

However, the mere moving to Harlem had not doused the rebellious flame. Upon arriving Cordelia had not only refused to go to school and refused to hold even the most easily held job, but had also victoriously defied her harassed parents so frequently when it came to matters of discipline that she soon found herself with a mesmerizing lack of home restraint, for the stress of trying to maintain themselves and their family in the new environment was far too much of a task for Mr. and Mrs. Jones to attend to facilely and at the same time try to control a recalcitrant child. So, when Cordelia had refused either to work or to attend school, Mrs. Jones herself had gone out for day's work, leaving Cordelia at home to take care of their five room railroad flat, the front room of which was rented out to a couple "living together," and to see that the younger children, all of whom were of school age, made their four trips daily between home and the nearby public school—as well as see that they had their greasy, if slim, food rations and an occasional change of clothing. Thus Cordelia's days were full—and so were her nights. The only difference being that the days belonged to the folks at home while the nights (since the folks were too tired or too sleepy to know or care when she came in or went

out) belonged to her and to—well—whosoever will, let them
come.

Cordelia had been playing this hectic, entrancing game for six
months and was widely known among a certain group of young
men and girls on the avenue as a fus' class chippie when she and I
happened to enter the theatre simultaneously. She had clumped
down the aisle before me, her open galoshes swishing noisily, her
two arms busy wriggling themselves free from the torn sleeve
lining of a shoddy imitation fur coat that one of her mother's wash
clients had sent to her. She was of medium height and build, with
overly developed legs and bust, and had a clear, keen light brown
complexion. Her too slick, too naturally bobbed hair, mussed by
the removing of a tight, black turban was of an undecided nature,
i.e., it was undecided whether to be kinky or to be kind, and her
body, as she sauntered along in the partial light had such a
conscious sway of invitation that unthinkingly I followed, slid into
the same row of seats and sat down beside her.

Naturally she had noticed my pursuit, and thinking that I was
eager to play the game, let me know immediately that she was
wise, and not the least bit averse to spooning with me during the
evening's performance. Interested, and, I might as well confess,
intrigued physically, I too became wise, and played up to her with
all the fervor, or so I thought, of an old timer, but Cordelia soon
remarked that I was different from mos' of des' sheiks, and when
pressed for an explanation brazenly told me in a slightly scandal-
ized and patronizing tone that I had not even felt her legs . . . !

At one o'clock in the morning we strolled through the snowy
bleakness of one hundred and forty-fourth street between Lenox
and Fifth Avenues to the walk-up tenement flat in which she lived,
and after stamping the snow from our feet, pushed through the
double outside doors, and followed the dismal hallway to the rear
of the building where we began the tedious climbing of the
crooked, creaking, inconveniently narrow stairway. Cordelia had
informed me earlier in the evening that she lived on the top
floor—four flights up east side rear—and on our way we rested at
each floor and at each halfway landing, rested long enough to
mingle the snowy dampness of our respective coats, and to hug
clumsily while our lips met in an animal kiss.

Finally only another half flight remained, and instead of pro-
ceeding as was usual after our amorous demonstration I abruptly
drew away from her, opened my overcoat, plunged my hand into
my pants pocket, and drew out two crumpled one dollar bills

which I handed to her, and then, while she stared at me foolishly, I muttered good-night, confusedly pecked her on her cold brown cheek, and darted down into the creaking darkness.

Six months later I was taking two friends of mine, lately from the provinces, to a Saturday night house-rent party in a well known whore house on one hundred and thirty-fourth street near Lenox Avenue. The place as we entered seemed to be a chaotic riot of raucous noise and clashing color all rhythmically merging in the red, smoke filled room. And there I saw Cordelia savagely careening in a drunken abortion of the Charleston and surrounded by a perspiring circle of handclapping enthusiasts. Finally fatigued, she whirled into an abrupt finish, and stopped so that she stared directly into my face, but being dizzy from the calisthenic turns and the cauterizing liquor she doubted that her eyes recognized someone out of the past, and, visibly trying to sober herself, languidly began to dance a slow drag with a lean hipped pimply faced yellow man who had walked between her and me. At last he released her, and seeing that she was about to leave the room I rushed forward calling Cordelia?—as if I was not yet sure who it was. Stopping in the doorway, she turned to see who had called, and finally recognizing me said simply, without the least trace of emotion—'Lo kid. . . .

And without another word turned her back and walked into the hall to where she joined four girls standing there. Still eager to speak, I followed and heard one of the girls ask: Who's the dicty kid? . . .

And Cordelia answered: The guy who gimme ma' firs' two bucks. . . .

Zora Neale Hurston (1903-1958)

Sweat

During her lifetime, Zora Neale Hurston earned respect both as a novelist and as a folklorist. Born in the all-Negro town of Eatonville, Florida, she worked as a maid and waitress and attended Morgan College and Howard University before earning a degree at Barnard, where she studied anthropology under Franz Boas while serving as personal secretary for Fannie Hurst. Supported by research grants, Miss Hurston collected Negro folklore in Florida, Louisiana, and, later, in Haiti and other parts of the Caribbean. Thus, she became the first black writer since Charles Chesnutt to give attention to the literary and cultural importance of folk material.

During the 1920's Miss Hurston began writing short stories about Southern Negroes, but she did not gain national prominence until the Thirties, when she published *Jonah's Gourd Vine* (1934), *Mules and Men* (1935), *Their Eyes Were Watching God* (1937), *Tell My Horse* (1938), and *Moses, Man of the Mountain* (1939). *Jonah's Gourd Vine* and *Their Eyes Were Watching God* are novels about Southern Negroes relatively unaffected by interracial conflicts. *Moses*, a satirical novel, draws delightful analogues between black Americans and "The Hebrew Children." *Mules and Men* and *Tell My Horse* are collections of folklore. After a long silence, Miss Hurston published her final novel, *Seraph in the Suwanee* (1948). When she died, she was reported to be working on another novel with a Biblical setting.

From *Fire,* I (November, 1926).

"Sweat," one of her first stories, reveals three major emphases of her work: skill in presenting the picturesque idiom of Southern Negroes, credible characterization, and her absorption with love and hatred in intrafamilial relationships. In her fiction, men and women love each other totally, or they hate vengefully.

Sweat

It was eleven o'clock of a Spring night in Florida. It was Sunday. Any other night, Delia Jones would have been in bed for two hours by this time. But she was a washwoman, and Monday morning meant a great deal to her. So she collected the soiled clothes on Saturday when she returned the clean things. Sunday night after church, she sorted them and put the white things to soak. It saved her almost a half day's start. A great hamper in the bedroom held the clothes that she brought home. It was so much neater than a number of bundles lying around.

She squatted in the kitchen floor beside the great pile of clothes, sorting them into small heaps according to color, and humming a song in a mournful key, but wondering through it all where Sykes, her husband, had gone with her horse and buckboard.

Just then something long, round, limp and black fell upon her shoulders and slithered to the floor beside her. A great terror took hold of her. It softened her knees and dried her mouth so that it was a full minute before she could cry out or move. Then she saw that it was the big bull whip her husband liked to carry when he drove.

She lifted her eyes to the door and saw him standing there bent over with laughter at her fright. She screamed at him.

"Sykes, what you throw dat whip on me like dat? You know it would skeer me—looks just like a snake, an' you knows how skeered Ah is of snakes."

"Course Ah knowed it! That's how come Ah done it." He slapped his leg with his hand and almost rolled on the ground in his mirth. "If you such a big fool dat you got to have a fit over a earth worm or a string, Ah don't keer how bad Ah skeer you."

"You aint got no business doing it. Gawd knows it's a sin. Some day Ah'm gointuh drop dead from some of yo' foolishness. 'Nother thing, where you been wid mah rig? Ah feeds dat pony. He aint fuh you to be drivin' wid no bull whip."

"You sho is one aggravatin' nigger woman!" he declared and stepped into the room. She resumed her work and did not answer him at once. "Ah done tole you time and again to keep them white folks' clothes outa dis house."

He picked up the whip and glared down at her. Delia went on with her work. She went out into the yard and returned with a galvanized tub and set it on the washbench. She saw that Sykes had kicked all of the clothes together again, and now stood in her way truculently, his whole manner hoping, *praying*, for an argument. But she walked calmly around him and commenced to resort the things.

"Next time, Ah'm gointer kick 'em outdoors," he threatened as he struck a match along the leg of his corduroy breeches.

Delia never looked up from her work, and her thin, stooped shoulders sagged further.

"Ah aint for no fuss t'night Sykes. Ah just come from taking sacrament at the church house."

He snorted scornfully. "Yeah, you just come from de church house on a Sunday night, but heah you is gone to work on them clothes. You ain't nothing but a hypocrite. One of them amen-corner Christians—sing, whoop, and shout, then come home and wash white folks clothes on the Sabbath."

He stepped roughly upon the whitest pile of things, kicking them helter-skelter as he crossed the room. His wife gave a little scream of dismay, and quickly gathered them together again.

"Sykes, you quit grindin' dirt into these clothes! How can Ah git through by Sat'day if Ah don't start on Sunday?"

"Ah don't keer if you never git through. Anyhow, Ah done promised Gawd and a couple of other men, Ah aint gointer have it in mah house. Don't gimme no lip neither, else Ah'll throw 'em out and put mah fist up side yo' head to boot."

Delia's habitual meekness seemed to slip from her shoulders like a blown scarf. She was on her feet; her poor little body, her bare knuckly hands bravely defying the strapping hulk before her.

"Looka heah, Sykes, you done gone too fur. Ah been married to you fur fifteen years, and Ah been takin' in washin' fur fifteen years. Sweat, sweat, sweat! Work and sweat, cry and sweat, pray and sweat!"

"What's that got to do with me?" he asked brutally.

"What's it got to do with you, Sykes? Mah tub of suds is filled yo' belly with vittles more times than yo' hands is filled it. Mah sweat is done paid for this house and Ah reckon Ah kin keep on sweatin' in it."

She seized the iron skillet from the stove and struck a defensive pose, which act surprised him greatly, coming from her. It cowed him and he did not strike her as he usually did.

"Naw you won't," she panted, "that ole snaggle-toothed black woman you runnin' with aint comin' heah to pile up on *mah* sweat and blood. You aint paid for nothin' on this place, and Ah'm gointer stay right heah till Ah'm toted out foot foremost."

"Well, you better quit gittin' me riled up, else they'll be totin' you out sooner than you expect. Ah'm so tired of you Ah don't know whut to do. Gawd! how Ah hates skinny wimmen!"

A little awed by this new Delia, he sidled out of the door and slammed the back gate after him. He did not say where he had gone, but she knew too well. She knew very well that he would not return until nearly daybreak also. Her work over, she went on to bed but not to sleep at once. Things had come to a pretty pass!

She lay awake, gazing upon the debris that cluttered their matrimonial trail. Not an image left standing along the way. Anything like flowers had long ago been drowned in the salty stream that had been pressed from her heart. Her tears, her sweat, her blood. She had brought love to the union and he had brought a longing after the flesh. Two months after the wedding, he had given her the first brutal beating. She had the memory of his numerous trips to Orlando with all of his wages when he had returned to her penniless, even before the first year had passed. She was young and soft then, but now she thought of her knotty, muscles limbs, her harsh knuckly hands, and drew herself up into an unhappy little ball in the middle of the big feather bed. Too late now to hope for love, even if it were not Bertha it would be someone else. This case differed from the others only in that she was bolder than the others. Too late for everything except her little home. She had built it for her old days, and planted one by one the trees and flowers there. It was lovely to her, lovely.

Somehow, before sleep came, she found herself saying aloud: "Oh well, whatever goes over the Devil's back, is got to come under his belly. Sometime or ruther, Sykes, like everybody else, is gointer reap his sowing." After that she was able to build a spiritual earthworks against her husband. His shells could no longer reach her. *Amen.* She went to sleep and slept until he announced his presence in bed by kicking her feet and rudely snatching the cover away.

"Gimme some kivah heah, an' git yo' damn foots over on yo' own side! Ah oughter mash you in yo' mouf fuh drawing dat skillet on me."

Delia went clear to the rail without answering him. A triumphant indifference to all that he was or did.

The week was as full of work for Delia as all other weeks, and Saturday found her behind her little pony, collecting and delivering clothes.

It was a hot, hot day near the end of July. The village men on Joe Clarke's porch even chewed cane listlessly. They did not hurl the cane-knots as usual. They let them dribble over the edge of the porch. Even conversation had collapsed under the heat.

"Heah come Delia Jones," Jim Merchant said, as the shaggy pony came 'round the bend of the road toward them. The rusty buckboard was heaped with baskets of crisp, clean laundry.

"Yep," Joe Lindsay agreed. "Hot or col', rain or shine, jes ez reg'lar ez de weeks roll roun' Delia carries 'em an' fetches 'em on Sat'day."

"She better if she wanter eat," said Moss. "Syke Jones aint wuth de shot an' powder hit would tek tuh kill 'em. Not to *huh* he aint."

"He sho' aint," Walter Thomas chimed in. "It's too bad, too, cause she wuz a right pritty lil trick when he got huh. Ah'd uh mah'ied huh mahseff if he hadnter beat me to it."

Delia nodded briefly at the men as she drove past.

"Too much knockin' will ruin *any* 'oman. He done beat huh 'nough tuh kill three women, let 'lone change they looks," said Elijah Moseley. "How Syke kin stommuck dat big black greasy Mogul he's layin' roun' wid, gits me. Ah swear dat eight-rock couldn't kiss a sardine can Ah done thowed out de back do' 'way las' yeah."

"Aw, she's fat, thass how come. He's allus been crazy 'bout fat women," put in Merchant. "He'd a' been tied up wid one long time ago if he could a' found one tuh have him. Did Ah tell yuh 'bout him come sidlin' roun' *mah* wife—bringin' her a basket uh pecans outa his yard fuh a present? Yessir, mah wife! She tol' him tuh take 'em right straight back home, cause Delia works so hard ovah dat washtub she reckon everything on de place taste lak sweat an' soapsuds. Ah jus' wisht Ah'd a' caught 'im 'roun' dere! Ah'd a' made his hips ketch on fiah down dat shell road."

"Ah know he done it, too. Ah sees 'im grinnin' at every 'oman dat passes," Walter Thomas said. "But even so, he useter eat some mighty big hunks uh humble pie tuh git dat lil' 'oman he got. She wuz ez pritty ez a speckled pup! Dat wuz fifteen yeahs ago. He useter be so skeered uh losin' huh, she could make him do some parts of a husband's duty. Dey never wuz de same in de mind."

"There oughter be a law about him," said Lindsay. "He aint fit tuh carry guts tuh a bear."

Clarke spoke for the first time. "Taint no law on earth dat kin make a man be decent if it aint in 'im. There's plenty men dat takes a wife lak dey do a joint uh sugar-cane. It's round, juicy an' sweet when dey gits it. But dey squeeze an' grind, squeeze an' grind an' wring tell dey wring every drop uh pleasure dat's in 'em out. When dey's satisfied dat dey is wrung dry, dey treats 'em jes lak dey do a cane-chew. Dey thows 'em away. Dey knows whut dey is doin' while dey is at it, an' hates theirselves fuh it but they keeps on hangin' after huh tell she's empty. Den dey hates huh fuh bein' a cane-chew an' in de way."

"We oughter take Syke an' dat stray 'oman uh his'n down in Lake Howell swamp an' lay on de rawhide till they cain't say 'Lawd a' mussy.' He allus wuz uh ovahbearin' niggah, but since dat white 'oman from up north done teached 'im how to run a automobile, he done got too biggety to live—an' we oughter kill 'im," Old Man Anderson advised.

A grunt of approval went around the porch. But the heat was melting their civic virtue and Elijah Moseley began to bait Joe Clarke.

"Come on, Joe, git a melon outa dere an' slice it up for yo' customers. We'se all sufferin' wid de heat. De bear's done got *me!*"

"Thass right, Joe, a watermelon is jes' whut Ah needs tuh cure de eppizudicks," Walter Thomas joined forces with Moseley. "Come on dere, Joe. We all is steady customers an' you aint set us up in a long time. Ah chooses dat long, bowlegged Floridy favorite."

"A god, an' be dough. You all gimme twenty cents and slice away," Clarke retorted. "Ah needs a col' slice m'self. Heah, everybody chip in. Ah'll lend y'll mah meat knife."

The money was quickly subscribed and the huge melon brought forth. At that moment, Sykes and Bertha arrived. A determined silence fell on the porch and the melon was put away again.

Merchant snapped down the blade of his jackknife and moved toward the store door.

"Come on in, Joe, an' gimme a slab uh sow belly an' uh pound uh coffee—almost fuhgot 'twas Sat'day. Got to git on home." Most of the men left also.

Just then Delia drove past on her way home, as Sykes was ordering magnificently for Bertha. It pleased him for Delia to see.

"Git whutsoever yo' heart desires, Honey. Wait a minute, Joe. Give huh two botles uh strawberry soda-water, uh quart uh parched ground-peas, an' a block uh chewin' gum."

With all this they left the store, with Sykes reminding Bertha that this was his town and she could have it if she wanted it.

The men returned soon after they left, and held their watermelon feast.

"Where did Syke Jones git da 'oman from nohow?" Lindsay asked.

"Ovah Apopka. Guess dey musta been cleanin' out de town when she lef'. She don't look lak a thing but a hunk uh liver wid hair on it."

"Well, she sho' kin squall," Dave Carter contributed. "When she gits ready tuh laff, she jes' opens huh mouf an' latches it back tuh de las' notch. No ole grandpa alligator down in Lake Bell ain't got nothin' on huh."

Bertha had been in town three months now. Sykes was still paying her room rent at Della Lewis'—the only house in town that would have taken her in. Sykes took her frequently to Winter Park to "stomps." He still assured her that he was the swellest man in the state.

"Sho' you kin have dat lil' ole house soon's Ah kin git dat 'oman outa dere. Everything b'longs tuh me an' you sho' kin have it. Ah sho' 'bominates uh skinny 'oman. Lawdy, you sho' is got one portly shape on you! You kin git *anything* you wants. Dis is *mah* town an' you sho' kin have it."

Delia's work-worn knees crawled over the earth in Gethsemane and up the rocks of Calvary many, many times during these months. She avoided the villagers and meeting places in her efforts to be blind and deaf. But Bertha nullified this to a degree, by coming to Delia's house to call Sykes out to her at the gate.

Delia and Sykes fought all the time now with no peaceful interludes. They slept and ate in silence. Two or three times Delia had attempted a timid friendliness, but she was repulsed each time. It was plain that the breaches must remain agape.

The sun had burned July to August. The heat streamed down like a million hot arrows, smiting all things living upon the earth. Grass withered, leaves browned, snakes went blind in shedding and men and dogs went mad. Dog days!

Delia came home one day and found Sykes there before her. She wondered, but started to go on into the house without speaking, even though he was standing in the kitchen door and she must either stoop under his arm or ask him to move. He made no room for her. She noticed a soap box beside the steps, but paid no particular attention to it, knowing that he must have brought it there. As she was stooping to pass under his outstretched arm, he suddenly pushed her backward, laughingly.

"Look in de box dere Delia, Ah done brung yuh somethin'!"

She nearly fell upon the box in her stumbling, and when she saw what it held, she all but fainted outright.

"Syke! Syke, mah Gawd! You take dat rattlesnake 'way from heah! You *gottuh*. Oh, Jesus, have mussy!"

"Ah aint gut tuh do nuthin' uh de kin'—fact is Ah aint got tuh do nothin' but die. Taint no use uh you puttin' on airs makin' out lak you skeered uh dat snake—he's gointer stay right heah tell he die. He wouldn't bite me cause Ah knows how tuh handle 'im. Nohow he wouldn't risk breakin' out his fangs 'gin *yo'* skinny laigs."

"Naw, now Syke, don't keep dat thing 'roun' heah tuh skeer me tuh death. You knows Ah'm even feared uh earth worms. Thass de biggest snake Ah evah did see. Kill 'im Syke, please."

"Doan ast me tuh do nothin' fuh yuh. Goin' 'roun' tryin' tuh be so damn asterperious. Naw, Ah aint gonna kill it. Ah think uh damn sight mo' uh him dan you! Dat's a nice snake an' anybody doan lak 'im kin jes' hit de grit."

The village soon heard that Sykes had the snake, and came to see and ask questions.

"How de hen-fire did you ketch dat six-foot rattler, Syke?" Thomas asked.

"He's full uh frogs so he caint hardly move, thass how Ah eased up on 'm. But Ah'm a snake charmer an' knows how tuh handle 'em. Shux, dat aint nothin'. Ah could ketch one eve'y day if Ah so wanted tuh."

"Whut he needs is a heavy hick'ry club leaned real heavy on his head. Dat's de bes 'way tuh charm a rattlesnake."

"Naw, Walt, y'll jes' don't understand dese diamon' backs lak Ah do," said Sykes in a superior tone of voice.

The village agreed with Walter, but the snake stayed on. His box remained by the kitchen door with its screen wire covering. Two or three days later it had digested its meal of frogs and literally came to life. It rattled at every movement in the kitchen or the yard. One day as Delia came down the kitchen steps she saw his chalky-white fangs curved like scimitars hung in the wire meshes. This time she did not run away with averted eyes as usual. She stood for a long time in the doorway in a red fury that grew bloodier for every second that she regarded the creature that was her torment.

That night she broached the subject as soon as Sykes sat down to the table.

"Syke, Ah wants you tuh take dat snake 'way fum heah. You done starved me an' Ah put up widcher, you done beat me an Ah took dat, but you done kilt all mah insides bringin' dat varmint heah."

Sykes poured out a saucer full of coffee and drank it deliberately before he answered her.

"A whole lot Ah keer 'bout how you feels inside uh out. Dat snake aint goin' no damn wheah till Ah gits ready fuh 'im tuh go. So fur as beatin' is concerned, yuh aint took near all dat you gointer take ef yuh stay 'roun' *me*."

Delia pushed back her plate and got up from the table. "Ah hates you, Sykes," she said calmly. "Ah hates you tuh de same degree dat Ah useter love yuh. Ah done took an' took till mah belly is full up tuh mah neck. Dat's de reason Ah got mah letter fum de church an' moved mah membership tuh Woodbridge—so Ah don't haftuh take no sacrament wid yuh. Ah don't wantuh see yuh 'roun' me atall. Lay 'roun' wid dat 'oman all yuh wants tuh, but gwan 'way fum me an' mah house. Ah hates yuh lak uh suck-egg dog."

Sykes almost let the huge wad of corn bread and collard greens he was chewing fall out of his mouth in amazement. He had a hard time whipping himself up to the proper fury to try to answer Delia.

"Well, Ah'm glad you does hate me. Ah'm sho' tiahed uh you hangin' ontuh me. Ah don't want yuh. Look at yuh stringey ole neck! Yo' rawbony laigs an' arms is enough tuh cut uh man tuh death. You looks jes' lak de devvul's doll-baby tuh *me*. You cain't hate me no worse dan Ah hates you. Ah been hatin' *you* fuh years.

"Yo' ole black hide don't look lak nothin' tuh me, but uh passle uh wrinkled up rubber, wid yo' big ole yeahs flappin' on each side lak up paih uh buzzard wings. Don't think Ah'm gointuh be run 'way fum mah house neither. Ah'm goin' tuh de white folks bout *you*, mah young man, de very nex' time you lay yo' han's on me. Mah cup is done run ovah." Delia said this with no signs of fear and Sykes departed from the house, threatening her, but made not the slightest move to carry out any of them.

That night he did not return at all, and the next day being Sunday, Delia was glad she did not have to quarrel before she hitched up her pony and drove the four miles to Woodbridge.

She stayed to the night service—"love feast"—which was very warm and full of spirit. In the emotional winds her domestic trials were borne far and wide so that she sang as she drove homeward,

> *"Jurden water, black an' col'*
> *Chills de body, not de soul*
> *An' Ah wantah cross Jurden in uh calm time."*

She came from the barn to the kitchen door and stopped.

"Whut's de mattah, ol' satan, you aint kickin' up yo' racket?" She addressed the snake's box. Complete silence. She went on into the house with a new hope in its birth struggles. Perhaps her threat to go to the white folks had frightened Sykes! Perhaps he was sorry! Fifteen years of misery and suppression had brought Delia to the place where she would hope *anything* that looked towards a way over or through her wall of inhibitions.

She felt in the match safe behind the stove at once for a match. There was only one there.

"Dat niggah wouldn't fetch nothin' heah tuh save his rotten neck, but he kin run thew whut Ah brings quick enough. Now he done toted off nigh on tuh haff uh box uh matches. He done had dat 'oman heah in mah house, too."

Nobody but a woman could tell how she knew this even before she struck the match. But she did and it put her into a new fury.

Presently she brought in the tubs to put the white things to soak. This time she decided she need not bring the hamper out of the bedroom; she would go in there and do the sorting. She picked up the pot-bellied lamp and went in. The room was small and the hamper stood hard by the foot of the white iron bed. She could sit and reach through the bedposts—resting as she worked.

"Ah wantah cross Jurden in uh calm time." She was singing again. The mood of the "love feast" had returned. She threw back the lid of the basket almost gaily. Then, moved by both horror and terror, she sprang back toward the door. *There lay the snake in the basket!* He moved sluggishly at first, but even as she turned round and round, jumped up and down in an insanity of fear, he began to stir vigorously. She saw him pouring his awful beauty from the basket upon the bed, then she seized the lamp and ran as fast as she could to the kitchen. The wind from the open door blew out the light and the darkness added to her terror. She sped to the darkness of the yard, slamming the door after her before she thought to set down the lamp. She did not feel safe even on the ground, so she climbed up in the hay barn.

There for an hour or more she lay sprawled upon the hay a gibbering wreck.

Finally she grew quiet, and after that, coherent thought. With this, stalked through her a cold, bloody rage. Hours of this. A period of introspection, a space of retrospection, then a mixture of both. Out of this an awful calm.

"Well, Ah done de bes' Ah could. If things aint right, Gawd knows taint mah fault."

She went to sleep—a twitchy sleep—and woke up to a faint gray sky. There was a loud hollow sound below. She peered out. Sykes was at the wood-pile, demolishing a wire-covered box.

He hurried to the kitchen door, but hung outside there some minutes before he entered, and stood some minutes more inside before he closed it after him.

The gray in the sky was spreading. Delia descended without fear now, and crouched beneath the low bedroom window. The drawn shade shut out the dawn, shut in the night. But the thin walls held back no sound.

"Dat ol' scratch is woke up now!" She mused at the tremendous whirr inside, which every woodsman knows, is one of the sound illusions. The rattler is a ventriloquist. His whirr sounds to the right, to the left, straight ahead, behind, close under foot— everywhere but where it is. Woe to him who guesses wrong unless he is prepared to hold up his end of the argument! Sometimes he strikes without rattling at all.

Inside, Sykes heard nothing until he knocked a pot lid off the stove while trying to reach the match safe in the dark. He had emptied his pockets at Bertha's.

The snake seemed to wake up under the stove and Sykes made a quick leap into the bedroom. In spite of the gin he had had, his head was clearing now.

"Mah Gawd!" he chattered, "ef Ah could on'y strack uh light!"

The rattling ceased for a moment as he stood paralyzed. He waited. It seemed that the snake waited also.

"Oh, fuh de light! Ah thought he'd be too sick"—Sykes was muttering to himself when the whirr began again, closer, right underfoot this time. Long before this, Sykes' ability to think had been flattened down to primitive instinct and he leaped—onto the bed.

Outside Delia heard a cry that might have come from a maddened chimpanzee, a stricken gorilla. All the terror, all the horror, all the rage that man possibly could express, without a recognizable human sound.

A tremendous stir inside there, another series of animal screams, the intermittent whirr of the reptile. The shade torn violently down from the window, letting in the red dawn, a huge brown hand seizing the window stick, great dull blows upon the wooden floor punctuating the gibberish of sound long after the rattle of the snake had abruptly subsided. All this Delia could see and hear from her place beneath the window, and it made her ill. She crept over to the four-o'clocks and stretched herself on the cool earth to recover.

She lay there. "Delia, Delia!" She could hear Sykes calling in a most despairing tone as one who expected no answer. The sun crept on up, and he called. Delia could not move—her legs were gone flabby. She never moved, he called, and the sun kept rising.

"Mah Gawd!" She heard him moan, "Mah Gawd fum Heben!" She heard him stumbling about and got up from her flower-bed. The sun was growing warm. As she approached the door she heard him call out hopefully, "Delia, is dat you Ah heah?"

She saw him on his hands and knees as soon as she reached the door. He crept an inch or two toward her—all that he was able, and she saw his horribly swollen neck and his one open eye shining with hope. A surge of pity too strong to support bore her away from that eye that must, could not, fail to see the tubs. He would see the lamp. Orlando with its doctors was too far. She could scarcely reach the Chinaberry tree, where she waited in the growing heat while inside she knew the cold river was creeping up and up to extinguish that eye which must know by now that she knew.

(James) Langston Hughes
(1902-1967)

Thank You, M'am, Last Whipping *and* Christmas Song

Langston Hughes was the most versatile and most productive Afro-American writer who ever lived. He wrote poetry, novels, plays, histories, librettos, short stories, a novel, and an opera. He edited collections of folklore, humor, and poetry.

Born in Joplin, Missouri, reared in Kansas and Ohio, Hughes traveled widely before he returned to America to earn a B.A. from Lincoln University (Pa.). After college he resumed the writing career which he had begun earlier.

Despite his frequent awards he never enjoyed the critical acclaim which came to such contemporaries as Countee Cullen, Richard Wright, and, later, James Baldwin and Ralph Ellison. But, in a forty-five year literary career he contributed significantly to black American literature. In his early poetry he was known for his experiments with jazz and blues rhythms. Forty years later, in *Montage of a Dream Deferred*, he was still experimenting—with the rhythm and idiom of a new generation. Continually interested in the theatre, he established several Negro theatrical groups and wrote a play, *Mulatto* (1934), which ran longer on Broadway than any Negro drama except *A Raisin in the Sun*.

He was not only concerned with diminishing bigotry in the world; he also wanted to arouse black Americans to more intense pride in themselves and in their cultural heritage. For this reason,

351

he traveled extensively on the Negro college circuit reading his poetry to the younger generations; and he anthologized and described the literary and musical achievements of black men in all parts of the world.

Hughes's most significant contribution to American literature, however, is his creation of the stories and sketches about Jesse B. Semple. A Virginian transplanted in Harlem, Jesse B. Semple is a folk hero. Intelligent despite his lack of formal education, proud to be American, and glad to be alive, "Simple" lives and speaks for the ordinary black man.

The first of the following pieces is a story from his early period. The last two are Simple sketches.

Thank You, M'am

She was a large woman with a large purse that had everything in it but a hammer and nails. It had a long strap, and she carried it slung across her shoulder. It was about eleven o'clock at night, dark, and she was walking alone, when a boy ran up behind her and tried to snatch her purse. The strap broke with the sudden single tug the boy gave it from behind. But the boy's weight and the weight of the purse combined caused him to lose his balance. Instead of taking off full blast as he had hoped, the boy fell on his back on the sidewalk and his legs flew up. The large woman simply turned around and kicked him right square in his blue-jeaned sitter. Then she reached down, picked the boy up by his shirt front, and shook him until his teeth rattled.

After that the woman said, "Pick up my pocketbook, boy, and give it here."

She still held him tightly. But she bent down enough to permit him to stoop and pick up her purse. Then she said, "Now ain't you ashamed of yourself?"

Firmly gripped by his shirt front, the boy said, "Yes'm."

The woman said, "What did you want to do it for?"

The boy said, "I didn't aim to."

She said, "You a lie!"

By that time two or three people passed, stopped, turned to look, and some stood watching.

"If I turn you loose, will you run?" asked the woman.

"Yes'm," said the boy.

"Then I won't turn you loose," said the woman. She did not release him.

"Lady, I'm sorry," whispered the boy.

"Um-hum! Your face is dirty. I got a great mind to wash your face for you. Ain't you got nobody home to tell you to wash your face?"

"No'm," said the boy.

"Then it will get washed this evening," said the large woman, starting up the street, dragging the frightened boy behind her.

He looked as if he were fourteen or fifteen, frail and willow-wild, in tennis shoes and blue jeans.

The woman said, "You ought to be my son. I would teach you right from wrong. Least I can do right now is to wash your face. Are you hungry?"

"No'm," said the being-dragged boy. "I just want you to turn me loose."

"Was I bothering *you* when I turned that corner?" asked the woman.

"No'm."

"But you put yourself in contact with *me*," said the woman. "If you think that that contact is not going to last awhile, you got another thought coming. When I get through with you, sir, you are going to remember Mrs. Luella Bates Washington Jones."

Sweat popped out on the boy's face and he began to struggle. Mrs. Jones stopped, jerked him around in front of her, put a half nelson about his neck, and continued to drag him up the street. When she got to her door, she dragged the boy inside, down a hall, and into a large kitchenette-furnished room at the rear of the house. She switched on the light and left the door open. The boy could hear other roomers laughing and talking in the large house. Some of their doors were open, too, so he knew he and the woman were not alone. The woman still had him by the neck in the middle of her room.

She said, "What is your name?"

"Roger," answered the boy.

"Then, Roger, you go to that sink and wash your face," said the woman, whereupon she turned him loose—at last. Roger looked at the door—looked at the woman—looked at the door—*and went to the sink.*

"Let the water run until it gets warm," she said. "Here's a clean towel."

"You gonna take me to jail?" asked the boy, bending over the sink.

"Not with that face, I would not take you nowhere," said the woman. "Here I am trying to get home to cook me a bite to eat, and you snatch my pocketbook! Maybe you ain't been to your supper either, late as it be. Have you?"

"There's nobody home at my house," said the boy.

"Then we'll eat," said the woman. "I believe you're hungry—or been hungry—to try to snatch my pocketbook!"

"I want a pair of blue suede shoes," said the boy.

"Well, you didn't have to snatch *my* pocketbook to get some suede shoes," said Mrs. Luella Bates Washington Jones. "You could of asked me."

"M'am?"

The water dripping from his face, the boy looked at her. There was a long pause. A very long pause. After he had dried his face, and not knowing what else to do, dried it again, the boy turned around, wondering what next. The door was open. He could make a dash for it down the hall. He could run, run, run, *run!*

The woman was sitting on the daybed. After a while she said, "I were young once and I wanted things I could not get."

There was another long pause. The boy's mouth opened. Then he frowned, not knowing he frowned.

The woman said, "Um-hum! You thought I was going to say *but*, didn't you? You thought I was going to say, *but I didn't snatch people's pocketbooks.* Well, I wasn't going to say that." Pause. Silence. "I have done things, too, which I would not tell you, son—neither tell God, if He didn't already know. Everybody's got something in common. So you set down while I fix us something to eat. You might run that comb through your hair so you will look presentable."

In another corner of the room behind a screen was a gas plate and an icebox. Mrs. Jones got up and went behind the screen. The woman did not watch the boy to see if he was going to run now, nor did she watch her purse, which she left behind her on the daybed. But the boy took care to sit on the far side of the room, away from the purse, where he thought she could easily see him out of the corner of her eye if she wanted to. He did not trust the woman *not* to trust him. And he did not want to be mistrusted now.

"Do you need somebody to go to the store," asked the boy, "maybe to get some milk or something?"

"Don't believe I do," said the woman, "unless you just want sweet milk yourself. I was going to make cocoa out of this canned milk I got here."

"That will be fine," said the boy.

She heated some lima beans and ham she had in the icebox, made the cocoa, and set the table. The woman did not *ask* the boy anything about where he lived, or his folks, or anything else that would embarrass him. Instead, as they ate, she told him about her job in a hotel beauty shop that stayed open late, what the work was like, and how all kinds of women came in and out, blondes, redheads, and Spanish. Then she cut him a half of her ten-cent cake.

"Eat some more, son," she said.

When they were finished eating, she got up and said, "Now here, take this ten dollars and buy yourself some blue suede shoes. And next time, do not make the mistake of latching onto *my* pocketbook *nor nobody else's*—because shoes got by devilish ways will burn your feet. I got to get my rest now. But from here on in, son, I hope you will behave yourself."

She led him down the hall to the front door and opened it. "Good night! Behave yourself, boy!" she said, looking out into the street as he went down the steps.

The boy wanted to say something other than, "Thank you, m'am," to Mrs. Luella Bates Washington Jones, but although his lips moved, he couldn't even say that as he turned at the foot of the barren stoop and looked up at the large woman in the door. Then she shut the door.

Last Whipping

When I went by his house one Sunday morning to pick up my Kodak that he had borrowed, Simple was standing in the middle of the floor in his shirttail imitating a minister winding up his Sunday morning sermon, gestures and all.

He intoned, " 'Well, I looked and I saw a great beast! And that great beast had its jaws open ready to clamp down on my mortal soul. But I knowed if it was to clamp, ah, my soul would escape and go to glory. Amen! So I was not afraid. My body was afraid, a-a-ah, but my soul was not afraid. My soul said whatsoever you may do to my behind, a-a-ah, beast, you *cannot* harm my soul. Amen! No, Christians! That beast *cannot* tear your immortal soul.

That devil in the form of a crocodile, the form of a alligator with a leather hide that slippeth and slideth through the bayous swamp —that alligator *cannot* tear your soul!' "

"You really give a good imitation of a preacher," I said. "But come on and get dressed and let's go, since you say you left my Kodak at Joyce's. I didn't stop by here to hear you preach."

"I am saying that to say this," said Simple, "because that is the place in the sermon where my old Aunt Lucy jumped up shouting and leapt clean across the pulpit rail and started to preaching herself, right along with the minister.

"She hollered, 'No-ooo-oo-o! Hallelujah, no! It cannot tear your soul. Sometimes the devil comes in human form,' yelled Aunt Lucy, 'sometimes it be's born right into your own family. Sometimes the devil be's your own flesh and kin—and he try your soul—but your soul he cannot tear! Sometimes you be's forced to tear his hide *before* he tears your soul. Amen!'

"Now, Aunt Lucy were talking about *me* that morning when she said 'devil.' That is what I started to tell you."

"Talking about you, why?" I asked.

"Because I had been up to some devilment, and she had done said she was gonna whip me come Monday. Aunt Lucy were so Christian she did not believe in whipping nobody on a Sunday."

"What had you done?"

"Oh, I had just taken one of her best laying hens and give it to a girl who didn't even belong to our church; to roast for her Sunday school picnic, because this old girl said she was aiming to picnic *me*—except that she didn't have nothing good to eat to put in her basket. I was trying to jive this old gal, you know—I was young—so I just took one of Aunt Lucy's hens and give her."

"Why didn't you pick out a pullet that wasn't laying?"

"That hen was the biggest, fattest chicken in the pen—and I wanted that girl to have plenty to pull out of her basket at that picnic so folks would make a great big admiration over her and me."

"How did your Aunt Lucy find out about the hen?"

"Man, you know womenfolks can't keep no secret! That girl told another girl, the other girl told her cousin, the cousin told her mama, her mama told Aunt Lucy—and Aunt Lucy woke me up Sunday morning with a switch in her hand."

"Weren't you too old to be whipped by then?"

"Of course, I was too old to whip—sixteen going on seventeen, big as a ox. But Aunt Lucy did not figure I was grown yet. And she took her duty hard—because she always said the last thing my mother told her when she died was to raise me right."

"What did you do when you saw the switch?"

"Oh, I got all mannish, man. I said, 'Aunt Lucy, you ain't gonna whip me no more. I's a man—and you ain't gonna whip me.' "

"Aunt Lucy said, 'Yes, I is, too, Jess. I will whip you until you gets grown enough to know how to act like a man—not just *look* like one. You know you had no business snatching my hen right off her nest and giving it to that low-life hussy what had no better sense than to take it, knowing you ain't got nowhere to get no hen except out of *my* henhouse. Were this not Sunday, I would whale you in a inch of your life before you could get out of that bed.' "

"Aunt Lucy was angry," I commented.

"She was," said Simple. "And big as I was, I was scared. But I was meaning not to let her whip me, even if I had to snatch that sapling out of her hand."

"So what happened on Monday morning?"

"Aunt Lucy waited until I got up, dressed, and washed my face. Then she called me. 'Jess!' I knowed it were whipping time. Just when I was aiming to snatch that switch out of her hand, I seed that Aunt Lucy was crying when she told me to come there. I said 'Aunt Lucy, what you crying for?' "

"She said, 'I am crying 'cause here you is a man, and don't know how to act right yet, and I done did my best to raise you so you would grow up good. I done wore out so many switches on your back, still you tries my soul. But it ain't *my* soul I'm thinking of, son, it's yourn. Jess, I wants you to carry yourself right and 'sociate with peoples what's decent and be a good boy. You understand me? I's getting too old to be using my strength like this. Here!' she hollered, 'bend over and lemme whip you one more time!' "

"Did she whip you?"

"She whipped me—because I bent," said Simple. "When I seen her crying, I would have let her kill me before I raised my hand. When she got through, I said, 'Aunt Lucy, you ain't gonna have to whip me no more. I ain't gonna give you no cause. I do not mind to be beat. But I do not *never* want to see you cry no more—so I am going to do my best to do right from now on and not try your soul. And I am sorry about that hen.' "

"And you know, man, from that day to this, I have tried to behave myself. Aunt Lucy is gone to glory this morning, but if she is looking down, she knows that is true. That was my last whipping. But it wasn't the whipping that taught me what I needed to know. It was because she cried—and cried. When peoples care for you and cry for you, they can straighten out your soul. Ain't that right, boy?"

"Yes," I said, "that's right."

Christmas Song

"Just like a Negro," said Simple, "I have waited till Christmas Eve to finish my shopping."

"You are walking rather fast," I said. "Be careful, don't slip on the ice. The way it's snowing, you can't always see it underneath the snow."

"Why do you reckon they don't clean off the sidewalks in Harlem nice like they do downtown?"

"Why do *you* reckon?" I asked. "But don't tell me! I don't wish to discuss race tonight, certainly not out here in the street, as cold as it is."

"Paddy's is right there in the next block," said Simple, heading steadily that way. "I am going down to 125th Street to get two rattles, one for Carlyle's baby, Third Floor Front, and one for that other cute little old baby downstairs in the Second Floor Rear. Also I aims to get a box of hard candy for my next-door neighbor that ain't got no teeth, poor Miss Amy, so she can suck it. And a green rubber bone for Trixie. Also some kind of game for Joyce to take her godchild from me during the holidays."

"It's eight o'clock already, fellow. If you've got all that to do, you'd better hurry before the stores close."

"I am hurrying. Joyce sent me out to get some sparklers for the tree. Her and her big old fat landlady and some of the other roomers in their house is putting up a Christmas tree down in the living room, and you are invited to come by and help trim it, else watch them trimming. Do you want to go?"

"When?"

"Long about midnight P.M., I'd say. Joyce is taking a nap now. When she wakes up she's promised to make some good old Christmas eggnog—if I promise not to spike it too strong. You might as well dip your cup in our bowl. Meanwhile, let's grab a quick beer here before I get on to the store. Come on inside. Man, I'm excited! I got another present for Joyce."

"What?"

"I'm not going to tell you until after Christmas. It's a surprise. But whilst I am drinking, look at this which I writ yesterday."

XMAS

I forgot to send
A card to Jennie—
But the truth about cousins is
There's too many.

I also forgot
My Uncle Joe,
But I believe I'll let
That old rascal go.

I done bought
Four boxes now.
I can't afford
No more, nohow.

So Merry Xmas,
Everybody!
Cards or no cards,
Here's HOWDY!

"That's for my Christmas card," said Simple. "Come on, let's go."

"Not bad. Even if it will be a little late, be sure you send me one," I said as we went out into the snow.

"Man, you know I can't afford to have no cards printed up. It's just jive. I likes to compose with a pencil sometimes. Truth is, come Christmas, I has feelings right up in my throat that if I was a composer, I would write me a song also, which I would sing myself. It would be a song about that black Wise Man who went to see the Baby in the Manger. I would put into it such another music as you never heard. It would be a baritone song."

"There are many songs about the Three Wise Men," I said. "Why would you single out the black one?"

"Because I am black," said Simple, "so my song would be about the black Wise Man."

"If you could write such a song, what would it say?"

"Just what the Bible says—that he saw a star, he came from the East, and he went with the other Wise Mens to Bethlehem in Judea, and bowed down before the Child in the Manger, and put his presents down there in the straw for that Baby—and it were the greatest Baby in the world, for it were Christ! That is what my song would say."

"You don't speak of the Bible very often," I said, "but when you do, you speak like a man who knew it as a child."

"My Aunt Lucy read the Bible to me all the time when I were knee high to a duck. I never will forget it. So if I wrote a Christmas song, I would write one right out of the Bible. But it would not be so much what words I would put in it as what my music would say—because I would also make up the music myself. Music explains things better than words and everybody in all kind of languages could understand it then. My music would say everything my words couldn't put over, because there wouldn't be many words anyhow.

"The words in my song would just say a black man saw a star and followed it till he came to a stable and put his presents down. But the music would say he also laid his heart down, too—which would be my heart. It would be *my* song I would be making up. But I would make it like as if I was there myself two thousand years ago, and *I* seen the star, and *I* followed it till I come to that Child. And when I riz up from bending over that Baby in the Manger I were strong and not afraid. The end of my song would be, *Be not afraid.* That would be the end of my song."

"It sounds like a good song," I said.

"It would be the kind of song everybody could sing, old folks and young folks. And when they sing it, some folks would laugh. It would be a happy song. Other folks would cry because—well, I don't know," Simple stopped quite still for a moment in the falling snow. "I don't know, but something about that black man and that little small Child—something about them two peoples—folks would cry."

Richard Wright (1908-1960)

The Man Who Was Almost a Man

Richard Wright has been described as the most influential Afro-American novelist who ever lived. Born in Natchez, Mississippi, he dreamed of becoming a writer even while he was undergoing the brutalizing experiences of discrimination in Mississippi and Tennessee. In 1927 he moved to Chicago, where, while working at various jobs, he studied and practiced the craft of fiction. His first book, *Uncle Tom's Children*, a collection of stories about Southern Negroes, appeared in 1938. Although it was well received, Wright feared that he had evoked only an ineffectual pity for black Americans rather than an anger which would incite readers to correct the oppressive conditions. In 1940, he earned international fame with *Native Son*, a shocking indictment of American racism revealed through the story of a black youth who accidentally murders his wealthy employer's daughter. The novel gave new direction to fiction by black Americans. The first novel of social protest by a Negro to be evaluated and praised as a work of art rather than merely as a social document, it encouraged and compelled subsequent black writers to concern themselves with their art rather than merely with their message.

During the remainder of his life, most of it spent in France, Wright published an autobiography—*Black Boy* (1945); an interpretive history of black Americans—*12 Million Black Voices*; nonfiction about Africa, Spain, and racial problems; four novels, and a collection of short stories—*Eight Men.*

In the following story Wright, with characteristic violence, tells of a black American youth who wants to affirm his manhood.

The Man Who Was Almost a Man

Dave struck out across the fields, looking homeward through paling light. Whut's the use talkin wid em niggers in the field? Anyhow, his mother was putting supper on the table. Them niggers can't understan nothing. One of these days he was going to get a gun and practice shooting, then they couldn't talk to him as though he were a little boy. He slowed, looking at the ground. Shucks, Ah ain scareda them even ef they are biggern me! Aw, Ah know whut Ahma do. Ahm going by ol Joe's sto n git that Sears Roebuck catlog n look at them guns. Mebbe Ma will lemme buy one when she gits mah pay from old man Hawkins. Ahma beg her t gimme some money. Ahm ol ernough to hava gun. Ahm seventeen. Almost a man. He strode, feeling his long loose-jointed limbs. Shucks, a man oughta hava little gun aftah he done worked hard all day.

He came in sight of Joe's store. A yellow lantern glowed on the front porch. He mounted steps and went through the screen door, hearing it bang behind him. There was a strong smell of coal oil and mackerel fish. He felt very confident until he saw fat Joe walk in through the rear door, then his courage began to ooze.

"Howdy, Dave! Whutcha want?"

"How yuh, Mistah Joe? Aw, Ah don wanna buy nothing. Ah jus wanted t see ef yuhd lemme look at tha catlog erwhile."

"Sure! You wanna see it here?"

"Nawsuh. Ah wans t take it home wid me. Ah'll bring it back termorrow when Ah come in from the fiels."

"You plannin on buying something?"

"Yessuh."

"Your ma lettin you have your own money now?"

"Shucks. Mistah Joe, Ahm gittin t be a man like anybody else!"

Joe laughed and wiped his greasy white face with a red bandanna.

"Whut you plannin on buyin?"

Dave looked at the floor, scratched his head, scratched his thigh, and smiled. Then he looked up shyly.

"Ah'll tell yuh, Mistah Joe, ef yuh promise yuh won't tell."

"I promise."

"Waal, Ahma buy a gun."

"A gun? Whut you want with a gun?"

"Ah wanna keep it."

"You ain't nothing but a boy. You don't need a gun."

"Aw, lemme have the catlog, Mistah Joe. Ah'll bring it back."

Joe walked through the rear door. Dave was elated. He looked around at barrels of sugar and flour. He heard Joe coming back. He craned his neck to see if he were bringing the book. Yeah, he's got it. Gawddog, he's got it!

"Here, but be sure you bring it back. It's the only one I got."

"Sho, Mistah Joe."

"Say, if you wanna buy a gun, why don't you buy one from me? I gotta gun to sell."

"Will it shoot?"

"Sure it'll shoot."

"Whut kind is it?"

"Oh, it's kinda old . . . a left-hand Wheeler. A pistol. A big one."

"Is it got bullets in it?"

"It's loaded."

"Kin Ah see it?"

"Where's your money?"

"Whut yuh wan fer it?"

"I'll let you have it for two dollars."

"Just two dollahs? Shucks, Ah could buy tha when Ah git mah pay."

"I'll have it here when you want it."

"Awright, suh. Ah be in fer it."

He went through the door, hearing it slam again behind him. Ahma git some money from Ma n buy me a gun! Only two dollahs! He tucked the thick catalogue under his arm and hurried.

"Where yuh been, boy?" His mother held a steaming dish of black-eyed peas.

"Aw, Ma, Ah just stopped down the road t talk wid the boys."

"Yuh know bettah t keep suppah waitin."

He sat down, resting the catalogue on the edge of the table.

"Yuh git up from there and git to the well n wash yosef! Ah ain feedin no hogs in mah house!"

She grabbed his shoulder and pushed him. He stumbled out of the room, then came back to get the catalogue.

"Whut this?"

"Aw, Ma, it's jusa catlog."

"Who yuh git it from?"

"From Joe, down at the sto."

"Waal, thas good. We kin use it in the outhouse."

"Naw, Ma." He grabbed for it. "Gimme ma catlog, Ma."

She held onto it and glared at him.

"Quit hollerin at me! Whut's wrong wid yuh? Yuh crazy?"

"But Ma, please. It ain mine! It's Joe's! He tol me t bring it back t im termorrow."

She gave up the book. He stumbled down the back steps, hugging the thick book under his arm. When he had splashed water on his face and hands, he groped back to the kitchen and fumbled in a corner for the towel. He bumped into a chair; it clattered to the floor. The catalogue sprawled at his feet. When he had dried his eyes he snatched up the book and held it again under his arm. His mother stood watching him.

"Now, ef yuh gonna act a fool over that ol book, Ah'll take it n burn it up."

"Naw, Ma, please."

"Waal, set down n be still!"

He sat down and drew the oil lamp close. He thumbed page after page, unaware of the food his mother set on the table. His father came in. Then his small brother.

"Whutcha got there, Dave?" his father asked.

"Jusa catlog," he answered, not looking up.

"Yeah, here they is!" His eyes glowed at blue-and-black revolvers. He glanced up, feeling sudden guilt. His father was watching him. He eased the book under the table and rested it on his knees. After the blessing was asked, he ate. He scooped up peas and swallowed fat meat without chewing. Buttermilk helped to wash it down. He did not want to mention money before his father. He would do much better by cornering his mother when she was alone. He looked at his father uneasily out of the edge of his eye.

"Boy, how come yuh don quit foolin wid tha book n eat yo suppah?"

"Yessuh."

"How you n ol man Hawkins gitten erlong?"

"Suh?"

"Can't yuh hear? Why don yuh lissen? Ah ast yu how wuz yuh n ol man Hawkins gittin erlong?"

"Oh, swell, Pa. Ah plows mo lan than anybody over there."

"Waal, yuh oughta keep yo mind on whut yuh doin."

"Yessuh."

He poured his plate full of molasses and sopped it up slowly with a chunk of cornbread. When his father and brother had left the kitchen, he still sat and looked again at the guns in the catalogue, longing to muster courage enough to present his case to his mother. Lawd, ef Ah only had tha pretty one! He could almost feel the slickness of the weapon with his fingers. If he had a gun like that he would polish it and keep it shining so it would never rust. N Ah'd keep it loaded, by Gawd!

"Ma?" His voice was hesitant.

"Hunh?"

"Ol man Hawkins give yuh mah money yit?"

"Yeah, but ain no usa yuh thinking bout throwin nona it erway. Ahm keepin tha money sos yuh kin have cloes t go to school this winter."

He rose and went to her side with the open catalogue in his palms. She was washing dishes, her head bent low over a pan. Shyly he raised the book. When he spoke, his voice was husky, faint.

"Ma, Gawd knows Ah wans one of these."

"One of whut?" she asked, not raising her eyes.

"One of these," he said again, not daring even to point. She glanced up at the page, then at him with wide eyes.

"Nigger, is yuh gone plumb crazy?"

"Aw, Ma—"

"Git outta here! Don yuh talk t me bout no gun! Yuh a fool!"

"Ma, Ah kin buy one fer two dollahs."

"Not ef Ah knows it, yuh ain!"

"But yuh promised me one—"

"Ah don care whut Ah promised! Yuh ain nothing but a boy yit!"

"Ma, ef yuh lemme buy one Ah'll *never* ast yuh fer nothing no mo."

"Ah tol yuh t git outta here! Yuh ain gonna toucha penny of tha money fer no gun! Thas how come Ah has Mistah Hawkins t pay yo wages t me, cause Ah knows yuh ain got no sense."

"But, Ma, we needa gun. Pa ain got no gun. We needa gun in the house. Yuh kin never tell whut might happen."

"Now don yuh try to maka fool outta me, boy! Ef we did hava gun, yuh wouldn't have it!"

He laid the catalogue down and slipped his arm around her waist.

"Aw, Ma, Ah done worked hard alla summer n ain ast yuh fer nothing, is Ah, now?"

"Thas whut yuh spose t do!"

"But Ma, Ah wans a gun. Yuh kin lemme have two dollahs outta mah money. Please, Ma. I kin give it to Pa ... Please, Ma! Ah loves yuh, Ma."

When she spoke her voice came soft and low.

"Whut yu wan wida gun, Dave? Yuh don need no gun. Yuh'll git in trouble. N ef yo pa jus thought Ah let yuh have money t buy a gun he'd hava fit."

"Ah'll hide it, Ma. It ain but two dollahs."

"Lawd, chil, whut's wrong wid yuh?"

"Ain nothin wrong, Ma. Ahm almos a man now. Ah wans a gun."

"Who gonna sell yuh a gun?"

"Ol Joe at the sto."

"N it don cos but two dollahs?"

"Thas all, Ma. Jus two dollahs. Please, Ma."

She was stacking the plates away; her hands moved slowly, reflectively. Dave kept an anxious silence. Finally, she turned to him.

"Ah'll let yuh git tha gun ef yuh promise me one thing."

"Whut's tha, Ma?"

"Yuh bring it straight back t me, yuh hear? It be fer Pa."

"Yessum! Lemme go now, Ma."

She stooped, turned slightly to one side, raised the hem of her dress, rolled down the top of her stocking, and came up with a slender wad of bills.

"Here," she said. "Lawd knows yuh don need no gun. But yer pa does. Yuh bring it right back t me, yuh hear? Ahma put it up. Now ef yuh don, Ahma have yuh pa lick yuh so hard yuh won fergit it."

"Yessum."

He took the money, ran down the steps, and across the yard.

"Dave! Yuuuuuh Daaaaave!"

He heard, but he was not going to stop now. "Naw, Lawd!"

The first movement he made the following morning was to reach under his pillow for the gun. In the gray light of dawn he held it loosely, feeling a sense of power. Could kill a man with a gun like this. Kill anybody, black or white. And if he were holding his gun in his hand, nobody could run over him; they would have to respect him. It was a big gun, with a long barrel and a heavy handle. He raised and lowered it in his hand, marveling at its weight.

He had not come straight home with it as his mother had asked; instead he had stayed out in the fields, holding the weapon in his hand, aiming it now and then at some imaginary foe. But he had not fired it; he had been afraid that his father might hear. Also he was not sure he knew how to fire it.

To avoid surrendering the pistol he had not come into the house until he knew that they were all asleep. When his mother had tiptoed to his bedside late that night and demanded the gun, he had first played possum; then he had told her that the gun was hidden outdoors, that he would bring it to her in the morning. Now he lay turning it slowly in his hands. He broke it, took out the cartridges, felt them, and then put them back.

He slid out of bed, got a long strip of old flannel from a trunk, wrapped the gun in it, and tied it to his naked thigh while it was still loaded. He did not go in to breakfast. Even though it was not yet daylight, he started for Jim Hawkins' plantation. Just as the sun was rising he reached the barns where the mules and plows were kept.

"Hey! That you, Dave?"

He turned. Jim Hawkins stood eying him suspiciously.

"What're yuh going here so early?"

"Ah didn't know Ah wuz gittin up so early, Mistah Hawkins. Ah wuz fixin t hitch up ol Jenny n take her t the fiels."

"Good. Since you're so early, how about plowing that stretch down by the woods?"

"Suits me, Mistah Hawkins."

"O.K. Go to it!"

He hitched Jenny to a plow and started across the fields. Hot dog! This was just what he wanted. If he could get down by the woods, he could shoot his gun and nobody would hear. He walked behind the plow, hearing the traces creaking, feeling the gun tied tight to his thigh.

When he reached the woods, he plowed two whole rows before he decided to take out the gun. Finally, he stopped, looked in all directions, then untied the gun and held it in his hand. He turned to the mule and smiled.

"Know whut this is, Jenny? Naw, yuh wouldn know! Yuhs jusa ol mule! Anyhow, this is a gun, n it kin shoot, by Gawd!"

He held the gun at arm's length. Whut t hell, Ahma shoot this thing! He looked at Jenny again.

"Lissen here, Jenny! When Ah pull this ol trigger, Ah don wan yuh t run n acka fool now!"

Jenny stood with head down, her short ears pricked straight. Dave walked off about twenty feet, held the gun far out from him at arm's length, and turned his head. Hell, he told himself, Ah ain afraid. The gun felt loose in his fingers; he waved it wildly for a moment. Then he shut his eyes and tightened his forefinger. Bloom! A report half deafened him and he thought his right hand was torn from his arm. He heard Jenny whinnying and galloping over the field, and he found himself on his knees, squeezing his fingers hard between his legs. His hand was numb; he jammed it into his mouth, trying to warm it, trying to stop the pain. The gun lay at his feet. He did not quite know what had happened. He stood up and stared at the gun as though it were a living thing. He gritted his teeth and kicked the gun. Yuh almos broke mah arm! He turned to look for Jenny; she was far over the fields, tossing her head and kicking wildly.

"Hol on there, ol mule!"

When he caught up with her she stood trembling, walling her big white eyes at him. The plow was far away; the traces had broken. Then Dave stopped short, looking, not believing. Jenny was bleeding. Her left side was red and wet with blood. He went closer. Lawd, have mercy! Wondah did Ah shoot this mule? He grabbed for Jenny's mane. She flinched, snorted, whirled, tossing her head.

"Hol on now! Hol on."

Then he saw the hole in Jenny's side, right between the ribs. It was round, wet, red. A crimson stream streaked down the front leg, flowing fast. Good Gawd! Ah wuzn't shootin at tha mule. He felt panic. He knew he had to stop that blood, or Jenny would bleed to death. He had never seen so much blood in all his life. He chased the mule for half a mile, trying to catch her. Finally she stopped, breathing hard, stumpy tail half arched. He caught her mane and led her back to where the plow and gun lay. Then he stooped and grabbed handfuls of damp black earth and tried to plug the bullet hole. Jenny shuddered, whinnied, and broke from him.

"Hol on! Hol on now!"

He tried to plug it again, but blood came anyhow. His fingers were hot and sticky. He rubbed dirt into his palms, trying to dry them. Then again he attempted to plug the bullet hole, but Jenny shied away, kicking her heels high. He stood helpless. He had to do something. He ran at Jenny; she dodged him. He watched a red stream of blood flow down Jenny's leg and form a bright pool at her feet.

"Jenny . . . Jenny," he called weakly.

His lips trembled. She's bleeding t death! He looked in the direction of home, wanting to go back, wanting to get help. But he saw the pistol lying in the damp black clay. He had a queer feeling that if he only did something, this would not be; Jenny would not be there bleeding to death.

When he went to her this time, she did not move. She stood with sleepy, dreamy eyes; and when he touched her she gave a low-pitched whinny and knelt to the ground, her front knees slopping in blood.

"Jenny . . . Jenny . . ." he whispered.

For a long time she held her neck erect; then her head sank, slowly. Her ribs swelled with a mighty heave and she went over.

Dave's stomach felt empty, very empty. He picked up the gun and held it gingerly between his thumb and forefinger. He buried it at the foot of a tree. He took a stick and tried to cover the pool of blood with dirt—but what was the use? There was Jenny lying with her mouth open and her eyes walled and glassy. He could not tell Jim Hawkins he had shot his mule. But he had to tell something. Yeah, Ah'll tell em Jenny started gittin wil n fell on the joint of the plow. . . . But that would hardly happen to a mule. He walked across the field slowly, head down.

It was sunset. Two of Jim Hawkins' men were over near the edge of the woods digging a hole in which to bury Jenny. Dave was surrounded by a knot of people, all of whom were looking down at the dead mule.

"I don't see how in the world it happened," said Jim Hawkins for the tenth time.

The crowd parted and Dave's mother, father, and small brother pushed into the center.

"Where Dave?" his mother called.

"There he is," said Jim Hawkins.

His mother grabbed him.

"Whut happened, Dave? Whut yuh done?"

"Nothin."

"C mon, boy, talk," his father said.

Dave took a deep breath and told the story he knew nobody believed.

"Waal," he drawled. "Ah brung ol Jenny down here sos Ah could do mah plowin. Ah plowed bout two rows, just like yuh see." He stopped and pointed at the long rows of upturned earth. "Then somethin musta been wrong wid ol Jenny. She wouldn ack right a-tall. She started snortin n kickin her heels. Ah tried t hol her, but she pulled erway, rearin n goin in. Then when the point of the plow was stickin up in the air, she swung erroun n twisted herself back on it . . . She stuck herself n started t bleed. N fo Ah could do anything, she wuz dead."

"Did you ever hear of anything like that in all your life?" asked Jim Hawkins.

There were white and black standing in the crowd. They murmured. Dave's mother came close to him and looked hard into his face. "Tell the truth, Dave," she said.

"Looks like a bullet hole to me," said one man.

"Dave, whut yuh do wid the gun?" his mother asked.

The crowd surged in, looking at him. He jammed his hands into his pockets, shook his head slowly from left to right, and backed away. His eyes were wide and painful.

"Did he hava gun?" asked Jim Hawkins.

"By Gawd, Ah tol yuh tha wuz a gun wound," said a man, slapping his thigh.

His father caught his shoulders and shook him till his teeth rattled.

"Tell whut happened, yuh rascal! Tell whut . . ."

Dave looked at Jenny's stiff legs and began to cry.

"Whut yuh do wid tha gun?" his mother asked.

"Whut wuz he doin wida gun?" his father asked.

"Come on and tell the truth," said Hawkins. "Ain't nobody going to hurt you . . ."

His mother crowded close to him.

"Did yuh shoot tha mule, Dave?"

Dave cried, seeing blurred white and black faces.

"Ahh ddinn gggo tt sshooot hher . . . Ah ssswear ffo Gawd Ahh ddin. . . . Ah wuz a-tryin t sssee ef the old gggun would sshoot—"

"Where yuh git the gun from?" his father asked.

"Ah got it from Joe, at the sto."

"Where yuh git the money?"

"Ma give it t me."

"He kept worryin me, Bob. Ah had t. Ah tol im t bring the gun right back t me . . . I was fer yuh, the gun."

"But how yuh happen to shoot that mule?" asked Jim Hawkins.

"Ah wuzn shootin at the mule, Mistah Hawkins. The gun jumped when Ah pulled the trigger . . . N fo Ah knowed anythin Jenny was there a-bleedin."

Somebody in the crowd laughed. Jim Hawkins walked close to Dave and looked into his face.

"Well, looks like you have bought you a mule, Dave."

"Ah swear fo Gawd, Ah didn go t kill the mule, Mistah Hawkins!"

"But you killed her!"

All the crowd was laughing now. They stood on tiptoe and poked heads over one another's shoulders.

"Well, boy, looks like yuh done bought a dead mule! Hahaha!"

"Ain tha ershame."

"Hohohohoho."

Dave stood, head down, twisting his feet in the dirt.

"Well, you needn't worry about it, Bob," said Jim Hawkins to Dave's father. "Just let the boy keep on working and pay me two dollars a month."

"Whut yuh wan fer yo mule, Mistah Hawkins?"

Jim Hawkins screwed up his eyes.

"Fifty dollars."

"Whut yuh do wid tha gun?" Dave's father demanded.

Dave said nothing.

"Yuh wan me t take a tree n beat yuh till yuh talk!"

"Nawsuh!"

"Whut yuh do wid it?"

"Ah throwed it erway."

"Where?"

"Ah ... Ah throwed it in the creek."

"Waal, c mon home. N firs thing in the mawnin git to tha creek n fin tha gun."

"Yessuh."

"Whut yuh pay fer it?"

"Two dollahs."

"Take tha gun n git yo money back n carry it t Mistah Hawkins, yuh hear? N don fergit Ahma lam you black bottom good fer this! Now march yosef on home, suh!"

Dave turned and walked slowly. He heard people laughing. Dave glared, his eyes welling with tears. Hot anger bubbled in him. Then he swallowed and stumbled on.

That night Dave did not sleep. He was glad that he had gotten out of killing the mule so easily, but he was hurt. Something hot seemed to turn over inside him each time he remembered how they had laughed. He tossed on his bed, feeling his hard pillow. N Pa says he's gonna beat me ... He remembered other beatings, and his back quivered. Naw, naw, Ah sho don wan im t beat me tha

way no mo. Dam em all! Nobody ever gave him anything. All he
did was work. They treat me like a mule, n then they beat me. He
gritted his teeth. N Ma had t tell on me.

Well, if he had to, he would take old man Hawkins that two
dollars. But that meant selling the gun. And he wanted to keep
that gun. Fifty dollars for a dead mule.

He turned over, thinking how he had fired the gun. He had an
itch to fire it again. Ef other men kin shoota gun, by Gawd, Ah
kin! He was still, listening. Mebbe they all sleepin now. The house
was still. He heard the soft breathing of his brother. Yes, now! He
would go down and get that gun and see if he could fire it! He
eased out of bed and slipped into overalls.

The moon was bright. He ran almost all the way to the edge of
the woods. He stumbled over the ground, looking for the spot
where he had buried the gun. Yeah, here it is. Like a hungry dog
scratching for a bone, he pawed it up. He puffed his black cheeks
and blew dirt from the trigger and barrel. He broke it and found
four cartridges unshot. He looked around; the fields were filled
with silence and moonlight. He clutched the gun stiff and hard in
his fingers. But, as soon as he wanted to pull the trigger, he shut
his eyes and turned his head. Naw, Ah can't shoot wid mah eyes
closed n mah head turned. With effort he held his eyes open; then
he squeezed. *Blooooom!* He was stiff, not breathing. The gun was
still in his hands. Dammit, he'd done it! He fired again. *Blooooom!*
He smiled. *Bloooom! Blooooom! Click, click.* There! It was empty.
If anybody could shoot a gun, he could. He put the gun into his
hip pocket and started across the fields.

When he reached the top of a ridge he stood straight and proud
in the moonlight, looking at Jim Hawkins' big white house, feeling
the gun sagging in his pocket. Lawd, ef Ah had just one mo bullet
Ah'd taka shot at tha house. Ah'd like t scare ol man Hawkins
jusa little . . . Jusa enough t let im know Dave Saunders is a man.

To his left the road curved, running to the tracks of the Illinois
Central. He jerked his head, listening. From far off came a faint
hoooof-hoooof; hoooof-hoooof; hoooof-hoooof. . . . He stood rigid.
Two dollahs a mont. Les see now . . . Tha means it'll take bout two
years. Shucks! Ah'll be dam!

He started down the road, toward the tracks. Yeah, here she
comes! He stood beside the track and held himself stiffly. Here she
comes, erroun the ben . . . C mon, yuh slow poke! C mon! He had
his hand on his gun; something quivered in his stomach. Then the
train thundered past, the gray and brown box cars rumbling and

clinking. He gripped the gun tightly; then he jerked his hand out of his pocket. Ah betcha Bill wouldn't do it! Ah betcha ... The cars slid past, steel grinding upon steel. Ahm ridin yuh ternight, so hep me Gawd! He was hot all over. He hesitated just a moment; then he grabbed, pulled atop of a car, and lay flat. He felt his pocket; the gun was still there. Ahead the long rails were glinting in the moonlight, stretching away, away to somewhere, somewhere where he could be a man ...

Frank Yerby (1916-   )

My Brother Went to College

One of the most popular contemporary novelists, Frank Yerby, a native of Augusta, Georgia, received a B.A. from Paine College in that city and an M.A. in English from Fisk University. After teaching briefly, he moved North to work in factories, which paid more money than he was earning as an instructor in Southern Negro colleges in the early Forties.

In his earliest stories, such as "Health Card," which won an O. Henry Award in 1944, Yerby protested against the discriminatory treatment of black Americans. After failing to sell a novel on the same theme, however, he turned to historical or "costume" romances. The first, *The Foxes of Harrow* (1946), told the story of an Irish immigrant who works his way to riches in nineteenth-century Louisiana. Each year since 1946 Yerby has published a novel. Most have been set in the South; all but one have been historical; and most have been best-sellers. Since the early 1950's he has lived in France and Spain.

Occasionally Yerby has been criticized for writing historical romances about white protagonists rather than telling the stories of contemporary Negroes. His detractors accuse him of refusing to assume a role as critic or interpreter of society. It is significant, however, that all of Yerby's novels are written about outcasts who, by intelligence and courage, prove themselves superior to a society which rejects them because of their alien, inferior, or illegitimate birth. It is also significant that, through his white Southern

protagonists, Yerby has ridiculed the most cherished myths identified with the antebellum South.

"My Brother Went to College" exemplifies his early work. It is
strongly contemporary in its treatment of the theme of a youth
who rebels against but later accepts the values of middle-class
society.

My Brother Went to College

When I was very young, the land was a hunger in me. I wanted
to devour it all: plains, mountains, cities teeming with men. Therefore I left the three rooms above the little shop where my father
cobbled shoes, crawling over the still sleeping form of my brother,
Matt, and tiptoeing past the great brass bed in which my father
snored. As I went by, he turned over and murmured, "Mark"; but
he was still sleeping, so I crept by him very quietly and stole down
the creaking stairs. Mark is my name. I suppose that father was
planning to have two more sons and name them Luke and John,
but mother died before he could accomplish it. Afterwards Matt
and I used to argue over whether father, if he had been blessed
with three more sons, would have called the fifth one, "The Acts,"
Matt holding that he would not, and I that he would. Acts of the
Apostles Johnson. It had a very satisfying sound.

I was ten when I ran away from home. When I came back, I was
twenty. For ten years I wandered upon the face of the earth,
hearing the long, sweet, sad, lost, lonesome cry of the train whis-
tles in the night until the sound was in my blood and part of me. I
wandered through the Delta while the sun soaked into my black
hide, and sat on Scott's Bluff near Baton Rouge and watched the
Mississippi run golden with the mud of half a continent. I grew a
lean belly and a knotty calf, and the black wool on my head
kinked tight as cockle burrs. I drank moonshine in the Georgia
swamp country, and rotgut in the Carolina hills. I worked for
spells until I would wake up in the night to hear the trains crying;
then I was off, pushing the earth backward under my feet. I
listened to the whippoorwill at night, and sang with the mocking-
bird in the morning.

I wasn't worth a damn and I didn't care. I was free. I couldn't
keep a job because of that. Sooner or later, the boss would find out
that I could jump to do his orders and still stay free, that I could

be polite and still be free, that you could kick me and cuss me and I could still stay free, because the freedom was inside me. I had soaked it up from the blazing sun in Texas; I had breathed it in with the cool mountain air in Tennessee; I'd drunk it down with all the tepid, muddy, fish-tasting river water. I'd devoured it along with ten thousand miles of timeless space.

I whored from New Orleans to Memphis, and gambled from Louisville to Miami. I was worthless, useless, a ne'er-do-well, a disgrace to my family and I didn't give a damn. But after a while, as I grew older, the hunger lessened in me, and in its place came the great longing to see again the face of my brother, and to walk down streets where people would call out to me as I passed, knowing me, knowing my name. Besides, I had decided to settle down, get me a good job, maybe in the post office, and take a wife.

It took me four days to get home. I didn't even stop to eat. I swung six freights and a fruit truck, and did twenty miles afoot. Then I was walking down the streets of my city, all the well-loved streets, sniffing the smell of the garbage like bouquets of roses, and laughing all over myself. A woman leaned out of a window and said:

"Where you going, pretty brown?"

"Home!" I laughed. "Home!"

"Come on up and I give you luck sho'. Just a dollar to you. Come on up, pretty brown."

"Hell," I said, "I'm black and I sure ain't pretty, and what you got ain't worth no dollar. Leave me be, sister, I'm going home!"

I went around the last corner very slow, making the pleasure last, and there was the old shop just as I'd left it, only a little more run down maybe. Then my heart stopped beating altogether, because the man hammering away at the thick, mostly cardboard, half soles sure Lord wasn't father, or even the half of him.

I walked to the door and I asked him where Deacon Johnson was, who used to keep this shop, and he looked up at me and said:

"He dead. Mighty near six years now since he was laid to rest."

I sat down weakly on one of the high stools.

"And his son—Matt Johnson?" I asked.

"Oh, he here awright. He Doctor Matt Johnson now. Finished up his schoolin' at Mo'house and taken up medicine at Meharry. Fine man, Doctor Johnson. He my doctor. Other night I was taken with a misery in my——"

"Where he live?" I demanded. "I got to see him."

"Way 'cross town. Over there on Westmoreland Drive. What's the matter, son, are you sick?"

"Naw," I said. "Naw, I ain't sick. I'm ever so much obliged to you, mister."

When I had left town, ten years before, only white people had lived on Westmoreland Drive, and big shots at that; so I wasn't at all sure that the new cobbler wasn't stringing me. But that other part sounded all right—all that about the schooling and being a doctor and all. That was just like Matt. There wasn't but one place for him, and that was at the top. That's the way Matt was.

It took me more than a half-hour to get over to Westmoreland Drive. I had to go past five points and through all the city traffic, and after ten years I wasn't exactly clear as to where it was. But I reached it at last, and stood on the corner looking down the shaded street at all the big brick houses sitting high on their green terraces with the automobile driveways curving up and around them, and I drew in my breath and let it out again in one big whoosh. Then I went up to the first house and rang the bell. A young girl came to the door. She had brown skin and soft black hair that curled down over her shoulders. She was so doggoned pretty that I couldn't get my mouth shut.

"Yes?" she said. "Yes?"

"Doctor Johnson," I said, "Doctor Matthew Johnson—do he live here?"

"No," she said, "he lives four houses down on the other side."

Then she smiled at me. I wanted to stand there and just look at her, but then I saw my old rusty shoes and the worn-out fringes at the bottom of my breeches, so I mumbled, "Thank you Ma'am," and went back down the walk to the street.

I stood in front of my brother's house a long time before I got up the nerve to climb up the inclined walk to the door. It was just about the biggest and the best-looking house on the street. Matt had got somewhere, he had. I pushed on the bell button and held my breath. Then the door popped open and a young woman, prettier'n an angel out of Glory, and so light complexioned that I looked at her three times and still I wasn't sure, stuck her head out and said:

"Good evening?"

"Howdy do," I said; "is Matt home?"

"Yes," she said, and her voice was puzzled. "Who shall I tell him is calling?"

"Just tell him, Mark," I said. "He'll know."

She went back in the house, leaving me standing there like a fool. The sunlight slanted through the shade trees on the walk. Where it hit the leaves, it made a kind of blaze. Then it came on through and touched the side of the house, making it a kind of salmon pink.

I heard Matt's big feet come hammering through the hall, then the door banged open, and there he was big as life and twice as handsome. He had on a dark blue suit that must have cost plenty, and his hair was cut close to his skull so that the kink didn't show so much, and his black face was shaved, steamed and massaged until the skin was like black velvet. He took the pipe out of his mouth and stood there staring at me, his Adam's apple bobbing up and down out of the collar of his silk shirt. Then he grinned and said:

"Mark, you crazy little bastard!"

I put out my horny paw, and he took it and wrung it almost off. I was ashamed of myself because all the time I had been standing there thinking that maybe he wouldn't want to see me now, but I should have known better. Matt wasn't like that at all.

He took me by the arm, rags and all, and drew me inside the house. It was a palace. I had seen houses like that in the movies, but nobody could have made me believe that there was a black man anywhere who owned one. The rugs were so soft and deep that they came up to my ankles, and the combination radio-phonograph filled up half of one wall. Sitting in one of the huge chairs was the light girl, and with her were two fat, copper-brown children with soft brown hair almost the color of their skins curling all over their little heads. I just stood there and I couldn't say a word.

It came to me then that Matt had done what I had tried to do, and that he'd done it the right way. He'd built himself a world, and he was free. I had run away from everything and slept in the open fields, hunting for something, and Matt had stayed at home and fought for the same thing and he had got it. I felt less than two inches high.

"Martha," Matt was saying, his voice full of laughter, "this bum you were telling me about is my little brother, Mark."

"Oh," she said. "Oh—I'm so sorry—I didn't know—"

"It's awright, Ma'am," I said. "You was right. I am a bum. I just wanted to see Matt one more time, and now that I have, I reckon I'll be on my way agin."

"Like hell you will!" Matt roared. "You come in the back and have some supper. I promised paw on his death bed that I'd find you, and now that I have, you aren't getting away. Come on now."

He took me to the kitchen, and began to pull stuff out of a huge electric refrigerator and pile it on the table. There was so much food there that I couldn't eat. For the life of me I couldn't. I barely tasted the cold chicken, and ate a tiny piece of cherry pie. And all the time, Matt sat there and looked at me.

"Why didn't you write?" he growled at me. "Any time in the last four years I could have had you back in school—well, it isn't too late now. You're gonna bone up, do you hear me—college preparatory—we'll skip over high—you're too damned old. You'll take pharmacy along with college, and when you're out we'll open a drug store. And Gawddammit, if you fail, I'll break every bone in your stupid body—running off like that!"

I just sat there like a fool and gulped and said, "Yes, Matt, no, Matt, that's right, Matt, that'll be swell." When I had finished, he took me upstairs to the bathroom and drew a tubful of water hot enough to scald the hide off of me.

"Get in," he said, "and give me those clothes." I did as I was told, and he took them out into the hall. I heard him calling the old woman who was his housekeeper. When she got there, I heard him say:

"Take these rags out back and burn them!"

When I got out of the tub he gave me his robe and slippers, and there on the bed was one of his suits and a white shirt and tie and handkerchief and socks and shoes and silk underwear—silk, mind you!

"Get dressed," he growled. "We're going for a walk."

I put on the things, and they fitted except for being a little too big here and there; then we went back down the stairs. Matt put on his hat and kissed his wife and the children, and then we went out on the street. By that time it was dark and the stars hung just above the street lamps. I tried to talk.

"The kids," I said, "Geez, Matt—"

"They're all right," he said. "Martha's swell, too—"

"I'll say," I said. "Where'd you find her?"

"College. You'd better do as well."

"Not me," I said. "She's too light. I wouldn't feel comfortable. I want me a tall brown with white teeth and wide hips. Fat chance, though."

"You get what you go after," Matt said, "and doggone it, I'm gonna see that you go after it! We go in here."

I looked up and saw that it was a barber shop. All the barbers grinned when Matt came in.

"Howdy, Doc," they said, "back so soon?"

"Tom," Matt said to the oldest barber, "this is my brother, Mark. Get out your clippers and give him a close cut. Take that rosary off his head!"

When they had finished with me, I was somebody else. I looked like Matt. I looked prosperous and well fed. I looked important— and just a little, I began to feel important, too.

"Tomorrow night," Matt said, "there's a dance. You're going with us. I want you to meet some nice girls. And for Christsake watch your grammar."

"That girl," I said, "four houses up the street on the other side. Will she be there?"

"Elizabeth? You catch on fast, don't you? Yes, I imagine so. But you won't get a look-in there—she's doggoned popular, I tell you."

"Ain't no harm in trying," I said.

They were nice to me, but I felt strange. Martha went out of her way to make me feel at home. Little Matt and little Martha crawled all over me and called me Uncle, but still I didn't feel right. The mattresses were too soft. I couldn't sleep. The food was so good and so rich that my stomach refused it. And every doggoned one of them, including Matt, talked English like Yankee white folks so that half the time I was saying, "Huh? Whatcha say?"

They said "Courthouse—courrrthouse"—not Co'thouse, like a body ought to do. They said "sure"—not sho'. And they never said "ain't." They talked like the people in pictures—like radio announcers. I admired their proper talk, but it didn't sound right. Martha—all right, she looked the part, but I couldn't get it through my thick skull that anybody black as Matt and I ought to talk like that.

And that dance! I stood by a pillar and looked at the girls—
they had on evening dresses that trailed the floor, and there were
flowers in their hair. And they were all the colors of the rainbow:
soft, velvety nightshade girls, chocolate-brown girls, coppery-
brown girls, gingerbread-brown girls, lemon-yellow girls, old-ivory
colored girls, just off-white girls, and snowy-skinned octoroons
with blond hair and blue eyes.

"Jesus!" I said. "Jesus! Old Saint Peter done gone to sleep and
left open the gates." But I didn't dance. The couples drifted past
me in stately waltzes. Nobody jitterbugged. If anybody had started to, they'd have been thrown out. I felt stiff. I felt frozen. I felt
like the deuce of spades against a king-high flush. I was a lost ball
in high grass. I was a cue ball smack up behind the eight, and the
side pocket was miles away.

I got to get out, I thought. I got to catch myself a freight and
highball it down the river. I can shuffle in a Beale Street juke
joint, where the girls are wide across the beam and you can count
every knee in the place; where you hang a cigarette out the corner
of your mouth and shove your hat back on your head and tickle
the ivories, while you squint your left eye so the smoke won't blind
you; where your sweet gal dances with you, up against you, till her
thighs scald you and you smell her hairgrease under your nose
along with the body sweat and cheap perfume. But in here I can't
breathe, not here, where they drift along like something you dream
about, and the perfume don't come from the dime store, and the
girls move on the air halfway out on your arm. No, by God!

I started toward the door. When I got there, I saw a black boy
in a zoot suit standing there looking in. I felt a great rush of fellow
feeling for him. I was outside looking in, too, although I was inside
the hall. But when I got close, I saw the white policeman that a
city ordinance required at all Negro dances, no matter how respectable they were, standing there breaking matches into little pieces
and flipping them into the broad brim of the boy's Big Apple hat.
And the boy was grinning all over his flat face. I turned around
and went back into the hall.

Then she was coming toward me, smiling. I wanted to run. I
wanted to hide. I wanted to kick a hole in the floor and pull it over
me.

"Hello," she said, "I've been looking all over for you."

"You—you been looking all over for me?"

"Yes—Doctor Matt told me you were here. My, but you've changed! Why you're positively handsome with a haircut."

I pulled out a handkerchief and mopped my brow.

"Well," Elizabeth teased, "aren't you going to dance with me?"

I took her in my arms and we moved off. It was like floating—like flying—like dreaming. And I didn't want to wake up. Matt had me. He'd won. The juke boxes in the river joints died away out of mind into silence. I was lost. I could never go back again and I knew it.

"Oh, my God!" I groaned. "Oh, my God!"

I took Elizabeth home after the dance and went through hell wondering whether or not I should try to kiss her, but in the end I decided against it and watched her running up the stairs laughing all over herself. Then I walked home through the gray dawn on Westmoreland Drive that was like no other dawn I'd ever seen. And I thought about how it was with Matt and Matt's crowd: the men in tuxedoes and tails, the women in evening gowns, all very correct, nobody laughing out loud or dancing with their entire bodies or yelling across the dance floor, or saying ain't, or ever doing anything that wasn't on page one of Emily Post, and I wondered if it really felt good to be like that. And while I was wondering, I pushed open the door to the bathroom and found Matt standing before the mirror shaving with a tiny, gold-plated safety razor, and cussing with quiet violence.

He turned around and saw me, and slowly his eyes lit up.

"You!" he said. "You can do it!"

"Do what?" I said.

He put his hand down in his pocket and came out with a ten dollar bill.

"You go downtown today and buy me an old-fashioned straight razor. I hate these damn little things!"

"All right," I said.

"I've been wanting a straight razor for five years," Matt said, touching his jaw with his fingertips.

"Yeah," I said, thinking about Elizabeth.

"I can't always wait to go to the barber shop," Matt said.

"Five years," I said. "Why didn't you just go and buy one?"

Matt turned and looked at me, one half of his face still covered with lather.

"You know I couldn't do that," he said.

"Why not?"

"You know what they'd think I wanted it for."

I looked at Matt and I began to laugh. I laughed so I lost my breath. When I went out into the hall, leaving him there, staring at me, I was still laughing. But I shouldn't have laughed. Even then I must have known it wasn't funny. Now, when I think about it (after all these years, watching my wife, Elizabeth, serving ice cream sodas over the counter of our drug store with her beautiful hands, remembering that Matt did this too), I realize that it was really sad, one of the saddest things, in fact, that I ever heard of.

Ralph W. Ellison (1914-   )

Mister Toussan

Although he has published only two books, Ralph Ellison is one of America's most respected writers. His novel, *Invisible Man* (1952) won the National Book Award when it was first published. Thirteen years later, a poll of more than two hundred authors, critics, and editors selected it as "the most distinguished work published during the past twenty years."

Born in Oklahoma City, Oklahoma, Ellison studied music for three years at Tuskegee Institute. When his college education was interrupted by the need to earn money, he studied sculpture, worked in a variety of occupations—including those of free-lance photographer and professional jazz musician, and wrote essays and reviews for major periodicals. Since publishing *Invisible Man*, he has lectured and taught at several colleges. In 1964, he published *Shadow and Act*, a collection of essays.

Ralph Ellison's short stories are uncollected and relatively unknown because, written while he was undergoing his apprenticeship as a writer, they appeared in magazines less frequently examined by anthologists. "Mister Toussan" comes from this early period. Although the story lacks the sophisticated style, the symbolism, and the satire now identified with Ellison, there is a charming freshness in the sketch of a black boy's first encounter with black history.

From *New Masses* (November 4, 1941). Copyright © 1941 by Ralph Ellison. Reprinted by permission of William Morris Agency, Inc.

Mister Toussan

Once upon a time
The goose drink wine
Monkey chew tobacco
And he spit white lime.
—Rhyme used as a prologue to Negro slave stories.

"I hope they all gits rotten and the worms git in 'em," the first boy said.

"I hopes a big wind storm comes and blows down all the trees," said the second boy.

"Me too," the first boy said. "And when ole Rogan comes out to see what happened I hope a tree falls on his head and kills him."

"Now jus' look a-yonder at them birds," the second boy said, "they eating all they want and when we asked him to let us git some off the ground he had to come calling us little nigguhs and chasing us home!"

"Doggonit," said the second boy, "I hope them birds got poison in they feet!"

The two small boys, Riley and Buster, sat on the floor of the porch, their bare feet resting upon the cool earth as they stared past the line on the paving where the sun consumed the shade, to a yard directly across the street. The grass in the yard was very green and a house stood against it, neat and white in the morning sun. A double row of trees stood alongside the house, heavy with cherries that showed deep red against the dark green of the leaves and dull dark brown of the branches. They were watching an old man who rocked himself in a chair as he stared back at them across the street.

"Just look at him," said Buster. "Ole Rogan's so scared we gonna git some his ole cherries he ain't even got sense enough to go in outa the sun!"

"Well, them birds is gitting their'n," said Riley.

"They mocking birds."

"I don't care what kinda birds they is, they sho in them trees."

"Yeah, ole Rogan don't see *them*. Man, I tell you white folks ain't got no sense."

They were silent now, watching the darting flight of the birds into the trees. Behind them they could hear the clatter of a sewing machine: Riley's mother was sewing for the white folks. It was quiet and as the woman worked, her voice rose above the whirring machine in song.

"Your mamma sho can sing, man," said Buster.

"She sings in the choir," said Riley, "and she sings all the leads in church."

"Shucks, I know it," said Buster. "You tryin' to brag?"

As they listened they heard the voice rise clear and liquid to float upon the morning air:

> *I got wings, you got wings,*
> *All God's chillun got a-wings*
> *When I git to heaven gonna put on my wings*
> *Gonna shout all ovah God's heaven.*
> *Heab'n, heab'n*
> *Everybody talkin' 'bout heab'n ain't going*
> *there*
> *Heab'n, heab'n, Ah'm gonna fly all ovah God's*
> *heab'n....*

She sang as though the words possessed a deep and throbbing meaning for her, and the boys stared blankly at the earth, feeling the somber, mysterious calm of church. The street was quiet and even old Rogan had stopped rocking to listen. Finally the voice trailed off to a hum and became lost in the clatter of the busy machine.

"Wish I could sing like that," said Buster.

Riley was silent, looking down to the end of the porch where the sun had eaten a bright square into the shade, fixing a flitting butterfly in its brilliance.

"What would you do if you had wings?" he said.

"Shucks, I'd outfly an eagle, I wouldn't stop flying till I was a million, billion, trillion, zillion miles away from this ole town."

"Where'd you go, man?"

"Up north, maybe to Chicago."

"Man, if I had wings I wouldn't never settle down."

"Me, neither. Hecks, with wings you could go anywhere, even up to the sun if it wasn't too hot...."

"... I'd go to New York...."

"Even around the stars...."

"Or Dee-troit, Michigan...."

"Hell, you could git some cheese off the moon and some milk from the Milkyway...."

"Or anywhere else colored is free...."

"I bet I'd loop-the-loop. . . ."

"And parachute. . . ."

"I'd land in Africa and git me some diamonds. . . ."

"Yeah, and them cannibals would eat the hell outa you too," said Riley.

"The heck they would, not fast as I'd fly away. . . ."

"Man, they'd catch you and stick soma them long spears in your behin'!" said Riley.

Buster laughed as Riley shook his head gravely: "Boy, you'd look like a black pin cushion when they got through with you," said Riley.

"Shucks, man, they couldn't catch me, them suckers is too lazy. The geography book says they 'bout the most lazy folks in the whole world," said Buster with disgust, "just black and lazy!"

"Aw naw, they ain't neither," exploded Riley.

"They is too! The geography book says they is!"

"Well, my ole man says they ain't!"

"How come they ain't then?"

" 'Cause my ole man says that over there they got kings and diamonds and gold and ivory, and if they got all them things, all of 'em cain't be lazy," said Riley. "Ain't many colored folks over here got them things."

"Sho ain't, man. The white folks won't let 'em," said Buster.

It was good to think that all the Africans were not lazy. He tried to remember all he had heard of Africa as he watched a purple pigeon sail down into the street and scratch where a horse had passed. Then, as he remembered a story his teacher had told him, he saw a car rolling swiftly up the street and the pigeon stretching its wings and lifting easily into the air, skimming the top of the car in its slow, rocking flight. He watched it rise and disappear where the taut telephone wires cut the sky above the curb. Buster felt good. Riley scratched his initials in the soft earth with his big toe.

"Riley, you know all them African guys ain't really that lazy," he said.

"I know they ain't," said Riley, "I just tole you so."

"Yeah, but my teacher tole me, too. She tole us 'bout one of them African guys named Toussan what she said whipped Napoleon!"

Riley stopped scratching in the earth and looked up, his eyes rolling in disgust:

"Now how come you have to start lying?"

"Thass what she said."

"Boy, you oughta quit telling them things."

"I hope God may kill me."

"She said he was a *African?*"

"Cross my heart, man. . . ."

"Really?"

"Really, man. She said he come from a place named Hayti."

Riley looked hard at Buster and seeing the seriousness of the face felt the excitement of a story rise up within him.

"Buster, I'll bet a fat man you lyin'. What'd that teacher say?"

"Really, man, she said that Toussan and his men got up on one of them African mountains and shot down them peckerwood soldiers fass as they'd try to come up. . . ."

"Why good-God-a-mighty!" yelled Riley.

"Oh boy, they shot 'em down!" chanted Buster.

"Tell me about it, man!"

"And they throwed 'em off the mountain. . . ."

" . . . Goool-leee! . . ."

". . . And Toussan drove 'em cross the sand. . . ."

". . . Yeah! And what was they wearing, Buster? . . ."

"Man, they had on red uniforms and blue hats all trimmed with gold, and they had some swords all shining what they called sweet blades of Damascus. . . ."

"Sweet blades of Damascus! . . ."

". . . They really had 'em," chanted Buster.

"And what kinda guns?"

"Big, black cannon!"

"And where did ole what-you-call-'im run them guys? . . ."

"His name was Toussan."

"Toussan! Just like Tarzan. . . ."

"Not *Taar*-zan, dummy, *Toou*-zan!"

"Toussan! And where'd ole Toussan run 'em?"

"Down to the water, man. . . ."

". . . To the river water. . . ."

". . . Where some great big ole boats was waiting for 'em. . . ."

". . . Go on, Buster!"

"An' Toussan shot into them boats. . . ."

". . . He shot into em. . . ."

". . . Shot into them boats. . . ."

"Jesus!! . . ."

"With his great big cannons. . . ."

". . . Yeah! . . ."

"... Made a-brass. ..."

"... Brass. ..."

"... An' his big black cannon balls started killin' them pecker-woods. ..."

"... Lawd, Lawd. ..."

"... Boy, till them peckerwoods hollowed *Please, Please, Mister Toussan, we'll be good!*"

"An' what'd Toussan tell em, Buster?"

"Boy, he said in his big deep voice, *I oughta drown all a-you bastards.*"

"An' what'd the peckerwoods say?"

"They said, Please, Please, *Please, Mister Toussan. ...*"

"... We'll be good," broke in Riley.

"Thass right, man," said Buster excitedly. He clapped his hands and kicked his heels against the earth, his black face glowing in a burst of rhythmic joy.

"Boy!"

"And what'd ole Toussan say then?"

"He said in his big deep voice: *You all peckerwoods better be good, 'cause this is sweet Papa Toussan talking and my nigguhs is crazy 'bout white meat!*"

"Ho, ho, ho!" Riley bent double with laughter. The rhythm still throbbed within him and he wanted the story to go on and on. ...

"Buster, you know didn't no teacher tell you that lie," he said.

"Yes she did, man."

"She said there was really a guy like that what called hisself Sweet Papa Toussan?"

Riley's voice was unbelieving and there was a wistful expression in his eyes which Buster could not understand. Finally he dropped his head and grinned.

"Well," he said, "I bet thass what ole Toussan said. You know how grown folks is, they cain't tell a story right, 'cepting real old folks like grandma."

"They sho cain't," said Riley. "They don't know how to put the right stuff to it."

Riley stood, his legs spread wide and stuck his thumbs in the top of his trousers, swaggering sinisterly.

"Come on, watch me do it now, Buster. Now I bet ole Toussan looked down at them white folks standing just about like this and said in a soft easy voice: Ain't I done begged you white folks to quit messin' with me? ..."

"Thass right, quit messing with 'im," chanted Buster.

"But naw, you-all all had to come on anyway. . . ."

". . . Jus' 'cause they was black. . . ."

"Thass right," said Riley. "Then ole Toussan felt so damn bad and mad the tears come a-trickling down. . . ."

". . . He was really mad."

"And then, man, he said in his big bass voice: Goddamn you white folks, how come you-all cain't let us colored alone?"

". . . An' he was crying. . . ."

". . . An' Toussan tole them peckerwoods: I been beggin' you-all to quit bothering us. . . ."

". . . Beggin' on his bended knees! . . ."

"Then, man, Toussan got real mad and snatched off his hat and started stompin' up and down on it and the tears was tricklin' down and he said: You-all come tellin' me about Napoleon. . . ."

"They was tryin' to scare him, man. . . ."

"Said: I don't give a damn about Napoleon. . . ."

". . . Wasn't studyin' 'bout him. . . ."

". . . Toussan said: Napoleon ain't nothing but a man! Then Toussan pulled back his shining sword like this, and twirled it at them peckerwoods' throats so hard it z-z-z-zinged in the air!"

"Now keep on, finish it, man," said Buster. "What'd Toussan do then?"

"Then you know what he did, he said: I oughta beat the hell outa you peckerwoods!"

"Thass right, and he did it too," said Buster. He jumped to his feet and fenced violently with five desperate imaginary soldiers, running each through with his imaginary sword. Buster watched him from the porch, grinning.

"Toussan musta scared them white folks almost to death!"

"Yeah, thass 'bout the way it was," said Buster. The rhythm was dying now and he sat back upon the porch, breathing tiredly.

"It sho is a good story," said Riley.

"Hecks, man, all the stories my teacher tells us is good. She's a good ole teacher—but you know one thing?"

"Naw; what?"

"Ain't none of them stories in the books! Wonder why?"

"Hell, you know why, Ole Toussan was too hard on them white folks, thass why."

"Oh, he was a hard man!"

"He was mean. . . ."

"But a good mean!"

"Toussan was clean. . . ."

". . . He was a good, clean mean," said Riley.

"Aw, man, he was sooo-preme," said Buster.

"Riiiley!!"

The boys stopped short in their word play, their mouths wide.

"Riley, I say!" It was Riley's mother's voice.

"Ma'am?"

"She musta heard us cussin'," whispered Buster.

"Shut up, man. . . . What you want, Ma?"

"I says I wants you-all to go round in the backyard and play, you keeping up too much fuss out there. White folks says we tear up a neighborhood when we move in it and you-all out there jus' provin' them out true. Now git on round in the back."

"Aw, ma, we was jus' playing, ma. . . ."

"Boy, I said for you-all to go on."

"But, ma . . ."

"You hear me, boy!"

"Yessum, we going," said Riley. "Come on, Buster."

Buster followed slowly behind, feeling the dew upon his feet as he walked upon the shaded grass.

"What else did he do, man?" Buster said.

"Huh? Rogan?"

"Hecks, naw! I'm talkin' 'bout Toussan."

"Doggone if I know, man—but I'm gonna ask that teacher."

"He was a fightin' son-of-a-gun, wasn't he, man?"

"He didn't stand for no foolishness," said Riley reservedly. He thought of other things now, and as he moved along he slid his feet easily over the short-cut grass, dancing as he chanted:

> *Iron is iron,*
> *And tin is tin,*
> *And that's the way*
> *The story. . . .*

"Aw come on man," interrupted Buster. "Let's go play in the alley. . . ."

> *And that's the way. . . .*

"Maybe we can slip around and git some cherries," Buster went on.

> *. . . the story ends,* chanted Riley.

James Baldwin (1924-   )

The Man Child

The best known Afro-American author of this generation, James Baldwin is recognized as a talented writer of fiction and as one of the most distinguished essayists of our time. For many readers his chief merit, demonstrated more effectively in his essays than in his fiction, is his ability to articulate persuasively what it means to be a Negro.

Born and reared in Harlem, Baldwin became a minister when he was fourteen. But, dissatisfied, he left the church to search for his identity, first in America and later in France, where he has lived since 1948. He first aroused critical attention with *Go Tell It on the Mountain* (1953), a semi-autobiographical novel about a youth's religious awakening. Since then he has published three novels, two plays, three collections of essays, and one collection of short stories. His best-known works are *Another Country* (1962), a novel focused on homosexuality and interracial conflicts; *The Fire Next Time* (1963), a long essay explaining the need for black Americans to pity rather than hate their white countrymen; and *Blues for Mr. Charlie* (1964), a dramatization of interracial conflict in the South.

In "The Man Child," Baldwin looks through a white child's eyes at the violent admixtures of love and hate in the world of white adults.

The Man Child

As the sun began preparing for her exit, and he sensed the waiting night, Eric, blond and eight years old and dirty and tired, started homeward across the fields. Eric lived with his father, who was a farmer and the son of a farmer, and his mother, who had been captured by his father on some far-off, unblessed, unbelievable night, who had never since burst her chains. She did not know that she was chained anymore than she knew that she lived in terror of the night. One child was in the churchyard, it would have been Eric's little sister and her name would have been Sophie: for a long time, then, his mother had been very sick and pale. It was said that she would never, really, be better, that she would never again be as she had been. Then, not long ago, there had begun to be a pounding in his mother's belly, Eric had sometimes been able to hear it when he lay against her breast. His father had been pleased. *I did that,* said his father, big, laughing, dreadful, and red, and Eric knew how it was done, he had seen the horses and the blind and dreadful bulls. But then, again, his mother had been sick, she had had to be sent away, and when she came back the pounding was not there anymore, nothing was there anymore. His father laughed less, something in his mother's face seemed to have gone to sleep forever.

Eric hurried, for the sun was almost gone and he was afraid the night would catch him in the fields. And his mother would be angry. She did not really like him to go wandering off by himself. She would have forbidden it completely and kept Eric under her eye all day but in this she was overruled: Eric's father liked to think of Eric as being curious about the world and as being daring enough to explore it, with his own eyes, by himself.

His father would not be at home. He would be gone with his friend, Jamie, who was also a farmer and the son of a farmer, down to the tavern. This tavern was called the Rafters. They went each night, as his father said, imitating an Englishman he had known during a war, *to destruct the Rafters, sir.* They had been destructing The Rafters long before Eric had kicked in his mother's belly, for Eric's father and Jamie had grown up together, gone to war together, and survived together—never, apparently, while life ran, were they to be divided. They worked in the fields all day together, the fields which belonged to Eric's father. Jamie had been forced to sell his farm and it was Eric's father who had bought it.

Jamie had a brown and yellow dog. This dog was almost always with him; whenever Eric thought of Jamie he thought also of the dog. They had always been there, they had always been together: in exactly the same way, for Eric, that his mother and father had always been together, in exactly the same way that the earth and the trees and the sky were together. Jamie and his dog walked the country roads together, Jamie walking slowly in the way of country people, seeming to see nothing, heads lightly bent, feet striking surely and heavily on the earth, never stumbling. He walked as though he were going to walk to the other end of the world and knew it was a long way but knew that he would be there by morning. Sometimes he talked to his dog, head bent a little more than usual and turned to one side, a slight smile playing about the edges of his granite lips; and the dog's head snapped up, perhaps he leapt upon his master, who cuffed him down lightly, with one hand. More often he was silent. His head was carried in a cloud of blue smoke from his pipe. Through this cloud, like a ship on a foggy day, loomed his dry and steady face. Set far back, at an unapproachable angle, were those eyes of his, smoky and thoughtful, eyes which seemed always to be considering the horizon. He had the kind of eyes which no one had ever looked into—except Eric, only once. Jamie had been walking these roads and across these fields, whistling for his dog in the evenings as he turned away from Eric's house, for years, in silence. He had been married once, but his wife had run away. Now he lived alone in a wooden house and Eric's mother kept his clothes clean and Jamie always ate at Eric's house.

Eric had looked into Jamie's eyes on Jamie's birthday. They had had a party for him. Eric's mother had baked a cake and filled the house with flowers. The doors and windows of the great kitchen all stood open on the yard and the kitchen table was placed outside. The ground was not muddy as it was in winter, but hard, dry, and light brown. The flowers his mother so loved and so labored for flamed in their narrow borders against the stone wall of the farmhouse; and green vines covered the grey stone wall at the far end of the yard. Beyond this wall were the fields and barns, and Eric could see, quite far away, the cows nearly motionless in the bright green pasture. It was a bright, hot, silent day, the sun did not seem to be moving at all.

This was before his mother had had to be sent away. Her belly had been beginning to grow big, she had been dressed in blue, and had seemed—that day, to Eric—younger than she was ever to seem again.

Though it was still early when they were called to table, Eric's father and Jamie were already tipsy and came across the fields, shoulders touching, laughing, and telling each other stories. To express disapproval and also, perhaps, because she had heard their stories before and was bored, Eric's mother was quite abrupt with them, barely saying, "Happy Birthday, Jamie" before she made them sit down. In the nearby village church bells rang as they began to eat.

It was perhaps because it was Jamie's birthday that Eric was held by something in Jamie's face. Jamie, of course, was very old. He was thirty-four today, even older than Eric's father, who was only thirty-two. Eric wondered how it felt to have so many years and was suddenly, secretly glad that he was only eight. For today, Jamie *looked* old. It was perhaps the one additional year which had done it, this day, before their very eyes—a metamorphosis which made Eric rather shrink at the prospect of becoming nine. The skin of Jamie's face, which had never before seemed so, seemed wet today, and that rocky mouth of his was loose; loose was the word for everything about him, the way his arms and shoulders hung, the way he sprawled at the table, rocking slightly back and forth. It was not that he was drunk. Eric had seen him much drunker. Drunk, he became rigid, as though he imagined himself in the army again. No. He was old. It had come upon him all at once, today, on his birthday. He sat there, his hair in his eyes, eating, drinking, laughing now and again, and in a very strange way, and teasing the dog at his feet so that it sleepily growled and snapped all through the birthday dinner.

"Stop that," said Eric's father.

"Stop what?" asked Jamie.

"Let that stinking useless dog alone. Let him be quiet."

"Leave the beast alone," said Eric's mother—very wearily, sounding as she often sounded when talking to Eric.

"Well, now," said Jamie, grinning, and looking first at Eric's father and then at Eric's mother, "it *is* my beast. And a man's got a right to do as he likes with whatever's his."

"That dog's got a right to bite you, too," said Eric's mother, shortly.

"This dog's not going to bite me," said Jamie, "he knows I'll shoot him if he does."

"That dog knows you're not going to shoot him," said Eric's father. "Then you *would* be all alone."

"All alone," said Jamie, and looked around the table. "All alone." He lowered his eyes to his plate. Eric's father watched him. He said, "It's pretty serious to be all alone at *your* age." He smiled. "If I was you, I'd start thinking about it."

"I'm thinking about it," said Jamie. He began to grow red.

"No, you're not," said Eric's father, "you're dreaming about it."

"Well, goddammit," said Jamie, even redder now, "it isn't as though I haven't tried!"

"Ah," said Eric's father, "that was a *real* dream, that was. I used to pick *that* up on the streets of town every Saturday night."

"Yes," said Jamie, "I bet you did."

"I didn't think she was as bad as all that," said Eric's mother, quietly. "*I* liked her. I was surprised when she ran away."

"Jamie didn't know how to keep her," said Eric's father. He looked at Eric and chanted: "*Jamie, Jamie, pumkin-eater, had a wife and couldn't keep her!*" At this, Jamie at last looked up, into the eyes of Eric's father. Eric laughed again, more shrilly, out of fear. Jamie said:

"Ah, yes, you can talk, you can."

"It's not my fault," said Eric's father, "if you're getting old— and haven't got anybody to bring you your slippers when night comes—and no pitter-patter of little feet—"

"Oh, leave Jamie alone," said Eric's mother, "he's *not* old, leave him alone."

Jamie laughed a peculiar, high, clicking laugh which Eric had never heard before, which he did not like, which made him want to look away and, at the same time, want to stare. "Hell, no," said Jamie, "I'm not old. I can still do all the things we used to do." He put his elbows on the table, grinning. "I haven't ever told you, have I, about the things we used to do?"

"No, you haven't," said Eric's mother, "and I certainly don't want to hear about them now."

"He wouldn't tell you anyway," said Eric's father, "he knows what I'd do to him if he did."

"Oh, sure, sure," said Jamie, and laughed again. He picked up a bone from his plate. "Here," he said to Eric, "why don't you feed my poor mistreated dog?"

Eric took the bone and stood up, whistling for the dog; who moved away from his master and took the bone between his teeth. Jamie watched with a smile and opened the bottle of whiskey and poured himself a drink. Eric sat on the ground beside the dog, beginning to be sleepy in the bright, bright sun.

"Little Eric's getting big," he heard his father say.

"Yes," said Jamie, "they grow fast. It won't be long now."

"Won't be long *what?*" he heard his father ask.

"Why, before he starts skirt-chasing like his Daddy used to do," said Jamie. There was a mild laughter at the table in which his mother did not join; he heard instead, or thought he heard, the familiar, slight, exasperated intake of her breath. No one seemed to care whether he came back to the table or not. He lay on his back, staring up at the sky, wondering—wondering what he would feel like when he was old—and fell asleep.

When he awoke his head was in his mother's lap, for she was sitting on the ground. Jamie and his father were still sitting at the table; he knew this from their voices, for he did not open his eyes. He did not want to move or speak. He wanted to remain where he was, protected by his mother, while the bright day rolled on. Then he wondered about the uncut birthday cake. But he was sure, from the sound of Jamie's voice, which was thicker now, that they had not cut it yet; or if they had, they had certainly saved a piece for him.

"—ate himself just as full as he could and then fell asleep in the sun like a little animal," Jamie was saying, and the two men laughed. His father—though he scarcely ever got as drunk as Jamie did, and had often carried Jamie home from The Rafters—was a little drunk, too.

Eric felt his mother's hand on his hair. By opening his eyes very slightly he would see, over the curve of his mother's thigh, as through a veil, a green slope far away and beyond it the everlasting, motionless sky.

"—she was a no-good *bitch*," said Jamie.

"She was beautiful," said his mother, just above him.

Again, they were talking about Jamie's wife.

"Beauty!" said Jamie, furious. "Beauty doesn't keep a house clean. Beauty doesn't keep a bed warm, neither."

Eric's father laughed. "You were so—poetical—in those days, Jamie," he said. "Nobody thought you cared much about things like that. I guess she thought you didn't care, neither."

"I cared," said Jamie, briefly.

"In fact," Eric's father continued, "I *know* she thought you didn't care."

"*How* do you know?" asked Jamie.

"She told me," Eric's father said.

"What do you mean," asked Jamie, "what do you mean, she told you?"

"I mean just that. She told me."

Jamie was silent.

"In those days," Eric's father continued after a moment, "all you did was walk around the woods by yourself in the daytime and sit around The Rafters in the evenings with me."

"You two were always together then," said Eric's mother.

"Well," said Jamie, harshly, "at least that hasn't changed."

"Now, you know," said Eric's father, gently, "it's not the same. Now I got a wife and kid—and another one coming—"

Eric's mother stroked his hair more gently, yet with something in her touch more urgent, too, and he knew that she was thinking of the child who lay in the churchyard, who would have been his sister.

"Yes," said Jamie, "you really got it all fixed up, you did. You got it all—the wife, the kid, the house, and all the land."

"I didn't steal your farm from you. It wasn't my fault you lost it. I gave you a better price for it than anybody else would have done."

"I'm not blaming you. I know all the things I have to thank you for."

There was a short pause, broken, hesitantly, by Eric's mother. "What I don't understand," she said, "is why, when you went away to the city, you didn't *stay* away. You didn't really have anything to keep you here."

There was the sound of a drink being poured. Then, "No. I didn't have nothing—*really*—to keep me here. Just all the things I ever knew—all the things—*all* the things—I ever cared about."

"A man's not supposed to sit around and mope," said Eric's father, wrathfully, "for things that are over and dead and finished, things that can't *ever* begin again, that can't ever be the same again. That's what I mean when I say you're a dreamer—and if you hadn't kept on dreaming so long, you might not be alone now."

"Ah, well," said Jamie, mildly, and with a curious rush of affection in his voice, "I know you're the giant-killer, the hunter, the lover—the real old Adam, that's you. I know you're going to cover the earth. I know the world depends on men like you."

"And you're damn right," said Eric's father, after an uneasy moment.

Around Eric's head there was a buzzing, a bee, perhaps, a blue-fly, or a wasp. He hoped that his mother would see it and brush it away, but she did not move her hand. And he looked out again, through the veil of his eyelashes, at the slope and the sky, and then saw that the sun had moved and that it would not be long now before she would be going.

"—just like you already," Jamie said.

"You think my little one's like me?" Eric knew that his father was smiling—he could almost feel his father's hands.

"Looks like you, walks like you, talks like you," said Jamie.

"*And* stubborn like you," said Eric's mother.

"Ah, yes," said Jamie, and sighed. "You married the stubbornest, most determined—most selfish—man I know."

"I didn't know you felt that way," said Eric's father. He was still smiling.

"I'd have warned you about him," Jamie added, laughing, "if there'd been time."

"Everyone who knows you feels that way," said Eric's mother, and Eric felt a sudden brief tightening of the muscle in her thigh.

"Oh, *you*," said Eric's father, "I know *you* feel that way, women like to feel that way, it makes them feel important. But," and he changed to the teasing tone he took so persistently with Jamie today, "I didn't know my fine friend, Jamie, here—"

It was odd how unwilling he was to open his eyes. Yet, he felt the sun on him and knew that he wanted to rise from where he was before the sun went down. He did not understand what they were talking about this afternoon, these grown-ups he had known all his life; by keeping his eyes closed he kept their conversation far from him. And his mother's hand lay on his head like a blessing, like protection. And the buzzing had ceased, the bee, the blue-fly, or the wasp seemed to have flown away.

"—if it's a boy this time," his father said, "we'll name it after you."

"That's touching," said Jamie, "but that really won't do me—or the kid—a hell of a lot of good."

"Jamie can get married and have kids of his own any time he decides to," said Eric's mother.

"No," said his father, after a long pause, "Jamie's thought about it too long."

And, suddenly, he laughed and Eric sat up as his father slapped Jamie on the knee. At the touch, Jamie leaped up, shouting, spilling his drink and overturning his chair, and the dog beside Eric awoke and began to bark. For a moment, before Eric's unbelieving eyes, there was nothing in the yard but noise and flame.

His father rose slowly and stared at Jamie. "What's the matter with you?"

"What's the matter with me!" mimicked Jamie, "what's the matter with me? what the hell do you care what's the matter with me! What the hell have you been riding me for all day like this? What do you want? what do you *want?*"

"I want you to learn to hold your liquor for one thing," said his father, coldly. The two men stared at each other. Jamie's face was red and ugly and tears stood in his eyes. The dog, at his legs, kept up a furious prancing and barking. Jamie bent down and, with one hand, with all his might, slapped his dog, which rolled over, howling, and ran away to hide itself under the shadows of the far grey wall.

Then Jamie stared again at Eric's father, trembling, and pushed his hair back from his eyes.

"You better pull yourself together," Eric's father said. And, to Eric's mother. "Get him some coffee. He'll be all right."

Jamie set his glass on the table and picked up the overturned chair. Eric's mother rose and went into the kitchen. Eric remained sitting on the ground, staring at the two men, his father and his father's best friend, who had become so unfamiliar. His father, with something in his face which Eric had never before seen there, a tenderness, a sorrow—or perhaps it was, after all, the look he sometimes wore when approaching a calf he was about to slaughter—looked down at Jamie where he sat, head bent, at the table. "You take things too hard," he said. "You always have. I was only teasing you for your own good."

Jamie did not answer. His father looked over to Eric, and smiled.

"Come on," he said. "You and me are going for a walk."

Eric, passing on the side of the table farthest from Jamie, went to his father and took his hand.

"Pull yourself together," his father said to Jamie. "We're going to cut your birthday cake as soon as me and the little one come back."

Eric and his father passed beyond the grey wall where the dog still whimpered, out into the fields. Eric's father was walking too fast and Eric stumbled on the uneven ground. When they had gone a little distance his father abruptly checked his pace and looked down at Eric, grinning.

"I'm sorry," he said. "I guess I said we were going for a walk, not running to put out a fire."

"What's the matter with Jamie?" Eric asked.

"Oh," said his father, looking westward where the sun was moving, pale orange now, making the sky ring with brass and

copper and gold—which, like a magician, she was presenting only
to demonstrate how variously they could be transformed—"Oh,"
he repeated, "there's nothing wrong with Jamie. He's been drinking a lot," and he grinned down at Eric, "and he's been sitting in
the sun—you know, his hair's not as thick as yours," and he
ruffled Eric's hair, "and I guess birthdays make him nervous.
Hell," he said, "they make me nervous, too."

"Jamie's *very* old," said Eric, "isn't he?"

His father laughed. "Well, butch, he's not exactly ready to fall
into the grave yet—he's going to be around awhile, is Jamie.
Hey," he said, and looked down at Eric again, "you must think
I'm an old man, too."

"Oh," said Eric, quickly, "I know you're not as old as Jamie."

His father laughed again. "Well, thank you, son. That shows
real confidence. I'll try to live up to it."

They walked in silence for awhile and then his father said, not
looking at Eric, speaking to himself, it seemed, or to the air: "No,
Jamie's not so old. He's not as old as he should be."

"How old *should* he be?" asked Eric.

"Why," said his father, "he ought to be his age," and, looking
down at Eric's face, he burst into laughter again.

"Ah," he said, finally, and put his hand on Eric's head again,
very gently, very sadly, "don't you worry now about what you
don't understand. The time is coming when you'll have to worry—
but that time hasn't come yet."

Then they walked till they came to the steep slope which led to
the railroad tracks, down, down, far below them, where a small
train seemed to be passing forever through the countryside, smoke,
like the very definition of idleness, blowing out of the chimney
stack of the toy locomotive. Eric thought, resentfully, that he
scarcely ever saw a train pass when he came here alone. Beyond
the railroad tracks was the river where they sometimes went swimming in the summer. The river was hidden from them now by the
high bank where there were houses and where tall trees grew.

"And this," said his father, "is where your land ends."

"What?" said Eric.

His father squatted on the ground and put one hand on Eric's
shoulder. "You know all the way we walked, from the house?" Eric
nodded. "Well," said his father, "that's your land."

Eric looked back at the long way they had come, feeling his
father watching him.

His father, with a pressure on his shoulder made him turn; he
pointed: "And over there. It belongs to you." He turned him
again. "And that," he said, "that's yours, too."

Eric stared at his father. "Where does it end?" he asked.

His father rose. "I'll show you that another day," he said. "But it's further than you can walk."

They started walking slowly, in the direction of the sun.

"When did it get to be mine?" asked Eric.

"The day you were born," his father said, and looked down at him and smiled.

"My father," he said, after a moment, "had some of this land— and when he died, it was mine. He held on to it for me. And I did my best with the land I had, and I got some more. I'm holding on to it for you."

He looked down to see if Eric was listening. Eric was listening, staring at his father and looking around him at the great countryside.

"When I get to be a real old man," said his father, "even older than old Jamie there—you're going to have to take care of all this. When I die it's going to be yours." He paused and stopped; Eric looked up at him. "When you get to be a big man, like your Papa, you're going to get married and have children. And all this is going to be theirs."

"And when *they* get married?" Eric prompted.

"All this will belong to *their* children," his father said.

"Forever?" cried Eric.

"Forever," said his father.

They turned and started walking toward the house.

"Jamie," Eric asked at last, "how much land has *he* got?"

"Jamie doesn't have any land," his father said.

"Why not?" asked Eric.

"He didn't take care of it," his father said, "and he lost it."

"Jamie doesn't have a wife anymore, either, does he?" Eric asked.

"No," said his father. "He didn't take care of her, either."

"And he doesn't have any little boy," said Eric—very sadly.

"No," said his father. Then he grinned. "But *I* have."

"*Why* doesn't Jamie have a little boy?" asked Eric.

His father shrugged. "Some people do, Eric, some people don't."

"Will I?" asked Eric.

"Will you what?" asked his father.

"Will I get married and have a little boy?"

His father seemed for a moment both amused and checked. He looked down at Eric with a strange, slow smile. "Of course you will," he said at last. "Of course you will." And he held out his arms. "Come," he said, "climb up. I'll ride you on my shoulders home."

So Eric rode on his father's shoulders through the wide green fields which belonged to him, into the yard which held the house which would hear the first cries of his children. His mother and Jamie sat at the table talking quietly in the silver sun. Jamie had washed his face and combed his hair, he seemed calmer, he was smiling.

"Ah," cried Jamie, "the lord, the master of this house arrives! And bears on his shoulders the prince, the son, and heir!" He described a flourish, bowing low in the yard. "My lords! Behold your humble, most properly chastised servant, desirous of your— compassion, your love, and your forgiveness!"

"Frankly," said Eric's father, putting Eric on the ground, "I'm not sure that this is an improvement." He looked at Jamie and frowned and grinned. "Let's cut that cake."

Eric stood with his mother in the kitchen while she lit the candles—thirty-five, one, as they said, to grow on, though Jamie, surely, was far past the growing age—and followed her as she took the cake outside. Jamie took the great, gleaming knife and held it with a smile.

"Happy Birthday!" they cried—only Eric said nothing—and then Eric's mother said, "You have to blow out the candles, Jamie, before you cut the cake."

"It looks so pretty the way it is," Jamie said.

"Go ahead," said Eric's father, and clapped him on the back, "be a man."

Then the dog, once more beside his master, awoke, growling, and this made everybody laugh. Jamie laughed loudest. Then he blew out the candles, all of them at once, and Eric watched him as he cut the cake. Jamie raised his eyes and looked at Eric and it was at this moment, as the suddenly blood-red sun was striking the topmost tips of trees, that Eric had looked into Jamie's eyes. Jamie smiled that strange smile of an old man and Eric moved closer to his mother.

"The first piece for Eric," said Jamie, then, and extended it to him on the silver blade.

That had been near the end of summer, nearly two months ago. Very shortly after the birthday party, his mother had fallen ill and had had to be taken away. Then his father spent more time than ever at The Rafters; he and Jamie came home in the evenings, stumbling drunk. Sometimes, during the time that his mother was away, Jamie did not go home at all, but spent the night at the farm house; and once or twice Eric had awakened in the middle of the night, or near dawn, and heard Jamie's footsteps walking up and down, walking up and down, in the big room downstairs. It had been a strange and dreadful time, a time of waiting, stillness, and silence. His father rarely went into the fields, scarcely raised himself to give orders to his farm hands—it was unnatural, it was frightening, to find him around the house all day, and Jamie was there always, Jamie and his dog. Then one day Eric's father told him that his mother was coming home but that she would not be bringing him a baby brother or sister, not this time, nor in any time to come. He started to say something more, then looked at Jamie who was standing by, and walked out of the house. Jamie followed him slowly, his hands in his pockets and his head bent. From the time of the birthday party, as though he were repenting of that outburst, or as though it had frightened him, Jamie had become more silent than ever.

When his mother came back she seemed to have grown older—old; she seemed to have shrunk within herself, away from them all, even, in a kind of storm of love and helplessness, away from Eric; but, oddly, and most particularly, away from Jamie. It was in nothing she said, nothing she did—or perhaps it was in everything she said and did. She washed and cooked for Jamie as before, took him into account as much as before as a part of the family, made him take second helpings at the table, smiled good night to him as he left the house—it was only that something had gone out of her familiarity. She seemed to do all that she did out of memory and from a great distance. And if something had gone out of her ease, something had come into it, too, a curiously still attention, as though she had been startled by some new aspect of something she had always known. Once or twice at the supper table, Eric caught her regard bent on Jamie, who, obliviously, ate. He could not read her look, but it reminded him of that moment at the birthday party when he had looked into Jamie's eyes. She seemed to be looking at Jamie as though she were wondering why she had not looked at him before; or as though she were discovering, with some surprise, that she had never really liked him but also felt, in her weariness and weakness, that it did not really matter now.

Now, as he entered the yard, he saw her standing in the kitchen doorway, looking out, shielding her eyes against the brilliant setting sun.

"Eric!" she cried, wrathfully, as soon as she saw him. "I've been looking high and low for you for the last hour. You're getting old enough to have some sense of responsibility and I wish you wouldn't worry me so when you know I've not been well."

She made him feel guilty at the same time that he dimly and resentfully felt that justice was not all on her side. She pulled him to her, turning his face up toward hers, roughly, with one hand.

"You're filthy," she said, then. "Go around to the pump and wash your face. And hurry, so I can give you your supper and put you to bed."

And she turned and went into the kitchen, closing the door lightly behind her. He walked around to the other side of the house, to the pump.

On a wooden box next to the pump was a piece of soap and a damp rag. Eric picked up the soap, not thinking of his mother, but thinking of the day gone by, already half asleep: and thought of where he would go tomorrow. He moved the pump handle up and down and the water rushed out and wet his socks and shoes—this would make his mother angry, but he was too tired to care. Nevertheless, automatically, he moved back a little. He held the soap between his hands, his hands beneath the water.

He had been many places, he had walked a long way and seen many things that day. He had gone down to the railroad tracks and walked beside the tracks for awhile, hoping that a train would pass. He kept telling himself that he would give the train one more last chance to pass; and when he had given it a considerable number of last chances, he left the railroad bed and climbed a little and walked through the high, sweet meadows. He walked through a meadow where there were cows and they looked at him dully with their great dull eyes and moo'd among each other about him. A man from the far end of the field saw him and shouted, but Eric could not tell whether it was someone who worked for his father or not and so he turned and ran away, ducking through the wire fence. He passed an apple tree, with apples lying all over the ground—he wondered if the apples belonged to him, if he were still walking on his own land or had gone past it—but he ate an apple anyway and put some in his pockets, watching a lone brown horse in a meadow far below him nibbling at the grass and flicking his tail. Eric pretended that he was his father and was walking through the fields as he had seen his father walk, looking it all over calmly, pleased, knowing that everything he saw belonged to him. And he stopped and pee'd as he had seen his father do, standing wide-legged and heavy in the middle of the fields; he pretended at the same time to be smoking and talking, as he had seen his father do. Then, having watered the ground, he walked on, and all the earth, for that moment, in Eric's eyes, seemed to be celebrating Eric.

Tomorrow he would go away again, somewhere. For soon it would be winter, snow would cover the ground, he would not be able to wander off alone.

He held the soap between his hands, his hands beneath the water; then he heard a low whistle behind him and a rough hand on his head and the soap fell from his hands and slithered between his legs onto the ground.

He turned and faced Jamie, Jamie without his dog.

"Come on, little fellow," Jamie whispered. "We got something in the barn to show you."

"Oh, did the calf come yet?" asked Eric—and was too pleased to wonder why Jamie whispered.

"Your Papa's there," said Jamie. And then: "Yes. Yes, the calf is coming now."

And he took Eric's hand and they crossed the yard, past the closed kitchen door, past the stone wall and across the field, into the barn.

"But *this* isn't where the cows are!" Eric cried. He suddenly looked up at Jamie, who closed the barn door behind them and looked down at Eric with a smile.

"No," said Jamie, "that's right. No cows here." And he leaned against the door as though his strength had left him. Eric saw that his face was wet, he breathed as though he had been running.

"Let's go see the cows," Eric whispered. Then he wondered why he was whispering and was terribly afraid. He stared at Jamie, who stared at him.

"In a minute," Jamie said, and stood up. He had put his hands in his pockets and now he brought them out and Eric stared at his hands and began to move away. He asked, "Where's my Papa?"

"Why," said Jamie, "he's down at The Rafters, I guess. I have to meet him there soon."

"I have to go," said Eric. "I have to eat my supper." He tried to move to the door, but Jamie did not move. "I have to go," he repeated, and, as Jamie moved toward him the tight ball of terror in his bowels, in his throat, swelled and rose, exploded, he opened his mouth to scream but Jamie's fingers closed around his throat. He stared, stared into Jamie's eyes.

"That won't do you any good," said Jamie. And he smiled. Eric struggled for breath, struggled with pain and fright. Jamie relaxed his grip a little and moved one hand and stroked Eric's tangled hair. Slowly, wondrously, his face changed, tears came into his eyes and rolled down his face.

Eric groaned—perhaps because he saw Jamie's tears or because his throat was so swollen and burning, because he could not catch his breath, because he was so frightened—he began to sob in great, unchildish gasps. "Why do you hate my father?"

"I love your father," Jamie said. But he was not listening to Eric. He was far away—as though he were struggling, toiling inwardly up a tall, tall mountain. And Eric struggled blindly, with all the force of his desire to live, to reach him, to stop him before he reached the summit.

"Jamie," Eric whispered, "you can have the land. You can have all the land."

Jamie spoke, but not to Eric: "I don't want the land."

"I'll be your little boy," said Eric. "I'll be your little boy forever and forever and forever—and you can have the land and you can live forever! Jamie!"

Jamie had stopped weeping. He was watching Eric.

"We'll go for a walk tomorrow," Eric said, "and I'll show it to you, all of it—really and truly—if you kill my father I can be your little boy and we can have it all!"

"This land," said Jamie, "will belong to no one."

"Please!" cried Eric, "oh, please! Please!"

He heard his mother singing in the kitchen. Soon she would come out to look for him. The hands left him for a moment. Eric opened his mouth to scream, but the hands then closed around his throat.

Mama. Mama.

The singing was further and further away. The eyes looked into his, there was a question in the eyes, the hands tightened. Then the mouth began to smile. He had never seen such a smile before. He kicked and kicked.

Mama. Mama. Mama. Mama. Mama.

Far away, he heard his mother call him.

Mama.

He saw nothing, he knew that he was in the barn, he heard a terrible breathing near him, he thought he heard the sniffling of beasts, he remembered the sun, the railroad tracks, the cows, the apples, and the ground. He thought of tomorrow—he wanted to go away again somewhere tomorrow. *I'll take you with me*, he wanted to say. He wanted to argue the question, the question he remembered in the eyes—wanted to say, *I'll tell my Papa you're hurting me.* Then terror and agony and darkness overtook him, and his breath went violently out of him. He dropped on his face in the straw in the barn, his yellow head useless on his broken neck.

Night covered the countryside and here and there, like emblems, the lights of houses glowed. A woman's voice called, "Eric! Eric!"

Jamie reached his wooden house and opened his door; whistled, and his dog came bounding out of darkness, leaping up on him; and he cuffed it down lightly, with one hand. Then he closed his door and started down the road, his dog beside him, his hands in his pockets. He stopped to light his pipe. He heard singing from The Rafters, then he saw the lights; soon, the lights and the sound of singing diminished behind him. When Jamie no longer heard the singing, he began to whistle the song that he had heard.

William Melvin Kelley
(1937-   )

The Only Man on Liberty Street

William M. Kelley is judged by many critics to be one of the most promising novelists of the past decade. Born in New York City, educated at Harvard University, he has won the Reed Literary Prize and the Rosenthal Foundation Award of the National Institute of Arts and Letters.

Kelley earned his first national recognition for *A Different Drummer* (1962), a novel describing the events of a memorable moment in history when all of the Negro residents emigrate from an unnamed Southern state. Since then, Kelley has published *Dancers on the Shore* (1964), a collection of short stories; and *Dem*, a second novel.

In his early work Kelley has been most effective when telling his story through a child, as he does in the following tale of miscegenation in the South.

The Only Man on Liberty Street

She was squatting in the front yard, digging with an old brass spoon in the dirt which was an ocean to the islands of short yellow grass. She wore a red and white checkered dress, which hung loosely from her shoulders, and obscured her legs. It was early

From *Dancers on the Shore* (Garden City, New York: Doubleday & Company, 1963). Copyright © 1963 by William Melvin Kelley. Reprinted by permission of Doubleday & Company, Inc.

spring and she was barefoot. Her toes stuck from under the skirt. She could not see the man yet, riding down Liberty Street, his shoulders square, the duster he wore spread back over the horse's rump, a carpetbag tied with a leather strap to his saddle horn and knocking against his leg. She could not see him until he had dismounted and tied his horse to a small, black, iron Negro jockey and unstrapped the bag. She watched now as he opened the wooden gate, came into the yard, and stood, looking down at her, his face stern, almost gray beneath the brim of his wide hat.

She knew him. Her mother called him Mister Herder and had told Jennie that he was Jennie's father. He was one of the men who came riding down Liberty Street in their fine black suits and starched shirts and large, dark ties. Each of these men had a house to go to, into which, in the evening usually, he would disappear. Only women and children lived on Liberty Street. All of them were Negroes. Some of the women were quite dark, but most were coffee-color. They were all very beautiful. Her mother was light. She was tall, had black eyes, and black hair so long she could sit on it.

The man standing over her was the one who came to her house once or twice a week. He was never there in the morning when Jennie got up. He was tall, and thin, and blond. He had a short beard that looked as coarse as the grass beneath her feet. His eyes were blue, like Jennie's. He did not speak English very well. Jennie's mother had told her he came from across the sea and Jennie often wondered if he went there between visits to their house.

"Jennie? Your mother tells me that you ask why I do not stay at night. Is so?"

She looked up at him. "Yes, Mister Herder." The hair under his jaw was darker than the hair on his cheeks.

He nodded. "I stay now. Go bring your mother."

She left the spoon in the dirt, and ran into the house, down the long hall, dark now because she had been sitting in the sun. She found her mother standing over the stove, a great black lid in her left hand, a wooden spoon in her right. There were beads of sweat on her forehead. She wore a full black skirt and a white blouse. Her one waist-length braid hung straight between her shoulder blades. She turned to Jennie's running steps.

"Mama? That man? My father? He in the yard. He brung a carpetbag."

First her mother smiled, then frowned, then looked puzzled. "A carpetbag, darling?"

"Yes, Mama."

She followed her mother through the house, pausing with her at the hall mirror where the woman ran her hand up the back of her neck to smooth stray black hair. Then they went onto the porch, where the man was now seated, surveying the tiny yard and the dark green hedge that enclosed it. The carpetbag rested beside his chair.

Her mother stood with her hands beneath her apron, staring at the bag. "Mister Herder?"

He turned to them. "I will not go back this time. No matter what. Why should I live in that house when I must come here to know what home is?" He nodded sharply as if in answer to a question. "So! I stay. I give her that house. I will send her money, but I stay here."

Her mother stood silently for an instant, then turned to the door. "Dinner'll be on the table in a half hour." She opened the screen door. The spring whined and cracked. "Oh." She let go the door, and picked up the carpetbag. "I'll take this on up." She went inside. As she passed, Jennie could see she was smiling again.

After that, Jennie's mother became a celebrity on Liberty Street. The other women would stop her to ask about the man. "And he staying for good, Josie?"

"Yes."

"You have any trouble yet?"

"Not yet."

"Well, child, you make him put that there house in your name. You don't want to be no Sissie Markham. That white woman come down the same day he died and moved Sissie and her children right into the gutter. You get that house put in your name. You hear?"

"Yes."

"How is it? It different?"

Her mother would look dazed. "Yes, it different. He told me to call him Maynard."

The other women were always very surprised.

At first, Jennie too was surprised. The man was always there in the morning and sometimes even woke her up. Her mother no longer called him Mister Herder, and at odd times, though still quite seldom, said, No. She had never before heard her mother say

No to anything the man ever said. It was not long before Jennie was convinced that he actually was her father. She began to call him Papa.

Daily now a white woman had been driving by their house. Jennie did not know who she was or what she wanted, but playing in the yard, would see the white woman's gray buggy turn the corner and come slowly down the block, pulled by a speckled horse that trudged in the dry dust. A Negro driver sat erect in his black uniform, a whip in his fist. The white woman would peer at the house as if looking for an address or something special. She would look at the curtained windows, looking for someone, and sometimes even at Jennie. The look was not kind or tender, but hard and angry as if she knew something bad about the child.

Then one day the buggy stopped, the Negro pulling gently on the reins. The white woman leaned forward, spoke to the driver and handed him a small pink envelope. He jumped down, opened the gate, and without looking at Jennie, his face dark and shining, advanced on the porch, up the three steps, which knocked hollow beneath his boots, opened the screen door and twisted the polished brass bell key in the center of the open, winter door.

Her mother came drying her hands. The Negro reached out the envelope and her mother took it, looking beyond him for an instant at the buggy and the white woman who returned her look coldly. As the Negro turned, her mother opened the letter, and read it, moving her lips slightly. Then Jennie could see the twinkling at the corners of her eyes. Her mother stood framed in the black square of doorway, tall, fair, the black hair swept to hide her ears, her eyes glistening.

Jennie turned back to the white woman now and saw her lean deeper into her seat. Then she pulled forward. "Do you understand what I will have them do?" She was shouting shrilly and spoke like Jennie's father. "You tell him he has got one wife! You are something different!" She leaned back again, waved her gloved hand and the buggy lurched down the street, gained speed, and jangled out of sight around the corner.

Jennie was on her feet and pounding up the stairs. "Mama?"

"Go play, Jennie. Go on now, *play!*" Still her mother stared straight ahead, as if the buggy and the white woman remained in front of the house. She still held the letter as if to read it. The corners of her eyes were wet. Then she turned and went into the house. The screen door clacked behind her.

At nights now Jennie waited by the gate in the yard for her father to turn the corner, walking. In the beginning she had been waiting too for the one day he would not turn the corner. But each night he came, that day seemed less likely to come. Even so, she was always surprised to see him. When she did, she would wave, timidly, raising her hand only to her shoulder, wiggling only her fingers, as if to wave too wildly would somehow cause the entire picture of his advancing to collapse as only a slight wind would be enough to disarrange a design of feathers.

That night too she waved and saw him raise his hand high over his head, greeting her. She backed away when he reached the gate so he might open it, her head thrown way back, looking up at him.

"Well, my Jennie, what kind of day did you have?"

She only smiled, then remembered the white woman. "A woman come to visit Mama. She come in a buggy and give her a letter too. She made Mama cry."

His smile fled. He sucked his tongue, angry now. "We go see what is wrong. Come." He reached for her hand.

Her mother was in the kitchen. She looked as if she did not really care what she was doing or how, walking from pump to stove, stove to cupboard in a deep trance. The pink envelope was on the table.

She turned to them. Her eyes were red. Several strands of hair stuck to her temples. She cleared her nose and pointed to the letter. "She come today."

Her father let go Jennie's hand, picked up the letter and read it. When he was finished he took it to the stove and dropped it into the flame. There was a puff of smoke before he replaced the lid. He shook his head. "She cannot make me go back, Josephine."

Her mother fell heavily into a wooden chair, beginning to cry again. "But she's white, Maynard."

He raised his eyebrows like a priest or a displeased school teacher. "Your skin is whiter."

"My mother was a slave."

He threw up his hands, making fists. "Your mother did not ask to be a slave!" Then he went to her, crouched on his haunches before her, speaking quietly. "No one can make me go back."

"But she can get them to do what she say." She turned her gaze on Jennie, but looked away quickly. "You wasn't here after the war. But I seen things. I seen things happen to field niggers that ... I was up in the house; they didn't bother me. My own father, General Dewey Willson, he stood on a platform in the center of town and promised to keep the niggers down. I was close by." She took his face in her hands. "Maynard, maybe you better go back, leastways—"

"I go back—dead! You hear? Dead. These children, these cowardly children in their masks will not move me! I go back dead.
That is all. We do not discuss it." And he was gone. Jennie heard
him thundering down the hall, knocking against the table near the
stairs, going up to the second floor.

Her mother was looking at her now, her eyes even more red than
before, her lips trembling, her hands active in her lap. "Jennie?"

"Yes, Mama." She took a step toward her, staring into the
woman's eyes.

"Jennie, I want you to promise me something and not forget
it."

"Yes, Mama." She was between her mother's knees, felt the
woman's hands clutching her shoulders.

"Jennie, you'll be right pretty when you get grown. Did you
know that? Promise me you'll go up North. Promise me if I'm not
here when you get eighteen, you'll go north and get married. You
understand?"

Jennie was not sure she did. She could not picture the North,
except that she had heard once it was cold and white things fell
from the sky. She could not picture being eighteen and her mother
not being there. But she knew her mother wanted her to understand and she lied. "Yes, Mama."

"Repeat what I just said."

She did. Her mother kissed her mouth, the first time ever.

From the kitchen below came their voices. Her father's voice
sounded hard, cut short; Jennie knew he had made a decision and
was sticking to it. Her mother was pleading, trying to change his
mind. It was July the Fourth, the day of the shooting match.

She dressed in her Sunday clothes and coming downstairs, heard
her mother: "Maynard, please don't take her." She was frantic
now. "I'm begging you. Don't take that child with you today."

"I take her. We do not discuss it. I take her. Those sneaking
cowards in their masks . . ." Jennie knew now what they were
talking about. Her father had promised to take her to the shooting
match. For some reason, her mother feared there would be trouble
if Jennie went downtown. She did not know why her mother felt
that way, except that it might have something to do with the
white woman, who continued to ride by their house each morning,
after her father had left for the day. Perhaps her mother did not
want to be alone in the house when the white woman drove by in

her gray buggy, even though she had not stopped the buggy since the day two months ago, when the Negro had given her mother the pink envelope.

But other strange things had happened after that. In the beginning she and her mother, as always before, had gone downtown to the market, to shop amid the bright stalls brimming with green and yellow vegetables and brick-red meats, tended by dark, country Negroes in shabby clothes and large straw hats. It would get very quiet when they passed, and Jennie would see the Negroes look away, fear in their eyes, and knots of white men watching, sometimes giggling. But the white women in fine clothes were the most frightening; sitting on the verandas or passing in carriages, some even coming to their windows, they would stare angrily as if her mother had done something terrible to each one personally, as if all these white women could be the one who drove by each morning. Her mother would walk through it all, her back straight, very like her father's, the bun into which she wove her waist-length braid on market days, gleaming dark.

In the beginning they had gone to the suddenly quiet market. But now her mother hardly set foot from the house, and the food was brought to them in a carton by a crippled Negro boy, who was coming just as Jennie and her father left the house that morning.

Balancing the carton on his left arm, he removed his ragged hat and smiled. "Morning, Mister Herder. Good luck at the shooting match, sir." His left leg was short and he seemed to tilt.

Her father nodded. "Thank you, Felix. I do my best."

"Then you a sure thing, Mister Herder." He replaced his hat and went on around the house.

Walking, her hand in her father's, Jennie could see some of the women of Liberty Street peering out at them through their curtains.

Downtown was not the same. Flags and banners draped the verandas; people wore their best clothes. The Square had been roped off, a platform set up to one side, and New Marsails Avenue, which ran into the Square, had been cleared for two blocks. Far away down the Avenue stood a row of cotton bales onto which had been pinned oilcloth targets. From where they stood, the bull's-eyes looked no bigger than red jawbreakers.

Many men slapped her father on the back, and furtively, looked at her with a kind of clinical interest. But mostly they ignored her. The celebrity of the day was her father, and unlike her mother, he was very popular. Everyone felt sure he would win the match; he was the best shot in the state.

After everyone shot, the judge came running down from the targets, waving his arms. "Maynard Herder. Six shots, and you can cover them all with a good gob of spit!" He grabbed her father's elbow and pulled him toward the platform, where an old man with white hair and beard, wearing a gray uniform trimmed with yellow, waited. She followed them to the platform steps, but was afraid to go any farther because now some women had begun to look at her as they had at her mother.

The old man made a short speech, his voice deep, but coarse, grainy-sounding, and gave her father a silver medal in a blue velvet box. Her father turned and smiled at her. She started up the steps toward him, but just then the old man put his hand on her father's shoulder.

People had begun to walk away down the streets leading out of the Square. There was less noise now but she could not hear the first words the old man said to her father.

Her father's face tightened into the same look she had seen the day the letter came, the same as this morning in the kitchen. She went halfway up the stairs, stopped.

The old man went on: "You know I'm no meddler. Everybody knows about Liberty Street. I had a woman down there myself . . . before the war."

"I know that." The words came out of her father's face, though his lips did not move.

The old man nodded. "But, Maynard, what you're doing is different."

"She's your own daughter."

"Maybe that's why . . ." The old man looked down the street, toward the cotton bales and the targets. "But she's a nigger. And now the talking is taking an ugly turn and the folks talking are the ones I can't hold."

Her father spoke in an angry whisper. "You see what I do to that target? You tell those children in their masks I do that to the forehead of any man . . . or woman that comes near her or my house. You tell them."

"Maynard, that wouldn't do any real good *after* they'd done something to her." He stopped, looked at Jennie, and smiled. "That's my only granddaughter, you know." His eyes clicked off her. "You're a man who knows firearms. You're a gunsmith. I know firearms too. Pistols and rifles can do lots of things, but they don't make very good doctors. Nobody's asking you to give her up. Just go back home. That's all. Go back to your wife."

Her father turned away, walking fast, came down the stairs and grabbed her hand. His face was red as blood between the white of his collar and the straw yellow of his hair.

They slowed after a block, paused in a small park with green trees shading several benches and a statue of a stern-faced young man in uniform, carrying pack and rifle. "We will sit."

She squirmed up onto the bench beside him. The warm wind smelled of salt from the Gulf of Mexico. The leaves were a dull, low tambourine. Her father was quiet for a long while.

Jennie watched birds bobbing for worms in the grass near them, then looked at the young, stone soldier. Far off, but from where she viewed it, just over the soldier's hat, a gliding sea gull dived suddenly behind the rooftops. That was when she saw the white man, standing across the street from the park, smiling at her. There were other white men with him, some looking at her, others at the man, all laughing. He waved to her. She smiled at him though he was the kind of man her mother told her always to stay away from. He was dressed as poorly as any Negro. From behind his back, he produced a brown rag doll, looked at her again, then grabbed the doll by its legs, and tore it part way up the middle. Then he jammed his finger into the rip between the doll's legs. The other men laughed uproariously.

Jennie pulled her father's sleeve. "Papa? What he doing?"

"Who?" Her father turned. The man repeated the show and her father bolted to his feet, yelling: "I will kill you! You hear? I will kill you for that!"

The men only snickered and ambled away.

Her father was red again. He had clenched his fists; now his hands were white like the bottoms of fishes. He sighed, shook his head and sat down. "I cannot kill everybody." He shook his head again, then leaned forward to get up. But first he thrust the blue velvet medal box into her hand. It was warm from his hand, wet and prickly. "When you grow up, you go to the North like your mother tells you. And you take this with you. It is yours. Always remember I gave it to you." He stood. "Now you must go home alone. Tell your mother I come later."

That night, Jennie tried to stay awake until he came home, until he was there to kiss her good night, his whiskers scratching her cheek. But all at once there was sun at her window and the sound of carts and wagons grating outside in the dirt street. Her mother was quiet while the two of them ate. After breakfast, Jennie went into the yard to wait for the gray buggy to turn the corner, but for the first morning in many months, the white woman did not jounce by, peering at the house, searching for someone or something special.

Kristin Hunter (1931-   )

Debut

Born in Philadelphia, Pennsylvania, Kristin Hunter is one of the promising novelists of the current decade. She began writing for *The Pittsburgh Courier* several years before she earned a Bachelor of Science in Education from the University of Pennsylvania in 1951. Since then, Mrs. Hunter has had varied experience as a copywriter, an information officer for the city of Philadelphia, and a free lance writer.

Kristin Hunter earned her first significant recognition as a writer when she was awarded a Fund for the Republic prize for her television documentary, "Minority of One," produced by Columbia Broadcasting System in 1956. She has published two novels, *God Bless the Child* (1964) and *The Landlord* (1965).

Rather than following some recent writers who promote "black literature for black people," Mrs. Hunter has interested herself in the interrelationships of white and black Americans and in the emotional crises of urban Negroes. In the following story, she focuses on the daughter of a social-climbing Negro woman, a subject rarely treated by current black authors.

Debut

"Hold *still*, Judy," Mrs. Simmons said around the spray of pins that protruded dangerously from her mouth. She gave the thirtieth

From *Negro Digest*, XVII (June, 1968). Copyright 1968 by Kristin Hunter. Reprinted by permission of Harold Matson Company, Inc.

tug to the tight sash at the waist of the dress. "Now walk over there and turn around slowly."

The dress, Judy's first long one, was white organdy over taffeta, with spaghetti straps that bared her round brown shoulders and a floating skirt and a wide sash that cascaded in a butterfly effect behind. It was a dream, but Judy was sick and tired of the endless fittings she had endured so that she might wear it at the Debutantes' Ball. Her thoughts leaped ahead to the Ball itself . . .

"*Slowly*, I said!" Mrs. Simmons' dark, angular face was always grim, but now it was screwed into an expression resembling a prune. Judy, starting nervously, began to revolve by moving her feet an inch at a time.

Her mother watched her critically. "No, it's still not right. I'll just have to rip out that waistline seam again."

"Oh, Mother!" Judy's impatience slipped out at last. "Nobody's going to notice all those little details."

"They will too. They'll be watching you every minute, hoping to see something wrong. You've got to be the *best*. Can't you get that through your head?" Mrs. Simmons gave a sigh of despair. "You better start noticin' 'all those little details' yourself. I can't do it for you all your life. Now turn around and stand up straight."

"Oh, Mother," Judy said, close to tears from being made to turn and pose while her feet itched to be dancing, "I can't stand it any more!"

"You can't stand it, huh? How do you think *I* feel?" Mrs. Simmons said in her harshest tone.

Judy was immediately ashamed, remembering the weeks her mother had spent at the sewing machine, picking her already tattered fingers with needles and pins, and the great weight of sacrifice that had been borne on Mrs. Simmons' shoulders for the past two years so that Judy might bare hers at the Ball.

"All right, take it off," her mother said. "I'm going to take it up the street to Mrs. Luby and let her help me. It's got to be right or I won't let you leave the house."

"Can't we just leave it the way it is, Mother?" Judy pleaded without hope of success. "I think it's perfect."

"You would," Mrs. Simmons said tartly as she folded the dress and prepared to bear it out of the room. "Sometimes I think I'll never get it through your head. You got to look just right and act just right. That Rose Griffin and those other girls can afford to be careless, maybe, but you can't. You're gonna be the darkest, poorest one there."

Judy shivered in her new lace strapless bra and her old, childish knit snuggies. "You make it sound like a battle I'm going to instead of just a dance."

"It is a battle," her mother said firmly. "It starts tonight and it goes on for the rest of your life. The battle to hold your head up and get someplace and be somebody. We've done all we can for you, your father and I. Now you've got to start fighting some on your own." She gave Judy a slight smile; her voice softened a little. "You'll do all right, don't worry. Try and get some rest this afternoon. Just don't mess up your hair."

"All right, Mother," Judy said listlessly.

She did not really think her father had much to do with anything that happened to her. It was her mother who had ingratiated her way into the Gay Charmers two years ago, taking all sorts of humiliation from the better-dressed, better-off, lighter-skinned women, humbly making and mending their dresses, fixing food for their meetings, addressing more mail and selling more tickets than anyone else. The club had put it off as long as they could, but finally they had to admit Mrs. Simmons to membership because she worked so hard. And that meant, of course, that Judy would be on the list for this year's Ball.

Her father, a quiet carpenter who had given up any other ambitions years ago, did not think much of Negro society or his wife's fierce determination to launch Judy into it. "Just keep clean and be decent," he would say. "That's all anybody has to do."

Her mother always answered, "If that's all *I* did we'd still be on relief," and he would shut up with shame over the years when he had been laid off repeatedly and her days' work and sewing had kept them going. Now he had steady work but she refused to quit, as if she expected it to end at any moment. The intense energy that burned in Mrs. Simmons' large dark eyes had scorched her features into permanent irony. She worked day and night and spent her spare time scheming and planning. Whatever her personal ambitions had been, Judy knew she blamed Mr. Simmons for their failure; now all her schemes revolved around their only child.

Judy went to her mother's window and watched her stride down the street with the dress until she was hidden by the high brick wall that went around two sides of their house. Then she returned to her own room. She did not get dressed because she was afraid of pulling a sweater over her hair—her mother would notice the difference even if it looked all right to Judy—and because she was afraid that doing anything, even getting dressed, might precipitate her into the battle. She drew a stool up to her window and looked out. She had no real view, but she liked her room. The wall hid the crowded tenement houses beyond the alley, and from its cracks and bumps and depressions she could construct any imaginary landscape she chose. It was how she had spent most of the free hours of her dreamy adolescence.

"Hey, can I go?"

It was the voice of an invisible boy in the alley. As another boy chuckled, Judy recognized the familiar ritual; if you said yes, they said, "Can I go with you?" It had been tried on her dozens of times. She always walked past, head in the air, as if she had not heard. Her mother said that was the only thing to do; if they knew she was a lady, they wouldn't dare bother her. But this time a girl's voice, cool and assured, answered.

"If you think your big enough," it said.

It was Lucy Mae Watkins; Judy could picture her standing there in a tight dress with bright, brazen eyes.

"I'm big enough to give you a baby," the boy answered.

Judy would die if a boy ever spoke to her like that, but she knew Lucy Mae could handle it. Lucy Mae could handle all the boys, even if they ganged up on her, because she had been born knowing something other girls had to learn.

"Aw, you ain't big enough to give me a shoe-shine," she told him.

"Come here and I'll show you how big I am," the boy said.

"Yeah, Lucy Mae, what's happenin'?" another, younger boy said. "Come here and tell us."

Lucy Mae laughed. "What I'm puttin' down is too strong for little boys like you."

"Come here a minute, baby," the first boy said. "I got a cigarette for you."

"Aw, I ain't studyin' your cigarettes," Lucy Mae answered. But her voice was closer, directly below Judy. There were the sounds of a scuffle and Lucy Mae's muffled laughter. When she spoke her voice sounded raw and cross. "Come on now, boy. Cut it out and give me the damn cigarette." There was more scuffling, and the sharp crack of a slap, and then Lucy Mae said, "Cut it out, I said. Just for that I'm gonna take 'em all." The clack of high heels rang down the sidewalk with a boy's clumsy shoes in pursuit.

Judy realized that there were three of them down there. "Let her go, Buster," one said. "You can't catch her now."

"Aw, hell, man, she took the whole damn pack," the one called Buster complained.

"That'll learn you!" Lucy Mae's voice mocked from down the street. "Don't mess with nothin' you can't handle."

"Hey, Lucy Mae. Hey, I heard Rudy Grant already gave you a baby," a second boy called out.

"Yeah. Is that true, Lucy Mae?" the youngest one yelled.

There was no answer. She must be a block away by now.

For a moment the hidden boys were silent; then one of them guffawed directly below Judy, and the other two joined in the secret male laughter that was oddly high-pitched and feminine.

"Aw man, I don't know what you all laughin' about," Buster finally grumbled. "That girl took all my cigarettes. You got some, Leroy?"

"Naw," the second boy said.

"Me neither," the third one said.

"What we gonna do? I ain't got but fifteen cent. Hell, man, I want more than a feel for a pack of cigarettes." There was an unpleasant whine in Buster's voice. "Hell, for a pack of cigarettes I want a bitch to come across."

"She will next time, man," the boy called Leroy said.

"She better," Buster said. "You know she better. If she pass by here again, we gonna jump her, you hear?"

"Sure, man," Leroy said. "The three of us can grab her easy."

"Then we can all three of us have some fun. Oh, *yeah*, man," the youngest boy said. He sounded as if he might be about 14.

Leroy said, "We oughta get Roland and J. T. too. For a whole pack of cigarettes she oughta treat all five of us."

"Aw, man, why tell Roland and J. T.?" the youngest voice whined. "They ain't in it. Them was *our* cigarettes."

"They was *my* cigarettes, you mean," Buster said with authority. "You guys better quit it before I decided to cut you out."

"Oh, man, don't do that. We with you, you know that."

"Sure, Buster, we your aces, man."

"All right, that's better." There was a minute of silence.

Then, "What we gonna do with the girl, Buster?" the youngest one wanted to know.

"When she come back we gonna jump the bitch, man. We gonna jump her and grab her. Then we gonna turn her every way but loose." He went on, spinning a crude fantasy that got wilder each time he retold it, until it became so secretive that their voices dropped to a low indistinct murmur punctuated by guffaws. Now and then Judy could distinguish the word "girl" or the other word they used for it; these words always produced the loudest guffaws of all. She shook off her fear with the thought that Lucy Mae was too smart to pass there again today. She had heard them at their dirty talk in the alley before and had always been successful in ignoring it; it had nothing to do with her, the wall protected her from their kind. All the ugliness was on their side of it, and this side was hers to fill with beauty.

She turned on her radio to shut them out completely and began to weave her tapestry to its music. More for practice than anything else, she started by picturing the maps of the places to which she intended to travel, then went on to the faces of her friends. Rose Griffin's sharp, Indian profile appeared on the wall. Her coloring was like an Indian's too and her hair was straight and black and glossy. Judy's hair, naturally none of these things, had been "done" four days ago so that tonight it would be "old" enough to have a gloss as natural-looking as Rose's. But Rose, despite her handsome looks, was silly; her voice broke constantly into high-pitched giggles and she became even sillier and more nervous around boys.

Judy was not sure that she knew how to act around boys either. The sisters kept boys and girls apart at the Catholic high school where her parents sent her to keep her away from low-class kids. But she felt that she knew a secret: tonight, in that dress, with her hair in a sophisticated upsweep, she would be transformed into a poised princess. Tonight all the college boys her mother described so eagerly would rush to dance with her, and then from somewhere *the boy* would appear. She did not know his name; she neither knew nor cared whether he went to college, but she imagined that he would be as dark as she was, and that there would be awe and diffidence in his manner as he bent to kiss her hand . . .

A waltz swelled from the radio; the wall, turning blue in deepening twilight, came alive with whirling figures. Judy rose and began to go through the steps she had rehearsed for so many weeks. She swirled with a practiced smile on her face, holding an imaginary skirt at her side; turned, dipped, and flicked on her bedside lamp without missing a fraction of the beat. Faster and faster she danced with her imaginary partner, to an inner music that was better than the sounds on the radio. She was "coming out," and tonight the world would discover what it had been waiting for all these years.

"Aw, git it, baby." She ignored it as she would ignore the crowds that lined the streets to watch her pass on her way to the Ball.

"Aw, do your number." She waltzed on, safe and secure on her side of the wall.

"Can I come up there and do it with you?"

At this she stopped, paralyzed. Somehow they had come over the wall or around it and into her room.

"Man, I sure like the view from here," the youngest boy said. "How come we never tried this view before?"

She came to life, ran quickly to the lamp and turned it off, but not before Buster said, "Yeah, and the back view is fine, too."

"Aw, she turned off the light," a voice complained.

"Put it on again, baby, we don't mean no harm."

"Let us see you dance some more. I bet you can really do it."

"Yeah, I bet she can shimmy on down."

"You know it, man."

"Come on down here, baby," Buster's voice urged softly dangerously. "I got a cigarette for you."

"Yeah, and he got something else for you, too."

Judy, flattened against her closet door, gradually lost her urge to scream. She realized that she was shivering in her underwear. Taking a deep breath, she opened the closet door and found her robe. She thought of going to the window and yelling down, "You don't have a thing I want. Do you understand?" But she had more important things to do.

Wrapping her hair in protective plastic, she ran a full steaming tub and dumped in half a bottle of her mother's favorite cologne. At first she scrubbed herself furiously, irritating her skin. But finally she stopped, knowing she would never be able to get cleaner than this again. She could not wash away the thing they considered dirty, the thing that made them pronounce "girl" in the same way as the other four-letter words they wrote on the wall in the alley; it was part of her, just as it was part of her mother and Rose Griffin and Lucy Mae. She relaxed then because it was true that the boys in the alley did not have a thing she wanted. She had what they wanted, and the knowledge replaced her shame with a strange, calm feeling of power.

After her bath she splashed on more cologne and spent 40 minutes on her makeup, erasing and retracing her eyebrows six times until she was satisfied. She went to her mother's room then and found the dress, finished and freshly pressed, on its hanger.

When Mrs. Simmons came upstairs to help her daughter she found her sitting on the bench before the vanity mirror as if it were a throne. She looked young and arrogant and beautiful and perfect and cold.

"Why, you're dressed already," Mrs. Simmons said in surprise. While she stared, Judy rose with perfect, icy grace and glided to the center of the room. She stood there motionless as a mannequin.

"I want you to fix the hem, Mother," she directed. "It's still uneven in back."

Her mother went down obediently on her knees, muttering, "It looks all right to me." She put in a couple of pins. "That better?"

"Yes," Judy said with a brief glance at the mirror. "You'll have to sew it on me, Mother. I can't take it off now. I'd ruin my hair."

Mrs. Simmons went to fetch her sewing things, returned, and surveyed her daughter. "You sure did a good job on yourself, I must say," she admitted grudgingly. "Can't find a thing to complain about. You'll look as good as anybody there."

"Of course, Mother," Judy said as Mrs. Simmons knelt and sewed. "I don't know what you were so worried about." Her secret feeling of confidence had returned, stronger than ever, but the evening ahead was no longer the vague girlish fantasy she had pictured on the wall; it had hard, clear outlines leading up to a definite goal. She would be the belle of the Ball because she knew more than Rose Griffin and her silly friends; more than her mother; more, even, than Lucy Mae, because she knew better than to settle for a mere pack of cigarettes.

"There," her mother said, breaking the thread. She got up. "I never expected to get you ready this early. Ernest Lee won't be here for another hour."

"That silly Ernest Lee," Judy said, with a new contempt in her young voice. Until tonight she had been pleased by the thought of going to the dance with Ernest Lee; he was nice, she felt comfortable with him, and he might even be the awe-struck boy of her dream. He was a dark, serious neighborhood boy who could not afford to go to college; Mrs. Simmons had reluctantly selected him to take Judy to the dance because all the Gay Charmers' sons were spoken for. Now, with an undertone of excitement, Judy said, "I'm going to ditch him after the first dance, Mother. You'll see. I'm going to come home with one of the college boys."

"It's very nice, Ernest Lee," she told him an hour later when he handed her the white orchid, "but it's rather small. I'm going to wear it on my wrist, if you don't mind." And then, dazzling him with a smile of sweetest cruelty, she stepped back and waited while he fumbled with the door.

"You know, Edward, I'm not worried about her any more," Mrs. Simmons said to her husband after the children were gone. Her voice became harsh and grating. "Put down that paper and listen to me! Aren't you interested in your child?—That's better," she said as he complied meekly. "I was saying, I do believe she's learned what I've been trying to teach her, after all."

A. Anthologies Including Short Stories

Brawley, Benjamin, ed. *Early Negro American Writers; Selections with Bibliographical and Critical Introduction.* Chapel Hill: University of North Carolina Press, 1935.

Brown, Sterling A., ed. *American Stuff.* New York: Viking, 1937.

———. Arthur P. Davis, and Ulysses Lee, eds. *The Negro Caravan.* New York: Dryden, 1941.

Calverton, Victor F., ed. *An Anthology of American Negro Literature.* New York: Modern Library, 1929.

Chapman, Abraham, ed. *Black Voices.* New York: Dell, 1968.

Clarke, John Henrik, ed. *American Negro Short Stories.* New York: Hill and Wang, 1967.

Cromwell, Otelia, Lorenzo D. Turner, and Eva B. Dykes, eds. *Readings from Negro Authors.* New York: Harcourt, Brace, 1931.

Cunard, Nancy, ed. *Negro Anthology.* London: Wishart, 1934.

Dreer, Herman, ed. *American Literature by Negro Authors.* New York: Macmillan, 1950.

Emanuel, James A., and Theodore Gross, eds. *Dark Symphony: Negro Literature in America.* New York: The Free Press, 1968.

Ford, Nick Aaron, and H. L. Faggett, eds. *Best Short Stories by Afro-American Writers, 1925-1950.* Boston: Meador, 1950.

Hill, Herbert, ed. *Soon, One Morning: New Writings by American Negroes, 1940-1962.* New York: Knopf, 1963.

Hughes, Langston, ed. *The Best Short Stories by Negro Writers: An Anthology from 1899 to the Present.* Boston and Toronto: Little, Brown, 1967.

Johnson, Charles S., ed. *Ebony and Topaz: A Collectanea.* New York: National Urban League, 1927.

Jones, LeRoi, and Larry Neal, eds. *Black Fire.* New York: Morrow, 1968.

Locke, Alain, ed. *The New Negro.* New York: Boni, 1925.

Watkins, Sylvester C., ed. *Anthology of American Negro Literature.* New York: Modern Library, 1944.

B. Collections of Stories by Individual Authors

Anderson, Alston. *Lover Man*. Garden City, New York: Doubleday, 1959.

Baldwin, James. *Going to Meet the Man*. New York: Dial, 1965.

Chesnutt, Charles W. *The Conjure Woman and Other Tales*. Boston: Houghton Mifflin, 1899.

_____. *The Wife of His Youth and Other Stories of The Color Line*. New York: Houghton Mifflin, 1899.

Dunbar, Paul Laurence. *Folks from Dixie*. New York: Dodd, Mead, 1898.

_____. *The Heart of Happy Hollow*. New York: Dodd, Mead, 1904.

_____. *In Old Plantation Days*. New York: Dodd, Mead, 1903.

_____. *The Strength of Gideon and Other Stories*. New York: Dodd, Mead, 1900.

Gaines, Ernest J. *Bloodline*. New York: Dial, 1968.

Hughes, Langston. *The Best of Simple*. New York: Hill and Wang, 1961.

_____. *Laughing to Keep from Crying*. New York: Holt, 1952.

_____. *Simple Speaks His Mind*. New York: Simon and Schuster, 1950.

_____. *Simple Stakes A Claim*. New York: Rinehart, 1957.

_____. *Simple Takes a Wife*. New York: Simon & Schuster, 1953.

_____. *Simple's Uncle Sam*. New York: Hill and Wang, 1965.

_____. *The Ways of White Folks*. New York: Knopf, 1934.

Jones, LeRoi. *Tales*. New York: Grove, 1967.

Kelley, William M. *Dancers on the Shore*. Garden City, New York: Doubleday, 1963.

McGirt, James E. *The Triumphs of Ephraim*. Philadelphia: McGirt, 1907.

McKay, Claude. *Gingertown*. New York: Harper, 1932.

Madden, Will A. *Five More*. New York: Exposition, 1963.

_____. *Two and One*. New York: Exposition, 1961.

Marshall, Paule. *Soul Clap Hands and Sing*. New York: Atheneum, 1961.

Toomer, Jean. *Cane*. New York: Boni & Liveright, 1923.

Walrond, Eric. *Tropic Death*. New York: Boni & Liveright, 1926.

Wright, Richard. *Eight Men*. New York: World, 1940, 1961.

_____. *Uncle Tom's Children, Five Long Stories*. New York: Harper, 1938.

Drama

Introduction

The Afro-American Playwright in the New York Professional Theatre, 1923-1959

Although professional theatre in the United States of America is more than two hundred years old, professional playwrights of African ancestry are relatively unknown because opportunities for black writers have been restricted far more severely in drama than in other literary fields. An African slave, Phillis Wheatley, published a collection of poems as early as 1773.[1] A fugitive slave, William Wells Brown, published an autobiography in 1847, a book of travels in 1852, and a novel in 1853.[2] But even though a few blacks wrote dramas in the nineteenth century,[3] no Afro-American had a full-length serious drama produced in a Broadway theatre in New York City until 1925,[4] and only ten additional plays written totally or partly by Afro-Americans were produced on Broadway from 1926 until 1959, when Lorraine Hansberry's *A Raisin in the Sun* began the longest run on Broadway ever experienced by a play of Afro-American authorship.

The dearth of black playwrights cannot be attributed to a lack of literary talent among Afro-Americans. Phillis Wheatley, Frederick Douglass, William Wells Brown, W. E. B. DuBois, and Paul Laurence Dunbar earned international fame in other fields of letters before 1920. Langston Hughes, Gwendolyn Brooks, Richard Wright, Chester Himes, James Baldwin, and Ralph Ellison are only a few of the Afro-American writers who have earned international acclaim since 1920.

---

[1] Phillis Wheatley, kidnapped from Senegal and taken to Massachusetts at the age of seven, published *Poems* in London.

[2] Born a slave in Lexington, Kentucky, Brown escaped in 1835. He published *The Narrative of William Wells Brown* (1847), *My Three Years in Europe* (1852), and *Clotel, or the President's Daughter* (1853).

[3] An original play by an Afro-American was produced in 1821, and William Wells Brown gave readings from his play *The Escape* in 1858.

[4] Garland Anderson's *Appearances,* 1925.

Instead, the shortage must be blamed on a lack of opportunity for recognition. A combination of economic, cultural, and social circumstances has restricted the black playwright.

In the United States, a reputation in drama is more expensive than in any other literary field. A poet may publish in magazines or on mimeographed sheets. He can read his work in lecture halls or on street corners. If he is heard or read by influential people, his work may be collected and published in book form at a reasonable cost. A fiction writer may publish in small literary magazines. His first novel may appear as a limited printing which does not represent a major financial gamble by a publishing house.

But a dramatist needs a cast of people and an auditorium with stage, lights, scenery, and seats. Even then, he is rarely recognized in the United States until his drama appears in one of the large theatres near Broadway in New York City, the theatrical capital of the United States.[5] A Broadway production, needless to say, is a costly experiment which producers approach cautiously. Unwilling to lose money, they rarely gamble on new materials; instead, they revive and reshape the traditional in an effort to pander to the tastes which they presume to be characteristic of their potential audience of middle-class and upper-class white Americans.

Even daring directors and producers recognize this fact. Joseph Papp, a respected director, has earned a reputation for presenting Shakespearean plays without charging admission and for staging artistic works by little-known dramatists. Yet he has written,

> With few exceptions the large theatres in New York attract theatregoers who both have money and are settled in their attitudes. These people . . . have no desire to spend money to hear their ideals assaulted. They cannot tolerate doubts, and if they have any they certainly do not want them exposed . . . It is perfectly human to cultivate, and cater to, the status quo. It is certainly more reasonable to mount a production for an audience that already exists than to do shows that must find their audience (or, indeed, create it.)[6]

This combination of economic and cultural circumstances is intensified by a social fact. Since Afro-Americans represent a minority of the entire population and an even less significant per-

---

[5] Only within the past few years have critics begun to say that the most exciting drama in America is found in the little New York theatres off Broadway. Significantly, these OB productions have been enriched since 1963 by the work of Afro-American playwrights, such as Le Roi Jones, Adrienne Kennedy, Douglas T. Ward, Lonnie Elder, and, most recently, Charles Gordone, winner of a Pulitzer Prize for *No Place to be Somebody.*

[6] *New York,* II (April 21, 1969), p. 55.

centage of the Broadway audience, Negro life is regarded as an exotic subject for the American theatre. Therefore, only a limited number of plays on Negro themes are approved. Furthermore, to please his predominantly white audience, the cautious producer wishes to have these themes developed in accordance with his customers' expectations. Too frequently, therefore, he wants the stereotypes of Negro life and character which white playwrights popularized and which many black playwrights refuse to perpetuate. For example, in the years between 1769, when the first black character appeared in a play in America, and 1923, when the first black playwright had a one-act play produced on Broadway, white playwrights established five major stereotypes: the Buffoon, a comically ignorant type; the Tragic Mulatto, the product of miscegenation, who is destined to tragic exclusion from white society, which will not accept her, and black society, which she will not accept; the Christian Slave, a docile individual who worships both his mortal white master and his immortal Master; the Carefree Primitive, an exotic, amoral savage; and the Black Beast, a villain who seeks equality with white people. And when white playwrights wrote of Negro life, they most frequently wrote folk comedy. By repetition, white playwrights had given reality to these stereotypes of Afro-American character and life for numerous white Americans who rarely experienced intimate personal relationships with black Americans. Therefore, producers did not seek plays written about the actual characters and lives of Afro-Americans; from black and white playwrights, they wanted dramas which would repeat the familiar.

Finally, playwrights, more than other writers, depend upon acquaintance with people who have money. Poets and novelists may submit manuscripts to publishing firms; a dramatist needs to know someone who knows a producer. In the segregated society of the United States, personal contact between black artists and wealthy producers has been very limited.

For all of these reasons, black American playwrights developed very slowly in the years before the work of Lorraine Hansberry in 1959. The first significant efforts in dramatic writing, in fact, were not serious dramas but "coon" shows, musical variety shows. Very popular in the years between 1895 and 1905, these attracted and utilized the talents of such black writers as Paul Laurence Dunbar, one of America's most popular poets at the beginning of the twentieth century, and James Weldon Johnson, a poet and novelist who later earned a reputation as an American consul and as secretary of the National Association for the Advancement of Colored People. In these shows, which emphasized comedy, singing, and dancing rather than a story, black poets and actors shamelessly pandered to the expectations of their white audiences. They wrote of Buffoons and Carefree Primitives. Afro-American performers put cork-black on their faces and painted red make-up around their lips to transform themselves into the grinning gargoyles popularized in the black-face minstrel shows which employed white actors. James Weldon Johnson later described the manner in which black song writers even avoided love duets for their heroes and heroines because American audiences, presuming sexual amorality to be characteristic of Negro life, refused to believe that romance could be a serious topic for Afro-Americans.

Although these all-black musical shows disappeared from Broadway for more than a decade while black writers and performers were refused opportunity, musical comedy about black people has remained popular in the American theatre. *Shuffle Along* (1921), an all-black musical, written by Miller, Lyles, Sisse, and Blake, is frequently praised as one of the works which revived American interest not only in black talent but also black culture during the 1920's. It was the first of many such musicals produced during that decade. *Porgy and Bess* (1935), a folk opera by George Gershwin based on a play by Dubose Heyward (both white), is so highly esteemed by white Americans that, during the 1950's, the United States government selected it to be presented in Europe as the theatrical work best exemplifying American art and culture. In each decade, musical comedies about black people have extraordinary success in the theatre. The continuation of the pattern is evidenced in the present by *Golden Boy* and *Hello, Dolly!* both written originally for white performers but adopted into musicals for blacks. The perennial popularity of such shows evidences both the talent of black performers and the persistence of white Americans' predilection for viewing black Americans primarily as gay, or occasionally pathetic, people continually expressing their emotions in song and dance.

In contrast to the success of musical shows is the relative failure of serious professional drama by black American playwrights from 1923 to 1959, the focus of this essay.

The first to be produced on Broadway was *The Chip Woman's Fortune* (1923), a one-act play by Willis Richardson. Because of debts, Silas Green, a porter in a store, is about to lose his job and the record player he has purchased on credit. He turns for assistance to Aunt Nancy, a chip woman, who has helped him previously. But Aunt Nancy plans to give her savings to her son Jim, just released from prison after serving a term for assaulting his

unfaithful sweetheart and her lover. When Jim arrives, he agrees
to give Silas enough money to pay the debts. As the opener on a
program which included a revival of Oscar Wilde's *Salome*, *The
Chip Woman's Fortune*, presented by the Ethiopian Art Players
of Chicago, lasted only two weeks on Broadway.

The first full-length play, Garland Anderson's *Appearances*, first
produced on October 13, 1925, treated a more serious subject — a
Negro bell-hop's successful defense of himself from a false charge
of rape.

Three years later, Frank Wilson, an actor, created an unusual
protagonist in *Meek Mose*, which opened February 6, 1928. Most
black playwrights have refused to write about docile blacks or have
portrayed them as villains who must either be converted to self-
respect or destroyed before the final curtain. Frank Wilson, however, not only made such a character a protagonist but even
rewarded him. When white community leaders propose to move the
blacks to a different section of town, peace-loving Mose, a leader
of the black community, advises the blacks to agree. The blacks
turn on him when disease and death result from the new living
conditions, but he is rewarded for his faith when oil is discovered on
the new property. Historically, of course, *Meek Mose* retells the
success of some American Indians who, driven from their fertile
farmland in the East, were forced to relocate in Oklahoma, where
oil was later discovered. Nevertheless, it is an unusual theme for
a black playwright. The play lasted only twenty-four performances.

Harlem, the final play to appear on Broadway during the 1920's,
was a collaboration between Wallace Thurman, a talented, satirical
black novelist, and a white playwright, William Jordan Rapp.
Thurman, who had written two novels about Harlem, blended
melodrama and the exoticism of Harlem into a play which continued for ninety-three performances. The plot of *Harlem* retraces
themes familiar to individuals who have read widely in literature
by blacks. After migrating from South Carolina to Harlem, the
Williamses find unhappiness instead of the anticipated opportunity.
Impoverished, they are forced to give parties to which they charge
admission so that they can pay the rent. The daughter Cordelia
becomes intoxicated by the wild life of the city. After rejecting a
West Indian suitor, Cordelia becomes the mistress of a Harlem
gambler. When he is killed, the West Indian is suspected but ac-
quitted. Cordelia and her family continue to search for happiness
in the cold city.

Paul Laurence Dunbar had told a comparable story in *The
Sport of the Gods* (1901) when he novelized the misfortunes of

Southern blacks who corrupt their souls in Harlem. In the 1920's, novelist Rudolph Fisher repeated the theme in fiction, and in the following decade Randolph Edmonds developed it in drama. Sometimes white American critics have misinterpreted this theme as evidence of the black author's willingness to perpetuate the myth that life is better for black people in the South than it is in the North. To the contrary, the black writer was often more concerned with dispelling the myth that white Americans created about Harlem — that it was a world where black people enjoyed a gay, carefree existence.

In these four Broadway productions, black playwrights worked within the framework set by white playwrights. *The Chip Woman's Fortune* tells of black peasants. *Meek Mose* presents docile blacks. While *Harlem* suggests actuality, it nevertheless perfumes the stage with exoticism and amorality, and it capitalizes upon the national popularity which Harlem enjoyed during the 1920's.

In 1929, a severe economic depression hit America, and in 1930 Marc Connelly adapted Roark Bradford's *Ol' Man Adam and His Children* into *Green Pastures*, a comic fantasy about religion as practised by blacks. These two events motivated four dramas by black playwrights on Broadway and two in the more experimental, less costly theatres off Broadway.

Marc Connelly's play is a white man's fantasy about black people's conceptions of Biblical stories. The central character is De Lawd, a magnificent, white-haired, cigar-smoking black man — excellently acted by Richard B. Harrison, a college teacher of speech who, according to Langston Hughes, required the services of a white actor to train him to speak the "Negro" dialect which Marc Connelly had written. The heavenly fish fries and carryings-on amused white audiences but both irritated and intrigued black playwrights, who capitalized upon the interest in Negroes' religion as background for their works.

Staged by the Negro Theatre Guild, Augustus Smith's *Louisiana* (1933), melodramatically but much more realistically than *Green Pastures*, depicted religious forces in a black community in Louisiana. The two most powerful community leaders are Amos Berry, minister of a Baptist church, and Aunt Hagar, who practices voodoo. When a disreputable tavern keeper attempts to force his attentions on the minister's niece, Berry and Aunt Hagar combine the powers of Christianity and voodoo to crush him.

This was not the first American drama to portray voodoo prominently. In 1922, Mary Wiborg, a white playwright, had presented *Taboo,* and within the same decade Em Jo Basshe had written

Earth. Despite its exoticism, however, voodoo has not excited American audiences. *Taboo* barely lasted through three performances; Smith's *Louisiana* lasted only eight.

Two days after *Louisiana* opened, Hall Johnson's *Run, Little Chillun* began a more successful run of 126 performances. It too told a story of different religious forces. This time, however, there is conflict between the pagan New Day Pilgrims and the Hope Baptists. Sulamai, a New Day Pilgrim, entices married Jim Jones, who is the son of the minister of the Baptist church. Finally, Christianity triumphs when Jim returns to his faith and Sulamai is stricken during a revival meeting.

Five years later, George Norford, in a theatre off Broadway, dramatized a different religious element in black life when he wrote about Father Divine, a black, self-proclaimed re-incarnation of God, who attracted a large following during the Depression.

The economic depression influenced black playwrights less directly than had *Green Pastures.* The severity of life during the 1930's prompted writers to question all aspects of life in the United States and to protest against conditions which mitigated against poor people. This concern spread even to the Broadway stages. Here again, however, black dramatists seem to have been granted opportunity to tell their stories only after paths had been prepared by white playwrights.

In 1932, white James Miller wrote *Never No More,* a protest against lynching. In 1934, white John Wexley presented *They Shall Not Die,* based on an actual incident in which nine Negro youths from Scottsboro, Alabama, were convicted of alleged rape of two white prostitutes; and in *Stevedore,* in the same year, George Sklar and Paul Peters, white playwrights, described the manner in which a militant black youth was made to seem responsible for a crime which he did not commit.

In 1934 also, Dennis Donoghue, a black playwright with a non-black name, wrote *Legal Murder,* another version of the case of the Scottsboro boys. In Donoghue's play, the nine youths have hopped aboard a freight train to ride to Chicago to seek work as singers. Their car is invaded by two white men and two women. One white man, who is armed, orders the youths to jump from the moving train, but the youths seize the gun. At the next stop, they are arrested and falsely accused of rape. In court, they and their Jewish lawyer are ridiculed, and they are convicted.

Legal Murder lasted only seven days, but in 1935, Langston Hughes' *Mulatto* began the longest Broadway run of any play by a black dramatist before Lorraine Hansberry. Produced in 1935, but written in 1930, *Mulatto* is an emotionally engaging drama, marred by melodrama, propaganda, and failings common to inexperienced playwrights. Developed from a short story, "Father and Son," *Mulatto* dramatizes the conflict between Colonel Norwood, a wealthy white man, and Robert, his yard child. Since the age of seven, Robert has hated his father for refusing to recognize their relationship, of which he himself had been proud. During his summer's vacation from college, Robert has strained tension to a breaking point by defying the morés of his father and of the Georgia town in which they live. Finally, on the day of Bert's scheduled return to college, the tension snaps. Incensed to learn that Bert has defied a white woman, has driven faster than a white man, and has entered the front door of the house regularly, Norwood threatens to kill Bert. Bert kills his father and flees; but, chased by a posse, he returns to the house, where he kills himself.

Much of the power of the play derives from the subject itself. A traditional subject in drama, father-son conflict inevitably generates excitement and frequently produces memorable characters and confrontations: Laius and Oedipus, Claudius and Hamlet, Theseus and Hippolytus are only a few. In this instance, the excitement was intensified for American audiences by the first professional dramatization of a conflict between a mulatto and his father.

The play gains strength also from Hughes' characterizations of Bert and his mother Cora. Although he is obviously modeled on the proud and noble slaves of Negro literary tradition, Bert is an interesting character. His contempt for other Negroes, his stubborn insistence that he be recognized as a man, and his arrogant defiance of custom symptomize a fatal *hubris*. In his deliberate provocation of trouble, a manifestation of what seems almost a suicidal complex, he anticipates James Baldwin's protagonist in *Blues for Mr. Charlie*, written a generation later (1964).

The theme of protest was continued off Broadway in Langston Hughes' *Don't You Want To Be Free?* (1937), a musical history of blacks in America, and in Theodore Ward's *Big White Fog* (1940). Although it lasted only sixty-four performances, *Big White Fog* dramatized a black man's frustrated and tragic existence more bitterly than any play previously presented professionally in the United States.

Set in Chicago and covering a period from 1922 to 1931, the play recounts the misadventures of Victor Mason and his family. Convinced that black people cannot live profitably in the United States, Victor Mason buys stock in the Black Star liner on which

Marcus Garvey, a West Indian, plans to help black people return to Africa, where they will re-establish themselves in a new community. Events intensify Mason's conviction that he must leave: His son Lester is denied a scholarship because of his race; his daughter Wanda abandons her education in hopes of earning money to purchase some of the luxuries she desires. But, despite the opposition of his wife, Mason idealistically clings to the hope that Garvey's plan will succeed. The hope collapses when Garvey is arrested and convicted of fraud.

Nine years later, the Masons have hit bottom. Wanda has become a prostitute. Les has become a Communist. Mason's wife, Ella, pawns their few valuables in order to feed the family. When bailiffs come to evict the family for failure to pay rent, Victor Mason is killed attempting to stop them. The play ends with the glimmering hope that union of blacks and whites may improve conditions in America, but one remembers more vividly Les's despairing cry: "Seems like the world ain't nothing but a big white fog, and we can't see no light no where."

Typically, in contrast to the short life of *Big White Fog* off Broadway, *Cabin in the Sky* in the same year titillated Broadway audiences for 156 performances. A comic fantasy written by whites, it repeated the familiar Negro stereotypes in a story heavily laden with primitive religious faith, comedy, and song.

The decade of protest reached its climax in Richard Wright's *Native Son* (1941), adapted for the stage by Paul Green, a white regional dramatist who had written more plays about Negroes than any other American dramatist. Written originally as a novel, *Native Son* tells the story of Bigger Thomas, a twenty-year-old black youth from Mississippi, who lives with his mother and his younger sister and brother in a rat-infested room in the slums of Chicago's black ghetto. A monster created by America's economic and social system, Bigger is characterized by envy, fear, and hatred. He envies, fears, and hates white people who control the society, own the houses and the stores in the slums, acquire education and jobs, and deny opportunity and free movement to black people. Bigger, however, also hates blacks because they occupy inferior positions in America. To stave off awareness of his impotence to assist his family, he even erects a wall of hate between himself and them. But, because he cannot completely conceal his impotence from himself, he also hates himself.

Hired as a chauffeur by the Daltons, white "liberals" who derive part of their fortune from slum houses such as Bigger's, Bigger is ordered to drive the Daltons' daughter, Mary, to her evening classes at the University of Chicago. Mary, however, insists that Bigger take her to an assignation with her Communist sweetheart, Jan, who attempts to enlist Bigger in the Party. At the end of the evening, Bigger assists the drunken girl to her room, where he is surprised by her blind mother. Fearing that he will be discovered and accused of rape, Bigger accidentally smothers the girl while trying to prevent her from responding to her mother's questions. After a melodramatic chase during which he rapes and kills his Negro sweetheart, Bigger is caught, tried, and executed.

As a novel, *Native Son* was a powerful and shocking indictment of America. Much of the emotional impact resulted from the subjective presentation of Bigger; readers saw the United States through his eyes, and for them also it became a world of white horror. The adaptation of the work into a drama transformed the character and the theme. Bigger was humanized and made less fearful, less brutal. In the novel, Bigger fights his black associates to prevent himself from realizing that he is too cowardly to rob a white man; in the play, his temper is the only reason for his fight. In the novel, he brutally assaults his sweetheart to prevent her betraying him to the police; in the play, she is killed by policemen. Although these character changes made Bigger a more sympathetic individual for a theatre audience, they erased Wright's major thesis: that American society has shaped this Bigger and other Biggers into monsters who are brutal because they are fearful. Furthermore, in the play, a white reporter, suspecting Bigger, skillfully proves Bigger's guilt. In contrast, emphasis in the novel is placed upon the fact that, as a result of his accidental murder, Bigger, for the first time, realizes that he can outwit white people. In the novel, his guilt is discovered accidentally by reporters who suspect him no more than Captain Delano suspected the innocent-looking black mutineers in Melville's "Benito Cereno." Finally, without the introspective examination of Bigger, *Native Son* is more a cops-and-robbers melodrama than a thesis play. Nevertheless, it ran for ninety-four performances and was even nominated for a Drama Critics Circle award for the year.

Protest did not disappear from the theatre during the 1940's, but the end of World War II and the apparent triumph of democracy revived idealistic hopes for brotherhood and understanding. While white dramatists wrote pleas for integration of Negroes into the opportunities, black dramatists sought to educate white audiences by writing more realistically about problems of the past and the present.

In *Our Lan'* (1947), Theodore Ward described the efforts of black freedmen after the Civil War. Although the play focuses on the United States' betrayal of freed slaves, who were promised land, then forced to sign away their rights, and finally driven off by Union troops, considerable attention is given to the character of the slaves themselves and to their problems not related to land.

In 1954, in a theatre off Broadway, William Branch presented *In Splendid Error*, the story of an important episode in the life of Frederick Douglass, who, after escaping from slavery, dedicated himself to abolishing that evil from the United States. For a period of time, Douglass supported John Brown's efforts to help slaves liberate themselves by flight and by guerilla attacks upon Southern planters. When Brown, however, decided to attack federal property at Harper's Ferry, Douglass was forced to choose between unpleasant alternatives: if he accompanied Brown, he would sacrifice his life in a mission which he considered suicidal; if he refused, some would suspect him of cowardly betrayal of the cause. The play is the story of Douglass's effort to make a choice.

In 1956, off Broadway, Loften Mitchell's *A Land Beyond the River* dramatized a more recent incident in the history of black Americans. It recounted the valiant efforts of Mr. Dulane, a minister in South Carolina, to help Negro children enroll in schools reserved for white children, where facilities, supplies, and equipment promised a higher quality of education than was possible in the antiquated structures assigned to black children. Historically, Mr. Dulane succeeded; his case was one of those which persuaded the Supreme Court to rule in 1954 that all publicly supported schools must admit students without restriction based on race or religion. Nonetheless, historically, as in the play, Mr. Dulane was forced to save his life by fleeing at night from embittered white neighbors resentful of the changing conditions.

Professional drama by Afro-Americans came of age on Broadway during the 1950's. In 1953, Louis Peterson told the story, in *Take a Giant Step*, of educated northern Negroes, who are neither primitive nor pathetic but who have problems. Spencer Scott, the protagonist, is a member of the only black family in a neighborhood in Philadelphia, Pennsylvania. When he reaches the age of sexual maturity, he becomes isolated from his former white friends, who no longer invite him to their homes or visit him. He attempts to discover companionship among members of his race, but he cannot adjust to the Negroes whom he sees in taverns. Isolated by race and by social position, he is alone except for a grandmother who loves him but cannot provide the companionship required by a teen-aged youth. Peterson did not pretend to have a solution. At the end of the play, Scott remains isolated.

Take a Giant Step continued for seventy-six performances and was followed in the next year by *Mrs. Patterson*, a happier tale of the daydreams of a black girl, co-authored by Charles Sebree, black, and Greer Johnson, white. Teddy Hicks wants to be a wealthy white woman, like Mrs. Patterson, her mother's employer; but she also dreams of an exciting life with "Mr. D." from Hell. Eventually, the dreams are crushed, and Teddy faces reality. This play lasted for 101 performances, undoubtedly benefitting from the casting of popular Eartha Kitt as Teddy.

The trend towards verisimilitude, however, was interrupted by Langston Hughes's *Simply Heavenly* (1957), which, designed for the commercial theatre, reached Broadway in a state weaker than Hughes's *Simple Takes a Wife*, the book upon which the play was based. The major sufferer in the adapatation is Jesse B. Semple himself. In the tales and dialogues of the Simple books, Jesse assumes the dimensions of a folk hero. Even though he drinks, cavorts with women, has difficulty paying rent, talks ungrammatically and excessively, his foibles never detract from his dignity; for, like the Greek gods and the heroes of various mythologies, he is larger than life. It may be appropriate even to say that he, like Joseph Conrad's Kurtz, is remembered primarily as a voice, in this instance a voice which utters common sense even when the speaker seems emotional and illogical. Reduced to actable dimensions, however, Simple loses his grandeur. In the play, he peeks beneath his legs to watch Joyce, his fiancée, change clothes; he turns somersaults; he is thrown from a car to land on his "sit-downer"; he is propped comically in a hospital bed with his legs in traction; sentimentally and pathetically, he tries to reform and to win Joyce. In short, Simple's reality as the embodied spirit of the Negro working class is reduced to the Harlem barfly; the Chaplinesque Comic Hero shrinks to a farcical fall guy of the model made familiar earlier by Stan Laurel and Lou Costello.

The second major injury resulting in the adaptation is suffered by the material itself. Even though incidents occur in the book, they generally serve merely as acceptable devices to generate Simple's philosophizing. Consequently, what is important is not the event itself but the reaction which it stimulates from Simple. For a Broadway show, however, Hughes needed to emphasize action and to minimize Simple's reflections. As a result, undue attention is given to Simple's unsuccessful efforts to seduce Joyce, to the Watermelon Man's pursuit of Mamie, and to the domestic difficulties of Bodidilly and Arcie. The effort to please Broadway failed; the show closed after sixty-two performances.

Two years later Lorraine Hansberry achieved the kind of success which earlier black American playwrights had dreamed of. Her drama, *A Raisin in the Sun*, won the Drama Critics Circle Award as the best play of 1958-59. It continued for 530 performances in its initial run.

Appropriately, *A Raisin in the Sun* is a play about the dreams of ghetto dwellers. Descended from five generations of slaves and sharecropper, the Youngers have moved North in the hope of realizing their dreams. In Chicago, however, their dreams are dying. Thirty-five-year-old Walter Lee Younger is merely a chauffeur who cannot support his family adequately, cannot even provide a bedroom for his young son, who sleeps on a couch in the living room. Beneatha, Walter Lee's sister, wants to be a doctor even though she realizes the financial strain that her education places upon the family. Walter Lee's wife, who is pregnant, suffers with the realization that the family cannot afford another child. Walter Lee's mother wants happiness for her children and a garden for herself; but she sees weariness and sorrow in her children, and in the concrete wasteland of Chicago's ghetto she can find space enough only for a window box plant for herself.

In order to earn money to support his family, Walter Lee wants to purchase a share of a liquor store with the money his mother has received from the insurance of his father, who died from overwork. His mother refuses because she believes liquor stores are immoral and because she wants to use the money to purchase a home for the family. Walter Lee steals part of the money but loses it in a swindle. The mother makes a down payment on a home, but it is in a neighborhood where black people have never lived: exorbitant costs have prevented her buying a home in Negro neighborhoods. Despite warnings of opposition by their new neighbors, the Youngers decide to move, hoping at last to realize one dream.

Lorraine Hansberry did not idealize the Younger family. Walter Lee Younger experiences bitter frustration because no one else in his family agrees to his scheme to invest his mother's insurance money in a liquor store. Far from epitomizing nobility, he searches for pride and for maturity. As he says, "I'm thirty-five years old; I been married eleven years and I got a boy who sleeps in the living room—and all I got to give him is stories about how rich white people live." He believes that the Negro who wishes to succeed must imitate white people.

In contrast, his sister, Beneatha (Bennie), inspired partly by racial pride and partly by the lectures of her African suitor, argues against the assimilation of the Negro race into the American culture. Whereas Walter materialistically concentrates upon acquiring money, Bennie wants to become a doctor because her desire since childhood has been to help other people.

Concerned neither with money nor with crusades, their mother desires merely to provide cleanliness and decency for her family. When she receives the insurance money left by her husband, she restrains herself from donating the ten thousand dollars to the church only because she wishes to help her children realize their dreams. She wants her children to respect themselves and to respect others.

The Youngers disagree even in their attitudes toward their race. Although Walter blames the backwardness of the race for the inferior economic status of the black, he responds to the rhythms of recordings of African music. Bennie recognizes the barrier which separates her from the snobbish Negroes who possess wealth; yet she considers herself a crusader for and a defender of her race. Individual in their characters and their attitudes towards life, the Youngers find unity only in their common belief in the importance of self-respect, a philosophy not unique to the black people.

The play also includes a wealthier Negro—well-dressed, well-educated, condescending toward lower-class blacks and ridiculed in turn by people of that lower economic class. Contrasted with him is an African, who is proud of his nationality and contemptuous of the assimilationist behavior of American blacks.

The play has been judged a comedy because it is amusing, but it remains the most perceptive presentation of Negroes in the history of American theatre.

It is encouraging to observe that Afro-American dramatists since the 1950's have had the freedom to people their plays with individualized blacks rather than stereotypes. Clearly, this indicates that the popular images are changing. Nevertheless, the Afro-American remains an exotic subject for American professional theatre. As long as this condition continues, the major opportunities for Afro-American dramatists will lie in the amateur theatricals of the colleges and in the semi-professional performances of black community groups. Despite recent awards, the black dramatist is not yet a significant force in American professional theatre.

The three plays included in this anthology represent work developed in three different arenas of training for black playwrights and performers—the professional Broadway theatre, the Afro-American college theatre, and the black community theatre. Although the current interest in Afro-American literature has stimulated the publishing and anthologizing of many of the better-known plays which have been produced professionally during recent years, relatively little effort has been made to preserve plays produced in black colleges and communities. Consequently, the work in these little theatres remains relatively unknown. It is important, however, that attention be given to such plays, for they often reflect Afro-American culture and thought more accurately than do the plays produced professionally in downtown New York. As I have pointed out in the essay, Afro-American writers frequently have chosen or have been required to adapt their plays to the interests and tastes of the white producers or predominantly white audiences of the downtown theatres. Depending on the times, they have been required to use stereotyped characters, to emphasize sensational aspects of interracial relationships, to insert comic or musical interludes, to modify the language, or to soften their criticism of America's treatment of Afro-Americans. In the predominantly black colleges and communities, however, the dramatists have had greater freedom to write as they saw fit, restricted only by their individual concepts of what constitutes good drama or what will appeal to a predominantly black audience.

There is no published history of the Afro-American college theatre, an important training ground for playwrights and performers. Under the talented and dedicated guidance of such director-teachers as Randolph Edmonds, Thomas Pawley, Owen Dodson, Melvin B. Tolson, and Baldwin Burroughs—only a few of the better known—dramatic groups have been developed at almost all of the black colleges. Although these groups frequently produced the standard fare, the classics typical of little theatres everywhere, they also staged original productions written by the director, by faculty members or students, or occasionally by black writers outside of the campus community. For example, James Baldwin's *The Amen Corner* was produced first at Howard University. Records suggest that the only productions of Jean Toomer's plays occurred on black campuses. Edmonds, Pawley, Dodson, and Tolson were among the more prolific writer-directors. Carlton E.

Moss, a talented writer for radio, television, and motion pictures, is one of many who earned their first applause as writers for efforts which were produced while they were students at black institutions.

Any brief account of the Afro-American college theatre will necessarily offend by omitting individuals whose contributions have been significant either on their own campuses or in the establish- ment of the National Association of Dramatic and Speech Arts or the national Intercollegiate Dramatic Association, two societies which have afforded black collegiate groups the opportunity to share theories and practices during their annual meetings. Even less possible in a brief account is the identification of the many individuals whose personal prominence as artists and performers has obscured memory of their work in college theatre. For example, Melvin Tolson's national literary reputation is that of a brilliant poet. On his own campus, however, he was respected equally for his work as a director and a playwright. Zora Neale Hurston, known as a novelist and folklorist, once directed drama at North Carolina College in Durham. For many years before he become interna- tionally famous as "De Lawd" in Marc Connelly's *Green Pastures*, Richard B. Harrison taught rhetoric and drama in such a black college as North Carolina A and T in Greensboro.

A history of this theatre is needed; yet one can sympathize with the scholars who hesitate to begin the study. The primary materials are scattered through more than one hundred colleges in sixteen states; the records of the history of dramatic activities are incom- plete even on the campuses where they occurred; secondary sources are virtually non-existent.

Black community theatres and theatrical groups have also been important to Afro-American drama, especially during the frequent periods when black writers and performers, denied opportunity in commercial downtown theatres in New York, kept their talents alive by working in community theatre. This too is a world which scholarly research has not illuminated. No published study explores in detail the important activities of the Lafayette and the Lincoln Companies at the time of World War I, the several theatrical groups — including the Harlem Suitcase Theatre — organized by Langston Hughes, the Rose McClendon workshop, the Krigwa Players, Karamu House, the American Negro Theatre, or the sev- eral other groups which have been significant in the past. For that matter, too little attention at present is given to documenting and recording the current activities of Douglas Turner Ward's Negro Ensemble Theatre, Le Roi Jones' Spirit House and Jihad Players, the New Lafayette Theatre in New York, or the various groups developing on the West Coast. The problems of research in the community theatre correspond with those in the college theatre.

Yet, someday the detailed history of the black little theatre movements and activities must be written. An adequate picture of the black man in the theatre cannot be drawn without attention to that world in which he has developed freely without regard for the censoring tastes of white producers and audiences.

Randolph Edmonds (1900-   )

Nat Turner

A native of Laurenceville, Virginia, Randolph Edmonds, educated at Oberlin College, Columbia University (where he earned a Master's degree) and Yale, is one of the pioneers in the Afro-American college theatre. Formerly a professor of drama at Dillard and Lincoln Universities, and for many years head of the speech and drama department of Florida A and M University, Mr. Edmonds founded the Negro Intercollegiate Drama Association and the National Association of Drama and Speech Arts. During World War II, he organized and directed theatrical activities for the USO. Influential both as a teacher and a director, he has twice been selected to present the Florida A and M players in a theatrical tour abroad as part of the government's effort to improve its relationships with other nations through presentation of American culture.

The author of many plays, Mr. Edmonds has published three collections of his plays: *Shades and Shadows, The Land of Cotton and Other Plays*, and *Six Plays for a Negro Theatre*. The plays in the latter collection reveal Mr. Edmonds' interest in using drama to reveal the Negro folk. "Nat Turner" reflects this interest in the effort to imitate folk dialect, the realistic presentation of attitudes, superstitions, and habits of rural Negroes, and the presentation of an important figure in the history of black people. In 1831 Nat

Published in *Six Plays for a Negro Theatre*, © 1934 by Randolph Edmonds (Boston: Baker, 1934). Reprinted by permission of the author. All rights reserved by the author.

Turner led a rebellion of slaves in southeastern Virginia. Here, in a drama written for a college audience, Mr. Edmonds sketches the story briefly with emphasis on the slaves' attitudes toward Nat and on Nat's religious convictions.

Nat Turner

Characters

HENRY PORTER
HARK TRAVIS
NELSON WILLIAMS
SAMUEL FRANCIS
JACK REESE
WILL FRANCIS
JESSEE HARRIS
BOB PORTERS
JOB WESTBROOK
LUCINDA MOORE
NAT TURNER

SCENE.—*A small clearing in the midst of leafy trees on the plantation of* JOSEPH TRAVIS *at Cross Keys, Virginia, in Southampton
County, on August 21, 1831. Here is gathered that small band of
slaves which started the famous Nat Turner Insurrection. It is about
ten o'clock. The low full moon coming up over the horizon casts
orange shadows through the trees down on the group. They are
winding up a barbecue feast which has lasted from three o'clock
in the afternoon. The small fire on which they roasted a pig has
died down to embers; and there is just light enough to see the slaves
as they eat their barbecue, and drink cider.*

(HENRY, *who has been walking around, suddenly exclaims:*)

HENRY. (*Pointing to the right*)　Look!

(*All spring up.*)

HARK.　Whut is hit, Henry?
HENRY.　Look at dat moon over dere through de trees.

455

SAM.   Hit sho' is gut a 'culiar color tuh hit.

JACK.   Hit's a blood moon, dat's whut.

HARK.   Hit means red blood is gwine be spilled.

HENRY.   So many things been happenin' round heah lately, judgment day mus' be coming soon.

HARK.   Hit is coming soon fuh a whole lot o' white folks in dis county.

WILL.   (*Sitting down*) Les' stop talkin' 'bout de moon and finish up dis barbecue.

(*They all sit down and start eating and drinking again.*)

HENRY.   (*Apparently not finished with the conversation*) Dis August is a funny month. Las' Sattiday on de thirteenth hit was de sun dat was funny, and now hit's de moon.

NELSON.   Ah never will fugit dat day ez long ez Ah lives.

HARK.   (*After draining a glass of cider*) Ah won't neither, Nelson. When de sun riz hit was a light green, 'bout nine o'clock hit had turned tuh blue, and at twelve o'clock hit had turned tuh grey wid a black spot on hit.

SAM.   "Prophet Nat" said hit was de last sign, and tuh git ready tuh strike fuh freedom.

HENRY.   And we is heah ready tuh strike.

JOB.   Whut is dis feast 'bout? Henry told me 'bout organizin' and fightin', but he didn't make hit clear. Ah been settin' heah eatin' and drinkin' since 'bout de middle o' de evenin' and nobody ain't said no mo'. Ah want tuh know why all us was tole tuh bring hoes, pitchforks, and clubs; and whut's all dis feast 'bout?

HENRY.   Yuh tell him, Hark.

HARK.   When Christ was gittin' ready tuh save de worl' by givin' His life, He had His las' supper, didn't He?

JOB.   (*Insisting*) Yeah, but Ah ain't gittin' ready tuh giv' ma life fuh nothin'.

BOB.   Ah'm lak yuh, Job. Ah wants tuh know dese things, too.

HARK.   (*To* JOB) Ef yuh'll jes hab de patience ob de Bible man dat yuh was named arter, Job, Prophet Nat will 'splain things when he gits heah.

BOB.   But hit's gittin' late. Ah don't b'lieve Ole Nat is coming.

HARK. He'll be heah all right. Ah's sure he jes' wanted de eatin' and drinkin' tuh git over. Yuh knows he never drank lak de res' ob us.

NELSON. (*Biting on a sandwich*) He ain't never touched a drap o' likker in his life. When everybody is drinkin' and habin' a good time, Prophet Nat is off prayin'. Ah bet he is somewhar prayin' now.

JOB. Dat part's all right; but ain't nobody yit told me jes' whut we is tuh do.

NELSON. We is gwine tuh organize a army and kill all de white folks and set all de black slaves free.

WILL. (*Getting up and stretching. He is a big, muscular, and athletic looking Negro*) Ah sho will be glad when hit's time tuh start, too.

HENRY. Ah knows yuh will be glad, Will. Yuh always did lak tuh fight.

HARK. Wait a minute! Ef yuh is gwine tuh talk 'bout fightin' and everythin' we'd better hab a guard. De bushes might have eahs. (*Looking around.*) Jessee, yuh seems tuh be 'bout de only one not eatin', s'pose yuh act as de guard and see dat no white folks sneak up on us.

(JESSEE *gets up. He is very young.*)

JACK. How did yuh ever leave yo' gal, Lucinda, Jessee? Wunder she ain't come tuh look fuh yuh by now.

JESSEE. (*Good-naturedly*) Ah jes' told huh Ah was gwine away. Dat's all Ah ever tells wimmin.

BOB. Yuh must 'a' told huh more'n dat 'cause she is wust dan de Moster on yuh.

NELSON. She'll hardly let him out huh sight. Hit is a wunder she ain't been heah.

JESSEE. Ah's been heah ez long ez anybody else, ain't Ah?

HARK. (*In a positive manner*) Aw, go on guard, and stop doin' so much talkin'.

JESSEE. Ah's gwine, Hark. (*He goes on guard.*)

JOB. (*Rising*) Ah's gwine on back tuh de house, Hark. All de rest can stay ez long ez yuh wants tuh.

BOB. (*Rising*) Ah's gwine wid yuh, Job.

SAM.   Ah jes' b'lieve dey want tuh do dat so dey can tell de white folks everything.

JOB.   (*Towering over* SAM *and threatening him*) Yuh watch out how yo' mouf talks, Sam. Hit must not want no mo' teef in hit.

SAM.   *(Rising)* Ain't no man gwine keep me frum talkin' when Ah wants tuh.

HARK.   Aw, cut out dat talk. We don't want no fightin' heah.

WILL.   Dere ain't gwine be no fightin' 'less Ah do some; and Ah don't be ready jes' yit.

HARK.   Aw, go on now. Le's everybody wait fuh Nat.

BOB.   Why should everybody wait fuh Ole Nat all dis time? Ah ain't never laked him nohow. He is a 'culiar slave.

NELSON.   (*Sharply*) He's gut mo' sense dan any slave in de county. Even de white folks says dat.

JOB.   Ah ain't been in dis county long nuff tuh know much 'bout him; but he don't act lak he's gut much sense tuh me. He stay by hisse'f all de time, and walks 'round lak he's gut his haid in de sky.

SAM.   Don't yuh fool yo'se'f. Old Nat, ez yuh calls him, gut plenty o' sense laid up in dat head o' hisen. Lemme tell yuh one thing. One day when he was jes' a little boy he was tellin' a story 'bout sompen dat happened on de farm heah befo' he was bawn. Nobody never told him nothin' 'bout hit. De Lawd shows him, dat's whut. De Lawd shows him many things. Dat's why we call him a prophet.

HENRY.   And he can read and write jes' lak de white folks.

NELSON.   Dat's why he is de best tuh lead us 'gainst de white folks.

JACK.   And he can make paper and gunpowder, too. And nobody ain't never teached him nothin'.

JOB.   Old Nat's gut yuh fooled, dat's all. He is jes' an ole conjurer, dat's all.

WILL.   Yuh don't know whut yuh is talkin' 'bout, Job. Me and Nat ain't never been good frens; but he ain't no conjure man. He is jes' a smart black slave, dat's all. Yuh can giv' him any ole pieces o' iron lak ole plow points and buggy tires, and he'll make yuh a good lookin' bell, or a sword. Ah knows dat 'cause he made some fuh ma Moster.

NELSON.   Ah tells yuh sompen else dat yuh don't know neither. He can spit blood whenever he wants tuh, and he can prophesy when strange things gwine tuh happen. He show'd us some plain leaves on de trees and told us dat some strange writin' would be on dem de next day. We went dere de next mawning, and sho nuff, dere 'twas. Nat ain't no conjurer. He's gut de sperit o' God in him, dat's all. He is a prophet.

HARK. Yuh ain't been 'round heah long, Job; but we who has, knows Nat Turner. We knows dat he was 'pinted by Gawd tuh lead de black slaves from dere bondage. Folks thinks he is crazy, 'cause he stays by hisse'f. He's been talkin' tuh de Lawd all day while we's been heah eatin' barbecue and drinkin' cider. When he fust told his plans tuh Henry, Nelson and me, we thought he was crazy. We don't think so now. We know de black slaves ain't never gwine tuh be free 'til dey raise a army and fight fuh demselves. De Lawd told Nat Turner dat.

JOB. Ole Nat jes' outer his head, dat's all. Ef yuh keep listenin' tuh him de white folks is gwine tuh hang yuh all.

BOB. He ain't gwine git me in no trouble.

HARK. Wal, yuh can wait a few minutes tull he gits heah, can't yuh? He ought tuh be heah any minute now.

BOB. Ah done waited long nuff. Come on, Job.

JOB. Yeah, let's go. Nat Turner mout be a prophet tuh yuh; but he is jes' a crazy buck tuh me. Ah ain't gwine let him make de white folks stretch ma nake on no limb.

SAM. Wal, ef he is scared tuh stay heah and fight, let him go on home and hide behind his ole 'lady's coat tails. Ah's gwine stick wid Prophet Nat.

NELSON. Ah'm stickin', too.

BOB. (*Angry*) Ah told yuh don't let yo' mouf talk so much, but yuh won't listen; ef you don't take back whut yuh said, Ah's gwine separate yo' teef and gums.

WILL. (*Rising*) Ah said nobody was gwine fight 'less Ah git in hit too. Ah says anybody dat leaves dis place befo' Nat Turner gits heah, gut tuh beat Will Francis. Is yuh and Bob leavin', Job?

HARK. Be quiet, all ob yuh. Ah told yuh we don't want no fightin'.

JESSEE. (*Before they can get things straight* JESSEE *yells out*) Be quiet, everybody! Ah heah somebody comin'.

HARK. Hit mus' be Prophet Nat.

JESSEE. Halt! Who's dere! Speak!

NAT. (*In a strong voice*) Dis is Nat Turner coming! (*He comes in with a firm step. There is a mystical appearance about him. All of his movements and words give the impression that he is a strange man, that he is a part of this world with a strong suggestion of the other. He stops abruptly when he sees* WILL.) How come yuh heah, Will?

WILL. (*Submissively*) Hark told me 'bout yo' plans tuh git free; and Ah thought ma life is no mo' dan de others, and liberty tuh me is jes' ez dear.

NAT. Do yuh think yuh can obtain liberty?

WILL. (*Proudly*) Ah can, or lose ma life in de attempt.

NAT. How 'bout dese others, Hark, Job and Bob and Jessee?

HARK. Jessee is all right. Ah thought Job and Bob was too; but dey was gittin' ready tuh leave jes' befo' yuh come.

NAT. Don't yuh and Bob want tuh be free, Job?

JOB. Cose we does; but we don't know nothin' 'bout whut yuh is gwine tuh do. Ef dere is a good chance, we wants tuh be free lak anybody else.

BOB. Le's heah yo' plans, Nat.

JOB. (*Eagerly*) Yeah, and ef we sees dere is a chance, we'll be wid yuh.

NAT. (*Apparently satisfied*) Dat's fair enuff; but Ah never starts tuh do anythin' 'til Ah acknowledge Him who guides us all, Him who made de worl', and Him who told me tuh carry out His plans. Le's bow our heads in prayer. (*They all get down on their knees.* NAT *stands above them. He prays fervently.*) Oh, Lawd Gawd ob Hosts, we is met heah tu-night tuh do Thy will as revealed tuh Thy servant. Come down from Yo' throne on high, and be wid us tu-night. Open Yo' pearly gates and let Yo' sperit flow down and warm our hearts tuh do Yo' task. Oh, Lawd, Yuh who stood by Jacob and Isaac, be wid us tu-night. Oh Lawd, Yuh who delivered Jonah from de belly o' de whale, and Daniel frum de lion's den, and walked in de fire wid de three Hebrew chilluns, come down and be wid us heah tu-night. (*In a less rhythmical voice.*) Be wid us, Lawd. Help us do de right thing. Show us de right path and guide our feet in de way ob righteousness fuh Jesus sake, Ahmen!

ALL. Ahmen! Ahmen! (*They all get up from their knees and sit around for further orders.* NAT *seats himself in the middle on an old stump with an equal number on each side.*)

NAT. Is everybody finished wid de feast, Hark?

HARK. Yeah, dey is jes' 'bout.

NAT. Wal, we is ready tuh start our plans den.

HARK. Yeah, we was waitin' fuh yuh.

NAT. Ah been communicating wid de Holy Sperit all day. Ah wanted tuh be sho we was right. Dis idea ob fightin' fuh our freedom ain't jes' come tuh me. Hit is been in ma head a long time. De Lawd put hit in ma mind yeahs ago.

BOB. Whut is yuh planning tuh do?

JACK. Be quiet, Bob.

NAT. De sperit revealed dis tuh me: dat tu-night is de best possible time tuh start dis insurrection. Most ob de white folks is gone over in North Ca'lina, tuh Winton and Murfreesboro, tuh tend de big meetings. Dat only leaves a few around; and dey won't bother us 'cause dey is so far apart. Even now dey thinks we is away having a meeting ob our own. We can kill dese few white folks, organize all de slaves in a large army and take Jeresulem, de county seat, git all de guns and ammunitions. We can den conquer de whole county, march tuh de Dismal Swamp and work frum dere. Soon we can overcome de whole state, den de whole country lak George Washington did from de British.

WILL. Dat sounds good. Let's start now.

JOB. (*Not convinced*) Whut yuh want tuh do all dat fuh?

NAT. (*Fiercely*) Because we wants tuh be free men. Because we wants tuh call de 'tention ob de whole worl' tuh de condition ob slavery. We can strike de blow dat will make de whole worl' tremble at our might. Dere ain't no better way ob declarin' tuh de worl' dat black men is gwine be free dan tuh rise up and fight. With de help ob Gawd we is gwine tuh do hit, too.

JOB. Ah hates tuh see de white folks all killed up lak dat. Our Mosters is treating us all right. We's gut plenty tuh eat, and dey don't whup us lak dey do way down south on de Mississippi.

NAT. (*A little intolerant at his lack of understanding*) Ah hates tuh kill folks, too; but war ain't no barbecue feast. Yuh thinks 'cause yuh is gut a belly full and a place tuh lay yo' head dat dat is nuff; but hit ain't nuff fuh men made in de image ob Gawd. No real man ain't willing tuh be wurked lak a mule in de fields, whupped lak a dog, and tied tuh one farm and one Moster. (*Eloquently.*) Is yuh willing tuh continue dis servitude, dis slavery? Is yuh willing fuh yo' chilluns tuh look back tuh de time we live, and say dat dey is slaves 'cause we ain't gut guts nuff tuh fight? Is yuh willing tuh be beaten, enslaved, debased? Is yuh willing everybody?

VOICES. No!! No!!

NAT. Den we mus' fight fuh our freedom. We mus' let dem know we's gut a backbone. We mus' let dem know dat jes' because our skins is black we is not afraid tuh die. Even ef death overtake us in dis struggle, we mus' say lak de 'posle Paul "Ah's fought a good fight, Ah's runned de course; and dere is a crown waiting up in glory fuh me."

JOB. How come yuh git all dis in yo' head? Yuh knows yuh can't do nothin' 'gainst de white folks. Look whut dey done tuh Gabriel Prosser, and Denmark Vesey.

HARK. (*Restless*) Don't answer him. Le's git gwine.

WILL. No matter whut yuh say he ain't gwine b'lieve yuh. Dere ain't but one way tuh make him see. Lemme hammer hit in in his thick haid.

NAT. (*Rising and restraining him*) Don't do dat, Will. Dat ain't de way. Ef he wants tuh know how Gawd works, let him larn; 'cause we ain't doin' dis fuh ourselves, we's doin' hit fuh Him. But Gawd's ways are mysterious. Every man can't understand dem; but He speaks tuh me lak He did tuh de prophets ob old —lak He did tuh Isaiah, Jeremiah, Amos, and Hosea. Gawd talks tuh me lak he did tuh dem. Ah's gwine tuh tell yuh whut He said.

JACK. Tell dem whut He said, Brother Nat!

VOICES. Ahmen! Ahmen!

NAT. Set down and listen! Set down 'round de embers ob de dying fire whar yuh part took ob earthly things and listen tuh whut de Lawd revealed unto me.

(*They all sit down but* BOB *and* JOB.)

HARK. (*Sharply*) He means yuh, too. Set down!

(*They obey.* NAT *remains standing. He goes into a kind of trance.*)

NAT. 'Bout six yeahs ago Ah was thinkin' 'bout de Bible text: "Seek ye fust de kingdom ob heaven, and all dese things will be added unto yuh." I thought and thought 'bout dat text. Ah wundered ef de Lawd meant black slaves. Ah said tuh mase'f, "Surely dis can't be true 'cause black slaves wants tuh be free."

Dis wurried me a whole lot, but one day while Ah was walkin' in de field behind de plow, all ob a sudden de sperit said, "Seek ye fust de kingdom ob heaven, and all dese things will be added unto yuh." Ah said, "Lawd, dat can't be Yuh talkin' 'cause Ah want de things ob dis worl'." So Ah ran away frum ma Moster. Ah wanted tuh make ma way tuh freedom lak me father befo' me. Ah tried tuh dodge de Moster's will; but one day de sperit came tuh me agen, and said in a loud voice, "For he who knoweth de Moster's will and doeth hit not shall be beaten wid many strikes." So Ah came back heah tuh ma Moster. Ah came back tuh yuh. Ah came back tuh do ma Father's will.

HENRY.   Yuh came back tuh lead us tuh freedom.

NAT.   (*Not noticing the interruption*) Ah wasn't heah long befo' one day de Lawd showed me a vision. Ah saw white sperits and black sperits engaged in battle, and de sun was darkened, de thunder rolled in heaven, and blood flowed in streams. Den de sperit spoke agen and said, "Such is yo' luck. Such yuh is called tuh see, and let hit come rough or smooth, yuh mus' surely bar hit."

HARK.   We'll he'p yuh bar hit! We'll he'p yuh!

VOICES.   Ahmen! Ahmen!

NAT.   After dis revelation ob de sperit, Ah sought more dan ever true holiness befo' de great day ob judgment should appear. And den Ah began tuh receive de true knowledge ob de faith. And frum de first steps ob righteousness tuh de las' was Ah made perfect, and de Holy Ghost was in me, and said, "Behold me as Ah stand in heaven!" And Ah looked up and saw men in different altitudes. And dere was lights in de sky tuh which de chilluns ob darkness gave other names dan whut dey really was—fuh dey was lights ob de Savior's hands stretched forth frum de east tuh de west, even as dey were extended tuh Calvary fuh de redemption ob sinners.

VOICES.   Ahmen! Ahmen!

NAT.   And Ah wundered greatly at dese miracles, and prayed tuh be informed ob a certainty ob de meaning thereob—and shortly afterwards while laboring in de fields Ah discovered drops ob blood on de corn as dough hit was dew frum heaven, and Ah found on de leaves hieroglyphic characters and numbers wid de forms ob men in different attitudes portrayed in blood, and representing de figgers Ah had seen befo' in de heavens. And

so de Holy Ghost revealed hisse'f tuh me and made plain de
miracles Ah had seen. For de blood ob Christ had been shed
on dis earth and had ascended tuh heaven fuh de salvation ob
sinners and was now returning tuh earth in de form ob dew.
Den Ah was baptised in de Holy Sperit.

VOICES.   Speak de truth! Tell de worl' 'bout hit!

NAT.   Ah still wasn't satisfied. Ah couldn't b'lieve Gawd had chosen
me fuh His instrument. So Ah axed de sperit fuh a futher sign;
and Gawd answered ez He always answers de prayers ob de
faithful. Las' February He blotted out de sun, and turned day
into night. When dis happened Ah began tuh b'lieve at last.
Den Ah had another vision. Ah heard a loud noise in de heaven
and de sperit instantly appeared tuh me and said, "De serpent
is loosed, and Christ is laid down de yoke dat He bore fuh de
sins ob men." De sperit said Ah should take hit up and fight
de serpent, fuh de time is at hand when de las' shall be fust and
de fust shall be las'. And de sperit said Ah should arise and
prepare mase'f, and slay ma enemies wid dere own weapon.
(*Pauses dramatically and sits upon stump.*)

WILL.   Le's start now! Le's git gwine!

NAT.   So Ah's heah not fuh mase'f, fuh Ah could 'a' stayed free when
Ah run away; but Ah's heah as an instrument ob Gawd. He
sent me heah tuh lead yuh forth in dis battle. He told me tuh
do lak He told Saul 'gainst de Hittites, tuh let not one escape.
We is tuh slay every man, woman, and child ob dose who held
us in bondage. Thus saith de Lawd, "Ah shall deliver dem tuh
yuh dis day." Is yuh ready? Is yuh willing tuh join de army ob
de Lawd? Is yuh ready tuh slay yo' enemies? Is yuh ready tuh
fight dat yo' black chilluns mout be free?

VOICES.   Yeah! We is ready! Lead us! Lead us into battle!

NAT.   (*Reaching down and picking up a bundle of red bands made
out of cloth that he has brought*) Who will wear one ob dese
bands tuh show dat yuh is ready tuh fight?

VOICES.   Ah will! Gimme one!

(*He rises and distributes them.*)

NAT.   Is yuh convinced now, Job? Will yuh wear one ob dese bands?

JOB.   Yeah, yuh'd better gimme one, too.

BOB.   Ah'll take one.

NAT. Everybody gut one?

(*They all drape these bands over their left shoulder and tie them on their right side.*)

HARK. We's ready! Le's move!

NAT. Git whut weapons yuh gut and fall in line. (*They get their axes, grubbing hoes, rusty swords, clubs and fall in two lines.*) Listen! Ah is no longer "Prophet Nat." From now on Ah is General Nat. Hark Travis heah is yo' second in command. Yuh understand?

ALL. We understand.

(HARK *falls out of line and stands before the two columns.*)

NAT. We's gut tuh do a little drillin' befo' we march tuh de fust house. Remember yuh is gut tuh obey orders. We'll git guns ez we go along. Ah'll set de example by strikin' de fust blow.

ALL. We is ready!

NAT. Salute!

(*They salute awkwardly.*)

HARK. Git yo' hand up.

NAT. Le's drill now. Squad right! March! Squad right! March! Squad right! March! Squad left! March! Squad left! March! Squad Front! March! Halt! (*They march around in obedience to these orders. They hold their weapons like guns.*) Ah didn't giv yuh de command tuh retreat, 'cause dere ain't gwine be no retreat. We is gwine now and fight; and we is gwine keep on fightin' and dyin' tull all slaves everywhar is free.

VOICES. We heah yuh, General Nat!

NAT. Squad right! Forward! Forward tuh de line o' battle! March!

ALL. (*While marching*) Tuh de line o' battle!

NAT. Tuh Jeresulem de County seat!

ALL. Tuh Jeresulem de County seat!

NAT. March, soldiers ob freedom, March!

(*The curtain goes down to indicate the passing of three days. During that time the many assassinations take place. From behind the curtain come the sounds of marching feet, the hoofbeats of horses and the thud of blows. There come, also, sharp commands, the sound of guns, the glee of the army and the moans of the dying. These sounds coalesce into an impression of the fearful days of Nat*

*Turner's Rebellion. Finally there is silence. Then the curtain rises
again on* SCENE II. *During this time no lights have been turned on
in the audience. They sit through the above interval in absolute
darkness.*)

Scene II

WEDNESDAY NIGHT

The same scene as SCENE I. *It is darker, however, for no moon rays
filter down through the leafy branches. Shadows seem to press in
with their ominous silence. Everything seems still and menacing.
Suddenly* NAT'S *voice rings out in the black night anxiously as if he
knows it is in vain to call.*)

NAT.   Hark! Henry! Nelson! (*There is silence.*) Speak, Hark! Dis
is General Nat comin'! (*There is no answer.* NAT *runs in panting
with exhaustion. Instead of the God-inspired person who knows
no failure, there is a hunted look about him as though he half
suspects the white troops to be there ready to capture him and
swing him from one of the limbs. He looks around.*) Ah thought
Ah heard voices; but dey ain't heah. Dere ain't nobody heah.
Dere ain't no sound 'cept ma own talk dyin' away in de dark
shadows ob de woods. (*Looking over where the moon was.*)
On Sunday night when we started we had de light ob de full
moon, even ef hit seem tuh drip blood down on dis wicked
world. But now on Wednesday everythin' is dark. Dere ain't
no light nowhar in dis wide world. Even de light ob God done
faded into de awful blackness which surrounds dis place. (*Rem-
niscently.*) When de white soldiers fired on ma army up dere
near Jeresulem, dey all deserted and run lak cowards. Dey
didn't hab guts enuff tuh fight; tuh stand up and be men. At
de fust sign ob real battle dey tucked dere tails lak scared dogs
and run away wid dere tails between dere legs. Dey ought tuh
knowed dey couldn't lose. Nobody can lose when dey fight de
battle ob de one true Gawd ob Hosts. (*Walking around.*) We
ain't licked yet. We is still gwine fight. Ah sent Jessee and Jack
tuh tell Henry and Hark, Nelson and Sam tuh meet me heah
last night, and we would raise another army and carry out our
plans. But dey didn't come. Ah stayed heah tull nearly daybreak waiting fuh dem. (*Half fearfully, then crying out.*) Ah
wunder ef anything happened tuh dem. Naw! Naw! Dat
couldn't be. De Lawd Gawd wouldn't let dat happen! Would
yuh, Lawd? Dere ain't no answer; but Ah know dey'll be heah
in a few minutes. Dey couldn't git heah last night; but dey'll

sho be heah tu-night. (*Pacing around like a lion in a cage.*) Hark! Dere ain't no answer. Ah can't do nothin' but wait! Wait! Dey gut tuh come soon. Dey can't stay way forever.

VOICE. (*Far off and faint*) General Nat!

NAT. (*Full of life*) What's dat? Somebody callin'!! Dat's Hark! He's comin'! Ah knowed he would come! Good old Hark! Now we'll git dis army together. We'll fight! We'll kill everybody in de worl' dat own slaves. We'll set all de black folks free! Ah feel lak Ah could kill a hundred white folks wid one blow!

VOICE. (*Closer and in pain*) General Nat!

NAT. Heah Ah is, Hark. Come right on. Bring de whole army heah. We'll drill dem twell dey learn tuh obey. We ain't gwine let dem drink cider dis time and git drunk. Dey is gut tuh fight and tend tuh business.

(JESSEE *drags in with great difficulty. He has been wounded and his whole body seems twisted with pain.*)

JESSEE. He'p me, General Nat! Dis is Jessee!

NAT. Jessee! Ah'll he'p yuh! Come on, whut's de matter?

JESSEE. (*In a halting manner*) Dey gut me! De white folks shoot me down lak a dawg when Ah tries tuh git heah and tell yuh. Ah fell down lak Ah was daid, den Ah gits up somehow and comes heah tuh let yuh know.

NAT. Whut happened? Whar is Hark?

JESSEE. (*In pain*) Ah's gwine in a few minutes. Ah can't las' much longer.

NAT. Whar is Hark? Did he git de army? (JESSEE *moans and drops to the ground.*) Don't go yit, Jessee! Tell me, whar is Hark? Is everthin' all ready tuh keep on?

JESSEE. (*Rambling*) Dis pain in ma belly is killin' me.

LUCINDA. (*Calling*) Jessee!! Jessee!! Whar is yuh?

NAT. Who is dat?

JESSEE. Hit's Lucinda.

LUCINDA. Jessee! Jessee!

NAT. Heah he is, poor boy!

(LUCINDA *comes in. She is a young slave girl dressed in dark clothes. She sees* JESSEE *on the ground moaning.*)

LUCINDA.   Whut's de matter, Jessee?

JESSEE.   De white folks gut me. Dey shoot me right in de belly.

LUCINDA.   (*Getting down and holding his head in her lap*) Does hit hurt much, honey?

JESSEE.   Yeah, hit hurts turrible. Ah's sinkin'.

NAT.   Don't go befo' yuh tells me, Jessee. Tell me 'bout de army. Tell ——

LUCINDA.   (*Cutting him off*) Ah thought sompen would happen tuh yuh. Dat's why Ah followed yuh.

JESSEE.   Ah had tuh carry out General Nat's orders.

NAT.   Whut did yuh find out, Jessee?

JESSEE.   (*Ignoring him*) Hold me in yo' arms, Lucinda. Ah ain't heah fuh long.

LUCINDA.   Is dat better, Jessee?

NAT.   Is dere anythin' somebody can do tuh ease yo' misery, Jessee?

JESSEE.   (*Coughing*) Naw, dere ain't nothin'. Ah's gwine tuh another worl'.

LUCINDA.   (*Crying out*) Yuh can't go. Yuh can't go. Yuh is gut tuh stay heah wid me.

JESSEE.   Ah can't stay. (*He raises up out of* LUCINDA's *arms, straightens up and salutes.*) General Nat, dere ain't no mo' army. De white folks done captured Hark and all de res'. Yuh's better hide yo'se'f in a safe place. Dey is lookin' fuh yuh.

NAT.   (*Bursting out*) No army! Everybody captured! Dis is sho sad news yuh brings tuh me, Jessee.

(JESSEE *crumples up and falls to the ground. He is seized with violent coughing. He shudders violently and lies still.*)

LUCINDA.   (*Shaking him*). Jessee! Jessee! Yuh can't go! Come back, Jessee. (*She bursts into tears*).

NAT.   Poor boy! He's gone!

LUCINDA.   (*Springing up, shrieking*) Yeah he is gone! And yuh killed him! Yuh did hit! Yuh killed him, Ah said. Yuh wid yo' fine notions 'bout slaves should be free. Yuh fooled dem all into jining an army tuh fight 'gainst de white folks. Yuh knowed yuh wa'n't gwine do nothin'! And yuh made dem shoot Jessee. (*Getting more vehement.*) But yuh'll git yours. See ef yuh don't! De

white folks is all 'round in dese woods. Dey is gwine ketch yuh
and stretch yo' nake on de gallows. Dey is gwine cut yo' body up
lak hawgs. Yuh ain't fittin' tuh live, dat's whut. Yuh said Gawd
tole yuh tuh git an army. Well, see whut Gawd tells yuh when
dey start stretchin' yo' nake. Ah'm gwine tuh tell de white folks
whar yuh is. Ah'm gwine tuh tell dem, Ah say! Yuh ain't nothin'
but a beast, dat's whut, a beast. *(She rushes off.)*

NAT.   *(Bursting out)* A beast! She called me a beast! Ef Ah's a
beast, who made me one? Ef dey buy and sell me, whip me lak
dawgs, and feed me dere leavin's, how can Ah be nothin' else but
a beast? How can dey blame me ef Ah turns on dem and rend
dem? *(Looking down at* JESSEE.*)* Jessee's daid. A few minutes
ago he was heah in dis worl' groaning in misery. Hark is captured, and dere ain't no army. What is Ah gwine tuh do now,
Lawd? What is Ah gwine tuh do? What can Ah do? Ah knows
whut Ah'll do. Ah'll go hide under dat pile ob fence rails 'til Ah
can git another army. Ah done put ma hands tuh de plow and
Ah can't turn back. *(The yellow light of the moon filters down
through the trees.)* Look at dat moon comin' back tuh light up
de worl'. Hit is big and round and yellow. Hit done dripped out
all hits blood. Ma hands is full o' blood, too. Will dey ever be
clean? Was Ah wrong, Lawd, to fight dat black men mout be
free? Whut is Ah gwine tuh do now? Show me a vision, Lawd,
lak yuh did when de sperits was fightin' in de air. Talk tuh me,
Holy Ghost, lak yuh did when yuh told me tuh seek de kingdom
of heaven. Didn't yuh say yuh was gwine reveal de secret ob de
planets? Speak tuh me and show me, Lawd. *(He stops suddenly.)* Whut's dat noise? Hit mus' be de soldiers lookin' 'bout
in de woods fuh me. Ah can't let dem catch me. Ah is gut tuh
git me a army and fight some mo' fuh freedom. Ah wants freedom! Ah mus' hab freedom fuh all de black slaves. Show me how
tuh git hit, Lawd! *(Shouting wildly as he goes out.)* Sperit ob
Gawd! Show me de way! Guide me! Lead me! Lead me!

*(He rushes off the stage. Everything is quiet. The yellow rays of the
moonlight filter down through the trees.)*

CURTAIN

Ossie Davis (1917-   )

Purlie Victorious

Born in Cogdell, Georgia, Ossie Davis, a graduate of Howard University in Washington, D. C., earned his theatrical reputation primarily as an actor on stage and, more recently, in motion pictures. He has appeared in such plays as *Jeb*, *No Time for Sergeants*, *Raisin in the Sun*, and *Purlie Victorious*. Although he has written several plays, he is best-known for *Purlie Victorious*.

First produced in 1961, *Purlie Victorious* (filmed as *Gone Are the Days*) is a spoof of all traditional stereotypes of black-white relationships in the South. The Ol' Cap'n, the Uncle Tom, the Mammy, the young white liberal, the self-educated black religious leader, the naive black country girl—all appear in what may seem to be merely a hilarious ridicule of both groups. The focus of Mr. Davis's sympathies, however, is unmistakable. The Southern white bigots are merely ridiculous; the black folk are redeemed from their occasional human absurdities by their serious attempts to find ways to live comfortably and with dignity. Beneath the unmistakable hilarity, a song of racial and individual pride swells in echo of the new confidence which had inspired black people in the year of nonviolent demonstrations, boycotts, and sit-ins which preceded the initial production of the play. Climactically, the play reaches a point at which the black folk have become so inspired by their leader's faith that they can sustain him when his confidence flags. When even Gitlow, like a modern Sancho Panza, sees and believes a vision of new life more clearly than his idealistic leader does, a reader also is persuaded to believe.

Purlie Victorious

Characters

PURLIE VICTORIOUS JUDSON
LUTIEBELLE GUSSIEMAE JENKINS
MISSY JUDSON
GITLOW JUDSON
CHARLIE COTCHIPEE
IDELLA LANDY
OL' CAP'N COTCHIPEE
THE SHERIFF
THE DEPUTY

"Our churches will say segregation is immoral because it makes perfectly wonderful people, white and black, do immoral things; . . .

Our courts will say segregation is illegal because it makes perfectly wonderful people, white and black, do illegal things; . . .

And finally our Theatre will say segregation is ridiculous because it makes perfectly wonderful people, white and black, do ridiculous things!"

—From "Purlie's I.O.U."

Act I

Scene 1

PLACE   *The cotton plantation country of the Old South*

TIME   *The recent past*

SCENE   *The setting is the plain and simple interior of an antiquated, run-down farmhouse such as Negro sharecroppers still live in, in South Georgia. Threadbare but warm-hearted, shabby but clean. In the Center is a large, rough-hewn table with three homemade chairs and a small bench. This table is the center of all family activities. The main entrance is a door in the Upstage Right corner, which leads in from a rickety porch which we cannot see. There is a small archway in the opposite corner, with some long strips of gunny-sacking hanging down to serve as a door, which leads off to the kitchen. In the center of the Right wall is a window that is wooden, which opens outward on hinges. Downstage Right is a small door leading off to a bedroom, and opposite, Downstage Left, another door leads out into the backyard, and on into the cotton fields beyond. There is also a smaller table and a cupboard against the wall. An old dresser stands against the Right wall, between the window and the Downstage door. There is a shelf on the Left wall with a pail of drinking water, and a large tin dipper. Various cooking utensils, and items like salt and pepper are scattered about in appropriate places.*

AT RISE   *The CURTAIN rises on a stage in semi-darkness. After a moment, when the LIGHTS have come up, the door in the Up Right corner bursts open: Enter* PURLIE JUDSON. PURLIE JUDSON *is tall, restless, and commanding. In his middle or late thirties, he wears a wide-brim, ministerial black hat, a string tie, and a claw hammer coat, which, though far from new, does not fit him too badly. His arms are loaded with large boxes and parcels, which must have come fresh from a department store.* PURLIE *is a man consumed with that divine impatience, without which nothing truly good, or truly bad, or even truly ridiculous, is ever accomplished in this world—with rhetoric and flourish to match.*

PURLIE.   (*Calling out loudly.*) MISSY! (*No answer.*) Gitlow!—It's me—Purlie Victorious! (*Still no answer.* PURLIE *empties his overloaded arms, with obvious relief, on top of the big Center table. He stands, mops his brow, and blows.*) Nobody home it seems. (*This last he says to someone he assumes has come in with him. When there is no answer he hurries to the door through which he entered.*) Come on—come on in!

(*Enter* LUTIEBELLE JENKINS, *slowly, as if bemused. Young, eager, well-built: though we cannot tell it at the moment. Clearly a girl from the backwoods, she carries a suitcase tied up with a rope in one hand, and a greasy shoebox with what's left of her lunch, together with an out-moded, out-sized handbag, in the other. Obviously she*

*has traveled a great distance, but she still manages to look fresh and
healthy. Her hat is a horror with feathers, but she wears it like a
banner. Her shoes are flat-heeled and plain white, such as a good
servant girl in the white folks' kitchen who knows her place absolutely is bound to wear. Her fall coat is dowdy, but well-intentioned
with a stingy strip of rabbit fur around the neck.* LUTIEBELLE *is like
thousands of Negro girls you might know. Eager, desirous—even
anxious, keenly in search for life and for love, trembling on the brink
of self-confident and vigorous young womanhood—but afraid to take
the final leap: because no one has ever told her it is no longer necessary to be white in order to be virtuous, charming, or beautiful.*)

LUTIEBELLE. (*Looking around as if at a museum of great importance.*) Nobody home it seems.

PURLIE. (*Annoyed to find himself so exactly echoed, looks at her
sharply. He takes his watch from his vest pocket, where he
wears it on a chain.*) Cotton-picking time in Georgia it's against
the law to be home. Come in—unload yourself. (*Crosses and
looks out into the kitchen.* LUTIEBELLE *is so enthralled, she
still stands with all her bags and parcels in her arm.*) Set your
suitcase down.

LUTIEBELLE. What?

PURLIE. It's making you lopsided.

LUTIEBELLE. (*Snapping out of it.*) It is? I didn't even notice. (*Sets
suitcase, lunch box, and parcels down.*)

PURLIE. (*Studies her for a moment; goes and gently takes off her
hat.*) Tired?

LUTIEBELLE. Not stepping high as I am!

PURLIE. (*Takes the rest of her things and sets them on the table.*)
Hungry?

LUTIEBELLE. No, sir. But there's still some of my lunch left if you—

PURLIE. (*Quickly.*) No, thank you. Two ham-hock sandwiches in
one day is my limit. (*Sits down and fans himself with his hat.*)
Sorry I had to walk you so far so fast.

LUTIEBELLE. (*Dreamily.*) Oh, I didn't mind, sir. Walking's good
for you, Miz Emmylou sez—

PURLIE. Miz Emmylou can afford to say that: Miz Emmylou got
a car. While all the transportation we got in the world is tied
up in second-hand shoe leather. But never mind, my sister,

never-you-mind! (*Rises, almost as if to dance, exaltation glowing in his eyes.*) And toll the bell, Big Bethel—toll that big, black, fat and sassy liberty bell! Tell Freedom the bridegroom cometh; the day of her deliverance is now at hand! (PURLIE *catches sight of* MISSY *through door Down Left.*) Oh, there she is. (*Crosses to door and calls out.*) Missy!—Oh, Missy!

MISSY.   (*From a distance.*) Yes-s-s-s-!

PURLIE.   It's me!—Purlie!

MISSY.   Purlie Victorious?

PURLIE.   Yes. Put that battling stick down and come on in here!

MISSY.   All right!

PURLIE.   (*Crosses hurriedly back to above table at Center.*) That's Missy, my sister-in-law I was telling you about. (*Clears the table of everything but one of the large cartons, which he proceeds to open.*)

LUTIEBELLE.   (*Not hearing him. Still awe-struck to be in the very house, in perhaps the very same room that* PURLIE *might have been born in.*) So this is the house where you was born and bred at.

PURLIE.   Yep! Better'n being born outdoors.

LUTIEBELLE.   What a lovely background for your home-life.

PURLIE.   I wouldn't give it to my dog to raise fleas in!

LUTIEBELLE.   So clean—and nice—and warm-hearted!

PURLIE.   The first chance I get I'ma burn the damn thing down!

LUTIEBELLE.   But — Reb'n Purlie! — It's yours, and that's what counts. Like Miz Emmylou sez—

PURLIE.   Come here! (*Pulls her across to the window, flings it open.*) You see that big white house, perched on top of that hill with them two windows looking right down at us like two eyeballs: that's where Ol' Cap'n lives.

LUTIEBELLE.   Ol' Cap'n?

PURLIE.   Stonewall Jackson Cotchipee. He owns this dump, not me.

LUTIEBELLE.   Oh—

PURLIE.   And that ain't all: hill and dale, field and farm, truck and tractor, horse and mule, bird and bee and bush and tree—

and cotton!—cotton by bole and by bale—every bit o' cotton you see in this county!—Everything and everybody he owns!

LUTIEBELLE.   Everybody? You mean he owns people?

PURLIE.   (*Bridling his impatience.*) Well — look! — ain't a man, woman or child working in this valley that ain't in debt to that ol' bastard! — (*Catches himself.*) bustard! — (*This still won't do.*) buzzard!—And that includes Gitlow and Missy—everybody—except me.—

LUTIEBELLE.   But folks can't own people no more, Reb'n Purlie. Miz Emmylou sez that—

PURLIE.   (*Verging on explosion.*) You ain't working for Miz Emmylou no more, you're working for me—Purlie Victorious. Freedom is my business, and I say that ol' man runs this plantation on debt: the longer you work for Ol' Cap'n Cotchipee, the more you owe at the commissary; and if you don't pay up, you can't leave. And I don't give a damn what Miz Emmylou nor nobody else sez—that's slavery!

LUTIEBELLE.   I'm sorry, Reb'n Purlie—

PURLIE.   Don't apologize, wait!—Just wait!—til I get my church; —wait til I buy Big Bethel back—(*Crosses to window and looks out.*) Wait til I stand once again in the pulpit of Grandpaw Kincaid, and call upon my people—and talk to my people —About Ol' Cap'n, that miserable son-of-a—

LUTIEBELLE.   (*Just in time to save him.*) Wait—!

PURLIE.   Wait, I say! And we'll see who's gonna dominize this valley!—him or me! (*Turns and sees* MISSY *through door Down Left.*) Missy—!

(*Enter* MISSY, *ageless, benign, and smiling. She wears a ragged old straw hat, a big house apron over her faded gingham, and low-cut, dragged-out tennis shoes on her feet. She is strong and of good cheer —of a certain shrewdness, yet full of the desire to believe. Her eyes light on* LUTIEBELLE, *and her arms go up and outward automatically.*)

MISSY.   Purlie!

PURLIE.   (*Thinks she is reaching for him.*) Missy!

MISSY.   (*Ignoring him, clutching* LUTIEBELLE, *laughing and crying.*) Well—well—well!

PURLIE.   (*Breaking the stranglehold.*) For God's sake, Missy, don't choke her to death!

MISSY.   All my life—all my life I been praying for me a daughter just like you. My prayers is been answered at last. Welcome to our home, whoever you is!

LUTIEBELLE.   (*Deeply moved.*) Thank you, ma'am.

MISSY.   "Ma'am—ma'am." Listen to the child, Purlie. Everybody down here calls me Aunt Missy, and I'd be much obliged if you would, too.

LUTIEBELLE.   It would make me very glad to do so—Aunt Missy.

MISSY.   Uhmmmmmm! Pretty as a pan of buttermilk biscuits. Where on earth did you find her, Purlie? (PURLIE *starts to answer.*) Let me take your things—now, you just make yourself at home—Are you hungry?

LUTIEBELLE.   No, ma'am, but cheap as water is, I sure ain't got no business being this thirsty!

MISSY.   (*Starts forward.*) I'll get some for you—

PURLIE.   (*Intercepts her; directs* LUTIEBELLE.) There's the dipper. And right out yonder by the fence just this side of that great big live oak tree you'll find the well—sweetest water in Cotchipee county.

LUTIEBELLE.   Thank you, Reb'n Purlie. I'm very much obliged.

(*Takes dipper from water pail and exits Down Left.*)

MISSY.   Reb'n who?

PURLIE.   (*Looking off after* LUTIEBELLE.) Perfection — absolute Ethiopian perfect. Hah, Missy?

MISSY.   (*Looking off after* LUTIEBELLE.) Oh, I don't know about that.

PURLIE.   What you mean you don't know? This girl looks more like Cousin Bee than Cousin Bee ever did.

MISSY.   No resemblance to me.

PURLIE.   Don't be ridiculous; she's the spitting image—

MISSY.   No resemblance whatsoever!

PURLIE.   I ought to know how my own cousin looked—

MISSY.   But I was the last one to see her alive—

PURLIE.   Twins, if not closer!

MISSY.   Are you crazy? Bee was more lean, loose, and leggy—

PURLIE.   Maybe so, but this girl makes it up in—

MISSY. With no chin to speak of—her eyes: sort of fickle one to another—

PURLIE. I know, but even so—

MISSY. (*Pointing off in* LUTIEBELLE's *direction.*) Look at her head —it ain't nearly as built like a rutabaga as Bee's own was!

PURLIE. (*Exasperated.*) What's the difference! White folks can't tell one of us from another by the head!

MISSY. Twenty years ago it was, Purlie, Ol' Cap'n laid bull whip to your natural behind—

PURLIE. Twenty years ago I swore I'd see his soul in hell!

MISSY. And I don't think you come full back to your senses yet— That ol' man ain't no fool!

PURLIE. That makes it one "no fool" against another.

MISSY. He's dangerous, Purlie. We could get killed if that old man was to find out what we was trying to do to get that church back.

PURLIE. How can he find out? Missy, how many times must I tell you, if it's one thing I am foolproof in it's white folks' psychology.

MISSY. That's exactly what I'm afraid of.

PURLIE. Freedom, Missy, that's what Big Bethel means. For you, me and Gitlow. And we can buy it for five hundred dollars, Missy. Freedom!—You want it, or don't you?

MISSY. Of course I want it, but—After all, Purlie, that rich ol' lady didn't exactly leave that $500 to us—

PURLIE. She left it to Aunt Henrietta—

MISSY. Aunt Henrietta is dead—

PURLIE. Exactly—

MISSY. And Henrietta's daughter Cousin Bee is dead, too.

PURLIE. Which makes us next in line to inherit the money by law!

MISSY. All right, then, why don't we just go on up that hill man-to-man and tell Ol' Cap'n we want our money?

PURLIE. Missy! You have been black as long as I have—

MISSY. (*Not above having her own little joke.*) Hell, boy, we could make him give it to us.

PURLIE. Make him—how? He's a white man, Missy. What you plan to do, sue him?

MISSY. (*Drops her teasing; thinks seriously for a moment.*) After all, it is our money. And it was our church.

PURLIE. And can you think of a better way to get it back than that girl out there?

MISSY. But you think it'll work, Purlie? You really think she can fool Ol' Cap'n?

PURLIE. He'll never know what hit him.

MISSY. Maybe—but there's still the question of Gitlow.

PURLIE. What about Gitlow?

MISSY. Gitlow has changed his mind.

PURLIE. Then you'll have to change it back.

GITLOW. (*Offstage.*) Help, Missy; help, Missy; help, Missy; help, Missy! (GITLOW *runs on.*)

MISSY. What the devil's the matter this time?

GITLOW. There I was, Missy, picking in the high cotton, twice as fast as the human eye could see. All of a sudden I missed a bole and it fell—it fell on the ground, Missy! I stooped as fast as I could to pick it up and—(*He stoops to illustrate. There is a loud tearing of cloth.*) ripped the seat of my britches. There I was, Missy, exposed from stem to stern.

MISSY. What's so awful about that? It's only cotton.

GITLOW. But cotton is white, Missy. We must maintain respect. Bring me my Sunday School britches.

MISSY. What!

GITLOW. Ol' Cap'n is coming down into the cotton patch today, and I know you want your Gitlow to look his level best. (MISSY *starts to answer.*) Hurry, Missy, hurry! (GITLOW *hurries her off.*)

PURLIE. Gitlow—have I got the girl!

GITLOW. Is that so—what girl?

PURLIE. (*Taking him to the door.*) See? There she is! Well?

GITLOW. Well what?

PURLIE. What do you think?

GITLOW. Nope ; she'll never do.

PURLIE. What you mean, she'll never do?

GITLOW. My advice to you is to take that girl back to Florida as fast as you can!

PURLIE. I can't take her back to Florida.

GITLOW. Why can't you take her back to Florida?

PURLIE. 'Cause she comes from Alabama. Gitlow, look at her: she's just the size—just the type—just the style.

GITLOW. And just the girl to get us all in jail. The answer is no! (*Crosses to kitchen door.*) MISSY! (*Back to* PURLIE.) Girl or no girl, I ain't getting mixed up in no more of your nightmares —I got my own. Dammit, Missy, I said let's go!

MISSY. (*Entering with trousers.*) You want me to take my bat to you again?

GITLOW. No, Missy, control yourself. It's just that every second Gitlow's off the firing line-up, seven pounds of Ol' Cap'n's cotton don't git gotten. (*Snatches pants from* MISSY, *but is in too much of a hurry to put them on—starts off.*)

PURLIE. Wait a minute, Gitlow. . . . Wait! (GITLOW *is off in a flash.*) Missy! Stop him!

MISSY. He ain't as easy to stop as he used to be. Especially now Ol' Cap'n's made him Deputy-For-The-Colored.

PURLIE. Deputy-For-The-Colored? What the devil is that?

MISSY. Who knows? All I know is Gitlow's changed his mind.

PURLIE. But Gitlow can't change his mind!

MISSY. Oh, it's easy enough when you ain't got much to start with. I warned you. You don't know how shifty ol' Git can git. He's the hardest man to convince and keep convinced I ever seen in my life.

PURLIE. Missy, you've got to make him go up that hill, he's got to identify this girl—Ol' Cap'n won't believe nobody else.

MISSY. I know—

PURLIE. He's got to swear before Ol' Cap'n that this girl is the real Cousin Bee—

MISSY. I know.

PURLIE. Missy, you're the only person in this world ol' Git'll really listen to.

MISSY. I know.

PURLIE.   And what if you do have to hit him a time or two—it's for his own good!

MISSY.   I know.

PURLIE.   He'll recover from it, Missy. He always does—

MISSY.   I know.

PURLIE.   Freedom, Missy—Big Bethel; for you; me; and Gitlow—!

MISSY.   Freedom—and a little something left over—that's all I ever wanted all my life. (*Looks out into the yard.*) She do look a little somewhat like Cousin Bee—about the feet!

PURLIE.   Of course she does—

MISSY.   I won't guarantee nothing, Purlie—but I'll try.

PURLIE.   (*Grabbing her and dancing her around.*) Everytime I see you, Missy, you get prettier by the pound!

(LUTIEBELLE *enters.* MISSY *sees her.*)

MISSY.   Stop it, Purlie, stop it! Stop it. Quit cutting the fool in front of company!

PURLIE.   (*Sees* LUTIEBELLE, *crosses to her, grabs her about the waist and swings her around too.*)
How wondrous are the daughters of my people.
Yet knoweth not the glories of themselves!

(*Spins her around for* MISSY'S *inspection. She does look better with her coat off, in her immaculate blue and white maid's uniform.*)

Where do you suppose I found her, Missy—
This Ibo prize—this Zulu Pearl—
This long lost lily of the black Mandingo—
Kikuyu maid, beneath whose brown embrace
Hot suns of Africa are burning still: where—where?
A drudge; a serving wench; a feudal fetch-pot:
A common scullion in the white man's kitchen.
Drowned is her youth in thankless Southern dishpans;
Her beauty spilt for Dixiecratic pigs!
This brown-skinned grape! this wine of Negro vintage—

MISSY.   (*Interrupting.*) I know all that, Purlie, but what's her name?

(PURLIE *looks at* LUTIEBELLE *and turns abruptly away.*)

LUTIEBELLE.   I don't think he likes my name so much—it's Lutiebelle, ma'am—Lutiebelle Gussiemae Jenkins!

MISSY. (*Gushing with motherly reassurance.*) Lutiebelle Gussie-mae Jenkins! My, that's nice.

PURLIE. Nice! It's an insult to the Negro people!

MISSY. Purlie, behave yourself!

PURLIE. A previous condition of servitude, a badge of inferiority, and I refuse to have it in my organization!—change it!

MISSY. You want me to box your mouth for you!

PURLIE. Lutiebelle Gussiemae Jenkins! What does it mean in Swahili? Cheap labor!

LUTIEBELLE. Swahili?

PURLIE. One of the thirteen silver tongues of Africa: Swahili, Bushengo, Ashanti, Baganda, Herero, Yoruba, Bambora, Mpongwe, Swahili: a language of moons, of velvet drums; hot days of rivers, red-splashed and bird-song bright!, black fingers in rice white at sunset red! — ten thousand Queens of Sheba—

MISSY. (*Having to interrupt.*) Just where did Purlie find you, honey?

LUTIEBELLE. It was in Dothan, Alabama, last Sunday, Aunt Missy, right in the junior choir!

MISSY. The junior choir—my, my, my!

PURLIE. (*Still carried away.*)
Behold! I said, this dark and holy vessel,
In whom should burn that golden nut-brown joy
Which Negro womanhood was meant to be.
Ten thousand queens, ten thousand Queens of Sheba:

(*Pointing at* LUTIEBELLE.)

Ethiopia herself—in all her beauteous wonder,
Come to restore the ancient thrones of Cush!

MISSY. Great Gawdamighty, Purlie, I can't hear myself think—!

LUTIEBELLE. That's just what I said last Sunday, Aunt Missy, when Reb'n Purlie started preaching that thing in the pulpit.

MISSY. Preaching it!?

LUTIEBELLE. Lord, Aunt Missy, I shouted clear down to the Mourners' Bench.

MISSY. (*To* PURLIE.) But last time you was a professor of Negro Philosophy.

PURLIE. I told you, Missy: my intention is to buy Big Bethel back; to reclaim the ancient pulpit of Grandpaw Kincaid, and preach freedom in the cotton patch—I told you!

MISSY. Maybe you did, Purlie, maybe you did. You got yourself a license?

PURLIE. Naw!—but—

MISSY. (*Looking him over.*) Purlie Victorious Judson: Self-made minister of the gospel-claw-hammer coattail, shoe-string tie and all.

PURLIE. (*Quietly but firmly holding his ground.*) How else can you lead the Negro people?

MISSY. Is that what you got in your mind: leading the Negro people?

PURLIE. Who else is they got?

MISSY. God help the race.

LUTIEBELLE. It was a sermon, I mean, Aunt Missy, the likes of which has never been heard before.

MISSY. Oh, I bet that. Tell me about it, son. What did you preach?

PURLIE. I preached the New Baptism of Freedom for all mankind, according to the Declaration of Independence, taking as my text the Constitution of the United States of America, Amendments First through Fifteenth, which readeth as follows: "Congress shall make no law—"

MISSY. Enough — that's enough, son — I'm converted. But it is confusing all the changes you keep going through. (*To* LUTIE- BELLE.) Honey, every time I see Purlie he's somebody else.

PURLIE. Not any more, Missy; and if I'm lying may the good Lord put me down in the book of bad names: Purlie is put forever!

MISSY. Yes. But will he stay put forever?

PURLIE. There is in every man a finger of iron that points him what he must and must not do—

MISSY. And your finger points up the hill to that five hundred dollars with which you'll buy Big Bethel back, preach freedom in the cotton patch, and live happily ever after!

PURLIE. The soul-consuming passion of my life! (*Draws out watch.*) It's 2:15, Missy, and Gitlow's waiting. Missy, I suggest you get a move on.

MISSY. I already got a move on. Had it since four o'clock this morning!

PURLIE. Time, Missy—exactly what the colored man in this country ain't got, and you're wasting it!

MISSY. (*Looks at* PURLIE, *and decides not to strike him dead.*) Purlie, would you mind stepping out into the cotton patch and telling your brother Gitlow I'd like a few words with him? (PURLIE, *overjoyed, leaps at* MISSY *as if to hug and dance her around again, but she is too fast.*) Do like I tell you now— go on! (PURLIE *exits singing.* MISSY *turns to* LUTIEBELLE *to begin the important task of sizing her up.*) Besides, it wouldn't be hospitable not to set and visit a spell with our distinguished guest over from Dothan, Alabama.

LUTIEBELLE. (*This is the first time she has been called anything of importance by anybody.*) Thank you, ma'am.

MISSY. Now. Let's you and me just set back and enjoy a piece of my potato pie. You like potato pie, don't you?

LUTIEBELLE. Oh, yes, ma'am, I like it very much.

MISSY. And get real acquainted. (*Offers her a saucer with a slice of pie on it.*)

LUTIEBELLE. I'm ever so much obliged. My, this looks nice! Uhm, uhn, uhn!

MISSY. (*Takes a slice for herself and sits down.*) You know—ever since that ol' man—(*Indicates up the hill.*) took after Purlie so unmerciful with that bull whip twenty years ago—he fidgets! Always on the go; rattling around from place to place all over the country: one step ahead of the white folks — something about Purlie always did irritate the white folks.

LUTIEBELLE. Is that the truth!

MISSY. Oh, my yes. Finally wound up being locked up a time or two for safekeeping — (LUTIEBELLE *parts with a loud, sympathetic grunt. Changing her tack a bit.*) Always kept up his schooling, though. In fact that boy's got one of the best second-hand educations in this country.

LUTIEBELLE. (*Brightening considerably.*) Is that a fact!

MISSY. Used to read everything he could get his hands on.

LUTIEBELLE. He did? Ain't that wonderful!

MISSY. Till one day he finally got tired, and throwed all his books to the hogs—not enough "Negro" in them, he said. After that he puttered around with first one thing then another. Remember that big bus boycott they had in Montgomery? Well, we don't travel by bus in the cotton patch, so Purlie boycotted mules!

LUTIEBELLE.   You don't say so?

MISSY.   Another time he invented a secret language, that Negroes could understand but white folks couldn't.

LUTIEBELLE   Oh, my goodness gracious!

MISSY.   He sent it C.O.D. to the NAACP but they never answered his letter.

LUTIEBELLE.   Oh, they will, Aunt Missy; you can just bet your life they will.

MISSY.   I don't mind it so much. Great leaders are bound to pop up from time to time 'mongst our people—in fact we sort of look forward to it. But Purlie's in such a hurry I'm afraid he'll lose his mind!

LUTIEBELLE.   Lose his mind—no! Oh, no!

MISSY.   That is unless you and me can do something about it.

LUTIEBELLE.   You and me? Do what, Aunt Missy? You tell me— I'll do anything!

MISSY.   (*Having found all she needs to know.*) Well, now; ain't nothing ever all that peculiar about a man a good wife—and a family—and some steady home cooking won't cure. Don't you think so?

LUTIEBELLE.   (*Immensely relieved.*) Oh, yes, Aunt Missy, yes. (*But still not getting* MISSY's *intent.*) You'd be surprised how many tall, good-looking, great big, ol' handsome looking mens —just like Reb'n Purlie—walking around, starving theyselves to death! Oh, I just wish I had one to aim my pot at!

MISSY.   Well, Purlie Judson is the uncrowned appetite of the age.

LUTIEBELLE.   He is! What's his favorite?

MISSY.   Anything! Anything a fine-looking, strong and healthy— girl like you could put on the table.

LUTIEBELLE.   Like me? Like ME! Oh, Aunt Missy—!

MISSY.   (PURLIE's *future is settled.*) Honey, I mind once at the Sunday School picnic Purlie et a whole sack o' pullets!

LUTIEBELLE.   Oh, I just knowed there was something—something —just reeks about that man. He puts me in the mind of all the good things I ever had in my life. Picnics, fish-fries, corn-shuckings, and love-feasts, and gospel-singings—picking huck-leberries, roasting groundpeas, quilting-bee parties and barbecues; that certain kind of—welcome—you can't get no-where else in all this world. Aunt Missy, life is so good to us—sometimes!

MISSY.   Oh, child, being colored can be a lotta fun when ain't no-body looking.

LUTIEBELLE.   Ain't it the truth! I always said I'd never pass for white, no matter how much they offered me, unless the things I love could pass, too.

MISSY.   Ain't it the beautiful truth!

(PURLIE *enters again; agitated.*)

PURLIE.   Missy—Gitlow says if you want him come and get him!

MISSY.   (*Rises, crosses to door Down Left; looks out.*) Lawd, that man do take his cotton picking seriously. (*Comes back to* LUTIEBELLE *and takes her saucer.*) Did you get enough to eat, honey?

LUTIEBELLE.   Indeed I did. And Aunt Missy, I haven't had potato pie like that since the senior choir give—

MISSY.   (*Still ignoring him.*) That's where I met Gitlow, you know. On the senior choir.

LUTIEBELLE.   Aunt Missy! I didn't know you could sing!

MISSY.   Like a brown-skin nightingale. Well, it was a Sunday after-noon—Big Bethel had just been—

PURLIE.   Dammit, Missy! The white man is five hundred years ahead of us in this country, and we ain't gonna ever gonna catch up with him sitting around on our non-Caucasian rumps talk-ing about the senior choir!

MISSY.   (*Starts to bridle at this sudden display of passion, but changes her mind.*) Right this way, honey. (*Heads for door Down Right.*) Where Cousin Bee used to sleep at.

LUTIEBELLE.   Yes, ma'am. (*Starts to follow* MISSY.)

PURLIE.   (*Stopping her.*) Wait a minute—don't forget your clothes! (*Gives her a large carton.*)

MISSY.   It ain't much, the roof leaks, and you can get as much September inside as you can outside any time; but I try to keep it clean.

PURLIE.   Cousin Bee was known for her clothes!

MISSY.   Stop nagging, Purlie—(*To* LUTIEBELLE.) There's plenty to eat in the kitchen.

LUTIEBELLE.   Thank you, Aunt Missy. (*Exits Down Right.*)

PURLIE.   (*Following after her.*) And hurry! We want to leave as soon as Missy gets Gitlow in from the cotton patch!

MISSY.   (*Blocking his path.*) Mr. Preacher—(*She pulls him out of earshot.*) If we do pull this thing off—(*Studying him a moment.*) what do you plan to do with her after that—send her back where she came from?

PURLIE.   Dothan, Alabama? Never! Missy, there a million things I can do with a girl like that, right here in Big Bethel!

MISSY.   Yeah! Just make sure they're all legitimate. Anyway, marriage is still cheap, and we can always use another cook in the family! (PURLIE *hasn't the slightest idea what* MISSY *is talking about.*)

LUTIEBELLE.   (*From Offstage.*) Aunt Missy.

MISSY.   Yes, honey.

LUTIEBELLE.   (*Offstage.*) Whose picture is this on the dresser?

MISSY.   Why, that's Cousin Bee.

LUTIEBELLE.   (*A moment's silence. Then she enters hastily carrying a large photograph in her hand.*) Cousin Bee!

MISSY.   Yes, poor thing. She's the one the whole thing is all about.

LUTIEBELLE.   (*The edge of panic.*) Cousin Bee—Oh, my!—Oh, my goodness! My goodness gracious!

MISSY.   What's the matter?

LUTIEBELLE.   But she's pretty—she's so pretty!

MISSY.   (*Takes photograph; looks at it tenderly.*) Yes—she was pretty. I guess they took this shortly before she died.

LUTIEBELLE.   And you mean—you want me to look like her?

PURLIE.   That's the idea. Now go and get into your clothes. (*Starts to push her off.*)

MISSY.   They sent it down to us from the college. Don't she look smart? I'll bet she was a good student when she was living.

LUTIEBELLE.   (*Evading* PURLIE.) Good student!

MISSY.   Yes. One more year and she'd have finished.

LUTIEBELLE. Oh, my gracious Lord have mercy upon my poor soul!

PURLIE. (*Not appreciating her distress or its causes.*) Awake, awake! Put on thy strength, O, Zion—put on thy beautiful garments. (*Hurries her Offstage.*) And hurry! (*Turning to* MISSY.) Missy, Big Bethel and Gitlow is waiting. Grandpaw Kincaid gave his life. (*Gently places the bat into her hand.*) It is a far greater thing you do now, than you've ever done before—and Gitlow ain't never got his head knocked off in a better cause. (MISSY *nods her head in sad agreement, and accepts the bat.* PURLIE *helps her to the door Down Left, where she exits, a most reluctant executioner.* PURLIE *stands and watches her off from the depth of his satisfaction. The door Down Right eases open, and* LUTIEBELLE, *her suitcase, handbag, fall coat and lunch box firmly in hand, tries to sneak out the front door.* PURLIE *hears her, and turns just in time.*) Where do you think you're going?

LUTIEBELLE. Did you see that, Reb'n Purlie? (*Indicating bedroom from which she just came.*) Did you see all them beautiful clothes—slips, hats, shoes, stockings? I mean nylon stockings like Miz Emmylou wears—and a dress, like even Miz Emmylou don't wear. Did you look at what was in that big box?

PURLIE. Of course I looked at what was in that big box—I bought it—all of it—for you.

LUTIEBELLE. For me!

PURLIE. Of course! I told you! And as soon as we finish you can have it!

LUTIEBELLE. Reb'n Purlie, I'm a good girl. I ain't never done nothing in all this world, white, colored or otherwise, to hurt nobody!

PURLIE. I know that.

LUTIEBELLE. I work hard; I mop, I scrub, I iron; I'm clean and polite, and I know how to get along with white folks' children better'n they do. I pay my church dues every second and fourth Sunday the Lord sends; and I can cook catfish — and hushpuppies—You like hushpuppies, don't you, Reb'n Purlie?

PURLIE. I love hushpuppies!

LUTIEBELLE. Hushpuppies—and corn dodgers; I can cook you a corn dodger would give you the swimming in the head!

PURLIE. I'm sure you can, but—

LUTIEBELLE. But I ain't never been in a mess like this in all my life!

PURLIE. Mess—what mess?

LUTIEBELLE. You mean go up that hill, in all them pretty clothes, and pretend — in front of white folks — that — that I'm your Cousin Bee—somebody I ain't never seen or heard of before in my whole life!

PURLIE. Why not? Some of the best pretending in the world is done in front of white folks.

LUTIEBELLE. But Reb'n Purlie, I didn't know your Cousin Bee was a student at the college; I thought she worked there!

PURLIE. But I told you on the train—

LUTIEBELLE. Don't do no good to tell ME nothing, Reb'n Purlie! I never listen. Ask Miz Emmylou and 'em, they'll tell you I never listen. I didn't know it was a college lady you wanted me to make like. I thought it was for a sleep-in like me. I thought all that stuff you bought in them boxes was stuff for maids and cooks and—Why, I ain't never even been near a college!

PURLIE. So what? College ain't so much where you been as how you talk when you get back. Anybody can do it; look at me.

LUTIEBELLE. Nawsir, I think you better look at me like Miz Emmylou sez—

PURLIE. (*Taking her by the shoulders, tenderly.*) Calm down— just take it easy, and calm down. (*She subsides a little, her chills banished by the warmth of him.*) Now—don't tell me, after all that big talking you done on the train about white folks, you're scared.

LUTIEBELLE. Talking big is easy—from the proper distance.

PURLIE. Why—don't you believe in yourself?

LUTIEBELLE. Some.

PURLIE. Don't you believe in your own race of people?

LUTIEBELLE. Oh, yessir—a little.

PURLIE. Don't you believe the black man is coming to power some day?

LUTIEBELLE. Almost.

PURLIE. Ten thousand Queens of Sheba! What kind of a Negro are you! Where's your race pride?

LUTIEBELLE. Oh, I'm a great one for race pride, sir, believe me—
it's just that I don't need it much in my line of work! Miz
Emmylou sez—

PURLIE. Damn Miz Emmylou! Does her blond hair and blue eyes
make her any more of a woman in the sight of her men folks
than your black hair and brown eyes in mine?

LUTIEBELLE. No, sir!

PURLIE. Is her lily-white skin any more money-under-the-mattress
than your fine fair brown? And if so, why does she spend half
her life at the beach trying to get a sun tan?

LUTIEBELLE. I never thought of that!

PURLIE. There's a whole lotta things about the Negro question
you ain't thought of! The South is split like a fat man's underwear; and somebody beside the Supreme Court has got to make
a stand for the everlasting glory of our people!

LUTIEBELLE. Yessir.

PURLIE. Snatch Freedom from the jaws of force and filibuster!

LUTIEBELLE. Amen to that!

PURLIE. Put thunder in the Senate—!

LUTIEBELLE. Yes, Lord!

PURLIE. And righteous indignation back in the halls of Congress!

LUTIEBELLE. Ain't it the truth!

PURLIE. Make Civil Rights from Civil Wrongs; and bring that ol'
Civil War to a fair and a just conclusion!

LUTIEBELLE. Help him, Lord!

PURLIE. Remind this white and wicked world there ain't been
more'n a dime's worth of difference twixt one man and another'n, irregardless of race, gender, creed, or color—since God
Himself Almighty set the first batch out to dry before the chim-
neys of Zion got hot! The eyes and ears of the world is on Big
Bethel!

LUTIEBELLE. Amen and hallelujah!

PURLIE. And whose side are you fighting on this evening, sister?

LUTIEBELLE. Great Gawdamighty, Reb'n Purlie, on the Lord's
side! But Miss Emmylou sez—

PURLIE. (*Blowing up.*) This is outrageous—this is a catastrophe!
You're a disgrace to the Negro profession!

LUTIEBELLE.   That's just what she said all right — her exactly words.

PURLIE.   Who's responsible for this? Where's your Maw and Paw at?

LUTIEBELLE.   I reckon I ain't rightly got no Maw and Paw, where-ever they at.

PURLIE.   What!

LUTIEBELLE.   And nobody else that I knows of. You see, sir—I been on the go from one white folks' kitchen to another since before I can remember. How I got there in the first place—whatever became of my Maw and Paw, and my kinfolks—even what my real name is—nobody is ever rightly said.

PURLIE.   (*Genuinely touched.*) Oh. A motherless child—

LUTIEBELLE.   That's what Miz Emmylou always sez—

PURLIE.   But—who cared for you—like a mother? Who brung you up—who raised you?

LUTIEBELLE.   Nobody in particular—just whoever happened to be in charge of the kitchen that day.

PURLIE.   That explains the whole thing—no wonder; you've missed the most important part of being somebody.

LUTIEBELLE.   I have? What part is that?

PURLIE.   Love — being appreciated, and sought out, and looked after; being fought to the bitter end over even.

LUTIEBELLE.   Oh, I have missed that, Reb'n Purlie, I really have. Take mens—all my life they never looked at me the way the other girls get looked at!

PURLIE.   That's not so. The very first time I saw you—right up there in the junior choir—I give you that look!

LUTIEBELLE.   (*Turning to him in absolute ecstasy.*) You did! Oh, I thought so!—I prayed so. All through your sermon I thought I would faint from hoping so hard so. Oh, Reb'n Purlie—I think that's the finest look a person could ever give a person—Oh, Reb'n Purlie! (*She closes her eyes and points her lips at him.*)

PURLIE.   (*Starts to kiss her, but draws back shyly.*) Lutiebelle—

LUTIEBELLE.   (*Dreamily, her eyes still closed.*) Yes, Reb'n Purlie—

PURLIE.   There's something I want to ask you—something I never —in all my life—thought I'd be asking a woman—Would you— I don't know exactly how to say it—would you—

LUTIEBELLE.   Yes, Reb'n Purlie?

PURLIE.   Would you be my disciple?

LUTIEBELLE.   (*Rushing into his arms.*) Oh, yes, Reb'n Purlie, yes! (*They start to kiss, but are interrupted by a NOISE coming from Offstage.*)

GITLOW.   (*Offstage; in the extremity of death.*) No, Missy. No— no!—NO!—(*This last plea is choked off by the sound of some solid object brought smartly into contact with sudden flesh. "CLUNK!"* PURLIE *and* LUTIEBELLE *stand looking off Left, frozen for the moment.*)

LUTIEBELLE.   (*Finally daring to speak.*) Oh, my Lord, Reb'n Pur- lie, what happened?

PURLIE.   Gitlow has changed his mind. (*Grabs her and swings her around bodily.*) Toll the bell, Big Bethel!—toll that big, fat, black and sassy liberty bell. Tell Freedom—(LUTIEBELLE *suddenly leaps from the floor into his arms and plants her lips squarely on his. When finally he can come up for air.*) Tell Freedom—tell Freedom—WOW!

CURTAIN

Act I

Scene 2

TIME   *It is a little later the same afternoon.*

SCENE   *We are now in the little business office off from the commis- sary, where all the inhabitants of Cotchipee Valley buy food, clothing, and supplies. In the back a traveler has been drawn with just enough of an opening left to serve as the door to the main part of the store. On Stage Left and on Stage Right are simulated shelves where various items of reserve stock are kept: A wash tub, an axe, sacks of peas, and flour; bolts of gingham and calico, etc. Downstage Right is a small desk, on which an ancient type- writer, and an adding machine, with various papers and necessary books and records of commerce are placed. There is a small chair at this desk. Downstage Left is a table, with a large cash register, that has a functioning drawer. Below this is an entrance from the street.*

AT RISE   *As the CURTAIN rises, a young white* MAN *of 25 or 30, but still gawky, awkward, and adolescent in outlook and behavior, is sitting on a high stool Downstage Right Center. His face is held in the hands of* IDELLA, *a Negro cook and woman of all work, who has been in the family since time immemorial. She is the only mother* CHARLIE, *who is very much oversized even for his age, has ever known.* IDELLA *is as little as she is old and as tough as she is tiny, and is busily applying medication to* CHARLIE'S *black eye.*

CHARLIE.   Ow, Idella, ow!—Ow!

IDELLA.   Hold still, boy.

CHARLIE.   But it hurts, Idella.

IDELLA.   I know it hurts. Whoever done this to you musta meant to knock your natural brains out.

CHARLIE.   I already told you who done it—OW!

IDELLA.   Charlie Cotchipee, if you don't hold still and let me put this hot poultice on your eye, you better! (CHARLIE *subsides and meekly accepts her ministrations.*) First the milking, then the breakfast, then the dishes, then the washing, then the scrubbing, then the lunch time, next the dishes, then the ironing— and now; just where the picking and plucking for supper ought to be—you!

CHARLIE.   You didn't tell Paw?

IDELLA.   Of course I didn't—but the sheriff did.

CHARLIE.   (*Leaping up.*) The sheriff!

IDELLA.   (*Pushing him back down.*) Him and the deputy come to the house less than a hour ago.

CHARLIE.   (*Leaping up again.*) Are they coming over here!

IDELLA.   Of course they're coming over here—sooner or later.

CHARLIE.   But what will I do, Idella, what will I say?

IDELLA.   (*Pushing him down.* CHARLIE *subsides.*) "He that keepeth his mouth keepeth his life—"

CHARLIE.   Did they ask for me?

IDELLA.   Of course they asked for you.

CHARLIE. What did they say?

IDELLA. I couldn't hear too well; your father took them into the study and locked the door behind them.

CHARLIE. Maybe it was about something else.

IDELLA. It was about YOU: that much I could hear! Charlie—you want to get us both killed!

CHARLIE. I'm sorry, Idella, but—

IDELLA. (*Overriding; finishing proverb she had begun.*) "But he that openeth wide his lips shall have destruction!"

CHARLIE. But it was you who said it was the law of the land—

IDELLA. I know I did—

CHARLIE. It was you who said it's got to be obeyed—

IDELLA. I know it was me, but—

CHARLIE. It was you who said everybody had to stand up and take a stand against—

IDELLA. I know it was me, dammit! But I didn't say take a stand in no barroom!

CHARLIE. Ben started it, not me. And you always said never to take low from the likes of him!

IDELLA. Not so loud; they may be out there in the commissary! (*Goes quickly to door Up Center and peers out; satisfied no one has overheard them she crosses back down to* CHARLIE.) Look, boy, everybody down here don't feel as friendly towards the Supreme Court as you and me do—you big enough to know that! And don't you ever go outta here and pull a fool trick like you done last night again and not let me know about it in advance. You hear me!

CHARLIE. I'm sorry.

IDELLA. When you didn't come to breakfast this morning, and I went upstairs looking for you, and you just setting there, looking at me with your big eyes, and I seen that they had done hurt you—my, my, my! Whatever happens to you happens to me—you big enough to know that!

CHARLIE. I didn't mean to make trouble, Idella.

IDELLA. I know that, son, I know it. (*Makes final adjustments to the poultice.*) Now. No matter what happens when they do come I'll be right behind you. Keep your nerves calm and your mouth shut. Understand?

CHARLIE.   Yes.

IDELLA.   And as soon as you get a free minute come over to the house and let me put another hot poultice on that eye.

CHARLIE.   Thank you, I'm very much obliged to you. Idella—

IDELLA.   What is it, son?

CHARLIE.   Sometimes I think I ought to run away from home.

IDELLA.   I know, but you already tried that, honey.

CHARLIE.   Sometimes I think I ought to run away from home— again!

(OL' CAP'N *has entered from the Commissary just in time to hear this last remark.*)

OL'CAP'N.   Why don't you, boy — why don't you? (OL' CAP'N COTCHIPEE *is aged and withered a bit, but by no means infirm. Dressed in traditional southern linen, the wide hat, the shoestring tie, the long coat, the twirling moustache of the Ol' Southern Colonel. In his left hand he carries a cane, and in his right a coiled bull whip: his last line of defense. He stops long enough to establish the fact that he means business, threatens them both with a mean cantankerous eye, then hangs his whip— the definitive answer to all who might foolishly question his Confederate power and glory—upon a peg.* CHARLIE *freezes at the sound of his voice.* IDELLA *tenses but keeps working on* CHARLIE's *eye.* OL' CAP'N *crosses down, rudely pushes her hand aside, lifts up* CHARLIE's *chin so that he may examine the damage, shakes his head in disgust.*) You don't know, boy, what a strong stomach it takes to stomach you. Just look at you, sitting there—all slopped over like something the horses dropped; steam, stink and all!

IDELLA.   Don't you dare talk like that to this child!

OL' CAP'N.   (*This stops him—momentarily.*) When I think of his grandpaw, God rest his Confederate soul, hero of the battle of Chicamauga—(*It's too much.*) Get outta my sight! (CHARLIE *gets up to leave.*) Not you—you! (*Indicates* IDELLA. *She gathers up her things in silence and starts to leave.*) Wait a minute —(IDELLA *stops.*) You been closer to this boy than I have, even before his ma died—ain't a thought ever entered his head you didn't know 'bout it first. You got anything to do with what my boy's been thinking lately?

IDELLA.   I didn't know he had been thinking lately.

OL' CAP'N.   Don't play with me, Idella — and you know what I mean! Who's been putting these integrationary ideas in my boy's head? Was it you—I'm asking you a question, dammit! Was it you?

IDELLA.   Why don't you ask him?

OL' CAP'N.   (*Snorts.*) Ask him! ASK HIM! He ain't gonna say a word unless you tell him to, and you know it. I'm asking you again, Idella Landy, have you been talking integration to my boy!?

IDELLA.   I can't rightly answer you any more on that than he did.

OL' CAP'N.   By God, you will answer me. I'll make you stand right there—right there!—all day and all night long, till you do answer me!

IDELLA.   That's just fine.

OL' CAP'N.   What's that! What's that you say?

IDELLA.   I mean I ain't got nothing else to do—supper's on the stove; rice is ready, okra's fried, turnip's simmered, biscuits' baked, and stew is stewed. In fact them lemon pies you wanted special for supper are in the oven right now, just getting ready to burn—

OL' CAP'N.   Get outta here!

IDELLA.   Oh—no hurry, Ol' Cap'n—

OL' CAP'N.   Get the hell out of here! (IDELLA *deliberately takes all the time in the world to pick up her things. Following her around trying to make his point.*) I'm warning both of you; that little lick over the eye is a small skimption compared to what I'm gonna do. (IDELLA *pretends not to listen.*) I won't stop till I get to the bottom of this! (IDELLA *still ignores him.*) Get outta here, Idella Landy, before I take my cane and— (*He raises his cane but* IDELLA *insists on moving at her own pace to exit Down Left.*) And save me some buttermilk to go with them lemon pies, you hear me! (*Turns to* CHARLIE; *not knowing how to approach him.*) The sheriff was here this morning.

CHARLIE. Yessir.

OL' CAP'N. Is that all you got to say to me: "Yessir"?

CHARLIE. Yessir.

OL' CAP'N. You are a disgrace to the southland!

CHARLIE. Yessir.

OL' CAP'N. Shut up! I could kill you, boy, you understand that? Kill you with my own two hands!

CHARLIE. Yessir.

OL' CAP'N. Shut up! I could beat you to death with that bull whip —put my pistol to your good-for-nothing head—my own flesh and blood—and blow your blasted brains all over this valley! (*Fighting to retain his control.*) If—if you wasn't the last living drop of Cotchipee blood in Cotchipee County, I'd—I'd—

CHARLIE. Yessir. (*This is too much.* OL' CAP'N *snatches* CHARLIE *to his feet. But* CHARLIE *does not resist.*)

OL' CAP'N. You trying to get non-violent with me, boy? (CHARLIE *does not answer, just dangles there.*)

CHARLIE. (*Finally.*) I'm ready with the books, sir—that is—whenever you're ready.

OL' CAP'N. (*Flinging* CHARLIE *into a chair.*) Thank you—thank you! What with your Yankee propaganda, your barroom brawls, and all your other non-Confederate activities, I didn't think you had the time.

CHARLIE. (*Picks up account book; reads.*) "Cotton report. Fifteen bales picked yesterday and sent to the cotton gin; bringing our total to 357 bales to date."

OL' CAP'N. (*Impressed.*) 357—boy, that's some picking. Who's ahead?

CHARLIE. Gitlow Judson, with seventeen bales up to now.

OL' CAP'N. Gitlow Judson; well I'll be damned; did you ever see a cotton-pickinger darky in your whole life?!

CHARLIE. Commissary report—

OL' CAP'N. Did you ever look down into the valley and watch ol' Git a-picking his way through that cotton patch? Holy Saint Mother's Day! I'll bet you—

CHARLIE. Commissary report!

OL' CAP'N. All right!—commissary report.

CHARLIE. Yessir—well, first, sir, there's been some complaints: the flour is spoiled, the beans are rotten, and the meat is tainted.

OL' CAP'N. Cut the price on it.

CHARLIE. But it's also a little wormy—

OL' CAP'N. Then sell it to the Negras—Is something wrong?

CHARLIE. No, sir — I mean, sir . . . , we can't go on doing that, sir.

OL' CAP'N. Why not? It's traditional.

CHARLIE. Yessir, but times are changing—all this debt— (*Indicates book.*) According to this book every family in this valley owes money they'll never be able to pay back.

OL' CAP'N. Of course — it's the only way to keep 'em working. Didn't they teach you nothin' at school?

CHARLIE. We're cheating them — and they know we're cheating them. How long do you expect them to stand for it?

OL' CAP'N. As long as they're Negras—

CHARLIE. How long before they start a-rearing up on their hind legs, and saying: "Enough, white folks—now that's enough! Either you start treating me like I'm somebody in this world, or I'll blow your brains out"?

OL' CAP'N. (*Shaken to the core.*) Stop it—stop it! You're tampering with the economic foundation of the southland! Are you trying to ruin me? One more word like that and I'll kill—I'll shoot—(CHARLIE *attempts to answer.*) Shut up! One more word and I'll—I'll fling myself on your Maw's grave and die of apoplexy. I'll—! I'll—! Shut up, do you hear me? Shut up! (*Enter* GITLOW, *hat in hand, grin on face, more obsequious today than ever.*) Now what the hell *you* want?

GITLOW. (*Taken aback.*) Nothing, sir, nothing!—That is—Missy, my ol' 'oman—well, suh, to git to the truth of the matter, I got a little business—

OL' CAP'N. Negras ain't got no business. And if you don't get the hell back into that cotton patch you better. Git, I said! (GITLOW *starts to beat a hasty retreat.*) Oh, no—don't go. Uncle Gitlow —good ol' faithful ol' Gitlow. Don't go—don't go.

GITLOW. (*Not quite sure.*) Well—you're the boss, boss.

OL' CAP'N. (*Shoving a cigar into* GITLOW's *mouth.*) Just the other day, I was talking to the Senator about you — What's that great big knot on your head?

GITLOW. Missy—I mean, a mosquito!

OL' CAP'N. (*In all seriousness, examining the bump.*) Uh! Musta been wearin' brass knuck—And he was telling me, the Senator was, how hard it was — impossible, he said, to find the old-fashioned, solid, hard-earned, Uncle Tom type Negra nowadays. I laughed in his face.

GITLOW. Yassuh. By the grace of God, there's still a few of us left.

OL' CAP'N. I told him how you and me growed up together. Had the same mammy—my mammy was your mother.

GITLOW. Yessir! Bosom buddies!

OL' CAP'N. And how you used to sing that favorite ol' speritual of mine: (*Sings.*) "I'm a-coming . . . I'm a-coming, For my head is bending low," (GITLOW *joins in on harmony.*) "I hear the gentle voices calling, Ol' Black Joe. . . ." (*This proves too much for* CHARLIE; *he starts out.*) Where you going?

CHARLIE. Maybe they need me in the front of the store.

OL' CAP'N. Come back here! (CHARLIE *returns.*) Turn around—show Gitlow that eye. (CHARLIE *reluctantly exposes black eye to view.*)

GITLOW. Gret Gawdamighty, somebody done cold cocked this child! Who hit Mr. Charlie, tell Uncle Gitlow who hit you? (CHARLIE *does not answer.*)

OL' CAP'N. Would you believe it? All of a sudden he can't say a word. And just last night, the boys was telling me, this son of mine made hisself a full-fledged speech.

GITLOW. You don't say.

OL' CAP'N. All about Negras — NeGROES he called 'em — four years of college, and he still can't say the word right—seems he's quite a specialist on the subject.

GITLOW. Well, shut my hard-luck mouth!

OL' CAP'N. Yessireebob. Told the boys over at Ben's bar in town, that he was all for mixing the races together.

GITLOW. You go on 'way from hyeah!

OL' CAP'N.   Said white children and darky children ought to go the same schoolhouse together!

GITLOW.   Tell me the truth, Ol' Cap'n!

OL' CAP'N.   Got hisself so worked up some of 'em had to cool him down with a co-cola bottle!

GITLOW.   Tell me the truth—again!

CHARLIE.   That wasn't what I said!

OL' CAP'N.   You calling me a liar, boy!

CHARLIE.   No, sir, but I just said, that since it was the law of the land—

OL' CAP'N.   It is not the law of the land no sucha thing!

CHARLIE.   I didn't think it would do any harm if they went to school together—that's all.

OL' CAP'N.   That's all—that's enough!

CHARLIE.   They do it up North—

OL' CAP'N.   This is down South. Down here they'll go to school together over me and Gitlow's dead body. Right, Git?!

GITLOW.   Er, you the boss, boss!

CHARLIE.   But this is the law of the—

OL' CAP'N.   Never mind the law! Boy—look! You like Gitlow, you trust him, you always did—didn't you?

CHARLIE.   Yessir.

OL' CAP'N.   And Gitlow here, would cut off his right arm for you if you was to ask him. Wouldn't you, Git?

GITLOW.   (*Gulping.*) You the boss, boss.

OL' CAP'N.   Now Gitlow ain't nothing if he ain't a Negra!—Ain't you, Git?

GITLOW.   Oh—two-three hundred percent, I calculate.

OL' CAP'N.   Now, if you really want to know what the Negra thinks about this here integration and all lackathat, don't ask the Supreme Court—ask Gitlow. Go ahead—ask him!

CHARLIE.   I don't need to ask him.

OL' CAP'N.   Then I'll ask him. Raise your right hand, Git. You solemnly swear to tell the truth, whole truth, nothing else but, so help you God?

GITLOW.   (*Raising hand.*) I do.

OL' CAP'N.   Gitlow Judson, as God is your judge and maker, do you believe in your heart that God intended white folks and Negra children to go to school together?

GITLOW.   Nawsuh, I do not!

OL' CAP'N.   Do you, so help you God, think that white folks and black should mix and 'sociate in street cars, buses, and railroad stations, in any way, shape, form, or fashion?

GITLOW.   Absolutely not!

OL' CAP'N.   And is it not your considered opinion, God strike you dead if you lie, that all my Negras are happy with things in the southland just the way they are?

GITLOW.   Indeed I do!

OL' CAP'N.   Do you think ary single darky on my place would ever think of changing a single thing about the South, and to hell with the Supreme Court as God is your judge and maker?

GITLOW.   As God is my judge and maker and you are my boss, I do not!

OL' CAP'N.   (*Turning in triumph to* CHARLIE.) The voice of the Negra himself. What more proof do you want!

CHARLIE.   I don't care whose voice it is—it's still the law of the land, and I intend to obey it!

OL' CAP'N.   (*Losing control.*) Get outta my face, boy—get outta my face, before I kill you! Before I—

(CHARLIE *escapes into the commissary.* OL' CAP'N *collapses.*)

GITLOW.   Easy, Ol' Cap'n, easy, suh, easy! (OL' CAP'N *gives out a groan.* GITLOW *goes to shelf and comes back with a small bottle and a small box.*) Some aspirins, suh . . . , some asaphoetida? (PURLIE *and* LUTIEBELLE *appear at door Left.*) Not now—later—later! (*Holds bottle to* OL' CAP'N's *nose.*)

OL' CAP'N.   Gitlow—Gitlow!

GITLOW.   Yassuh, Ol' Cap'n—Gitlow is here, suh; right here!

OL' CAP'N.   Quick, ol' friend—my heart. It's—quick! A few passels, if you please—of that ol' spiritual.

GITLOW.   (*Sings most tenderly.*) "Gone are the days, when my heart was young and gay . . ."

OL' CAP'N. I can't tell you, Gitlow—how much it eases the pain —(GITLOW *and* OL' CAP'N *sing a phrase together.*) Why can't he see what they're doing to the southland, Gitlow? Why can't he see it, like you and me? If there's one responsibility you got, boy, above all others, I said to him, it's these Negras—your Negras, boy. Good, honest, hard-working cotton choppers. If you keep after 'em.

GITLOW. Yes, Lawd. (*Continues to sing.*)

OL' CAP'N. Something between you and them no Supreme Court in the world can understand—and wasn't for me they'd starve to death. What's gonna become of 'em, boy, after I'm gone—?

GITLOW. Dass a good question, Lawd—you answer him. (*Continues to sing.*)

OL' CAP'N. They belong to you, boy—to you, evah one of 'em! My ol' Confederate father told me on his deathbed: feed the Negras first—after the horses and cattle—and I've done it evah time! (*By now* OL' CAP'N *is sheltered in* GITLOW's *arms. The LIGHTS begin slowly to fade away.* GITLOW *sings a little more.*) Ah, Gitlow ol' friend—something, absolutely sacred 'bout that speritual—I live for the day you'll sing that thing over my grave.

GITLOW. Me, too, Ol' Cap'n, me, too! (GITLOW's *voice rises to a slow, gentle, yet triumphant crescendo, as our LIGHTS fade away.*)

BLACKOUT
CURTAIN

Act II

Scene 1

TIME   *A short while later.*

SCENE   *The scene is the same: the little commissary office.*

AT RISE   *The Stage is empty. After a moment* GITLOW *hurries in from the commissary proper, crosses down to the little back door and opens it.*

PURLIE. (*Entering hurriedly.*) What took you so long?

GITLOW. S-sh! Not so loud! He's right out there in the commissary! (PURLIE *crosses over and looks out into the commissary, then crosses back to the little back door and holds out his hands.* LUTIEBELLE *enters. She is dressed in what would be collegiate style. She is still full of awe and wonder, and—this time—of fear, which she is struggling to keep under cover.*) Ain't she gonna carry no school books?

PURLIE. What are they doing out there?

GITLOW. The watermelon books don't balance.

PURLIE. What!

GITLOW. One of our melons is in shortage!

PURLIE. You tell him about Lutiebelle—I mean, about Cousin Bee?

GITLOW. I didn't have time. Besides, I wanted you to have one more chance to get out of here alive!

PURLIE. What's the matter with you!? Don't five hundred dollars of your own lawful money mean nothing to you? Ain't you got no head for business?

GITLOW. No! The head I got is for safekeeping, and—besides— (PURLIE *lifts* OL' CAP'N's *bull whip down from its peg.*) don't touch that thing, Purlie! (GITLOW *races over, snatches it from him, replaces it, and pats it soothingly into place, while at the same time looking to see if* OL' CAP'N *is coming—and all in one continuous move.*)

PURLIE. Why not? It touched me!

GITLOW. (*Aghast.*) Man, ain't nothing sacred to you!?

OL' CAP'N. (*Calling from Off in the commissary.*) Gitlow, come in here!

GITLOW. (*Racing off.*) Coming, Ol' Cap'n, coming!

OL' CAP'N. (*Offstage.*) Now! We are going to cross-examine these watermelons one more time—one watermelon—

GITLOW. (*Offstage.*) One watermelon!

CHARLIE. (*Offstage.*) One watermelon!

OL' CAP'N. Two watermelons—

GITLOW. Two watermelons—

CHARLIE. Two watermelons—

(*The sound of the watermelon count-down continues in the background.* PURLIE, *finding he's got a moment, comes over to reassure* LUTIEBELLE.)

PURLIE. Whatever you do, don't panic!

LUTIEBELLE. (*Repeating after him: almost in hypnotic rote.*) Whatever you do, don't panic!

PURLIE. Just walk like I taught you to walk, and talk like I taught you to talk—

LUTIEBELLE. Taught like I walked you to—

PURLIE. (*Shaking her shoulders.*) Lutiebelle!

LUTIEBELLE. Yes, Reb'n Purlie!

PURLIE. Wake up!

LUTIEBELLE. Oh my goodness, Reb'n Purlie—was I sleep?

PURLIE. Alert.

LUTIEBELLE. Alert!—

PURLIE. Wide awake!—

LUTIEBELLE. Wide awake!—

PURLIE. Up on your toes!

LUTIEBELLE. (*Starting to rise on toes.*) Up on your—

PURLIE. No. No, that's just a figure of speech. Now! You remember what I told you—?

LUTIEBELLE. No, sir. Can't say I do, sir.

PURLIE. Well—first: chit-chat—small-talk!

LUTIEBELLE. Yessir—how small?

PURLIE. Pass the time of day—you remember? The first thing I taught you on the train?

LUTIEBELLE. On the train—Oh! "Delighted to remake your acquaintance, I am sure."

PURLIE. That's it—that's it exactly! Now. Suppose he was to say to you: (PURLIE *imitates* OL' CAP'N.) "I bet you don't remember when you wasn't kneehigh to a grasshopper and Ol' Cap'n took you by the hand, and led you down on your first trip to the cotton patch?"

LUTIEBELLE.   Just like you told me on the train?

PURLIE.   Yes!

LUTIEBELLE.   "I must confess—that much of my past life is vague and hazy."

PURLIE.   (*Imitating.*) Doggone my hide—you're the cutest li'l' ol' piece of brown skin sugar I ever did see!

LUTIEBELLE.   Oh, thank you, Reb'n Purlie.

PURLIE.   I ain't exactly me, saying that—it's Ol' Cap'n. (*Continues imitation.*) And this is my land, and my cotton patch, and my commissary, and my bull whip—still here, just like you left us. And what might be your name, li'l gal?

LUTIEBELLE.   (*Warming to the game.*) Beatrice Judson, sir.

PURLIE.   And what is your daddy's name, li'l gal?

LUTIEBELLE.   Horace Judson, sir.

PURLIE.   And what did they teach you up in that college, li'l gal?

LUTIEBELLE.   It was my major education, Ol' Cap'n.—

PURLIE.   You mean you majored in education. (*Resumes imitation.*) Well—nothing wrong with Negras getting an education, I always say—But then again, ain't nothing right with it, either. Cousin Bee—heh, heh, heh—you don't mind if I call you Cousin Bee, do you, honey?

LUTIEBELLE.   Oh, sir, I'd be delighted!

PURLIE.   Don't! Don't be delighted until he puts the money in your hands. (*Resumes imitation.*) And where did you say your Maw worked at?

LUTIEBELLE.   In North Carolina.

PURLIE.   Where is your maw at now?

LUTIEBELLE.   She's at the cemetery: she died.

PURLIE.   And how much is the inheritance?

LUTIEBELLE.   Five hundred dollars for the next of kin.

PURLIE.   (*Delighted at her progress.*) Wonderful, just — just — wonderful! (*Enjoying his own imitation now.*) (OL' CAP'N *enters from the commissary, followed by* GITLOW. LUTIEBELLE *sees* OL' CAP'N, *but* PURLIE *is so wrapped up in his own performance he does not.*) Say, maybe you could teach a old dog

like me some new tricks. (*He tries to get a rise out of* LUTIE-
BELLE *but she is frozen in terror.* OL' CAP'N *becomes aware of*
PURLIE's *presence, and approaches.*) By swickety—a gal like
you could doggone well change a joker's luck if she had a mind
to—see what I mean? (PURLIE *punches what he expects to be
an invisible* GITLOW *in the ribs. His blow lands upon* OL' CAP'N
with such force, he falls onto a pile of sacks of chicken feed.)

OL' CAP'N. (*Sputtering.*) What! What in the name of—(GITLOW
and PURLIE *scramble to help him to his feet.*)

PURLIE. My compliments, sir—are only exceeded by my humblest
apologies. And allow me, if you please, to present my Aunt
Henrietta's daughter, whom you remember so well: Beatrice
Judson—or as we call her—Cousin Bee.

OL' CAP'N. (*He is so taken by what he sees he forgets his anger.*)
Well, I'll be switched!

PURLIE. Come, Cousin Bee. Say "howdo" to the man.

LUTIEBELLE. How do to the man. I mean—(*Takes time to correct
herself, then.*) Delighted to remake your acquaintance, I'm
sure.

OL' CAP'N. What's that? What's that she's saying?

PURLIE. College, sir.

OL' CAP'N. College?

PURLIE. That's all she ever talks.

OL' CAP'N. You mean Henrietta's little ol' button-eyed pickaninny
was in college? Well bust my eyes wide open! Just LOOK at
that! (*Gets closer, but she edges away.*) You remember me,
honey. I'm still the Ol' Cap'n round here.

LUTIEBELLE. Oh, sir, it would not be the same without you being
the Ol' Cap'n around here.

OL' CAP'N. You don't say! Say, I'll bet you don't remember a long
time ago when—

LUTIEBELLE. When I wasn't but knee high to a hoppergrass, and
you took me by the hand, and led me on my first trip to the
cotton patch.

OL' CAP'N. (*Ecstatic.*) You mean you remember that!

LUTIEBELLE. Alert, wide awake, and up on my toes—if you please,
sir! (*Rises up on her toes.*)

OL' CAP'N.   (*Moving in.*) Doggone my hide. You're the cutest li'l ol' piece of brown sugar I ever did see—

LUTIEBELLE.   (*Escaping.*) And this is your land, and your cotton patch, and your commissary, and your bull whip—

OL' CAP'N.   What's that?

LUTIEBELLE.   Just a figure of speech or two—

OL' CAP'N.   Well, Beatrice—you wouldn't mind if Ol' Cap'n was to call you Cousin Bee?

LUTIEBELLE.   Oh, positively not, not!—since my mother's name was Henrietta Judson; my father's name was Horace Judson—

OL' CAP'N.   But most of all, I remember that little ol' dog of yours —"Spicey," wasn't it?

LUTIEBELLE.   Oh, we wasn't much for eating dogs, sir—

OL' CAP'N.   No, no! Spicey was the name—wasn't it?

(LUTIEBELLE *looking to* PURLIE *for help, but* PURLIE *cannot help. He looks to* GITLOW, *who also cannot remember.*)

LUTIEBELLE.   You, er, really think we really called him "Spicey"?

OL' CAP'N.   Not him—her!

PURLIE.   HER!

LUTIEBELLE.   Oh, her! Her! I am most happy to recollect that I do.

OL' CAP'N.   You do! You don't say you do!

LUTIEBELLE.   I did, as I recall it, have a fond remembrance of you and "Spicey," since you-all went so well together—and at the same time!

OL' CAP'N.   You do? Well hush my mouth, eh, Git?

GITLOW.   Hush your mouth indeed, sir.

LUTIEBELLE.   Cose soon it is my sworn and true confession that I disremembers so many things out of my early pastime that mostly you are haze and vaguey!

OL' CAP'N.   Oh, am I now!

LUTIEBELLE.   Oh, yes, and sir — indeedy.

OL' CAP'N.   Doggone my hide, eh, Git?

GITLOW.   Doggone your hide indeed, suh.

LUTIEBELLE.   You see of coursely I have spount—

PURLIE.   Spent—

LUTIEBELLE. Spunt so much of my time among the college that hardly all of my ancient maidenhead—

PURLIE. Hood.

LUTIEBELLE. Is a thing of the past!

OL' CAP'N. You don't say!

LUTIEBELLE. But yes, and most precisely.

OL' CAP'N. Tell me, Li'l Bee—what did they teach you up at that college?

LUTIEBELLE. Well, mostly they taught me an education, but in between I learned a lot, too.

OL' CAP'N. Is that a fact?

LUTIEBELLE. Reading, writing, 'rithmetic—oh, my Lord—just sitting out on the rectangular every evening after four o'clock home work and you have your regular headache—

OL' CAP'N. You know something, I been after these Negras down here for years: Go to school, I'd say, first chance you get—take a coupla courses in advanced cotton picking. But you think they'd listen to me? No sireebob. By swickety! A gal like you could doggone well change a joker's luck if she was a mind to. (*Gives* GITLOW *a broad wink and digs him in his ribs.* GITLOW *almost falls.*) See what I mean?

LUTIEBELLE. Oh, most indo I deed.

OL' CAP'N. Look — anything! Ask me anything! Whatever you want—name it and it's yours!

LUTIEBELLE. You mean—really, really, really?

OL' CAP'N. Ain't a man in Cotchipee County can beat my time when I see something I want—name it! (*Indicates with a sweep the contents of the commissary.*) Some roasted peanuts; a bottle of soda water; a piece of pepmint candy?

LUTIEBELLE. Thank you, sir, but if it's all the same to you I'd rather have my money.

OL' CAP'N. (*As if shot.*) Your WHAT?

LUTIEBELLE. (*Frightened but determined to forge ahead under her own steam.*) Now I'm gonna tell you like it was, Your Honor: You see, Reb'n Purlie and Uncle Gitlow had one aunty between them, name of Harrietta—

PURLIE. Henrietta!

LUTIEBELLE.   Henrietta—who used to cook for this rich ol' white lady up in North Carolina years ago; and last year this ol' lady died—brain tumor—

PURLIE.   Bright's disease!

LUTIEBELLE.   Bright's disease — leaving five hundred dollars to every servant who had ever worked on her place, including Henrietta. But Henrietta had already died, herself: largely from smallpox—

PURLIE.   No!

LUTIEBELLE.   Smally from large pox?

PURLIE.   Influenza!

LUTIEBELLE.   Influenza—and since Henrietta's husband Harris—

PURLIE.   Horace!

LUTIEBELLE.   Horace—was already dead from heart trouble—

PURLIE.   Gunshot wounds!—

LUTIEBELLE.   (*Exploding.*) His heart stopped beating, didn't it?!

PURLIE.   Yes, but—

LUTIEBELLE.   Precisely, Reb'n Purlie, precisely! (*Turning back to* OL' CAP'N.) Since, therefore and where-in-as Cousin Bee, her daughter, was first-in-line-for-next-of-kinfolks, the five hundred dollars left in your care and keep by Aunt Henrietta, and which you have been saving just for me all these lonesome years—

OL' CAP'N.   I ain't been saving no damn sucha thing!

PURLIE.   (*Stepping swiftly into the breach.*) Oh, come out from behind your modesty, sir!

OL' CAP'N.   What!

PURLIE.   Your kindness, sir; your thoughtfulness, sir; your unflagging consideration for the welfare of your darkies, sir: have rung like the clean clear call of the clarion from Maine to Mexico. Your constant love for them is both hallmark and high water of the true gentility of the dear old South.

OL' CAP'N.   Gitlow, Gitlow—go get Charlie. I want him to hear this. (GITLOW *exits Upstage Center.*) Go on, boy, go on!

PURLIE.   And as for your faithful ol' darkies themselves, sir—why, down in the quarters, sir, your name stands second only to God Himself Almighty.

OL' CAP'N.   You don't mean to tell me!

PURLIE.   Therefore, as a humble token of their high esteem and their deep and abiding affection, especially for saving that five hundred dollar inheritance for Cousin Bee, they have asked me to present to you . . . this plaque! (PURLIE *unveils a "sheepskin scroll" from his inside coat pocket.* OL' CAP'N *reaches for it, but* PURLIE *draws it away.* CHARLIE *appears in the doorway Upstage Center followed by* GITLOW.) Which bears the following citation to wit, and I quote: "Whereas Ol' Cap'n has kindly allowed us to remain on his land, and pick his cotton, and tend his cattle, and drive his mules, and whereas Ol' Cap'n still lets us have our hominy grits and fat back on credit and whereas Ol' Cap'n never resorts to bull whip except as a blessing and a benediction, therefore be it resolved, that Ol' Cap'n Cotchipee be cited as the best friend the Negro has ever had, and officially proclaimed Great White Father of the Year!"

OL' CAP'N.   (*Stunned.*) I can't believe it—I can't believe it! (*Sees* CHARLIE.) Charlie, boy—did you hear it? Did you hear it, Charlie, my boy—GREAT WHITE FATHER OF THE YEAR!

PURLIE.   (*Like a professional undertaker.*) Let me be the first to congratulate you, sir. (*They shake hands solemnly.*)

OL' CAP'N.   Thank you, Purlie.

LUTIEBELLE.   And me. (*They shake hands solemnly.*)

OL' CAP'N.   Thank you, Cousin Bee.

GITLOW.   And me, too, Ol' Cap'n.

OL' CAP'N.   (*On the verge of tears, as they shake hands.*) Gitlow— Gitlow. I know this is some of your doings—my old friend. (*He turns expectantly to* CHARLIE.) Well, boy— (CHARLIE *is trapped.*) ain't you gonna congratulate your father?

CHARLIE.   Yessir. (*Shakes his hand.*)

OL' CAP'N.   This—is the happiest day of my life. My darkies—my Negras—my own—(*Chokes up; unable to continue.*)

PURLIE.   Hear, hear!

GITLOW AND LUTIEBELLE.   Hear, hear!
   (CHARLIE *tries to sneak off again, but* OL' CAP'N *sees him.*)

OL' CAP'N.   I am just too overcome to talk. Come back here, boy. (CHARLIE *comes back and stands in intense discomfort.*) Silent — speechless — dumb, my friends. Never in all the glorious hoary and ancient annals of all Dixie—never before—(*Chokes up with tears; blows nose with big red handkerchief, and pulls himself together.*) My friends, in the holy scripture—and I could cite you chapter and verse if I was a mind to—"In the beginning God created white folks and He created black folks," and in the name of all that's white and holy, let's keep it that way. And to hell with Abraham Lincoln and Martin Luther King!

PURLIE. I am moved, Ol' Cap'n—

GITLOW AND LUTIEBELLE. Uhn!

PURLIE. Moved beyond my jurisdiction; as for example, I have upon my person a certificate of legal tender duly affixed and so notarized to said itemized effect—(*Hands over an official-looking document.*) a writ of Habeas Corpus.

OL' CAP'N. (*Taking the document.*) Habeas who?

PURLIE. Habeas Corpus. It means I can have the body.

OL' CAP'N. Body—what body?

PURLIE. The body of the cash—the five hundred dollars—that they sent you to hold in trust for Cousin Bee.

OL' CAP'N. (*Pauses to study the eager faces in the room; then*) Charlie—

CHARLIE. Yessir.

OL' CAP'N. Bring me—five hundred dollars—will you? (CHARLIE *starts for safe.*) No, no, no—not that old stuff. Fresh money, clean money out of my private stock out back. Nothin's too good for my Negras.

CHARLIE. Yessir—yessir! (*Starts out, stops.*) And Paw?

OL' CAP'N. Yes, son?

CHARLIE. All I got to say is "Yessir!" (*Crosses to cash register.*)

OL' CAP'N. Just wait—wait till I tell the Senator: "Great White Father of the Year."

CHARLIE. (*Returns with roll of bills which he hands to his father.*) Here you are, Paw.

OL' CAP'N. Thank you, boy.

(*Enter* IDELLA, *followed by the* SHERIFF *and the* DEPUTY.)

IDELLA. Here everybody is, back in the office.

OL' CAP'N. (*Overjoyed to see them.*) Just in time, Sheriff, for the greatest day of my life. Gentlemen—something has happened here today, between me and my Negras, makes me proud to call myself a Confederate: I have just been named Great White Father of the Year. (*To* PURLIE.) Right?

PURLIE. Right. And now if you'll just—

SHERIFF AND DEPUTY. Great White Father of the Year! Congratulations. (*They shake his hands warmly.*)

OL' CAP'N. True, there are places in this world where the darky is rebellious, running hog wild, rising up and sitting down where he ain't wanted, acting sassy in jail, getting plumb out of hand, totally forgetting his place and his manners—but not in Cotchipee County! (*To* PURLIE.) Right?

PURLIE. Right! And now perhaps we could get back to the business at hand.

OL' CAP'N. (*Finishing his count.*) All right—five hundred dollars. (PURLIE *impulsively reaches for the money, but* OL' CAP'N *snatches it back.*) Just a moment. There's still one small formality: a receipt.

PURLIE. A receipt? All right, I'll—

OL' CAP'N. Not you—You! (*Thrusts a printed form toward* LUTIE-BELLE.) . . . just for the record. (*Offers her a fountain pen.*) Sign here. Your full and legal name—right here on the dotted line.

PURLIE. (*Reaching for the pen.*) I'll do it—I have her power of attorney.

LUTIEBELLE. (*Beating* PURLIE *to the pen.*) It's all right, Reb'n Purlie, I can write. (*Takes pen and signs paper with a flourish.*)

OL' CAP'N. (*Takes up paper and reads the signature.*) Sheriff, I want this woman arrested!

PURLIE. Arrested?! For what?

OL' CAP'N. She came into my presence, together with him—(*Indicates* PURLIE.) and with him—(*Indicates* GITLOW.) And they all swore to me that she is Beatrice Judson.

PURLIE. She IS Beatrice Judson!

OL' CAP'N. (*Pouncing.*) Then how come she to sign her name: Lutiebelle Gussiemae Jenkins!

PURLIE.   Uhn-uhn!

GITLOW.   Uhn-uhn!

LUTIEBELLE.   Uhn-uhn!

GITLOW.   (*Starting off suddenly.*) Is somebody calling my name
out there—

OL' CAP'N.   Come back here, Gitlow—(GITLOW *halts in his tracks.*)
You'll go out of that door when the Sheriff takes you out. And
that goes for all of you. (*The* SHERIFF *starts forward.*) Just a
minute, Sheriff. Before you take 'em away there's something
I've got to do. (*Crosses to where the whip is hung.*)

GITLOW.   (*Horrified at the thought of the whip.*) I'll make it up
to you in cotton, Ol' Cap'n—

LUTIEBELLE.   (*Stepping between the* SHERIFF *and* PURLIE.) Don't
you dare!

SHERIFF.   What!

LUTIEBELLE.   Insultin' Reb'n Purlie, and him a man of the cloth!
(*Grabs his gun arm and bites it.*)

SHERIFF.   Owwww! (*She kicks him in the shin.*) Owwwwwwww!
(*The* DEPUTY *charges in to the rescue. He attempts to grab* LUTIE-
BELLE, *but she eludes him and steps down hard on his corns.*)

DEPUTY.   Owwwwwwwwwww!

PURLIE.   (*Going for the* DEPUTY.) Keep your hands off her, you
hypothetical baboon, keep your hands OFF her! (*Grabs the*
DEPUTY, *spins him around and knocks him across the room,
starts to follow, but the* SHERIFF *grabs him and pins his arms
behind him.*)

CHARLIE.   (*Breaks loose from* IDELLA, *snatching at the* SHERIFF.)
You let him go, dammit, let him go! (*With one arm the* SHERIFF
pushes CHARLIE *away.*)

SHERIFF.   (*Still holding* PURLIE'S *arms pinned back.*) All right,
Dep, he's all yours. Throw him your fast ball—high, tight and
inside!

DEPUTY.   Glad to oblige you, Sheriff! (*He draws back like a big
league baseball pitcher.*)

CHARLIE.   (*Rushing into the breach.*) Stop! Stop — stop in the
name of the—(*The* DEPUTY *swings from the floor,* PURLIE
ducks and rolls his head sharply to one side. CHARLIE *runs full
into the force of the blow. Collapsing heavily.*) Idella—aaaaaaa!

OL' CAP'N. (*Rushing to him.*) Charlie—!

IDELLA. Charlie—!

(PURLIE, *taking advantage of the confusion, snatches* LUTIEBELLE *by the arms and dashes with her out the back door.*)

OL' CAP'N. After them, you idiots, after them!

SHERIFF. (*To the* DEPUTY.) After them, you idiot! (*They both run off after* PURLIE *and* LUTIEBELLE.)

(OL' CAP'N *and* IDELLA *are kneeling beside the prostrate* CHARLIE. GITLOW, *after a moment, comes into the picture.*)

OL' CAP'N. His eyes, Idella, his eyes! Where are his eyes?

IDELLA. Gitlow, fetch me the asaphoetida, Ol' Cap'n, you rub his hands.

GITLOW. Yess'm.

IDELLA. (*Slapping his face.*) Charlie, honey, wake up—wake up! It's me, Idella.

(OL' CAP'N *is too disorganized to be of any assistance.* GITLOW *has returned with a bottle which he hands to* IDELLA. *He then kneels and starts rubbing* CHARLIE's *hands.*)

GITLOW. Mr. Charlie, wake up—

(*With* GITLOW *and* IDELLA's *help,* CHARLIE *slowly rises to his feet. Still unsteady, his eyes glazed and vacant.*)

OL' CAP'N. (*Snapping his fingers in front of his eyes.*) It's me, Charlie, me—It's your daddy, boy! Speak to me—talk to me— say something to me!

CHARLIE. (*Snaps suddenly into speech—but still out on his feet.*) Fourscore and seven years ago, our fathers brought forth—

OL' CAP'N. Shut up!

CURTAIN

Act II

Scene 2

TIME *Two days later.*

SCENE *Back at the shack, outside in the yard area.*

AT RISE   MISSY *is discovered, busy working on some potted plants.*
She is preoccupied, but we feel some restlessness, some anticipa-
tion in the manner in which she works. PURLIE *enters.*

PURLIE.   (*The great prophet intones his sorrows.*) Toll the bell—
Big Bethel; toll the big, black, ex-liberty bell; tell Freedom
there's death in the family.

MISSY.   Purlie—

PURLIE.   All these wings and they still won't let me fly!

MISSY.   Where you been these last two days, Purlie? We been
lookin' for you. All this plotting and planning—risking your
dad-blasted neck like a crazy man! And for what — FOR
WHAT! (IDELLA *enters.*) Oh, come in, Miz Idella.

IDELLA.   Is anybody here seen Charlie Cotchipee this morning?

MISSY.   No, we haven't.

PURLIE.   Is something wrong, Miz Idella?

IDELLA.   He left home this morning right after breakfast—here it
is after lunch and I ain't seen him since. I can't find Charlie—
first time in forty-five years I been working up there in that
house I ever misplaced anything! You don't suppose he'd run
away from home and not take me—?

MISSY.   Oh, no, Miz Idella! Not li'l Charlie Cotchipee.

IDELLA.   Well, I guess I'd better be getting back. If you should see
him—

MISSY.   Miz Idella, we all want to thank you for keeping Purlie
out of jail so kindly. (*Hands her flowers.*)

IDELLA.   Oh, that was nothing; I just told that ol' man if he didn't
stop all that foolishness about chain gangs and stuff, I would
resign from his kitchen and take Charlie right along with me!
But now I've lost Charlie. First time in forty-five years I ever
misplaced anything! (*She exits.*)

MISSY.   (*Turns to* PURLIE.) Don't you know there's something
more important in this world than having that broken down
ol' ex-church of a barn to preach in?

PURLIE.   Yeah—like what?

MISSY.   Like asking Lutiebelle to marry you.

PURLIE.   Asking Lutiebelle to marry me?

MISSY.   She worships the ground you walk on. Talks about you all
the time. You two could get married, settle down, like you ought

to, and raise the cutest little ol' family you ever did see. And she's a cookin', po' child — she left you some of her special fritters.

PURLIE. Freedom, Missy, not fritters. The crying need of this Negro day and age is not grits, but greatness; not cornbread but courage; not fat-back, but fight-back; Big Bethel is my Bethel; it belongs to me and to my people; and I intend to have it back if I have to pay for it in blood!

MISSY. All right—come on in and I'll fix you some dinner.

GITLOW. (*Enters front door, singing.*) "I'm comin', I'm comin'—"

MISSY. (*Entering house.*) Not so loud, Gitlow. You want to wake up the mule?

GITLOW. Not on his day off. "For my head is bendin' low—" (GIT-LOW *sits, unfolds comic section and reads.*)

MISSY. Where's Lutiebelle, Gitlow?

GITLOW. "The history of the War Between the States will be continued next week." That sure is a good story—I wonder how that's gonna come out?

MISSY. Grown man, deacon in the church, reading the funny-paper. And your shirt. You sneaked outta here this morning in your clean white shirt, after I told you time and time again I was saving it!

GITLOW. Saving it for what?

MISSY. It's the only decent thing you got to get buried in! (*Exits side door.*)

GITLOW. Don't you know that arrangements for my funeral has been taken over by the white folks? (*To* PURLIE.) Besides, I got the money!

PURLIE. What kinda money?

GITLOW. The five hundred dollar kinda money.

PURLIE. Five hundred dollars! You mean Ol' Cap'n give the money to you?

GITLOW. "Gitlow," he said. "Ain't another man in this valley, black, white, or otherwise, I would trust to defend and protect me from the N double ACP but you."

PURLIE. Is that a fact?

GITLOW. Well, now. Whatever become of you? All them gretgawd-amighty plans your mouth runneth over—all that white folks' psychology?

PURLIE.   Gitlow! Er, Deacon Gitlow—Big Bethel is waiting!

GITLOW.   So you're the good-for-nothing, raggedy ass high falute 'round here that goes for who-tied-the-bear!

PURLIE.   Naw, Git, man—ain't nothing to me.

GITLOW.   Always so high and mighty—can't nobody on earth handle white folks but you—don't pay no 'tention to Gitlow; naw —he's a Tom. Tease him—low-rate him—laugh at ol' Gitlow; he ain't nothing but a fool!

PURLIE.   Aw, Git, man, you got me wrong. I didn't mean nothing like that!

GITLOW.   Who's the fool now, my boy—who's the fool now?

PURLIE.   Er—I'm the fool, Gitlow.

GITLOW.   Aw, man, you can talk plainer than that.

PURLIE.   I'm the fool, Gitlow.

GITLOW.   Uh-huh! Now go over to that window, open it wide as it will go and say it so everybody in this whole damn valley can hear you! Go on! Go on, man—I ain't got all day!

PURLIE.   (*Goes to window.*) I'm the fool, Gitlow!

GITLOW.   Nice. Now beg me!

PURLIE.   What!

GITLOW.   I said if you want to see the money, beg me! Do it like you do white folks.

PURLIE.   I'd rather die and go to hell in a pair gasoline drawers— (GITLOW *starts to put money away.*) No, wait. Holy mackerel, dere, Massa Gitlow—hee, hee, hee. Hey! Boss, could I possible have a look at that there five hundred dollars dere, suh? Hyuh, hyuh, hyuh!

GITLOW.   Man, you sure got style! You know together you and me could make the big time! (PURLIE *reaches for money.*) Come in and see me during office hours! As Deputy-For-The-Colored, I'll just sort of step outside for a minute and let that low September sun shine down on a joker as rich as he is black!

PURLIE.   Gitlow—Gitlow! (GITLOW *starts for side door.*) If slavery ever comes back I want to be your agent!

GITLOW.   Now that was a snaggy-toothed, poverty-struck remark if I ever heard one.

MISSY.   (*Enters side door.*) Youall wash your hands and git ready —Gitlow! Where's Lutiebelle?

GITLOW. (*Evasive.*) She didn't get back yet.

MISSY. We know she didn't get back yet.

PURLIE. Where is Lutiebelle, Gitlow?

GITLOW. What I mean is—on our way home from church, we stopped by Ol' Cap'n's awhile, and he asked me to leave her there to help with the Sunday dinner.

PURLIE. And you left her!

MISSY. With that frisky ol' man?

GITLOW. For goodness' sakes, she's only waiting on table.

PURLIE. The woman I love don't wait on table for nobody, especially Ol' Cap'n; I know that scoun'. I'm going and get her!

GITLOW. Wait a minute—you can't get her right now!

PURLIE. (*Studying him.*) What you mean, I can't get her right now?

GITLOW. Not right this minute—that'll spoil everything. Ol' Cap'n wouldn't like it.

MISSY. How low can you git, Gitlow!

GITLOW. I mean she's got to stay and bring us the $500.00.

MISSY. What 500 dollars?

PURLIE. I thought you already had the money?

GITLOW. Well, not exactly. But he promised me faithful to send it down by Lutiebelle.

PURLIE. I'm going and get Lutiebelle—

GITLOW. Wait a minute, wait a minute; you want to buy Big Bethel back or don't you?

PURLIE. (*A glimmering of truth.*) I hope I misunderstand you!

GITLOW. You said it yourself: It is meet that the daughters of Zion should sacrifice themselves for the cause.

PURLIE. (*Grabbing up* MISSY's *bat.*) Gitlow, I'll kill you—!

GITLOW. Wait a minute, wait a minute, wait a MINUTE!

(*The door opens suddenly, and there stands* LUTIEBELLE. *She, too, has on her Sunday best, but it is disheveled. She has a work apron over her dress, with her hat completely askew, the once proud feather now hanging over her face. In her hands she still clutches a rolling pin.*)

MISSY. Lutiebelle—Lutiebelle, honey!

LUTIEBELLE.   I think I am going to faint. (*She starts to collapse, and they rush toward her to help; but suddenly she straightens up and waves them off.*) No, I ain't, either—I'm too mad! (*She shudders in recollection.*) I was never so insulted in all my dad-blamed life!

PURLIE.   Lutiebelle!

LUTIEBELLE.   Oh, excuse me, Reb'n Purlie—I know I look a mess, but—

MISSY.   What happened up there?

LUTIEBELLE.   (*Boiling again.*) I'm a maid first class, Aunt Missy, and I'm proud of it!

MISSY.   Of course you are.

LUTIEBELLE.   I ain't had no complaints to speak of since first I stepped into the white folks' kitchen. I'm clean; I'm honest, and I work hard—but one thing: I don't stand for no stuff from them white folks.

PURLIE.   Of course you don't. You don't have to—

LUTIEBELLE.   I mean, I KNOW my job, and I DO my job—and the next ol' sweaty, ol' grimey, ol' drunkeny man puts his hands on me—so much as touch like he got no business doing—God grant me strength to kill him! Excuse me, Reb'n Purlie.

GITLOW.   Well, Ol' Cap'n do get playful at times—did he send the money?

LUTIEBELLE.   Money! What money? There ain't none!

GITLOW.   What! Naw, naw! He wouldn't do that to me—not to good ol', faithful ol' Gitlow, nawsir!

LUTIEBELLE.   The whole thing was a trick—to get you out of the house—

GITLOW.   Not to ME he didn't!

LUTIEBELLE.   So he could—sneak up behind me in the pantry!

MISSY.   What I tell you!—what I tell you!

LUTIEBELLE.   I knowed the minute I—Come grabbing on me, Reb'n Purlie; come grabbing his dirty ol' hands on me!

PURLIE.   He did!

LUTIEBELLE.   And twisting me around, and — and pinching me, Reb'n Purlie!

PURLIE.   Pinching you—where? Where?

LUTIEBELLE.   Must I, Reb'n Purlie—?

PURLIE.   I demand to know—where did he pinch you!

(LUTIEBELLE *diffidently locates a spot on her left cheek. They all examine it anxiously.*)

MISSY.   That's him all right!

GITLOW.   Aw, Missy—

MISSY.   I'd know them fingerprints anywhere!

LUTIEBELLE.   Right in the pantry—and then he, he—Oh, Reb'n Purlie, I'm so ashamed!

PURLIE.   What did he do? Tell me, woman, tell me: what did he do? WHAT DID HE DO?

LUTIEBELLE.   He kissed me!

PURLIE AND MISSY.   No!

LUTIEBELLE.   He kissed me—right here.

MISSY.   (*Squinting, it is a very small spot indeed.*) Right where? (LUTIEBELLE *is so broken up, she can only point to her other cheek.*)

GITLOW.   Aw, for Pete's sakes.

PURLIE.   (*Almost out of control.*) He kissed my woman, Gitlow—he kissed the woman I love!

GITLOW.   So what!

PURLIE.   So what do you mean, "So what"? No man kisses the woman I love and lives! (GITLOW *laughs.*) Go ahead, laugh! Laugh. Let's have one last look at your teeth before I knock 'em down your throat!

GITLOW.   Aw, man, git off my nerves.

PURLIE.   I'm going up that hill, and I'm gonna call that buzzardly ol' bastard out, and I wouldn't be surprised if I didn't beat him until he died.

LUTIEBELLE.   (*Suddenly not so sure.*) Reb'n Purlie—

GITLOW.   (*Also wondering about* PURLIE.) Now looka here, Purlie —don't you be no fool, boy—you still in Georgia. If you just got to defend the honor of the woman you love, do it somewhere else.

PURLIE.   Kissing my woman—kissing my woman! (*Runs to window, flings it open and shouts out.*) Man, I'll break your neck off!

LUTIEBELLE. (*Helping* GITLOW *and* MISSY *to wrestle* PURLIE *away from the window.*) Please, Reb'n Purlie!

PURLIE. (*Breaks away and goes to window and shouts again.*) I'll stomp your eyeballs in!

LUTIEBELLE. (*They snatch him from the window again.*) Don't, Reb'n Purlie—oh my goodness!—

PURLIE. (*Breaks away still again and shouts from window.*) I'll snatch your right arm outta the socket, and beat the rest of you to death!

LUTIEBELLE. (*This time they get him away, and close the window.*) Don't talk like that, Reb'n Purlie!

MISSY. (*Standing at the window, arms widespread to block him.*) Have you gone crazy?

GITLOW. (*Still struggling with* PURLIE.) You go up that hill to-night, boy, and they'll kill you!

PURLIE. Let 'em kill me, it won't be the first time.

LUTIEBELLE. Aunt Missy, stop him—

GITLOW. Listen, boy! This is your Deputy-For-The-Colored telling you you ain't gonna leave this house, and that's an order!

PURLIE. You try and stop me!

GITLOW. Good gracious a life, what's the matter with you? The man only kissed your woman.

PURLIE. Yeah! And what you suppose he'd a done to me if I'd a kissed his? (*The one question too obvious to answer.*) And that's exactly what I'm gonna do to him!

LUTIEBELLE. Please, Reb'n Purlie. I beg you on bended knees. (*She throws her arms around him.*)

PURLIE. (*Holds her close.*) For the glory and honor of the Negro National Anthem; for the glory and honor of brown-skin Negro womanhood; for the glory and honor of—(LUTIEBELLE *suddenly kisses him big and hard.*)—for LUTIEBELLE! (*His emotions explode him out of the door which slams shut behind him.*)

GITLOW. (*Singing.*) "I hear them gentle bloodhounds callin'— Old Black Joe." . . .

(LUTIEBELLE *finds the deepest spot in* MISSY'S *shoulder to bury her head and cry, as:*)

CURTAIN

Act III

Scene 1

SCENE   *The shack.*

TIME   *Later that same night.*

AT RISE   *There is light only from a KEROSENE LAMP turned down low. The air of Sunday is gone from the room. The table-cloth has been changed, and things are as they were before.* LUTIEBELLE *enters Down Right.*

LUTIEBELLE.   Is it him, Aunt Missy, is it him?

MISSY.   No, honey, not yet.

LUTIEBELLE.   Oh, I could have sworn I thought it was him. What time is it?

MISSY.   About four in the morning from the sound of the birds. Now, why ain't you sleep after all that hot toddy I give you?

LUTIEBELLE.   I can't sleep. The strangest thing. I keep hearing bells —

MISSY.   Bells?

LUTIEBELLE.   Wedding bells. Ain't that funny? Oh, Lord, please don't let him be hurt bad, please! Where can he be, Aunt Missy?

MISSY.   Now don't you worry 'bout Purlie. My! You put on your pretty pink dress!

LUTIEBELLE.   Yes, ma'am. It's the only thing I got fitting to propose in.

MISSY.   Oh?

LUTIEBELLE.   I thought, to sort of show my gratitude, I'd offer him my hand in matrimony — it's all I've got.

MISSY.   It's a nice hand, and a nice dress — just right for matrimony.

LUTIEBELLE.   You really think so, Aunt Missy: really, really, really?

MISSY.   I know so, and wherever Reb'n Purlie is this morning, you can bet your bottom dollar he knows it, too.

LUTIEBELLE.   Ten thousand Queens of Sheba! Aunt Missy —

MISSY.   Yes —

LUTIEBELLE.   (*Letting it out in a gush.*) I wanted him to get mad; I wanted him to tear out up that hill; I wanted him to punch that sweaty ol' buzzard in his gizzard—You think I was wrong?

MISSY. I should say not!

LUTIEBELLE. Course I coulda punched him myself, I reckon.

MISSY. Why should you? Why shouldn't our men folks defend our honor with the white folks once in a while? They ain't got nothing else to do.

LUTIEBELLE. You really, really, really think so?

MISSY. (*Shrugs.*) Ten thousand Queens of Sheba —

LUTIEBELLE. Oh, my goodness, when he walks through that door, I'm just gonna —

(*Door Down Left suddenly swings open to reveal* GITLOW.)

GITLOW. (*Entering*) Well, well, Lutiebelle.

LUTIEBELLE. Did you find him, Uncle Git?

MISSY. Don't depend on Gitlow for nothing, honey — (*Exits to kitchen.*)

LUTIEBELLE. Where can he be, Uncle Gitlow, where can he be?

GITLOW. Oh — good wind like this on his tail oughta put him somewhere above Macon long 'bout now, if his shoes hold out!

LUTIEBELLE. You mean — running!

GITLOW. What's wrong with running? It emancipated more people than Abe Lincoln ever did.

LUTIEBELLE. How dare you! The finest, bravest man —

GITLOW. The finer they come, the braver they be, the deader these white folks gonna kill 'em when they catch 'em!

MISSY. (*Entering from the kitchen.*) Gitlow, I'll skin you!

GITLOW. All that talk about calling that man out, and whipping him —

MISSY. A man is duty-bound to defend the honor of the woman he loves, and any woman worth her salt will tell you so.

LUTIEBELLE. Love can make you do things you really can't do — can't it, Aunt Missy?

GITLOW. Look. That man's got the president, the governor, the courthouse, and both houses of the congress — on his side!

MISSY. Purlie Judson is a man the Negro woman can depend on!

LUTIEBELLE. An honor to his race, and a credit to his people!

GITLOW. (*Not to be sidetracked.*) The army, the navy, the marines; the sheriff, the judge, the jury, the police, the F.B.I.—all on his side. Not to mention a pair of brass knucks and the hungriest dogs this side of hell! Surely youall don't expect that po' boy to go up against all that caucasiatic power empty-handed!

MISSY. O, ye of little faith!

LUTIEBELLE. Didn't my Lord deliver Daniel?

GITLOW. Of course he did—but lions is one thing and white folks is another!

MISSY. Where there's a will there's a woman—

LUTIEBELLE. And where there's a woman there's a way!

GITLOW. (*Exasperated.*) Great Gawdamighty! All right—go ahead and have it your way. But I'll lay you six bits 'gainst half my seat on the heavenly choir, Purlie ain't been up that hill. And the minute he walks in that door — if he ever shows up again around here — I'm gonna prove it! Oh, damn — I can make better time out there talkin' to that mule.

MISSY. Why not — it's one jackass to another.

(GITLOW *exits to the kitchen.* MISSY *and* LUTIEBELLE *look at each other, both determined not to give way to the very real fright they feel. There is a long, uncomfortable pause.*)

LUTIEBELLE. It sure is a lovely year — for this time of morning, I mean. (*There is a pause.*) I can't tell you how much all this fresh air, wine-smoke, and apple-bite reminds me of Alabama.

MISSY. Oh, yes — Ol' Georgia can sure smile pretty when she's of a mind to —

PURLIE. (*Bursts in.*) "Arise and shine for thy light has come."

MISSY. Purlie — Purlie Victorious! (*They embrace.*)

LUTIEBELLE. Oh, you Reb'n Purlie you!

PURLIE. "Truth and Mercy are met together, Righteousness and Peace have kissed each other!" (*They embrace.*)

MISSY. Let me look at you — behold the man! — knee-deep in shining glory. Great day the righteous marching! What happened to you?

PURLIE. Mine enemy hath been destroyed!

MISSY. What!

PURLIE. I told that ol' man twenty years ago, Missy, that over his dead body, Big Bethel would rise again!

MISSY. Purlie —! You mean you done —

PURLIE. "Have I any pleasure that the wicked should die, saith the Lord, and not turn from his ways and live!" Lutiebelle, put on your hat and coat, and hurry!

LUTIEBELLE. Yessir!

PURLIE. Missy, throw us some breakfast into a paper sack, and quick!

MISSY. Yessir!

PURLIE. Gitlow, I'm calling on you and your fellow mule to write a new page in the annals of Negro History Week.

GITLOW. (*Entering.*) Well, if it ain't ol' little black riding hood, dere! How was the mean ol' peckerwolf tonight, dere, kingfish?

MISSY. Tell him, Purlie boy, what you told us: how you sashayed up that hill with force and fistfight!

GITLOW. Hallelujah!

MISSY. How you fit Ol' Cap'n to a halt and a standstill!

GITLOW. Talk that talk!

MISSY. And left him laying in a pool of his own Confederate blood!

GITLOW. For Pete sakes, Missy — quit lying!

MISSY. Don't you dare call Purlie Judson a liar!

LUTIEBELLE. No man calls Reb'n Purlie a liar and lives!

GITLOW. What's the matter with you people? Purlie ain't been up that hill; Purlie ain't seen Ol' Cap'n; Purlie ain't done doodley squat! And all that gabble about leaving somebody in a pool of his own Confederate blood ain't what the bull left in the barnyard!

PURLIE. Five hundred dollars says it is! (*Draws roll of bills from his pocket, for all to see.*)

ALL. Five hundred dollars!

PURLIE. In cool September cash!

GITLOW. Money! (*Lunges forward, but* PURLIE *slaps his hand.*)

PURLIE. And that ain't all I got — (*Opens bag he has brought. They look in.*)

GITLOW. (*Almost choking in awe.*) Oh, my goodness, Missy —
   great day in the morning time — Missy — Missy!

MISSY. (*Also impressed.*) Gitlow, that's *it!*

GITLOW. That's *it*, Missy — that's *it!*

MISSY. Of course that's *it!* — ain't nothing in the world but *it!*
   (PURLIE *slowly pulls out* OL' CAP'N'S *bull whip.*)

GITLOW. Ain't but one way — one way in all this world — for nobody to get that bull whip off'n Ol' Cap'n!

MISSY. And that's off'n his dead body!

GITLOW. And that's the everlovin' truth, so help me.

PURLIE. Here, take it—and burn it in a public place. Lutiebelle—

LUTIEBELLE. Yes, Reb'n Purlie.

PURLIE. This money belongs to the Negro people —

GITLOW. Reb'n Purlie, my boy, I apologize from the bottom of my
   knees. (*Kneels and starts to sing.*) "Gone are the days —"

MISSY. (*Snatching him to his feet.*) Get up and shut up!

PURLIE. (*Deliberately continuing to* LUTIEBELLE.) Take it, and
   wear it next to your heart.

LUTIEBELLE. (*Very conscious of the great charge laid upon her,
   turns her back to* GITLOW *and hides the money in her bosom.*)
   Until death us do part.

MISSY. (*To* GITLOW.) If I ever catch you with that song in your
   mouth again I'll choke you with it!

PURLIE. And go wake up the mule. We due in Waycross to buy
   Big Bethel.

GITLOW. I'm going, I'm going. (*Starts, but can't tear himself
   away.*) Cash—five hundred dollars in cash. And a bull whip,
   from Ol' Cap'n Cotchipee himself — Man, I'd give a pretty
   piece of puddin' to know how you did it!

MISSY. You go and wake up that mule! (*Turning back to* PURLIE.)
   Me, too! How did you do it, Purlie?

LUTIEBELLE. What happened when you first got there?

PURLIE. (*Almost laughing.*) Now wait a minute — don't rush me!

MISSY. That's what I say: don't rush him — let the man talk!

PURLIE. Talk! Missy, I told you. I haven't got time —

GITLOW.   That's all right, Purlie, we'll listen in a hurry.

LUTIEBELLE.   What happened when you called him out and whipped him?

PURLIE.   I didn't call him out and whip him!

GITLOW.   What!

MISSY.   You didn't!

LUTIEBELLE.   Reb'n Purlie—?

PURLIE.   I mean, I did call him out —!

LUTIEBELLE.   (*In ecstatic relief.*) Oh — You did call him out!

PURLIE.   Yeah — but he didn't come.

ALL.   What!

PURLIE.   So — er — I went in to get him!

ALL.   You did! Sure enough! What happened then?

PURLIE.   (*Still seeking escape.*) Well, like I told you —

LUTIEBELLE.   Tell us, Reb'n Purlie — please!

PURLIE.   (*No escape.*) Well — here was me; and there was him — twisted and bent like a pretzel! Face twitchified like a pan of worms; eyes bugging out; sweat dreening down like rain; tongue plumb clove to the roof of his mouth! (*He looks to his audience, and is impelled to go on.*) Well — this thief! This murderer; this adulterer — this oppressor of all my people, just sitting there: Stonewall Jackson Cotchipee, just a sitting there. (*Begins to respond to his own fantasy.*) "Go to, rich man, weep and howl, for your sorrows shall come upon you." And-a "Wherefore abhor yourself, and repent Ye in sackcloth and ashes!" 'cause ol' Purlie is done come to get you!

LUTIEBELLE.   (*Swept away.*) Oh, my Lord!

MISSY.   What he do, Purlie — what he do!?

PURLIE.   Fell down on bended knees and cried like a baby!

MISSY.   Ol' Cap'n Cotchipee on his knees!?

GITLOW.   Great day in the morning time!

PURLIE.   (*Warming to the task.*) Don't beg me, white folks, it's too late. "Mercy?" What do you know about mercy?! Did you have mercy on Ol' Uncle Tubb when he asked you not to cheat him out of his money so hard, and you knocked him deaf in his left ear? — Did you have mercy on Lolly's boy when he sassed you back, and you took and dipped his head in a bucket of syrup! And twenty years ago when little Purlie, black and manly as he could be, stood naked before you and your bull whip and pleaded with tears in his li'l ol' eyes, did you have mercy!?

GITLOW. Naw!

PURLIE. —And I'll not have mercy now!

ALL. Amen! Help him, Lawd! Preach it, boy, preach it! (*Etc.*)

PURLIE. Vengeance is mine saith the Lord! (*Hallelujah!*) Ye serpents; ye vipers; ye low-down sons of—! (*Amen!*) How can ye escape the damnation of hell!

MISSY. Throw it at him, boy!

PURLIE. And then, bless my soul, I looked up — up from the blazing depths of my righteous indignation! And I saw tears spill over from his eyeballs; and I heard the heart be-clutching anguish of his outcry! His hands was both a-tremble; and slobber a-dribblin' down his lips!

GITLOW. Oh, my Lawd!

PURLIE. And he whined and whimpered like an ol' hound dog don't want you to kick him no more!

LUTIEBELLE. Great goodness a mighty!

PURLIE. And I commenced to ponder the meaning of this evil thing that groveled beneath my footstool — this no-good lump of nobody! — not fit to dwell on this earth beside the children of the blessed — an abomination to the Almighty and stench in the nostrils of his people! And yet — (*Pause for effect.*) And yet — a man! A weak man; a scared man; a pitiful man; like the whole southland bogged down in sin and segregation crawling on his knees before my judgment seat — but still a MAN!

GITLOW. A man, Lawd!

PURLIE. He, too, like all the South, was one of God's creatures —

MISSY. Yes, Lawd!

PURLIE. He, too, like all the South, could never be beyond the reach of love, hope, and redemption.

LUTIEBELLE. Amen!

PURLIE. Somewhere for him — even for him, some father's heart was broken, some mother's tears undried.

GITLOW. Dry 'em, Lawd!

PURLIE. I am my brother's keeper!

ALL. Yes, Lawd.

PURLIE. And thinking on these things, I found myself to pause, and stumble in my great resolve — and sorrow squeezed all fury from my heart — and pity plucked all hatred from my soul — and the racing feet of an avenging anger slowed down to a halt and a standstill — and the big, black, and burly fist of my strong correction — raised on high like a stroke of God's own lightning — fell useless by my side. The book say, "Love one another."

MISSY. Love one another!

PURLIE. The book say, "Comfort ye one another."

LUTIEBELLE. Comfort ye one another.

PURLIE. The book say, "Forgive ye one another."

GITLOW. Forgive Ol' Cap'n, Lord.

PURLIE. Slowly I turned away — to leave this lump of human mess and misery to the infinite darkness of a hell for white folks only, when suddenly —

MISSY. Suddenly, Lord.

PURLIE. Suddenly I put on my brakes — Purlie Victorious Judson stopped dead in his tracks — and stood stark still, and planted his feet, and rared back, asked himself and all the powers-that-be some mighty important questions.

LUTIEBELLE. Yes, he did, Lawd.

MISSY. And that is the truth!

PURLIE. How come — I asked myself, it's always the colored folks got to do all the forgiving?

GITLOW. Man, you mighty right!

PURLIE. How come the only cheek gits turned in this country is the Negro cheek!

MISSY. Preach to me, boy!

PURLIE. What was this, this — man — Ol' Cap'n Cotchipee —
that in spite of all his sins and evils, he still had dominion over
me?

LUTIEBELLE. Ain't that the truth!

PURLIE. God made us all equal — God made us all brothers —

ALL. Amen, amen.

PURLIE. "And hath made of one blood all nations of men for to
dwell on the face of the earth." — Who changed all that!?

GITLOW. (*Furious*) Who changed it, he said.

PURLIE. Who took it and twisted it around!

MISSY. (*Furious*) Who was it, he said!

LUTIEBELLE. (*Furious.*) And where's that scoun' hiding?!

PURLIE. So that the Declarator of Independence himself might
seem to be a liar?

GITLOW. Who, that's what I want to know, who?

PURLIE. That a man the color of his face — (*Pointing up Cotchipee Hill.*) could live by the sweat of a man the color of mine!

LUTIEBELLE. Work with him, Lawd, work with him!

PURLIE. — Could live away up there in his fine, white mansion,
and us down here in a shack not fitting to house the fleas upon
his dogs!

GITLOW. Nothing but fleas!

PURLIE. —Could wax hisself fat on the fat of the land; steaks, rice,
chicken, roastineers, sweet potato pies, hot buttered biscuits
and cane syrup anytime he felt like it and never hit a lick at a
snake! And us got to every day git-up-and-git-with-it, sunup-
to-sundown, on fatback and cornmeal hoecakes — and don't
wind up owning enough ground to get buried standing up in!

MISSY. Do, Lord!

PURLIE. — And horses and cadillacs, bull whips and bourbon, and
two for 'leven dollar seegars — and our fine young men to serve
at his table; and our fine young women to serve in his bed!

LUTIEBELLE. Help him, Lawd.

PURLIE. Who made it like this — who put the white man on top?

GITLOW.   That's what I wants to know!

PURLIE.   Surely not the Lord God of Israel who is a just God!

MISSY.   Hah, Lord!

PURLIE.   And no respecter of persons! Who proved in the American Revolution that all men are created equal!

GITLOW.   Man, I was there when he proved it!

PURLIE.   Endowed with Civil Rights and First Class Citizenship, Ku Klux Klan, White Citizens Council notwithstanding!

MISSY.   Oh, yes, he did!

PURLIE.   And when my mind commenced to commemorate and to reconsider all these things —

GITLOW.   Watch him, Lawd!

PURLIE.   And I thought of the black mother in bondage — (*Yes.*) and I thought of the black father in prison — (*Ha, Lawd!*) And of Momma herself — Missy can tell how pretty she was —

MISSY.   Indeed I can!

PURLIE.   How she died outdoors on a dirty sheet cause the hospital doors said — "For white folks only." And of Papa, God rest his soul — who brought her tender loving body back home — and laid her to sleep in the graveyard — and cried himself to death among his children!

MISSY.   (*Crying.*) Purlie, Purlie —

PURLIE.   (*Really carried away.*) Then did the wrath of a righteous God possess me; and the strength of the host and of ten thousand swept into my good right arm — and I arose and I smote Ol' Cap'n a mighty blow! And the wind from my fist ripped the curtains from the eastern walls — and I felt the weight of his ol' bull whip nestling in my hands — and the fury of a good Gawd-almighty was within me; and I beat him — I whipped him — and I flogged him — and I cut him — I destroyed him!

(IDELLA *enters.*)

GITLOW.   Great day and the righteous marching—Whoeeeee! Man, I ain't been stirred that deep since the tree caught fire on a possum hunt and the dogs pushed Papa in the pot.

MISSY.   Idella, you shoulda heard him!

IDELLA.   I did hear him—all the way across the valley. I thought he was calling hogs. Well, anyway: all hell is broke loose at the big house. Purlie, you better get outa here. Ol' Cap'n is on the phone to the sheriff.

MISSY.   Ol' Cap'n Cotchipee is dead.

IDELLA.   The hell you preach.

ALL.   What!

IDELLA.   Ol' Cap'n ain't no more dead than I am.

LUTIEBELLE.   That's a mighty tacky thing to say about your ex-fellow man.

MISSY.   Mighty tacky.

LUTIEBELLE.   Reb'n Purlie just got through preaching 'bout it. How he marched up Cotchipee hill —

GITLOW.   (*Showing the bull whip.*) And took Ol' Cap'n by the bull whip —

MISSY.   And beat that ol' buzzard to death!

IDELLA.   That is the biggest lie since the devil learned to talk!

LUTIEBELLE.   I am not leaving this room till somebody apologizes to Reb'n Purlie V. Judson, the gentleman of my intended.

IDELLA.   Purlie Judson! Are you gonna stand there sitting on your behind, and preach these people into believing you spent the night up at the big house whipping Ol'Cap'n to death when all the time you was breaking into the commissary!

MISSY.   Breaking into the commissary!

GITLOW.   Something is rotten in the cotton!

PURLIE.   It's all right, Miz Idella — I'll take it from there —

MISSY.   It is not all right —!

PURLIE.   While it is true that, maybe, I did not go up that hill just word for word, and call that ol' man out, and beat him to death so much on the dotted line—!

MISSY.   (*Snatching up the paper bag.*) I'm goin' to take back my lunch!

PURLIE.   Missy! Wait a minute!

LUTIEBELLE.   You know what, Aunt Missy?

MISSY.   Yes, honey?

LUTIEBELLE.   Sometimes I just wish I could drop dead for a while!

PURLIE.   Wait, Lutiebelle, give me a chance to —

LUTIEBELLE.   Here's your money!—(*Puts roll into* PURLIE'S *hand.*)
   And that goes for every other great big ol' handsome man in the
   whole world!

PURLIE.   What you want me to do? Go up that hill by myself and
   get my brains knocked out?

MISSY.   It's little enough for the woman you love!

LUTIEBELLE.   Why'd you have to preach all them wonderful things
   that wasn't so?

GITLOW.   And why'd you have to go and change your mind?

PURLIE.   I didn't mean for them not to be so: it was a—a parable!
   A prophecy! Believe me! I ain't never in all my life told a lie
   I didn't mean to make come true, some day! Lutiebelle —!

IDELLA.   Purlie: unless you want to give heartbreak a headache,
   you better run!

PURLIE.   Run —run for what!

MISSY.   You want Ol' Cap'n to catch you here!?

PURLIE.   Confound Ol' Cap'n! Dad-blast Ol' Cap'n! Damn, damn,
   damn, and double-damn Ol' Cap'n!

   (*The front door swings open and in walks* OL' CAP'N *steaming with
   anger.*)

OL' CAP'N.   (*Controlling himself with great difficulty.*) Somebody
   — I say somebody — is calling my name!

GITLOW.   Ol' Cap'n, you just in time to settle a argument: is
   Rudolph Valentino still dead?

OL' CAP'N.   Shut up!

GITLOW.   (*To* MISSY.) See—I told you.

OL' CAP'N.   One thing I have not allowed in my cotton patch since
   am-I-born-to-die! And that's stealin'! Somebody broke into
   my commissary tonight — took two cans of sardines, a box of
   soda crackers, my bull whip! — (*Picks up whip from table.*)
   And five hundred dollars in cash. And, boy — (*Walking over
   to* PURLIE.) I want it back!

LUTIEBELLE.   Stealing ain't all that black and white.

MISSY.   And we certainly wasn't the ones that started it!

GITLOW.   Who stole me from Africa in the first place?

LUTIEBELLE. Who kept me in slavery from 1619 to 1863, working me to the bone without no social security?

PURLIE. And tonight — just because I went up that hill, and disembezzled my own inheritance that you stole from me —!

OL' CAP'N. (*Livid.*) I have had a belly full of your black African sass —!

(*The door bursts open again; this time it is the* SHERIFF *who comes in with pistol drawn.*)

SHERIFF. All right, everybody, drop that gun!

PURLIE. Drop what gun?

OL' CAP'N. So there you are, you idiot — what kept you so long?

SHERIFF. Like you told us to do on the phone, suh, we was taking a good, long, slow snoop 'round and 'bout the commissary looking for clues! And dog-gone if one didn't, just a short while ago, stumble smack into our hands!

OL' CAP'N. What!

SHERIFF. We caught the culprit red-handed — bring in the prisoner, Dep!

DEPUTY. Glad to oblige you, Sheriff.

(*Enter* DEPUTY, *dragging* CHARLIE, *who has his hands cuffed behind him; wears heavy leg shackles, and has a large white gag stuck into his mouth.*)

SHERIFF. Southern justice strikes again!

OL' CAP'N. Charlie! — oh, no!

IDELLA. Charlie, my baby!

OL' CAP'N. Release him, you idiots! Release him at once! (*Everybody pitches in to set* CHARLIE *free.*) What have they done to you, my boy?

IDELLA. What have they done to you!

CHARLIE. (*Free from the gag.*) Hello, Paw — Idella — Purlie —

OL' CAP'N. I'll have your thick, stupid necks for this!

SHERIFF. It was you give the orders, suh!

OL' CAP'N. Not my son, you idiot!

DEPUTY. It was him broke into the commissary.

OL' CAP'N. What!

SHERIFF. It was him stole the five hundred dollars — he confessed!

OL' CAP'N. Steal? A Cotchipee? Suh, that is biologically impossible! (*To* CHARLIE) Charlie, my boy. Tell them the truth — tell them who stole the money. It was Purlie, wasn't it, boy?

CHARLIE. Well, as a matter of fact, Paw — it was mostly me that broke in and took the money, I'd say. In fact it WAS me!

OL' CAP'N. No!

CHARLIE. It was the only thing I could do to save your life, Paw.

OL' CAP'N. Save my life! Idella, he's delirious —!

CHARLIE. When Purlie come up that hill after you last night, I seen him, and lucky for you I did. The look he had on his face against you was not a Christian thing to behold! It was terrible! I had to get into that commissary, right then and there, open that safe, and pay him his inheritance — even then I had to beg him to spare your life!

OL' CAP'N. (*To* PURLIE.) You spare my life, boy? How dare you? (*To* CHARLIE.) Charlie, my son, I know you never recovered from the shock of losing your mother — almost before you were born. But don't worry — it was Purlie who stole that money and I'm going to prove it. (*Starts to take out gun.* GITLOW *grabs gun.*) Gitlow, my old friend, arrest this boy, Gitlow! As Deputy-For-The-Colored—I order you to arrest this boy for stealing!

GITLOW. (*With a brand new meaning.*) "Gone are the days —" (*Still twirls pistol safely out of* OL' CAP'N's *reach.*)

PURLIE. "Stealin," it is? Well, I'm gonna really give you something to arrest me for. (*Snatches bull whip.*)

OL' CAP'N. Have a care, boy: I'm still a white man.

PURLIE. Congratulations! Twenty years ago, I told you this bull whip was gonna change hands one of these days!

MISSY. Purlie, wait —!

PURLIE. Stay out of my struggle for power!

MISSY. You can't do wrong just because it's right!

GITLOW. Never kick a man when he's down except in self-defense!

LUTIEBELLE. And no matter what you are, and always will be — the hero of Cotchipee Hill.

PURLIE. Am I?

LUTIEBELLE. Ten thousand queens!

PURLIE. I bow to the will of the Negro people . (*Throws whip away. Back to* OL' CAP'N.) But one thing, Ol' Cap'n, I am released of you — the entire Negro people is released of you! No more shouting hallelujah! every time you sneeze, nor jumping jackass every time you whistle "Dixie"! We gonna love you if you let us and laugh as we leave if you don't. We want our cut of the Constitution, and we want it now: and not with no teaspoon, white folks — throw it at us with a shovel!

OL' CAP'N. Charlie, my boy — my own, lily-white, Anglo-Saxon, semi-confederate son. I know you never recovered from the shock of losing your mother, almost before you were born. But don't worry: there is still time to take these insolent, messy cotton-picking ingrates down a peg—and prove by word and deed that God is still a white man. Tell 'em! Boy, tell 'em!

CHARLIE. Tell 'em what, Paw?

OL' CAP'N. Tell 'em what you and me have done together. Nobody here would believe me. Tell 'em how you went to Waycross, Saturday night, in my name —

CHARLIE. Yes, sir — I did.

OL' CAP'N. Tell 'em how you spoke to Ol' Man Pelham in my name —

CHARLIE. Yes, sir — I spoke to him.

OL' CAP'N. And paid him cash for that ol' barn they used to call Big Bethel!

CHARLIE. Yes, sir; that's what I did, all right.

OL' CAP'N. And to register the deed in the courthouse in my name —

CHARLIE. Yes, sir, that's exactly what you told me to do —

OL' CAP'N. Then —ain't but one thing left to do with that ramshackle dung-soaked monstrosity—that's burn the damn thing down. (*Laughs aloud in his triumph.*)

CHARLIE. But, Paw —

OL' CAP'N. First thing, though—let me see the deed: I wouldn't want to destroy nothing that didn't — legally — belong to me. (*Snatches deed from* CHARLIE's *hand. Begins to mumble as he reads it.*)

IDELLA.   Twenty years of being more than a mother to you!

CHARLIE.   Wait, Idella, wait. I did go to Waycross, like Paw said; I did buy the barn — excuse me, Purlie: the church — like he said; and I registered the deed at the courthouse like he told me—but not in Paw's name—

OL' CAP'N.   (*Startled by something he sees on the deed.*) What's this?

CHARLIE.   (*To* IDELLA.) I registered the deed in the name of —

OL' CAP'N.   (*Reading, incredulous.*) "Purlie Victorious Judson —" No!

IDELLA.   PURLIE VICTORIOUS Judson?

OL' CAP'N.   (*Choking on the words.*) Purlie Victorious Judssss — aaaarrrrgggghhhhh! (*The horror of it strikes him absolutely still.*)

CHARLIE.   (*Taking the deed from* OL' CAP'N's *limp hand.*) It was the only thing I could do to save your life. (*Offering deed to* PURLIE.) Well, Purlie, here it is.

PURLIE.   (*Counting out the five hundred dollars.*) You did a good job, Charlie — I'm much obliged!

CHARLIE.   (*Refuses money; still holds out deed to* PURLIE.) Thank you, Purlie, but —

PURLIE.   Big Bethel is my Bethel, Charlie: it's my responsibility. Go on, take it.

CHARLIE.   No, no! I couldn't take your money, Purlie —

IDELLA.   Don't be a fool, boy — business is business. (*She takes the deed from* CHARLIE *and gives it to* PURLIE, *while at the same time taking the money from* PURLIE.)

CHARLIE.   Idella — I can't do that!

IDELLA.   I can! I'll keep it for you.

CHARLIE.   Well — all right. But only, if — if —

IDELLA.   Only if what?

CHARLIE.   (*To* PURLIE.) Would you let me be a member of your church?

MISSY.   You?

GITLOW.   Li'l Charlie Cotchipee!

LUTIEBELLE.   A member of Big Bethel?

CHARLIE. May I? That is — that is, if you don't mind — as soon as you get it started?

PURLIE. Man, we're already started: the doors of Big Bethel, Church of the New Freedom for all Mankind, are hereby declared "Open for business!"

GITLOW. Brother Pastor, I move we accept Brother Charlie Cotchipee as our first candidate for membership to Big Bethel on a integrated basis —

MISSY. I second that motion!

PURLIE. You have heard the motion. Are you ready for the question?

ALL. (*Except* OL' CAP'N.) Question!

PURLIE. Those in favor will signify by saying "Aye." (EVERYBODY, *except* OL' CAP'N, *crowds around* CHARLIE, *saying "Aye" over and over, in such a crescendo of welcome that* PURLIE *has to ride over the noise.*) Those opposed? (*Looks at* OL' CAP'N, *who is still standing, as if frozen, as we last saw him. He does not answer.*) Those opposed will signify by saying —

(*He stops . . . all eyes focus on* OL' CAP'N *now, still standing in quiet, frozen-like immobility. There is a moment of silence, an unspoken suspicion in everybody's face. Finally,* GITLOW *goes over and touches* OL' CAP'N, *still standing rigid. Still he does not move.* GITLOW *feels his pulse, listens to his heart, and lifts up his eyelids. Nothing.*)

GITLOW. The first man I ever seen in all this world to drop dead standing up!

BLACKOUT

Act III

Epilogue

TIME   *Immediately following.*

SCENE *We are at Big Bethel at funeral services for* OL' CAP'N.

AT RISE *We cannot see the coffin. We hear the ringing of the CHURCH BELL as we come out of the blackout.* PURLIE *is in the pulpit.*

PURLIE. And toll the bell, Big Bethel, toll the bell! Dearly beloved, recently bereaved, and friends, we welcome you to Big Bethel, Church of the New Freedom: part Baptist; part Methodist; part Catholic — with the merriness of Christmas and the happiness of Hanukkah; and to the first integrated funeral in the sovereign, segregated state of Georgia. Let there be no merriments in these buryments! Though you are dead, Ol' Cap'n, and in hell, I suspect — as post-mortal guest of honor, at our expense: it is not too late to repent. We still need togetherness; we still need each otherness — with faith in the futureness of our cause. Let us, therefore, stifle the rifle of conflict, shatter the scatter of discord, smuggle the struggle, tickle the pickle, and grapple the apple of peace!

GITLOW. This funeral has been brought to you as a public service.

PURLIE. Take up his bones. For he who was my skin's enemy, was brave enough to die standing for what he believed. . . . And it is the wish of his family — and his friends — that he be buried likewise—(*The* PALLBEARERS *enter, carrying* OL' CAP'N's *ornate coffin just as he would have wished: standing up! It is draped in a Confederate flag; and his hat, his bull whip, and his pistol, have been fastened to the lid in appropriate places.*) Gently, gently. Put kindness in your fingers. He was a man — despite his own example. Take up his bones. (*The* PALLBEARERS *slowly carry the upright coffin across the stage.*) Tonight, my friends— I find, in being black, a thing of beauty: a joy; a strength; a secret cup of gladness; a native land in neither time nor place— a native land in every Negro face! Be loyal to yourselves: your skin; your hair; your lips, your southern speech, your laughing kindness—are Negro kingdoms, vast as any other! Accept in full the sweetness of your blackness—not wishing to be red, nor white, nor yellow: nor any other race, or face, but this. Farewell, my deep and Africanic brothers, be brave, keep freedom in the family, do what you can for the white folks, and write me in care of the post office. Now, may the Constitution of the United States go with you; the Declaration of Independence stand by you; the Bill of Rights protect you; and the State Commission Against Discrimination keep the eyes of the law upon you, henceforth, now and forever. Amen.

CURTAIN

Kingsley B. Bass, Jr.

We Righteous Bombers

In *New Plays from the Black Theatre*, Kingsley B. Bass, Jr., is identified as a twenty-four-year old Blackman killed by Detroit police during the uprising in 1967.

We Righteous Bombers is a product of a movement frequently described as the Black Arts or Black Revolutionary Movement. A movement among younger writers during the 1960's, it is characterized by rejection of traditional European styles of drama, an appeal to black rather than white audiences, and emphasis upon themes related to revolution of black people against white oppressors. Le Roi Jones was among the first of such playwrights, earning recognition for *Dutchman, The Toilet,* and *The Slave.* Presently the most productive are Ed Bullins and Jimmy Garret. Others who have earned particular recognition are William W. Mackey, Sonja Sanchez, and Marvin X. Needless to say, because of the bitter denunciations of American society, most of these dramas have been produced only in black community theater.

The experimentation with dramatic technique, the interweaving of past with present, the characterization, and the vital thought reveal the author of the play to be an individual of considerable talent as a playwright. More consciously than most others, he explored and presented the differing psychologies motivating the diverse elements banded together in a black revolutionary movement. In this manner, he seems to develop for black revolutionary drama

---

From *New Plays from the Black Theatre,* ed. Ed Bullins (New York: Bantam, 1969).

some of the "universality" too frequently sought by white American critics, who generally discover it in revolutionary drama only in the efforts of the Irish Nationalists and the German Expressionists.

To comprehend the play, it is necessary only to project oneself into a world ominously predicted in John A. Williams' *The Man Who Cried I Am*—an America, which, to protect the interests of its leaders, has imprisoned black people in the wall-less concentration camps of the inner cities. This is the world of *We Righteous Bombers*.

We Righteous Bombers

(The stage is black. Noise begins low and gradually builds. The noise is of varied things: engines, buses, jets, trains, gunfire, explosions, dogs barking, men fighting, human moans, women screaming, human hysteria—Black music counterpoints. Simultaneously, faint lights show on the several screens arranged around and in the playing areas. The lights are red, blue and orange. They change into and swirl together in abstract shapes and patterns as the sound rises and the red becomes more pronounced. An effect of rapid accelera- tion starts and increases, created through sound, lights and screen projections. Upon the screen are fuzzy images suggesting crowd activity—rioting, disorder, large groups being detained in wired, outside enclosures. Images of fences, walls, closed gates. Of bomb craters, gutted buildings, weed-choked railroad tracks, overturned cars. Of social and political chaos.
Lights rise and show the dim shape of MURRAY JACKSON *sitting in his cell. The cell is merely an iron grate that* JACKSON *remains behind, but is open on the sides and back so that other actors can freely move around and with him. In other areas numerous less distinguishable shapes move, and make sounds—choking, gagging, hisses, laughter, whimpers, coughs, etc.*
A VOICE *begins to speak over the loudspeaker. As the loudspeaker broadcasts, the stage should be vibrating with dark, sinister move- ment in the shadows; with the combined effects of light, sound, film and motion. One of the screens lights up and a* BLACKMAN *speaking in the voice of a whiteman and wearing a uniform suggestive of a military auxiliary unit appears.)*

ANNOUNCER. And folks . . . this about ends our daily bulletin from your government information bureau. To sum up: there is evi- dence of increased guerrilla activity in the Western Sector of the Northeastern Command . . . near the 9th Military Pacification Area that was formerly known as Pittsburgh. In the ensuing

action there were four hundred twenty-three enemy Black Revolutionary bandits killed, and our loyal government forces lost
a total of forty-one whitemen killed and wounded . . . and
ninety-seven of our loyal negro mercenaries killed in combat
with the enemy Blacks. Of course, most of the latter casualties
were caused by sniping and by bombs . . . thrown by Black
Revolutionary suicide personnel and planted in various loca-
tions in the Black pacified areas that negro mercenaries police
. . . For as everyone knows . . . it is your government's policy
. . . Black and white do not mix . . . Even the negro mercenary
combat units that are loyal to your government work and live
exclusively in Black areas that are totally surrounded by electrified barbed wire and policed by combat veterans, white police
and military detachments and dogs. By the Black controlling
their areas and manning their own military, police and bureau-
cratic positions of government under our present martial law
and apartheid system of government . . . they have the fullest
range of freedom . . . that is allowed to any man in these times
. . . Black or white.

*(The moans and wails in the shadows rise as if in protest. There
is automatic gunfire, punctuated by flashes of light, and the picture
on the screen momentarily goes out of focus.)*

To complete our news summary . . . the Controlling Military
Council announced today that all Black Revolutionaries would
soon be captured and destroyed and the government would
in the near future be handed back to the free peoples of America
and free elections would be reinstated . . . and the end of official
apartheid and martial law is soon in sight for our peoples. But
in these times of crisis it is vital that all citizens understand that
the negroes must lose their civil and constitutional rights, so
not to give aid and comfort to the Black terrorists and rebels
that seek comfort in their midst. But rest assured people of
America . . . both negro and white . . . These vicious beasts that
trample American freedom, the American flag itself, will soon
be brought to bay, and they will feel the full weight of American
justice and vengeance.

VOICE OF GUARD (*off*).   ATTENTION ON DECK! ATTENTION!
ALL RADIOS AND VIDEOS OFF! ALL RADIOS AND VID-
EOS OFF!

ANNOUNCER.   And the Controlling Military Council wishes to praise
today the inspired leadership of the negro prefects of the Black
sectors who police their districts so thoroughly . . .

VOICE OF GUARD (*coming closer*). ALL HANDS OFF YOUR SEATS AND ON YOUR FEETS! THAT'S ALL HANDS, YAWHL HARE? YOU MAHTHAFUKKERS OVER THERE IN DEATH ROW HIT YO FEETS . . . YAWHL HEAR WHAT I SAID! . . . WRING IT OUT . . . BLACK MAHTHAFUKKERS!

(MURRAY JACKSON *stirs. The lights slowly rise to reveal him in black pajama-like dress. His shirt should suggest a cheap, black dashiki; his pants are large and loose fitting. His head is shaven. The sounds and movements of the others on stage counterpoint the action of the scene.*)

ANNOUNCER. And we congratulate our courageous and loyal negro Seek and Kill teams whose job it is to enter the dreaded Black no-man's-land and rout out the Black enemies of American Freedom.

GUARD (*comes on; light on him*). STAND BY FOR COUNT. STAND BY. WHEN I CALL YOUR NAME, SPEAK UP! (GUARD *freezes in tableau.*)

BONNIE BROWN (*faint light in shadows; unreal*). Speak up when you're called . . . he says. Well, you can call me Bonnie Brown . . . I'm just a sister . . . (*Soft snort.*) Huh huh . . . a sister, really . . . a stone revolutionary soul sister . . . ha ha . . . an' kinda foxy . . . yeah, that's me. (*Walks forward a few steps into light.*) Yeah . . . I'm just a down to the nitty Blackbitch . . . I can't even stand fancy clothes. Look at what I'm wearing now . . . Look! Some ole jive actress's ole thrown-away buba. Not even naturally Afro . . . really . . . nothin' like that . . . Just my nappy wig, that's natural . . . like me . . . nothin' jive. And I'm gonna be with yawhl this evening as we go through some Black Revolutionary changes . . . But yawhl remember . . . I'm just plain ole me . . . Sister Bonnie Mae Brown. (*She moves out of the light.*)

GUARD (*reality*). STAND BY FOR COUNT. STAND BY. WHEN I CALL YOUR NAME, SPEAK UP!

(GUARD *freezes; lights change.*)

ELTON "L" CLEVELAND (*unreality; steps from the shadows*). We are righteous Blackmen, brothers and sisters. Righteous bombers. We do not fear death as the whiteman does. Each moment of our lives we build until the second of death . . . That way we meet death like the Black heroes we are . . . fighting to the end.

(*Images on the screen speed up as the speeches go on; sound and movement continue. Lights change.*)

GUARD (*reality*). STAND BY FOR COUNT, PRISONERS. STAND BY. WHEN I CALL . . . SPEAK UP!

(GUARD *freezes; unreality.*)

SISSIE WILLIAMS (*reciting at attention*). Black Revolutionary Codes of War: . . .

(MURRAY JACKSON, BONNIE BROWN, ELTON CLEVELAND, HARRISON BANES *and* KENNETH BURK *snap to attention.*)

SISSIE WILLIAMS. Article Eight: sub-section four (Terrorists, Spies, Saboteurs, Special Forces, Assassins and related Black Liberation Freedom Fighters): . . .

(MURRAY JACKSON, BONNIE BROWN, ELTON CLEVELAND, HARRISON BANES *and* KENNETH BURK *speak the lines with* SISSIE, *at attention. The* GUARD *remains frozen, in the shadows.*)

THE REVOLUTIONARIES (*together*). . . . THE OATH: We Righteous Bombers . . . Righteous in the Grace of the Supreme Black Spirit, Oneness, Allah, We do His bidding so as to liberate the BLACK PEOPLES of the Conscious Universe, of this planet, Earth . . . *by any means necessary.*

(*Lights change;* GUARD *moves.*)

GUARD. STAND BY. WHEN I SAY . . . SAY YOUR NAME.

SISSIE WILLIAMS. Sissie Williams . . . sir.

HARRISON BANES. Harrison goddammit . . . it's Harrison Banes . . .

(GUARD *moves among them, acknowledging their presence, but the atmosphere is not quite real.*)

. . . And yeah . . . I know it's hard and brutal . . . murder, maimings and death . . . and all that. But I'm brutal cause that's the way it is. For me hatred is not a game. Brothers! . . . and sisters . . . we haven't joined together to admire each other's blackness . . . But to bring our people freedom, justice and self-determination. We have joined together to *get something done.* To get something done for Black people . . . *by any means necessary.*

SISSIE. All praises due to the Blackman!

GUARD. YOUR NAMES!

HARRISON. Sorry . . . but I don't have a tender heart. That kinda shit cuts no ice with *me!* . . . tender heart . . . for the whiteman and his pet negroes? . . . WE HAVE A WAR TO WIN, BROTH-ERS! . . . And not until the day comes when we stop sentimentalizing about a golden past that niggers never had here in America will the revolution triumph. This is the last half of the last century for the whiteman, brothers! We have to start takin' care of business.

GUARD.   SPEAK UP . . . YOU BLACK BASTARDS!

(*The group weave in and around the playing area; the movement surrounds* MURRAY JACKSON'S *cage. Music, screen projections, moans and whimpers accompany the action.*)

KENNETH BURK (*humble*).   I've always been afraid . . .

(BONNIE BROWN *laughs hysterically.* SISSIE WILLIAMS *weeps.*)

I'm just not made for this. I'm not a terrorist. I realize that now. The best thing for me to do is to make it . . . to split. I'll do my thing in propaganda, on revolutionary committees . . . and shit like that.

BONNIE (*straining it out, pleading*).   I want the next bomb, brothers.

BURK.   You don't see what happens on a committee. It's far from slicing throats. It's easy to attend meetings, work out plans, and then pass orders for the carrying out of those orders. You risk your life, of course, for the penalty is death for *any* revolutionary activity, but there's a sort of shield between you and the . . . the blood and flesh.

BONNIE.   Give me the next bomb.

GUARD.   I WANT NAMES! . . . SPEAK UP!

BURK.   It's somethin' else again. . . goin' down into the street when night is fallin' on Harlem, takin' your stand among the crowds of people out on the corners or hurrying from the subway exits and buses to their evenin' meals, their children, the wife who's waitin' and watchin' from her window — and havin' to stand there, evil lookin' and silent, with the pull of the bomb on your arm — and knowin' that in only minutes, perhaps in seconds, you'll race out toward a car, bomb in your hand.

BONNIE.   Give it to me.

BURK.   That's what terrorist activity means and I know now that I couldn't start it all over again without feeling all the blood drained from my veins.

GUARD.   GET READY FOR ROLL CALL . . . WHEN I SAY YOUR NAME . . . ANSWER UP! . . .AN' I BETTER HEAR

YA SAY "SIR" ON THE END . . . OR I'LL COME INTO
YOUR CELL TONIGHT AN' KICK YO' ASS 'TIL I GET
TIRED . . . YA UNDERSTAND?

(*Silence.*)

I SAID DID YOU UNDERSTAND?

ALL (*together*).   YES, SIR!

GUARD.   GOOD! . . . THEN LISTEN UP! . . . BONNIE MAE
BROWN!

BONNIE BROWN.   Here, sir.

GUARD.   SISSIE ANN WILLIAMS!

SISSIE.   Here, sir.

GUARD.   ELTON "L" CLEVELAND!

CLEVELAND.   Here, sir.

GUARD.   KENNETH BURK!

BURK.   Here, sir.

GUARD.   HARRISON BANES!

BANES.   Here . . . sir.

GUARD.   WHAT DID YOU SAY?

(*Lights change; they dim to dark around the edges as the group
moves away into the shadows, except for* MURRAY JACKSON. *Sound
and screen projections subside. Lights gradually come up on* JACK-
SON's *cell. He relaxes and sits. The others are in the shadows now,
moving and speaking.*)

BANES.   I said . . . here, sir.

GUARD.   Repeat.

BANES.   Here, sir.

GUARD.   Louder!

BANES (*a bit louder*).   Here, sir!

GUARD.   I can't hear you!

BANES.   HERE, SIR!

GUARD.   Fall out.

(*Silence. Lights change. Images on screen of night skies. Stars.
The moon in varied phases. Clouds scudding through night/lit
space. Images out.* JACKSON *rises and looks toward the cell door.
The* GUARD *enters, followed by a prisoner carrying a mop and
bucket.*)

GUARD (*opens cell door, to* PRISONER). Okay now. Get with it.

(*The* GUARD *takes a seat nearby and takes out a copy of* Playboy *magazine with a Black bunny on the cover, and begins reading.* FOSTER, *the prisoner, begins to wash the floor; he takes no notice of* JACKSON. *A short silence.*)

JACKSON. What's your name, brother?

FOSTER. Foster.

JACKSON. Are you a convict?

FOSTER. Am I a water buffalo? What the hell else do you think I could be?

(*Short silence.*)

JACKSON. What are you in for?

FOSTER. I killed a black mathafukker who was messin' round with my ole lady.

JACKSON. You mean he was attacking her . . . And you protected her?

GUARD. Sssssh. Hey, not so loud.

JACKSON. What?

GUARD. What did you say?

JACKSON (*confused, then understanding*). . . . I said, "What, sir?"

GUARD (*satisfied*). Okay . . . Now don't speak so loud. It's against the rules for you to be talkin' at all. So I'd advise you to talk quietly, like ole man Foster.

JACKSON. Yes, sir . . . (*Pause, to* FOSTER.) Is that why you killed . . . to protect your loved one?

FOSTER. Protect hell . . . they had been foolin' round together for years.

JACKSON. They had?

FOSTER. Sho had. I got drunk one day and came in and she was gone somewhere . . . hadn't even left supper on the stove.

JACKSON. Yeah? And then?

FOSTER. So I figured where the bitch was. Some little afterhour joint usta be over on Seventh Avenue and 137th Street. I had an ole cane knife . . . a long curved thing. Usta use it when I was in Louisiana. Well, I just picked it up, and went over there . . . walked in and just started swingin' at anything that moved.

Killed six of 'em, they tell me, her included. But the nigger she was with got away.

(JACKSON *stares at him.*)

Ohhh . . . my young friend, I see you don't call me brother no more. My little story cooled you out?

JACKSON (*hurriedly*).   No, it hasn't. I've killed too.

FOSTER.   How many?

JACKSON.   I'll let you know, brother, if you want to know. But tell me . . . well . . . you're sorry for what you did, aren't you?

FOSTER.   Sure, I'm sorry. Seventy-five years hard labor, that's quite a stretch, youngblood. I've been here thirty years already. That's enough to make anybody feel sorry.

JACKSON.   Seventy-five years! I come here when I'm twenty-three — and when I go out . . . even with time off for . . .

FOSTER.   Oh, cheer up . . . there's ways of getting a lot of time cut off your sentence. And there's no knowing what a judge will do; if his ole lady was nice to him the night before that means a lot. Maybe he'll be in a good mood and let you off easy. And then you look pretty smart. Well educated and all that. If you have some pull . . . you know, juice . . . you know it ain't the same when you got connections outside, not like me. You'll get off with almost no time.

JACKSON.   I doubt that. And anyhow I don't want to. Feeling guilt and shame for all those years. That would be horrible.

FOSTER.   Guilt! Shame! Where does all that come in? That's just one of those bullshit notions you young studs have . . . How many people did you kill?

JACKSON.   One man.

FOSTER.   One man? Hummmp! . . . was he Black or white?

JACKSON.   Black.

FOSTER.   Why, that's nothin'. You'll be out in no time. They might even give you a medal . . . if it was the right nigger.

JACKSON.   He was the Grand Prefect.

FOSTER.   He was?

JACKSON.   Yeah.

FOSTER.   The *Grand* Prefect?

JACKSON. Yeah.

(*Lights off* JACKSON, FOSTER *and* GUARD.)

(*Up on* HARRISON, CLEVELAND, SISSIE *and* BONNIE.)

HARRISON (*looks at* CLEVELAND). We gonna kill that mathafukker, ain't we?

CLEVELAND. We gonna kill him.

SISSIE. You heard what I said, Harrison, about them nasty white girls up there in Canada.

BONNIE. Quiet, sister. Let the brothers talk. You know better than to be runnin' your mouth all the time like that.

HARRISON. We gonna kill that Uncle Tom nigger, right! Dammit to hell! You're the leader, Big L, and anything you say, man, is good enough by me. Just as long as we kill that (*Derisive.*) *negro.*

CLEVELAND. I don't need your promise, man. We're all brothers.

SISSIE. Don't forget us sisters.

HARRISON. But discipline's essential. That's something I learned for myself at the concentration camp. The Black Revolutionary Organization cannot do without discipline. We all must be disciplined if we're gonna kill the Prefect and set back tyranny and terrorism of Harlem and the Black peoples of America and the world.

BONNIE (*goes to him*). Sit down, brother. You must be tired after that long trip.

HARRISON. I ain't never tired. I'd walk from Canada if I had to be able to be in on this kill.

SISSIE. Haven't you eaten, brother? I got some bean pie I made yesterday.

HARRISON. Yeah . . . that sounds boss, sister.

(*She goes for the pie.* BONNIE *sits.* HARRISON *and* CLEVELAND *face each other.*)

CLEVELAND. Now.

HARRISON. Is everything ready, man?

CLEVELAND (*in a brisker manner*). Yeah, everything's ready. We've been waiting too long for us to fuck-up from lack of planning.

BONNIE.   Yes, we have been waiting so long.

HARRISON.   Yeah, I was just a kid back in the sixties when the riots . . .

BONNIE.   Riots?

HARRISON.   Sorry, sister, I forget sometimes. You know I meant to say the revolution. You know how they tried to brainwash us in those white schools . . . and I can't even describe the horror of the camps to you.

BONNIE.   Yes, I remember . . . I remember how they tried to turn all us Black children into white things in their schools . . .

HARRISON.   And they succeeded sometimes . . .

BONNIE.   Yes . . . yes . . . but don't push yourself too far now, brother.

CLEVELAND.   Go on, Harrison.

HARRISON.   I will, brother. Like I was sayin' . . . I was only a kid . . . like all of us who are old enough to remember when the revolution began for real back in the mid-sixties.

BONNIE (*murmurs*).   I was born in Watts, remember? I remember my mother holding me by the hand when I was a little girl while the city burned around us.

HARRISON.   And each summer the intensity of the revolution picked up.

CLEVELAND.   Yeah.

HARRISON.   And the power structure became frightened for they were fighting a foreign war in Vietnam then . . . and preparing for their war with China.

BONNIE.   Go on, brother, teach.

HARRISON.   And first there was the silencing of the artists, the Black artists . . .

SISSIE.   Brother LeRoi.

BONNIE.   Remember Malcolm, brother.

CLEVELAND.   Yes, remember.

HARRISON.   I won't abandon him.

BONNIE.   Thank you, brother.

HARRISON.   And then the leaders were systematically tracked down and . . . and . . .

CLEVELAND. *Exterminated* . . . exterminated by *beasts* as if they were beasts.

SISSIE. So terrible . . . so terrible . . . what they did to our people.

BONNIE. They were killed like Jews . . . like niggers in the Georgia night.

HARRISON. And after that came what the whiteman called martial law and community pacification.

BONNIE. Yes, we had to have passes to go from one neighborhood to another.

CLEVELAND. In the following years walls of electrified barbed wire were put up around every Black community in America.

SISSIE. Like pigs . . . like filthy . . . foul swine in pens . . . that's how those beasts tried to make us.

BONNIE. We in Harlem couldn't even go to the Bronx . . . or to Brooklyn . . .

SISSIE. My mother tells me that the bridges that go to the Bronx didn't have guards or gates . . .

BONNIE. . . . We couldn't visit our families and friends without official papers from the police.

HARRISON. Yeah . . . the military pacified the entire nation. Blacks were physically separated from whites by walls and fences.

CLEVELAND. American apartheid became official government policy soon after the burning of Washington and the razing of the White House.

(SISSIE *begins to softly chant a Moslem prayer. From the dark surrounding areas cries and groans come.*)

BONNIE. And the Black purges were instituted and the Black concentration camps were activated immediately after the assassination attempt upon the President.

(*Images upon the screen document the narration.*)

CLEVELAND. All the measures were legal and constitutional under the whiteman's law . . . the McCarran Act . . .

BONNIE. And the Presidential decrees.

HARRISON. And after each and every Black community came under federal military law Blackmen were placed over each community to govern it by whiteman's law.

BONNIE.   Yea, negroes were appointed to carry out the slavemaster's will. Negroes who are called prefects . . .

(SISSIE *appears to be in a semi-trance as she recites. Images upon the screen of various Hollywood negro comedians: Rochester, Stepin Fetchit, Man Tan Morland, Kingfish, Pig Meat Markham, Hattie McDaniels, etc.*)

BONNIE.   . . . negroes who are more white than the whitest whiteman, negroes who grind the blood, marrow and juices from the Black people to feed the vampire whiteman.

CLEVELAND.   Hell must be policed by Black prefects.

HARRISON.   The only hell we'll ever know is this one here on earth, brother. But our children will inherit the heaven that we build the foundations for now in our revolution against the whiteman.

BONNIE.   Teach, brother.

SISSIE (*moans, coming back*).   Prefects . . . Black killers of their own . . . evil . . . the most evil, the most unrighteous.

BONNIE.   Yes, sister, and Harlem has the most evil and unrighteous one . . . we have the *Grand* Prefect.

(*Lights down on group; up on* JACKSON, FOSTER *and the* GUARD. *Images on screen go off.*)

FOSTER (*chuckles*).   Well, I'll be goddamned. You young squirts don't know where to leave off, do you?

JACKSON.   No, I guess we don't.

FOSTER.   Yeah, it sho looks black for you, son. Ha ha ha . . .

JACKSON.   Black?

FOSTER.   Uumhmmm . . . very black.

JACKSON.   Oh . . . I see. Yeah, very black. But really white, wouldn't you say, brother?

FOSTER (*slowly perceiving*).   . . . Aha . . . aha . . . oh, yeah . . . Hey, you's quite a card, sonny . . . Ha ha . . . But why'd you have to go kill *him* for?

JACKSON.   But I had to do it. It had to be done.

FOSTER.   Oh . . . so you believe you got the right nigger after all. Why? What business does a fine young man like you have in gettin' hisself into a mess like this? Oh, yeah . . . now I know. It was over some bitch, huh? A black bitch, I bet.

JACKSON (*indignant*). A what?

FOSTER. You know ... a woman ... a black gal. A good-lookin' boy like you ... I can see it all now. She was his daughter, wasn't she? ... Or his niece ...

JACKSON. Sir, I am a Revolutionary! Our beautiful sisters shouldn't be spoken of ...

FOSTER. Shssss ... not so loud, boy.

JACKSON (*deliberately raising his voice*). I am a Black Revolutionary!

GUARD. And if I have to come in there ... you gonna be a quiet one.

JACKSON. Yes, sir.

FOSTER (*low*). What kinda bullshit is dat? What did you have to be that for ... whatever you just said you were? All you had to do was be cool, little sucker, and you would have had it made. The world is okay for you boys who got some education ... you could'a been an administrator ... or sumpten' ... in civil service ... with a good lifetime job.

JACKSON. An administrator? Work for the whiteman all my life? You mean be in the pay of the white power structure and help keep my own Black people imprisoned and enslaved ... No, never!

FOSTER. But you would have had it made, son.

JACKSON. No. Not me. It's made for *you*, old uncle. There are too many crimes against our people, too many submerged in poverty, starvation and ignorance caused by the whiteman. But when that day comes when there will be only a world by, for and of Blackmen, then my brother ...

FOSTER (*ridicule*). Save it, please.

JACKSON. If Black people were free you would not be here, old man.

FOSTER. Maybe so ... maybe not. But one thing's sure: whether free or no, you better always be able to hold your liquor. Even a slave should hold his liquor ... And I couldn't.

JACKSON. Yeah, that's right. But a man usually gets caught up in alcohol or drugs because he is oppressed. A day will come when there's no more point in getting drunk or being on the needle, when no Blackman will feel ashamed for being Black ... or being anything but what he is, a brother. We will all be brothers and freedom, justice and self-determination will make our souls glow. Do you know what I'm talking about, brother?

FOSTER.   Yeah, I think I know what you're talking about. (*Ridicule.*) You're talkin' about dreams.

JACKSON (*hurt*).   Brother . . . not dreams.

FOSTER.   Yeah. The Kingdom of God, they call it.

GUARD.   Shut your fucken mouths. I'm not gonna tell ya any more, ya hear?

JACKSON.   No, you're wrong, brother. God can't do anything to help; unless we recognize who God is. I follow Allah . . . the spirit and soul of the Black people. Freedom, justice and self-determination is *our* concern.

(*A short silence.*)

Don't you understand? Do you know that old Africa tale about the most high prince and the great spirit?

FOSTER.   Nawh . . . I don't know nothin' bout no Africans.

JACKSON.   The most highest and greatest prince of all Africa . . . this was before the European came to Africa . . . the prince had made an appointment to meet the great spirit . . . the greatest spirit of them all. When he was on his way to keep the appointment he came upon a great elephant who was stuck in a mudhole. And the great prince stopped to help the great elephant. The mud was deep and thick and the elephant's whole body was submerged, legs, tail and all, and it took the great prince, as great as he was, the better part of the day helping to get the elephant out. When this was done the great prince hurried to the meeting place. But it was too late. Allah had gone.

FOSTER.   And then what?

JACKSON.   What? . . . well there are those who always get there too late. Too many elephants in their path, too many brothers to help out of the mire.

(FOSTER *fidgets uneasily.*)

What's the matter?

GUARD.   That's the way I want it in there . . . quiet. And you, old man, stop bullshitting around. You've had time enough size him up.

FOSTER.   Somethin' ain't right. It ain't natural, all that stuff about African princes and spirits and elephants and whatnot. Sounds crazy to me, and you got yourself put in prison for stuff like that. And then, there's somethin' else.

JACKSON (*looks at him*).   Something else? What is it?

FOSTER.   Now what's done to people who kill prefects, grand or no?

JACKSON.   They're hanged.

FOSTER.   You've said it, not me.

(*He begins to move away. The* GUARD, *who has been grinning, moves closer and gives a loud guffaw.*)

JACKSON.   Stop! What have you got against me, brother?

FOSTER.   Nothin'. Only, fine young men like you are, well, I don't like to make a fool of you. It's okay talkin' like we've been doin' just to pass the time—but if you're goin' to be hung, and, no, it ain't right, it ain't playin' fair, as I see it.

JACKSON.   Why not?

GUARD (*laughs*).   C'mon, grandpa. Sock it to him.

FOSTER.   Because all this talk about you and me bein' brothers and all just won't wash, lil ole chump. I'm the hangman, ya see?

JACKSON.   Oh. I thought you were a prisoner, like me.

FOSTER.   Yeah, I am. But they've given me that job, and I get a year knocked off my sentence for every man I hang. It's gravy for nothin'.

JACKSON.   So, to atone for your crimes, they make you commit new ones?

FOSTER.   Ahhh . . . c'mon now . . . you can't call them crimes; I'm only carrying out mah orders. And, anyway, crimes or not, they don't care. If you want to know what I think . . . they ain't Christians.

JACKSON.   How many times have you hung a Blackman since you came here?

FOSTER.   Well, like I said . . . I came in thirty years ago with seventy-five years on me. That was before I could work off my time like I do now . . . that started about twelve years ago. But when I tie the knot on you, son, I'll only have five more to go. You a smart youngster . . . figure it out for yourself.

JACKSON.   Each man's life is worth a year to you.

FOSTER.   Actually, somebody's else's life ain't worth nothin' to me . . . I just am able to cash it in for a year's worth . . . ya understand?

(JACKSON *shrinks away from him. The* GUARD *guides* FOSTER *toward the door.*)

JACKSON. So you're the grim reaper? . . . An old *negro.*

FOSTER (*from the doorway*). And you, mister . . . who do you think you is? (FOSTER *goes out.*)

(*Lights change.*)

GUARD'S VOICE (*off*). STAND BY FOR DRILL! . . . READY ON DECK FOR DRILL! . . . THREE MINUTES 'TIL DRILL! . . . STAND BY!

(CLEVELAND *and* HARRISON *enter.*)

HARRISON (*fiercely*). I want to throw the bomb.

CLEVELAND. No, Harrison. It's already been decided.

HARRISON. Hey, man . . . don't pull those rules and codes of bombers on me . . . you know it's bullshit as well as me. L, I beg you to let me throw it — you know how much it means to me.

CLEVELAND. No. We have our orders.

(*Pause.*)

I'm in the same shoes as you; I have to stay here while others are on the firing line. It's tough, but discipline must be maintained.

HARRISON. Who's gonna throw the first bomb?

JACKSON. I am. And Burk's gonna throw the second.

HARRISON. You?

JACKSON. Why d'ya sound like that? What's the matter . . . don't you trust me?

HARRISON. Experience is needed.

JACKSON. Experience? Hey, what kinda jive is that? . . . After you throw a bomb, baby, that's it . . . No one has ever had a second chance. It's not like if we had a time fuse or could use a high-powered rifle. That's why we bomber units in the Black Revolutionary Organization are listed as "Suicide Squads" and are composed of only true revolutionaries. It's . . .

HARRISON. A steady hand is needed.

JACKSON (*stretches out a hand*). Look! Does that look like it's shaking?

(HARRISON *looks away.*)

Steady as she goes. Don't you get shook, brother? When the time comes . . . it's goin'a be all over 'cept for the shoutin'. But do you think I'd cop out, if I had that mathafukker in front of me? Nawh, an' I ain't goin'a go fo that. And even if for some reason my arm might start shakin', I'd know a sure way of killin' the Grand Prefect.

CLEVELAND. What way?

JACKSON. I'd jump out in front of his car and we'd all go up. BOOOMMM!!! Just like that!

(HARRISON *paces about the cell.*)

CLEVELAND. No, man, that's not on the program. Your orders are to try to get away. The group needs you, and you must save your life, if you can.

JACKSON. Well . . . if that's how it goes down. I realize my great responsibility, brother. And I'm honored by it. I also promise to be worthy of it.

CLEVELAND. You, Harrison, will be in the street while Jack and Ken are waiting for the Grand Prefect's car. I want you to stroll up and down in front of our windows; we'll decide on the signal you're to give. Bonnie and I will wait here, ready to launch our manifesto when the moment comes. With luck we'll do the Grand Prefect in.

JACKSON (*excitedly*). Yeah, I'll do him in. And how good that will be if it comes off. But, he's really nothing, the Grand Prefect. We must strike higher.

CLEVELAND. The Grand Prefect to begin with. We have to get the whiteman's stooges first. We must cleanse our communities.

JACKSON. And what if we fail? Then, L, we must act like the Japanese.

CLEVELAND. Like the Japanese? What do you mean?

JACKSON. During the war the Japanese never surrendered. They killed themselves.

CLEVELAND. No. Jack, don't think of suicide. Even though we're classified as a high risk suicide unit . . . suicide is against the Black Revolutionary Codes. We must live, if we can, so that we can fight for the liberation of Black people.

JACKSON. But the reason I volunteered for this unit is because it is an absolute unit. There's no turning back here . . . we are absolute revolutionaries . . . and our commitment is based upon death.

CLEVELAND. Yeah . . . perhaps . . . yeah . . . but you shouldn't think of suicide.

JACKSON. What should I think of, then?

CLEVELAND. Of carrying on our work, of terrorism.

HARRISON (*from behind* JACKSON). To commit suicide a man must have a great love for himself. A true Black Revolutionary cannot love himself. His life is the Black people's.

JACKSON (*swings around*). A true Black Revolutionary? Why are you fucking with me like this? What have you got against me?

HARRISON. I don't like niggers who fuck around with revolution because they're bored.

CLEVELAND. Harrison!

HARRISON (*rises to his feet and faces them*). Yeah, it's hard and brutal. And I'm brutal. But for me hatred is not just a game. We haven't joined together to admire each other. But to bring our people freedom, justice and self-determination. We have joined together *to get something done*. To get something done for Black people . . . *by any means necessary.*

(*A shrill, piercing police whistle shrieks. Lights change.*)

GUARD'S VOICE (*coming nearer*). FALL IN FOR DRILL! . . . THAT MEANS PRONTO, GODDAMMIT! . . . FALL IN FOR DRILL!

(BURK, BONNIE *and* SISSIE *enter. The* REVOLUTIONARIES *line up, one behind the other,* BONNIE *at the front,* SISSIE *behind her, the* MEN *behind them with* MURRAY JACKSON *at the rear of the line. Behind* BONNIE, *each marcher has his right hand upon the right shoulder of the one in front; and they march back and forth across the stage in close lockstep. The* GUARD *enters blowing his whistle. The screens light up and show scenes of firing squads, electric chairs, gallows, gas chambers, guillotines, funerals, morgues, mass starvation, etc.*)

GUARD. KEEP IN STEP, YA CLUMSY BASTARDS! . . . PICK 'EM UP 'N PUT 'EM DOWN! . . . SOUND OFF . . . 'N BRING IT ON DOWN FRONT! . . . I SAID DOWN FRONT!

BONNIE. BONNIE MAE BROWN, SIR! . . . DOWN FRONT!

GUARD. YA HARE ME! . . . I SAID DOWN FRONT!

Sissie. SISSIE ANN WILLIAMS, SIR! . . . DOWN FRONT!

Guard. RIGHT! . . . THAT'S THE WAY! . . . NOW DOWN FRONT LIKE I SAID . . . DOWN FRONT!

Cleveland. ELTON "L" CLEVELAND, SIR! . . . DOWN FRONT!

Guard. 'N AGAIN!

Harrison. HARRISON BANES, SIR! . . . DOWN FRONT!

Guard. LIKE I SAID!

Burk. KENNETH BURK, SIR! . . . DOWN FRONT!

Guard. SHO 'NUF!

Jackson. MURRAY JACKSON, SIR! . . . DOWN FRONT!

Guard. 'NUF SAID! . . . DOWN FRONT!

The Revolutionaries (*together*). DOWN FRONT!

Guard. WHAT CHOU SAY!

Revolutionaries. DOWN FRONT!

Guard. AGAIN!

Revolutionaries. DOWN FRONT!

Guard. SING FOR YOUR SUPPER . . . NIGGERS!

Revolutionaries. DOWN FRONT, SIR! DOWN FRONT, SIR! DOWN FRONT, SIR!

Guard. WELL . . . ALL RITE DEN! . . . NOW GIT WIT' IT 'N DON'T MISS A BEAT!

(Guard *marches them off, blowing whistle. Lights go down. Images brighten upon screens to show a few last stark realities of late 20th century America, then stage goes black.*)

Act II

(*In the dark there are sounds: footsteps, words of command, clanging prison doors and the hum of high voltage electric wires and the whirr of well-oiled motors. Lights up showing* Sissie *downstage, center, in a spot.* Murray Jackson *sits in his cell, unaware of* Sissie.)

SISSIE (*out front*).   I'm sorry . . . I'm sorry, brothers and sisters . . .
Oh, please forgive me. Allah will bless you if you have pity on
one of his humblest children.

But it was the eyes . . . the electric eyes . . . I could feel them
on me as I stood on look-out. All the time I could feel them . . .
look at me . . . through me . . . as if I didn't have no clothes on.
They could see through my disguise . . . could see my skin, brothers and sisters.

And when the car came up and nothin' happen . . . no explosion . . . no screams or fighting . . . I knew the electric things had
gotten them . . . and would get me . . . so I ran. I ran. I deserted
under fire . . . and ran and ran . . . I found myself on 129th Street
close to where I was born . . . near Park Avenue . . . and I ran.
Ran more. Tried to run off into the river, brothers and sisters.
Tried to jump in the Harlem River and drown . . . But I couldn't
. . . I couldn't . . . there was barbed wire in front of me . . . and
it stretched north and south as far as I could see. And it was so
quiet. No cars down the streets or the East Side Highway or on
Harlem River Drive . . . no trains running overhead on the Park
Avenue elevated . . . no boats or tugs in the river . . . Just the
steady electric hum of the barbed wire that would kill me if I
touched it. And I was a deserter . . . and I wanted to throw
myself on the wire . . . but I couldn't. I couldn't. So I came here
so that you could give me the punishment I deserve . . . Please
execute me . . . give me the coward's death I deserve, Black people. (*Crying.*) Please help me . . . help me, please . . . execute
me . . . now. I can't stand this condition of living death dragging
on into each morning. I have failed my brothers and sisters . . .
and I am unworthy and unrighteous in the sight of myself and
my god, Allah, the righteous Black Spirit of our people.

(*Light off* SISSIE. *A noise.* JACKSON *is alert.* SMITH *enters, followed
by the* GUARD. SMITH *is spick and span.*)

SMITH (*to the* GUARD).   You can go.

(GUARD *exits.*)

(*To* JACKSON.) Good morning, or evening . . . or whatever it
may be. You don't know me . . . now, do you? But I know you.
(*Laughs.*) Quite a celebrity, aren't you? May I introduce myself?

(JACKSON *remains silent.*)

Oh, you don't feel like talking—yes, I understand. That's the
effect of solitary confinement: seven days and nights. It gets

you down, doesn't it? Your mind tends to wander sometimes, right? You may even feel that you're hallucinating ... hummm? But that's all right as long as you're not hurting yourself ... Ha ha ... We've sorta fixed it so that you won't be hurting anyone else ... *physically* ... Well, your days of being entirely alone except for our gracious representative, the guard, are over. That's all over now. From now on you can have visitors. Your friends, perhaps? ... We'd love to accommodate them ... ha ha ... And, of course, the press. The press especially. They are actually slavering to get at our young blood splattered Black Revolutionary ... And in fact, you've had a visitor already—that old gentleman, Foster. He's kinda weird, isn't he? I thought that he might interest you ... He's a very old acquaintance of mine. Yes, indeed, he is. But you must be happy over the change; it's good to see a human face again after a week's solitary confinement, right?

JACKSON.   That depends on the face.

SMITH.   Ah, that's good. If you're worrying about Foster's face ... well, it won't be around here for long.

JACKSON.   That's right ... five more after me ... then he gets out.

SMITH.   Gets out? ... Oh, ha ha ha ... Of course, he told you that he'd be getting out ... But he doesn't know what we know. You see, we know that he'll be our new executioner's first client.

JACKSON.   But I thought ...

SMITH.   So does he ... but, alas, his old head carries too many secrets ... knowledge is dangerous, you know.

JACKSON (*violently*).   You people are more evil than my wildest imaginings could fathom! ...

SMITH (*mimics*).   "You people are more evil than my wildest imaginings could fathom! ..." (*Relaxed.*) Ha ha ha ... your language is so quaint ... so gauche ... give some more samples ... won't you, please?

JACKSON.   You'll get nothin' from me but contempt!

SMITH.   Splendid! ... Ha ha ha ... I see you know your own mind, my young friend. (*A short silence.*) So, unless I'm a fool, my face displeases you too?

JACKSON.   Yes.

SMITH.   That's too bad. Sorry about that, my young friend ... ha ha ... sorry about that. Still, I have hopes that you may change your mind. For one thing, the light here is poor; these basement cells make everything smell and look like shit . . . excuse the expression, but that is the reality we are confronted by. And then, too, you don't know me, do you? Sometimes a man's face puts one off at first, later, when one gets to know the man himself . . .

JACKSON. THAT'S ENOUGH! Who are you?

SMITH (*snaps to attention*). Smith here! . . . Chief of Security.

VOICE OVER LOUDSPEAKER. ATTENTION ON DECK! . . . ATTENTION! . . . STANDBY FOR INSPECTION!

SMITH. Yes, my young friend, it's me . . . ha ha . . . just ole Brother Smith.

LOUDSPEAKER. STANDBY FOR SMITH! . . . FOR (*Echo chamber effect.*) SMITHSMITHSMITHSMITHSMITHSMITH-SMITH . . .

JACKSON. A Blackman . . . Chief of Security . . . the secret police?

(*Lights change;* CLEVELAND *and* BURK *enter the cell.*)

CLEVELAND. There's no such place for any of us where peace waits except death. All our paths lead to the same end: the concentration camp, the prison cell, the gallows.

BURK. Yeah, but you don't see the secret police as you see the man you have to kill. You gotta imagine them. And, lucky for me, I have no imagination where that's concerned. (*Brief, nervous laugh.*) Do you know, I've never really believed in the secret police? Absurd, isn't it, for a terrorist? I'll believe they exist only when I get my first kick in the stomach. Not before.

CLEVELAND. And when you're in prison? In prison you can't help knowing, and seeing. There's no more shutting your eyes to the facts.

BURK. In prison you have no more decisions to make. What a relief to feel that everything's decided for you. You ain't got to tell yourself: "Now it's up to you, you must decide on the moment when to strike." One thing I'm sure of now is that I won't try and escape; for escaping, too, you got to make decisions, you got to take the lead. If you don't try to escape, the others keep the initiative—they do all the work.

CLEVELAND. Sometimes the work they do is—hanging you, brother.

(*Lights change;* CLEVELAND *and* BURK *withdraw into the shadows.*)

SMITH (*to* JACKSON). Black people need security as well as whites . . . wouldn't you say, my young man? Ha ha ha . . .

JACKSON. You know what you can do with "my young man." In other words you're saying that you're a flunky. A flunky murderer for the whiteman.

SMITH. My . . . my . . . your language just isn't inspiring. But have it your own way. Still, if I were in your position, I wouldn't be so cocky. You haven't been tortured, you know . . . not yet, anyway. But maybe you'll learn your lesson before too long. You know . . . one begins by wanting justice—and one ends by setting up a security force . . . secret police, in this case . . . to restore and protect justice, of course . . . and guarantee law and order, naturally. Anyhow, I'm not backing away from the truth, and let me talk to you very frankly, young man. Oh, you don't like that, do you? Let me say, brother, then.

JACKSON. Brother? From you?

SMITH. Let's not examine labels, shall we? Or get hung up in semantics. You interest me. I'd like to help you get off.

JACKSON. What do you mean?

SMITH. Certainly, it's obvious. I can get you a pardon. I am bringing you a chance for your life.

JACKSON. Who asked you for it?

SMITH. One doesn't ask for life, my friend. One's given it. Have *you* never let anybody off?

(*A short silence.*)

Think hard.

(*Lights change.* BONNIE *and* CLEVELAND *enter.*)

JACKSON (*anguish*). Brothers . . . forgive me . . . I couldn't do it . . .

(BONNIE *goes to him and clasps his hand.*)

BONNIE (*soothing*). That's all right. Don't worry . . .

CLEVELAND. What happened?

BONNIE (*to* JACKSON). Don't take it so hard, Jack. Sometimes it's like that, you know; at the last minute everything goes wrong.

CLEVELAND. No, I can't believe my ears.

BONNIE. Leave him alone. You're not the only one, Jack. Some of our old brothers couldn't bring it off the first time.

CLEVELAND. Jack, were you . . . afraid?

JACKSON (*indignant*). Afraid? Certainly not—and you haven't the right . . .

(HARRISON *enters.*)

CLEVELAND. THEN WHAT THE HELL DO I HAVE RIGHT TO?

JACKSON (*pleads*). There were children in the Grand Prefect's car.

HARRISON. Yeah, the Grand Prefect's niece and nephew.

CLEVELAND. But our spies told us that the Grand Prefect would be by himself.

HARRISON. There was the Grand Prefect's old lady too. Too many people, I guess, for our young poet. Good thing the police spies didn't notice anything.

(*All stare at* JACKSON *and back out of the lights, except for* SMITH *who remains.*)

JACKSON (*to* SMITH). Well, I don't want your pardon, and that's an end to it.

SMITH. Anyhow, please hear what I have to say. Appearances notwithstanding, I am not your enemy. I won't even say that your ideas are wrong. Except when they lead to murder.

JACKSON. I forbid you to use that word.

SMITH. Ah, your nerves are out of order, that's the trouble? (*Pauses.*) Quite honestly, I want to help you.

JACKSON. Help me?

SMITH. Yes. The Grand Prefect and I . . . how should I say it . . . we weren't exactly buddy buddy, you know?

JACKSON. Leave me alone. I'm ready to pay the price of what I've done. But I refuse to tolerate this familiarity on your part. Leave me in peace.

SMITH. The accusation you have to face . . .

JACKSON. That's wrong.

SMITH. I beg your pardon?

JACKSON. Accusation is not the word. I am a prisoner of war, not an accused person.

SMITH. Put it that way, if you prefer. Still, there's been damage done, you must admit. Let's leave politics out of it and look at the human side. A man has been killed—and killed in a particularly horrible way.

JACKSON. I threw the bomb at your tyranny, not at a man.

SMITH. Perhaps, but a man got in the way. It was a living Black human being that your bomb blew to bits. And being the Blackman's policeman I'm concerned about crimes perpetrated against Blacks by Blacks . . .

JACKSON. And what of crimes of whitemen against your Black brothers?

SMITH. Let's not change the subject just now, please . . . It wasn't a pretty sight, let me tell you, my young friend. When they had pieced the body together, the head was missing. Completely disappeared. And as for the rest, an arm and a bit of leg were all that escaped undamaged.

JACKSON. I carried out a verdict.

SMITH. Maybe you did. Nobody blames you for the verdict, son. What's in a verdict, as the saying goes. It's just a word that's all . . . and we don't want to hassle about words, do we? What you're accused of—sorry, I know you don't like that word— is, let's say, a sort of amateurishness, doing a messy job, in fact. The results, anyhow, were plain enough to see; there's no disputing *them*. Ask the Grand Madame Prefect. There was blood, you know, a lot of blood.

JACKSON. Shut up, damn you!

SMITH. Very well. All I want to say is that if you persist in talking about a "verdict" and asserting that it was the organization, and the organization alone that tried and executed the victim— that, in short, the Grand Prefect was killed not by a bomb but by an idea—well, in that case, you don't need a pardon. Say, suppose, however, we get down to brass tacks; suppose we say that it was you, Murray Jackson, who blew the Grand Prefect's head to bits—that puts a rather different complexion on the matter, doesn't it? Then undoubtedly you stand in need of pardon. And that's where I can be of aid, out of pure Black fellow feeling, I assure you. (*Smiles.*) That's how I'm built; I am not interested in ideas, I'm interested in human beings.

JACKSON (*furiously*). But, damn it, I don't recognize your right or the right of your masters to sit in judgment of me. You can kill me if you think fit, and that is the only right you have over my person. Oh, I can see what you're leading up to. You are trying to find a chink in my armor, you are hoping to make me feel ashamed of myself, burst into tears, repent of what you call my crime. Well, you won't get anywhere; what I am is no concern of yours. What concerns me is our hatred, mine and my brothers'. And you are welcome to it.

SMITH. That, too, is an idea, or rather, an obsession, young man.

JACKSON. Do you have to talk like that?

SMITH. But murder isn't just an idea; it is something that takes place. And, obviously, so do its consequences. Which are repentance for the crime, and punishment. Now we get down to the heart of the matter, and that in fact is why I joined the secret police. I like being at the heart of things. But you don't want to hear me talking about myself . . . (*Pauses. Then moves slowly toward* JACKSON.) All I wish to say is that you should not forget, or profess to forget, the Grand Prefect's head. If you took it into account, you would find that mere ideas lead nowhere. For instance, instead of feeling pleased with yourself, you'd be ashamed of what you did. And, when once you felt ashamed, you would want to live, in order to atone. So the great thing is that you decide to live.

JACKSON. And suppose I decided to live, what then?

SMITH. A pardon for you and for your brothers . . . and the two sisters.

JACKSON. I don't know what you're talking about.

SMITH. Yes . . . of course we know . . . we have recorded your group's every breath for months.

(*Lights change.*)

SISSIE (*from the shadows*). I can feel them . . . I can feel the machines watching and listening to us.

BONNIE (*in shadows*). Oh . . . stop scarin' yourself, sister. That electronic equipment of his can't reach us . . . nor stop us . . . You know that. We're too far away . . . That's why we work, live and are in the center of our people . . . so we can be more effective in reaching Black people and have protection from the beast.

SISSIE (*walks forward into light*). But it was the eyes . . . the electric eyes, brothers and sisters.

(*The screens show images of the areas surrounding the theater, and the local Black community: the people upon the streets, in bars, in barber shops, attending meetings, of well-known local figures photographed unsuspectedly, etc.*)

SISSIE. I could feel the eyes on me. All the time I feel them look at me . . . through me . . . as if I don't have no clothes on. They can see me . . . *see me* . . . and I am discovered.

(*Images out.* SISSIE *moves off. Lights change.*)

JACKSON. But why didn't you . . .

SMITH. Stop you? Ha ha ha . . . stop you from what?

JACKSON. The execution . . . the bomb . . . I . . .

SMITH. How could I pardon you . . . if you had committed no crime. Ha ha ha . . . Besides . . . have you ever really looked at the Grand Prefect? . . . I mean from up close . . . say, as close as I stand to you?

(JACKSON *peers at* SMITH, *then backs away.*)

JACKSON. But it can't be.

SMITH. But it is . . . ha ha . . . saves the Black taxpayers money, doesn't it? Getting a Grand Prefect and a Chief of Security in one head.

JACKSON. But . . . but . . .
(*Successive images of* SMITH's *face appear upon the screens showing varied expressions — wearing different official headgear — policeman's cap, government official's homburg, and bareheaded with changing eye glasses and without them.*)

SMITH. The poor chap you murdered? . . . Oh, well, just another double . . . some ignorant actor that took pleasure in dressing up as me . . . ha ha ha . . . Those sweet little Black children were doubles too. Their parents were able to afford a second car and live in New Jersey from the money they make by hiring their babies out . . . ha ha ha . . . very shrewd people. They know that not even one of those *dreadful* Black Revolutionaries would even touch a kink of their little pickaninnies' naps . . . Ha ha ha . . .

(JACKSON, *hands over ears, rushes from the cell area and staggers before the screen images of* SMITH, *like an insect defying a candle's flame. Lights change. Images fade. Shapes move out of the shadows. The* REVOLUTIONARIES, *except for* SISSIE, *surround* JACKSON. *All are gazing at him, who now looks up and fixes his eyes on* HARRISON.)

JACKSON (*wildly*).   I'd never imagined anything like that. Children, children especially. Have you ever noticed children's eyes— that grave, intent look they often have? Somehow I never can face it. I have to look away . . . And, to think, only a moment before I was so extremely happy, standing at the corner of that little street, in a patch of shadow. The moment I saw the car's lights winking in the distance, my heart began to race. With joy, I can assure you. And as the hum of the motor came nearer, my heart beat faster and faster. Drumming inside of me like a drum. I wanted to leap into the air. I was also laughing and crying . . . laughing and crying with joy. And I kept on saying: "Yes . . . yes . . ." Don't you understand? (*Averting his gaze from* HARRISON, *he relapses into his dejected attitude.*) I ran forward. The car almost stopped to make its turn in the narrow street. And then I saw them from the light of the streetlamp. I saw the children. They weren't laughing, not them. Just staring into emptiness, and holding themselves very straight. They looked so sad and wise. Dressed in their Sunday go meetin' best, with their hands resting on their legs, like two little Afri- can statues framed in the windows on each side of the door. I didn't see the Grand Prefect or his woman, only them. I saw only them. If they had turned my way, I think I might have thrown the bomb—if only to put out that sad look of theirs. But they kept staring straight ahead. (*Raising his head, he looks at the others. Silence. Then, in a still lower voice.*) I can't explain what happened to me then. My arms went limp. My legs seemed to be giving way beneath me. And, a moment afterwards, it was too late. (*Another silence; he is staring at the floor.*) Bonnie, was I dreaming, or was there bells ringing then?

BONNIE.   No, brother, you didn't dream it.

(*She lays her hand on his arm.* JACKSON *looks up and sees their eyes intent on him.*)

JACKSON.   Yeah, look at me, brothers, look at me . . . But I'm no coward, L, I didn't flinch. Only I wasn't expecting them. And everything went too fast. Those two serious little black faces, and in my hand that thing of death. I'd have had to throw it at the *children*. Like that. Straight at them. No, I just couldn't bring myself to destroy black children . . . (*He scans their faces.*) In the old days when I used to go out driving on the freeway outside our town in California, I always drove like hell.

I had a Jaguar then. I wasn't afraid of shit, man, nothin' except for running over a kid—that was my only fear. I . . . I could imagine a dull thump as my fender smashed a small head, and the thought of it sent shivers all over me. (*He is silent for some moments.*) Help me, brothers . . . (*Another silence.*) I wanted to kill myself just now. I came back only because I felt it was my duty; you are the only people who can judge me. I have to know whether I am right or wrong, and suffer the sentencing that you hand down. So here I am—say something, please.

(BONNIE *moves beside him, her hand brushing his shoulder. He looks round, then continues in a toneless voice.*)

This is what I mean. If you decide that those children—those Black children—must be killed, I will go to the theater where the Grand Prefect is sitting this very minute, The New Lafayette Theatre, and wait till they are coming out. Then I will take care of the situation by myself, without help; I'll throw the bomb and I can swear to you that I won't miss. So make your choice; I'll do whatever the group wants.

HARRISON. The group gave you orders to kill the Grand Prefect.

JACKSON. That's right. But I wasn't told to murder children.

CLEVELAND. Jack's right. That wasn't on the program.

HARRISON. His only duty was to obey his orders.

CLEVELAND. I'm in charge of operations and I'm to blame. I should have anticipated every unforeseen possibility so that everyone would know how to jump without the least hesitation. Well, we gotta decide whether we let this chance slip by, or tell Jack to wait outside the New Lafayette for them to come out. You, Ken, what do you think?

BURK. I don't know what to think. I guess I'd have done the same thing that Jack did. But I'm not that sure . . . my hands . . . I can't trust them always not to shake.

CLEVELAND. Bonnie? How about you?

BONNIE (*emphatically*). I'd done the same as Jack! I couldn't blow to bits young life that could have sprung from me.

BURK. What of the Grand Prefect and his woman . . . they were once children?

BONNIE. Don't confuse things, Brother Ken.

HARRISON.   I wonder if you folks understand what this means? Two hard months gone. Two months of shadowing, of barely escaping with our asses—two wasted months! Ahmed busted for no purpose. Chaka hanged for what? And we have to start all over again, do we? Weeks and weeks of terror without a break; of nights with no sleep, of plotting and scheming, before the day that that opportunity gives us the signal on our door. Have you all gone mad?

CLEVELAND.   You know he'll be goin' to the theatre in two more days.

HARRISON.   Two days in which we might get caught at any moment. I know that well as I know anything.

JACKSON (*starting to go*). Well, that's that.

BONNIE.   No, wait, brother. (*To* HARRISON.) You, Harrison, could you fire point blank on a Black child? I don't have to ask you about a white one. But a Black child. With your eyes open?

HARRISON.   I could, if it was ordered by the group.

BONNIE.   You just shut your eyes now, why?

HARRISON.   Huh? Did I shut my eyes?

BONNIE.   Yeah, you shut them, brother.

HARRISON.   Well, I know why . . . it was to picture . . . picture my answer so that I could make no mistake. I wanted only the true picture, sister.

BONNIE.   Open your eyes, brother, and try and realize that the group would be torn apart if we allowed this to happen, even by accident. Open your eyes to the picture of innocent Black babies blown apart by *our* righteous bombs.

HARRISON.   Sorry, but I don't have your tender heart; that kind of shit cuts no ice with *me* . . . Not until the day comes when we stop sentimentalizing about children will the revolution triumph. Yeah, they're Black kids, but they are on the other side. On the side of the whiteman.

BONNIE.   Children have no side, fool! They are born into what they are born into. When they are men then they may choose what side . . .

HARRISON.   We will be masters of the earth, even if we must destroy children, sister.

BONNIE. When the day comes when Black people see you destroy their children, the revolution will be hated by all Black people. As brother Mao said: "To treat a brother as an enemy is to go on the side of the enemy," brother. And to slaughter innocent Black children is to become the butchering whiteman.

HARRISON. If we love Black people enough to force our revolution on them, then we rescue Black people from themselves and from their enslavement.

BONNIE. And what if the Black people at large don't want the revolution? Suppose our people for whom you are fighting won't stand for the killing of their children, however wrong or lazy or Uncle Tomish they are. All Black people recognize Black children, whatever their father's allegiances. What then if they include you among the Mississippi sheriffs, and the Alabama highway patrol and the white citizens councils of America? What if they held your power of terror in awe second only to the Grand Prefect's himself, or, of course, his successor. What then, my brave Black brother? Would you turn on the Black people themselves then?

HARRISON. YES! If necessary. I would strike and strike and strike. And I would go on striking until they understood . . . Now, don't misunderstand me; I, too, love our people. But . . .

BONNIE. Love? You call that love? That's not how love shows itself.

HARRISON. WHO SAYS SO?

BONNIE. I say so.

HARRISON. You're a woman, and your idea of love is . . . well, let's say, unscientific.

BONNIE (*passionately*). In spite of what you think, brother, I have a very good idea of what shame means.

HARRISON. Only one time. Really, only one single time did I feel ashamed of myself. It was when I was beaten with the cat-o'-nine-tails in the concentration camp.

JACKSON. You were beaten?

HARRISON. Yeah, I was whipped. The cat—you know what that is, don't you? Reba . . . she was my soulmate . . . she was there beside me . . . even throwing herself in the way . . . her tears mixing with my blood as she supported me so I wouldn't fall at the whiteman's feet. She killed herself, as a protest. And the camp blew up in a revolt and more Blackmen died that day. But I . . . in spite of everything, I lived. So why should I be ashamed of anything, now?

CLEVELAND.   Harrison, all of us love and respect you, brother. But whatever private reasons you may have for feeling as you do, I can't allow you to say that everything's permitted. Thousands of our brothers have died to prove that everything is *not* permitted.

HARRISON.   Nothing that can serve our cause should be ruled out.

CLEVELAND (*angrily*).   Is it permitted for one of us to join the police and play a double game, as Ennis suggested doing? Would *you* do it?

HARRISON.   Yeah, if I felt it was necessary.

CLEVELAND.   Harrison, we will forget what you've just said, for the sake of all that you have done for us and with us . . . Now, let's keep to the matter at hand. The question is whether, presently, we are to throw bombs at those two children.

HARRISON.   Children! There you go again, always talking about children. Can't you realize what is at stake? Just because Jack couldn't bring himself to kill those two, thousands of Black children from the masses will go on dying of starvation for years to come. Have you ever seen children dying of starvation? I have. And to be killed by a bomb is a pleasant death compared with that. But Jack never saw children starving to death. He saw only the Grand Prefect's pair of innocent little puppies. What can you be thinking of? Not the future? Only of now? In that case then deal in charity and cure each petty suffering that meets your eye; but don't fuck around with the revolution, for its task is to cure *all* sufferings . . . present and to come.

BONNIE.   Jack's ready to kill the Grand Prefect because his death may help to bring nearer the time when Black children will no longer die of hunger. That in itself is none too easy for him. But the death of the Grand Prefect's niece and nephew won't prevent any child from dying of hunger. Even in destruction there's a right way and a wrong way—and there are limits.

HARRISON (*vehemently*).   There are no limits! The truth is that you don't believe in the revolution, any of you.

(*All, except* JACKSON, *react to this and surround* HARRISON.)

No, you don't believe in it. If you did believe in it sincerely, with all your hearts; if you felt sure that, by dint of our struggles and sacrifices, some day we shall build up a new Black nation, torn from the body of the whiteman that has consumed so much of our blood, a land of freedom, justice and self-determination that will spread out over the whole earth; and if you felt convinced that then and only then, freed from the whiteman and the slave's mind and religion, Blackmen will at last look up toward the heavens, a god in his own land—how, I ask you, could the deaths of two children be weighed in the balance against such a faith? Surely you would claim for yourselves the right to do anything and everything that might bring that great day nearer! So now, if you draw the line at killing these two children, well, it simply means you are not sure you have that right. So, I repeat, you do *not* believe in the revolution.

(*There is a short silence.* JACKSON, *too joins them.*)

JACKSON. Harrison, I am ashamed of myself—yet I can't let you go on. I am ready to shed blood, so as to overthrow the whiteman. But, behind your words, I see the threat of another sort of oppression which, if ever it comes into power, will make of me a murderer—and what I want to be is a righteous Blackman, not a man of blood.

HARRISON. Provided justice, freedom and self-determination are achieved—even if it's achieved by assassins—what does it matter which you are, brother? You and I mean nothing to the total.

JACKSON. We are more than nothing, brother. If we are nothing then what are we killing for? If we are nothing then we should lie still like a filthy pig and allow the whiteman to continue standing upon our heads. For you it's pride, just pride, that makes you talk as you are talking now.

HARRISON. My pride is my business. But Blackmen's pride, their rebellion, the injustice that is done them—these are the concern of all of us.

JACKSON. Blackmen do not live by freedom, justice and self-determination alone. We have survived this alien place for five hundred years.

HARRISON. When their bread and freedom are stolen, what else have they to live by, brother?

JACKSON.   By justice, and, don't forget, by innocence.

HARRISON.   Innocence? Yeah, maybe I know what that means. But I prefer to think that no Black man is innocent anymore . . . at least not to the facts of the white beast. But I prefer to shut my eyes to innocence—and to shut others' eyes to it, for the time being—so that one day it may have a Third World meaning.

JACKSON.   Well, you must feel very sure that day is coming if you repudiate everything that makes life worth living today, on its account.

HARRISON.   I am certain that that day is coming.

JACKSON.   No, you can't be as sure as that . . . Before it can be known which of us, you or me, is right, perhaps three generations will have to be sacrificed; there will have been more bloody wars, and no less bloody revolutions. And by the time that all this blood has dried off the earth, you and I will long since have turned to dust.

HARRISON.   Then others will come—other Blackmen—and I salute them as my brothers.

JACKSON (*excitedly*).   Others, you say! Other Blackmen. Well, you might be very right, brother. But those *I* love are the men who are alive today, and walk this same earth. It's they whom I salute, it is for them I am fighting and dying, yes, for them I am ready to lay down my life. But I shall not strike my brothers in the face for the sake of some far-off city, which, for all I know, may not exist. I refuse to add to the living injustice of the whiteman . . . that he has spread all around me, in the hearts of some so-called Black Revolutionaries, just for the sake of a dead justice. (*In a lower, but firmer voice.*) Brothers, I want to speak to you quite frankly and to tell you something that any brother out on the corner would say if you asked him his opinion. Killing children is a crime against a man's honor. The spirit of the race would rebel and move against the hand that destroyed its children, as it is doing to the whiteman now. And if one day the Black Revolution thinks to break with honor, well, I'm through with the Black Revolution. Remember what brother Jones said: "We are preaching a new virtue . . . ethics and aesthetics are one." Yes, brothers, a new virtue . . . a new ethic . . . a new Black morality, understand? If you decide that I must do it, well and good; I will go to the New Lafayette Theatre when they're due to come out—but I'll throw myself under the car wheels.

HARRISON. You fool! You fool! Honor is a luxury reserved for people who have limousines and chauffeurs.

JACKSON. No. It's the one wealth left to a poor Black man. You know it, and you also know that the revolution has its code of honor.

HARRISON. Honor to the whiteman?

JACKSON. No. It's far more involved than just with the whiteman. We should stop harping on the whiteman. He is not our reason for existing, is he? You know it, and you also know that the Black Revolution has its code of honor that it uses in regards to Black people. It's what we all are ready to die for. It's what made you hold your head up, Harrison, when they beat you; it's what made your woman, your Black woman, embrace you and lift you up so you would not fall at the whiteman's feet. And it's behind what you have been saying to us today.

HARRISON (*shrilly*). Shut up! Don't you ever speak of that again, understand?

JACKSON (*angrily*). Why must I keep quiet?

HARRISON. If you ever mention Reba again ... I'll break your back.

CLEVELAND. Enough of this.

JACKSON. I took it lying down when you said I didn't believe in the revolution. Which was as good as telling me that I was ready to kill the Grand Prefect for nothing; that I was a common killer. I let you say that—and somehow I kept my hands off you—and now you talk of breaking *my* back!

CLEVELAND. Jack!

HARRISON. It's killing for nothing, sometimes, not to kill enough.

CLEVELAND. Harrison, none of us here agree with you. And we have made our decision.

HARRISON. Then I submit to the will of the group. But, let me tell you once again that there is no place in work like ours for chicken heartedness. No bullshit about it. We're killers, plain and simple, and we've chosen to be killers . . . Special killers . . . bombers! . . .

CLEVELAND. That's a lie. We are not murderers!

HARRISON.   Not only do we murder . . . but our special way maims the flesh and shatters the senses . . . Think of it: gouged out eye sockets . . . exploded ear drums . . . limbs shredded from the body . . . WE ARE KILLERS, BROTHERS!

JACKSON (*screams, loses all self-control*). Stop the lies! I have chosen death so as to prevent murder from triumphing in the world. I've chosen to be innocent, to be righteous!

CLEVELAND.   Jack! Harrison! That's all. The group has decided that the slaughter of these children would serve no purpose. We must start again from the beginning, and be ready for another try at it in two days from now.

HARRISON.   And what if the children are with him again?

JACKSON.   Then we will wait for another chance.

HARRISON.   And supposing the Grand Prefect is with his woman?

JACKSON.   *Her* . . . I will not spare.

(*Lights change, then down. And up again showing* JACKSON *in his cell with* SMITH.)

Her . . . I will not spare. *I will not spare.*

SMITH.   Did I hear you right? . . . Who won't you spare?

JACKSON (*realization*).   Oh . . . God . . . Oh most merciful Allah . . . strike me down where I stand.

SMITH.   Now . . . now . . . don't allow your poet's nature to get the best of you.

JACKSON.   But you said that you and the Grand Prefect were enemies.

SMITH.   Not enemies, really . . . more like antagonists . . . two sides of the same coin, you might say. Both of us are determined to come up heads, always.

JACKSON.   But what about the others our group has liquidated?

SMITH (*near hysterical laughter*).   The supply of hungry actors is almost inexhaustible!

JACKSON (*after a pause, weary*).   Have the others been arrested?

SMITH.   Your friends? No. As a matter of fact they haven't. But if you decide to die, we shall arrest them. And that would be a shame, you see. They are so amusing . . . and useful . . . they keep us busy . . . they keep us prepared . . . what would we do

with martial law if we had nobody to martial? . . . Ha ha ha
. . . Yes, life would be much duller . . .

JACKSON.   I wonder if I've really understood . . .

SMITH.   Why, of course you have. Don't lose your temper—at least
not yet. Think about it. Obviously from the standpoint of the
idea—the ideal, if you would like to use that word—you cannot
hand them over to us. But it doesn't matter . . . we already have
them. If we want to reach out. But from a practical point of
view you'd be doing them a service if you helped us to tie all
the loose ends. You would be preventing them from getting
into further trouble . . . and from suffering. Yes, and that's
what I said . . . suffering, and by the same token, you'd be
saving them from the gallows, and worse, if you are co-operative.
And, best of all, you would regain your peace of mind and
serve a necessary function in this life.

JACKSON.   What do you mean?

SMITH.   We'll get to that eventually. But, from whatever angle
you look at it, you'd be doing the best thing, if you do things
our way. Well?

JACKSON.   My brothers will give you the answer before long.

SMITH.   Another crime! Decidedly, it's a vocation! Very well, I
have had my say. And I confess I'm disappointed. It's all too
obvious that you cling to your ideas like a leech; there's no
pulling you off them.

JACKSON.   You cannot separate me from my brothers.

SMITH.   Well, so long then. (*He starts to go, then turns back.*)
Why then did you spare the Grand Prefect's madame and her
fake niece and nephew?

JACKSON.   Who told you about that?

SMITH.   I told you. We know everything . . . well, almost everything. You have been under surveillance before *you* even knew
you would become a so-called Black Revolutionary. Your every
breath has been recorded and filed away for future reference.
Great revolutionaries you are . . . You should have listened to
that little girl you have with you . . . Sister Sissie . . . But, tell
me, why did you let them go?

JACKSON.   That's none of your business.

SMITH (*laughs*).   Ah, come off it . . . Well, let me tell you why. Your ideals can murder a Grand Prefect, but it hesitates at murdering women and children, if they are Black. That was a discovery you made, wasn't it? But let's go on. If your ideals won't allow you to murder Black children, how can they demand that you murder a Black Grand Prefect? You Black Revolutionaries are forever fantasizing about killing white people . . . but all I find evidence of is your willingness to destroy Blackmen.

No, don't answer *that*. I don't care one way or another. You will save your answers for the Grand Prefect's madame. Yes, tell Madame Prefect what is none of my business . . . but it is certainly hers.

JACKSON.   The Grand Madame Prefect?

SMITH.   Yes, she demands to see you. And my real reason for coming here was to make sure that that would be all right. It is. It may even cause you to think about some of your decisions. The Grand Madame Prefect is a very Christian lady. Yes, indeed, I've heard some people say that she makes a hobby of the soul. (*Laughs*.)

JACKSON.   I refuse to see her . . . But . . . wait a minute . . . aren't you her husband?

SMITH.   But she doesn't recognize me, dear fellow. She hasn't recognized me for years. She doesn't even recognize her sons or daughters . . . or grand-nephews or nieces . . . ha ha ha. Every so often one of my doubles is unfortunate enough to meet a young hot-head like yourself . . . And then she wears her black outfit for a while. Seems to be a great pleasure for her . . . dragging out that musty black uniform. And now it's your turn to suffer with her . . . (*Softly*.) Be kind to her, young man, be patient as you would with your own mother. Remember, some of you even pretend to repent to her god . . . and some of you lose your souls to the cross . . . Alas, it's all in how you handle yourself . . . all in how you feel that day.

JACKSON.   I'll have none of it!

SMITH.   Oh, yes you will . . . you have no other choice. You are guilty . . . so be guilty and accept the punishment meted out by those who decide your guilt . . . And you are not to tell the Madame Prefect our secrets . . . right?

JACKSON. And if I do?

SMITH. All your friends will die immediately, except for the women. The two women, young Bonnie, especially, will be taken to this very prison and first turned over to the guards . . .

JACKSON. No! No!

SMITH. When my comrades are finished . . . then they will be available to the prisoners . . . first to Foster . . . and then we shall torture them slowly . . . Attaching live wires to the sensitive and private parts of their bodies is a method we refined in Vietnam, remember?

JACKSON. Oh . . . please . . . why are you doing this?

SMITH. Begging for mercy already? You see I must get results. Madame Prefect commands. I'm sorry, but she will not take no for an answer. And you do owe her something. And not only that, since the incident, since her husband's death, she has become—how shall I say it?—more mentally unbalanced. It is a periodic condition, of course, but she is getting more senile. So we thought it better not to stop her. (*He waits.*) If you change your mind, don't forget my proposal. I'll be seeing you soon . . . I have some other things to discuss with you. (*Short silence, he listens.*) Here she comes. You can't complain about being neglected! But it all hangs together, doesn't it? Imagine God—oh, pardon me—Allah, without prisons . . . or prisoners . . . or guards. One would be lost without the other.

(*He exits laughing. Voices and words of command off. The* GRAND MADAME PREFECT *enters. Pause.*)

JACKSON. What do you want?

MADAME PREFECT (*lifts her veil*). Look!

(JACKSON *says nothing.*)

Do you know that many things die with a man?

JACKSON. I know that.

MADAME (*in weary voice*). No, murderers and beasts do not know that. If they did, how could they do nothing but kill?

(*A short silence.*)

JACKSON. Okay, I've seen you. Now leave me alone.

MADAME. No. I must look at your face.

(JACKSON *shrinks away. The* MADAME *moves beside him; she seems exhausted.*)

I'm so lonely. I can't stay by myself any longer. In the old days he'd be there when I was sad, he used to share my sorrow —and I didn't mind it so much . . . then. But now . . . No, I can't stand being alone and keeping quiet. But who can I speak to? Nobody else *knows*. They pretend to mourn. And perhaps they really care, for an hour or two. Then they go off to eat, or drink—or to sleep. To sleep really. In some way, I felt you must be like me. You don't sleep, do you? I know that for sure. And who else can I speak of the murder except to you, the murderer?

JACKSON.   What murder? All I know of is an act of justice.

MADAME.   The same voice! You have the same voice as his. But, I guess, all men use the same voice when they speak of justice. He used to say "This is just," and no one had a right to question it. And yet perhaps you, too, are mistaken.

JACKSON.   He was an incarnation of that supreme, unholy injustice under which the Blackman has been slaving and groaning for centuries and centuries. And in return for this . . . this Super Tom, *the Grand Prefect* of all the enslaved Blacks of northeastern America . . . this super Black vampire made in the devil's image was given privileges, rewards, and honors. But, as for me, even if I am mistaken, the wages I am due are imprisonment and death.

MADAME.   Yes, young man, you are suffering. But he is dead, you killed him.

JACKSON.   Did I?

MADAME.   What? . . . Are you pleading innocence?

JACKSON (*remembers his role*).   He died suddenly. He never knew what hit him. A death like that is nothing.

MADAME.   Nothing? (*Lower voice.*) That's true. They took you away right afterwards. I'm told that you made speeches while the police officers were closing in on you. Yes, I can understand that. That must have helped you face what you are facing now. But it was different for me. I came sometime later, and I *saw*. I took all that I could collect. What a lot of blood there was. (*Pauses.*) I was wearing white . . . like an old nun.

JACKSON.   Keep quiet.

MADAME. Why? I am telling the truth, only the truth. Do you know what he was doing two hours before he died? He was sleeping. In an armchair in front of the TV with his feet propped up on a hassock . . . as he did so often. He was sleeping, and you . . . you were waiting for him down in those mean streets. *(She is crying.)* Oh, help me now, please help me!

(He stiffens and moves away.)

You are young, so young, surely you can't be all wicked.

JACKSON. Wicked? I've never had time to be young, lady.

MADAME. Oh, why are you so hard, so cold? Do you never feel pity for yourself?

JACKSON. No.

MADAME. You're wrong. It's better that way. Yes, that's right, better . . . to see you as you are. And that too is my penalty. To see a dream that never was . . .

JACKSON. I am not a dream, you wife of a super nigger fantasy . . . The Grand Prefect . . . jailer of his people, consular of the whiteman's law . . . You went to bed, old slut . . . with the slavemaster's slave . . . the man who sold you into bondage . . . and I'm a dream . . . a . . . a dream of some poor Black lady's who kept quiet and had the slavemaster's children . . . and had the master's best nigger . . . fashioned in his own image . . . you were so quiet with your children.

MADAME. But it kept them alive, son . . . it kept them alive . . . alive . . . so that you could be here . . . the dream that is you could be here.

JACKSON. I am not a dream, I am a man . . . a Blackman . . . a righteous Blackman . . .

MADAME. And an assassin.

JACKSON. A bomber . . . one through whom the will of the Black people is launched and explodes as murders and terrorists . . . and deaths to the enemies of the Black people . . . whether they are Black or white.

MADAME (*ironic*). A righteous assassin . . . all you righteous bombers are mirror images of your fathers . . . My husband was exactly like you when . . .

JACKSON. We righteous bombers are the mirror of the future reality. We stand without souls . . . without hearts. The best of us have been invested with the spirits of the people . . . and we offer up ourselves to the people . . . No, Madame Prefect . . . we righteous bombers who began by looking into the single reflections of our fathers have shattered that surface and millions of splinters of Black recognition smile blackly back from the African frames . . . We righteous bombers, we righteous ones are the new, not something that we are killing and have killed.

MADAME. But your smug illusions do not stop my suffering. Why didn't you kill me with him, instead of sparing me?

JACKSON. I didn't spare you, mother . . . I've only given you the most difficult task, as usual.

MADAME. And you allowed me to live . . . how terribly you hate me.

JACKSON. It was not you I saved, but the children you had with you. That part of the future that you had with you.

MADAME. I know . . . But I don't like them much. (*Pauses.*) They were the Grand Prefect's favorites . . . not mine. Aren't they guilty, like us?

JACKSON. No.

MADAME. How can you be so sure? My grand-niece is an evil little Black bitch. When she's told to give something to the poor colored people, the poor Black people that she sees, she refuses, and spits from the limousine window at them. She won't go near them, except to spit upon them. Is she not unrighteous? Of course she is. And my poor husband was so fond of her; she was the light of his eyes. And he was very fond of Black people too, no matter what you might think. He used to drink and laugh with them. And now you've killed him! Surely you, too, are unrighteous. The world is bleak . . . a savage waste stretching before us until . . .

JACKSON. Stop the pity! You're wasting your time. You want to drain me of my soul and empty my Black heart of the rightness of my act. But you won't get to first base. So leave me alone.

MADAME. Won't you join with me in prayer, and repent? Then we would not be alone.

JACKSON.   Let me get ready to die my own way. If I do not die
. . . then I am a murderer.

MADAME.   To die? You want to die? No. I forbid it. (*Goes to* JACK-
SON, *with rising emotion.*) It is your duty to accept being a
murderer. You killed him, didn't you? Don't hesitate! . . . Well,
didn't you? . . . Good! . . . I want to tell you that God is the
only one who can justify your . . .

JACKSON.   Whose God? Yours or mine?

MADAME.   The God of our Holy Church.

JACKSON.   What has the church to do with it? Besides . . . there is
a new holiness in this land . . . the Black holiness of Allah.

MADAME.   A love whose only link is ignorance of itself. What kind
of love is that?

JACKSON.   The only sort of love that the whiteman and you, his
slave, allow us.

MADAME.   I loved the man you killed. And it wasn't ignorance
that brought us together.

JACKSON.   I know. That is why I forgive you for the wrong that
you and your kind have done me. You cannot perceive the degree of your misunderstanding. Now go, please. Please.

MADAME.   Yes, I'll go. I came here to reintroduce you to God, my
son, but now I understand that you see yourself as our own
judge. So save yourself, unaided. That is beyond all powers,
even your own, save the Lord's. But God can do it, if you live.
I will ask that you are allowed to live, my son.

JACKSON.   No! Don't do that! I beg of you, don't do that. Let me
die—or else I will hate you, I'll despise and curse you forever.

MADAME.   I shall ask that you be allowed to live—you must have
time to think of all that has happened. You must have lots of
time.

JACKSON.   No, no! I won't let you. I won't let you! Don't!

(*She moves away. Lights change. Short silence, then images of*
SMITH *appear on screens.* SMITH *enters.*)

JACKSON.   I am glad to see you.

SMITH.   You are? I must compliment you on your fine act.

JACKSON.   Act?

SMITH.   Yes . . . Well, it makes my heart beat fast your being glad to see me. But tell me why?

JACKSON.   Because I wanted something to hate again.

SMITH.   You did? . . . Tsk tsk tsk . . . Well, I've come for your answer.

JACKSON.   You have it.

SMITH *(different tone.)*   No, you're wrong. Now, listen to me. The reason why I allowed the Madame Prefect to see you is because I can now publish a report of the meeting in the papers. This report will say that a certain young man known to his Black Revolutionary friends as Murray Jackson will have repented out of pity for the widow prefect and betrayed them! Betrayed his brothers and sisters! They will be screaming curses to your name as they are tortured, executed and raped. They will spread the infamy of Murray Jackson across the revolutionary consciousness of humanity . . . Your name will be spoken of to dwarf Benedict Arnold's . . . to ridicule Judas' . . .

JACKSON.   So be it! . . . I shall not betray them.

SMITH.   Which is it better to be, man . . . Judas or Jesus! . . . To live a life among men . . . or die like a dog for an impossible dream?

JACKSON.   To be a man . . .to uphold the truth of freedom . . . justice . . . not a coward and traitor.

SMITH.   Would you see your brothers and sisters die at one swoop . . . all their visions and work extinguished by the rope . . . at the same moment. Let them go on . . .one at a time they will die . . . Who knows . . . they might even advance your revolution . . . they might have time to overcome me . . . Brother Jackson . . . if they are to die let them have some lease on life . . . grant them this . . . for this is your function to be from now on. The true harbinger of death.

JACKSON.   I don't understand what you are saying.

SMITH.   You are our next hangman . . . our next executioner.

(JACKSON *backs away terrified.*)

JACKSON.   This is not real . . . this cannot happen . . . Why no one could believe this . . . or could they make it up. Tell me I'm mad.

SMITH.   Your friends will not believe anything . . . Why kill them tomorrow. You hold the life of dear little Bonnie in your hands for six more years . . . I swear to you . . . I'll not touch her for six years, whatever she does . . . Give her these years, brother, then it will be her time to go . . .

JACKSON. But Bonnie . . . Cleveland, Harrison and the rest would never believe it. You don't know their love for me. They'd die gladly for me and know I'd never betray them.

SMITH. But, brother . . . brotherhood wears thin as a worn blanket in the middle of a cool night . . . when it is measured by the rope. Think about it. I'll wait. *(Starts to leave.)* Take your time, young friend. Take your time. I'd hate to lose you. We shall have many long conversations in the years to come. And I've watched your chess game . . .yes, your game is well developed . . . especially that unorthodox opening you use. You learned to play in youth prison, didn't you? . . . Ha ha . . . no need to answer . . . our records are complete. So, just call when you want me.

JACKSON *(crying)*. But you have an executioner.

SMITH. Have you forgotten that he will be your first client?

JACKSON *(mutters)*. But seventy-five . . . seventy-five of my brothers and sisters.

SMITH. One hundred and fifty . . .One hundered and fifty, Murray Jackson . . . You see . . . we believe that you are twice the man that Foster ever was.

(SMITH *exits; his image continues upon the screens until the* GUARD *enters.*)

GUARD. LIGHTS OUT!

(*Lights off, except for the image that gradually dims.*)

I SAID LIGHTS OUT, DAMMIT! I AIN'T GONNA SAY IT AGAIN! ALL LIGHTS OUT!

(*Lights down.*)

Act III

(*Under an eerie light* MURRAY JACKSON *prepares for the execution ritual. He slowly, ceremoniously dons his executioner's garb and tests his equipment: the rope, the white, sterile tape for masking the victim's mouth, the leather thong for tying the hands and binding the arms next to the body. Simultaneously, as the above action goes on,* MURRAY JACKSON *and* BONNIE *appear on the screens.*)

BONNIE. What's the matter, brother?

JACKSON. It's Harrison. We've fallen out. He doesn't like me.

(Pause.)

BONNIE. Harrison doesn't like anybody; that's how he is. But he'll be glad when everything is through. Don't let it make you sad, Jack.

JACKSON. But I *am* sad, sister. I want you all to love me. When I joined the group I cut myself away from everything, and if my brothers turn against me, how can I stand it? Time and again I feel they do not understand me. Perhaps it's my fault. I know I'm often clumsy, I don't say the right things, I . . .

BONNIE. They love you and they understand you. Only, Harrison's different.

JACKSON. No. I can guess what he thinks; I heard somebody say almost the same thing: "Jack's too shaky, too jive time to be a revolutionary." I'd have them know that I'm not at all weak. I imagine I seem to them as being not together, dizzy very likely. But I believe in the revolution as strongly as they do. Like them, I'm ready to give my life up for the revolution. I, too, can be slick, silent, sharp, when it's called for. Only, I'm still convinced that life is a great thing, I'm in love with beauty, happiness. That's why I hate the Black people's position here in America and the world. The trouble is to make my brothers understand this. Revolution, by all means. But revolution for the sake of life—to give life a chance, if you see what I mean.

BONNIE *(impulsively)*. Yes, I do! *(Short silence, in lower voice.)* Only—what we're going to give isn't life, but death.

JACKSON. We? Oh, I see what you mean. But that's not the same thing at all. When we kill, we're killing so as to build up a Black world in where there will be no more killing. We have to be murderers so that at last the innocent and righteous, and only they, will inherit the earth.

BONNIE. And suppose it doesn't work out that way?

JACKSON. How can you say such a thing? It's unthinkable. Then Harrison would be right—and we'd have to spit in the face of grace.

BONNIE. I've had more experience than you in this work, and I know that nothing's so simple as you imagine. But you have faith, brother, and faith is what we need, all of us.

JACKSON. Faith? No. Only one man had faith in that sense. Malcolm.

BONNIE. Well, let's say then that you have a whole lotta soul, and you'll do your job, no matter what the cost. Why did you ask to throw the first bomb?

JACKSON. When one's a terrorist one can talk of direct action without taking part in it?

BONNIE. No.

JACKSON. And one must be in the forefront, of course . . .

BONNIE (*musing*). Yes, there's the forefront—and there's also the last moment. We all should think of that. That's where courage is at, and the selfless passion we all need . . . you, too, need.

JACKSON. For a year now that has never left my thoughts; I've been living for that moment day by day, hour by hour. And I know now that I'd like to die on the spot, beside the Grand Prefect. To shed my blood to the last drop, or blaze up like napalm in the flash of the explosion and leave not an ash of me behind. Do you understand why I asked to throw the bomb? To die for an ideal — that's the only way of proving oneself worthy of it. It's our only justification.

BONNIE. That's the death I, too, want.

JACKSON. Yeah, the happiest end of all. Sometimes at night when I'm lying awake on the thin straw mattress that I sleep on, I'm worried by the thought that they have forced us into being murderers. But then I remind myself that I'm going to die, too, and everything's all right. I smile to myself like a child and go peacefully to sleep.

BONNIE. That's how it should be, Jack. To kill, and to die on the spot. But, to my mind, there's a still greater happiness.

(*Pause.*)

The scaffold!

(*As the scene plays upon the screen, down in the stage area,* JACKSON *continues to prepare himself for the execution ritual, until two black-clad* GUARDS *drag in* FOSTER *who struggles silently when* JACKSON *plunges a hypodermic into his arm which relaxes him. Then* JACKSON *prepares* FOSTER *for execution.*)

JACKSON. Yeah, yeah, the scaffold. Since martial law was first declared and the pacification began that long ago summer the penalty for terrorism and rebellion has been public hanging.

Yeah, I, too, have thought of that. There's something missing about dying on the spot. While between the moment the bomb is thrown and the scaffold, there is an eternity, perhaps the only eternity a man can know.

BONNIE (*earnest*).   And that's the thought which must help you through. We are paying more than we owe.

JACKSON.   What do you mean?

BONNIE.   We're forced to kill, aren't we? We deliberately sacrifice a life, a single life?

JACKSON.   Yes.

BONNIE.   But throwing the bomb and then climbing the scaffold—that's giving one's life *twice*. That way we pay more than we owe.

JACKSON.   Yeah, it's dying twice over. Thank you, Bonnie. There's nothing with which anyone can reproach us. Now, I'm sure of myself.

(*A short silence.*)

What is it, Bonnie? Why are you silent?

BONNIE.   I'd like to help you in another way as well. Only . . .

JACKSON.   Only . . . what?

BONNIE.   No, I'd better not . . .

JACKSON.   Don't you trust me?

BONNIE.   It's not that I don't trust *you*, darling; I don't trust myself. Ever since one of our old brothers dropped a bomb and died . . . I've been having . . . strange ideas. I have to tell you about it sometime. And anyhow it's not for me to tell you what will be so difficult.

JACKSON.   But I like things that are difficult. Unless you have a very low opinion of me, say what you have in mind, sister.

BONNIE (*gazes at him*).   I know. You're brave. That, in fact, is what makes me anxious. You laugh, you work yourself up, you go ahead and sacrifice yourself like you almost enjoy it. But in a few hours' time you'll have to come out of your dreams and face reality, and the terrible thing you are to do. Perhaps it's best to speak of this beforehand—so that you won't be taken by surprise, and flinch.

JACKSON.   That's nonsense! I shall *not* flinch. But please explain . . .

BONNIE. Throwing the bomb, the scaffold, dying twice over—that's the easier part. Your heart will see you through. But standing in the front line . . . (*She pauses, scans him again and seems to hesitate.*) You'll be standing in front, you'll see him . . .

JACKSON. Who'll I see?

BONNIE. The Grand Prefect.

JACKSON. Oh, only for a moment at most.

(SMITH'S *image is superimposed over* BONNIE *and* JACKSON'S *upon the screen.*)

BONNIE. A moment during which you'll look at him. Oh, Jack, it's best for you to know, to be forewarned! A man is a man. Perhaps the Grand Prefect has gentle eyes . . .

(*Maniacal laughter and strange music starts and surrounds them.*)

. . . perhaps you'll see him smiling to himself, scratching his ear. Perhaps—who knows?—you'll see a little scar on his cheek where he cut himself shaving. And, if he looks at you, at that moment . . .

JACKSON. It's not he I'm killing. I'm killing the tyranny.

BONNIE. That's quite true. And tyranny must be killed. I'll get the bomb ready and when I'm screwing in the fuse—that's the moment when it's touch and go, and one's nerves are taut— I'll feel a strange little thrill . . . of joy. But, then, I don't know the Grand Prefect; it wouldn't be anything so easy if while I was screwing in the fuse he were sitting in front of me, looking at me.

(SMITH *enters upon stage and watches* JACKSON *complete his preparations for the execution.*)

But you'll see him quite near, Jack, from only a yard or two away.

JACKSON (*vehemently*). I shall *not* see him!

(*More laughter.*)

BONNIE. Why? Will you shut your eyes?

JACKSON. No. But, with Allah's aid, my hatred will surge up just in time, and blind me.

(*The* GUARD *enters on stage and silently signals* JACKSON *that the time of execution has come. Images fade upon the screen. Music and laughter down. With the* GUARD *leading,* JACKSON, *the two* STRONG-ARM MEN *on each side of* FOSTER *and* SMITH *form a proces-*

sion and march silently off. Lights change and up on BONNIE *and*
CLEVELAND *onstage.*)

CLEVELAND.   Try and get some rest, sister Bonnie.

BONNIE (*paces*).   My feet are numb.

CLEVELAND.   C'mon, put this coat over you.

BONNIE (*still pacing*).   Time never ends . . . the night . . . then
sun comes up showing us our despair. L, this cold is no good.

(HARRISON *and* BURK *enter. They greet warmly.*)

Did you find out, Ken?

HARRISON.   We think it's tonight. All the junior officers have been
ordered to report to their stations . . . They can watch the execution on their televisions. The announcements came over the air
last night of a TV special this morning . . . and you know what
that means.

BURK.   It's a requirement that all off-duty junior officers watch
when a Black Revolutionary is executed.

BONNIE.   Are you going to . . .

CLEVELAND.   Yes . . . we will turn the television on and watch it
too . . . when the times comes. But you don't have to.

BONNIE.   It's for dawn . . . this dawn.

CLEVELAND.   There's still a chance, sister. It depends upon the
Chief of Security's decision.

HARRISON.   It depends on the Security Chief. What if Jack has
asked for a pardon . . . what if . . .

BONNIE.   He hasn't. He wouldn't.

HARRISON.   Why did he see the Madame Prefect if it wasn't to confess . . . if it wasn't to ask for a pardon? She's told everybody
that he's repented . . . become a fucken Christian, even. How
do we know what went on? This very moment he's probably
writing our names down and handing them . . .

BONNIE.   Shut up! You damn . . .

CLEVELAND.   Brother! Sister! We cannot become hysterical . . . we
are professional revolutionaries . . . and we will not break . . .
understand, we will not!

BONNIE.   We know what Jack said at the trial, and we have the
letter he smuggled out. Didn't he say that if he had another

life he would offer that too, he would spit in the faces of the Black and white tyrants. Could the man who said that go on living . . . and . . . and repent . . . and ask for forgiveness like a dog? No, he will die . . . as we watch our television screen. Our Black and beautiful hero Jack is going to die because it is impossible for him to go back on what he's done . . . on what he is.

HARRISON. That's swell, baby, but he saw that Madame Prefect bitch.

BONNIE. He is the judge of what he had to do.

HARRISON. No. According to the code . . .

BONNIE. What code!

HARRISON. Our code . . . the code of the Black Revolutionary . . .

BONNIE. So you make up rules on the spot.

HARRISON. They may not be written down like the whiteman writes down everything but the truth in the alphabet he stole from our Arabic brothers in Africa before . . .

CLEVELAND. Please . . . please . . . no history.

HARRISON. It was his duty not to see her!

BONNIE. Our duty is to commit murder . . . nothing else . . . murder . . . pure and clean as death!

HARRISON. Let's not be subjective, sister.

BONNIE. Fuck you and that shit you spout out. We are human . . . Black Revolutionaries or not . . . My man is free! . . . Do you hear . . . Free! Jack is free . . . and don't you lick his corpse with your foul tongue coated with that bullshit you never put into practice . . . (*Ridicule.*) brother.

HARRISON. He's not free yet. In ten minutes, yeah . . . but not yet.

BONNIE. He's free, nigger! Now that death is holding his hand, he has the right to pull down his pants in the face of life . . . if he wants to. He owes nothing to life . . . and this piss poor life owes him nothin' but a kind burial. He is going to die, my brothers and there's nothing you can do about it or would if you could . . . Don't worry . . . you won't be cheated out of your circus.

CLEVELAND. Bonnie!

BONNIE.   Why lie, niggers! Why hide behind the Black Revolution
when it is your dry, flaking lips that wait to taste blood and
bone splinters whether they belong to a Grand Prefect . . . or
a brother. Admit it, weak, selfish, cowardly nigger men . . .
Murder is your last resort. You throwers of paper bombs and
exploding bullshit. Your best you lead out into the monster's
jaws and then desert him . . . your best! Jack is nothing. But
a poor, scared nigger boy like yourselves . . . just an unambitious
soul brother who scribbled poems . . . not a Malcolm . . . or
Martin Luther King even . . . or a LeRoi . . . just a poor beaten
Black boy who should have been busy giving me babies so that
he would have someone to listen to his poems. That's all he
was . . . and how he will end is part of the sport of defeat . . .
a martyr to the God of Vengeance . . . a sacrifice to the God
Assassination . . . a victim, my poor victim. Brothers, why
shouldn't our poor little Black Revolutionary nigger poet repent and cry in the dark circle of the noose? He has committed
the act. He has gotten his man. What more can he do? What
other service can he do you, brothers? What? Nothing. He would
only be good to father my children . . . and that stage of the
revolution has passed already, right? So he will die . . . and
you will believe in his death . . . and in the revolution . . . for
men only die for the most profound reasons, right? And you
will love his memory . . . and perhaps sing songs to his corpse
and one day toast him . . . Toast his act that is nothing but
stupidity and ignorance . . . Your love has a heavy price.

BURK.   That's not right, sister. We always believed in him.

BONNIE.   Did you? Well, maybe you did . . . So, I'm sorry. But it
doesn't matter. We shall see the truth in a few minutes . . . in
livid color . . . in our own home. But, Ken, my poor brother,
why did you come back? I thought you had left us to work on
revolutionary committees.

BURK.   To take his place. When I heard what he'd said at the trial
I cried I was so proud. You know his words by heart: "Black
deaths by the millions will smother your animal breaths and
you whitemen will fall and become fertilizer from which a new
people will spring and grow, after the death of you beasts."
When I heard that I shook all over, I could hardly stand . . .

CLEVELAND.   So you raced back to die?

BURK.   No, brother. I am here to serve.

BONNIE. "Whitemen will fall and become the fertilizer from which a new Black people will spring and grow." Yes, he said that. Very poetic.

BURK. Yes, he did. Bonnie . . . he had so much courage. And at the end he said . . . he said those words that sounded like the ghost of our African fathers echoing from across the seas and ages: "If my Black soul has caused me to be worthy of the duty placed upon me, of destroying violence and tyranny with all my manhood, may death take me, I throw my Black self into the teeth of history, and may it be a Black history, and may it judge me as merely a Blackman." I heard these words and returned to you to complete my duty.

BONNIE (*burying her face in her hands*). It was truth he wanted above all else. But it was such a cruel path he chose to reach it.

BURK. Please don't cry, sister.

(*Lights change.* JACKSON *enters, unnoticed by them, and goes to* BONNIE, *places his arms about her, attempting to comfort her.*)

Remember what he asked — that none of us show anything except our revolutionary determination to go on. Oh, I understand him so well—now. How could I have doubted him before? I was miserable because I was a coward. And the coward me handed the bomb back to Cleveland. But I am a Jack too . . . and I take back my legacy . . . a righteous Black assassin . . .

BONNIE (*whispers*). A righteous bomber . . . How sad.

(JACKSON *nods.*)

BURK. When I read that he was going to be executed . . . I couldn't help myself. I had to come as soon as possible and take my place beside him.

BONNIE. Who can take Jack's place tonight? Tonight he is alone with death, Ken.

BURK. We must keep him in our pride, as he keeps us by his example. Don't cry, sister.

BONNIE. But I'm not crying. I am not proud either.

HARRISON. Bonnie, forgive me. I want Jack to live. We need him.

BONNIE. But Jack does not want to live. And it's our duty to see him die.

CLEVELAND. Don't talk crazy, Bonnie.

BONNIE.   But it's our duty, L. I know Jack. Only death will bring him peace. Please . . . let him die without our whimpers. Let it happen quickly . . . let it be quick.

HARRISON.   Okay, L, I'm makin' it. C'mon, Ken. Let's make the rounds once more before it's time to turn on the TV.

BONNIE.   Stop by Sister Sissie's watch station . . . and bring the little sister here with you.

HARRISON.   Who will take the duty?

BONNIE.   I don't give a damn if nobody does . . . I need her here with me.

(HARRISON *sighs and shrugs.*)

CLEVELAND.   Yeah, you'd better make it if you're goin'a get back in time. But get back in time, okay?

(HARRISON *and* BURK *start to leave.* HARRISON *looks at* BONNIE.)

HARRISON.   In a few minutes, sister, we will know everything . . . Take care of her, L.

(HARRISON *and* BURK *exit. Lights change.* CLEVELAND *moves away into the shadows, leaving* BONNIE *and* JACKSON.)

BONNIE.   Yes . . . but why then are you so depressed? Not so long ago you looked so cheerful. Like a schoolboy going on vacation. But now . . .

JACKSON (*with bitterness.*)   Today I know something I did not know before. You were right, Bonnie; it's not so simple as it seems. I thought it was quite easy to kill, provided one has courage and is lifted up by a dream. But now I've lost my wings. I have realized that hatred brings no happiness. I can see the poison in myself, and in the others, too. Murderous instincts, cowardice, injustice. I've got to kill—there are no two ways about it. But I shall see it through to the end. I shall go beyond hatred.

BONNIE.   Beyond? There's nothing beyond.

JACKSON.   Yeah. There's love.

BONNIE.   Love? No, that's not what is needed, brother.

JACKSON.   Oh, Bonnie, how can you say that? You of all people, you whose heart I know so well!

BONNIE.   Too much blood, too much brutal violence—there's no escape for us. Those whose hearts are set on justice have no right to love. They're on their toes, as I am, holding their heads up, their eyes fixed on the heights. What room for love is there in such proud hearts? Love bows heads, gently, compassionately. We, Jack, are stiff-necked.

JACKSON.   But we love our Black people.

BONNIE.   Yes, we love them—in our own way. With a vast love that has nothing to support it; that brings only sadness. The Black people? We live so far away from them, shut up in our thoughts. And do they love us? Do they even guess we love them? No, they hold their tongues. And that silence, that deep silence.

JACKSON.   But surely that's exactly what love means—sacrificing everything without expecting anything in return?

BONNIE.   Perhaps. Yes, I know that love, an absolute, ideal love, a pure and solitary joy—and I feel it burning in my heart. Yet there are times when I wonder if love isn't something else; something more than a lonely voice, a monologue, and if there isn't sometimes a response. And then I see a picture floating up before my eyes. The sun is shining, pride dies from the heart, one bows one's head gently, almost shyly, and every barrier is down! Oh, Jack, if only we could forget, even for an hour, the ugliness and misery of this world we are in, and let ourselves go—at last! One little hour or so of thinking of ourselves, just you and me, for a change. Can you see what I mean?

JACKSON.   Yeah, Bonnie, I can; it's what is called love—baby—in the simple, Black sense.

BONNIE.   Yes, honey, you've guessed what I mean—but does that kind of love mean anything to you, really, darling? Do you love justice with that kind of love?

(JACKSON *is silent.*)

Do you love our Black people with that love—all tenderness and gentleness and self-forgetting?

(JACKSON *says nothing.*)

You see. (*She goes toward him—her voice low.*) And how about *me*, baby? Do you love me—as a lover?

JACKSON.   No one will ever love you as I love you, woman.

BONNIE.   I know. But wouldn't it be better to love—like an ordinary man?

JACKSON.   I'm not an ordinary man. Whatever I am, I love you.

BONNIE.   Do you love me more than freedom, justice and self-determination, more than the Black Revolutionary Organization?

JACKSON.   For me, you, freedom and the rest, the organization are one. I don't make differences between you.

BONNIE.   Yes. But do, please, answer me, brother. Do you love me all for yourself . . . selfishly . . . possessively? . . . Oh, you know what I mean! Would you love me if I were unrighteous?

JACKSON.   If you were unrighteous and I could love you it wouldn't be you I loved.

BONNIE.   That's no answer. Tell me only this; would you love me if I didn't belong to the organization?

JACKSON.   Then what would you belong to, baby?

BONNIE.   I remember the time when I was a student. I was pretty then. I used to spend hours walking around town, dreaming all kinds of silly daydreams. I was always laughing. Would you love me if I were like that now—carefree, sweet, like a young girl?

JACKSON (*hesitantly, in low voice*).   I'm wanting to, oh damn, how I'm wanting to say yeah.

BONNIE (*eagerly*).   Then say yes, honey—if you mean it, if it's true. In spite of everything: of freedom, justice and self-determination, of our suffering Black people, of human slavery. Try and forget for a moment all the suffering—the hangman, the agony of little Black children, of Black men and women whipped until they die . . . the meat hanging from their bones.

JACKSON.   Bonnie! Please, baby.

BONNIE.   No, surely for once we can let our hearts take charge. I'm waiting for you to say the word, to tell me you want me— Bonnie, the living Black woman—and I mean more to you than this world, this fucked-up white world that is around our throats like a noose.

JACKSON (*brutally*).   Shut up! My heart wants you, and you alone . . . But, a few minutes from now I'll need a clear head and a strong hand.

BONNIE.   A few minutes from now. Oh, yes, I was forgetting. (*Laughs and sobs at once.*) No, darling, I'll do as you want. Don't be angry with me—I was talking nonsense. I promise to be sensible. I'm too tired, that's all. I, too, I couldn't have said—what I wanted you to say. I love you with the same love as yours: a love that's half frozen, because it's stuck in justice and raised in concentration camps . . . Summer, baby, do you remember what that's like, a real summer's day? But—no, it's a winter without end for us here. We don't belong to the world of living men. We are the righteous ones. Part spirits of beautiful Blackness, part dreadful ghosts of destruction and death. We are the righteous bombers. And outside there is sun and light; but not for us, never for us. Only the tomb and the concentration camp awaits us. (*Averts her eyes.*) May the pity of Allah shine on we the righteous.

JACKSON.   Yeah, that's what we get out of this life, baby; love is . . . just not possible. But I will do what I must, and then at last there will be peace for you and me.

BONNIE.   Peace? Oh, brother, you don't think that. When can we find peace?

JACKSON.   Each of us will find peace soon . . . in his own way.

(*Lights change.* JACKSON *moves away and* CLEVELAND *enters and replaces* JACKSON.)

BONNIE.   Death. The hangman. Always death . . . L, L . . . what are we going to do?

CLEVELAND.   Nothing, little sister. There's no other way.

BONNIE.   Don't talk like that. If death is the only way then we are on the wrong path. The right one leads to life, to sunlight . . . We can't only feel cold and then die.

CLEVELAND.   The path we are on, also, leads to life, sister. To Black life. Black people will live, our children's children will live. Remember what Jack used to say? "Black people will seize the land of their dreams."

BONNIE.   Our children's children, always others—yes. But Jack is in prison and the rope hangs down waiting. He is facing it this very minute. Maybe he is already dead—so that other Black people, after him, will go on, and live. And, L, suppose . . . suppose that, after all, the others did not live? Suppose he is dying for nothing?

CLEVELAND.   Shut up!

BONNIE.   Oh, it's so cold! And spring is here. I can see the trees blooming out on 7th Avenue. He must be able to see trees from his cell window.

CLEVELAND.   No. His cell is in the lower basement of the prison. Security reasons.

BONNIE.   But if he gets a chance I know he would look at the trees . . . and smell the changing of the air.

CLEVELAND.   Don't let your imagination get away from you, Bonnie. And please try and stop shivering. Here, let me put my coat around you . . . I'll hold you.

BONNIE.   I'm so cold I must be already dead. This life is only a way of death, isn't it, brother? We will never feel young again. With the first murder our youth ends forever. And it is so sorrowful . . . our predicament. Here . . . we are committed to murdering Black men. Blackmen . . . not the whites we know we must destroy . . . but Blackmen like ourselves. Oh, brother, I'm glad it is over . . . life is such an evil game.

CLEVELAND.   Shhh . . . shhh . . . don't upset yourself anymore.

BONNIE.   We throw a bomb and in the next instance everything in our existence and even our history has changed . . . A whole life time dissolved . . . and all that's left is death. Always death.

CLEVELAND.   We are righteous Blackmen, sister. We do not fear death as the whiteman does. Each moment of our lives we build until the second of death. That way we meet death like heroes, fighting to the end.

BONNIE.   You have gone about it too fast. You are no longer men . . . you have taken on the ways of the beast . . . and have become the monsters he has projected you to be.

CLEVELAND.   But Black misery and injustice go fast as well. In today's world there's no time for patience and quiet progress. Our fathers had patience for four hundred years. Black people are in a hurry. And all the universe will step aside, if need be.

BONNIE.   I know, Brother L. We have taken to our breasts all the sorrow of Black America. Jack took those sorrows and went out alone and did something . . . committed an act. That called for bravery. Yet I sometimes think that such pride will be punished.

CLEVELAND.   It's Black pride, a pride we pay for with our lives. No one can do more. It's a pride to which we own entirely.

BONNIE.   Are you sure that no one can do more? Sometimes when I hear what Harrison says I fear for the future. Others may replace us who might take our authority for killing; and will *not* pay with their lives. Only go on killing one after another Blackmen . . . for the savor of the kill.

CLEVELAND. Blackmen are not insane like the white beasts. And if we are our insanity takes human form . . . not animal.

BONNIE. We have long thought that the whites would exterminate us . . . and they have had some success. Is that why we only kill other Blacks at this stage, brother, not whitemen?

CLEVELAND. BONNIE!

BONNIE. Who knows? Do you make the decisions as who is to die? . . . No, you don't, do you? The orders come from a committee that none of us have ever seen . . . or know. And they give orders to kill only Blackmen, *brother*. Would they be so diabolical as to make up a committee of themselves and order us to destroy ourselves?

CLEVELAND. They? . . . What are you talking about, woman?

BONNIE. You know what I'm talking about. Wouldn't it be possible for the whites to be directing us?

CLEVELAND. Woman! How dare you! How dare you to blaspheme? You have lost your mind. The strain of your lover going to his death has been too much for you. You have lost the faith. I've never known you like this before . . . and would have never believed it. I wish I was dead rather than have heard what you just said. If I had a gun in my hand right now I'd lay it aside your head, sister, and put an end to your mad, miserable ravings.

BONNIE. Elton . . . L . . . I'm so cold, so cold. Hold me. And I'm thinking of him—and so many strange visions, dreams and images flood my mind, trying to block him out. I see him shivering . . . he's trying to hold himself upright, so not to be afraid. He seems to be dressed in black . . . Oh, L, it's so horrible . . . not the gray of the executed but the black . . . the black that the executioner wears. He's covered his head now . . . and he takes the rope in his hands and holds it tight to keep from shivering.

CLEVELAND. Are you no longer with me, sister?

BONNIE (*flings herself at him.*) Oh, no, L, don't say that! I am here with you, whatever my mind holds I know that I am really here. That I am standing in the real world . . . in your arms. I will be with you to the end. I hate the world . . . the world the whiteman has created through destruction. And I know the only way to destroy the whiteman and his world is for us to be together. I cannot act any other way than together with my brothers. I was so happy when I began this adventure of world liberation . . . and it's so sad, sorrowful and lonely to keep it up. But continue I must. This life of death is the only life I have, brother. It's so horrible that it's beautiful . . . we are prisoners.

CLEVELAND.   All Black people are prisoners . . . and all America is a prison. But we will blow down the prison walls one day.

BONNIE.   Yes, one day. Only give me the bomb to throw, or to plant. I shall walk through the flames and bodies laughing. I will not shiver then. It's easy to die . . . not live. And I will give my life to the death we serve. L . . . tell me, have you ever loved anyone? Really loved?

CLEVELAND.   Yeah. It was so long that I've forgotten all about it.

BONNIE.   How long?

CLEVELAND.   Six years.

BONNIE.   What happened?

CLEVELAND.   She was white.

BONNIE.   I see . . . Couldn't you have left the country, or done something?

CLEVELAND.   When I found out what white means and what it means to be Black there was nothing I could do but live my life the way it has become.

BONNIE.   How long have you been head of the organization for Harlem?

CLEVELAND.   Three years. Now it's my only love.

BONNIE.   Loving, that's strange . . . and to be loved, that's even more scary. No! We have too much work to do. It would be good to rest. But we have work to do. We haven't time to be in love with love because we love such things as freedom, justice, self-determination, liberation, righteousness . . . so many things other than people.

CLEVELAND.   But we love Black people.

BONNIE.   No, no . . . let's not go into that. For we would only find blind alleys and lies. We love what we love, that's all. There's nothing else. Keep on pushin', sister Bonnie. Keep the faith, brother L. (*She bursts into tears.*) But, for him, he is dead.

CLEVELAND (*takes her in his arms*).   He'll be pardoned.

BONNIE.   Oh, shut your mouth. You know that's impossible. You know that could not happen . . . It would be terrible. I can't see him in my mind anymore. He has escaped me. Perhaps he is walking to the gallows now. Oh, please turn on the television, L.

CLEVELAND.   Are you sure you want to see this, Bonnie?

BONNIE.   It is my duty! Isn't it my duty as a senior member of our revolutionary cell? (*He turns the television on.*) The picture isn't in focus yet . . . hurry, brother. I know the people will be there, standing silent as he approaches. I hope he's not cold like me . . . Hurry, L, get it. Do you know how men are hanged?

(*Picture of an* ANNOUNCER *comes into focus.*)

CLEVELAND.   With a rope. Men are hanged by ropes . . . I can't, Bonnie.

(*He turns it off.*)

BONNIE (*wildly rushes him*).   And the hangman leaps onto his shoulder, his beautiful Black shoulders, right? His neck cracks, his feet jerk and dance. And they say Christian prayers over what's left of him.

CLEVELAND (*restraining her*).   And he finds happiness . . . peace and happiness, sister.

(*She breaks away, and turns the television on.*)

BONNIE.   HAPPINESS!

CLEVELAND.   To feel free that last second as you drop . . . just after feeling another man's hand upon you. (*He stands before the screen.*) Let's go away for a while, Bonnie . . . I can get forged passes and we can slip over to Jersey for a month.

BONNIE.   Get out of the way.

CLEVELAND.   We all need a rest. And I need you. I've loved you so long.

BONNIE.   Get out of the way, brother.

(*He does. The picture shows the procession to the gallows. There is no sound.*)

CLEVELAND. I am your brother in revolution. But I need to be your man, as well.

BONNIE (*looks intently at the screen*). And all my brothers want to do nothing but love me . . . Between killing they want to love me.

(*It is raining in the television picture. There is a patter of rain from offstage. Daylight is growing on the screen and on the outer area of the stage. Whispering.*)

How I hate brotherhood, sometimes.

(HARRISON, BURK *and* SISSIE *enter in rain gear. All stand watching the screen.* BONNIE'S *knees sag;* CLEVELAND *supports her;* SISSIE *weeps.*)

They have their heads covered . . . Both him . . . and the executioner. How strange . . . He looks so strange in gray . . . so small and shrunken . . . and frightened . . . And the executioner . . . Oh, how horrible . . . he looks like the Jack of my dreams . . . after he had put his hood on, Cleveland.

(SISSIE *kneels and prays.*)

CLEVELAND. Steady, sister. Steady . . . Jack has been through hell in the past month . . . they probably starved him . . . I'm so glad it'll be over soon.

(HARRISON *steps forward and turns up the sound.*)

TV ANNOUNCER (*Blackman with white voice*). Yes, folks . . . the procession is now at the foot of the gallow steps. Up to this point there have been no upsetting actions by the accused. These so-called Black Revolutionaries are cold, ruthless characters. They're fanatics, folks . . . and it's lucky that we are systematically wiping them out. Too bad we didn't get this monster before the unfortunate killing of that Black official up there in Harlem.

HARRISON. Wow, man . . . look how straight Jack is walkin'.

BURK. Yeah . . . that's a real man we're lookin' at . . . Man, I wouldn't have missed this for the world.

CLEVELAND. Let me turn it off, Bonnie.

BONNIE. No, I have to see. His death belongs to me . . . understand? . . . to me.

TV ANNOUNCER. They're reading the judgment of the court now, folks. Let's zoom in and catch this shot with our "right-there" lens.

VOICE FROM SCREEN (*white voice*).　You have been tried by your approximate peers in the courts of lower Manhattan and found guilty of criminal acts against the state and city of New York, and for breaking the national anti-law and order codes. It is true that your jury was entirely white . . . but as you know Blackmen are not allowed any longer to serve on juries since their constitutional rights have been suspended . . . And the court finds you guilty and sentences you to death by hanging . . . And may God have mercy on your soul.

BONNIE.　Oh, Jack . . . say something. Say something, Jack. Give the world words that we can create slogans which will inflame all revolutionaries of the world.

BURK.　He can't say nothin', sister. They tape their mouths and drug them.

BONNIE.　What beasts whitemen are . . . I can't look at any more.

HARRISON.　Ahhh, please, don't turn it off, L.

ANNOUNCER.　Like all the other Black Revolutionaries who are hanged this one doesn't seem like he's going to say anything, folks. But just before he left his cell he did give a speech: "I have given up my Black life, for Black people, and welcome death knowing that I am righteous in Blackness."

　　　　(SISSIE *begins chanting "Allah Akbar."*)

BONNIE.　Did you hear that! Did you hear what the announcer said?

HARRISON.　It's a good thing we kept it on.

CLEVELAND.　Quick, Ken, write it down.

ANNOUNCER.　And now the accused is walking up the steps of the gallows . . . straight and certain. You have to admit . . . these Black fellows have a certain style about them. Someone from beyond the wall is singing an old time negro spiritual . . . and . . . yes, and I can hear dogs barking from way off . . . A soft rain is falling as dawn arrives. And the accused is still climbing the long stairway to heaven or hell . . . or wherever Black Revolutionaries go . . . supported by two red-hooded guards and followed by the dreaded man in black. Remember, folks, that we will be with you on instant replay of the actual hanging . . . just seconds afterwards . . . and tonight we will bring you by video tape the more stirring segments of this historic program.

And now they have reached the top. There are only seconds before the military tribunal can intervene and give a pardon. All eyes who are not on the accused now are looking across the courtyard, waiting to see if that little door will open and a messenger will come rushing out bringing news of . . .

BONNIE.   Turn if off! Turn it off!

CLEVELAND.   Get ahold of yourself, sister.

> (*She turns the set off.* SISSIE's *wails rise.*)

HARRISON.   Sissie! . . . cut out all that noise.

BURK.   Let her pray, man.

HARRISON.   But it gets to me, man. I don't want this broad buggin' me while I'm trying to concentrate.

SISSIE.   I can't stand it. I can't stand it here in the house of the unrighteous. (*She rises and rushes off.*)

CLEVELAND.   Now I want everybody to control themselves . . . Remember who you are.

BONNIE.   He's happy. There's nothing more to do but cry.

HARRISON.   Are you crazy? Happy?

BONNIE.   Didn't you see him? How calmly he walked? He was happy in death. He is getting what he wanted. What we all want.

BURK.   But he was drugged, sister . . . he . . .

BONNIE (*screams*).   Do not cry, brothers. He wouldn't have it. Don't you realize this is a day of celebration.

> (*Bells begin ringing.*)

Do you hear the bells? It is over. All the revolutionaries of the world know what day this is. Jack is not a murderer but a man of important deeds. A revolutionary. And what confirmed it was a terrible crash that we didn't hear. But the bells tell us about it. And he was so young. L.

CLEVELAND.   Yeah?

BONNIE.   You're my friend, my brother? Take me away for a while. Take me to Jersey . . . and play my man . . . and I'll be your woman.

CLEVELAND.   Whatever you say, sister.

BONNIE.   And when we return . . . give me the bomb . . . the next bomb.

(*All stare at her.*)

Give it to me. I want to throw it. I want to be the first to throw.

CLEVELAND.   You know it's against our policy for women to be on the direct firing line. You can be a lookout like Sissie.

BONNIE.   A woman! You say I'm a woman after this?

BURK.   Let her have it, L.

HARRISON.   Give it to her.

CLEVELAND.   It was your turn, Harrison.

HARRISON.   Say yeah, man. She's the one.

BONNIE.   It is mine, isn't it? And I can throw it. And after that . . .

CLEVELAND.   Okay. Okay. It's yours, but first Jersey, okay?

BONNIE.   Yes, yes, anything. Anything! Jack! One dawn not so long from now I will join you on TV . . . and the same rope . . . the same rope will bind us forever . . . Oh, the sun is out, brothers, it is spring . . . and how suddenly happy I am.

A. Selected Anthologies Including Dramas by Afro-Americans

Alhamisi, Ahmed and Harun K. Wangara, eds. *Black Arts: Anthology of Black Creations*. Detroit: Broadside, 1970.

Brasmer, William and Dominick Consolo, eds. *Black Drama: An Anthology*. Columbus, Ohio: Merrill, 1970.

Brown, Sterling A., Arthur Davis and Ulysses Lee, eds. *The Negro Caravan*. New York: Dryden, 1941.

Bullins, Ed, ed. *New Plays from the Black Theatre*. New York: Bantam, 1969.

Couch, William, ed. *Black Playwrights; an Anthology*. Baton Rouge, La., Louisiana State UP, 1968.

Jones, LeRoi and Larry Neale, eds. *Black Fire*. New York: Morrow, 1968.

Locke, Alain and Montgomery Gregory, eds. *Plays of Negro Life: A Source-Book of Native American Drama*. New York: Harper, 1927.

Richardson, Willis, ed. *Plays and Pageants from the Life of the Negro*. Washington, D. C.: Associated Pub., 1930.

Richardson, Willis and May Miller, eds. *Negro History in Thirteen Plays*. Washington, D. C.: Associated Pub., 1935.

B. Selected Published Dramas by Afro-Americans

Baldwin, James. *The Amen Corner*. New York: Dial, 1968.
_____. *Blues for Mister Charlie*. New York: Dial, 1956.

Bullins, Ed. *How Do You Do?* California: Illuminations Press, 1969.

————.*Five Plays*. Indianapolis: Bobbs-Merrill, 1969.

Davis, Ossie. *Purlie Victorious: A Comedy in Three Acts*. New York: French, 1961.

Edmonds, Randolph. *Shades and Shadows*. Boston: Meador, 1930. (Reprinted, Ann Arbor, Mich.: University Microfilms).

————. *Six Plays for a Negro Theatre*. Boston: Bakers, 1934. (Reprinted, Ann Arbor, Mich.: University Microfilms).

————. *The Land of Cotton and Other Plays*. Washington, D. C.: Associated Pub., 1942.

Elder, Lonnie. *Ceremonies in Dark Old Men*. New York: Farrar, Straus & Giroux, 1969.

Gordone, Charles. *No Place To Be Somebody*. Indianapolis: Bobbs-Merrill, 1969.

Hansberry, Lorraine. *A Raisin in the Sun*. New York: Random, 1959.

————. *The Sign in Sidney Brustein's Window*. New York: Random, 1965.

Hughes, Langston. *Five Plays by Langston Hughes,* ed. Webster Smalley. Bloomington, Ind.: Indiana UP, 1963.

Jones, LeRoi. *The Baptism and the Toilet*. New York: Grove 1966.

————. *Dutchman and the Slave*. New York: Morrow, 1964.

————. *Four Black Revolutionary Plays*. Indianapolis: Bobbs-Merrill, 1969.

Mackey, William W. *Behold! Cometh the Vanderkellans*. New York: Azazel, 1966.

Mitchell, Loften. *A Land Beyond the River*. Cody, Wyoming: Pioneer Drama Service, 1963.

Peterson, Louis S. *Take a Giant Step*. New York: French, 1954.

Richardson, Willis. *The King's Dilemma and Other Plays for Children*. New York: Exposition, 1956.

Ward, Douglas T. *Happy Ending and Day of Absence*. New York: Dramatists Play Service, 1968.